BENJAMIN SPOCK, M.D. is best known for his book *Baby and Child Care,* which has been translated into thirty-nine languages and has sold over thirty million copies since its first publication in the 1940s. He attended Yale Medical School before receiving his M.D. from Columbia University's College of Physicians and Surgeons. Dr. Spock practiced pediatrics from 1933 to 1947. Then he became a medical teacher and researcher at the Mayo Clinic, the University of Pittsburgh, and Western Reserve University. He has written ten books. He and his wife, Mary Morgan, have lived in Rogers, Arkansas, since 1976.

MICHAEL B. ROTHENBERG, M.D. is a pediatrician and child psychiatrist who has combined these two fields in his work with children and their families for over thirty years. He has a national reputation as a children's advocate, working with legislators, parents, schools, hospitals, and other health care providers. He has three children and two grandchildren. Dr. Rothenberg and his wife, Jo, live in Seattle, Washington. He and Dr. Spock first met in 1955.

Baby and Child Care

BENJAMIN SPOCK, M.D. AND
MICHAEL B. ROTHENBERG, M.D.

CONSULTANTS:
Lawrence R. Berger, M.D.
Kathryn A. Mikesell, M.D.

Illustrations by
DOROTHEA FOX

POCKET BOOKS
New York London Toronto Sydney Tokyo

Revised and Updated Edition

POCKET BOOKS, a division of Simon & Schuster Inc.
1230 Avenue of the Americas, New York, N.Y. 10020

ISBN: 0-671-67355-6

First Pocket Books revised edition printing November 1985

15 14 13 12 11 10 9 8 7 6

Printed in the U.S.A.

Contents

Why This Revision of Baby and Child Care

"I" or "we"? Even single authors speak as "we," and so do co-authors, of course. But in the spots in this book where the authors use the first person pronoun, Dr. Rothenberg and I will continue to say "I" because we think alike and because "we" sounds to us less personal, more pompous.

There have been pediatric consultants for all previous editions, to get a wide perspective, but this time they are listed on the title page. Lawrence R. Berger and Kathryn A. Mikesell each read through the previous edition and provided a multitude of detailed comments and suggestions. Larry Berger provided a special perspective on the public health aspects of the lives of children and their parents. Kathy Mikesell brought the particularly valuable viewpoint of the pediatrician who is also a mother.

New Material and Emphases

More space has been given to the problems of divorce, single-parent families, and the difficulties of the step-parent relationship, because these situations are still increasing. There are expanded sections on breast-feeding for working mothers and the new role of fathers in childbirth. There are entirely new sections, such as the one on child abuse and neglect. Some diseases have been omitted or de-emphasized because they are no longer prevalent, and a few others have been added. (There has never been room for more than the commonest of the hundreds of diseases that exist.) All of the factual material in the book has been brought up to date. The traditional egg, for example, is no longer recommended as part of the diet for babies during the first year of life, because of the recent discovery that the iron in egg yolk cannot be absorbed by them and in fact interferes with their absorption of iron from other sources.

I want to call special attention to two other points by including them in this introduction:

Children's Fear of Nuclear War

In these times of rising international tensions, a realistic fear of nuclear war is almost universal among children and adolescents. Young children express it as fear that their parents will be killed and worry about who will take care of them then. Older children see the direct danger to themselves. Adolescents are moved to pessimism, asking what is the use of studying or maintaining their health if they are to die before they become workers and parents.

Parents can give their children partial reassurance if they can say, "Yes, there is a danger but it need not happen if we will all work for peace. We vote for the candidates for president, senator, and congressman who are for a nuclear freeze, disarmament, and peaceful settlement of disputes. We write to our officials, not just once but often. We belong to peace groups and attend demonstrations. You can help by writing letters and attending demonstrations too."

The Question of Permissiveness

I don't consider myself permissive and almost all the people who've used this book feel the same way. The people who call me permissive say indignantly that they haven't read it, wouldn't use it. The accusation came for the first time in 1968—22 years after the book came out—from several prominent individuals who objected strongly to my opposition to the war in Vietnam. They said that my advice to parents to give "instant gratification" to their babies and children was what made so many young men who opposed the war "irresponsible, undisciplined, and unpatriotic." There is no instant gratification in this book. I've always advised parents to respect their children but to remember to ask for respect for themselves, to give firm, clear leadership and to ask for cooperation and politeness.

[illegible]

[illegible] of [illegible] [illegible] [illegible] [illegible] [illegible] [illegible] [illegible] [illegible] [illegible] [illegible] [illegible] selves, [illegible] [illegible] [illegible] [illegible] [illegible] the [illegible] [illegible] [illegible] and parents.

Parents [illegible] [illegible] [illegible] [illegible] [illegible] [illegible] [illegible] [illegible] [illegible] [illegible] [illegible] [illegible] [illegible] [illegible] demonstrations, [illegible] [illegible] [illegible] and [illegible] [illegible]

[illegible]

[illegible] [illegible] [illegible] [illegible] [illegible] [illegible] [illegible] [illegible] [illegible] [illegible] [illegible] [illegible] [illegible] [illegible] [illegible] [illegible] [illegible] [illegible] [illegible] [illegible]

A Letter to the Reader

Most of you have a doctor you can consult. The doctor knows your child, and therefore is the only person in a position to advise you wisely. By glancing at a rash or asking a couple of questions over the telephone, the doctor can usually get to the solution of a problem that reading would only get you more mixed up about. This book is not meant to be used for diagnosis or treatment; it's only meant to give you a general understanding of children, their troubles and their needs. It is true that in certain sections there is emergency advice for those very few parents who are out of reach of a doctor. It's better for them to have book advice than no advice at all. But book advice is never so helpful or so safe as real medical assistance.

The most important thing I have to say is that you should not take too literally what is said in this book. Every child is different, every parent is different, every illness or behavior problem is somewhat different from every other. All I can do is describe the most common developments and problems in the most general terms. Remember that you know a lot about your child and I don't know anything.

Warning: Salesmen for children's encyclopedias, sets of books on child care, nursery furniture, children's clothing, and equipment may claim that Dr. Spock or Dr. Rothenberg is intimately connected with their enterprises in some way, or at least endorse their products. All such claims are fraudulent and entitle you to threaten to call the authorities in order to get rid of the salesman. We have no connection with any such enterprise and never endorse a commercial product. Dr. Spock writes a regular column for *Redbook* magazine, and he has authored or co-authored several separate books but they are sold only through regular bookstores or paperback outlets, never door-to-door.

Acknowledgments

From Dr. Spock: My debt is now tremendous to all the physicians and other experts, including parents, who have advised me through four previous editions of the book, and the skillful editors and secretaries who have brought the manuscripts to publication.

C. Anderson Aldrich, M.D.; Barbara Biber, Ph.D.; Sylvia K. Bingham; Dale Bland, B.S.; David Bland, M.S.S.A.; Abram Blau, M.D.; Gordon M. Bruce, M.D.; Marjorie Charney; Clement B.P. Cobb, M.D.; John R. Cobb, M.D.; Carol Colbert, B.A.; Elizabeth S. Cole, M.S.W.; Frances Connor, Ph.D.; Michael Cook, B.A.; Velma Davies, R.N.; Ralph De Palma, M.D.; Lucy Helen Dunn, M.A.; Edwin Eigner, M.D.; Mary S. Fisher, Ph.D.; Mary Hamm Flumerfelt, B.A.; Lewis Fraad, M.D.; David Friedman, M.D.; Edwin Gerrish, M.D.; Harry Gold, M.D.; Sidonie M. Gruenberg; Hiram Hardesty, M.D.; William W. Heroy, M.D.; Jiri Herrmann; G.K. Hourwich, B.S.; Frederick C. Hunt, M.D.; Frances L. Ilg, M.D.; Donald Jackson, M.D.; John Kaster, M.D.; John Kennell, M.D.; Mary Lescaze; Milton I. Levine, M.D.; Samuel Z. Levine, M.D.; Jean Marzollo, M.A.T.; Diane Meslin; Fran Miller, B.A.; John Montgomery, M.D.; Hamden C. Moody, M.D.; Gisela Moriarty; Frank Mueller; Marjorie Mueller; Norma Nero; Pearl Nickels; Robert Nickels, M.S.W.; Charles O'Regan, M.D.; Peggy Daly Pizzo, M.Ed.; Marian Putnam, M.D.; John Reinhart, M.D.; Oscar M. Schloss, M.D.; Milton J.E. Senn, M.D.; Betty R. Shreve, M.S.; Carl H. Smith, M.D.; Norma Spector; Samuel Spector, M.D.; Jessie Stanton; Linda Steckelberg; Marion Stranahan, M.D.; Rebecca S. Straus, M.A.; Irving Sunshine, M.D.; Sophie van S. Theis, L.H.D.; K.E. Thomsett; William Wallace, M.D.; Myron E. Wegman, M.D.; E.R. Woodyatt; Lois Woodyatt; Caroline B. Zachry, Ph.D.

* * *

ACKNOWLEDGMENTS

From Dr. Rothenberg: I am very grateful to the following colleagues and friends for their generous support and technical assistance: Molly Bennett-Kaufman, C.R.N., P.N.P.; Edwin L. Bierman, M.D.; Lawrence Corey, M.D.; Treuman Katz, Chief Executive Officer, and the Board of Trustees of Children's Orthopedic Hospital and Medical Center; Lauri Lowen; Edgar K. Marcuse, M.D.; Tona McGuire, Ph.D.; Bette O'Donnell, R.D.; Linda Quan, M.D.; Mark A. Richardson, M.D.; John L. Short, M.D.; David Tapper, M.D.; and Jerome Roth.

My warmest thanks go to my Administrative Secretary, Ms. Barbara K. Lovseth, for her endless endurance, patience, skill, and good humor—and her many helpful suggestions—in the preparation of the manuscript.

My thanks to Beverly Lewis, our editor, and all the other Pocket Books staff who provided expert advice and guidance for this fifth edition.

I want to thank Dr. Ben Spock, my teacher, colleague, and friend. He has patiently guided me through this project with an extraordinary blend of humility, simplicity, and wisdom.

My wife, Jo, with her emotional and technical support, has made my participation in this work possible.

To Jane

In the first of the three years it took to write this book in the 1940s, Jane typed the original draft of the manuscript from my slow, slow dictation, from 9 P.M. when we finished dinner (after a full day of practice) until 1 A.M. She figured out such details as how many diapers, sheets, pads, nighties, shirts, bottles, and nipples should be recommended. She tested the various ways to prepare formulas, to make sure they worked.

When it became apparent that the job would never be done if we continued our social life, she suggested we give it up immediately—a real deprivation.

In the second year of writing, when I was in the Navy stationed outside New York City and couldn't get off duty in the daytime, Jane held consultations with specialists and publishers.

In the third year, when I was transferred to California and the book was near completion, it was Jane who spent hundreds of hours on the last-minute revisions and indexing. She took down the changes I spelled out over the long-distance phone at 2 A.M. (I couldn't get my calls through to New York until then), and later in the morning rushed them to the publisher. She was endlessly resourceful. Her advice was always practical and wise. The book couldn't have been what it is without her.

B.S.

Mary Morgan made special contributions to this 5th edition. It was she who first suggested Dr. Rothenberg as a collaborator, because she had read and admired his writings on the harmful effects on children of television violence. She took part in the interviewing of the four final candidates, in the selection of Dr. Rothenberg, and in all the endless discussion with the lawyers about the details of the agreement between the collaborating authors.

B.S.

Baby and Child Care

The Parents' Part

TRUST YOURSELF

1. You know more than you think you do. Soon you're going to have a baby. Maybe you have one already. You're happy and excited, but if you haven't had much experience, you wonder whether you are going to know how to do a good job. Lately you have been listening more carefully to your friends and relatives when they talk about bringing up a child. You've begun to read articles by experts in the magazines and newspapers. After the baby is born, the doctors and nurses will begin to give you instructions, too. Sometimes it sounds like a very complicated business. You find out all the vitamins a baby needs and all the immunizations. One mother tells you that egg should be given early because of its iron, and another says that egg should be delayed to avoid allergy. You hear that a baby is easily spoiled by being picked up too much but also that a baby must be cuddled plenty; that fairy tales make children nervous, and that fairy tales are a wholesome outlet.

Don't take too seriously all that the neighbors say. Don't be overawed by what the experts say. Don't be afraid to trust your own common sense. Bringing up your child won't be a complicated job if you take it easy, trust your own instincts, and follow the directions that your doctor gives you. We know for a fact that the natural loving care that kindly parents give their children is a hundred times more valuable than their knowing how to pin a diaper on just right or how to make a formula expertly. Every time you pick your baby up—let's assume it's a girl—even if you do it a little awkwardly at first, every time you change her, bathe her, feed her, smile at her, she's getting a feeling that she belongs to you and that you belong to her. Nobody else in the world, no matter how skillful, can give that to her.

It may surprise you to hear that the more people have studied different methods of bringing up children, the more they have come to the conclusion that what good mothers and fathers instinctively feel like doing for their babies is usually best, after all. Furthermore, all parents do their best job when they have a natural, easy confidence in themselves. Better to make a few mistakes from being natural than to do everything letter-perfect out of a feeling of worry.

Prenatal classes for expectant mothers and fathers are provided in many communities by the Visiting Nurse Association, the Red Cross, or the city or county health department. They are very helpful in discussing the questions and problems that all expectant parents have concerning pregnancy, delivery, and care of the baby.

In Section 106 I talk about alternative birthing methods and how to find out more about them.

2. How you learn to be a parent. Fathers and mothers don't really find out how to care for and manage children from books and lectures, though these may have value in answering specific questions and doubts. They learned the basics from the way they themselves were handled while they were children. That's what they were always practicing when they "played house" and cared for their dolls.

You'll find that you learn the rest gradually through the experience of caring for your children. It's taking care of your baby, finding out that you can feed, change, bathe, and burp successfully, and that your baby responds contentedly to your ministrations that gives you the feelings of familiarity, confidence, and love. A solid relationship and a mutual trust are established very early. Then when your baby, let's say a girl, begins to feel like a separate person with ideas and a will of her own, at about a year, you and she will have a solid basis for coping with such common problems as excessive explorativeness or negativism.

All parents expect to influence their children, but many are surprised to find that it's a two-way street and that they learn and gain from their parenting and their children. In other words, parenting is an enormously influential developmental step for adults in their own lives.

ENJOY YOUR BABY

3. Don't be afraid of your baby. You'd think from what some people—including some doctors—say about babies demanding attention that they come into the world determined to get their parents under their thumbs by hook or by crook. This isn't true. Your baby is born to be a reasonable, friendly human being.

Don't be afraid to feed her when you think she's really hungry. If you are mistaken, she'll merely refuse to take much.

Don't be afraid to love her and enjoy her. Every baby needs to be smiled at, talked to, played with, fondled—gently and lovingly—just as much as she needs vitamins and calories. That's what will make her a person who loves people and enjoys life. The baby who doesn't get any loving will grow up cold and unresponsive.

Don't be afraid to respond to other desires of hers as long as they seem sensible to you and as long as you don't become a slave to her. When she cries in the early weeks, it's because she's uncomfortable for some reason or other—maybe it's hunger or indigestion, or fatigue, or tension. The uneasy feeling you have when you hear her cry, the feeling that you want to comfort her, is meant to be part of your nature, too. Being held, rocked, or walked may be what she needs.

Spoiling doesn't come from being good to a baby in a sensible way, and it doesn't come all of a sudden. Spoiling comes on gradually when parents are too afraid to use their common sense or when they really want to be slaves and encourage their babies to become slave drivers.

Everyone wants the child to turn out to be healthy in her habits and easy to live with. But each child herself wants to eat at sensible hours and later to learn good table manners. Her bowels (as long as the movements don't become too hard) will move according to their own healthy pattern, which may or may not be regular; and when she's a lot older and wiser, you can show her where to sit to move them. She will develop her own pattern of sleep according to her own needs. In all these habits she will sooner or later want to fit into the family's way of doing things, with only a minimum of guidance from you.

4. Enjoy children as they are—that's how they'll grow up best. Every baby's face is different from every other's. In the same way, every baby's pattern of development is different. One may be very advanced in her general bodily strength and coordination, an early sitter, stander, walker—a sort of infant athlete. And yet she may be slow in doing careful, skillful things with her fingers, or in talking. Even babies who are athletes in rolling over, standing, and creeping may turn out to be slow to learn to walk. Babies who are advanced in their physical activities may be very slow in teething, and vice versa. Children who turn out later to be smart in schoolwork may have been so slow in beginning to talk that their parents were afraid for a while that they were dull; and children who have just an ordinary amount of intelligence are sometimes very early talkers.

I am purposely picking out examples of children with mixed rates of development to give you an idea of what a jumble of different qualities and patterns of growth each individual person is composed.

One baby is born to be big boned and square and chunky, while another will always be small boned and delicate. Some individuals really seem to be born to be fat. If they lose weight during an illness, they gain it back promptly afterward. The troubles that they have in the world never take away their appetites. The opposite kind of individuals stay on the thin side, even when they have the most nourishing food to eat, even though life is running smoothly for them.

Love and enjoy your children for what they are, for what they look like, for what they do, and forget about the qualities that they don't have. I don't give you this advice just for sentimental reasons. There's a very important practical point here. The children who are appreciated for what they are, even if they are homely, or clumsy, or slow, will grow up with confidence in themselves—happy. They will have a spirit that will make the best of all the capacities that they have, and of all the opportunities that come their way. They will make light of any handicaps. But the children who have never been quite accepted by their parents, who have always felt that they were not quite right, will grow up lacking confidence. They'll never be able to make full use of what brains, what skills, what physical attractiveness they have. If they start life with a handicap, physical or mental, it will be multiplied tenfold by the time they are grown up.

5. Babies aren't frail. "I'm so afraid I'll hurt her if I don't handle her right," a parent often says about her first baby. You don't have to worry; you have a pretty tough baby. There are many ways to hold her. If her head drops backward by mistake, it won't hurt her. The open spot on her skull (the fontanel) is covered by a tough membrane—tough as canvas—that isn't easily injured. The system to control body temperature is working quite well by the time she weighs 7 pounds if she's covered halfway sensibly. She has good resistance to most germs. During a family cold epidemic, she's apt to have it the mildest of all. If she gets her head tangled in anything, she has a strong instinct to struggle and yell. If she's not getting enough to eat, she will probably cry for more. If the light is too strong for her eyes, she'll blink and fuss. (You can take her picture with a flashbulb, even if it does make her jump.) She knows how much sleep she needs, and takes it. She can care for herself pretty well for a person who can't say a word and knows nothing about the world.

6. A baby at birth is usually disappointing looking to a parent who hasn't seen one before. Her skin is coated with a soft white wax, which, if left on, will be absorbed slowly and will lessen the chance of rashes during the hospital stay. Her skin underneath is apt to be very red. Her face tends to be puffy and lumpy, and there may be black-and-blue marks from forceps. The head is misshapen from "molding" during labor—low in the forehead, elongated at the back, and quite lopsided. Occasionally there may be, in addition, a hematoma, a localized bleeding under the scalp that sticks out as a distinct bump and takes weeks to go away. A couple of days after birth there may be a touch of jaundice—a yellowish tint of the skin—which is visible for about a week. (Jaundice that comes the first day or is very noticeable or lasts more than a week should be reported to the doctor.) At the base of the spine, there is often a bluish-gray spot, the "Mongolian spot," which fades gradually.

The baby's body is covered all over with fuzzy hair, which is usually shed in about a week. For a couple of weeks afterward there is apt to be a dry scaling of the skin, which is also shed. Some babies have black hair on the scalp at first, which may come far down on the forehead. The first hair, whatever its color or texture, comes out, and the new hair that grows in, sooner or later, may be quite different in all respects.

BODILY CONTACT AND OTHER BONDS

7. We've put distance between mothers and babies. Before birth, babies are not only enveloped and warmed and nourished by their mothers, they participate in every bodily movement their mothers make.

After birth, in many of the more natural, nonindustrial parts of the world, most babies are held against their mothers all day long by cloth carriers of one kind or another. They continue to share in all their mothers' movements as their mothers go about their regular jobs whatever they may be: food gathering and preparing, tilling, weaving, house care. The babies are breast-fed the instant they whimper. They not only hear but feel the vibrations of their mothers' words and songs.

In many societies, as babies get a little older, they are carried about most of the day on the hips of their slightly older sisters.

Our society has thought up a dozen ingenious ways to put distance between mothers and their babies.

It invented anesthetized childbirth, so a mother misses the

dramatic evidence of having carried and borne her baby herself. Babies are whisked away to a nursery where other people care for them, leaving mothers with the impression they are not very competent. Babies are fed cow's milk from bottles, so mothers and babies lose the opportunity for the most intimate bond in child rearing.

We've thought up the idea of propping bottles on babies' chests so that parents can be tending to other chores during the relatively short periods when young babies are awake and feeding.

To us it seems natural to put our babies on flat firm mattresses, in immobile cribs, preferably in quiet rooms.

We have infant seats in which babies can be strapped so that they don't have to be held when they're awake or restless or being moved about.

We put babies in pens where they can be kept out of trouble without having to be picked up, moved, or carried.

Two doctor friends of mine, John Kennell and Marshall Klaus, who have spent months observing natural baby care in an Indian village in Guatemala, point out that there appears to be no spitting, no crying, no fretfulness, no colic there. Yet mothers have never heard of burping.

Drs. Kennell and Klaus have also watched what mothers in America naturally do when allowed to have their babies with them soon after birth. They don't just look at them. They spend a lot of time touching their limbs and bodies and faces with their fingers. Months later these mothers have easier relations with their babies and their babies are more responsive than is the case where mothers don't have these opportunities to touch soon after birth.

I think that parents in our society should be aware of how different—or even peculiar—our methods are compared to what comes naturally in simpler societies.

8. How to be natural. I'd draw the following conclusions:

Natural childbirth and rooming-in should be available for all who want them. (If the parents who would like them will all make a point of asking for them, all hospitals, doctors, and nurses will eventually get the message.)

Mothers and fathers should have their baby to hold and

fondle for an hour after the baby is born, especially if rooming-in is not available.

Breast-feeding should be encouraged, especially by nurses and doctors, and relatives.

Bottle propping should be avoided—except when it can't be avoided, as when a mother of twins has no help and has to prop for one baby, at least, at each feeding.

Mothers and fathers should try to use a cloth carrier more than the infant seat for going places with the young baby and for comforting the baby when fussy or colicky. The carrier is even more valuable when used to carry the baby on the chest rather than on the back.

STRICTNESS OR PERMISSIVENESS?

9. This looms as a big question for many new parents. A great majority of them find the right answer in a little while. For a few parents it remains a worrisome question, no matter how much experience they've had.

I may as well let the cat out of the bag right away as far as my opinion goes and say that strictness or permissiveness is not the real issue. Good-hearted parents who aren't afraid to be firm when it is necessary can get good results with either moderate strictness or moderate permissiveness. On the other hand, a strictness that comes from harsh feelings or a permissiveness that is timid or vacillating can each lead to poor results. The real issue is what spirit the parent puts into managing the child and what attitude is engendered in the child as a result.

10. We've been through a big transition. It's hard to get any perspective on this topic without taking a historical view. Styles in strictness vary from one period to another. The Victorian Age was quite strict, for instance, about manners and modesty. In the twentieth century, especially after World War I, a reaction set in. Several factors pushed it along. The great American pioneers in educational research, like John

Dewey and William Kilpatrick, showed that a child learns better and faster with a method of teaching that makes allowance for individual readiness to progress and that recognizes that all children are eager to learn if the subject matter is suitable. Freud and his followers showed that harsh toilet training or frightening a child about sex can distort personality and lead to neurosis. Studies of delinquents and criminals revealed that most of them had suffered more from lack of love in childhood than from lack of punishment. These discoveries, among others, encouraged a general relaxation in child discipline and a greater effort to give children what they seemed to need as individuals. Several wise leaders in American pediatrics, Aldrich and Powers and Gesell, began to introduce a similar philosophy into the medical care of babies and children. But physicians remained strict about infant feeding right into the 1940s, because they still feared that irregular schedules and irregular amounts of formula might bring on the severe diarrheal diseases that used to cause so many infant deaths. Then the experiments of Dr. Preston McLendon and Ms. Frances P. Simsarian with the "self-demand" schedule, published in 1942, helped to convince doctors that most babies can do very well choosing their own feeding times and will remain healthy. Since then, there has been a rapid and widespread shift in medical practice. Today a majority of American babies are being put on more or less flexible schedules from the beginning.

Doctors who used to conscientiously warn young parents against spoiling are now encouraging them to meet their baby's needs, not only for food, but for comforting and loving.

These discoveries and these changes of attitudes and methods have benefited most children and parents; as a result, there are fewer tense ones, more happy ones.

But it's not possible for a civilization like ours to go through such a change of philosophy—it really amounts to a revolution—without raising doubts in many parents' minds and without getting some parents thoroughly mixed up. It's basic human nature to tend to bring up your children in about the same way as you were brought up. It's easy enough to pick up new ideas about vitamins and immunizations. But if your upbringing was fairly strict in regard to obedience, manners, sex, truthfulness, then it's natural, it's almost inevitable, that you will feel strongly inside about such matters when raising your own children. You may have changed your theories because of what you've studied or read or heard, but when your child does something that would have been considered bad in your own childhood, you'll probably find yourself becoming more tense, or anxious, or angry than you imagined possible. This is nothing to be ashamed of. This is the way Nature expects human beings to learn child care—from their own childhood. This is how different civilizations have managed to remain stable and carry on their ideals from generation to generation.

The reason that most parents have been able to do a good job with their children during the past fifty years of changing theory is that they themselves had been brought up to be reasonably happy, were comfortable about raising their children the same way, and didn't follow any new theory to extremes. When doctors were emphasizing regularity, confident parents followed a regular schedule in general (and **most** babies adjusted to it **most** of the time), but they weren't afraid to make an occasional exception when the baby became painfully hungry ahead of time, because they felt in their bones that this was right.

When doctors more recently have been emphasizing flexibility, confident parents haven't carried this to extremes, either. They don't let a sleepy but obstinate baby refuse to be put to bed, because they know very well (mostly from their own childhood) that bedtime is bedtime and that theories of flexibility have very little to do with this situation.

11. Parents who become confused with new theories are often of two kinds. There are, first of all, those who have been brought up with too little confidence in their own judgment. If you don't dare trust yourself, you **have** to follow what someone else says, willy-nilly. A second group are those parents who feel that they were brought up too severely. They remember the resentment they felt toward their parents at times, and they don't want their children to feel that way about them. But this is a very difficult situation. If you want to raise your children the way you were raised, you have a definite pattern to follow. You know just how obedient, how helpful, how polite, you want them to be. You don't have to stop and think. But if you want to treat them quite differently from the way you were treated—more indulgently, for instance, or more as equals—you don't have any pattern of how far to carry it. If things begin to get out of hand—if, for example, your child begins to take advantage of your permissiveness—it's harder to find your way back onto the right track. The child makes you mad, all right, but the madder you get the guiltier you feel for fear you'll step into the very pattern you were determined to avoid.

Of course, I'm making all this sound too black or white. We all start out as young parents partly agreeing, partly disagreeing, with the methods our parents used. It's a matter of degree. And most of us find a compromise that works reasonably well. I have been exaggerating in order to make clear the difficulty that some parents have had.

12. Stick to your convictions. I think that good parents who naturally lean toward strictness should stick to their guns and raise their children that way. Moderate strictness—in the sense of requiring good manners, prompt obedience, orderliness—is not harmful to children so long as the parents are basically kind and so long as the children are growing up happy and friendly. But strictness is harmful when the parents are overbearing, harsh, chronically disapproving, or make no allowances for a child's age and individuality. This kind of severity produces children who are either meek and colorless or mean to others.

Parents who incline to an easygoing kind of management, who are satisfied with casual manners as long as the child's attitude is friendly, or who happen not to be particularly strict—for instance, about promptness or neatness—can also raise children who are considerate and cooperative, as long as the parents are not afraid to be firm about those matters that do seem important to them.

When parents get unhappy results from too much permissiveness, it is not so much because they demand too little, though this is part of it. It is more because they are timid or guilty about what they ask or because they are unconsciously encouraging the child to rule the roost.

WHAT ARE YOUR AIMS IN RAISING A CHILD?

The rearing of children is more and more puzzling for parents in the twentieth century because we've lost a lot of our old-fashioned convictions about what kind of morals and ambitions and characters we want them to have. We've even lost our convictions about the purpose of human existence. Instead we have come to depend on psychological concepts. They've been helpful in solving many of the smaller problems but they are of little use in answering the major questions.

You may not be conscious of these changes—because you are so much a part of these times or because you grew up in an unusually stable family.

13. Other countries and times. In the past it was assumed in many countries that humanity's main function in the world—over and above making a living—was to serve God, by carrying out his purposes as revealed by religion. That's why in the Middle Ages the churches were by far the most imposing buildings. Much the same was true in America in the Colonial period. Children never had any idea that life was for their fulfillment. They were constantly exhorted to overcome their base natures in order to grow up to be pleasing in God's eyes.

In other places, especially in the past hundred years or so, it has been taught that people's purpose is to serve their country. This was true to a degree of France in Napoleon's time, and during the British empire and the German empire. It has been even more true of some modern states, not only of a Communist state like the Soviet Union but of a democratic one like Israel.

In those places, parents and teachers are in agreement with leaders about what virtues are to be encouraged in children:

cooperativeness, studiousness, dedication to the specific principles of the nation. Parents don't have to keep wondering and worrying about whether they are doing the right thing.

In even more parts of the world, it has always been assumed that children are born and raised to serve the aims of the family—what sociologists call the extended family or the clan. In childhood and youth they are to prepare themselves for work at the jobs which are considered the valuable ones by their particular family. They must, as children and later as grown-ups, revere and defer to their elders. Even in marrying, in many countries, they must accept marriages that are arranged by their parents for the purpose of advancing the family's welfare.

14. Child-centered United States. In our country today, very few children are raised to believe that their principal destiny is to serve their family, their country or God. Generally we've given them the feeling that they are free to set their own aims and occupations in life according to their inclinations. In a majority of cases these aims are visualized mainly in material terms.

The tendency is for American parents to consider the child at least as important as themselves—perhaps potentially more important. An English anthropologist said that whereas in other countries children are taught to look up to their parents as rather distinguished superior people, whatever their actual place in the society, the remarkable thing about the United States is that parents will say to their child, "If you don't do better than I've done, I won't think much of you." This is an upside-down respect. This is why the United States has often been called child-centered.

In other lands young parents gain confidence about aims and methods for rearing their children from family traditions and from having the grandparents nearby to advise and help them. These comforts have often been lacking in America. Our ancestors left their homelands because they were impatient with old ways and had the courage to try the unknown. Their descendants ever since have been restlessly moving from place to place in search of opportunity, often raising their children hundreds of miles away from any relatives. So they've had to turn to professional advisers and books and new theories for the help they needed.

I want to give a couple of small examples of how the child-centered, psychological approach can leave parents in the lurch unless it is backed up by a moral sense. Jealous quarreling among brothers and sisters has recently been tolerated **much more** than it was in previous generations. The psychological reasoning has been that jealousy is normal; if it is inhibited too severely, by making a child feel excessively guilty, it can cause various distortions of the personality. Parents shouldn't be badgering their children over **every little** thing anyway. There is considerable truth in these concepts. But when parents have followed them too exclusively, without consideration for the rights of the family or the ethics of society, the jealous child has been allowed to be much too mean to the younger one, has kept the family in an uproar and ended up with a guilty conscience anyway, because of the cruelty she has gotten away with.

A student of 19 is becoming increasingly rude and even verbally abusive toward his mother, who is a highly conscientious person. She has come to the guilty conclusion—incorrectly—that she must have failed him somehow, so she responds submissively to his reproaches. He senses that it is not right for him to pick on his mother just because he is out of sorts in some other department of his life; yet, instinctively, he behaves worse and worse in order to get her to crack down.

You can see that psychological concepts don't help unless they are backed up by a sense of what's right and proper; they can seriously interfere with the operation of the parents' good sense; they can create further problems.

I doubt that parents here will ever want their children's ambitions to be subordinated to the wishes of the family or the needs of the country. However, I think that more of our children would grow up happier and more stable if they were acquiring a conviction, all through childhood, that the most important and most fulfilling thing that human beings can do is to serve humanity in some fashion and to live by their ideals. (This does not preclude their earning a living or seeking advancement.) This is why human beings behave better, feel more purposeful, have better mental health during wartime, for example, when they have a common purpose. And statistics show that there is less crime and less suicide during financial depressions, when people face a greater challenge. It's also **much easier** for the parents themselves, in meeting the hundred issues that come up every day with children—for instance, about politeness, chores, quarreling, schoolwork, dating—if they have their own principles. Then the answers to the detailed questions come more readily.

15. We are disillusioned. Fortunate are the parents with a strong religious faith. They are supported by a sense of conviction and serenity in all their activities. Usually they can pass on their faith to at least a majority of their children.

Many of the people who have no religious faith are doubly deprived today, because they don't have much belief in humankind either. We live in a disenchanted, disillusioned age—not about things, but about human beings.

This has been evident in the increasing tendency in literature, plays, and movies in the past fifty years to play down the kindly and spiritual aspects of humanity and to focus on its crude, animal side. Manners in social life have been coarsened. Even greeting cards, instead of wishing invalids and relatives well, jeer at them. Art has rarely shown attractive people; it has omitted them altogether or made them hideous. Many youths have cultivated dishevelment as if they were ashamed to be human and a few of them have withdrawn from society altogether.

The disenchantment has been caused in part by the rapid strides in the sciences of biology, psychology, and sociology, which have seemed to stress the human being's closeness to other animals, the crudeness of basic instincts, the mechanicalness of behavior patterns. Perhaps even more basic has been the weakening of the authority of religion in the minds of many people, caused by the increased authority of the sciences. This has greatly diminished people's former feeling that they were very special and noble creatures created in God's image.

The realization that the Biblical description of Creation

cannot be taken literally has made many people question whether religious teachers have a solid basis for prescribing people's conduct and aims.

I believe that this disillusionment is based on a misunderstanding of human nature. It's true we are related by evolution to other animals. But we are also vastly different. We are idealistic in our aspirations. Our relationships are predominantly spiritual. Our capacity for abstract reasoning has enabled us to discover much of the meaning of the universe. We have invented fantastic machines. We have created beauty in all the arts. All this has been made possible by the aspirations kindled in us in early childhood by adoration of our parents. Whether or not people have religious faith, they can believe in the power of love and in their potentialities for good, if they understand the spiritual development of a child.

16. How human beings get their aspirations. In the 3- to 6-year-old period children mature by means of an intense adoration of their parents—not the parents as the neighbors see them but glorified. They overestimate their parents' wisdom, power, and attractiveness. The boy yearns to be like his idealized father and spends all day practicing, in activities and manner. At the same time he develops a strong romantic attachment to his mother and idolizes her as his feminine ideal. As such she will strongly influence his choice of a wife when he grows up.

For the girl it's the other way around. She yearns to be like her mother—in occupation and in having babies of her own. She forms a possessive romantic attachment to her father.

Because children are so very aware at this dependent age of how much their parents' love means to them, they are now inspired with a similar capacity to love generously their parents and other people. Out of this will eventually grow their devotion to their own children and their altruism toward humanity.

In this same age period several other significant psychological developments take place. Both girls and boys become fascinated with marriage and having babies. It is hard to convince boys that they can't grow babies inside themselves. Their frustrated rivalry with girls about this is believed to be one of the sources of creativity in the arts, inventions, and machines.

In Nature's scheme of things the intense attachments to the two parents, having served their purpose of setting the children's ideals and advancing their maturity, must then be greatly diminished, so that they can begin the next big step—between 6 and 12 years—of becoming emotionally more independent of parents and oriented instead toward the outside community and its ways of doing things. This is brought about by a dramatic shift in feelings toward each parent.

Children's romantic attachment to the parent of the opposite sex gradually arouses increasingly uncomfortable feelings of rivalry with the parent of the same sex. This forces them eventually, by about the age of 6 or 7, to suppress guiltily their possessiveness toward the parent of the opposite sex and, along with it, fascination with marriage, with having babies, and with sex differences. They are able to sublimate (transform) these interests into impersonal, abstract pursuits such as the three R's, science, nature study. They turn away impatiently from both parents as idols. Instead they revere God, government authorities, laws, and the heroes of history, fiction, and the comics.

It is fascinating to realize that what distinguishes human beings so sharply from other creatures are these attitudes developed soon after the age of 5: inhibition and sublimation of sexuality; interest in symbols, abstractions, systems, and rules; capacity for being inspired by heroes, God, and spiritual ideals. These very human characteristics are brought out first by the special loves for each parent and then by having to give up the romantic attachment to one because of fear of rivalry with the other.

The glandular pressures of adolescence break up this impersonal, middle-childhood adjustment. The child's sexual and romantic drive now insists on some form of expression and it gradually breaks through the old inhibitions. Nevertheless, part of it will still be held in reserve and invested in idealistic aspirations—to the degree that the parents have these. The boy's romantic adoration of his mother, suppressed for years, veiled, disembodied, now lends mystery, chivalry, and spirituality to his awakening love for a girl. He will want to protect, please, idolize her. Similarly, the girl's adoration of her father now invests her awakening love for a boy with the same qualities.

Human beings' idealization of the opposite sex also combines with their drive to create (Section 564) and this is a major inspiration for their creativity in architecture, engineering, technical inventiveness, scientific discovery, literature, drama, music, painting. A classic example is Dante's *Divine Comedy* which was inspired by and dedicated to Beatrice, a woman the poet had only seen, never known. To tie together this spiritual sequence: human beings can build a magnificent reality in adulthood out of what was only an illusion in early childhood—their loving, joyous, trusting, ingenuous, unrealistic overidealization of their two parents.

These capacities in people are developed highly in a few individuals, moderately in many, hardly at all in others. The capacity—for idealism, creativity, spirituality—is latent in all children. Whether they will realize them all will depend on their parents. At 3 and 4 years they will overidealize their parents anyway. If parents have aspirations, if they have a respect for themselves, for each other and for their children, then their offspring will continue to be inspired by their pattern, even after they appear to turn away from their parents in later childhood. If, on the other hand, parents have no interests beyond their bodily needs, their children's estimation of them will gradually shrink down to life size and they won't try to go beyond their parents' level.

17. Why we need idealistic children. A child raised to have ideals will have no lack of opportunities to apply them. There are enormous, frightening problems in our country and in the world. Through our reliance on initiative and materialism we have accomplished technological miracles. But as our physical needs are met it becomes embarrassingly evident that we have made no progress in human relations, in spiritual serenity, or in world security. Our rates of divorce, suicide, and crime are among the highest in the world. Our race relations are barbaric—a disgrace to a nation that pretends to believe in freedom, equality, and God. We have areas of poverty and demoralization in our own country that could be well on the way to solution in a year if we had the tendency to face our responsibilities. Millions of dollars are spent persuading us to buy automobiles with five times the necessary horsepower, and to buy cigarettes, which cause cancer.

We know how to produce food with fantastic efficiency but have held production down in spite of the fact that there are more hungry people in the world than ever before in history.

We have an overwhelming supply of the most powerful weapons the world has ever known. Yet we are in imminent danger of annihilation, with no solution remotely in sight and no sense of security. Because of our power we are interfering arrogantly in the affairs of other nations and arousing worldwide resentment. We are still spending billions each year on a race into space.

Our only realistic hope as I see it is to bring up our children with a feeling that they are in this world not for their own satisfaction but primarily to serve others. Children are proud to think that they can be truly useful and will rise to the challenge. This can begin very young. Babies of 9 months shouldn't be allowed to get the impression that it's all right to pull their mother's hair or bite her cheek but that they owe her respect. Between 1 and 2 years they shouldn't be allowed deliberately to break their own possessions nor to make a deliberate mess with them. By 2 they can be expected to go through the motions of helping pick up the playthings. By 3 they should have such small chores as helping to set the table or empty the wastebaskets, even though they don't save parents much work. By 7 or 8 they should be carrying out genuinely useful jobs each day.

In family conversations children should hear their parents' concern about problems of the community, the nation, the world. They should see that their parents are contributing directly to the solutions—by participating in the work of local groups and committees.

In school, children should be studying not only the great accomplishments of their nation but its deficiencies and mistakes. Their schools should contain children from various races and backgrounds, not just out of fairness to minority groups but so that all kinds of children can learn to appreciate and get along with each other. High school and university students, while they are preparing for their eventual occupations, should spend time analyzing the unsolved problems in their own chosen fields—the human as well as the technical problems. It's also important, I think, for youths while they are still in school to volunteer or work for pay in part-time jobs where they can serve people who have serious, unmet needs, then discuss these problems in class so that they won't acquire critical or condescending attitudes toward those different from themselves.

18. Can you make superkids? When children are neglected or consistently ignored ("How many times have I told you? Stop bothering me with your questions."), their spirits and their minds will fail to develop fully.

At the other extreme, it has been discovered by certain psychologists that if you try hard enough you can teach a 3-year-old to write with a special ($10,000) typewriter and you can even teach your 1-year-old to recognize flashcards. Such discoveries have inspired some parents with the hope that with the right playthings from infancy, the right mental stimulation at home and in school, a child can be developed into a genius and be well on the way to a brilliant career. I think that this particular kind of parental ambition, though understandable in a country where intelligence is so highly prized and at a time when computer experts seem to hold the key to the future, is mistaken and apt to backfire. Mental capacity is only one aspect of a person and may well fail to make him or her a success in life unless it is balanced with warmth and common sense. When parents concentrate on the intellect alone, they may make their child a somewhat lop-sided person who won't fit into any job or won't get any joy out of life.

What stimulates normal, well-rounded development—emotional, social and intellectual? Babies and children, by their inborn nature, keep reaching out to people and to things. Fond parents, watching and coaxing, respond enthusiastically to their baby's first smiles with smiles of their own, head noddings and declarations of love. Repetitions of this scene, every waking hour for months, along with hugs, comforting during misery, and the offering of food at times of hunger keep reinforcing feelings of love and trust. These form the foundation on which the child's future relationships with all the other people in her life will be built. Even her interest in things, and her later capacity to deal with ideas and concepts, in school and in occupation, will depend on this foundation of love and trust.

At 1 and 2 years of age children mature by striving to copy their parents' actions, and parents foster this by showing their pleasure at each tiny accomplishment. That's how vocabulary expands at 2, for example. By 3 years, children become intensely curious about everything they see or hear and they turn to their parents for explanations and encouragement. Between 3 and 6, children mature emotionally and intellectually by striving to pattern themselves after their beloved parents.

This natural interplay between the children reaching out and the parents responding has been sufficient through the ages to produce plenty of bright, capable, sociable, loving young people. Special drills and special equipment are not necessary, at least until the school years.

If you try to make children "super" through **your** interest and initiative, you may rub them the wrong way and create aversion to your plan. Or you may succeed and make them one-sided robots.

The same risks apply, I think, in overemphasizing a little girl's prettiness or in trying too hard to make a boy into an athlete. Children should grow up feeling that they are appreciated and loved for their whole person or personality, not primarily for their brains or their looks or their muscle or their musical ability. It's all right to appreciate a child's special gift, as long as it is considered of secondary importance.

PARENTS ARE HUMAN

19. They have needs. Books about child care, like this one, put so much emphasis on all the needs that children have—for love, for understanding, for patience, for consistency, for firmness, for protection, for comradeship, for calories and vitamins—that parents sometimes feel physically and emotionally exhausted just from reading about what is expected of them. They get the impression that they are meant to have no needs themselves. They can't help feeling that an author who seems to be standing up for children all the time must be critical of parents when anything goes wrong.

It would be only fair if this book had an equal number of pages about the genuine needs of parents, the frustrations they constantly meet not only in the home but outside it, how tired they get, how much help their children could be if they were more considerate. The fact is that child rearing is a long, hard job and that parents are just as human as their children.

20. Some children are a lot more difficult than others. There is considerable evidence that different children are born with quite different temperaments. Parents can't order what they want. They take what they get. But parents have well-formed personalities, too, which they can't change overnight. One gentle couple might be ideally suited to raise a boy with a gentle, sensitive nature, able to give him the freedom he needs in order to develop into an independent, capable person. They may not be nearly so ready for an energetic, assertive boy. They may find him uncomfortable, baffling, and challenging, no matter how much they love him. Another couple may handle a spunky son they call Butch with ease and joy but be quite disappointed with a quiet one. Parents do the best they know how with the kind of child they receive.

21. At best, there's lots of hard work and deprivation. There is an enormous amount of hard work in child care—preparing the proper diet, washing clothes, changing diapers, cleaning up messes that an infant makes with food and that an older child makes with play, stopping fights and drying tears, listening to stories that are hard to understand, joining in games and reading stories that aren't very exciting to an adult, trudging around zoos and museums and carnivals, responding to pleas for help with homework, being slowed down in housework, yardwork, and cellar work by eager helpers, going to parent–teacher association meetings on evenings when parents are tired.

Children's needs account for a good part of the family budget, from the high rent or mortgage on a large enough house to the shoes that wear out or are outgrown in no time at all.

Children keep parents from parties, trips, theaters, meetings, games, friends. The fact that you prefer having children, wouldn't trade places with a childless couple for anything, doesn't alter the fact that you still miss your freedom.

Of course, parents don't have children because they want to be martyrs, or at least they shouldn't. They have them because they love children and want some of their very own. They also love children because they remember being loved so much by their parents in their own childhood. Taking care of their children, seeing them grow and develop into fine people, gives most parents—despite the hard work—their greatest satisfaction in life. This is creation. This is our visible immortality. Pride in other worldly accomplishments is usually weak in comparison.

22. Needless self-sacrifice and excessive preoccupation. Many conscientious young people facing the new responsibility of parenthood feel inside that they are called on to give up all their freedom and all their former pleasures, not as a matter of practicality, but almost as a matter of principle. Others just get obsessed. They forget their hobbies and interests. Even if they do sneak off when a good chance comes, they feel too guilty to get full enjoyment. They come to bore their friends and each other. In the long run, they chafe at the imprisonment. They can't help resenting the baby unconsciously.

I think that the temptation to become totally absorbed in the baby should be strenuously resisted. After you have made all the necessary sacrifices of time and effort, even things up by going out together. You can squeeze in your hobbies and reading and see friends (make a Herculean effort not to talk to them about the baby). Remember to look at each other, smile at each other, and say loving things often. This will all be good for the child as well as for yourselves.

23. Parents should expect something from their children. Since having children does mean giving up so much, good parents naturally do, and should, expect something from their children in return: not spoken thanks for being born or being cared for—that's too much—but considerateness, affectionateness, and willingness to accept the parents' standards and ideals. The parents want these qualities in their children not only selfishly, for themselves, but because they want their children to grow up to live cooperatively and happily with others.

If parents are too hesitant in asking for reasonable behavior —because they have misunderstood theories of self-expression, because they are self-sacrificing by nature, or because they are afraid of making their children dislike them—they can't help resenting the bad behavior that comes instead. They keep getting angrier underneath, without knowing what to do about it. This bothers the children, too. It makes them feel guilty and scared, but it also makes them meaner and all the more demanding. If, for example, babies acquire a taste for staying up in the evening and the parents are afraid to deny them this pleasure, they may, over a period of several months, turn into disagreeable tyrants who keep their mothers and fathers walking for hours. Parents are bound to dislike them for their tyranny. If parents can be encouraged to be firm, it's amazing how fast the children will sweeten up and the parents will, too.

In other words, parents can't feel right toward their children in the long run unless they can make them behave reasonably, and children can't be happy unless they are behaving reasonably.

24. Parents are bound to get cross. I think that idealistic young people approaching parenthood assume that if they are the right sort they will have unlimited patience and love for their innocent baby. But this is not humanly possible. When your baby girl has been crying angrily for hours, despite all your patient efforts to comfort her, you can't go on feeling sympathetic. She seems like a disagreeable, obstinate, unappreciative creature and you can't help feeling angry—really angry. Or your older son has done something that he knows very well he shouldn't have done. Maybe he was so fascinated with a breakable object of yours or so eager to join some children on the other side of the street that he couldn't resist the temptation. Or maybe he was cross at you for having denied him something or angry at the baby for receiving so much attention. So he misbehaved from simple spite. When a child disobeys a well-understood and reasonable rule, you can't simply be a cool statue of justice. Any good parent feels strongly about right and wrong. You were taught to feel that way back in your own childhood. It's your rule that has been broken. It's probably your possession that has been damaged. It's your child, about whose character you care a great deal, who has done wrong. It's inevitable that you feel indignant. The child naturally expects this and is not hurt by it if your reaction is fair.

Sometimes it takes you a long time to realize that you are losing your temper. The boy may have been putting on a series of irritating acts from the time he appeared at breakfast —making disagreeable remarks about the food, half deliberately knocking over a glass of milk, playing with something forbidden and breaking it, picking on a younger child—all of which you have tried to ignore in a supreme effort to be patient. Then at the final act, which perhaps isn't so bad, your resentment suddenly boils over, and it shocks you a little with its vehemence. Often when you look back over such a series of exasperating actions, you can see that the child has really been asking for firmness or punishment all morning and that it was your well-intentioned effort at overpatience that made him go from one provocation to another, looking for a check.

We all get cross with our children, also, because of the pressures and frustrations we are feeling from other directions altogether. A sort of comic-strip example that's true to life concerns the father who comes home on edge from troubles that he's having in his work; he criticizes his wife, who then snaps at the older boy for something that ordinarily brings no disapproval, and he in turn picks on his younger sister.

25. Better to admit crossness. So far we have been discussing the inevitability of parental impatience and resentment from time to time. But it's just as important to consider a related question: Can the parents comfortably accept their cross feelings? Parents who aren't excessively strict with themselves are always able to admit their irritation. A natural, outspoken good mother whose little boy has been bedeviling her is able to say to a friend, half jokingly, "I don't think I can stand being in the house with him for another minute," or "I'd enjoy giving him a thorough walloping." She may not carry out any of these thoughts, but she isn't ashamed to admit them to a sympathetic friend or to herself. It relieves her feelings to recognize them so clearly and to blow them off in talk. It also helps her to see what she has been putting up with and to be firmer in putting a stop to it.

It's the parents who set impossibly high standards for themselves, the parents who have angry feelings at times but can't believe that good parents should, who really suffer from them. When they detect such emotions stirring in themselves, they either feel unbearably guilty or try strenuously to deny them. But if a person tries to bury such feelings they only pop up somewhere else—as tenseness, for example, or tiredness or headache. Another indirect expression is overprotectiveness. A mother who can't ever admit that she feels antagonism toward her children imagines instead all the awful things that could beset them from other directions; she worries excessively about germs, or traffic. She tries to ward off these dangers by hovering over the children, and this tends to make them too dependent.

I'm not pointing out the problems created by denying crossness in order merely to relieve the uncomfortable feelings of parents. In general, what makes a parent miserable makes the child miserable, too. When a parent believes that antagonistic feelings are too horrible to admit, the child absorbs the same dread of them. In child guidance clinics, we see children who develop fears of imaginary dangers—fear of insects, fear of going to school, fear of being separated from their parents—that prove on investigation to be disguises for ordinary angry feelings toward their parents that these perfectionistic children dare not recognize.

To put it the other way around, children are happier around parents who aren't afraid to admit their anger, because then they can be more comfortable about their own. And justified anger that's expressed tends to clear the air and leave everyone feeling better. I am talking not about being rough on children but about admitting your feelings. And I don't mean that all the antagonism expressed toward children is justified. Here and there you see a harsh, unloving parent who abuses a child all hours of the day, verbally or physically, with little excuse and no shame. What I have been discussing is the irritation of parents whose conscientiousness and devotion to their children is plain to see.

A loving parent who feels angry **most** of the time (whether it's expressed openly or not) is suffering from a real emotional strain and deserves help from a psychiatrist or a social worker (Section 633). The anger may be coming from some entirely different direction.

26. Parents' quarrels. Arguments aren't shameful. Parents who disagree often make a great point of trying to conceal their arguments from their children and even imagine that they don't suspect that anything is up. It is certainly better to carry on heated fights when the children are out of the way, but it's a mistake to think that they aren't aware of family tensions. When a child stumbles in unexpectedly on a scene, I think it's much better for the parents to admit humanly that they have been having an argument than to suddenly become silent and severe and order the child out of the room. It helps to clear the air for everyone to admit that fights are one of the facts of life, even among grown-ups, that people can fight at times and still love and respect each other, that a fight doesn't mean the end of the world.

27. Children like to be kept on their good behavior. I've probably given a false impression by focusing so much on irritation. Most of us, when family life is running with fair smoothness, get cross or angry only during occasional crises, though, as we all know, there are more of these on some days than others. The way we avoid irritation the rest of the time, whether we realize it or not, is by keeping our children under reasonable control and by being extra firm or sufficiently disapproving when things first threaten to go wrong. Such firmness is one aspect of parental love. Firmness, by keeping children on the right track, keeps them lovable. And they love us for keeping them out of trouble.

PARENTAL DOUBTS ARE NORMAL

28. Mixed feelings about pregnancy. We have an ideal about motherhood that says that a woman is overjoyed when she finds that she is going to have a baby. She spends the pregnancy dreaming about the baby. When it arrives she slips into the maternal role with ease and delight. This is all true to a degree—more in one case, less in another. But it is of course only one side of the picture. Medical studies have brought out (what wise women have known all along) that there are normal negative feelings connected with a pregnancy, too, especially the first one.

To some degree, the first pregnancy spells the end of carefree youth—very important to Americans. The maidenly figure goes gradually into eclipse, and with it goes sprightly grace. Both eclipses are temporary but very real. The woman realizes that after the baby comes there will be distinct limitations of social life and other outside pleasures. No more hopping into the car on the spur of the moment, going anywhere the heart desires and coming home at any odd hour. The same budget has to be spread thinner, and her husband's attention, all of which has gone to her at home, will soon be going to two.

29. Feelings are different in every pregnancy. The changes to be expected because of the arrival of one more child do not look so drastic after you have had one or two, but medical experience shows that a mother's spirit may rebel at times during any pregnancy. There may be obvious reasons why one pregnancy is more strained—perhaps it came unexpectedly soon, or one of the parents is having tensions at work, or there is serious illness on either side of the family, or there is disharmony between mother and father. On the other hand, there may be no explanation visible to the naked eye.

An obstetrician I know says he sometimes senses an inner crisis with the second or third pregnancy in parents who had been happily looking forward to a family of that size. A mother who really wants more than one child may still be disturbed subconsciously, during the next pregnancy, with sudden doubts about whether she will have the time, the physical energy, or the unlimited stores of love that she imagines will be called for in taking care of another and another. Or the inner doubts may start with the father, who feels somewhat neglected as his wife becomes more and more preoccupied with the children. In either case, the blueness or grumpiness of one spouse soon has the other one feeling disappointed, too. To put it another way, each person, in order to keep on giving, must feel he or she is receiving something, too.

I don't want to make these reactions sound inevitable. I only want to reassure you that they do occur in the very best of parents and that in the great majority of cases they are temporary. The child's arrival proves to be less of a challenge than the parents had anticipated subconsciously, probably because they have grown in spirit in response to the need.

30. Love for the baby comes gradually. Many a woman who is pleased and proud to be pregnant finds it hard to feel a personal love for a baby she's never seen or felt. But when it begins to move, it helps her to believe that it's a real person, after all. As the pregnancy progresses, her thoughts turn more realistically to the baby, to what it will mean to care for it.

A great majority of those who admit that their first reaction to pregnancy was predominantly one of dismay (and there are plenty of good people who feel this way) are reassured to find that their acceptance of the pregnancy and their fondness for the baby reaches a comfortable level before the birth.

But even when the anticipation is all that could be desired, there is often a letdown for the inexperienced mother when the baby actually arrives. She expects to recognize the baby immediately as her own flesh and blood, to respond to the infant with an overwhelming rush of maternal feeling. But in many cases this doesn't happen the first day or even the first week. Instead it is a gradual process that isn't complete until they have been home together for a little while. This gradual process applies to fathers, too.

Most of us have been taught that it's not fair to a coming baby to hope and expect that it will be a girl or a boy, in case it turns out to be the opposite. I wouldn't take this too seriously. We can't really begin to imagine and love a future baby without picturing it as being one sex or the other. That's the very first step. I think that all expectant parents have a preference for a girl or boy during each pregnancy, even though most of them will be quite ready to love a baby who turns out to be the opposite. So enjoy your imaginary baby and don't feel guilty if another kind arrives.

31. Why feelings are different for different children. Are parents meant to love all their children equally? This question worries a lot of conscientious parents because they suspect that in some ways they don't. When they reproach themselves about this, I think they are expecting the impossible of themselves. Good parents love their children equally in the sense that they are equally devoted to each. They want the best out of life for each and will make any necessary sacrifice to achieve this. But since all children are quite different, no parent can **feel** just the same about any two of them, either in the sense of enjoying their special charms or being displeased by their special faults.

It's the feeling of particular irritation toward one child that makes parents feel most guilty, especially if there is no clear reason for it. A mother says, "This one **always** rubs me the wrong way. Yet I'm constantly trying to be sweeter to her and to overlook her bad behavior."

32. Some causes of dissatisfaction. The reasons why parents sometimes get off on the wrong foot with one child are quite varied and are usually hidden under the surface. Two possible factors were mentioned in Section 29: the parents may not have felt ready for this pregnancy or there may have been unusual family tensions during it. The baby himself may have got the parents off to the wrong start by being completely different from what they had been secretly expecting—a boy when they were looking for a girl, or a very homely baby when they were anticipating a beauty, or a frail infant compared to their other husky children. The infant may cry for several months with colic and seem to spurn her parents' efforts to comfort her. The father may be disappointed when his son turns out to be no athlete, no scrapper; the mother because he's no student. It doesn't matter that the parents are intelligent people who well know that they can't order the kind of baby they want most. Being human, they have irrational expectations and can't help feeling let down.

As children become a little older they may remind us,

consciously or unconsciously, of a brother, sister, father, or mother who made life hard for us at times. A mother's daughter may have traits like her younger sister, who used to be always in her hair—and yet she may have no conscious realization that this is the cause of a lot of her irritation.

A father may be excessively bothered by some particular characteristic in his young son—timidity, for instance—and never connect it with the fact that as a child he himself had a terrible time in overcoming timidity. You'd think that a person who has suffered a lot in trying to overcome what he considers a fault would be more sympathetic with it in his child. Usually it doesn't work that way.

33. Impatience and approval are part of child rearing. The very human tendency to react intensely to our children's behavior works positively for us, too: we strongly foster in our children the good traits that our parents fostered in us. We do it automatically, without having to think, because we learned our ideals so thoroughly in childhood. Otherwise, rearing our children would be ten times as hard as it is.

So it's human and normal and inevitable that we should feel quite differently about each of our children, that we should be impatient with certain characteristics in certain ones of them and proud of others. All these mixed attitudes are only different aspects of our deep feeling of obligation to bring up our children properly.

But if we feel too guilty about our chronic impatience with one child or another, it may produce increasing complications in our relations with her. Our guiltiness then gets to be harder on her than our irritation. This is discussed in Section 532.

34. The blue feeling. It's possible that you will find yourself feeling discouraged for a while when you first begin taking care of your baby. It's a fairly common feeling, especially with the first. You may not be able to put your finger on anything that is definitely wrong. You just weep easily. Or you may feel very bad about certain things. One woman whose baby cries quite a bit feels sure that he has a real disease, another that her husband has become strange and distant, another that she has lost all her looks.

A feeling of depression may come on a few days after the

baby is born or not till several weeks later. The commonest time is when a mother comes home from the hospital, where she has been waited on hand and foot, and abruptly takes over full care of baby and household. It isn't just the work that gets her down. She may even have someone to do all the work, for the time being. It's the feeling of being responsible for the whole household again, plus the entirely new responsibility of the baby's care and safety. Then there are all the physical and glandular changes at the time of birth, which probably upset the spirits to some degree.

The majority of mothers don't get discouraged enough in this period to ever call it depression. You may think it is a mistake to bring up unpleasant things that may never happen. The reason I mention it is that several mothers have told me afterward, "I'm sure I wouldn't have been so depressed or discouraged if I had known how common this feeling is. Why, I thought that my whole outlook on life had changed once and for all." You can face a thing much better if you know that a lot of other people have gone through it, too, and if you know that it's just temporary.

If you begin to feel at all depressed, try to get some relief from the constant care of the baby in the first month or two, especially if the child cries a great deal. Go to a movie, or to the beauty parlor, or to get yourself a new dress. Work on some new or unfinished project—writing, painting, sewing, building—something creative and satisfying. Visit a good friend occasionally. Take the baby along if you can't find anyone to baby-sit. Or get your old friends to come and see you. All of these are tonics. If you are depressed, you may not feel like doing these things. But if you make yourself do them, you will feel a lot better. And that's important for the baby and your husband as well as yourself. If the depression does not lift in a few days or if it is becoming worse, you should promptly get in touch with a psychiatrist, through your regular doctor. A psychiatrist can be of great assistance and comfort at such a time.

When a mother feels blue and thinks that her husband seems indifferent, there are two sides to consider. On the one hand, anyone who is depressed feels that other people are less friendly and affectionate. But on the other hand, it's natural for a father, being human, to feel left out when his wife and the rest of the household are completely wrapped up in the baby. So it's a sort of vicious circle. The mother (as if she didn't have enough to do already!) has to remember to pay some attention to her husband. And she should encourage him to share in the care of the baby.

35. Other feelings. Most parents find that they are more anxious than usual the first few weeks at home. They worry about the baby's crying and fretful spells, suspecting that something is seriously wrong. They worry about every sneeze and every spot of rash. They tiptoe into the baby's room to see whether she is still breathing. It's probably instinctive for parents to be overly protective at this period. I suppose it's Nature's way of being sure that the millions of new parents throughout the world, some of whom may be immature and inexperienced, take their new responsibility seriously. A little worrisomeness might be a good thing for some irresponsible types. But of course it hits hardest the very conscientious ones who need it least. Fortunately it wears off.

Another kind of mood shift sometimes occurs. At first, in the hospital, a woman may feel very dependent on the nurses and grateful for the care they give the baby. Then comes a quick change of heart: she becomes confident she can take care of the baby herself and secretly resents the fact that the nurses don't let her take over. If she has a practical nurse at home, she may go through these two stages again. It certainly is normal for a mother to want to take care of her own baby by herself. The main reason she may not have this feeling at the start is that she is convinced she is inadequate. The stronger the sense of inferiority, the stronger will be the determination to assert her competence when she gains the courage.

THE SUPPORTIVE FATHER IN PREGNANCY AND DELIVERY

36. A man reacts to his wife's pregnancy with various feelings: protectiveness of the wife, increased pride in the marriage, pride about his virility (that's one thing men always worry about to some degree), anticipatory enjoyment of the child. But there can also be, way underneath, a feeling of being left out (just as small children may feel rejected when they find mother is pregnant), which can be expressed as grumpiness toward his wife, wanting to spend more evenings with his men friends, or flirtatiousness with other women. These reactions are no help to his wife, who craves extra support at the start of this unfamiliar stage of her life.

The father is apt to feel particularly left out during the hospital period with his first baby. He helps to get his wife safely to the hospital, where there are dozens of people to take care of her. Then, unless he's permitted to be in the labor and delivery rooms, he's really alone. He sits in the waiting room with some old magazines and worries about how the labor is going, and after the delivery, he goes to his unbelievably lonely home. It's no wonder that a man may take this occasion to drink in company at a bar. Where he works he gets some attention, but an awful lot of it is kidding. When he goes to see his wife and baby, the hospital doesn't make him feel like the head of the family; he's just another visitor who's tolerated at certain hours. When the time comes to take the family home, the concern of the mother (and of the grandmother or other helper, if any) is all for the baby, and the father's function seems to be mainly that of porter. I don't mean by all this that a father expects the limelight or should have it at this time, but that he's apt to feel less important than usual and therefore let down. There's much less chance of a man feeling this way if he's been able to actively participate in his wife's labor and delivery. (See Section 106 on Alternative Birthing Methods.)

37. A father can now be an integral and essential part of the pregnancy and labor. He may go to prenatal doctor visits and attend childbirth classes with his wife. He may be an active participant in the labor and in some hospitals may "catch" the infant as it is born, cut the cord or carry the child to the nursery, watching over him while the mother is being cared for in the delivery room. He may have unlimited access to mother and infant during the hospitalization. If the mother is unwell or if the baby has special problems, he may be the

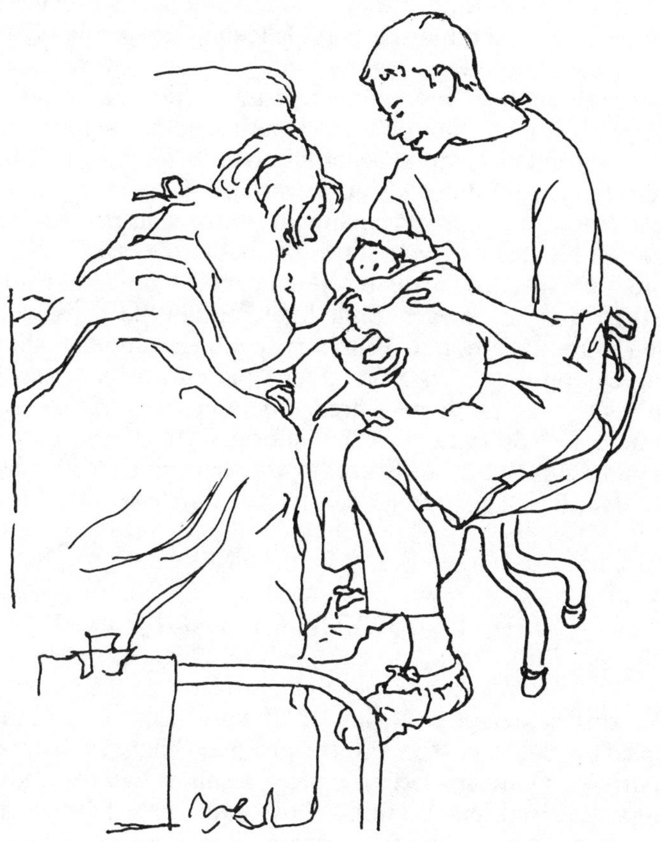

A father can now be an integral and essential part of the pregnancy and labor.

parent most actively involved with the baby in the early hours after the baby's birth. He no longer has to be the lonely, disgruntled onlooker.

38. The father's opportunity in the early weeks at home. A father shouldn't be surprised if he finds that he has mixed feelings at times toward his wife and toward his baby—during the pregnancy, during all the commotion of the labor and delivery stage, and after they are all home again. Nevertheless, he can remind himself that his feelings are probably not nearly so churned up as his wife's, especially after the homecoming. She has been through an intense glandular change. If it's her first baby, she can't help feeling anxious. Any baby will make great demands on her strength and spirits at first. What all this adds up to is that most women need a great deal of support and comfort from their husbands at this time. To be able to give a lot to the baby, they must receive more than usual. Partly it's the need of the father's full participation in the care of the baby, and in the housework. Even more it's emotional support: patience, understanding, appreciation, affection. The father's job may be complicated by the fact that if his wife is tired and upset she won't have the spirit to be appreciative of his efforts. In fact, she may be complaining. But if he realizes how much she needs his help and love, it will encourage him to give it anyway.

THE FAMILY IS CHANGING

In this subchapter I want to discuss—because of their impact on children—some of the profound changes that have occurred and are still occurring as a result of two trends: the progressive industrialization of our society, with men and women working away from home, and the efforts of the women's liberation movement to secure justice for their sex.

39. Discrimination is still rampant. Women in our society had to fight for half a century to get education for their sex, the vote, the right to enter at least some of the professions. Yet even in the 1980s they have to face the fact that they are still being grossly discriminated against—having difficulty getting into professional schools, being ignored for the higher-paying jobs in most fields, receiving lower pay for the same work, as well as facing unjust laws and biased social customs. The women's movement has won some gains. But there is still a long way to go.

Of the women who stay at home to care for their children,

many are proud of their occupation, and happy. Others feel sharply the lack of respect shown by a materialistic society to an occupation that pays no salary and in which there are no higher positions for which to compete. Many mothers feel cut off during the day, by our pattern of relatively isolated homes, from the stimulation and fun of adult companionship. This is so different from the intimate communities of simpler societies.

Most ignominious to all women who have the courage to face the fact consciously is the realization that they are considered—by many men and by many women—a second-class sex as far as capabilities and influence are concerned.

40. The subordination of women is brought about by countless small acts beginning in early childhood. Some are consciously intended to be belittling. Most are thoughtless expressions of prejudice or of old tradition.

People are apt to show admiration for the accomplishments of little boys and for the cuteness of little girls. Girlish clothes are designed to make an adult say, "How pretty you look!" which is complimentary in one sense, but which also gives girls a sense that they are primarily appreciated for their appearance rather than for their achievements. Children's books show boys building things or going on adventures; girls watch the boys or play with dolls. Girls are commonly warned not to climb into trees or onto garage roofs because they are not strong enough or will get hurt more easily. Boys are given toy cars, construction sets, sporting equipment, or doctor kits. Girls are given dolls, sewing sets, nurse kits, or articles of adornment. There's nothing wrong with any of these gifts in themselves, especially if the child asks for them. The harm comes when adults consistently impose these distinctions, which imply that females are only good at a limited number of occupations.

Boys are assigned chores in the garage, in the basement, or on the lawn, girls in the house. Of course housework is important to the welfare of the whole family so it should be accorded dignity; but when it is done only by females, in a society that gives so much prestige to males, it will be considered menial by both sexes.

Many boys, because of their own particular sense of

inferiority, taunt girls that they are not able to run fast or throw a ball, and so can't be on the team.

Some parents and teachers tell girls that, by their nature, they won't be able to study advanced mathematics or physics, or function as engineers. Many girls become convinced by adolescence that they will be inferior to men in such capabilities as abstract reasoning, executive ability, and emotional control.

The acceptance of these aspersions in itself destroys self-confidence and thus brings about the very impairment of abilities that are alleged (by many men and some women) to be inborn in females.

41. Men need liberating, too. Perceptive women, in trying to liberate themselves, have realized that men, too, are victims of sexist assumptions—sexual stereotyping. Boys are taught that they mustn't show their feelings when they are hurt or frightened or unhappy. To the extent that they absorb this belief they lose some of their sensitivity to all feelings—other people's and their own—even positive feelings like tenderness and joy. (I've seen this in trying to help medical students to understand the feelings of their patients.) They become emotionally restricted. They are less understanding—as husbands, as fathers, as friends, and as workers dealing with the public—and therefore more difficult to live with or deal with.

Boys learn early that men in our society are supposed to be tough, dauntless, aggressive, competitive, and successful. They must go into only the occupations that are traditional for men. Most of the males who can fit readily into this kind of pattern are at least slightly rigidified in personality as a result. They will hesitate to branch out beyond what's conventional in their interests, in their friendships, as well as in their jobs.

The boys and men who don't enjoy toughness and competition are made to feel inferior or even peculiar. This may impair their effectiveness, whether they get into traditional or unconventional work. It will lessen their sense of fulfillment.

When individuals feel obliged to conform to a conventional male or female sex stereotype, they are all cramped to a degree, depending on how much each has to deny and suppress his or her natural inclinations. Thus, valuable traits are lost to the society. And each person is made to feel inadequate to the degree that she or he fails to conform to the supposed ideal.

42. What is work, anyway? The recognition—by women and men—that both sexes need liberation from old, arbitrary restrictions has brought into question not only women's rights but men's roles within the home, the basic relationship between the sexes, the meaning of outside work and—crucial for this book—how the children are to be cared for. Another question for me is how children can be raised without fixed ideas and prejudices about the capabilities and roles of the two sexes. These varied questions can't be answered in isolation from each other.

Before we discuss how families can try to solve these problems, I think it will give us a better perspective to stop for a minute and think how complex, artificial, and frustrating our industrial civilization is compared to simpler societies.

In most simple, nonindustrial societies (the kind for which our species was designed, through evolution) all adults and older children work right in their own community at farming or fishing, at weaving, cooking, the making of pots, and so on.

The work is carried on cooperatively, companionably, by extended family groups (the wider family that includes three generations—grandparents, aunts, uncles, and cousins) or by the community-wide group. The purpose of work is to serve the group—not to make money or to get ahead of others.

Children are always near their parents, but their care is incidental to the other work. A mother may carry a young infant in a sling while she works. Later she may entrust the baby to a 4-year-old sister. Parents, aunts, and uncles are the teachers. Children begin to assist in serious adult work at an early age.

43. But in industrialized societies like ours the demands of industry have drastically artificialized and fragmented our home lives as well as our work lives. Many fathers and mothers go off to a job miles away. It may consist of dull, repetitive, impersonal work that gives no gratification in itself. Then the satisfaction has to come from the money earned and the position held. This has been true for so long now that we assume that these are the normal satisfactions. Actually they are narrow, meager substitutes for the joy of creating something useful and beautiful the way a craftworker does. The focus on money and position tends to foster rivalry between workers, between neighbors, and at times between working husbands and wives in place of the warm glow that comes from working cooperatively for the benefit of family or community.

Couples who are ready to move in order to get the work or pay or advancement they want or because regular moves for junior executives are a policy of the corporation, must leave behind the love and security of the extended family. They usually live in houses that are more or less isolated from each other, commonly without close ties to neighbors. They're often obliged to move so frequently, because of shifts in position, that they have no time to put down roots in the community or draw sustenance from it. This isolation and mobility put particular strain on the parent who stays at home, as well as on the children.

It may seem, in our society, that the main way for women to gain fulfillment would be for the society to recognize their right to equality with men through jobs with equal pay and prestige. Certainly women should have this kind of equality.

But I hope that men and women will also be imagining—as an alternative aim for the future—the liberation for both sexes through a more relaxed, more whole existence in which much less importance is given to the outside job and more to the activities of the close community and family.

Idealistic young people have been pointing the way. They've been asking, "Why should we put such emphasis on individualism and competitiveness? Why not work cooperatively, in a loving spirit?"

And, "Why give such a high priority to earning more money and then buying more and more possessions? Why not try to see how we can live simply and enjoyably?" (The depletion of resources, pollution, and the energy crisis are going to force us eventually to live more simply anyway.)

Young people have been trying various ways to achieve these ideals. Quite a few have shied away from careers in big industry because of the monotony at the lower levels, the competitiveness and the frequent moves at the upper levels, and the impersonalness at all levels. They have turned in greater numbers toward the helping professions—teaching, counseling, medicine, nursing, social work, legal work representing disadvantaged people. They have also gone into handcrafts.

A few have formed communes or collectives organized around a particular activity such as running a food-buying co-op, a child care center, a medical or counseling clinic, a farm, a publication. As far as possible they avoid specialization and hierarchy; they rotate the jobs so that everyone works at the less and the more creative ones.

I myself think that on the political level we should divide our cities into neighborhoods that would run their own affairs just as far as possible, to avoid the sense of isolation, impotence, and irresponsibility that so many citizens acquire in a large metropolis. Each neighborhood, with laws to prevent segregation, would run its own health facilities, its police, its housing, zoning, and recreation facilities, its child care, and its schools. Industry also, I think, should be divided into local units, with local consumers and workers constituting a majority of the board of directors, so that the environment can be protected and the jobs made as creative and fulfilling as possible.

While we're waiting and working for a more humane society I hope that there will always be men and women who feel that the care of children and home is at least as important and soul-satisfying as any other activity, and that neither men nor women will feel the need to apologize for deciding to make that their main career.

44. Outside work may improve parents. There are women and men who say frankly that, though they want children, it would make them tense and irritable if they stayed at home cooped up with them for many hours each day. They know that they are better parents for being away from their children a good part of the time. They are right in saying that it's not good for children to be cared for by adults who are always impatient with them.

And parents who know that they need a career or a certain kind of work for fulfillment should not simply give it up for their children. Their children would not benefit from such a sacrifice. Instead, I think such parents should work out some kind of compromise between their two jobs and the needs of their children, usually with the help of other caregivers, especially during the crucial first three years of development.

All irritability with children is not due to career frustration. Irritable parents may be able to modify the irritability—which is usually a carry-over from childhood tensions—by consulting with a worker in a family social agency or with a psychiatrist.

45. Both parents' rights to outside careers. Both parents have an equal right to a career if they want one, it seems to me, and an equal obligation to share in the care of their children, with or without the help of others. (If they want others to do it all, I'd advise against their having children.)

Since many couples want to limit their children to two and are having them in their twenties, many of the women who have felt totally fulfilled in caring for their children when young nevertheless are left feeling restless as their children become progressively more independent. Then it's more difficult—for most individuals—to start a meaningful career. The education, training, and perhaps some work experience would have come more easily in youth; and the skill could then have been kept fresh by part-time work through the intervening years.

There may be difficult problems that may have to be worked out when both parents have serious careers. Because of the strength of the tradition that mothers are meant to give priority to child care, they often feel guilty going to work. This is minimized if the mother's husband and other relatives approve. If the mother has resolved her guilt and doubts, her children will not only accept but be proud of her working.

If an unusually good job offer comes from another city to one parent and the other parent is well satisfied with the present position, who sacrifices? If they are in the same field and one proves much more successful, what does this do to the marriage? But the question that concerns me is how the care of the children is arranged.

When I said I thought fathers and mothers had an equal

responsibility in child care I didn't mean that they must necessarily put in exactly the same number of hours at it. That decision would depend on several considerations, e.g., family finances, flexibility of each parent's work schedule, as well as the mother's and father's preferences. I meant that the discussion (which had better begin when a couple first considers marriage) should start with the assumption that they have an equal **right** to a career with the least possible interruption, whether or not they both want to exercise that right, and at what stage.

When both parents have outside jobs and are trying to arrange work schedules that will give them maximum time with their young children, they can use various compromises. One parent at a time can be quite satisfying to children. Preschool children can be regularly allowed to stay up late in the evenings if it is possible for them to regularly sleep late in the mornings. The number of hours of companionship is less important than the quality, the spirit. From a practical point of view, "quality" time can be spent with children by taking advantage of driving time, mealtimes (no reading, no TV, no arguing over food or other issues of family life) and other routine times together. Regular time can be scheduled with all of the children or with each child individually. Local trips to favorite parks or museums or sports activities and special event trips can be planned. "Chore" trips to the doctor or to buy clothes can be dressed up with a meal out and time for talking—and listening. When both parents work outside, they may feel guilty enough to be inclined to overindulge their child, let her be too demanding of their time, of presents, of treats, of privileges, perhaps allowing her to be rude. This won't make her happy; quite the contrary. (See Section 532.)

CHILDREN'S EMOTIONAL NEEDS

Before we discuss further how mothers and fathers can work out their careers, we should discuss children's needs, particularly in the earliest years.

46. It's in the first 2 to 3 years of life that children's personalities are being most actively molded—by the attitudes of the parents or of the others who provide most of their care.

In earlier times, the babies who lived in understaffed orphanages or who spent their days lying neglected in their cribs in day nurseries used to wither—in body, in intellect, and in emotions, never fully to recover.

Whereas a baby, let's say it's a girl, who's cared for mainly by loving, enthusiastic parents (perhaps with the help of others) surges ahead. Some of the things they give her are their visible love, their pride and joy in her tiny accomplishments, thoughtful playthings, answers to her questions, and a willingness to let her play freely as long as she does no damage. They read to her, show her pictures. These are the attitudes and activities that foster emotional depth and keen intelligence.

Whether children will grow up to be lifelong optimists or pessimists, whether warmly loving or cool, whether trustful or suspicious, will depend to a considerable extent on the attitudes of the individuals who have taken responsibility for a major portion of their care in their first two years. Therefore, the personalities of parents and caregivers are of great importance.

One person acts toward children as if they were basically bad, always doubting them, always scolding them. Such children grow up doubting themselves, full of guilt. A person with more than average hostility finds a dozen excuses every hour for venting it on a child; and the child acquires a corresponding hostility. Other people have the itch to dominate children and unfortunately they can succeed.

In the first year, a baby has to depend mainly on the attentiveness, intuition, and helpfulness of adults to get her the things that she needs and craves. If the adults are too insensitive or indifferent to serve her (within sensible limits—they shouldn't be submissive slaves) she will become somewhat apathetic or depressed.

A very particular need of young children is continuity in their caregivers. From the age of a few months they come to love, and count on, and get their security from the one or two people who take the major part of their care. Even at 6 months babies will become seriously depressed, losing their smile, their appetite, their interest in things and people, if the parent who has cared for them disappears. There will be a depression, lesser in degree, if that person who assists the parent on a regular basis leaves. Small children who have been moved from one foster home to another, several times, will lose some of their capacity to love or trust deeply, as if it's too painful to be disappointed again and again.

So, it's important that the parent or other person who has taken the major part of a child's care not give it up during the first 2 or 3 years or give it up only after a substitute has very gradually taken over. It's important to be as sure as possible that a substitute plans to stick with the job. It's important, in the group care of young children, that if there are two or more staff people assigned to one group of children, each child be assigned to one person so that there will be a relationship more like that of child and parent.

47. Emotional needs after 3 years. Now I want to discuss the more general emotional needs of children of all ages, especially after 3 years.

Children know that they are inexperienced and dependent. They count on their parents for leadership, love, and security.

They are always watching their parents, instinctively, and patterning themselves after them. This is how they get their own personalities, their strength of character, their assurance, their ability to cope. They are learning—in childhood—how to be adult citizens, workers, spouses, and parents, by identifying with their parents. (See Section 563.)

The greatest gift from parents is love, which they express in countless ways: a fond facial expression, spontaneous demonstrations of physical affection, pleasure in their children's accomplishments, comforting them when they are hurt or frightened, controlling them to keep them safe and to help them become responsible people, giving them high ideals.

It's the parents' (or caregivers') love that creates an answering love in children. It's from this lovingness toward parents that children go on to form all their positive relations in life—with friends, teachers, spouses, offspring, neighbors, and fellow workers.

Children gain trust in themselves from being respected—as human beings—by their parents (or caregivers). This self-assurance helps them to be comfortable with themselves and with all kinds of people, for the rest of life.

Respect from parents is what teaches children to give respect to their parents in turn.

Boys and girls, by 3 years, focus on their parents' roles. A boy, by the age of 3 years, senses that his destiny is to be a man, so he watches his father particularly—his interests, manner, speech, pleasures, his attitude toward work, his relationships with his wife and with his sons and daughters, how he gets along with and copes with other men.

A girl's need of a father is not as obvious on the surface but is just as great underneath. Half her relationships throughout life will be with males. She gets her ideas about what males are supposed to be primarily from watching her father. The kind of man she eventually falls in love with and marries will probably reflect in one way or another the personality and attitudes of her father—for example, whether he's dominating or gentle, loyal or straying, pompous or humorous.

A mother's personality will be copied in many respects by her admiring daughter. How the mother feels about being a woman, a wife, a mother, a worker will make a strong impression on her daughter. How she gets along specifically with her husband will influence her daughter's future relationship with her husband.

A mother is her son's first great love. In obvious or subtle ways this will set his romantic ideal. It will influence not only his eventual choice of a wife but how he gets along with her.

48. Two parents are preferable. I feel, from pediatric and psychiatric experience, that, if possible, it is preferable for children to live with two parents (one may be a stepparent), if the parents love and respect each other. Then children will know both sexes realistically as well as idealistically, and will have a pattern of marital stability to guide them when they are adults. The two parents will be able to support each other emotionally. They will be able to balance or counteract each other's unjustified worries and obsessions about the children.

This is not to say that children can't grow up to be normal

without two parents; many do. If they lack a father, they create one—in their imagination—out of what they remember, what their mother has told them, and the appealing characteristics of friendly men they see from time to time. This synthetic father supplies fairly well the masculine image they need to grow on. Similarly a child without a mother creates one from memory, family stories, and relationships with other women. Certainly it would be a great mistake for a parent to make a hasty, unsuitable marriage just to provide a child with a second parent.

49. Is it necessary to reinforce sex roles? I used to assume that it was wise for parents to strengthen the maleness of their boys and the femaleness of their girls by differentiating between the clothes and playthings they bought for them and the chores they assigned them.

But parents' concerns about reinforcing their child's sex identity may really come from their anxiety about their own adequacy as women or men. When one of my sons, at the age of 3, asked for a doll (as most boys do) and his mother talked about getting one for him, I was horrified.

I realize now that the main thing that gives a boy a strong sex identity is not the toy cars or cowboy suits he's given, but primarily his positive relationship with his father in early childhood that makes him want to grow up to be the same kind of person.

If a father anxiously turns down his son's request for a doll—or otherwise shows his worry that the boy has "girlish" tastes—it doesn't reinforce the child's masculinity. It gives him a sense that his own and his father's masculinity are doubtful or inadequate.

I think it is normal for little boys to want to play with dolls and for little girls to want to play with toy cars, and it's quite all right to let them have them. A boy's desire to play with dolls is parental rather than effeminate, and it should help him to be a good father. There is no harm in boys and girls wearing unisex clothes—jeans and T-shirts, for example, if that's what they want—or for girls to have dresses, if that's their preference.

As for chores, I believe now that it's sound for boys and girls to have basically the same ones, just as I think it's wise for men and women to share in the same occupations, at home and outside. Boys can do as much bed making, room cleaning, dishwashing as their sisters. And girls can take part in yard work and car washing—as I hope their mothers will. I don't mean that boys and girls can't swap certain chores or that it all has to come out exactly even, only that there should not be obvious discrimination or differentiation. The example of the two parents will have a strong influence.

I wouldn't be complacent under all circumstances. If a boy wanted exclusively dresses and dolls and preferred to play only with girls, I would assume that something had gotten mixed up in his identification, as a result of misunderstandings and anxieties, and that this should be looked into by a child guidance clinic or a child psychiatrist. If a girl wanted to play a lot with boys and occasionally wished she were a boy, but also enjoyed playing with girls, I wouldn't be concerned. If she would play only with boys and was **always** unhappy about being a girl, I'd want a consultation.

It's good to remember that boys, though they identify predominantly with their fathers, also identify to a lesser degree with their mothers. This gives them understanding of the opposite sex as they grow up, and a richer, more flexible personality. It is only relatively few males who identify predominantly with the opposite sex. Similarly all girls have some identification with their fathers, but only a few have a predominant misidentification. So it's a matter of quantity, not of absolutes.

Since there is no such thing as a 100 percent identification with one's own sex, it's better to let children grow up with the mixture of identifications, attitudes, and interests that have developed in them, as long as they can accept comfortably what they are, rather than make them ashamed and anxious because of parental disapproval.

WHO WILL CARE FOR THE CHILDREN?

50. Various alternatives. Who will provide them with the affection, the firm guidance, and the responsiveness to their questions and achievements that good parents naturally give?

Best of all is when the mother's and father's work schedules can be dovetailed so that both can work a reasonably full shift, and yet one or the other can be at home for most of the day. This can be done much more easily when industrial workers can arrange to work different shifts, or when parents have occupations such as university student, teacher, insurance salesperson, artist, or writer. Also, nurses, physicians, social workers, and other professionals can often find work at untraditional schedules. An appropriate caregiver would fill in the hours not covered by the parents. Of course, it's critically important that the parents are together for sleeping times, as well as some waking hours.

Another solution is for one or both parents to cut down to less-than-full-time jobs for 2 to 3 years, until the child is mature enough to be able to attend nursery school one-half or two-thirds of the day, or a child care center.

A relative with whom the parents see eye-to-eye may be an ideal caregiver; but the relative who lives close by and is willing to take on such a heavy responsibility is hard to find these days.

Some working parents engage a housekeeper or sitter or caregiver (caregiver seems a more meaningful word than sitter) to come to their home to care for a baby or small child for part of the day. If it's for most of the day this person may well become the most formative influence on the young child's developing personality. So the parents should want to find a person who shows much the same kind of love, interest, responsiveness, and control as they do.

51. Family day care. Less expensive than a caregiver in the child's home, and sounder in theory, is to place a small child during the day with another parent, one who is not trying to care for more than four children under the age of 5, and not more than two under the age of 2, her own included. This is usually called family day care. In some cities there is a family and children's social agency that recruits and supervises day care parents. This gives added assurance that these parents are suitable people. In other cities thoughtful, resourceful working parents have worked together in organizing a family day care unit—or a small network of units. Some have come to prefer an arrangement in which **two** people take care of up to eight young children, not more than four under the age of 2, in a home setting, so that the caregiver will not become discouraged by the combination of the demandingness of the job and the isolation from other adults.

Supervised family day care is distinctly different from the common situation in which a person takes in many babies and small children with the idea of making as much money as possible, and with no idea of what children's needs are.

Parents should take great care in observing the way a prospective caregiver or family day care parent takes care of their child and other children—over a period of several weeks—before making a long-term commitment of this importance.

52. Family day care for children under the age of 2 or 3. I think it is preferable for children under the age of 2 or 3 years not to be in the fairly large groups of nursery schools or day care centers, where they may feel lost and confused, but to be in a family atmosphere where there are not more than three (or at the most four) children under the age of 5 to each adult, including the leader's own child if any; six to eight children for two leaders gives the adult some companionship and an opportunity to go to the toilet.

Children at this young age need a lot of the kind of care that good parents give spontaneously—playing with them occasionally, talking with them, keeping them out of trouble, comforting them, showing pleasure in their small accomplishments, responding to their friendly overtures, holding them and hugging them at times. There need to be suitable playthings of course.

Infants under walking age need to have even more attention brought to them because they can't go after it or ask for it. (It's all too easy to neglect them by leaving them alone in their cribs. That's why I use the expression, "the care that good parents give.") Infants of creeping age need to be out of their cribs and playpens most of the time when not asleep. Younger babies in cribs need to be within sight of children and adults, need to be visited and talked to often. All infants need to be held, hugged, fed in the lap, smiled at.

Some family and children's social agencies in cities select, recommend, and supervise suitable families who give good quality day care to babies and children under 2 or 3 years. The same health and safety standards should be met by family day care as by nursery schools and day care centers.

53. Qualities in a parent substitute. Far and away the most important aspect is the person's disposition. Most likely it will be a woman. Toward children she should be affectionate, understanding, comfortable, sensible, self-confident. She should love and enjoy them without smothering them with attention. She should be able to control them without nagging or severity. In other words, she should get along with them happily. It is a help when interviewing a prospective caregiver to have your child with you. You can tell how she responds to a child better by her actions than by what she says. Avoid the person who is cross, reproving, fussy, humorless, or full of theories.

A common mistake that parents make is to look first of all for a person with a lot of experience. It's natural that they should feel more comfortable leaving a child with someone who knows what to do for the colic or the croup. But illnesses and accidents are a very small part of a child's life. It's the minutes and hours of every day that count. Experience is fine when it's combined with the right personality. With the wrong personality, it's worth hardly anything.

Cleanliness and carefulness are a little more important than experience. You can't let someone make the baby's formula who refuses to do it correctly. Still, there are many rather untidy people who are careful when it's important. Better a person who is too casual than one who is too fussy.

Some parents focus on the education of a caregiver, but I think it's unimportant compared with other qualities, especially for young children. Even if they learn to say "ain't," they'll surely drop it later if it's not used by their parents and friends.

A common problem is that a grandmother or other caregiver may favor the youngest child in the family, especially one who was born after she joined the household. She calls that one **her** baby. If she can't understand the harm in doing this, she should not stay. It does irreparable harm to leave children in the care of a person who does not give them security.

Sometimes, inexperienced young parents settle for a caregiver about whom they don't really feel right because they've decided they can't do any better, or because the prospective person talks a good line, for example, about giving security to the child. The parents should keep looking until they find someone they really like.

There's the very common—and human—problem of whose child it is. Some caregivers have a great need to take over the child, to push the parents aside, and to show that they always know best. They may be quite unconscious of this need. They can rarely be reformed.

On the other hand, it's natural that parents should be unconsciously jealous when they see how dependent and affectionate their child has become toward a caregiver. This may make them excessively critical—even disrespectful—of the caregiver.

Certainly, if a caregiver is any good, a child will become attached, and parents will have twinges of jealousy. But if they can be conscious of this and face it honestly, they can adjust to it.

In a sense, then, the most important questions for caregivers and parents are whether they can be honest with themselves, listen to each other's ideas and criticisms, keep the lines of communication open, respect each other's good points and good intentions, and cooperate for the benefit of the child.

54. Care after the age of 3, for children whose parents work outside the home. Most children, somewhere between 2 and 3 years, gain enough independence and outgoingness to be able to profit from a good group situation—nursery school, day care center, Montessori school—and enjoy it. These three types of preschool are discussed in Sections 593–596.

After 6 years, and particularly after 8, children seek and enjoy independence, turn more to outside adults (especially to good teachers) and children for their ideals and companionship. They can get along comfortably for hours at a time without having to turn to a close adult for support. After school they still ought to have a feeling they belong somewhere. A motherly or fatherly neighbor may be able to substitute until one of the working parents comes home. After-school play centers are valuable for all children, but particularly for those whose parents work.

55. The temptation to spoil. Working parents may find that because they are starved for their child's company (and perhaps because they feel guilty about seeing her so little), they are inclined to shower her with presents and treats, bow to all her wishes regardless of their own, and generally let her get away with murder. When a child finds that her parents are appeasers, it doesn't satisfy her—it's apt to make her more greedy. It's fine for working parents to show their child as much agreeableness and affection as comes naturally, but they should feel free to stop when they're tired, consider their own desires, spend only what money is sensible, expect reasonable politeness and consideration—in other words, act like self-confident, all-day parents. The child will not only turn out better, but will enjoy their company more.

THE FATHER AS PARENT

56. A father's capability and responsibility. Men, especially the husbands of women with outside jobs, have been participating increasingly in all aspects of home and child care. There is no reason why fathers shouldn't be able to do these jobs as well as mothers, and contribute equally to the children's security and development. But the benefit is lost if this work is done as a favor to their wives, since that implies that it's really not their work but just an unusual degree of generosity on their part. The work should be done in the spirit of equal partnership. In fact there are increasing numbers of fathers married to mothers with full-time outside jobs who take the major share of the care of children and home while their children are small.

Some fathers who are not used to the idea of participating

in baby care say, "I'll wait until the child is more like a human being." But valuable time is lost that way. While the father is waiting, the mother becomes the expert. Then it's harder for the father to achieve an equal status as parent later.

Most mothers are also anxious about assuming the care of their first baby in the beginning. But they aren't able to postpone it. They have to start immediately and so learn quickly.

I think that a father with a full-time job—even where a mother is staying at home—will do best by his children, his wife, and himself if he takes on half or more of the management of the children (and also participates in the housework) when he gets home from work and on weekends. The mother's leadership and patience will probably have worn thin by the end of the day. (The father's would, too, if he alone had had the children all day.) The children will profit from experiencing a variety of styles of leadership and control.

When a father does his share as a matter of course when at home, it does much more than simply lighten his wife's work load and give her companionship in the work that she has had to do alone all day. It shows that he believes this work is crucial for the welfare of the family, that it calls for judgment and skill, and that it's his responsibility as much as it is hers when he is at home. This is what sons and daughters need to see in action if they are to grow up without sexist attitudes.

In child care, fathers can give bottles and solid foods, change diapers and clothes, wipe tears and noses, bathe and put to bed, read stories, fix toys, break up quarrels, help with questions about homework, explain rules and assign duties and see that they are carried out, correct and reprove.

Fathers can participate in the whole gamut of domestic work: shopping, food preparation, cooking and serving, dishwashing, bed making, house cleaning, laundry. (My mother taught me these jobs beginning when I was around age 7.)

It will be a great day when fathers:

Consider the care of their children to be as important **to them** as their jobs and careers.

Seek out jobs and work schedules that will allow them ample time to be with their wives and children.

Give first consideration, when discussing with their wives where to live, to what favors family life.

Will resist their companies' attempts to move them frequently.

Will let it be known at their work places that they take their parental responsibilities very seriously and may have to take time off when their children need them—just as working mothers have always done.

Will try to get other fathers at their work places to take the same stands.

57. The parent who shies away from leadership. There are quite a few parents in America—fathers much more often than mothers—who shy away from the guidance and control of their children (though they may play often with them), leaving most of this to their spouses. I think of fathers who are hidden behind the paper or glued to the television set when the crises occur.

Some of the nonparticipating fathers explain, when their wives reproach them, that they don't want their children to resent them the way they often resented **their** fathers. They want to be pals instead. It's good for children to have friendly parents who will play with them. However, they'll have many friends but only one father and one mother. They need parents to act like parents, however friendly they are too.

When a parent is timid or reluctant to give leadership, the children—especially those of the same sex—feel let down. They are like vines without a pole to grow on.

When parents are afraid to be definite and firm, their children keep testing the limits—making life difficult for the parents and also for themselves—until the parents are finally provoked into cracking down. Then the parents are apt to feel ashamed, and back off again.

The father who avoids the leadership role simply forces his wife to discipline for two. In many such cases, the father does not end up with just a pally relationship. Children know that adults get irritated when children keep misbehaving. When they are dealing with a father who pretends not to notice, it makes them uneasy. Child guidance clinic experience shows that children may fear this kind of father more than the one who participates freely in their management and lets his irritation show on occasion. With this latter father they have opportunities to learn just what his displeasure means. They find out that they can survive it. This gives them a kind of self-assurance, just as they gain confidence when they overcome their fears and learn to swim or ride a bike or walk home in the dark. Whereas with the father who dodges child management and hides his displeasure, the children imagine that he is concealing an anger that is much more dangerous than it really is.

RELATIONS WITH GRANDPARENTS

58. Grandparents can be a great help to young parents in all kinds of ways. They can also derive enormous pleasure from their grandchildren. They often ask wistfully, "Why couldn't I have enjoyed my own children the way I enjoy my grandchild? I suppose I was trying too hard and feeling only the responsibility."

In many parts of the world grandmothers are considered experts, and a young mother takes it for granted that when she has a question about her baby or needs a little help, she'll ask her mother. When a mother has this kind of confidence in the grandmother, she can get not only advice but comfort. In our country, though, a new mother is often more inclined to turn to her doctor first, and some women don't ever think of consulting their mothers. This is partly because we are so used to consulting professional people about our personal problems—doctors, guidance counselors in school, marriage counselors, social workers, psychologists, ministers. Also, we take it for granted that knowledge advances rapidly, and so we often think that anyone who knew how to do a job twenty years ago is behind the times today. A more basic reason is that many young parents still feel too close to adolescence. They want to prove to the world and to themselves that they can manage their own lives. They may be afraid that the grandparents will want to tell them what to do, as if they were still dependent, and they don't want to put themselves back in that position.

59. Tensions are normal. In some families, all is harmony between parents and grandparents. In a few, disagreements are fierce. In others, there is a little tension, most commonly concerning the care of the first child, but it wears off with time and adjustment.

The fortunate young woman who has lots of natural, comfortable self-confidence can turn easily to her mother for help when she needs it. And when the grandmother makes a suggestion on her own, the mother finds that she can accept it if it seems good, or she can tactfully let it pass and go her own way.

But most young parents don't have that amount of assurance at first. Like almost everybody else in a new job, they are sensitive about possible inadequacies, touchy about criticism.

Most grandparents remember this well from their earlier days and try hard not to interfere. On the other hand, they **have** had experience, they feel they've developed judgment, they love their grandchildren dearly, and they can't help having opinions. They see surprising changes from the time when they cared for babies—flexible feeding schedules, early feeding of solid foods, perhaps later toilet training—and these are hard to get used to. Even when they accept new methods, they may be bothered by what seems to them to be excessive zeal in carrying them out. (When you are a grandparent yourself, you'll probably understand better what I mean.)

I think that if young parents have the courage, they can keep relations most comfortable by permitting or even inviting the grandparents to speak up about their opinions. Frank discussions are usually, in the long run, more comfortable than veiled hints or uneasy silences. A mother who is pretty sure she is managing the baby properly can say, "I know that this method doesn't seem quite right to you, and I'm going to discuss it again with the doctor to be sure that I've understood his directions." This doesn't mean the mother is giving in. She certainly reserves the right to make her own decision in the end. She is only recognizing the grandmother's good intentions and evident anxiety. The young mother who shows reasonableness will reassure the grandmother not only in regard to the present problem but also in regard to the future in general.

A grandmother can help the mother do a good job by showing her confidence in her and fitting in with her methods as far as possible. This puts the mother in a mood to ask advice when she is in doubt.

When the children are left in the care of the grandparents, whether for half a day or for two weeks, there should be frank understanding and reasonable compromising. (See Section 65.) The parents must have confidence that the children will be cared for according to their beliefs in important matters (that, for instance, they won't be compelled to eat food they don't like, be shamed for bowel accidents, or be frightened about policemen). On the other hand, it's unfair to expect grandparents to carry out every step of management and discipline as if they were exact replicas of the parents. It won't hurt children to be a little more respectful to the grandparents (if that's what they want), or to have their meals on a different schedule, or to be kept cleaner or dirtier. If the parents don't feel right about the way the grandparents care for the children, of course they shouldn't ask them to take care of them.

Some parents are sensitive about advice. More than average tension may arise if the young mother (or father) has felt a lot of parental criticism throughout her childhood. This inevitably leaves her inwardly unsure of herself, outwardly impatient of disapproval, and grimly determined to prove her independence. She may take to new philosophies of child rearing with unusual enthusiasm and push them hard. They seem like a wholesome change from what she remembers. They are also a way to show the grandparents how old-fashioned they are and to bother them a bit. It's really fun to battle about theory when you're mad at the opponent. The only trouble is that it's the child's upbringing that provides the ammunition on both sides. All I'm suggesting is that parents who find that they are constantly upsetting grandparents should at least ask themselves whether they might be doing some of it on purpose, without realizing it.

60. The managerial grandmother. Occasionally there is a grandmother so constituted that she has always been too managerial with her own child and she can't stop now even though the child is now a parent. Such a young parent may have a tough time at first keeping a perspective. For instance, a daughter dreads advice. When it comes, it makes her angry, but she dare not express her feelings. If she accepts the advice, she feels dominated. If she turns it down, she feels guilty. How, then, can the beginning mother in this situation protect herself? It sounds as if she'd have to lift herself by her bootstraps. In a way she does have to, but it **can** be done gradually, with practice. In the first place, she can keep reminding herself that **she** is the mother now and that the baby is hers to take care of as she thinks best. She should be able to get support from the doctor or the public health nurse when she has been made to doubt her own method. She is surely entitled to the support of her husband, especially if it's his mother who is interfering. If he thinks that in a certain situation his mother is right, he should be able to say so to his wife, but at the same time he can show his mother that he stands with his wife against interference.

The young mother will come out better if she can learn gradually not to run away from the grandmother and not to be afraid to hear her out, because both these reactions reveal, in a way, that she feels too weak to stand up to her. Harder still, she can learn how not to get boiling mad inside or how not to explode outwardly in a temper. You might say she's entitled to get angry, which is true. But pent-up anger and explosions are both signs that she has already been feeling submissive for too long, out of fear of making the grandmother mad. A dominating grandmother usually senses these indirect signs of timidity and takes advantage of them. A mother shouldn't feel guilty about making her mother mad, if it must come to that. Actually, it shouldn't be necessary to blow up at the grandmother—or at least not more than once or twice. The mother can learn to speak up for herself right away, in a matter-of-fact, confident tone, **before she gets angry.** ("Well, the doctor told me to feed her this way." "You see, I like to keep him as cool as possible." "I don't want her to cry for long.") This calm, assured tone is usually the most effective way to convince the grandmother that the mother has the courage of her convictions.

In these occasional situations that contain a lot of continual tension, it is often helpful for the parents, and perhaps the grandparents, to consult a professional person—wise family doctor, psychiatrist, social worker, sensible minister—in group or separate interviews, so that each can present the picture as she or he sees it. Eventually they could all come together for a final discussion. In any case it should be understood that, in the end, the responsibility and the right to make the decision belong to the parents.

PLANNING THE HOMECOMING

61. Callers and visitors. The birth of a baby is an occasion that brings relatives and friends flocking, to congratulate the parents and to see the baby. This is gratifying to the parents and fills them with pride. However, too much of it may be exhausting to the mother. How much is too much? It's very different in different cases. Most mothers tire easily the first few weeks at home. They have just felt the effects of some intense glandular changes. Perhaps more important still are the emotional shifts that are called for, especially with the first baby, which are discussed in Section 34.

Visitors are pure pleasure to some people—relaxing, distracting, rejuvenating. To most of us, however, only a few old friends have such a good effect. Other visitors, to a greater or lesser degree, make us somewhat tense, even when we enjoy seeing them, and leave us somewhat fatigued, especially if we aren't feeling well. When a new mother becomes tired out, it gets her off on the wrong foot at the time of the most important transition in her life, and this is too bad for everybody. I think a new mother should set strict limits for visitors right from the start, see how it goes, and then increase the number very gradually if she finds she has plenty of strength left over. It helps a mother to get the doctor's agreement to strict limits. Then she doesn't have to feel that she's being inhospitable; she's just following doctor's orders. I'd tell each person who calls up, "The doctor says I can see only one visitor a day for fifteen minutes, beginning tomorrow. Can you come Tuesday, about 4 P.M.?" There are lots of additional reasons that can be thrown in to strengthen the point: extra-long labor, breast-feeding, slowness in getting strength back.

To people who appear at the house without a telephone call, you can act pleased but guilty: "The doctor wants me to see only one visitor a day for the next week, but come in for just a minute, anyway."

One mother found it helped to tack on her front door a notice saying she didn't want life insurance for the baby, photographs of the baby, nursery equipment, or sets of books, so she would not have to answer the door for salesmen.

62. Visitors playing with the baby. Most visitors get all excited when they see babies. They want to hold them, joggle them, tickle them, jounce them, waggle their heads at them, and keep up a blue streak of baby talk. Some babies can take a lot, some can't take any, and most are in between. A parent has to use her or his judgment about how much is wise and then be very firm. This is hard to carry out, though, because it's one of the great pleasures of parenthood to have people enjoy the baby. Most babies are easily tired, too, by strange places and strange happenings, as visits to the doctor's office prove.

63. Arranging for extra help in the beginning. If you can figure out a way to get someone to help you the first few weeks you are taking care of the baby during the hours when your husband is at work, by all means do so. If you try to do everything by yourself and get exhausted, you may **have** to get help and have it for longer in the end. Besides, getting tired and depressed starts you and the baby off on the wrong foot.

Your mother may be the ideal helper, if you get along with her easily. If you feel she is bossy and still treats you like a child, this is not the time to have her. You will want to feel that the baby is your own and that you are doing a good job. It will help to have a person who has taken care of babies before, but it's most important of all to have someone whom you enjoy having around.

If you can afford to hire a houseworker or a practical baby nurse for a few weeks, there will be the advantage over a relative that you can let her go if she doesn't work out right. In one way, a houseworker is best—the mother can have the satisfaction of taking complete care of her baby from the start—but a houseworker is hard to find. Next best is a practical nurse who will do part of the housework, who is willing to fit in with your way of doing things, who will let you feel that the baby is yours, and who has a relaxed, agreeable personality. If you find that you have a practical nurse who acts as if the baby were hers rather than yours and criticizes everything you do, for goodness' sake get rid of her right away and take a chance on finding a better one.

How long should you engage a helper for? It will depend, of course, on your finances, on your desire to take over, and on your strength. Each day as your strength increases, take over a little more of the work. If, when 2 weeks are nearly up, you find that you still get tired easily, then by all means keep the helper, whether you can really afford her or not. She is not a luxury, under these circumstances, but a necessity. If you take over before you are strong enough, it will cost more in the end, financially and spiritually, than if you keep her on for another week or two.

Most expectant parents feel a little scared at the prospect of taking sole charge of a helpless baby for the first time. If you have this feeling, it doesn't mean that you won't be able to do a good job or that you **have** to have a nurse to show you how. But if you feel **really** panicky, you will probably learn more comfortably with an agreeable practical nurse—or relative, if this can be arranged.

If you can't have regular help, you may be able to afford and find a person to come in once or twice a week to do the cleaning, help you catch up on the housework, and watch the baby for a few hours while you go out for a visit.

Whether or not you have your own help, you should arrange to have a visiting nurse come in for a visit or two. (See Section 107.)

64. Practical aids. Especially if you are going to be washing the baby's diapers yourself, now is the time to get an automatic washer and dryer if you can possibly afford them.

They save hours of work each week, and precious energy. They are somewhat less essential if you will be using disposable diapers or a diaper service but still very worthwhile.

New mothers find it a great help to send out the regular laundry, at least temporarily, during the early months of baby care. This is a good time to simplify housework by putting unnecessary furniture and furnishings in a storeroom for a couple of months or a couple of years. Learn to use more of the easily prepared foods for a while.

65. Sitters are a boon to parents and can help a child to develop independence. You and your child should know your sitter well. Let's assume for the discussion that it's a woman, though there is no reason why it should not be a man. For night sitting with a baby who doesn't waken, it may only be necessary for her to be sensible and dependable. But for babies who waken and for children above the age of 5 months who might waken, it's important for the sitter to be a person they know and like. It is frightening to most children to waken and find a stranger. If the sitter is to care for the children or even just put them to bed, you should be sure from seeing her in action with your children that she understands and loves children and can manage them with kindliness and firmness. So try to engage the sitter a few times while you and she will be there together for a while. Then the young children can get used to her before she has to do too much for them directly. As the children gradually accept her, she can do more for them.

It is certainly important that you stick to one or two sitters as much as possible. You can learn about capable sitters or about a reliable agency through a friend whose judgment you trust.

Young or old? It's a matter of maturity and spirit rather than years. I've occasionally seen a child as young as 14 who was extremely capable and dependable, but it's unfair to expect such qualities in most children that age. And some adults may prove unreliable or harsh or ineffectual. One older person has a knack with children. Another is too inflexible to adapt to a new child or is too nervous.

To keep things straight, it's sensible to have a permanent notebook for the sitter, listing the child's routine, some of the things she may ask for (in her words), the telephone numbers of the doctor and of a neighbor to call in an emergency if you can't be reached, bedtime hours, what the sitter may help herself to in the kitchen, the whereabouts of linen, night-clothes, and other things that may be needed, how to turn the furnace up or down.

But most of all, know your sitter and know that your child trusts her.

There is more on the qualities of a parent substitute in Section 53.

Equipment and Clothing

EQUIPMENT YOU'LL NEED

66. Getting things ahead of time. Some parents don't feel like buying anything until they have their baby. The only reason I know for this hesitation is the superstition that buying things ahead of time might cause the pregnancy to come to a bad end. The advantage of getting and arranging everything ahead of time is that it lightens the burden later. A certain number of mothers feel tired and easily discouraged at the time they begin taking care of the baby themselves. Then a little job like buying half-a-dozen nipples looms as a real ordeal. Mothers who have gotten depressed have said to me afterward, "The next time, I'm going to buy everything that I need way ahead. Every pin and nightie is going to be in its place."

What do you really have to have, in the way of equipment, to take care of a new baby (let's say it's a girl)? There are no exact rules, but here are some suggestions:

67. A place to sleep. You may want to get a beautiful bassinet, lined with silk. But the baby doesn't care. All she needs is sides to keep her from rolling out, and something soft but firm in the bottom for a mattress. Sometimes there's a cradle that's been in the family for many years, or the parents want to make a cradle, especially for their first child. Most parents start with a crib with a bumper pad to go all around the inside. Cribs should have slats less than 2⅜ inches apart, a snug-fitting mattress, childproof side locking mechanisms, no sharp edges or lead paint, and at least 26 inches from the top of the rail to the mattress set at its lowest level. Most mattresses are now constructed of foam-wrapped, coiled innersprings with a waterproof covering or high-density foam with a moisture-repellent covering. Mattresses filled with animal hair can still occasionally be found and have been known to cause allergies in a susceptible child in an allergic family. (This risk can be avoided by enclosing the mattress in an airtight casing made for this purpose.) You can make a mattress by folding up an old blanket and tufting it, or by obtaining the proper size foam and covering it with a waterproof enclosure. The sides of a small bassinet will probably have to be lined to protect your baby from injury. She doesn't need a pillow for her head, and it's better not to use one.

68. Something to bathe her in and dress her on. The baby can be bathed in the kitchen sink, a plastic tub (get one with a wide edge to rest your arm on), a dishpan, or a washstand. Molded plastic bathing tubs and contoured tubs of sponge material to fit the baby's body are available and generally inexpensive. You can bathe and dress the baby on a low table, at which you sit (a card table with steady legs is a good size), or on the top of a fairly high bureau, at which you stand. You can sit on a high stool at the sink.

Convenient is a dressing or changing table with a waterproof pad, safety straps, and storage shelves. Some types fold.

69. Other equipment.

Diaper pins. Rustproof, stainless steel with a lock head for safety.

Vitamin drops, usually containing vitamins A, C, and D. Ask your doctor which preparation to get.

Diaper pail. This should hold 3 gallons. Polyethylene is the usual material. If you are going to wash your own diapers, you may want two, one for wet and another, containing soapy water, for soiled diapers. If you are going to use a diaper service, they will provide a container.

An inclined plastic seat in which the baby can be strapped, carried short distances, set down almost anywhere, and from which she can watch the world go by, is a most useful accessory. (Some infant carriers can be used as seats.) The base should be larger than the seat; otherwise it will tip over when the baby gets active.

The seat tends, however, to be overused in the sense that the baby is apt to be always in it and so is deprived of bodily contact with people. A baby should be held for feedings, comforting, and at other times.

70. Carriers to carry a baby on the parent's chest, back, or side are useful for shopping, walks, visits, housework, and fretful periods. They provide physical and emotional closeness. The chest carrier may look awkward but it is favored by more parents because it is easy to get the baby in and out, you can see and check on her, and the physical and emotional contact is the closest. Chest carriers need to be used early and regularly or neither the parent nor infant may be able to tolerate them. People who do use them regularly soon find them indispensable. The side carrier has almost the same advantages.

Framed backpacks are satisfactory, and are easy to carry on long walks, for older babies who can sit straight. The top rim needs to be padded for when a sleeping baby's face rests on it. You cannot sit comfortably—on a bus, for example. Some types can be propped up as infant seats.

71. Government-approved, dynamically tested automobile restraints—a carrier for a baby, a seat for a child—are essential pieces of equipment for all children who ever ride in a car—and what child doesn't.

A baby should be able to ride reclining strapped into a carrier. A child between 20 and 45 pounds should be strapped into a special seat that protects from side crashes as well as head-on crashes.

In buying (or borrowing) a car carrier or seat, don't take one unless it conforms to a Federal Motor Vehicle Safety

Standard of 1981 or later, and has been dynamically (crash) tested. It's a good idea to take your car seat along when you are going to visit friends or relatives by plane or bus, so that you'll have it with you when you go on automobile trips after you have reached your destination.

I think the best way to teach children good safety habits in the car is to have a rule that the car doesn't get started up until the children are in their car seats and the older children (over 45 pounds) and grown-ups have their seat belts on. If you absolutely have to take a child in a car without a car seat, the best place for the child is in the back seat, not in the arms of a passenger in the front seat or loose on the rear deck of a station wagon or truck bed.

There are now many free or low-cost loan, rental, or purchase programs for carriers and car seats, and you can find out about them from your doctor or local public health nurse.

For up-to-date information on car seats, you can write to the Office of Public Education, American Academy of Pediatrics, 1801 Hinman Avenue, Evanston, IL 60204.

If you are using a car seat that requires a top anchor, never use it without that anchor.

THE CLOTHES BABIES NEED

The labels on babies' clothes warn against using soap, liquid bleach, or liquid softener, all of which remove the fire retardant protection. Currently, manufacturers recommend low-sudsing detergent and perborate bleach (non-chlorine).

Remember that your baby will be growing very rapidly during the first year, so be sure you buy her clothing to fit loosely. Except for plastic pants, it's generally better to begin with 3–6 month size clothes instead of newborn or "layette-sized" clothing.

72. Knitted nightgowns are entirely practical and can be worn also during babies' periods of wakefulness and even during visits.

The mittens on the ends of the sleeves, which are to keep

babies from scratching themselves, can be worn open or closed. The long gowns make it harder for babies to kick off their coverings; the short ones may be preferable for a hot climate. Buy three or four anyway. It would be convenient to have two or three more, especially if you don't have a washer and dryer.

73. Shirts. There are two styles of undershirt: pullover and snap closing. The latter is slightly easier to put on a small, limp baby. Medium weight and short sleeves should be sufficient unless a baby will live in an unusually cold house. Some brands have tabs to pin diapers to, which will help an inexperienced parent keep the diapers from falling down. Start with the 1-year size; or, if you are fussy about fit, the 6-month size. Buy three or four anyway. It would be convenient to have two or three more, especially if you don't have a washer and dryer.

74. Stretch suits of polyester, sometimes combined with cotton, or of terry, are increasingly popular for daytime wear for babies, but can also be used for sleeping. They snap or zip from the neck down one or both legs.

75. Sacks and kimonos are short jackets and long gowns, front opening, usually of flowered cotton flannelette, to be worn over shirt or nightie for a dressier appearance; not essential, often a shower present.

76. Sweaters, generally made of acrylic, are useful in a cold house, a cold sleeping room, or outdoors in cold weather, to add extra warmth over or under the other clothes when the baby is up, under other coverings when in bed. Be sure that the neck opening has sufficient give or that there are shoulder snaps or well-secured buttons.

77. Outer clothes for outings in cold climates.

A snowsuit, bunting, or pram bag is a zippered bag in which the baby is encased up to the shoulders.

A pram suit has a coverall shape and also encloses the feet and may come in one or two pieces. It should zip or snap from neck to foot.

These outer garments are usually made of water-repellent, synthetic layers, oftentimes quilted for insulation.

78. Bibs. Small round bibs are useful for keeping drool off the clothes. For the mess that babies or children always make with their solid food they need a large bib of plastic or terry (or a combination), preferably with a pocket along the lower edge to catch the food that comes running down. Plastic is easily rinsed, but just looks uncomfortable to the adult. Be sure there is a cloth binding around the neck. A terry bib can also be used for wiping the face if you can find a dry corner. Bibs are gift items.

79. Diapers. More parents now use disposable diapers that come in various sizes and thicknesses for day and night. They have attached adhesive tapes so do not require pins. They are particularly useful for traveling and visiting. Ask your friends about their preferences in brands and sizes. Generally, disposable diapers are expensive, their use may bring a higher incidence of diaper rash, and they tend to be an ecological nightmare because practically no one follows the disposal instructions.

Diaper service is available in some cities. The company supplies the diapers as well as launders them, and supplies a container.

If you are going to wash your own, you can save money.

The most popular materials for diapers are gauze, cotton flannel, and bird's-eye. The gauze diapers are quicker drying but do not hold as much of the urine when the baby is larger. Two dozen will cover your needs if you wash them every day and don't use too many for sheets, towels, etc. Six dozen will cover all possible needs. Get the large size.

Some parents prefer to use disposable diaper liners with the cloth diapers.

80. Waterproof pants over cloth diapers are a special help when you are going places with the baby. (Disposable diapers have a waterproof interlining.) Whether you use waterproof pants at home depends on how well the baby's skin stands up. When a baby has no waterproof pants on, a lot of the urine in the cloth diaper is absorbed into the surrounding clothing and evaporated. With waterproof pants the diapers stay much wetter and warmer. This favors diaper rash. As long as your baby's skin is clear in the diaper region, you can use pants as much as is convenient. When there is diaper rash, leave them off. Wash them each day.

Pants come in pull-on and snap-on styles. Waterproof silk or nylon pants stay soft longer than plastic pants. The elastic at the edges is less irritating when enclosed in a soft binding. Make sure the fit is not confining or tight around your baby's legs.

81. Bed or sleep bags and walkers. By 6 months, when babies can move about in their cribs, most parents find it more practical to put them to bed in sleep bags or walkers than to try to keep blankets over them. (They simply crawl out from under their covers.) The bags are shaped like long nighties, which cover the feet and have sleeves. The bed walkers are shaped like coveralls or snowsuits, enclosing each leg separately, including the foot. (The sole of the foot may be of tough, non-skid material.) These bags are generally made of polyester, frequently combined with cotton. Many of the bags can be let out in the length and shoulders as the child grows. Federal law requires that all sleepwear be flame-resistant, from infant through size 14. Read the washing instructions, to retain the flame-retardant properties.

If a baby or child is going to sleep in a room which is warm enough so that you would be comfortable wearing a cotton dress or shirt or sleeping under a cotton blanket, the baby's bag or walker shouldn't be warmer than cotton blanketing. If the room is cold enough so that an adult would require a good wool or acrylic blanket for covering, the baby will need a polyester bag or walker.

Incidentally, a baby or child doesn't need more in the way of clothing or covering than an adult; if anything, less.

It is most convenient when the zipper on a bed walker goes from neck to foot.

82. Other clothes. Knitted acrylic caps are all right for going outdoors in the kind of weather that makes grown-ups put on overcoats, or for sleeping in an equally cold room. For milder weather, caps are unnecessary; most babies don't like them anyway. You don't need booties and stockings, at least until your baby is sitting up and playing around in a cold house. Dresses make a baby look pretty, but are unnecessary otherwise, and bothersome to the baby and the parent. A sun hat, with a chin strap to keep it on, is useful for the baby who will tolerate it.

BEDCLOTHES

83. Blankets are usually a polyester–cotton combination or are made of acrylic. These are easy to wash and nonallergenic. Even if you use bed bags or walkers as the baby's principal bed covering, you will probably need a couple of blankets for certain occasions or for extra covering when it's cold. A knitted shawl is a particularly convenient form of blanket for babies because it wraps around them so easily when they are up, and stays tucked when it is over them in bed. Acrylic blankets and shawls are both warm and washable. Blankets should be large enough to tuck well under a crib mattress.

Cotton "receiving blankets," which have little warmth, are useful for wrapping around the baby who would otherwise kick off the bed coverings or for tightly swaddling the young baby who is only comfortable and secure when held immobile. (See Section 334.)

84. Waterproof sheeting of plastic or rubber. Most popular is sheeting that has a flannelette backing on both surfaces. It stays in place, and the sheet does not slip on it. It is more comfortable in case the baby happens to get in contact with it. Since it allows some circulation of air under the baby, there is usually no need to cover it with a quilted pad, and this makes a saving in laundry. However, in hot weather you may still need a pad, too. The sheeting should be washed (it will go in the machine) each day if it gets wet with urine, so you will need two.

The waterproof sheeting should preferably be large enough to tuck in around the mattress. Otherwise the edges of the mattress may get wet at times. Incidentally, the plastic cover that comes on most new mattresses is not sufficient by itself. Sooner or later urine gets into the air holes and makes it smell.

Additional small squares of flannel-backed sheeting will save more laundry. Place one under the baby's hips. It will keep the bedsheet dry if the baby stays in one place. You can use one as a lap protector.

A thin plastic bag such as that used to cover clothes from the dry cleaner should never be used in a crib because of the danger of suffocation if the baby's head gets tangled in it.

85. Pads. If you are using plain waterproof sheeting (without flannel backing), you will need to cover it with a quilted pad. This is to absorb moisture and allow some circulation of air under the baby's body; otherwise the skin stays too hot and wet. The number of pads you will need will depend on how often the laundry is done, how much the baby wets or spits up. You will need three anyway, and six are more convenient.

86. Sheets. You will need three to six sheets. If you are using a small bassinet at first, you can use diapers for sheets. For anything larger, the best sheets are made of cotton stockinette. They are easy to wash, quick to dry, spread smoothly without ironing, and do not feel clammy when wet. Fitted sheets can be bought to cover the crib mattress.

EQUIPMENT THAT MAY OR MAY NOT BE NECESSARY

87. Scales. If a baby is doing well and is seen by the doctor regularly, there is no real need to have scales at home. You can rent good scales at a children's store or hospital equipment store if your doctor thinks them necessary. Spring scales are not accurate enough. I think that scales generally are a waste of money and space and tend to cause worry rather than prevent it.

88. A carriage (pram) is used primarily by parents in cities in the northeastern part of the United States to take their babies on daily outings or to give them naps in, on the porch. They get a lot of satisfaction and use out of it. But in most parts of this country parents don't think about carriages—or outings.

A stroller is a handy way to take a young child shopping and on other errands, especially for those in cities who don't have a car at their disposal. A folding "umbrella" stroller can be easily carried on a bus or in a car.

89. Harnesses. The use of harnesses with toddlers is controversial. Some parents feel that they will be accused of treating their toddler like a dog if they're out in public with a harness on the child and are holding a "leash" which is attached to the harness. It seems to me that the parent who happens to have an especially active toddler, particularly if there is also a younger child in the family, can use such a harness arrangement as a very effective safety measure while shopping in supermarkets or other places where toddlers can easily do damage to themselves or the merchandise! Naturally, the harness lead should never be used to tie the toddler to something while the parent goes off in another direction.

90. Bottle warmer. It isn't considered necessary any longer to warm a baby's bottle. It can of course be warmed in any kind of container. An electric warmer is very handy when the hot water supply is undependable. There is a special warmer that plugs into an automobile cigarette lighter.

91. Bath thermometer. Not necessary, but a comfort to the inexperienced parent.

92. Pacifiers. If you decide to use them. (See Sections 394–396.)

93. Playpens are controversial. Some parents and psychologists disapprove of the imprisonment of a baby in a pen, fearing that it may cramp the desire to explore and cramp the spirit. I see what they mean. But I've known many babies who spent several hours a day in pens and who still ended up demon explorers with high spirits. But neither of these opinions proves anything definite.

As a practical matter it's hard for me to see how a parent can cook a meal, or do much else, after a baby has learned to crawl around, unless the baby is in a pen part of the time.

If you are going to use a pen, you must start putting the baby in it each day from about 3 months. Babies differ—some tolerate playpens well, some poorly. If you wait until a baby starts to crawl (6 to 8 months), the pen will surely seem like a prison and will be met with persistent howls.

94. Carryall bassinet. This is a combination of a carrying bassinet and diaper bag, in which the baby can sleep while you are visiting friends. It folds up for storage.

95. A bed strap that will hold a baby on a bed, yours or a friend's. It clips to the bed frame.

96. A food grinder or blender, to puree cooked meats, vegetables, and fruits, so that the baby can have what the family has, and so that you can get around the expense of canned baby foods and the further disadvantage that many of them are diluted with starches and water. To avoid the expense of an electric blender you can get a dishwashable, hand-operated grinder for babies' foods.

97. Toiletries.

Child's nose syringe, made of rubber with a soft tip or molded plastic tip, to remove mucus during colds.

Rectal thermometer, to take rectal or axillary (armpit) temperatures. Also available are heat-activated products you place on the baby's forehead which give a general read-out, letting you know if your baby is feverish. (See Section 682 for differences in readings.)

Absorbent cotton. A pound roll of sterile absorbent cotton. You make soft swabs for removing dried mucus from the nose and for cleaning the outer ear by firmly rolling a small piece of cotton between moist finger and thumb. Cotton balls and cotton already wrapped on flexible sticks can be bought for these purposes.

Soap. Any mild soap is satisfactory.

Baby lotion. Not really necessary unless the skin is dry, though parents enjoy applying it. Many parents now prefer to use creams and lotions which don't have scent or color added and which most often cost less than the usual baby products.

Baby oils, most of which are made of mineral oil, have been used extensively for dry or normal skin or for diaper rash. But tests have shown that mineral oil itself may cause a very mild rash in some babies. So it is sensible not to use it routinely unless you find by testing that it has more advantage than disadvantage in your baby's case.

Baby powder helps a little to avoid chafing, but it is not necessary in most cases. (Zinc stearate powder is not considered safe for babies because it is irritating when breathed into the lungs.) Ordinary kitchen cornstarch powder is the least expensive of all and has no known harmful effects for the baby. Any powder should be applied fairly carefully (shake it into your hand first), so that there isn't a cloud of it around the baby's face.

An ointment containing lanolin and petrolatum, in tube or jar, to protect the skin when there is a diaper rash.

Infant nail scissors. These have blunted ends to prevent injuring a squirming baby.

See Section 119 for other items to keep in your medicine cabinet.

FORMULA EQUIPMENT

98. Nursing bottles. Some parents can afford the expense of prepared formula which comes in disposable bottles.

If you know ahead of time that your baby is not going to be breast-fed, buy at least nine of the 8-ounce bottles. You will use six to eight a day in the beginning for the formula, and you will surely break a few eventually. If you expect to breast-feed, buy at least three, for occasional formula feedings, water, and juice.

The nipple fits into a plastic screw-on ring. Except when the baby is nursing, the nipple is stored upside down in the bottle and a plastic cap covers the opening.

Pyrex bottles are more expensive but don't break because of too rapid heating or chilling. In the long run they are probably an economy for most parents.

Plastic bottles don't break when adults or babies drop them.

Water and juice can be given just as well from 8-ounce bottles, even though they are unnecessarily large. But some parents prefer 4-ounce bottles for this purpose. Two or three of these will be enough.

There are also disposable bottles of thin flexible plastic that come in a long strip already sterilized, ready to be used with a rigid plastic holder, which is bought separately. The parents who use them swear by them.

99. Nipples. A dozen if the baby will be bottle-fed, a half dozen if breast-fed. You should have a few extra in case you drop one on the floor or are having trouble making the nipple holes the right size.

Nipples made with silicone are more expensive but don't deteriorate from boiling and milk fat.

Most people use nipples with one or more holes in the top. If you have trouble with clogged nipples, you can buy those with "crosscut" openings or you can crosscut your own (Section 232).

100. A pail, kettle, or roaster with lid for sterilizing the bottles, preferably 8 inches high and 9 inches in diameter so that it will hold 8 bottles vertically in a wire bottle rack. There are electric sterilizers that turn themselves off. Most parents won't need to sterilize, so this equipment won't be necessary. (See Section 205.)

101. A container for mixing formula, marked in ounces. A glass quart measure marked in ounces is very convenient. But you can use any measuring cup marked in ounces and then mix in any saucepan or pitcher that holds a quart.

102. Other equipment.

Long-handled spoon for stirring.

Set of measuring spoons for measuring the sugar or syrup if you are going to make your own formula or use powdered milk or powdered formula.

A bottle brush and a **nipple brush** are essential.

Can opener. A punch-type opener is easiest.

Tongs, plastic or rubber-coated in the part that grips a bottle, are good for handling hot bottles; but if you follow the method in Section 223, you'll let the bottles cool before handling them.

Medical and Nursing Care

HAVING THE BABY

103. Prepared ("natural") childbirth. More and more women want to have their babies by prepared childbirth. This means they want the least possible anesthesia—so that they can participate actively in the delivery and see the baby being born. The lack of anesthesia is good for the baby, also. Most of the women who have had this experience consider it the most moving and creative experience in their lives. Many of them want their husband to be present if he has the same desire and if the obstetrician is willing. (Some obstetricians don't want a nonprofessional visitor in the delivery room; it distracts their attention from their job. Some husbands don't want to be present. And some women don't want their husbands there when they have so much hard work to do.)

If parents want to participate in prepared childbirth, they must find an obstetrician who is in sympathy. Then they should receive instruction in classes, during the last 2 to 3 months of the pregnancy, in the anatomy, physiology, and psychology of pregnancy and delivery, so that they will understand all that goes on. The woman will also practice exercises in breathing and pushing so that she can cooperate actively during labor and delivery.

One of the basic concepts of prepared childbirth is that the anxiety about childbirth, which is so common in our society, is a major cause of the wrong kinds of muscular tension and of the pain. With sound education and muscular training, much of the fear and a certain amount of the pain can be avoided. Then the woman can cooperate in every way with the birth process. And she can get the joyful sense of achievement from giving birth to a new person, a joy she deserves after nine months of pregnancy.

104. Hospital impressions. Nowadays most babies in this country are born in a hospital. There the doctor is closer at hand when needed, and is assisted by interns, nurses, technicians, and consultants. A hospital offers all the complicated equipment, like incubators and oxygen tents, to cope with sudden emergencies. All this makes the mother feel very safe and well cared for. But this setting also has drawbacks, which are part and parcel of its virtues. The babies may be in a nursery some distance from the mothers, where they can be efficiently watched and cared for by the nurses and won't disturb their mothers' rest. But it isn't quite natural, from the new mother's point of view, to have her baby somewhere else and taken care of so completely for a number of days. It may give her a feeling underneath of being somewhat ignorant and useless. A mother who has had several children might laugh at this and say, "It's **wonderful** to have that long rest in the hospital and not to have to worry about the baby." But it's different for her; she has a lot of confidence in herself as a mother and takes the hospital in stride.

A man, too, may get the wrong impression of himself as a father when his baby is born in a hospital, depending on the policies of that hospital. The mother at least knows that she is the center of attention. The poor father may be a complete outsider. If he wants to see his baby, he may have to stand outside a nursery window and look beseechingly at the nurse. Viewing a baby through glass is a poor substitute for holding the baby in your arms. Of course, the hospital is right in guarding his baby and all the others from any outside germs. But it gives the father the feeling that he is not considered a suitable companion for his child. See Section 37 for the role the father increasingly may have nowadays.

105. Rooming-in. In an effort to overcome some of the unnatural drawbacks of traditional maternity care, some hospitals have introduced the so-called rooming-in plan. The baby's bassinet, instead of being in a nursery, is close to the mother's bed. She is encouraged by the nurses to begin taking care of her baby, let's suppose it's a boy, as soon as she is able—holding him, feeding him, diapering him, bathing him. She has the chance to practice these things while she is among experienced people who can explain things to her and help her. She learns about her baby's hunger patterns, his sleep, his cry, his bowel movements, so that he is not a stranger when she takes him home. This is of particular advantage to the inexperienced mother. An irregular feeding schedule, governed by the baby's need, is no problem, and this favors the success of breast-feeding. The father when visiting feels he is a part of the family, and he can hold the baby and practice baby care himself.

Though rooming-in has always been practiced in some other parts of the world and though it was practiced in the United States many years ago, it has only been revived here in the past thirty years. It is safe. Most first-time mothers who have rooming-in are very enthusiastic and many want to have subsequent babies the same way.

If you hoped to have rooming-in but find it unavailable, don't feel that all is lost. You'll be able to make up for the lack of it after going home, especially in these days when the hospital stay is so short.

Prepared childbirth and rooming-in have come as much from the pressure of parents as from changing concepts in the medical and nursing professions and in hospital administration. So, if you want these procedures, ask for them from your doctor and from the hospital where you will deliver. (Go to see the administrator or at least write a letter.) Even if you can't get these procedures for yourself, you will have helped to get them for future parents.

106. Alternative birthing methods. In recent years, there has been an increasing interest in methods of delivering one's baby that are different from the usual practice of going to a hospital and spending most of one's labor in a labor room or ward and then being taken into a delivery room which essentially is a surgical suite. Many parents having their first or subsequent babies are choosing to have their babies at home, or in special "birthing centers," or birthing rooms in hospitals; and the babies are delivered by certified nurse midwives or obstetricians. In all of these alternatives, the emphasis is on creating a homelike environment in which the father and brothers and sisters can participate to varying degrees. If your obstetrician doesn't agree with this approach, you will have to decide between what he or she recommends and finding an obstetrician who's comfortable with the new methods. You can obtain detailed information about childbirth education and family life education classes and the various alternative birthing methods from the International Childbirth Education Association (ICEA), P.O. Box 20048, Minneapolis, MN 55420-0048, telephone (612)854-8660. Many medium- and large-sized cities have branches of the ICEA and they can be found in your local phone book.

Sometimes a woman feels that if she has taken childbirth preparation classes and doesn't go all the way through labor and delivery without any pain medication at all, then she has "failed" in what she set out to do. I don't think that is the case at all. The objective of the alternative birthing methods is to make the birth of a new baby as natural a family experience as possible. That usually includes a certain amount of pain and sometimes the need for medication to relieve the pain, but this won't cancel out the family benefit.

THE VISITING NURSE

107. Whether or not you have help at home, you ought to try to get a visiting nurse or public health nurse to come in once or twice in the early days. The nurse will show you how to make the formula, bathe the baby, and follow other directions of the doctor. And you can always call the nurse later when you have questions and problems. There are visiting nurses or public health nurses in most cities and in many country districts. Ask the doctor or the nurse in the hospital, telephone the Visiting Nurse Association or local health department, or write the state health department.

THE BABY'S DOCTOR

108. Who's to be the doctor? In many cases the family physician who has delivered the baby will go on seeing her afterward. A family doctor who is used to taking care of babies can do just as good a job as the specialist, unless some unusual problem comes up. In large cities, the child may have been delivered by a specialist in obstetrics who doesn't take care of the baby afterward. Then the parents will want to find a children's specialist (known as a pediatrician). About 40 percent of current trainees in pediatrics are women. Some parents get along best with a doctor who is casual, not too fussy about details. Others feel right only if they get every direction down to the last period. You may have more confidence in an older person or feel that you are imposing less on a younger one. If you have definite feelings about what kind of doctor you want, discuss the matter with your obstetrician who will know the children's specialists who are available. Some parents visit several doctors before the baby is born, until they find someone with whom they feel comfortable.

109. The child-health clinic. A city baby whose parents can't afford regular visits to a private doctor can and should attend a "well-baby clinic" or "child-health conference" at a hospital or child-health clinic. These have been established in many country districts, too. If you live in the country, write ahead of time to the state health department to find where the nearest clinic is. In a city you can find the nearest clinic by telephoning the city health department or the Visiting Nurse Association. On the staff of the well-baby clinic or child-health conference are doctors and nurses who work as a team. The doctor examines the baby at regular intervals, and advises the parents. The nurse helps the parents in carrying out the doctor's recommendations and in dozens of other practical child-care matters. The nurse can make a home visit soon after the mother and baby leave the hospital, and at other times when the parents have a problem that won't wait until the next clinic visit.

110. The nurse practitioner or physician's assistant. Certain schools of nursing in collaboration with pediatric training hospitals are offering special additional training to registered nurses to qualify them to be physicians' assistants (or nurse practitioners). They work in child-health conferences and also in pediatricians' offices, particularly in well-baby and well-child care. They take histories of children's progress since the last visit, examine them, advise the parents.

111. Regular visits. The way to be sure that your baby is doing well, let's say it's a girl, is to have her checked by a doctor regularly. The commonest schedule is once a month for 2 months, every 2 months for the next 4 months, then every 3 months through the second year. I believe that many parents would benefit from more frequent visits, at least with their first child. If you'd like more visits, ask for them. The doctor will want to weigh and measure the baby to see how she's growing, examine her to see that she's developing well, give her immunizations. You will have five or ten questions that you want to ask, with a first baby anyway. It's a good idea to have a little notebook that's always handy for writing down questions when they come to your mind at home, and also for noting developments, such as teething or a rash, that you may want to know the date of later. Of course, some families live so far away from a doctor that they can't plan a monthly visit. In some cases the parents and doctor can keep in touch by telephone. Naturally, every baby won't get into trouble just because the doctor doesn't see her regularly. But experience has shown that the monthly visit is vitally important for the occasional baby who is not doing well and a worthwhile and comforting precaution for all the rest.

112. Getting along with a doctor. In most cases the parents and the doctor soon come to know and trust each other and get along fine. But occasionally, since they are all human beings, there may be misunderstandings and tensions. Most of these are avoidable or easily cleared up with frankness on both sides.

Unless expense is no concern, it's a good idea to discuss charges when first engaging a physician. It's easier at the start than later. Though this may embarrass you, remember that it's an old story with the doctor and she or he should be able to take it. Many physicians will lower their fees for people with less-than-average incomes and are glad to know of the need ahead of time.

Most new parents are bashful in the beginning about asking questions about baby care that they are afraid are too simple or silly. It's foolish to worry about this. If there's any kind of question on your mind, you're entitled to an answer—that's what doctors are for. Most doctors are pleased to answer any questions that they can; the easier, the better.

Even if you feel sure that your doctor will be grumpy about something that is probably not serious but that you are nonetheless concerned about, call anyway. Your child's health is more important than the doctor's feelings or your own feelings.

It often happens that a parent, say it's the mother, asks about a problem and the doctor explains part of it but gets sidetracked before having answered the mother's most important question. If the mother is bashful, she may hesitate about coming back to that point and go home somewhat unsatisfied. She should encourage herself to be bold, to make clear exactly what she wants to know, so that the doctor can give her the answer or, if it is out of that doctor's line, refer her to some other professional person.

Often, on getting home from an office visit, parents find that they forgot to bring up their most important question or questions, and are ashamed to call back so soon. Doctors are not bothered by this; they are quite used to it.

113. Office visits for illness. Most parents remember that when they were sick as children the doctor made home visits. It seems wrong to them to take a sick child out to the doctor's office. Of course, the office visit is more convenient for the busy doctor. But doctors wouldn't advise it if it had not proved entirely safe, in these days of heated cars, and definitely beneficial in many illnesses. With many throat infections it is now important to take a throat culture to discover whether a streptococcus is the cause. If it is, the use of antibiotic medication is essential. If not, it is better not to prescribe it. It is often helpful during an illness which is still undiagnosed to get a urine specimen or a blood count. After an injury an X-ray is often desirable. In these situations and many others, doctors can do a better job in their offices or a hospital emergency room.

114. Asking for a consultation. If your child has some illness or condition that worries you intensely and you would like another expert opinion, it is always your right to ask freely for a consultation. Many parents are hesitant about doing so, fearing that this would express lack of confidence in, and hurt the feelings of, their present doctor. But it is a regular procedure in the practice of medicine, and the doctor should be able to take it in stride. Actually, doctors, like any other human beings, sense uneasiness in the people they deal with, even when it is unspoken, and it makes their job harder. A consultation usually clears the air for them as well as for the family.

115. Frankness works best. I think the main point in all these situations is that if you are unsatisfied with your doctor's advice or care, you should try to bring it out into the open right away, in the most matter-of-fact manner you can muster. An early meeting of minds is easier for both of you than allowing your tension and irritation to accumulate inside you.

Sometimes, though, a parent and doctor find that they just can't get along together, no matter how frank and cooperative they try to be, and then it's better all around to admit it openly. Every doctor, including the most successful, has learned that she or he doesn't suit everybody and takes this philosophically.

116. The time for telephone calls. Find out what time of day your doctor prefers phone calls, particularly about new illness that may require a visit to his or her office. A majority of illnesses in children first show definite symptoms during the afternoon, and most doctors would like to know about them as early in the afternoon as possible so that they can plan these visits efficiently. Naturally, if the symptoms that worry you don't come on till later, that's the time you have to call the doctor.

117. When to call the doctor. After you've raised a couple of babies, you'll have a good idea of which symptoms or questions require prompt contact with the doctor and which can wait till tomorrow or the next visit. But new parents often ask for a list. Even if they never consult the list, they feel more comfortable having one.

No list can be anywhere near complete. There are, of course, hundreds of different diseases and injuries. You always have to use your own common sense. The following discussion contains only a few general guides.

By far the most important rule, as I see it, is to consult the doctor promptly, at least by telephone, if a baby or child **looks different** (in general appearance) or **acts differently.** By this I mean such signs as unusual paleness, unusual tiredness, unusual drowsiness, lack of interest, unusual irritability, anxiousness, restlessness, prostration. This is particularly true in the first 2 or 3 months of life when a baby can be seriously ill without fever or other specific symptoms and signs of illness.

Fever is discussed in Section 682. How high or low it is is less important than whether the child seems really sick. A high fever often accompanies a mild infection after the age of 1 or 2 years, and a young baby can be quite sick with little or no fever. As a general rule, consult the doctor if the baby has a temperature of 101°F or more. You don't have to call in the middle of the night if the baby has only a mild cold with 101°F and otherwise seems happy; call in the morning. But if the baby looks sick, even without any fever, call promptly, especially in the first 2 or 3 months.

Colds. In general, you call the doctor if the cold is more than mild, or if there are any new symptoms, or if the child looks sicker. What to be concerned about in **colds** is discussed in Sections 707–709; **coughs,** in Section 715; **earaches,** in Section 714.

Hoarseness of voice, difficulty in breathing (Sections 718–720, 730, 731) should always be reported immediately.

Pain or suspicion of pain should be reported when it first appears. (Colic that occurs every evening for weeks doesn't need to be reported every time, of course.) **Ear infection** is discussed in Section 714; **stomachache,** in Sections 774, 775; pain in the **urinary tract,** Sections 767–770; **headache** should be reported promptly in a small child.

Sudden decrease in appetite is sometimes a sign of illness. It doesn't need to be reported if it occurs only once and if the child is as comfortable and happy as ever. But if the child acts differently in other respects, the doctor should be called.

Vomiting of any unusual type should be reported promptly, especially if the child looks sick or different in any other way. This does not apply, of course, to the spitting up after meals that is so common at first. See Sections 350, 351, 774, 775.

Diarrhea of the more serious sort, in infants, which should be reported to the doctor immediately, and the milder kinds, which should be reported within a few hours, are discussed in Section 361. Diarrhea of children should be reported soon (Section 774).

Blood in the bowel movements (Sections 310, 361) or blood in the vomitus should be reported promptly.

Inflammation of the eye or injury to the eye should be reported promptly (Section 780).

Injury to the head should be reported if the baby isn't happy and healthy looking in 15 minutes (Section 802).

Bulging of the soft spot should be reported, as should a sunken soft spot.

Injury to a limb should be reported if the baby is not inclined to use it normally or shows pain on using it (Sections 800, 801).

Burns should be reported if blisters appear (Section 797).

Poisons. If your child has eaten anything that **might** possibly be dangerous (Sections 807–809), you should reach your doctor or Poison Control Center immediately. It's a good idea to keep the phone numbers of your doctor and Poison Control Center posted beside your telephone.

Cuts are discussed in Sections 790–795.

Nosebleeds are discussed in Section 796.

Rashes. Of course, the commonest rashes in the first year are diaper rash (Section 366) and rough patches on the cheeks or a few small raised pink spots on the face (Section 367), none of which is an emergency. Babies are protected against contagious diseases like measles, rubella (German measles), chicken pox, and scarlet fever for the first half year anyway, if the mother has had them. Cradle cap is very common but unimportant (Section 369). Eczema occurs occasionally (Section 733) and should be reported within a day or so. Impetigo should be reported the first day (Section 740). If a child seems sick with a rash or if the rash is extensive, you should call the doctor right away.

X-rays. X-rays were sometimes used routinely for diagnosis, for example at semiannual dental checkups or to determine the normality of pregnancies or for the intensive treatment of acne—until it was realized that they could be harmful. Since then, thoughtful people have become cautious and some have resisted any X-rays, no matter how necessary. A minute amount of radiation such as we get regularly from living on the earth will give cancer to one particularly susceptible person in a million, which is much less risk than what we take every time we cross a busy street. And an individual with unusual resistance may take many intense exposures without apparent harm. So it's a matter of balancing risks. The risk from an undiagnosed infection of a tooth or the lungs is much greater than from a single X-ray picture. If you have a particularly strong fear of radiation, you should say so to your doctor or dentist so that she or he can take this into account. But if she or he still urges the X-ray, I myself would go along, as parent and patient.

118. Finding a doctor in a strange city. If you need a doctor for your child in a strange town, find the name of the best hospital. Telephone, and ask for the name of a pediatrician on the staff or a general practitioner who takes care of children. If there is any hitch, ask to speak to the physician-in-chief (who will probably not be a children's specialist), who will give you the names of one or two suitable doctors.

119. Things to have in your medicine cabinet. A box of sterile gauze squares, or "dressings," 3 inches square (each dressing remains sterile in a separate envelope). Two rolls of sterile stretchable bandage 2 inches wide, two rolls 1 inch wide. A roll of adhesive tape 1 inch wide. You can make narrower strips by cutting the end with scissors and then tearing. A box of prepared bandages of various sizes. A good pair of tweezers to remove splinters.

Ask your doctor to recommend an antiseptic. A package of bicarbonate of soda (baking soda). A bottle of antifever tablets (acetaminophen, not aspirin) for babies (each tablet contains 1¼ grains). A 1-ounce bottle of syrup of ipecac to cause vomiting in a case of poisoning. A rectal thermometer. A hot-water bottle. A rubber nose syringe with a plastic tip for clearing out a baby's nose during a cold.

When you have a small child in the home, all medicines—and particularly aspirin—should be in "childproof" containers that are difficult to open.

Infant Feeding

WHAT FEEDING MEANS TO THE BABY

120. A baby knows a lot about diet. She is the one who knows how many calories her body needs and what her digestion can handle. If she's regularly not getting enough, she'll probably cry for more. If there's more in the bottle than she feels like, let her stop when she wants to. Take her word for it.

Think of the baby's first year this way: She wakes up because she's hungry, cries because she wants to be fed. She is so eager when the nipple goes into her mouth that she almost shudders. When she nurses, you can see that it is an intense experience. Perhaps she breaks into perspiration. If you stop her in the middle of a nursing, she may cry furiously. When she has had as much as she wants, she is groggy with satisfaction and falls asleep. Even when she is asleep, it sometimes looks as if she were dreaming of nursing. Her mouth makes sucking motions, and her whole expression looks blissful. This all adds up to the fact that feeding is her great joy. She gets her early ideas about life from the way feeding goes. She gets her first ideas about the world from the person who feeds her.

When parents constantly urge their babies to take more than they want, they are apt to become steadily less interested. They may try to escape from it by going to sleep earlier and earlier in the feeding, or they may rebel and become more balky. They're apt to lose some of their active, positive feeling about life. It's as though they got the idea: "Life is a struggle. Those people are always after you. You have to fight to protect yourself."

So don't urge babies to take more than they are eager for. Let them go on enjoying their meals, feeling that you are their friend. This is one of the principal ways in which their self-confidence, their joy in life, and their love of people will be firmly established during the first year.

121. The important sucking instinct. Babies nurse eagerly for two separate reasons. First, because they're hungry. Second, because they **love** to suck. If you feed them plenty but don't give them enough chance to suck, their craving for sucking will go unsatisfied and they will try to suck something else—their fists, or their thumbs, or the clothes. It is also true that the sucking need varies greatly in different babies. It's important to give them a long enough nursing period at each feeding and to have a sufficient number of feedings each day. All this is taken up in detail in Sections 385–396, on thumb-sucking. The thing to watch for in the beginning is not whether babies are actually sucking their thumbs, but whether they look as if they are trying to.

122. Babies normally lose weight in the beginning. Good-sized babies who get formula from the start usually begin to gain it back in 2 or 3 days, because they can drink and digest well. Small or premature babies lose weight longer and regain it more slowly, because they can take only small feedings at first. It may take them several weeks just to get back to birth weight. This delay doesn't handicap them. Eventually they will gain rapidly to make up for it.

Some parents worry unnecessarily about the initial weight loss. They can't help feeling that it's unnatural and dangerous for the weight to be going down instead of up. They also may have heard that if babies lose **excessive** amounts of weight, they may develop fever from becoming dehydrated (dried out). It's for this reason that some hospitals give water for the first few days to the babies who get no formula and whose mothers' milk has not come in yet. But the chance of dehydration fever is small, and it can always be cured immediately by giving fluid.

Concern about the early weight loss not only may upset a

mother needlessly but may also cause her to abandon breast-feeding before it has been given a fair chance. Some hospitals, to keep the mother from worrying, don't tell her the daily weight of the baby, but this method doesn't always work. The mother who is anxious imagines the worst. It's better for the mother to realize how natural the weight loss is and to resolve to leave the whole matter in the doctor's hands.

SCHEDULES

123. What regularity and flexibility are all about. During the first half of this century, babies were usually kept on very strict, regular schedules. Doctors did not know for sure the cause of the serious intestinal infections that afflicted tens of thousands of babies yearly. It was believed that these infections were caused not only by the contamination of milk but also by wrong proportions in the formula **and** by irregularity in feeding.

Strict regularity worked well enough with a majority of babies. When they took an ample feeding at breast or bottle, it lasted them for **about** 4 hours just because that is the way a young baby's digestive system usually works.

But there were always a few babies who had trouble adjusting to regularity in the first month or two—babies whose stomachs couldn't seem to hold 4 hours' worth of milk, babies who went to sleep halfway through feedings, restless babies, colicky babies. They would cry miserably for shorter or longer periods each day, but their mothers and doctors dared not feed them (or even pick them up) off schedule. It was hard enough on the babies. I think it was harder still on the parents.

Anyway, the serious diarrheal diseases almost disappeared. The chief factor was the pasteurization of milk in the commercial dairy. But it took many more years before doctors dared to begin experimenting with flexible schedules.

The first experiments were carried out by Dr. Preston McLendon and Ms. Frances P. Simsarian, a psychologist and a new mother, with Ms. Simsarian's new baby. They wanted to find out what kind of schedule babies would establish if they were breast-fed whenever they seemed hungry. The baby waked rather infrequently the first few days. Then, from just about the time the milk began to come in, he waked surprisingly often—about 10 times a day—in the second half of the first week. But by the age of two weeks he had settled down to six or seven feedings a day, at rather irregular intervals. By 10 weeks he had arrived at approximately a 4-hour schedule. They called this an experiment in "self-demand" feeding. Since that experiment led the way, in 1942, there has been a general relaxation in infant feeding schedules, which has had a wholesome effect on babies and parents. (It's now realized that the average number of hours between feedings for a breast-fed baby in the first two weeks of life is two. That means that some babies will be nursing every 3 hours and some as often as every hour and a half.)

124. Misunderstandings about self-demand. I think, though, that there has been a certain amount of misunderstanding. Some young parents, eager to be progressive, have assumed that if they wanted to get away from the rigid scheduling of the past they must go all the way in the opposite direction, feed their baby **any** time she woke and **never** wake her for a feeding, just as if **they** were conducting a scientific experiment, or as if there were a fundamental superiority in irregularity.

This may work out well enough if the baby is a peaceful one with a good digestion, if the parents don't have to worry about their own schedule, and if they don't mind being waked between midnight and 6 A.M. But if the baby happens to be a restless, fretful one, it can lead to a great many feedings and very little rest for the parents, for several months. And in a few cases it encourages the baby to be still waking for a couple of night feedings even at the end of the first year.

The main purpose of any schedule is to do right by the baby. But another purpose is to enable the parents to care for their child in a way that will conserve their strength and spirits. This usually means getting down to a reasonable number of feedings at predictable hours, and omitting the night feeding as soon as the baby is ready.

If parents **prefer** to feed their baby on an irregular schedule for many months, there is no harm done to the baby's nutrition. It does no harm to the parents, either, if they're people who just hate to do anything by the clock. But if they're fairly regular about the rest of their lives and have other things to get done, I only worry that they have gotten the idea that the more they give up for the baby the better it is for the child, or that they have to prove they are good parents by ignoring their own convenience. These attitudes tend to create difficulties in the long run.

I have seen happy families with babies on schedules of 2, 3½, 4, or 6 hours, and no schedule at all.

125. General guide to scheduling. The main consideration for babies is that they not have to cry with hunger for long periods. They don't mind at all being waked up for a feeding after an interval of 3 or 4 hours.

All babies have a tendency to develop regular habits of becoming hungry, and these will come much more rapidly if the parents guide them a bit.

Also, babies tend to lengthen gradually the interval between feedings as they grow bigger and older. A 5- or 6-pounder usually needs to be fed about every 3 hours. Most 8- and 9-pounders are happy to average 4 hours between feedings. They come to realize that they don't need the late-night feeding and most of them give it up by 1, 2, or 3 months of age. Somewhere between the fourth and eighth months, a majority of babies show a preference for a 5-hour interval, and during this period they become able to sleep through the evening feeding, too.

In all these tendencies—to more regular feedings and to fewer feedings—the baby can be greatly influenced by the parents' management. Suppose a mother wakes her baby boy whenever he's still asleep 4 hours after the last feeding; she is helping him to establish a 4-hour hunger habit. If, when he stirs and whimpers a couple of hours after the last feeding, she holds back for a few minutes and gives him a chance to go to sleep again, or if, when he gets crying steadily, she tries to comfort him with a pacifier or a bottle of water, she helps his stomach adjust to a longer interval. If, on the other hand, she always picks him up and feeds him promptly when he stirs, even though it's only a couple of hours after the last feeding, she keeps him accustomed to short intervals and small feedings.

Individual babies differ widely in how soon they can comfortably settle down to regular schedules. A great majority of the ones who are good feeders, who are reasonably relaxed, and who are getting plenty to drink from breast or bottle can be eased into a smooth 4-hour schedule and will give up the 2 A.M. feeding a month or two after birth. On the other hand, if a baby is a listless, sleepy feeder at first, or a restless, fretful waker (Sections 174, 234–236, 334–336), or if the breast-milk supply is not yet well established, it will be more comfortable for all concerned to go more slowly. But even in these cases, there will be less perplexity on the part of the parents every day—about whether to give a feeding right away or to wait—and an earlier settling down on the part of the baby, if the parents are always working gently toward more regular feedings, as close as possible to every 4 hours for bottle-fed babies and 3 hours for breast-fed babies. (Bottle-fed babies can all be gotten onto an average 4-hour schedule eventually, if that's what the parents need.)

126. Specific suggestions for working toward a regular schedule. A relaxed baby girl who weighed 7 or 8 pounds at birth usually is able to last 3½ to 4 hours on a full stomach and wants 6 or 7 feedings in the 24 hours at the start. The parents can keep in mind, as a rough guide, a 4-hour schedule (6 A.M., 10 A.M., 2 P.M., 6 P.M., 10 P.M., 2 A.M.), but be quite willing to feed her early if she really seems hungry—1 hour early if she is taking good amounts from the bottle; as much as 2 hours early if she is breast-fed and the supply is not yet well established.

If your baby is still asleep when one of these regular feeding hours comes around, you can wake her up. You won't have to urge her to eat. A baby who is waked up 4 hours after her last feeding will usually be starving hungry in a few minutes. But suppose she wakes an hour early for her next feeding. You don't have to feed her the first minute she whimpers. She's not sure herself she's hungry. But if in 10 or 15 minutes she's crying hard with hunger, I wouldn't wait any longer. What happens to the 4-hour schedule? She may make up the difference and sleep long enough before the next feeding to get back on schedule. If she doesn't make up the time during the day, she may make it up at night. If she's always waking early, nearer to every 3 hours, maybe she isn't getting enough to last 4 hours. If she is being breast-fed, let her nurse more often—even after 2 hours if she seems very hungry—expecting that the more frequent emptying of the breast and stimulation of the nipple and areola will lead to more milk supply in the next few days. When she gets a larger amount, she will be able to last longer. If she is on the bottle, draining every one, and regularly waking early, consult the doctor about increasing the formula.

127. Just how early should you give another feeding? I have been saying that if the baby who generally can go 4 hours wakes after 3 or 3½ hours and seems really hungry, it is all right to feed her then. But suppose she wakes an hour or so after her last feeding. If she finished her usual bottle at her last feeding, the chances are against her being hungry again so soon. It is more likely that she has been waked by indigestion or colic. You can try burping her again, or see whether she will be comforted by a couple of ounces of water or a pacifier. I would not be in a rush to feed her again, though you may decide to try it in a little while if nothing else works. You can't be sure it's hunger just because a baby tries to eat her hand or starts to take the bottle eagerly. Often a baby who is having colic will do both these things. It seems the baby herself can't distinguish between colic pains and hunger pains. This is discussed in Section 336.

In other words, you don't **always** feed a baby when she cries. If she is crying at the wrong times, you have to study the situation and perhaps discuss it with your doctor.

128. Other hours for a 4-hour schedule. Can you aim for a 4-hour schedule with hours other than the usual 6 A.M., 10 A.M., 2 P.M., 6 P.M., 10 P.M., 2 A.M.? You certainly can, if the baby is willing. The commonest substitute is 7 A.M., 11 A.M., 3 P.M., 7 P.M., 11 P.M. (with or without 3 A.M.). The only hitch is that most young babies always want to start the day between 5 and 6 A.M., no matter when they were last fed during the night. Once in a while, lucky parents get a baby who is on the usual 6-10-2-6-10 schedule but is willing to wait until 7 A.M. for the first feeding, even when quite young. This is all right, too.

129. A 3-hour schedule. If your baby is getting all the milk she wants but usually wakes in about 3 hours in the daytime, it will probably be more convenient to stick to a 3-hour schedule for the time being.

It's mostly babies weighing under 7 pounds who need to be on a 3-hour schedule. But this is not an absolute rule. Some 6-pounders are willing and able to go 4 hours. And an occasional 8-pounder can't hold enough to last more than 3 hours for the first couple of weeks.

Most babies who need a 3-hour schedule during the daytime are able to go 4 hours at night if they weigh as much as 5 pounds. The feedings usually work out about as follows: 6 A.M., 9 A.M., 12 noon, 3 P.M., 6 P.M., 10 P.M., 2 A.M.

130. The 2 A.M. feeding. The easiest rule for the 2 A.M. feeding is not to wake the babies but to let them wake you if they want to. Babies who still need that feeding usually wake surprisingly close to the hour of 2. Then some night, probably when they're between 2 and 6 weeks old, they will sleep through until 3 or 3:30 A.M. You feed them then, and count it as a 2 A.M. feeding. They'll probably be awake and hungry again between 6 and 7 A.M. The next night they may sleep till 4:30 or 5 A.M. You feed them then, but this time you count it as a 6 o'clock feeding and hope that they'll be happy until somewhere near 10 A.M. When babies get ready to give up the 2 A.M. feeding, they usually do it in a hurry, within two or three nights. Then you divide the total formula into five bottles instead of six.

131. Omitting the 2 A.M. feeding. If babies reach the age of 1 month and weigh 9 pounds and still wake for a 2 A.M. feeding, I think it's sensible for the parents to try to influence them to give it up. Instead of hurrying to them as soon as they stir, you can let them fuss for 15 or 30 minutes and see if they won't go back to sleep. If they don't quiet down, try a couple of ounces of warm water. If they're crying furiously at the end of half an hour, it will be easier all around to give them breast or formula, but try again in another week or two. From a nutritional point of view, a 9-pounder who's eating well during the day doesn't really need a 2 A.M. feeding.

132. The 10 P.M., or evening, feeding is the one that you can probably time to your own convenience. Most babies, by the time they are a few weeks old, are perfectly willing to wait until 11 or even midnight for it. If you want to get to bed early, wake the baby at 10 or even a little before. If a later feeding is more convenient, suit yourself, as long as the baby is willing to stay asleep.

For those babies who are still waking for 2 A.M. feedings, I would advise against letting them sleep through the 10 or 11 P.M. feedings, even though they're quite willing. When they're ready to give up one of them, you'll want them to give up the 2 A.M. feeding first, so that your sleep won't be interrupted.

For those babies who are already off the 2 A.M. feeding but are still quite irregular about their daytime feeding hours, I'd continue to wake them at 10 or 11 P.M., provided they're willing to be fed. This at least ends the day on schedule, helps very much to avoid a feeding between midnight and 4 A.M., and tends to start them off somewhere between 5 and 6 the next morning.

Omitting the 10 P.M. feeding is discussed in Section 266.

GIVING THE FEEDING

The details of giving breast feedings are discussed in Sections 148–164. Some of the problems of babies who do not nurse well in the early weeks and are slow to settle into a schedule are described in Section 174.

Giving the bottle is discussed in Sections 228–238. This includes some of the difficulties in the early weeks.

133. Refusal to nurse in later months. Once in a while a baby between 4 and 7 months old acts queerly at feeding time. The mother will say that her baby boy nurses hungrily at breast or bottle for a few minutes. Then he becomes frantic, lets go of the nipple, and cries as if in pain. He still seems very hungry. But each time he goes back to nursing he becomes uncomfortable sooner. He takes his solid food eagerly. I think that this distress is caused by teething. I suspect that as the baby nurses, the suction engorges his painful gums and makes them tingle unbearably. You can break each nursing period into several parts and give the solid food in the intervals, since the distress comes on only after a number of minutes of sucking. If he is on a bottle, you can experiment with enlarging the holes in a few nipples so that he finishes the bottle in a shorter time with less strenuous sucking. If the baby's discomfort is excessive and comes on very promptly, you could, for a few days, give up the bottle altogether. Give him his milk from the cup, if he is skillful enough, or from a spoon, or mix a large amount of it with his cereal and other foods. Don't worry if he doesn't get his usual amount.

An ear infection, complicating a cold, may cause enough pain in the jaw joint so that babies will refuse to nurse even though they may be able to eat solids pretty well.

Occasionally, babies will decline to take the breast during the mothers' menstrual periods. They can be offered the breast more often during those days. It will be necessary for the mother to express the breast milk manually to relieve the fullness and to keep the supply going. Babies will resume their usual breast-feeding when the period is over and will be able to revive the breast-milk supply.

134. Getting up the air bubble. You have to hold the bottle with the bottom high enough so the nipple is always full of formula. But all babies swallow some air while they are drinking their milk. It collects as a bubble in the stomach. Some babies' stomachs become uncomfortably full before they're halfway through their feeding, and they have to stop. Most never swallow enough air to interrupt the meal. A few, especially breast-fed babies, don't even have a bubble at the end of a feeding. There are a couple of ways to bubble babies, and you can find which works best for you. The first is to sit them upright in your lap and gently rub their stomach. The other is to hold them up against your shoulder and massage or pat them in the middle of the back. It's a good idea to put a diaper over your shoulder in case they spit up a little. One kind of stomach lets go of the bubble very easily and promptly. The other kind seems to want to hang on to it. When the bubble doesn't come up easily, it sometimes helps to put these babies in a lying position for a second and then bring them back to your shoulder again.

You need to bubble babies in the middle of a feeding only if they swallow so much air that it stops their nursing. But you should at least try to get the bubble up at the end of the feeding. Most babies will become uncomfortable in a little while if put to bed with the bubble still in the stomach. Some babies even get colic pains from it. On the other hand, if your baby is hard to bubble and always seems just as comfortable whether burped or not, there is no need for you to try for more than a few minutes.

This is as good a place as any to mention the fact that when a young baby has taken a full feeding, the abdomen bulges to an extent that's apt to worry the inexperienced parent. This is only because the amount the baby needs to drink at each feeding is much larger in comparison to the size of the abdomen than it is in an adult. You'd look full if you weighed 110 pounds and drank 2 quarts of milk at a meal!

GETTING ENOUGH AND GAINING WEIGHT

135. Infants usually know how much food they need. If they are outgrowing their present formula, or if their mother's breast-milk supply has decreased temporarily because of fatigue or tension, they will probably begin to wake earlier and earlier before each feeding and cry with a cry that you now recognize as one of hunger. They will be finishing all their bottles to the last drop and looking around for more. They may try to eat their hands. Sometimes babies who are getting hungry will become constipated, also. If they are getting **really** hungry, they may cry at the end of some of their feedings, too.

If your baby is showing some of these signs of dissatisfaction and is on a formula, it is time to add an ounce to each bottle.

If your baby is being breast-fed and waking early, you can nurse early, even though this might mean an extra feeding a day. The more frequent feedings will help to satisfy the baby, and the more frequent emptying of the breasts will stimulate them to produce a larger supply. If you have been nursing at only one breast a feeding, give both breasts at each feeding for a while.

136. How much weight should babies gain? The best that you can say is that they should gain at the rate that they seem to want to gain at. Most babies know. If they are offered more food than they need, they refuse it. If they are given less, they show their hunger by waking earlier before feedings and eating their fists.

We can talk about average babies if you remember clearly that no baby is average. When doctors talk about an average baby, they mean only that they have added together the fast gainers and the slow gainers and the medium gainers. One baby is **meant** to be a slow gainer, and another is **meant** to be a fast gainer.

If babies are gaining slowly, that doesn't mean for sure that they were meant to. If they are hungry all the time, that is a pretty good sign that they are meant to be gaining faster. Once in a while slow gaining means that a baby is sick. Slow gainers particularly need to be seen regularly by a doctor to make sure that they are healthy. Occasionally you see exceptionally polite babies who are gaining slowly and who don't seem too hungry. But if you give them more to eat, they take it quite willingly and gain more rapidly. In other words, not all babies yell when they are being fed too little.

The average baby's weight is a little over 7 pounds at birth, and 14 pounds between 3 and 5 months. That is to say, the average baby doubles birth weight between 3 and 5 months. But in actual practice, babies who are small at birth are more apt to grow faster, as if trying to catch up, and babies who are born big are less apt to double their birth weight by 3–5 months.

The average baby gains close to 2 pounds a month (6 or 8

ounces a week) during the first 3 months. Of course, some healthy ones gain less, and others more. Then the baby slows down. **By 6 months the average gain is down to a pound a month** (4 ounces a week). That's quite a drop in a 3-month period. In the last quarter of the first year, the average gain is down to ⅔ pound a month (2 or 3 ounces each week), and during the second year to about ½ pound a month.

As babies grow older, you can see that they gain more slowly. They also gain more irregularly. Teething, for instance, may take their appetite away for several weeks, and they may hardly gain at all. When they feel more comfortable, their appetite revives and their weight catches up with a rush.

You can't decide too much from how babies' weights change from week to week. What they weigh each time will depend on how recently they have urinated, how recently they have moved their bowels, how recently they have eaten. If you find, one morning, that your baby boy has gained only 4 ounces in the past week, whereas before he had always gained 7, don't jump to the conclusion that he is starving or that something else is wrong. If he seems perfectly happy and satisfied, wait another week to see what happens. He may make an extra large gain to make up for the small one. For the breast-fed baby, wetting the diapers at least every 6–8 hours, being alert and happy when awake, sleeping well, and having a weight gain from week to week are good indications that he's getting enough to eat. Always remember, though, that the older he gets, the slower he will gain.

137. How often do you need to weigh the baby? Of course, most parents don't have scales, and most babies get weighed only when they go to see their doctor, which is plenty often. When a baby is happy and doing well, weighing more frequently than once a month serves no purpose but to satisfy curiosity. If you have scales, don't weigh more often than once a week. Once in 2 weeks is even better. If you weigh your baby every day, you encourage yourself to get too wrapped up in the weight. On the other hand, if your baby is crying a lot, or having indigestion, or vomiting a great deal, more frequent weighing at the doctor's office may help you and your doctor in deciding what is the matter. For instance, excessive crying combined with rapid weight gaining points toward colic, not hunger.

138. Fatness may become lifelong. There is evidence—though not proof yet—from human and animal growth records that fatness in infancy tends to foster fatness for the rest of life. (See "Fat Children," Sections 674–678.)

So it's not a kindness to babies to get them fattened up; it's almost a curse in a society that dislikes and ridicules fatness. Adult obesity was not always scorned. Rubens's plump nudes, with their many dimples, were obviously considered beautiful.

It seems to be harder for us to change our feeling that obesity in babies is attractive and desirable. Relatives and friends still compliment parents on it as if it were proof of superior care. I think, also, that in parts of the world where mass starvation is still remembered, parents think of baby fat as a reserve against it, like money in the bank.

Anyway, I hope we can get over the idea that obesity is desirable in infancy.

Breast-feeding

THE VALUES OF BREAST-FEEDING

139. Breast-feeding is valuable in a number of ways. Careful studies in recent years have shown that babies receive immunity to a variety of infections through the colostrum (the fluid that comes in before the real milk) and through the milk.

A big advantage of breast-feeding is that the milk is always pure; a baby can't catch an intestinal infection from it. From a purely practical point of view, it saves hours of time every week, because there are no bottles to sterilize, no formulas to mix and cook, no refrigeration to worry about, no bottles to warm. You appreciate this particularly if you ever have to travel. Of course, breast-feeding saves money, too. It is more adapted to satisfying the baby's sucking instinct. At the breast he can suck as long as he feels the need. I think that there is less thumb-sucking among breast-fed babies, for that reason.

The most convincing evidence of the value of breast-feeding comes from mothers who have done it. They tell of the tremendous satisfaction they experience from knowing that they are providing their babies with something no one else can give them, from seeing their devotion to the breast, from feeling their closeness.

It is too seldom mentioned that, after a couple of weeks, breast-feeding becomes definitely pleasurable for the mother. Many nursing mothers say that the pleasure sensations which they feel in their breasts and in their genital region while they are nursing are very similar to the sensations they experience during sexual excitement. Some women feel confused and guilty about the similarity in these sensations because they don't realize that they are entirely normal. Many nursing mothers have the experience of beginning to leak milk from their breasts when another woman's baby cries hungrily nearby, and this is embarrassing to mothers who don't understand that this, too, is entirely normal.

Parents don't get to feel like parents, or come to enjoy being parents, or feel the full parental love for their child just from the fact that a baby has been born to them. With their first infant particularly, they become real parents only as they take care of their child. The more success they have in the beginning in doing their part, and the more visibly their baby is satisfied by their care, the sooner and more enjoyably they slip into the role. In this sense, breast-feeding does wonders for a young mother and for her relationship with her baby. She and her baby are happy in themselves and feel more and more loving to each other.

Fewer babies have been breast-fed in the twentieth century—all over the world. But in recent years, breast-feeding has been on the increase in America, particularly among women who have attended college. This is partly due to the new knowledge about the physical and emotional advantages, partly to the general respect, among the young, for Nature and the desire to do things the natural way.

140. Different feelings about breast-feeding. A few women, usually because of the way they were brought up, feel deeply uncomfortable at the prospect of breast-feeding—it may seem too immodest or too animal-like.

Quite a few fathers, including some very good ones, object to breast-feeding—they can't help feeling jealous. Many other fathers feel great pride in their wives' nursing their babies. So the mother has to use her judgment.

Some mothers and fathers are embarrassed by milk leaking during lovemaking, while others find this quite arousing. So you can see that it's really important for the parents to try to openly discuss their feelings about nursing with each other. Sometimes, having this discussion with the doctor present can help the parents get over their trouble in getting started.

QUESTIONS ABOUT BREAST-FEEDING

141. The mother's figure. Some mothers shy away from breast-feeding for fear it will spoil their figures. You certainly don't have to eat excessively or get fat in order to make milk. A nursing mother needs enough extra to keep her own body from being depleted. She does not need to gain an ounce above her regular weight.

But what about the effect of nursing on the shape and size of the breasts? They enlarge during pregnancy and even more during the first days after birth, whether or not the baby is nursed. Physicians believe that this preliminary enlargement —rather than continued nursing—is what causes some breasts to flatten and sag. Certainly the breasts become much less prominent and firm by the time a baby is a week old, even if the mother continues to nurse successfully, so much so that she may wonder whether her milk has gone.

An important factor—whether nursing is never started or is ended at 1, 3, 6, or 12 months—is the character of the supporting tissue of the breasts in each individual. There are women whose breasts have flattened without their ever having nursed a child. I know from my own medical experience that many women breast-feed several babies with no deleterious effect on their figures. Others end up with even better figures.

There are two precautions that are probably important. First, the mother should wear a well-fitting brassiere that supports the breasts, not only when she is nursing but also during the later part of pregnancy, day and night, when the breasts are definitely enlarged. This is to prevent stretching of the skin and of the supporting tissues in the breasts during the time the breasts are heavier. For many women it is advisable to change to a larger brassiere by the seventh month of pregnancy. It is well worthwhile to buy nursing brassieres that have changeable, washable pads in them to absorb any milk that may leak between feedings (of course, cotton pads may be used instead), and the fronts of which can be opened for nursing (get the kind that can be opened easily with one hand).

The other precaution during pregnancy and nursing is to

avoid putting on excess weight. After all, the breasts may sag from obesity, quite apart from pregnancy.

142. Size of breasts is of no importance. Some women with small breasts assume that they will be less able to produce milk in sufficient quantity. There is no basis for this belief. When a woman is not pregnant and not nursing, the glandular tissue is quiescent and constitutes only a minor part of the breast. The greater part is composed of fat tissue. The larger breast has more fat tissue; the smaller breast has less. As a woman's pregnancy progresses, secretions from the ovaries stimulate the glandular, milk-producing tissue to develop and enlarge. The arteries and veins that serve the glandular tissue enlarge, too, so that the veins become prominent on the surface of the breasts. The milk, when it comes in a few days after delivery, causes further enlargement of the breasts. Doctors who have cared for nursing mothers agree that even women who have unusually small breasts before pregnancy can produce copious amounts of milk.

143. Does it tire the mother? You occasionally hear it said that breast-feeding "takes a lot out of a woman." Many women do feel fatigued in the early weeks of nursing, but so do many who are feeding by bottle. They are getting their strength back after the delivery and hospitalization. The nervous tension from caring for a new baby is tiring. But it's also true that the breasts are providing a goodly number of calories each day for the baby, and a mother must eat considerably more than usual just to keep her weight up. In the long run there is no more reason for a woman to feel exhausted from breast-feeding than from a vacation on which she is taking a lot of exercise in the form of walks or swimming. Our bodies soon adapt to increasing or decreasing energy needs, and our appetites go up or down accordingly in order to keep our weight stationary. If a nursing mother is healthy and happy, her appetite will naturally take care of the need for extra calories for the baby's milk. Some nursing mothers are amazed at the amount of food they crave and can eat without gaining weight. Sometimes the appetite overdoes it, though, and then the woman has to call on her willpower and the help of the doctor, public health nurse, and perhaps nutritionist to keep from gaining too much.

A woman who feels that nursing takes too much out of her may be a worrisome person whose concern about the new baby depresses her appetite or her spirits. Or she may be an individual who has never had much confidence in her health and strength and therefore feels that any unusual demand on her system is a threat, even though her body is actually handling the situation well. Or, least likely of all, she may be in poor physical health. Needless to say, a nursing mother who is not feeling well or is losing weight should consult her doctor promptly.

144. The working mother. What about the woman who hesitates to nurse because she has to go back to work? The answer depends on her working hours and how soon she must get back to the job. If she has to be out of the home only 8 hours a day, she can still nurse her baby except for one feeding. Even if she can't nurse after she resumes work, it would still be worthwhile to breast-feed the baby temporarily if she has a month or two at home.

You'll probably find it really helpful to talk to some mothers who have nursed after going back to work, before you have your baby. Here are some suggestions given to me by experienced mothers who have nursed after going back to work:

1. Wait until the baby is about 6 weeks old to begin introducing the bottle. By 6 weeks the baby should be used to nursing, on somewhat of a schedule, and your milk flow should be well established.
2. Begin by giving a bottle of breast milk three times a week. Many babies won't take the bottles from their mothers—they know the difference—so the father or older brother or sister or sitter may need to take over.
3. Warm milk works best. Breast-fed babies aren't used to cold temperatures yet. Some babies will have no difficulty accepting a bottle, but with others it's a real struggle and requires patience.
4. For the baby who is reluctant to take the bottle, the mother should try leaving the room (or even the

house), since some babies will refuse the bottle if they can even hear the mother talking. You can also try holding the baby in a "non-nursing" position—for example, she can be lying in your lap with her feet toward you and her head toward your knees while you offer her the bottle. Sometimes, babies who really seem to like a sweet taste will at first accept apple juice, diluted half and half with water, from the bottle better than milk.

5. Before the mother returns to work, the baby should be taking at least one bottle a day well. It's important to express your milk during the bottle feedings to keep your supply up.
6. Try to nurse right before and right after work, and to express your milk at least once if you're working longer than 6 hours.
7. One easy way to express and store milk is to nurse the baby on one breast and use the breast pump on the other. This really helps because the "let down" reflex from nursing seems to allow the milk to pump easier. Breast milk keeps several days in the refrigerator and two weeks in the freezer. But smell and taste it, to be sure it's not sour, before giving it to the baby, and discard any unused portion after 24 hours. You can buy ice cube trays with individual cubes. Then you can freeze the breast milk (wrapped in plastic wrap) in 1½-ounce portions for use by the sitter when a bottle is given. Even totally breast-fed babies seem to do fine with one bottle of breast milk and maybe one bottle of diluted apple juice during a normal working day, so that the mother only misses one feeding.

Of course, you'll find what works best for you and your baby within a few weeks.

145. Success depends partly on the help of others. The attitudes of the doctor who delivered the baby, the hospital nurses, the doctor who's looking after the baby, will have a powerful effect in encouraging or discouraging breast-feeding. So will the attitudes of the mother's relatives and friends. A supportive father can make the difference between a positive experience or an early end to breast-feeding.

146. The mother can lead a normal life. Some mothers hesitate to nurse their babies because they have heard that they will have to give up too much. Generally speaking, this is not so. There is no evidence that it will harm the baby if the mother drinks coffee or tea in moderation, smokes in moderation (this is a good time to stop smoking forever, though), uses alcoholic beverages in moderation, or goes in for athletics. The nursing mother can usually continue to eat all the foods she is accustomed to. There is no reason to believe, for instance, that if she eats prunes it will make the baby's bowels loose, or that if she eats fried food it will give the baby indigestion. Once in a while, it is true, a baby seems to get upset every time the mother eats a certain food. Naturally, if this happens several times in succession, she can give up that particular food. Some drugs get into the milk, but usually not in large enough quantities to affect the baby. A mother can take milk of magnesia, mineral oil, aspirin and aspirin-substitutes, barbiturates, codeine, sulfa drugs, antibiotics, without affecting the baby. She should not take bromides, atropine, cascara, ergot, radioactive substances, or steroids. Heroin, morphine, and methadone come through in the milk in amounts sufficient to cause addiction. Check with your doctor about which drugs are safe or unsafe.

When a nursing mother becomes nervously upset, it sometimes cuts down, for the time being, the amount of milk she can produce. Occasionally it seems to make the baby feel out of sorts, too. Some women never menstruate so long as they continue to nurse. Others menstruate regularly or irregularly. Once in a while a nursing baby will be mildly upset during the mother's menstruation or refuse to nurse.

There is no reason a nursing mother shouldn't let the baby have a bottle once in a while, even once a day, in case she wants to be away from home for longer than 4 hours.

Breast-feeding does not prevent pregnancy. It's important to consult your doctor about when to resume the family planning method of your choice.

147. The mother's diet. A nursing mother does need to be sure that her diet contains plenty of the elements that the baby is withdrawing through her milk. A large amount of calcium (lime) is excreted in the milk, to enable the baby's bones to grow rapidly. If the mother takes in too little, it will be withdrawn from her bones. It used to be thought that she would lose calcium from her teeth, too, but this is probably not so. She should take as much milk as the baby is getting from her, plus a little extra for her own needs, in any beverage that she likes, or cooked into cereals, soups, puddings, or in the form of cheese (Section 489).

Her daily diet should include the following nutrients (even if she has to limit her diet otherwise to keep her weight down): **milk**—a quart a day, preferably a quart and a half. It can be the usual fresh milk or it can be low-fat, fat-free, evaporated, powdered, or skimmed, and it can be served in any form. **Fruits and vegetables**—six servings a day. (This may sound like too much until you realize that the juice of two oranges, a salad, a green or yellow vegetable, and potatoes twice add up to six servings.) To include enough vitamin C, two of these servings should be raw and two should be oranges, grapefruit, tomatoes, raw cabbage, or berries. For the sake of vitamin A, there should be one dark-green, leafy vegetable or a deep-yellow one. Potatoes are valuable aside from their calories. Fruits and vegetables can be fresh, canned, frozen, or dried. **Meat, poultry, fish**—at least one generous portion, preferably two. Liver is especially valuable and should be included occasionally. **Eggs**—one a day unless there is a family history of coronary heart disease. **Cereal and bread**—3 servings a day, whole grain to contain the B vitamins. **Butter or fortified margarine** for vitamin A. If your weight won't stand these, eat more green, leafy vegetables and deep-yellow ones. **A vitamin-D preparation,** prescribed by the doctor, to make sure you are utilizing the calcium in your diet. **Vitamins**—you should avoid using any vitamin in a daily dose larger than the one recommended by the United States government agency responsible for setting these standards, unless your doctor has recommended it. Some mothers will have used extra-large doses of vitamin C, for example, to prevent or treat colds and other conditions, before they were pregnant or became nursing mothers. This should never be done during pregnancy or when nursing, without consulting the doctor first. This is because extra-large doses of some vitamins can make babies seriously ill.

If a nursing mother is gaining unwelcome weight, she can drink low-fat or fat-free milk, hold down on butter, keep the cereal and bread portions small (but use whole-grain products to provide B vitamins), omit such high-calorie foods as candy, pastries, cakes, cookies, soda-fountain drinks. (It's too bad that these high-calorie sweets are the foods that weight-gainers crave most.) But she should not cut down on the milk, vegetables, fruit, meat, and vitamin D.

GETTING STARTED AT BREAST-FEEDING

148. The mother's position and relaxation. Some mothers prefer, even in bed in the hospital, to nurse sitting up. Others find it easier, while still in bed, to nurse lying down. Stitches in the perineum may be a factor, up to 6 weeks. To nurse lying down, lay the baby beside you on the bed and lie on your side, facing her. Move closer until the nipple touches her lips. You may need to prop yourself up on your elbow or on pillows to bring the nipple to the right position. When she feels the nipple near her mouth she will "root around," trying to get hold of it. At times you may need to put a finger on the breast to give her breathing space for her nose, though this isn't usually necessary. If you let your finger touch her face, she may go for it.

When you are able to sit up, in the hospital or later at home, you can find the position that suits you best. Most sit up. Those who have used a rocking chair for nursing swear by it. The height of the arm of the chair is really important for resting your arms. A pillow or cushion there may help. Anyway, get comfortable so that you can relax and rest your muscles.

You'll probably notice that the state of your feelings has a lot to do with how easily the milk comes. Worries and tenseness can hold the milk back. So try to get troubles off your mind before beginning. If possible, lie down for 15 minutes before you expect the baby to wake and do what is most relaxing, whether it's shutting your eyes, or reading, or watching TV.

After you have been nursing for a few weeks, you may notice a distinct sensation of the milk being "let down" or "coming in" at nursing time. It may start leaking from the breasts when you hear the baby beginning to cry in the next room. This shows how much feelings have to do with the formation and release of the milk.

(There are nursing pads, either disposable or reusable, to place inside the brassiere.)

149. Getting the entire areola into the baby's mouth. Babies do not get the milk simply by taking the nipple into their mouths and sucking. The milk is formed in the glandular tissue throughout the breast. It then passes through small ducts toward the center of the breast, where it collects in a number of "sinuses." These sinuses, or storage spaces, are located in a circle right behind the areola, the dark area around the nipple. A short duct leads from each sinus through the nipple to the outside (there are a number of openings in each nipple). When babies are nursing properly, most or all of the areolar area is in their mouths, and the principal action is the squeezing of the sinuses (behind the areola) by the babies' gums. This forces the milk, which has collected in the sinuses, through the nipple and into the mouth. The sucking action of the baby's tongue is not so much to draw the milk through the nipple as to keep the areola drawn into the mouth and also to get the milk from the front of the mouth back into the throat. If babies take only the nipple into their mouths, they get almost no milk. And, if they chew on the nipple, they are apt to make it sore. But if they take the entire areola into their mouths, their gums squeeze the areola and cannot hurt the nipple. It may help them get the entire areola into the mouth if the mother or nurse will compress it or flatten it a little between thumb and finger. (Some mothers have areolas which are too large for a newborn infant to fit entirely into her mouth.) If babies start to mouth and chew on the nipple alone, they should be stopped promptly. Slip your finger into the corner of the mouth to break the suction, or between the gums if necessary. (Otherwise you would have to pull the baby off the breast, which is hard on the nipple.) Then reinsert the areola into the mouth. If the baby persists in chewing the nipple, stop that feeding.

It's common for the breasts to become engorged when the milk first comes in. This may pull the nipple flat and in combination with a firm breast may make it difficult for a newborn to "latch on." The baby may get extremely angry and frustrated. Hot compresses and expressing some milk for a few minutes before nursing will pull the nipple out enough to help the baby get the areola into her mouth. (See Section 178.)

150. Different babies behave differently at the breast. A physician, with a sense of humor, who has studied the behavior of hundreds of babies when first put to breast has pointed out the different types. The **eager beavers** draw the areola in avidly and suck vigorously until satisfied. The only problem is that they may be too hard on the nipple if they are allowed to chew it. **Excitable** babies may become so agitated and active that they keep losing the breast and then, instead of trying again, they scream. They may have to be picked up and comforted for several minutes before they are calm enough to try again. After a few days they usually settle down. The **procrastinators** can't be bothered to nurse the first few days; they are waiting until the milk comes in. Prodding them only makes them balky. They do well when the time comes. The **tasters** must, for a little while, mouth the nipple and smack their lips over the drop of milk they taste, before they settle down to business. Efforts to hurry them only make them angry. The **resters** want to nurse a few minutes and then rest a few minutes before starting again. They can't be rushed. They usually do a good job in their own way, but it takes them longer.

151. There are two things that often make balky babies angrier. The first is holding the head, in trying to direct it toward the breast. Babies hate to have their heads held; they fight to get free. The other is to squeeze them across the cheeks to get the mouth open. Babies have an instinct to turn toward anything that touches their cheeks. This is to help them find the nipple. When you squeeze them on both cheeks at the same time, you baffle and annoy them.

When a baby is refusing to take the breast and carrying on, a mother can't help feeling spurned, frustrated, and irritated. She shouldn't let her feelings be hurt by this inexperienced but apparently opinionated newcomer. If she can keep trying for a few more feedings, the chances are that the baby will find out what it's all about.

152. The early natural schedule. Even though the milk usually doesn't come in for a few days, early, frequent feedings encourage the milk supply and help to prevent engorgement, so rooming-in is of enormous help to a mother in getting started at breast-feeding. Though some babies may be agreeable in adapting to a schedule set by the nursery, others are quite irregular at first in their wakefulness and hungriness. If they wake and cry at a time when they can't be brought from the nursery to their mothers, they may have cried themselves into a deep sleep by the time the schedule calls for a feeding. Whereas with rooming-in, a mother only has to reach over and put her baby to breast whenever she thinks her child is hungry. So the baby never has to cry for long or get overly tired.

The tendency in hospitals that favor rooming-in and breast-feeding is to let babies be put to breast soon after birth. If allowed, it could even be done in the delivery room, ideally during the time when mothers and fathers have a chance to examine and fondle their new babies.

Some hospitals still set an arbitrary interval of 12 or 18 hours after birth before the first feeding. This is no longer a recommended practice. If more mothers asked to have their babies earlier, such hospitals might give in.

Some babies tend to be relatively sleepy and unhungry for the first 2 or 3 days, waking only at long intervals. This is particularly apt to be so when their mothers have had a lot of sedation or anesthetic. Then babies are apt to shift over to a pattern of frequent waking, as often as every 2 hours for a few days, before gradually settling down to an interval averaging 3½ or 4 hours.

Other babies, though, are hungry and wakeful from the start. They may want to be fed ten or a dozen times in 24 hours for the first week or two, before settling down to something like six or seven feedings in the second, third, or fourth week.

153. When babies have to be on regular schedules because of hospital rules, it's important that they be brought to their mothers at 2 A.M. and 6 A.M., to get in enough feedings spread over the 24 hours to stimulate the breasts. In some hospitals it is possible to have a hungry baby on a 3-hour schedule during the day and a 4-hour schedule at night (6 A.M., 9 A.M., 12 noon, 3 P.M., 6 P.M., 10 P.M., 2 A.M.).

Nowadays, when the lying-in period is usually less than a week, the mother who has not yet been able to supply enough milk to satisfy her baby on a strict 4-hour schedule can shift to a flexible (self-demand) schedule just as soon as she gets home, and it will not be too late for the breasts to respond to the more frequent nursing.

154. When the milk comes in. There is considerable variation in the time and manner in which the milk comes in. It most often starts to come in on the third or fourth day of the baby's life. It tends to come earlier in mothers who have had a child before, later in new mothers. Sometimes it comes so suddenly that the mother can name the hour. In other cases the progress is much more gradual. And it's on about the third or fourth day that many babies become distinctly more wakeful and hungry. This is one of the many examples of how smoothly Nature works things out. Studies of babies who have been breast-fed whenever they appeared hungry have shown that a majority of them want to nurse unusually often between the third and sixth days, commonly up to ten or twelve times a day. (The stools may become frequent on these days, too.) Mothers who are particularly anxious to make a success of breast-feeding are apt to feel disappointed by this frequency, assuming that it means the breast-milk supply is inadequate. This is unnecessarily pessimistic. It's more sensible to think that the baby is now settling down to the serious business of eating and growing, and is providing the breasts with the stimulation they must have if they are to meet the increasing needs. It is during this latter half of the first week, too, that the breasts are receiving the strongest stimulation from the hormones (the glandular secretions that make the milk come in in the first place). It is no wonder that in the first few days the breasts sometimes become too full, and that sometimes there isn't enough to satisfy the newly hungry baby. Still, the system is generally efficient, much better than you or I could design. The hormone factor calms down at the end of the first week. Then it is how much the baby demands that determines how much the breasts produce. In the changeover period (the second week) there may not be quite enough until the breasts adjust to the demand. The baby's hunger teaches the breast how much to produce, not just in the second or third week, but on through the succeeding months. In other words, the supply may still be increasing when the baby is several months old, if she wants more.

155. How long to nurse at each feeding. It used to be assumed, since in some cases the nipples became sore, that it's better for the mother to limit the nursing time at first and then gradually increase it as the nipples show they have adjusted. But experience has shown that it's better to let the babies decide from the beginning. If they are always allowed to nurse promptly when hungry and about as long as they wish, they don't get so frantically hungry that they make the nipples sore.

This longer nursing from the start allows the let-down reflex, which is slower to respond at first, to come into play. (See Section 148.) I would still hold babies to 20–30 minutes per feeding for the first week or two, because they may be feeding every 2 hours and the longer duration of nursing would leave the mother with little time to do much else.

156. How often can you nurse? In one sense the answer is: As often as your baby appears hungry and as often as you feel able to accommodate the baby.

Mothers in natural societies may occasionally nurse again as soon as a half hour after the last feeding, though the baby will probably nurse only briefly at one or the other of these feedings.

The mother in our society who has successfully nursed a previous baby and has plenty of self-assurance might not hesitate to nurse occasionally after an hour, if she thought there was a special reason for hunger.

But there are several reasons why it wouldn't be helpful for me to say: Nurse as often as the baby cries. Babies cry for other reasons than hunger—colic, other forms of indigestion, spells of irritability that we don't understand, fatigue that for some reason doesn't bring sleep.

An anxious, inexperienced mother can get to a point of frantic fatigue if she's worrying and nursing all day and half the night. (This worrying can cut down on the milk supply and interfere with the let-down reflex, too.)

So in one way the answer is: Nurse as often as you wish. But in another way I think it helps the inexperienced mother to say: Protect yourself by generally trying to keep 2 hours between feedings. Let the baby fuss a bit in hopes that she'll go back to sleep. If not, try a pacifier or a bottle of water. Try rocking her for a few minutes or carrying her in a carrier on your chest. If you still think she's hungry nurse her again, but not more than 20 minutes this time.

With a baby who seems to be demanding feedings too frequently, limit each feeding to preferably 20 or at most 30 minutes.

But when your nipples have shown they are invulnerable and when you feel confident about your milk supply and your ability to judge your baby's hunger and other discomforts, nurse as often and as long as you decide it's sensible—at each feeding.

157. One or both breasts? In very natural, nonindustrial parts of the world, where nursing is the only way babies are fed, where mothers carry their babies around with them in slings while they work, and where schedules are unknown, babies tend to wake and be put to breasts frequently. They nurse relatively briefly, at one breast, and then fall asleep again. In our civilization, which runs pretty much according to the clock and in which babies are put in a crib in a quiet room after a feeding, the tendency is toward fewer and larger feedings. If a mother produces ample amounts of milk, her baby may be quite satisfied with one breast at each feeding. Each breast receives the stimulation of very complete emptying, even though this occurs only once in about 8 hours. In many cases, however, the amount in one breast does not satisfy the baby, and both breasts are given at each feeding, the left breast being offered first at one feeding, the right breast first at the next. Some mothers and doctors advocate both breasts anyway. To ensure complete emptying of one breast, the baby might be kept on the first breast for 12 to 15 minutes, if willing, and then allowed to nurse on the second breast for as short or as long a period as desired. A baby who sticks to business will take the greatest part of the milk in 5 or 6 minutes and will have pretty well emptied the breast in 10 or 15 minutes. (The breasts will always be producing a little new milk, so the baby will always taste something.) Therefore, there is no need for a mother to prolong breast-feeding beyond a total of 20 to 40 minutes, depending on how eager the baby is to continue and how much time the mother has to spare. Stop after 30 minutes if your baby is willing. Bringing up the bubble is discussed in Section 134.

158. How do you know whether the baby is getting enough? This question is likely to baffle the new mother. You certainly can't tell from the length of time the baby nurses. She goes on nursing after she's already obtained most of the milk—sometimes for 10 more minutes, sometimes for 30—because she's still getting a small trickle of milk, or because she enjoys sucking, or because she's still awake and having a good time. Careful observations of slightly older babies have shown that the same baby will appear to be entirely satisfied by 3 ounces at one feeding and by 10 ounces at another.

159. You can't tell from the appearance of breasts or milk. Most women with experience have decided that they can't tell from the apparent fullness of the breasts before feeding how much milk is there. In the first week or two, the breasts are noticeably full and firm as a result of glandular changes, but after a while they normally become softer and less prominent, even though the milk supply is **increasing.** A baby can get 6 or more ounces from a breast that to the mother does not seem full at all. You can't tell anything from the color and appearance of the milk. Breast milk always looks thin and bluish compared to cow's milk, and there are no important variations in the composition of the milk from time to time in the same mother, or from one mother to another.

160. You can't tell by the baby's crying alone. You can't be sure that the baby who fusses a lot after feeding is hungry, because in the early weeks babies who are fretful or colicky or have what I call "irritable crying" characteristically cry after certain feedings, even when these feedings are unusually large.

161. A more reliable guide is the combination of weight gain and satisfaction. Generally speaking, you and the doctor decide the question on the basis of the baby's behavior over a number of weeks and on the basis of weight-gaining. Neither alone is conclusive. A baby who is happy and gaining fast is obviously getting enough. A baby who cries hard every afternoon or evening but is gaining weight at the average rate is probably getting plenty to eat but having colic. A baby who gains slowly but is quite contented is, in most cases, a baby who is meant to be a slow gainer. However, there are a few babies who don't protest even when they are not gaining at all. It's the baby who is gaining **very** slowly and acting hungry most of the time who's **probably** not getting enough. A baby who is sleeping for longer than 4 hours in the first week or two of life, and is not gaining weight well, should be awakened. Babies who are sleepy at the breast can be encouraged to feed by being burped and switched to the other breast when they fall asleep. If this routine is repeated four or five times during a feeding most babies will be gaining weight and nursing more vigorously after 5 to 7 days.

So it's best to assume that the baby is getting enough in the long run unless the baby and the doctor definitely tell you differently. Certainly at any one feeding you should be satisfied if the baby seems satisfied.

162. Don't throw away your confidence. The doubt about sufficiency of the milk supply is common in the new mother, who has had no proof yet of her adequacy in our upside-down society which considers bottle feeding normal and makes breast-feeding the exception. The doubt also arises in mothers who have had more experience but who have **never** had much self-confidence. Usually when the mother is worrying about the amount, the doctor finds that there is no insufficiency of milk, only an insufficiency of confidence. Worry only discourages the milk supply.

It's good to remember that throughout the largest part of the world, in which there are no scales and no doctors, the mother simply assumes that her baby is receiving plenty if the child acts contented and looks well, and that this system works well in at least nine out of ten cases.

163. Care of nipples. Some doctors recommend regular massage of the nipples during the last month of pregnancy, to toughen them. Or, the husband can do this orally. After the baby is born and begins to nurse, no particular care of the nipples, no wiping or ointment, should ordinarily be necessary. (Many women who have breast-fed have a favorite ointment and there is quite a list.) It is sensible for the mother to wash her hands with soap before fingering her nipples (to massage or examine them), since infection can enter the breast through the nipple and since babies can easily pick up thrush, a mild fungus infection of the mouth. But hand washing should not be necessary before an ordinary nursing.

Some experienced mothers are convinced that the most helpful step in healing sore nipples, and in keeping them healthy, is to allow them to dry in the air for 10 or 15 minutes before closing the nursing flaps of the brassiere, or to leave the flaps open between feedings. Nipples will also stay drier and healthier if there is no waterproof lining in the brassiere.

Anything that causes drying and cracking of the nipples should be avoided, such as soaps or alcohol-containing preparations.

If soreness starts to develop, the frequency of nursing should be increased to promote the emptying of the breast and to prevent the baby becoming too hungry. Changing nursing positions so that the pressure of the baby's jaws is distributed in different areas of the areola is also helpful.

164. How to give breast-feeding a fair trial. You hear of women who want to nurse their babies but don't succeed. People talk about how complicated our civilization is and how it makes mothers too tense to nurse. There's no doubt that nervousness works against breast-feeding, but I don't think most women are nervous. Breast-feeding most often fails because it isn't given a good trial.

There are three factors that make a big difference: (1) keeping away from formula; (2) not getting discouraged too early; (3) sufficient stimulation of the breasts.

If a baby is given formula for the first 3 or 4 days of life, the chance of successful breast-feeding is diminished. The baby who is satisfied by plenty of formula doesn't try so hard at breast. (Water, which is sometimes given during this period to make sure she doesn't become too dried out, is not likely to interfere with her hunger at breast.) After the mother's milk has begun to come in, it's wise to avoid formula, too, if the baby can be kept fairly well satisfied and is not continuing to lose weight.

Sometimes a mother becomes discouraged just at the moment when her milk is coming in, or a day or two later, because she isn't producing very much. This is no time for her to quit. She hasn't given herself half a chance. If a mother has a practical or baby nurse at this stage, it's a great help to have one who is encouraging and cooperative.

The night nursings, which will probably come at about 10 P.M. and 2 A.M., are as important as the daytime nursings in giving the breasts regular stimulation at first.

If the breasts are not supplying a sufficient amount of milk to keep the baby satisfied for 3 or 4 hours, it helps to let the mother empty them more frequently, as often as every 2 hours (including both breasts at each feeding). This is the way the baby and the breasts would adjust to each other in a faraway spot where there was no cow's milk. The frequent emptying of the breasts stimulates them to produce more milk. Then the baby is able to go for longer periods again.

Of course, babies cannot be kept off formula indefinitely if they remain miserably hungry for several weeks, or continue to lose weight.

If a mother is able to keep in frequent touch with the doctor, the doctor will help her decide at each step such questions as how many days the baby can go on an insufficient amount of breast milk without resorting to formula, how much nursing the mother's nipples can stand, how frequently to nurse. The point is, though, that the doctor is influenced in many of these decisions by the mother's attitude toward nursing. If she makes it clear that she is eager to succeed, this encourages the doctor to give the directions that will make it possible.

La Leche League is composed of mothers who have succeeded at breast-feeding and are eager to give advice and support to inexperienced mothers. Consult your phone book or ask a nurse at the local health department.

WHEN THE BREAST MILK SEEMS INSUFFICIENT

165. Trying to increase it after getting home (if you cannot consult the doctor regularly). Suppose that in the hospital your baby was nursed as frequently as possible and received both breasts at each feeding, but still did not get enough. The doctor decided that the baby had to have some formula, too. Let's say that the baby was averaging less than 2 ounces from both breasts and required a 2-ounce bottle in addition at each nursing. You decided after talking it over with the doctor that you wanted to continue the breast-feeding after going home, with the hope of eventually getting the baby entirely breast-fed.

Sometimes the mother feels so much more relaxed and natural after a couple of days at home that the breast-milk supply increases without any other encouragement, and the satisfied baby is no longer particularly interested in the bottle. In that case the mother should stop offering the bottle right away. Usually, however, babies enjoy the bottle so much that they continue to take it and so have less appetite for the breast. Therefore, in most cases the mother must deliberately cut down on the formula and count on the baby's increasing hunger to give more stimulation to the breasts.

Here is one method: For the first couple of days at home continue to give the formula after nursing, as in the hospital, but don't give a drop more than the baby demands. (The breast-milk supply often does not increase the first day or two at home, and it sometimes decreases temporarily because of the mother's fatigue.) After 2 days, begin to reduce the amount in each bottle by ¼ ounce each day until you are down to no bottle at all. What will happen? As you cut down the formula, the baby will probably get hungry earlier. You nurse her when she becomes hungry, whether it's after 4, or 3, or even 2 hours. This sounds like an awful lot of work, but it won't be forever. You are hoping that the frequent emptying of the breasts will stimulate them to produce more and more milk. When this happens, the baby will begin to sleep for longer and longer periods again. In a week or two she may work herself back onto approximately a 4-hour schedule. (I remember one baby who never got more than an ounce at a time from the breast in the hospital, and who worked up to 5 ounces in 2 weeks at home.) If you try it for 5 or 6 days and the baby gets hungrier all the time and fails to gain weight, then you may have to go back to the formula temporarily. But even then, if you want to keep on trying, you can offer only 2 ounces of formula after each breast-feeding, and in a few days, when you feel more rested, try gradually reducing this amount again.

As a general rule it is not sensible to nurse more often than about every 2 hours. The mother is apt to become tired and irritable from the nervous strain.

Some doctors recommend manual expression of any milk that remains in the breast after the baby has finished nursing, as an excellent temporary method of increasing the supply (Sections 184 and 185).

166. Fluids for the mother. It's most important during this trial period that the mother take wonderful care of herself, avoid getting tired at all costs, let the housework go, forget about outside worries and obligations, keep visitors down to one or two comfortable friends, eat and drink well. A good time to drink something is 10 or 15 minutes before you expect a nursing. Some women who enjoy beer find it a very pleasant means of taking extra fluid and achieving relaxation, and it doesn't affect the baby.

There are two sides to the matter of fluids. There is no good to be gained from drinking more fluid than feels comfortable, because the body promptly gets rid of excess water through the urine. On the other hand, a new, excited, busy mother may forget to drink as much as she needs and go thirsty through absentmindedness. This will cut down the milk supply.

167. Don't let friends discourage you. Perhaps this is as good a time as any to mention that a mother who is attempting breast-feeding may occasionally be subjected to a surprising amount of skepticism on the part of friends and relatives who are otherwise quite sympathetic. There are remarks like: "You aren't going to breast-feed, are you?" "Very few can make the grade." "Why in the world are you trying to do that?" "With breasts like yours you'll never succeed." "Your poor baby is hungry. Are you trying to starve the child to prove a point?" The milder remarks can perhaps be blamed on surprise, but the meaner ones strongly suggest jealousy. Later on, if there is any question about continuing to nurse, you'll find several friends who'll urge you to stop.

168. When the breast milk seems to decrease later. A good percentage of mothers who are eager to breast-feed are successful in the hospital and for a number of days or weeks afterward (with the possible exception of the first day or two at home when the supply often decreases temporarily). Then, too many of them feel that they are failing and give up. They say, "I didn't have as much milk," or "My milk didn't seem to agree with the baby," or "As the baby grew bigger my milk was no longer sufficient."

Why is it that throughout most of the world a mother's milk takes care of the baby for many months and that it's only in bottle-feeding countries like ours that the breast-milk supply seems to fail so early in a majority of cases? I don't believe that American mothers are that nervous. They are certainly as healthy as any. I think there is one main reason. The mother here who is trying to breast-feed, instead of feeling that she is doing the most natural thing in the world and assuming that she'll succeed like everyone else, feels that she's attempting to do the unusual, the difficult thing. Unless she has tremendous self-confidence she keeps wondering whether she won't fail. In a sense, she's looking for signs of failure. If her baby cries one day a bit more than usual, her first thought is that her milk has decreased. If the baby develops indigestion or colic, or a rash, she is quick to suspect her milk. Her anxiety makes her feel sure that the bottle is the answer. And the trouble is that the bottle is always available. Probably she was given formula directions or packs of prepared formula when she left the hospital ("just in case"), or she can call the doctor or the public health nurse and get directions. Babies on the breast who begin to receive ample amounts of formula several times a day practically always nurse less eagerly at the breast. And milk left in the breast is Nature's method of signaling to the glands, "Make less, make less."

In other words, the combination of a mother lacking confidence in her ability to breast-feed and the availability of bottles of formula is the most efficient method of discouraging breast-feeding.

To put it positively: The way to make breast-feeding a success is to go on breast-feeding and keep away from formula (except possibly for one relief bottle a day after the breast supply is well established. See Sections 170 and 171).

Under normal conditions the amount of milk supplied by the breasts is not a stationary quantity. The breasts are ready at any time gradually to decrease or increase the amount, depending on whether the baby wants less or more. As a baby grows and her appetite increases, she empties the breasts more completely and sometimes more frequently. This is the stimulation that encourages a larger supply.

169. Hunger is not the commonest reason for crying. The most common reason for a mother to start worrying is that her baby begins to fret right after feedings, or between feedings. Her first thought is that her milk supply is failing. But this assumption is not correct. The fact is that almost all babies—especially first babies—have fretful spells, most often in the afternoon or evening. Bottle-fed babies fuss as much as breast-fed babies. Babies who are getting all the milk they can possibly hold have crying spells just the same as babies who are receiving less. These fretful spells are discussed in Section 337, on colic, and Section 334, on general fretfulness. If a mother realizes clearly that most of the fussing in the early weeks is not caused by hunger, she won't be so quick to lose confidence in her breast-milk supply.

Though it is much less likely, it is, of course, possible that a baby is beginning to fret because she's hungry. However, hunger is much more apt to wake a baby a little earlier for the next feeding than to bother her in the first hour or two after the last feeding. If she **is** hungry it may be because her appetite has taken a sudden spurt or it may possibly mean that her mother's milk has decreased slightly because of fatigue or tension. In either case the answer is the same: Take it for granted that she'll wake and want to nurse more frequently and more vigorously for a day or for a few days until the breasts have adjusted to the demand. Then she will probably go back to her previous schedule.

In case the fussing was **not** due to hunger at all, the extra nursing has done no harm.

The treatment of fretfulness seems clear to me. Any thought of giving a bottle of formula should be postponed for at least a couple of weeks. The baby should be allowed to nurse as often as every 2 hours (counting from the beginning of one feeding to the beginning of the next), for 20 to 40 minutes. If she makes a reasonable weight gain in that week or two, consideration of formula should again be put off, for at least 2 more weeks. The baby can be comforted during her fretful periods with a pacifier or with a bottle of water or possibly sugar water (Sections 242 and 243). The mother may occasionally want to nurse her even more frequently than every 2 hours. It certainly won't do the baby any harm. I'm only thinking of the mother: She can't help becoming frantic if she's nursing all day long, and it won't do that much good. Emptying the breasts 10 times a day will give them about as much stimulation as they can use. It is also necessary for the mother to have some rest and relaxation.

170. A relief bottle is all right. Does all this mean that a mother who wants to continue breast-feeding must never give a bottle under any circumstances? No, it isn't that critical. Most of the mothers who want to give a relief bottle regularly once a day find that they can do so without discouraging the breast-milk supply, provided the supply has been well established for a few weeks and provided it's only one bottle a day. And certainly a mother who has not been giving a bottle regularly can give one occasionally. Perhaps she must be away for a feeding. Or perhaps she has become extremely tired or upset and the baby has acted entirely dissatisfied with one feeding. One bottle doesn't stop breast-feeding. What I have been advising against is regularly giving a complementary bottle (a bottle given **in addition** to a breast-feeding) two or three times a day, if you hope to continue with breast-feeding.

171. A relief bottle. The relief bottle (breast milk or formula) can be given every day if desired, at the 10 A.M., 2 P.M., or 6 P.M. feeding. (When the baby is off the 2 A.M. feeding, the mother will usually be too uncomfortable to omit either the 10 P.M. or the 6 A.M. nursing, since this would leave the breasts full for 12 hours. Also, such a long interval might discourage the breast-milk supply.)

If a mother plans to wean her baby from breast to bottle sometime between 2 and 6 months, it's a good idea to offer a relief bottle at least once a week, even though she could nurse just as well. The reason is that some babies become so set in their ways during this age period that they will refuse to take a bottle of milk if they have not been used to it, and this may make quite a struggle. A baby rarely gets this opinionated before the age of 2 months, and after 6 months she will probably be weaned directly to the cup.

It is sometimes recommended that **all** breast-fed babies get a bottle once or twice a week, even though the mother is planning to nurse until her infant is weaned to the cup. This is on the theory that the mother might have to stop nursing for some unexpected reason. You can decide for yourself, balancing the inconvenience of making the bottle against risking the baby's putting up a struggle if weaned suddenly.

The simplest formula by far is prepared formula, ready to use, in a disposable bottle. (See Section 208.) It's relatively expensive, but doesn't add up to much in a week. Less expensive is a bottle made from prepared powdered formula. (See Section 215.)

172. Breast and bottle both. If a mother who can't produce enough milk to completely satisfy the baby wants to go on with a combination of breast and bottle, there is no reason why she shouldn't. However, in many cases of mixed feedings, the breast-milk supply gradually decreases. Also, the baby may come to prefer the bottle and reject the breast altogether.

Most women don't want to go on with both, because it means all the trouble of formula making **and** being tied down by the nursing schedule. The most sensible thing to do when the mother is producing a reasonable amount of milk (say half or more of what the baby needs) is to first make a real effort to dispense with the formula altogether (Section 165). If this does not increase the breast-milk supply sufficiently, then she can wean the baby completely to the bottle, knowing that she has tried as hard as she could.

173. How to supplement the breast with the bottle (if you cannot consult a doctor). Let's say that you have tried to get along on breast-feeding alone. You've tried nursing more frequently and doing all the things that help you relax and get as much rest as possible. But the baby is not gaining weight well. You have to give some formula to satisfy the baby, but you want to do it in the way that is least likely to decrease the breast-milk supply. I will discuss the subject in different paragraphs depending on how much extra the baby needs, and use the word **complemental** to mean a bottle that is given right after (in addition to) a breast-feeding and **supplemental** to mean a bottle that is given **instead** of a breast-feeding. In a general way, it may be more convenient to omit certain breast-feedings altogether and give supplemental bottles instead. On the other hand, there's more chance of keeping up the breast-milk supply if you continue to give the breast at every feeding, with a complemental bottle at certain feedings when the baby doesn't get enough at breast.

Suppose the breasts are supplying enough at all but one feeding. Six P.M. is apt to be the scantiest due to anxiety and fatigue, 3 P.M. the next. You could try giving a complemental bottle after the 6 P.M. nursing. Or you could give a supplemental bottle instead of the 3 P.M. nursing.

Suppose the breasts are supplying less than enough at two or more feedings. You could give complemental bottles after the breast-feedings at noon, 3 P.M. and 6 P.M. The 6 A.M. breast-feeding is apt to be the largest of the day and may supply all that the baby needs at that time. The 10 P.M. breast-feeding is also apt to be fairly large. Another method, if the breasts are supplying less than enough at several feedings, would be to breast-feed alone at 6 A.M., 3 P.M., 10 P.M., and give supplemental bottles alone at 10 A.M. and 6 P.M. (also at 2 A.M. if the baby still needs to be fed then).

If the breast-milk supply is insufficient at all feedings, you will need a bottle at all feedings, whether you give the breast first or not.

How much formula do you put in each bottle, whether it is a complemental or a supplemental bottle? The answer is: as much as the baby seems to need. Babies who weigh 9 pounds or more may want 6 ounces in the supplemental bottle; smaller babies may want less. If it's a complemental bottle after a breast-feeding, they may want 2 to 3 ounces. If so, offer 3 ounces and let them take what they want.

For formulas, see Section 205 and beyond.

SPECIAL PROBLEMS OF BREAST-FEEDING

174. The fiddler, the fusser, the sleeper, and the waker. There are several patterns of behavior in the early weeks of nursing that complicate the mother's job and may nearly drive her mad. The first is that of the babies who never seem to nurse very vigorously and fall asleep 5 minutes or so after starting. You don't know whether they have taken a reasonable amount or not. (Babies usually get a major part of what's in the breast in 5 minutes of steady nursing.) It wouldn't be so bad if they'd sleep for 2 or 3 hours, but they may wake and cry again in a few minutes after they're put back to bed. We don't really know what causes this inefficient nursing **or** the prompt waking. One possibility is that the baby's nervous system and digestive system are not yet working well enough together. Perhaps the comfort of their mothers' arms and the breast in the mouth is enough to put them back to sleep. When they're a little older and know what it's all about, their hunger will keep them awake until they're well satisfied. In the bottle-fed baby, a contributory cause of falling asleep may be nipple holes that are too small. In the breast-fed baby, it may be that although the mother has plenty of milk, the baby cannot get it easily enough.

It's probable that a mother's feelings control the ease with which the milk flows. Many mothers after a few weeks of nursing notice that as soon as they hear the baby cry with hunger, the milk starts to leak from the breasts. And feelings of anxiety or other tension probably hold the milk in. (Farmers know that cows can't "let down" the milk if they are tense.)

Some babies who find that they're getting little result from nursing go back to sleep. Then when they're put back into the harder, cooler bed, their hunger wakes them up again. Other babies, hungrier or more wide awake or more assertive, react with irritation when they find they can't get enough milk. They jerk their heads away from the breast and yell, try again, get mad again.

The fact that the baby doesn't nurse well only increases the mother's uneasiness, so a vicious cycle sets in. If a mother understands this mechanism, she can use all her ingenuity in finding her own best way to relax before and during nursing. It's different with each individual. Music, a magazine, a glass of beer, television—whatever works best is what she should adopt.

If your baby girl gets sleepy or restless after a few minutes at one breast, you can try shifting right away to the other breast, to see if the easier flow of milk will help. Of course, you'd like her to work at least 15 minutes on one breast to be sure that it is well stimulated, but if she won't, she won't.

If your baby is one of those "resters," who doze, off and on, but suck well in between, let her continue. But if she doesn't resume nursing, it works better not to prolong the nursing or to keep trying to wake her up again. In the long run you only take away her enthusiasm and make her an indifferent eater.

What do you do if she wakes as soon as you put her to bed or a little later? I think it's better to assume first that if she has nursed for 5 minutes she's had enough to keep her satisfied for a couple of hours, and try not to feed her again right away. Let her fuss for a while if you can stand it. Give her a pacifier if you and your doctor approve. See if a hot-water bottle will make her feel cozier (Section 337).

The purpose is to teach her that feedings come every few hours and that it's her eagerness that brings the satisfaction. To keep feeding her off and on for an hour and a half tends to teach her that feedings are always chasing her and that sometimes the only way to escape them is to go to sleep. However, the chances are that the baby will outgrow this inconvenient pattern in a few weeks, no matter how you handle it. So if she wakes as soon as she's in bed and can't be comforted and gets to crying frantically, you'd better feed her again anyway, and never mind the theory. You can at least give her a second chance. But don't go on to a third and a fourth feeding if you can help it. Make her wait an hour or two anyway.

175. Retracted nipples. If a mother's nipples are flat or retracted (drawn back into the breast by the supporting tissue), it may further complicate the business of getting a baby started at the breast, especially if the baby is the excitable type. If she searches around and can't find the nipple, she may cry angrily and pull her head back. There are several tactful things you can try. If possible, put her to breast when she first wakes up, before she gets too cross. If she starts crying at the first attempt, stop right away and comfort her before trying again. Take your time. It sometimes makes a nipple stand out better to massage it lightly with the fingers first. A few women have truly inverted nipples which don't become erect, but this doesn't prevent nursing. They sometimes benefit from the use of **breast shields.** (See Section 187.) Your doctor or her nurse will explain how to use them.

Actually, the nipple is not so important in nursing (as explained in Section 149) as it is in guiding the baby to draw the entire areola into her mouth. However, the supporting tissues that retract the nipple also make it more difficult for the baby to draw the areola forward and shape it to her mouth. Probably the most valuable procedure is for the mother (or nurse) to squeeze some of the milk from the sinuses by manual expression (Sections 184 and 185) so that the areolar region will be softer and more compressible. Then press the areola into a flatter shape, between thumb and finger, when putting it into the baby's mouth.

176. Pains during nursing. You may be bothered the first week or so by cramps in your lower abdomen as soon as the baby starts nursing. This is the normal reflex action by which nursing causes the uterus to contract. It is intended to help the uterus get back to its nonpregnant size. These cramps disappear after a while.

Twinges of pain in the nipple that last a few seconds after the baby begins to nurse, for the first few days or weeks, are very common, mean nothing and will soon go away.

177. Sore or cracked nipples. Pain that persists throughout the nursing may point to a cracked nipple, and a careful search should be made. (A very few mothers are unusually sensitive and continue to feel pain even though the nipples remain healthy.) If a nipple is cracked (often because a baby has chewed on it instead of taking the whole areola into her mouth), it is usually recommended that a combination of more frequent nursing, frequent changes of the baby's nursing position, and applications of ice packs be used. The physician may prescribe an ointment for the sore nipple. Another method is to let the nipples dry for 15 minutes before closing the flaps of the brassiere; or leave them open. Remove the waterproof lining from the brassiere. One mother found successful a small tea strainer (the kind that can be detached from the handle) over the nipple, inside an ample brassiere.

More frequent nursing will provide continued stimulation of the breast and relieve fullness.

178. Distended breasts; areolar engorgement. There are three different ways in which the breasts may become over-distended or engorged. The commonest and simplest is caused by overfilling of the sinuses, the storage spaces located behind the areola. This is not uncomfortable for the mother, but it may make the areolar region so firm and flat that the baby cannot take it into her mouth in order to compress it with her gums. The only thing she can get hold of is the nipple, and she is apt to chew on it and perhaps make it sore. It is important, therefore, for the mother or nurse to express sufficient milk from the sinuses so that the areolar region will become soft enough and compressible enough for the baby to take it into her mouth (Sections 184 and 185).

It is not necessary to express much milk to soften the areolar region. Two to 5 minutes on each breast should be sufficient. Then the mother can compress the areolar region from above and below as she puts the breast into the baby's mouth, to help her get started. This type of engorgement is most likely to occur in the latter half of the first week, to last 2 or 3 days, and not to return, as long as nursing continues normally.

179. Peripheral engorgement. Another type of engorgement involves not just the areolar region but the whole breast. The entire breast becomes firm and uncomfortable. Most cases are mild, but in the infrequent case that becomes severe, the breast is enlarged, surprisingly hard and very painful.

The usual mild case can be relieved promptly by having the baby nurse. It may be necessary to soften the areolar region first by manual expression if it is too firm for the baby to get into her mouth.

The severe case may require several different kinds of treatment. If the baby cannot consume enough milk to relieve the distension, the entire breast needs to be massaged, starting at the outer edges and working toward the areola. An ointment with lanolin and petrolatum in it or a vegetable oil should be used during the massage to avoid irritating the skin, but the ointment should be kept off the areola, because it makes it too slippery for areolar expression, which comes next. Massage of the entire breast is tiring to the mother and should be carried on only long enough to partially relieve the engorgement. It may be performed once or several times a day. The difficulty usually lasts only 2 or 3 days. The application of cloths wet with comfortably hot water seems to help prepare the breasts for massage. If massage and manual expression cannot be used successfully because there is no one available to do it or to teach the mother how, a breast pump can be tried (Section 186). Between nursings or treatments, a firm support should be given to the breasts from all sides by a large, firm brassiere or by a binder that gives support from the shoulders. The binder should be used not to flatten the breasts against the chest but to support them firmly from below and both sides. An ice bag or hot water bottle can be applied for short periods. There are various medications that the physician may prescribe. This total engorgement practically always occurs, if at all, in the latter half of the first week. It is rare after that.

180. Caked breast and breast abscess. A third type of engorgement is similar to total engorgement in that it is outside the areolar region and is painful. But it is confined to only one segment of the breast. This type is sometimes called caked breast. It is more likely to occur after the hospital period. Treatment is similar to that of total engorgement: hot applications followed by massage of the engorged area, support by an efficient brassiere or a binder, ice bag or hot-water bottle between treatments, increased frequency of nursing, frequent changes of the baby's nursing position, and adequate rest for the mother.

If a sore spot develops inside the breast, this may be an infection, or breast abscess. The skin may become red over it. Fever and chills may develop. You should take your temperature and get in touch with your doctor. However, with modern methods of treating infections, it should not be necessary to keep the baby from nursing at that breast, even temporarily.

181. When the mother is ill. In the ordinary illnesses during which the mother stays at home, it is customary to allow the baby to continue to nurse as usual. To be sure, there is a chance of the baby's catching the ailment, but this would be true even if the infant weren't being nursed. Besides, most infections are contagious before any symptoms are noticed.

Babies on the average have milder colds than older members of the family.

182. Biting the nipple (when the baby gets teeth). You can't blame the baby for trying a few bites when her gums are tingling during teething or when a couple of teeth have come in. She doesn't realize it hurts. But it's not only painful; it may make the nipples so sore that nursing has to be stopped.

Most babies can be taught quickly not to bite. Instantly slip your finger between her gums and gently say "No." If she does it again, put your finger in again, say "No" and end the feeding. It's usually late in the feeding anyway when a baby starts to bite.

MANUAL EXPRESSION AND BREAST PUMPS

183. The purpose. Manual expression or breast pumps are used to obtain milk for the baby who cannot or will not nurse at the breast, although the mother has plenty of milk. A small, premature baby may be too weak to nurse, or to be taken out of the incubator, but can be fed breast milk from a bottle or medicine dropper or by a stomach tube. When an ill mother is away in a hospital, or when it is considered unwise, in the home, to expose the baby to her directly, her milk can be collected and given to the baby from a bottle (or discarded) until she can nurse again.

When it is desired to obtain plenty of milk or to keep the breasts functioning, they are emptied at regular intervals. When the breasts are partially emptied to spare the mother pain during weaning, it is done only as often as necessary and only long enough to relieve the pressure.

The best way to learn manual expression is from an experienced person while you are in the hospital. It's a good idea to get some instruction even though you don't anticipate using it. Or a public health nurse or a visiting nurse can teach you at home. A mother can learn by herself, but this takes a little longer. In any case, it seems like an awkward business at first, and several practice sessions will be necessary before you become very efficient. Don't be discouraged.

The milk produced in the glandular tissue throughout the breast flows through tiny tubes toward the center of the breast and is stored in 15 to 20 sinuses, or sacs, which are located behind the areola, the dark-colored skin around the nipple. In manual expression, the breast is massaged first and then the milk is squeezed out of the sinuses, each of which has a small tube leading through the nipple to the outside.

If you are going to express only a small amount of milk—for instance, to relieve engorgement in the areolar area—you can use any handy cup or nursing bottle to catch it. If you are going to express as much as you can and will be giving it to the baby right afterward, you should wash the cup with soap, rinse it, and dry it with a clean towel. After expressing the milk, you pour it into a nursing bottle and cap with a nipple, both of which should have been washed with soap and rinsed since the last use. If you are going to save the milk for a number of hours—for instance, if you are delivering it once a day to the hospital for a premature baby—it should be kept refrigerated.

184. The finger-and-thumb method. First, of course, you wash your hands with soap. Then you massage the breast to bring the breast milk to the sinuses. In the commoner method of manual expression, the sinuses are then repeatedly squeezed between thumb and finger. To apply the pressure where the sinuses lie, deep behind the areola, it is necessary to place the tips of thumb and finger on opposite sides of the areola (just at the edge where the dark skin meets the normally colored skin). Then press thumb and finger in deeply until they meet the ribs. In this position, squeeze them rhythmically together. The right hand is usually used to express the left breast, and in this instance the left hand holds the cup that catches the milk.

The main thing is to press in deeply enough and at the edge of the areola. The nipple itself is not squeezed or fingered. You may be able to get more milk with each squeeze if you not only press thumb and finger toward each other but pull slightly outward with them (toward the nipple) at the same time, to complete the milking motion.

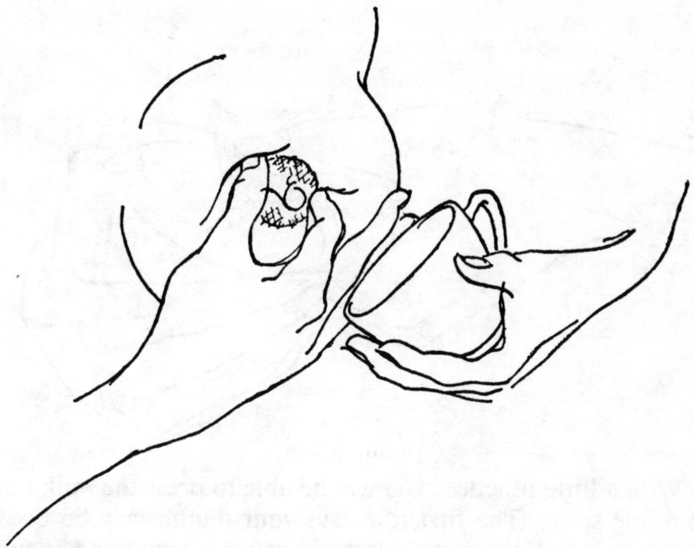

After a bit, the thumb and finger can be shifted, part way "around the clock," to be sure that all the sinuses are being pressed. If the finger and thumb become tired—and they will at first—you can shift back and forth from side to side.

185. The thumb-and-cup method. Another method, less commonly used but very efficient when learned, is to press the sinuses between the thumb and the inside edge of a teacup that has a flared edge (it's too hard to get the areola and the thumb down inside a cup with straight sides).

First, wash your hands with soap and water. Tuck the lower edge of the cup **deep** into the left breast, at the lower edge of the areola, and tip the cup up part way, holding it with the left hand. Place the thumb of the right hand on the **upper** edge of the areola. Now the areola is being pressed between the right thumb and the rim of the cup. Press the right thumb firmly inward (toward the rim) and then downward (toward the nipple). This squeezes the milk from the sacs into the tubes running through the nipple. When you press toward the nipple, don't slide your thumb across the dark skin; the skin moves with the thumb. It is not necessary to squeeze or even touch the nipple.

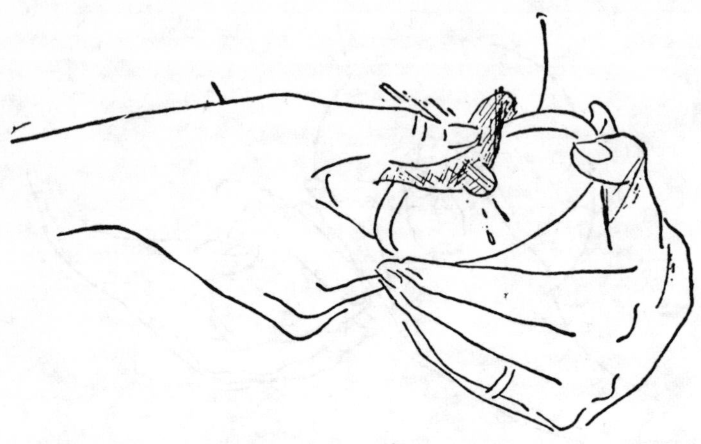

With a little practice, you will be able to press the milk out in a fine spray. The first few days your thumb may be tired and lame, but this won't last. If you are emptying a full breast, it may take 20 minutes—more if you are just learning. If you are attempting to empty the breasts completely after the baby has finished nursing, it will take only a few minutes. When the breast is full, the milk comes in a spray. When it is partly empty, it comes in drops. Stop when no more milk comes. Naturally, if you wait 10 minutes the breast will have made more milk, but you don't have to empty it again.

186. Breast pumps. Many mothers who have to express their milk regularly—especially working mothers who may be doing it for many weeks or months—prefer to use a breast pump. The simplest of these costs less than $10 and has a plastic cone which fits over the nipple and areola and a rubber bulb, with both the cone and the bulb attached to a rim which can screw on to an ordinary nursing bottle so that the mother can see how many ounces she is getting. Some experienced mothers can use this pump with one hand. There's a newer type of pump which consists of two plastic cylinders, one inside the other. It comes with adapters for smaller or larger nipples and requires both hands. The outer cylinder is marked off in ounces and with a collar and a nipple attached to the top can be used as a nursing bottle. This one costs between $20–$30, but many mothers and doctors feel that it's more efficient and less likely to hurt the breast tissue. There are electric breast pumps which can be rented from some hospitals and surgical-supply stores and are very efficient.

187. A breast shield consists of a single piece of soft rubber in the shape of a flat cone with a nipple protruding at the top of the cone. The cone fits over the front of the breast. As the baby sucks on the rubber nipple a vacuum is created in the cone and this draws the areola into the cone and draws out some of the milk. A breast shield is used temporarily when the mother's nipples are retracted. A **nipple shield** consists of a rubber nipple attached to a plastic cone that fits over the front of the breast. This is more likely to hurt the breast tissue than the breast shield.

Best of all is a "Swedish Milk Cup and Breast Shield" which many women have found valuable in making retracted or inverted nipples stand erect, in lessening engorgement by pressing on the areolar region, and in keeping the nipple dry. It is worn under the bra except when nursing. An inner dome with a hole in it fits over the nipple. A more prominent dome, attached to it, protects the nipple from the bra and creates a space which will contain any milk that leaks from the nipple. (Milk leaking directly into a bra keeps the nipple wet.) The pressure of the inner dome and the rim on the sinuses is believed to lessen engorgement; also, the pressure makes the nipple protrude and the protrusion continues for a while after the cup is removed. They are widely available.

WEANING FROM THE BREAST

Weaning is important not only for the baby but for the mother, and not only physically but emotionally. A mother who has set great store by nursing may feel mildly let down and depressed after she stops—as if she has lost some of her closeness to the baby or as if she has become a less worthwhile person. This is an additional reason for making weaning a gradual process whenever possible. Weaning doesn't have to be an all-or-nothing phenomenon. A woman can nurse one or two times a day until her baby is two years old or discontinue nursing entirely.

188. Weaning when there is little breast milk. Weaning from the breast is quite easy when the mother is producing only a **small** amount of milk. It's usually not necessary for her to bind her breasts or limit her own fluids. She can just stop putting the baby to breast and wait. If the breasts get so full that they are uncomfortable, she can nurse for 15 or 30 seconds. This will relieve the pressure without really stimulating the breast. If the breasts should become uncomfortable again, she can repeat this. If she is producing a **moderate** amount of milk, she should plan to wean more gradually. It still isn't necessary to bind the breasts or to limit fluids. Try omitting every other breast-feeding. If, in a day or two, the breasts have not become uncomfortably full, stop all regular nursing, but put the baby to breast for a short period if the breasts then become uncomfortable.

If you have no doctor to advise you, use one of the prepared commercial formulas mentioned in Section 206 or the evaporated milk formula in Section 217.

189. Sudden weaning from the breast (if you cannot consult a doctor). You may have to wean the baby from the breast suddenly if, for instance, you become seriously ill or you have to go out of town for an emergency. (It is not usually necessary to wean the baby because of mild or moderately severe illness in the mother. Your doctor is the one to decide this.) One method is to limit the fluids that the mother drinks and to apply a tight binder and ice bags to her breasts. This is a pretty uncomfortable business. A better way is to relieve the breasts whenever they become uncomfortably full, either with a breast pump or by manual expression.

If you have no doctor to advise you, use one of the prepared commercial formulas mentioned in Section 206 or the evaporated milk formula in Section 217.

190. Gradual weaning from breast to cup between 9 and 15 months. If a mother is producing plenty of milk, how long should she plan to nurse? Best of all, most natural of all, is to nurse until the baby is ready for weaning to the cup.

I think that a majority of babies are showing signs of decreased need for the breast between 9 and 12 months. They stop nursing several times during a feeding and want to play with their mothers. They may have to be nudged back onto the breast. With encouragement they will learn how to take more milk from the cup, and will switch over completely in a few weeks without any signs of deprivation or regret.

I make this point about readiness for weaning in the second half of the first year for the benefit of mothers who want to breast-feed for as long as their babies need suckling. (They don't want to have to shift to the bottle.) But they don't want to go on breast-feeding beyond what is necessary for "complete" breast-feeding.

But there are many breast-feeding mothers who definitely want to go to at least a year of age or to 2 years. They cite the frequency, in natural, simple societies, of breast-feeding until 2 years of age or longer. (It's my understanding that the commonest motive for this in these societies is the belief that it provides birth control. See Section 146.)

Anyway, I see no reason for not nursing until the age of 2 years if mother and baby want to.

It's a good idea to begin offering a sip of milk or other liquid from the cup from the age of 6 months, so that your baby gets used to it before she is too opinionated. By 9 months encourage her to hold the cup herself (Sections 272–274). If by 9 months she is nursing for shorter periods, I would assume she may be ready for gradual weaning. Now offer her the cup at all her meals and increase the amount as she shows her willingness to take more, but continue to breast-feed her at the end of the meal. Next, leave out one of her daily breast-feedings, the one that she seems the least interested in, giving her only the cup. This is usually at breakfast or lunch. In a week, omit another breast-feeding if she seems willing, and in another week, the last one. Her willingness to be weaned may not progress steadily. If she gets into a period when she is miserable from teething or illness, she may want to retreat a little. This is natural enough, and there is no danger in accommodating her.

When weaning is carried out this gradually, there is usually no problem about the mother's breasts. If, however, they become uncomfortably full at any time, the mother only needs to allow the baby to nurse for 15 to 30 seconds to relieve the pressure. Don't let her nurse for 5 minutes—that will encourage the breasts too much.

Most mothers are surprised to find they are reluctant to end this emotional tie and some will put off weaning, week after week.

Sometimes a mother will be afraid to give up nursing altogether, because the baby is not taking as much milk from the cup as she used to take from the breast. This may postpone the weaning indefinitely. I would stop the nursing if the baby is taking an average of 4 ounces from the cup at each meal, or a total of 12 to 16 ounces a day. After the nursing is stopped, she will probably increase the amount from the cup up to a total of 16 ounces or more. This is usually enough, with all the other things she is eating.

Some other points about weaning are taken up in Sections 272–277.

191. Gradual weaning from breast to bottle in the first 4 months. There are lots of mothers who either aren't able or don't want to nurse until a baby is ready to be weaned to the cup at about 6 to 9 months. In one case the milk supply becomes insufficient. The baby cries from hunger and fails to gain sufficient weight. A hungry baby like this seldom puts up any fuss over weaning to the bottle. How fast the weaning to the bottle goes will depend on how much the mother is producing.

If you find that your breast-milk supply is failing rapidly and the baby is quite hungry, and if you have no doctor to consult, make up a complete formula. Give her a bottle at each feeding, after the breast, letting her take as much or as little of it as she wants. Omit first the breast-feeding when you're least engorged. Two days later also omit the breast-feeding when you're next-to-the-least engorged. Discontinue the remaining breast-feedings, one every 2 or 3 days. (If the mother's milk is decreasing only gradually and the baby is only slightly dissatisfied, it will work better to introduce the bottles one feeding at a time, as in the third paragraph below.)

But suppose there is no problem of the milk supply giving out. Let's say a mother wants to nurse for a few months to give her baby a good start, but not for most of the year. How long is it important to nurse? There's no hard-and-fast answer to this, of course. The physical advantages of breast milk, its purity, its easy digestibility, are most valuable to the baby at first. But there is no age at which they suddenly become of no benefit. The emotional advantages of breast-feeding will not cease at any definite period, either. One sensible time to wean to the bottle is at about 3 months. By this age the baby's digestive system will have settled down. She will be about over any tendency to colic. She will be pretty husky and still gaining rapidly. But if a mother would like to stop at 1 or 2 months, those are satisfactory times to wean, too.

If you plan to wean to the bottle at some age beyond 1 month, it is wiser to keep the baby accustomed to the bottle from the age of 1 month on, by giving one bottle regularly 2 or 3 times a week, every day if you prefer.

If the breasts have been producing a good amount of milk, the weaning should preferably be gradual from the beginning. First, omit one breast-feeding a day, the one when you're least engorged, and give a bottle instead. Let the baby take as much or as little of this as she wants. Wait 2 or 3 days until the breasts become adjusted to the change, then omit another breast-feeding, too, and substitute a second daily bottle. Again wait 2 or 3 days, and then omit another breast-feeding. Now the baby is getting the breast only at two feedings and a bottle at each of the other three feedings. You will probably need to wait 3 or even 4 days each time before omitting these last two nursings. Any time the breasts become uncomfortable, even though it isn't time for a scheduled nursing, let the baby nurse for a few seconds, or use manual expression or a breast pump for a few minutes, just to relieve the pressure. Then it should not be necessary to limit your fluids.

192. If the baby won't take the bottle. A baby of 2 months or more who has not regularly had a bottle may balk completely. Try for a week offering a bottle once or twice a day, before the breast or solid food. Don't force it; don't get her angry. Take it away if she refuses, and give her the rest of her meal, including the breast. In a few days' time, she may change her mind.

If she's still adamant, omit the 2 P.M. breast-feeding altogether and see if this makes her thirsty enough so that she will try the bottle at 6 P.M. If she still holds out, you will probably have to give her the breast anyway at the 6 P.M. feeding, because it will be uncomfortably full. But continue to omit the 2 P.M. nursing for several days. It may work on a subsequent day, though it didn't on the first.

The next step is to try omitting every other breast-feeding throughout the 24 hours (nurse at 6 A.M., 2 P.M., 10 P.M.) and hold down on the solid foods so that she's pretty hungry—or omit solids altogether.

See Section 144 on leaving the room and having someone else offer the bottle.

The only alternative left is to stop breast-feeding entirely and starve the baby into capitulation. I put this last, because it is drastic for both baby and mother.

The mother can use a breast pump or manual expression (Sections 184–186) just enough to relieve the pressure and discomfort.

Bottle Feeding

VARIOUS MILKS

193. Pasteurized homogenized vitamin D milk. Most fresh milk sold in the United States is pasteurized, homogenized, vitamin D milk.

Pasteurized means that the milk has been heated high enough, long enough, to kill the bacteria dangerous to human beings, but not enough to sterilize it (kill all the germs), which would give it that boiled taste.

Homogenized means that the fat droplets have been divided into very small particles. This makes them easier for babies to digest and keeps the cream from rising to the top of the container—the cream stays mixed.

Vitamin D milk means that 400 units of vitamin D have been added to the quart of milk.

194. Raw milk is unpasteurized. It is milk just as it comes from the cow. Except for Certified Raw Milk—which comes from cows which have been certified to be free of tuberculosis by a government inspector—it cannot be sold in markets in the United States, but you may be offered it during travels. Whether it's Certified or not, it should be boiled, not only for babies but for children of all ages. This is to be sure that it does not contain bacteria that cause diarrhea, sore throat, or other infections besides tuberculosis. Bring the milk quickly to a full boil in a lightly covered saucepan and then immediately take the pan off the heat. This will kill the bacteria without allowing so much water to boil off that the milk becomes too concentrated with minerals.

Raw milk from Jersey and Guernsey cows is apt to be richer in cream than ordinary commercial milk, and so may upset a baby's digestion. If you use this rich milk, you should pour off a little of the cream so that what's left looks about like commercial milk.

195. Low-fat milks. There are various categories of low-fat milk: skim milk which has less than ½ percent of butterfat; low-fat milks with ½ percent of butterfat, 1 percent, 1½ percent, and 2 percent. Some are fortified with extra protein.

196. Powdered milk. Powdered whole (nonskimmed) milk is useful if you are traveling with your baby or child, or if you are going to live in a country where you can't get evaporated or safe fresh milk. (With a small baby you would be adding sugar or syrup. See Section 286.) You can carry a large supply with you, and it won't weigh too much. It may be more expensive than fresh or evaporated milk. You turn it back into liquid whole milk by mixing in the proportion of 1 level tablespoonful of powdered milk to 2 ounces of water.

If your older baby has been taking fresh pasteurized milk, the equivalent would be 16 level tablespoonfuls of powdered whole milk and 32 ounces of water.

197. Powdered skim milk. You can probably buy nonfat dry milk in cartons at the grocery or drugstore. Most brands are converted back to liquid skim milk by mixing in water in the ratio of 2 ounces of water to 1 level tablespoonful of powder (consult the label), as in Section 196.

198. Evaporated milk. (This should not be confused with **sweetened condensed milk** which is heavily sweetened and is not suitable for children.) Evaporated milk is canned, concentrated cow's milk that has **not** been modified to make it more like mother's milk. (**You** dilute it and add the sugar, to make the formula.) A little more than half the water has been removed by evaporation. (Twenty-eight ounces of average cow's milk has been evaporated down to 13 ounces of evaporated milk.)

The advantages of evaporated milk over pasteurized fresh milk, for the baby and older child, are several. It is thoroughly sterilized in the process of canning, so it is free of germs when you open it. It is, in some localities, cheaper than fresh milk. It can be kept indefinitely in the unopened can without refrigeration. It's the same wherever you buy it, so a baby who travels doesn't have to adjust to different kinds of milk. It is a little easier to digest than fresh milk and less apt to cause allergies, like eczema. An evaporated milk formula is considerably less expensive than a prepared formula.

When you have listed all these advantages, you wonder why anyone uses fresh milk. The main reasons are custom and taste. The taste of evaporated milk doesn't appeal to some older children and adults who have become accustomed to fresh milk. But babies love it and rarely object to changing back and forth. There's no reason why a baby shouldn't go on drinking evaporated milk for years (Section 271).

Since evaporated milk is about twice the strength of fresh milk, you always dilute it with at least an equal amount of water.

There are many brands of evaporated milk. All are of about the same composition. You do not have to worry about switching from one brand to another.

199. Artificial milks, for babies and children who are allergic or react to real milk, are made from a mixture of foods, such as soybean flour and granulated sugar. They require larger nipple holes.

VARIOUS SUGARS

200. Corn syrup is commonly used in formulas. It contains a mixture of sugar and dextrins. A dextrin is halfway between a sugar and a starch. In the intestine, it is only slowly converted into sugar, so that at any one time there is less sugar in the intestine to make gas. That's why a dextrin mixture is thought to be better for a baby who is forming lots of gas or has a tendency to looseness. However, it can be used for babies with good digestions, too. It is inexpensive. You use the same number of tablespoonfuls of it as you would of granulated sugar. The amount for a 24-hour formula is usually 2 tablespoonfuls. The light syrup is ordinarily used, unless there is a tendency to constipation. The dark syrup, being less refined, is slightly more laxative.

201. Ordinary granulated sugar (cane sugar, sucrose) is commonly used in formula making because it is cheap, available, and usually satisfactory. Being highly refined, it has nothing in it to counteract constipation, if a baby has that tendency. The largest amount usually added to a 24-hour formula is 2 tablespoonfuls.

202. Brown sugar is a less refined sugar. It is useful when the baby's stools are too dry and firm. A tablespoonful has the same food value as a tablespoonful of granulated sugar.

203. Lactose is the sugar that naturally occurs in human and cow's milk. It is satisfactory for formulas, but expensive. It takes 1½ tablespoonfuls of it to equal 1 tablespoonful of corn syrup.

FORMULAS

204. Sterilization. Sterilization of formula and bottles is no longer routinely recommended for people using reliable city or town water supplies and having adequate refrigeration in their homes. If you use well water or for any other reason have any question about your water supply, or if you're not sure about your refrigeration, check with your doctor or public health nurse or health department to see whether or not you have to sterilize.

Those who still have to sterilize will find detailed directions in Sections 205–224. Those who don't have to sterilize can substitute thorough soap and water washing and rinsing for sterilization. You can use your dishwasher for bottles and bottlecaps after you've rinsed them but nipples should be washed by hand.

205. What is a formula? Most are a mixture of cow's milk, water, and sugar. The purpose of the water is to dilute the protein and fat because cow's milk is more concentrated in these than mother's milk. But mother's milk is much sweeter than cow's milk, so sugar is added.

You may use an already prepared commercial formula, or make one with evaporated milk or powdered milk.

The reason you may have to sterilize carefully the ingredients and the bottles is that germs thrive on milk, just the way babies do. If a few bacteria get into the formula when you make it on Tuesday, they may have multiplied a lot by the time the baby drinks the last of it on Wednesday, especially if the formula has not been well refrigerated. Boiling the formula also makes it more digestible.

In the following five sections—206–210—is an overall view of the kinds of formulas in use today and the choices of how to sterilize and bottle them. Then, in Sections 211–224, come the actual directions for sterilization.

206. Prepared commercial formulas. Prepared formulas (which have brand names such as Similac, Enfamil, and SMA) are the most popular in the United States at present. They come in cans or bottles, already sterilized. In order to make them somewhat more like human milk in effect, the percentage of protein has been reduced, the sugar has been increased with the addition of lactose (milk sugar), and the cow's butterfat has been replaced with vegetable oils.

Vitamins A, C, and D have been added. Prepared formulas can be bought with or without iron, according to the doctor's advice.

These prepared formulas come in four forms:

1. **ready-to-use in a 32-ounce can**
2. **ready-to-use in disposable bottles**
3. **concentrated** form in **13-ounce cans,** which must be diluted with an equal amount of water.
4. **powdered** form in **16-ounce cans:** 1 level tablespoon of powdered formula for every 2 ounces of water.

207. Ready-to-use prepared formula comes in 32-ounce (1-quart) cans. No water needs to be added, so the formula is poured directly from the can into the bottles. The convenience is great, especially for the inexperienced parent.

The cost is one and a half times as much as the concentrated prepared formula, three times the cost of evaporated milk or fresh pasteurized milk.

You have **three choices of how to bottle the formula:**

1. You can **sterilize** the nursing bottles, nipples, and caps in a kettle or sterilizer and then fill them directly from the can.

   See Sections 213, 214, and 219 for the details.

But some parents hate the bother of sterilizing the bottles. You can get around this in either of two ways:

2. You can use **sterilized, disposable thin plastic containers** that come in rolls. This method is described in Section 221.
3. Another way to avoid sterilizing the bottles is—just before each feeding—to **fill one clean bottle** that has merely been washed carefully. This method and the reasoning behind it are explained in Section 220. You can use the same method for prepared **powdered** formula.

208. Ready-to-use formula in disposable bottles comes in six-packs, in three sizes of bottle: 4-ounce, 6-ounce, and 8-ounce. Formula in this form avoids all the work and fuss of formula bottling as well as formula making, which makes it particularly helpful for the inexperienced parent at the start, for the breast-fed baby who only needs an occasional bottle, and for the baby who is traveling. The bottles require no refrigeration. The expense is one and a half times as much as for the ready-to-use prepared formula in 32-ounce cans, more than twice as much as for the concentrated prepared formula, and four and a half times as much as for evaporated milk.

You can also buy these bottles with disposable nipples already attached and capped.

209. Concentrated prepared formula comes in 13-ounce cans and must be diluted with an equal amount of water before it can be used. Though this concentrated formula is less convenient to use than the ready-to-use formula in 32-ounce cans, it costs only about two thirds as much, and the cans are less bulky to store or to travel with.

You can choose between two ways to get the formula diluted if you need to sterilize:

1. **Boiling the water in a saucepan,** then adding the can of concentrated formula.

   With the above method of sterilizing the water and then adding the can of concentrated formula, you have three different ways to bottle the mixture. One appeals to one person, another to another. I'll list them as A, B, and C.

   A. **Sterilized nursing bottles:** You pour the mixture of formula and sterilized water into nursing bottles that have already been sterilized. This is the commonest method. It is described in Section 219.

   B. **The quart bottle of formula and the single clean nursing bottle:** If you want to avoid sterilizing all the nursing bottles, you can pour the mixture of concentrated formula and sterilized water into one sterilized quart bottle or jar, which you keep in the refrigerator. Whenever feeding time comes around you pour the right amount of formula into a nursing bottle and attach a nipple, both of which have merely been washed carefully but not sterilized. This method saves the trouble of boiling all the bottles, but takes a little longer at each feeding.

      The method and the reasoning behind it are explained in Section 220.

   C. **Disposable thin plastic nursing containers:** After boiling the water and adding the can of concentrated formula, you put this diluted formula into disposable thin plastic nursing containers that come in rolls (Playtex or Evenflo). You only have to boil the nipples and the caps. This method is described in Section 221.

These disposable containers add to the cost of feedings, of course.

2. **Terminal sterilization.** Up to now I've been discussing the method of sterilizing the water in a saucepan and then adding the can of concentrated formula, and the three different ways of bottling the mixture.

   There is also a different method: sterilizing the formula right in the bottles (the bottles get sterilized at the same time) in a large kettle or sterilizer. It is called terminal because all the sterilization is done at once, at the end.

   It appeals to some parents because there is only one sterilization process and this makes it seem simpler and surer; they don't have to worry about getting germs into the formula while they're measuring and mixing the ingredients because these germs will get killed anyway.

   The only disadvantage of terminal sterilization is that the heating of milk causes scum which may clog the holes in the nipples unless precautions are taken.

   Terminal sterilization is described in more detail in Sections 222–224.

210. Evaporated milk formulas. Evaporated milk is a little more than twice as concentrated as the average fresh milk, so it should be diluted with at least an equal amount of water. Like all cow's milk it needs added syrup or sugar to make the proportion more like human milk for babies in the early months.

Basically there are two different ways to get the formula diluted, sweetened, and sterilized:

1. **Boiling the water and syrup in a saucepan,** and then adding the can of evaporated milk. Then you are ready for bottling.

   (The reason you don't boil the whole mixture is that heating milk makes scum which sometimes plugs the nipple holes if you don't take precautions.)

Bottling. You have a choice of three quite different ways to bottle this evaporated milk formula. One appeals to one person, another to another. They're listed as A, B, and C in Section 209.

2. **Terminal sterilization.** This is described in Section 209.

PREPARING BOTTLE FEEDINGS

There are three steps to preparing bottle feedings, though two of the steps may be carried out together in certain methods.

1. Washing and sterilizing the bottles, nipples, screw rings that hold the nipples on, small caps of hard plastic, or large caps of rubber that cover certain kinds of nipples.
2. Mixing and sterilizing the formula.
3. Bottling the formula.

211. Washing the bottles, nipples, caps, etc. You can do a quicker and more efficient job of washing the equipment—the bottles, nipples, screw rings that hold the nipples on, and caps—if you will wash them with soap or detergent, and brush, soon after your baby has finished each bottle, before the milk has dried. However, this is not essential.

You can use your dishwasher if it really gets the bottle equipment clean.

But in the end you must sterilize the equipment unless you are using the single-bottle method (Section 220).

A bottle brush is important for washing the insides of the bottles. A nipple brush is important for getting the insides of the nipples clean. Then a toothpick should be twisted in each nipple hole.

Careful washing of the bottles, nipples, screw rings, and caps is particularly important if you are using the method of not sterilizing the bottles but filling one bottle just before each feeding.

Rinse with clean water.

Stand the bottles, upside down, to drain in a bottle rack or dish drainer.

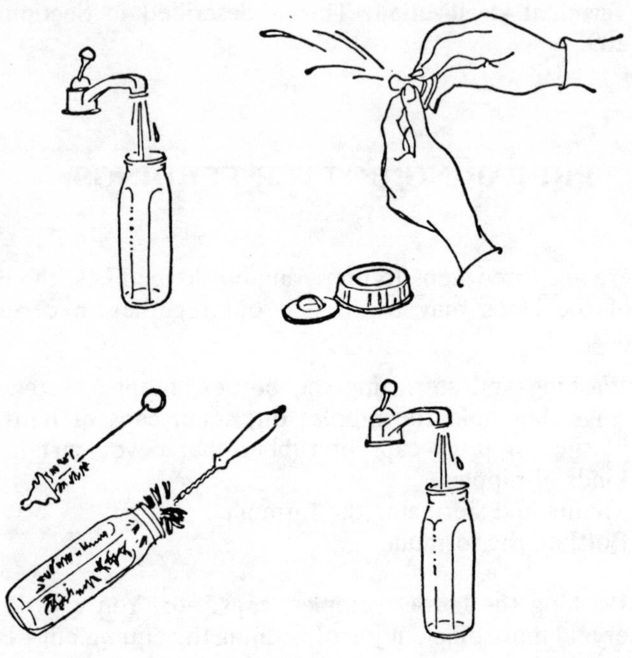

212. Sterilizing the bottles, nipples, screw rings, and caps. Most bottles now are wide mouthed. Until feeding time, the nipple is held in the bottle upside down, by a screw-on ring with an opening in the top, closed by a small cap. For feeding, the nipple is reversed and protrudes through the opening in the screw-on ring. (The nipples for disposable nursing containers are different.)

There are two methods of sterilizing this equipment. One is the method of **terminal sterilization** (Sections 222–224), in which you put formula made with unsterilized water into unsterilized bottles and then sterilize them all together. This is one of the methods used for prepared concentrated formulas and for evaporated milk, both of which must be diluted with water that has been sterilized.

The other method (sometimes called **aseptic**) is to sterilize the equipment by itself and then put sterile formula into it. This method is particularly suitable for prepared ready-to-use formula that comes out of the can already diluted and sterilized. But it is also used for prepared concentrated formulas and for evaporated milk formulas.

213. The aseptic method. You can use any container for sterilizing that is large enough to hold all the **8-ounce bottles** you'll need for formula for 24 hours (usually six, seven, or eight bottles in the early weeks), or perhaps two **4-ounce bottles** for water if your baby likes water, perhaps a jar with big holes punched in the top to hold more conveniently the nipples, caps, and rings. If there is no room in the jar for the screw-on rings, don't worry. They can be fitted anywhere in the sterilizer.

It's much more practical to put the bottles for formula and the nipple jar upright in a **wire rack** that can be easily lifted out of the kettle.

You can buy a **kettle** large enough to hold the bottles in a rack, or a stove-top sterilizer (which is essentially the same thing as a kettle), or even an electric sterilizer that turns itself off. Sterilizers usually come equipped with rack, bottles, caps, measure, and tongs.

Put the bottles in the rack upside down so that the steam can more easily get into them and the water can run out. The same goes for the jar containing the nipples and other equipment.

Put a couple of inches of hot water in the bottom of the kettle or sterilizer, put the top on, bring to a boil, and boil hard for 5 minutes. Let cool.

A pair of **tongs** sterilized with the rest of the equipment will be helpful in lifting the bottles out of the rack if they are still hot; they will also be helpful in placing the nipples upside down in the bottles after the bottles have been filled with formula, so that you won't handle them where they may come in contact with the formula. If you don't use tongs, handle the nipples by the edges, not by the tip that may dip into the formula and that will later go into the baby's mouth.

If you want a sterile place to lay nipples, screw rings, and caps while you are bottling the formula, put them on the inverted top of the kettle or sterilizer.

The bottles are now ready for the formula.

214. Diluting a prepared concentrated formula (Enfamil, SMA, or Similac) with sterilized water. The can holds 13 ounces of formula and you want to dilute it with 13 ounces of boiled water. Measure 15 ounces of hot or cold water into a saucepan. This allows 2 ounces for evaporation at gentle boiling for 5 minutes. (Hard boiling would evaporate 5 ounces in 5 minutes.)

Put a **long-handled cooking spoon** in the water, too, so that the bowl of the spoon will be sterilized. Bring to a boil and boil gently for 5 minutes. (Having the water steaming is not enough.) Use a timer.

Briefly wash the top of a can of formula with soap on a brush or on a piece of paper towel. Rinse the soap off. Wash and rinse a punch-type can opener.

Punch two holes on opposite sides of the top of the can, one to let the formula out, one to let air in.

When the water has boiled for 5 minutes, take the saucepan off the flame and pour the formula from the can into the water. Stir to mix.

Suggestions for bottling are in Sections 218–221.

(A prepared concentrated formula can also be diluted and sterilized by the terminal sterilization method (Section 224). In that case you add only 13 ounces of water because there will be no evaporation.)

215. A prepared powdered milk formula. In general the ratio is 1 level tablespoonful of the powdered formula for every 2 ounces of boiled water.

You add 15 level tablespoons of prepared powdered formula to 30 ounces of boiled water. But you start with 32 ounces of water, to allow 2 ounces for evaporation. Boil the water for 5 minutes and allow to cool. Beat in the powdered formula with a whisk or eggbeater which has been sterilized by leaving its lower end in the formula water while it boils. (The handle doesn't need to be sterilized.) Pour into bottles that have been sterilized (Section 219) or into disposable thin plastic nursing containers (Section 221).

To make a single bottle of 6 ounces, for example, you need 6 ounces of boiled water and 3 level tablespoonfuls of powdered formula. But you start with 8 ounces of water, to allow 2 ounces for evaporation, and proceed as in the last paragraph. If you are going to give the bottle right away, the bottle and nipple don't need to have been sterilized, only washed carefully. (See the explanation in Section 220.)

Prepared powdered milk formula has the following advantages:

1. It's the cheapest of the prepared formulas.
2. It's very convenient for an occasional bottle for a breast-fed baby, eliminating waste.
3. It's also very convenient for travel. You can take along premeasured amounts of water and formula powder and mix when you need them—this avoids the need for refrigeration.

216. Making an ordinary powdered whole milk formula. A suitable formula for a young baby would be 13 level tablespoonfuls of powdered whole milk, 32 ounces of water, and 2 tablespoonfuls of corn syrup.

You boil the required amount of water for 5 minutes, having added 2 extra ounces to allow for evaporation, and dissolve the syrup in it. When this has cooled at least to body heat, place the powder on top and beat it in with a sterilized eggbeater or whisk. The beater or whisk can be sterilized by leaving its lower end in the formula water while it boils.

Powdered milk should be kept in the refrigerator or a cool, dry place after the carton has been opened.

You can make a **single 8-ounce bottle** for an older baby, who has been drinking fresh pasteurized milk, by boiling for 5 minutes 10 ounces of water. (Two ounces of this is for evaporation.) Add a teaspoonful of corn syrup. When cool, beat in 4 level tablespoonfuls of powdered milk.

For a younger baby who has been on an evaporated milk formula or who has been on the breast, you can make a single bottle with powdered milk as follows: Boil 9 ounces of water for 5 minutes. (Two ounces of this is for evaporation.) Add a teaspoonful of corn syrup. When cool beat in 3 level tablespoonfuls of powdered milk.

217. Making an evaporated milk formula. A can of evaporated milk holds 13 ounces. It is a little more than twice the strength of the average fresh milk sold by dairies and stores. So in making the formula you use more water than evaporated milk.

A suitable formula could be:

Evaporated milk . . . . .13 ounces
Water . . . . .19 ounces
Corn syrup . . . . 2 tablespoonfuls

Measure 21 ounces of hot or cold water into a saucepan. (A quart-size glass pitcher marked in ounces is most convenient but a 16-ounce or 8-ounce measure will do.) You are allowing 2 extra ounces for evaporation during gentle boiling for 5 minutes. (Hard boiling would evaporate 5 ounces.)

Add 2 tablespoonfuls of corn syrup and stir briefly. Leave a **long-handled spoon** in the water while it boils, so that the bowl of the spoon will be sterilized too, for stirring in the milk. Bring to a boil and boil gently (having the water just steaming is not enough) for 5 minutes. Use a timer.

Briefly wash the top of a can of evaporated milk with soap on a brush or on a piece of paper toweling. Rinse the soap off. Wash and rinse a punch-type can opener. Punch two holes—one to let the milk out, the other to let air in.

Pour the milk into the saucepan which contains the sterilized water and syrup, and stir briefly to mix.

* * *

Now the formula is ready to bottle, either by pouring into sterilized nursing bottles (Section 219) or a sterilized quart bottle (Section 220) or into disposable thin plastic nursing containers (Section 221).

(You can also dilute and sterilize evaporated milk with the terminal method, Sections 222, 223. In that case you use only 19 ounces of water because there will be no evaporation.)

BOTTLING THE FORMULA

218. How much in each bottle? Most babies want to be fed more frequently at first, especially if they start small (under 7 pounds). Bottle-fed babies may want to be fed six, seven, or eight times in 24 hours. You may have discovered your baby's needs in the hospital if you had rooming-in. On the other hand, some babies become more wakeful and hungry after 3 or 4 days, so don't be surprised.

Most 7-pound babies will want less than a total of 21 ounces of formula in the 24 hours, 8-pounders less than 24 ounces.

The formulas discussed here provide 26 to 32 ounces, which should be more than enough in the early weeks.

If you are using **prepared ready-to-use formula** (Section 207) or the **evaporated milk formula** (Section 210) you have a total of 32 ounces. Put 4 ounces into each of eight bottles for a start, but don't expect your baby to finish 4 ounces unless she is large, with a large appetite. If you find you sometimes need nine bottles, put 3½ ounces in each. Later the baby will want fewer bottles and more in each. A 32-ounce formula will provide 4½ ounces in seven bottles, 6½ ounces in five bottles.

If you are making your formula from a **prepared concentrated formula,** you will have a total of 26 ounces. This will make approximately 3¼ ounces in eight bottles, 3¾ ounces in seven bottles, 4⅓ ounces in six bottles, or 5¼ ounces in five bottles. (Don't worry about these approximate fractions. The baby won't know the difference. A breast-fed baby will take 3 ounces at one feeding and 8 at another, and seem equally happy with both.)

219. Filling all the sterilized bottles at once. Pour the right amount into each bottle from your saucepan. Place the nipples upside down in the bottle necks. Handle them with tongs, or with your fingers on the outside edges. Screw the rings on loosely so that air can enter as the bottle cools. Refrigerate.

220. Storing the formula in a quart bottle or jar and filling one clean nursing bottle at each feeding. You can use any glass quart container: a bottle that orange juice comes in or a jar for preserving. (Most plastic containers becomes mis-shapen when boiled.) Boil the container in a saucepan for 5 minutes.

When the bottle is cool enough to handle, pour the entire sterilized formula into it. Seal loosely, so that air can enter during the cooling of the formula. Refrigerate.

When each feeding time comes around, pour the required number of ounces into a nursing bottle that has been carefully washed with soap or detergent on a bottle brush. Rinse.

It may have been washed and drained many hours before, or just before the feeding.

The nipple should have been carefully washed with soap or detergent on a nipple brush, and a toothpick twirled in the hole or holes. Rinse.

Put the quart bottle back in the refrigerator.

The reason the glass bottles (or firm plastic bottles) have to be merely washed but not sterilized is because any germs that may have been left in the bottles from the previous use won't have a chance to multiply between the time you fill each bottle and the time the baby empties it.

221. Filling disposable, sterilized thin plastic nursing containers that come in rolls. (Two commercial brands are Playtex and Evenflo.) These appeal to parents who are willing to pay a little more to avoid the fuss of sterilizing the bottles every day. You still have to boil the nipples and caps for 5 minutes.

You tear a clear plastic container off the roll, just as you tear off the small plastic bags you store food in. The open end is cut so that there are two tabs, for stretching it over the edge of the holder.

The holder is a cylinder of hard plastic, open at both ends. It has slits on two sides, with ounce markings at the edges, so that you can look through to see how much formula you have put in the inner container or how much the baby has drunk. You can't use these ounce markings for **diluting** formula—they're not accurate enough.

You slip a container into the holder, slightly folding it lengthwise so that it will go in, and then use the tabs to stretch open the open end of the container and fold it back over the upper end of the holder. (This is something like pulling the cuff of a shirt sleeve down and folding it back over the cuff of a jacket sleeve.)

When all the containers are in their holders you fill them with the right amount of formula.

Then stretch a nipple over the open edge of each container and holder. Try to avoid touching the inside of the nipple and the part that goes into the baby's mouth. In other words, try to handle the nipple by the outside edges.

There are rings to slip down over the shoulders of the nipples to keep an older, stronger baby from pulling the nipples off. They are not necessary at first.

There are large rubber caps that fit over the nipples while the containers are in the refrigerator or during trips.

222. Terminal sterilization of an evaporated milk formula. Let's, for example, assume that the formula will be:

Evaporated milk . . . . .13 ounces
Water . . . . .19 ounces
Corn syrup . . . . 2 tablespoonfuls

You should expect to make seven bottles of about 4½ ounces each. The steps are as follows:

Run faucet water (hot or cold) into the quart measure up to the 19-ounce mark.

Put the 2 level tablespoonfuls of corn syrup into the water and stir until dissolved (syrup or sugar dissolves faster in warm water).

Briefly wash the top of a 13-ounce can of evaporated milk with soap; rinse; then make two openings with the can opener on opposite sides of the top, one to let the milk out, the other to let air in.

Pour the can of evaporated milk into the quart measure, bringing the total to 32 ounces.

Stir with the tablespoon and pour about 4½ ounces into each of 7 bottles.

223. Sterilizing the formula. Insert the nipples upside down in the caps, cover with the disks, then screw the caps partly on. Leave the caps only partly screwed on so that there will be a space for hot air to escape as the bottles heat up, and for air to re-enter as the bottles cool again.

Place the bottles in the wire rack in the sterilizing pail, put an inch or two of hot water in the bottom, put the pail on the stove, and heat. The water should boil for a full 25 minutes.

It has been discovered that there will be the least clogging of the nipple holes if the formula is allowed to **cool slowly without being shaken** at all. (This allows the scum to form into one large firm piece which sticks to the inside of the bottle.) So leave the sterilizing pail (with its cover on) right on the stove (with the heat off) for an hour or two.

When the bottles are lukewarm, screw the caps down and place the bottles in the refrigerator.

224. Terminal sterilization of a prepared concentrated formula. This is the same as the previous section except that you will be using a 13-ounce can of prepared concentrated formula, 13 ounces of water, and no syrup. This will make about 3⅔ ounces in each of seven bottles.

So the steps are as follows (see Sections 222 and 223 for details):

Run 13 ounces of water into the measure.
Wash top of can of formula, punch holes, empty it into measure, stir.
Pour 3⅔ ounces into seven bottles.
Insert nipples and caps, and screw rings partly on.
Place bottles in rack and rack in kettle. Put 1 or 2 inches of water in kettle.
Bring to boil and boil for 25 minutes.
Let everything cool for an hour or two.
Tighten the screw rings and refrigerate.

FORMULA REFRIGERATION

225. Insufficient space in refrigerator. If you don't have room in your refrigerator for five or six bottles, you can sterilize your formula in a quart bottle. Just before each feeding pour the required amount of formula into a clean nursing bottle. The nursing bottle doesn't have to be sterilized if it's been well scrubbed and if the formula will be drunk right away. Formula shouldn't remain for hours in an unsterilized bottle.

226. Saving the unused milk. When you use less than a full can of prepared formula or evaporated milk, you can save what is left for the next day. Leave it in the can and cover the top to keep bacteria, mold, and dust particles from drifting in. Keep the covered can in the refrigerator, and use it all up the next day.

227. If you cannot keep the formula cold. If you ever get into a situation where you can't keep the baby's bottles cold until feeding time—for instance, if your refrigerator stops working—you will be pretty safe if you heat each bottle before giving it. Unscrew the cap partly, put the bottle in hot water, bring to a boil, boil 25 minutes, then cool it down to body temperature before giving it. The easiest solution is to use prepared powdered formula, mixing it with water before each use—one bottle at a time. (See Section 215.)

GIVING THE BOTTLE

228. The first few days. Usually the first bottle is offered about 4–6 hours after babies are born, though it can be started earlier if they seem hungry. Babies are apt to want little the first few feedings. Even if they take only half an ounce, don't try to get more into them. It's often 3 or 4 days before they want the amounts you expect them to need, and it may take a week or more. Don't worry; it may be better for their digestion to start gradually. They'll find out what they need when they become more active in a few days.

229. Giving the formula. You don't need to shake the bottle when you remove it from the refrigerator unless the formula is made from unhomogenized fresh milk—in which case the cream needs mixing in.

It has been discovered that babies enjoy just as much and do just as well on formula that is either warmed or at room temperature or right out of the refrigerator, as long as it comes at the same temperature at each feeding. I think the main reason why many parents still warm the bottles is that they have always thought of bottles as being warmed and breast milk is warm, so it seems unkind to give a baby cold milk. If I were a new parent I'd take advantage of the convenience of the new knowledge and feed always at room or refrigerator temperature, whichever was convenient.

You can warm the bottle in a saucepan or pitcher of hot water or in a washbasin. It's more convenient, if there is no hot water near the baby's room, to use an electric bottle warmer. Body temperature is the right temperature to aim for. The best way to test this is to shake a few drops on the inside of your wrist. If it feels hot, it is too hot.

If you make your formula with granulated sugar or lactose, it's a good habit to taste it before using it each day to avoid the dangerous accident that sometimes occurs of using salt or bicarbonate of soda instead. Or taste the drop of milk you shake on your wrist, at the first feeding after making formula.

Sit in a comfortable chair and hold the baby cradled in your arm. Most parents want a chair with arms, and perhaps a pillow under the elbow. Some find a rocking chair is perfect.

Keep the bottle tilted up, so that the nipple is always full. Most babies want to work steadily until they have taken all the formula they need. There are some, though, who swallow a lot of air during nursing, and if the air bubble in the stomach gets too big, they feel uncomfortably full and stop nursing in the middle of the bottle. If this happens, bring up the bubble (see Section 134) and go on with the feeding. A few babies need to be bubbled two or even three times in the course of a bottle—others not at all. You will soon find out which type your baby is.

As soon as your baby stops nursing and seems satisfied, let that be the end of the feeding. Babies know better than anyone else how much they need.

230. Can you prop the bottle? It's good for the parent to hold the baby in the arms during bottle feedings. This is the position that Nature intends. The baby and parent are as close as can be, and they can watch each other's faces. Feeding is a baby's greatest joy, by far, and it's good for the baby to link this with the parent's presence and face.

On the other hand, the father may not be home and the mother may be busy with other children or chores, and it may be necessary to prop the bottle at certain feedings. Most parents of twins find it essential frequently to prop the bottle for one or both babies. These parents point out that there are a number of chances every day for mothers and fathers to talk to their babies and cuddle them and that these other times may be calmer and happier than certain hectic feeding times. I agree that there are a hundred different ways to show a baby your love and that no single one of them is essential in itself. I agree that it does no harm for loving but busy parents to prop some of the bottles if they can make it up to the baby in other ways. I'd still advise parents who are not too busy not to prop.

Most parents prop with a folded diaper, but there are bottle holders that are more efficient.

Many babies by the time they are 6 or 7 months old feel so

grown up that they don't want to take the bottle cuddled in their parents' arms. They want to sit up straight and hold the bottle themselves. Of course, there's no point insisting on a baby's being in your lap who'd prefer something else. (See Section 238.)

For sitting babies who want to hold their bottles, there is an attachment consisting of a tube which runs from the nipple to the bottom of the bottle. By this means, milk can be drawn from the bottom of the bottle even when the bottle is held upright.

231. Making the nipple holes right. If the nipple holes are too small, the baby will get too little and start fussing, or become tired and go to sleep long before finishing the bottle. If the holes are too large, the baby may choke or get indigestion and, in the long run, may get too little sucking satisfaction and thumb-suck more. For most babies, the right speed is when the bottle takes about 20 minutes of straight sucking time. The holes are generally right for a young baby if, when you turn the bottle upside down, the milk comes out in a fine spray for a second or two and then changes to drops. If it keeps coming in a spray, it is probably too fast. If it comes in slow drops from the beginning, it is probably too slow.

There are probably small holes in the rubber shoulders of the nipples you use, or some other channel for letting air into the bottle as the baby withdraws milk, to prevent a vacuum, which would collapse the nipple. (After a while babies learn by themselves to release a collapsed nipple so that air can bubble in.) This air passage is usually designed so that if you screw the nipple cap down tighter, the passage is decreased in size (or closed altogether); so there is a partial vacuum and the baby has to suck harder and take longer to finish the bottle. A looser cap allows faster drinking. See Section 388 on relationship to thumb-sucking.

Many new nipples are too slow for a young baby but are right for an older, stronger one. If they are too slow for your baby, enlarge them carefully as follows: Stick the dull end of a fine (No. 10) needle into a cork. Then, holding the cork, heat the needle point in a flame until it's red-hot. Stick it a short distance into the top of the nipple. You don't have to poke it into the old hole. Don't use too large a needle or poke it in too far, until you can test your results. If you make the holes too large, you'll have to throw the nipple away. You can make one, two, or three enlarged holes. If you have no cork, you can wrap a piece of cloth around the dull end of the needle or hold it in pliers.

232. Nipple holes clogged with scum. If you have trouble with clogged nipple holes, you can buy nipples that, instead of having small holes, are "crosscut." This means that a small cross has been cut in the tip of the nipple. The milk does not pour out, as you might expect, because the edges of the cut stay together until the baby sucks. You can make small crosscuts in your regular nipples with a razor blade. First pinch the nipple tip to make a narrow ridge, then cut across it. Then pinch again (at a right angle to the first pinch) and make another cut.

233. Don't urge babies to take more than they want. The main trouble with bottle feeding, to my mind, is that the mother can see how much formula is left. Some babies always want the same quantity at every feeding of the day. But there are others whose appetites are much more variable. You mustn't get the idea that your baby has to have a certain amount at each feeding. It may help you acquire a more relaxed feeling about this to realize that breast-fed babies may get as much as 10 ounces at the 6 A.M. nursing and as little as 4 ounces at the 6 P.M. feeding and be perfectly happy with each. If you can trust breast-fed babies to take what they need, you can trust your bottle-fed baby, too.

It is necessary to make this point because quite a number of children develop feeding problems. They lose the natural appetite that they were born with and balk at all or many of their foods. These problems develop, in nine out of ten cases, because the parents have been trying, sometimes since infancy, to get their child, say a girl, to eat more than she wants. When you succeed in getting a baby or child to take a few more mouthfuls than she is eager for, it looks to you as if you have gained something. But this isn't so. She will only cut down at her next feeding. Babies know the amounts and they even know the different kinds of foods that their bodies are calling for. Urging children isn't necessary, doesn't get you anywhere. It is harmful because it begins, after a while, to take away their appetites, and makes them want to eat **less** than their systems really need.

In the long run, urging does more than destroy appetite and make thin children. It robs them of some of their positive feeling for life. Babies are meant to spend their first year getting hungry, demanding food, enjoying it, reaching satisfaction—a lusty success story, repeated at least three times a day, week after week. It builds into them self-confidence, outgoingness, trust in their parents. But if meal-time becomes a struggle, if feeding becomes something that is done **to** them, they go on the defensive and build up a balky, suspicious attitude toward life and toward people.

I don't mean that you have to snatch the bottle away for good the first time your baby pauses. Some babies like to rest a bit several times during a feeding. But if she seems indifferent when you put the nipple back in her mouth (and it's not due to a bubble), then she's satisfied, and you should be, too. You may say, "If I wait 10 minutes, she'll sometimes take a little bit more." Better not.

234. The babies who wake in a few minutes. What about the babies who go to sleep after they've taken 4 of their 5 ounces and then wake up and cry a few minutes later? This is more apt to be due to an air bubble or colic or periodic irritable crying than to hunger. Babies won't notice a difference of an ounce, especially if they've gone to sleep. In fact, babies will often sleep just as well when they've taken only half their usual amount, though they may wake a **little** early.

It's perfectly all right occasionally to give the rest of the formula a little later, if you feel sure that your baby's hungry for it. But I think it's better to assume first that it's not really hunger and give the child a good chance to go back to sleep—with or without a pacifier. In other words, try to postpone the next feeding for 2 or 3 hours.

235. The young baby who only half finishes. A mother may bring a baby, perhaps a boy, home from the hospital and find that he stops taking his bottle and falls asleep when it's still half full. Yet they said in the hospital that he was taking it all.

The mother keeps trying to rouse him, to wedge another quarter of an ounce in, but it's slow, hard, frustrating work. What's the trouble? He may be a baby who hasn't quite "come to" yet. (An occasional baby stays sluggish like that for the first 2 or 3 weeks and then comes to life with a bang.)

The constructive thing to do is to let the baby stop when he wants to, even if he's taken only an ounce or two. Won't he get hungry, then, long before it's time for the next feeding? He may, or he may not. If he does, feed him. "But," you say, "I'd be feeding him all day and night." It probably won't be that bad. The point is that if you let a baby stop when he feels like it and let him come to feel his own hunger, he will gradually become more eager for his feedings and take larger amounts. Then he will be able to sleep for longer periods. You can help him to learn to wait longer and be hungrier by trying to stretch out the interval to 2, 2½, then 3 hours. Don't pick him up just as soon as he starts fussing but wait a while. He may go back to sleep. If he gets to crying hard, you'll probably have to feed him.

If you keep urging him to finish, there's a chance that he'll go right on being indifferent.

236. The baby who fusses soon after starting a bottle or who promptly goes to sleep may be frustrated by a nipple hole that is clogged or too small. See if the milk comes in a fine spray when the bottle is first inverted. Try enlarging the nipple hole a little anyway, as an experiment (Section 231).

The older baby who refuses to nurse is discussed in Section 133.

237. How long after a bottle has been taken out of the refrigerator can you still use it? During the time when a bottle is at drinking temperature or room temperature or pleasant outdoor temperature, any bacteria that may have gotten into the formula will be able to multiply rapidly. That is why it is unwise to give a baby a bottle that has been sitting around the house or carriage or car for several hours, whether it's a full bottle or one that has been partly consumed.

If you will need to feed the baby a couple of hours after leaving home, put the bottle, as soon as you take it out of the refrigerator, into an insulated bag designed to keep things cold or wrap it in ten layers of newspaper (which is a pretty good insulator).

If you have a young baby who sometimes goes to sleep after half a bottle and then wakes up in a couple of hours for the rest, you can promptly put the half-finished bottle back into the refrigerator. I wouldn't use such a bottle more than twice.

238. Avoiding the bottle-in-bed, to expedite weaning. There are four reasons for weaning babies from the bottle at about the age of a year. In some cases they develop serious caries (decay) of the teeth as a result of ending every meal—especially when they fall asleep drinking the bottle—with milk in the mouth.

Some parents are bothered by the sight of a toddler wandering around or playing with a bottle in the hand, taking a swig now and then—it looks babyish or "dopey."

Falling asleep with milk in the mouth can lead to an ear infection. Some milk can run down the eustachian tube which connects the back of the throat to the part of the ear behind the eardrum. Then bacteria can grow in the milk behind the eardrum and start an infection.

After 6 months, many babies come to feel so grown up that they don't want to be cradled in their parents' arms at feeding time; they want to sit up. And they also want to take the bottle away from the parent and hold it themselves. Practical parents, seeing they're not much use, are apt to put such babies in their cribs, where they drink their bottles and put themselves to sleep all in one operation. This pattern is a handy one for putting babies to sleep, but in the long run it makes it impossible for some of them to go to sleep without a bottle. (Read Section 272.) When the parent tries to withhold the bedtime bottle at 9, 15, or 21 months, such babies will cry frantically and be unable to fall asleep for a long time. So, if you want your baby to be weaned from the bottle by a year of age—and I think this is preferable—let the child continue to take the bottle on your lap.

Adding Vitamins and Water

VITAMINS IN INFANCY

239. Babies may need extra vitamin D and vitamin C. (They are discussed in Sections 479 and 480.) There are only small amounts of these in milk as it comes from the cow and in solid foods that are given early.

Breast milk may contain sufficient vitamin C if the mother's diet is rich in citrus fruits and certain vegetables (Section 147), but breast milk doesn't contain enough vitamin D. Babies on an evaporated milk formula should receive 25–50 milligrams per day of vitamin C in a commercial preparation until they are receiving 2 ounces of orange juice daily. It does no harm for breast-fed babies to take this too as an extra precaution.

In the United States, pasteurized milk or ready-to-use formulas contain 400 units of vitamin D to the quart, and a can of concentrated prepared formula or evaporated milk contains the same amount. This should be sufficient to prevent rickets in a normal baby. A breast-fed baby should receive 400 units daily in a commercial preparation.

Most bottle-fed babies in the United States are given commercially prepared formulas which are vitamin-fortified so they don't need any added vitamins in infancy. Your doctor can tell you whether or not your baby needs extra vitamins.

If you have no doctor to advise you, you can buy a 3-vitamin preparation that contains C, D, and A. The dropper that comes with the bottle has lines showing 0.3 cc and 0.6 cc (three-tenths, and six-tenths of a cubic centimeter). Draw the fluid up to the line that's marked 0.3 cc and squirt it directly into the baby's mouth at the beginning of one of the feedings of the day, once a day, winter and summer, starting at one month or earlier. Some doctors prescribe 0.6 cc, but you should not go beyond this amount, since excessive doses of vitamin D can be harmful.

240. "Multivitamin" preparations contain a number of B vitamins in addition to A, D, and C. However, milk, cereals, and other foods that babies and children eat usually provide sufficient B vitamins. The main reason for not using one of these products routinely for children, aside from the fact that the added B vitamins are not necessary, is that they are more expensive.

241. Orange juice. Orange juice is not now routinely given until 9–12 months because some babies don't handle it well and may even be allergic to it. Babies get enough vitamin C in their formula or added vitamins. When your doctor suggests adding orange juice to the diet it can be fresh, frozen, or canned. Orange juice is usually mixed with an equal amount of water so that it won't taste too strong. One way is to start with 1 teaspoonful of orange juice and 1 teaspoonful of water. The next day give 2 teaspoonfuls of orange juice and 2 teaspoonfuls of water. The third day, 3 teaspoonfuls of each. And so on, up to an **ounce of each.** Then gradually decrease the water and increase the orange juice, until you are giving **2 ounces of straight orange juice.** If your baby is still on the bottle, you strain the orange juice so that the pulp won't clog the nipples. As soon as the baby starts using a cup or glass, you can offer her the orange juice that way. Orange juice is often given before the bath, because this is a time when the baby is always awake for about an hour before the next feeding. You can give it cold, at room temperature, or slightly warmed. Don't let it get hot. Heat destroys vitamin C.

Orange juice is not essential and is a luxury because it costs more than vitamin C in drops, and the drops can be continued indefinitely. The only advantage of orange juice is its pleasant taste. For the baby who doesn't take orange juice, continue with drops that contain vitamin C.

See Section 419 for a discussion of **Fluoride.**

DRINKING WATER FOR A BABY

242. Some want water; others don't. It is often recommended that a baby be offered a few ounces of water between meals, once or twice a day. It is not absolutely necessary, because the amount of fluid in the formula is calculated to satisfy the baby's ordinary needs. It is more important to offer water if the baby has fever, or during excessively hot weather, especially if his urine turns dark yellow and he appears extra thirsty. Babies who ordinarily refuse water often take it at these times. Some mothers have found that adding small amounts of apple juice to the water gets the baby more interested.

As a matter of fact, a lot of babies don't want any water from the time they are a week or two old until they are about a year. During this age they fairly worship anything with nourishment in it, but they feel insulted by plain water. If your baby boy likes it, by all means give it to him once or several times a day when he is awake between meals (not just before the next meal). You can give him as much as he wants. He probably won't want more than 2 ounces. But don't urge him to take water if he doesn't want it. There's no point in getting him mad. He knows what he needs.

If your baby takes water and you're in a situation where you have to sterilize, boil for 3 minutes a sufficient quantity for the day; keep it in a sterilized bottle. When you need some, pour 2 ounces into another bottle.

Boil the water that your baby drinks through the first year anyway, and through the second year also if you aren't sure that the water from your faucet or well is absolutely pure.

If you are using well water, it is important to have it tested for bacteria and for nitrates before the baby arrives. (Nitrate salts in well water cause blueness of the lips and skin of babies.) Write or call your state health department.

243. Sugar water. If your baby won't take his water plain, you can try him on sugar water. You may particularly want him to take water if you are trying to get him off a night feeding or if he is taking little milk because of an illness or if the weather is very hot.

Add 1 level tablespoonful of granulated sugar or corn syrup to a pint of water before boiling it for 3 minutes.

244. You don't have to boil everything. You sterilize the formula and nursing equipment because germs multiply in milk. You boil drinking water because there is a chance that harmful germs will get into the reservoir or well, or into your pipes through faulty plumbing. Sometimes parents get so scared by the care that they take in preparing the formula and drinking water that they think they have to sterilize everything that goes into the baby's mouth. You don't have to be so fussy with all the other things that your baby will eat and drink. You don't have to boil dishes and cups and feeding spoons, because germs don't get a chance to grow on clean, dry utensils.

You can wash with soap, when you first buy them, the teething rings, pacifiers, and toys that babies put in their mouths. But there is no need to keep on washing them afterward, unless they fall on the floor, because the only germs on them will be the babies' own germs that they're used to.

Changes in Diet and Schedule

ADDING SOLID FOODS

245. Keep a good balance of valuable foods and avoid obesity. Nutritionists (and I) are alarmed at the progressive deterioration of the diet of a majority of American adults and children. They are consuming more and more sweets and refined, deprived starches. These favor obesity and decay of the teeth. In those with a strong family history, early obesity may favor the later development of diabetes. They quickly satisfy the appetite so that children then eat too little of the valuable foods—vegetables, fruits, meats, and milk—and are thereby deprived of vitamins, minerals, high-quality protein, and roughage.

Food tastes are formed early in life and then tend to persist, so now is the time to get your child started on good eating habits. For example, an individual's preference for how much table salt she or he wants—and the amount plays a significant role in the causation of high blood pressure—is set in infancy and early childhood. (There are other factors in high blood pressure such as race and heredity.) So when you begin adding salt to your baby's foods (because you like added salt in yours, not because the baby asks for it), you are, in certain cases, encouraging high blood pressure and a shortened life on that account.

There is a growing suspicion among students of child development that many cases of lifelong obesity are started in infancy by an unnecessarily high caloric diet—too much sugar and starch (Section 138).

Surgeons concerned with cancer of the large intestine in older adults are now convinced that the main cause of this disease of civilization is the very slow passage of the intestinal contents in people whose diet all their lives has been deprived of roughage because they have eaten so little whole grain cereal and bread, and so few vegetables and fruits.

In the future, who knows what other diseases will be found to be caused by our artificially distorted diets?

When baby foods in jars were first produced, they consisted of single vegetables, single fruits, and single meats. Since then, the companies have tended toward mixtures of vegetables and starches, fruits and starches, and "dinners" consisting of starches, vegetables, and meats. Most often, the starches are refined rice, refined corn, and refined wheat. Rice and corn are less valuable starches to begin with because of the incompleteness of their proteins. And the refining of **any** grain further reduces its vitamins, proteins, and roughage.

Since most babies are getting cereal as a separate dish twice a day anyway, it makes their diets lopsidedly starchy to give them also starches mixed with their vegetables, their fruits, and their meats. The fact that the starches in the mixtures are mostly the less valuable ones, and also refined, makes for a further dietary imbalance.

Baby food companies, in order to make their foods appealing to babies and their parents, added sugar and salt for many years. Because of the complaints of doctors, nutritionists, and parents, this practice has been largely discontinued.

So, when buying baby food in jars, read carefully the fine print on the label. (When the big print says "creamed beans," the small print may say "beans with cornstarch.") Buy plain fruits, plain vegetables, and plain meats—in jars—to be sure that your baby is getting enough of these valuable foods and is not being overloaded with deprived starches. Decline to buy jars that contain added sugar or salt.

Don't get started on cornstarch puddings and gelatin desserts—they don't have the right food values. They both contain a lot of sugar. Cornstarch is a doubly deprived starch—because it's corn and because it's refined.

Serve your baby the suitable vegetables, fruits, and meats you prepare for the rest of the family, fresh, frozen, or canned. When serving canned fruit, pour off that syrup.

Put cooked vegetables and fruit through your food processor, blender, hand grinder, or a sieve. Serve mainly fruits, not puddings or cookies or cake, for dessert. Serve only whole-grain cereals after the age of 6 months, concentrating on whole wheat and oats. For meats and fish mince fine the ones considered suitable for babies. If they are too dry for the baby's taste, mix with broth, milk, vegetable, or yogurt.

246. There's no set age when it's important to start solid food. Eighty-five years ago it was begun when a baby was a year old. As the years have passed, doctors have experimented with giving it earlier and earlier, and found that babies took it and prospered. There are two definite advantages in starting in the first half year. Babies take to the idea more easily than when they are older and more opinionated. And a variety of solid foods adds to the diet substances, particularly iron, that are scanty in milk.

Nowadays doctors customarily recommend the first solid food sometime between 4 and 6 months. There is no great advantage in extreme earliness. A baby usually gets all the calories needed from milk for the first 6 months. The immature digestive system doesn't make much use of starch for several months; much of it comes out in the bowel movement.

When there is a family history of allergy, the doctor may wait considerably longer to introduce foods other than milk, because the older a baby is when receiving a new food, the less apt the child is to develop an allergy to it.

The baby's hunger and digestive system may both influence the age at which the doctor suggests starting solids. Breastfed babies of 8 weeks who are not gaining weight well or who seem to be hungry should be nursed more frequently. If that doesn't work you can try a supplementary formula. On the other hand, if babies have been on the edge of looseness all the time they were on formula alone, the doctor may prefer to wait longer than usual before introducing solids, for fear of upsetting the digestion further. A big factor in giving solids earlier has been the eagerness of parents who don't want their baby to be one day later than the baby up the street. They put strong pressure on doctors. I think it's sensible to wait till at least 4 months.

247. Solids before or after the milk? Most babies who are not used to solids expect their milk and want their milk first when it's feeding time. They become indignant if offered a spoonful of something solid instead. So start with the formula or the breast-feeding. A month or two later, when a baby has learned that solid foods can ward off starvation just as well as milk, you can experiment with moving the solids up to the middle or the beginning of the meal. Eventually almost all babies are happy to take all their solid food first and then top it off with the beverage, the way so many adults do. Shortcuts are mentioned in Section 833.

248. What kind of spoon? A teaspoon is pretty wide for a small baby's mouth, and most spoons have a bowl so deep that the baby can't scoop all the contents out. A small coffee spoon (demitasse spoon) is better, preferably one with a shallow bowl. Some parents like to use a flat butter spreader or wooden tongue blades—the kind that doctors use—which can be bought in bulk at the drugstore. There is a spoon with a rubber coating on the bowl for a teething baby who wants to bite on the spoon. For the 1-year-old self-feeder there's one in which the bowl swivels to stay level and a wide-bowled, short-handled type that works well.

249. Cereal. The exact order in which solids are introduced is not important. Cereal is commonly given first. The only disadvantage is that its taste doesn't have great appeal for many babies. Different babies prefer different ones. There is some advantage in getting a baby used to variety. Sometimes it helps to add a little fruit to the cereal.

250. Give the baby time to learn to like it. A doctor usually recommends starting with a teaspoonful or less and working up gradually to 2 or 3 tablespoonfuls if the baby wants it. This gradualness is to make sure the baby learns to like it and won't be upset. Just give a taste for several days, until the baby shows signs of enjoying it. There's no rush.

A baby girl (or boy) taking her first teaspoonful of solid food is quite funny and a little pathetic. She looks puzzled and disgusted. She wrinkles up her nose and forehead. You can't blame her. After all, the taste is new, the consistency is new, the spoon may be new. When she sucks on a nipple, the milk gets to the right place automatically. She's had no training in catching hold of a lump of food with the front of her tongue and moving it back into her throat. She just clacks her tongue against the roof of her mouth, and most of the cereal gets squeezed back out onto her chin. You will have to shave it off her chin and scoop it back into her mouth. Again a lot will be oozed out frontward, but don't be discouraged—some goes down inside, too. Be patient until she is more experienced.

It doesn't matter much at which meals you start the solids. Just don't give it at the feeding when she's least hungry. Cereal is usually given at the 10 A.M. and 6 P.M. feedings.

It's a good idea, if you are starting with cereal, to mix it (with formula or milk) thinner than the directions on the box say. Then it will seem more familiar to the baby and be easier to swallow. Also, babies and small children dislike food with a sticky consistency. If your baby is on a formula, you will use some of that to mix with the cereal. Some babies, however, miss any formula that is taken out of the bottle. In that case, or if the baby is on the breast, use pasteurized milk to make the cereal. You do not need to boil it, if your doctor agrees it is safe enough. If you have no fresh milk, use equal parts of evaporated milk and water to mix with the cereal. Of course, you can use plain boiled water, but this is less likely to appeal to the baby.

251. Which cereals? At first, most parents give the precooked cereals made especially for babies, of which there is a wide variety. They are ready for eating as soon as mixed, which is a great convenience. Most of them are fortified with iron, which is otherwise apt to be lacking in a baby's diet. Anemia from insufficient iron is fairly common during the first year. It's wise to start one cereal at a time, for 4–5 days. Sometimes, if the baby belongs to an allergic family, the doctor may prefer to start cereals at a later age than usual. Then cereals may start with rice, oats, corn, or barley, omitting wheat for several more months, because wheat causes allergy more often than other cereals. Also, the doctor may delay the mixed cereals until the baby has shown a capacity to take each of the separate kinds without trouble.

Or give the baby the same cooked cereals as the other members of the family. You can start with a white (refined) wheat cereal. This has small grains and little roughage. By the time the baby is 6 months old, it's wise to shift to the most valuable cereals—whole wheat and oatmeal—which have the best proteins, vitamins, and roughage.

252. The baby who balks at cereal. You will know within a few days after starting how your baby is going to take to cereal. Some babies seem to decide, "It's queer, but it's nourishment, so I'll eat it." As the days go by they grow more and more enthusiastic. They open their mouths for it like birds in the nest.

But there are other babies who decide on the second day of cereal that they don't like it at all. And on the third day they dislike it more than on the second. If your baby feels this way, be careful. Take it easy. If you try to push the cereal into babies against their will, they will get more and more rebellious. You will get exasperated, too. In a week or two they may become so suspicious that they balk at the bottle also. Offer the cereal just once a day. Give only enough to cover the tip of the teaspoon until they are used to it. Add a little fruit to see if they like it better that way. If in 2 or 3 days they are getting more set against it in spite of all these precautions, then stop altogether for a couple of weeks. If they still balk when you try again, report it to your doctor.

I think it's a great mistake to get into an argument with babies about their first solid food. Sometimes a long-lasting feeding problem starts in this way. Even if it doesn't last, it's bad for parents and babies to go through an unnecessary fight.

If you have no doctor to advise you, I suggest that you start with fruit instead of cereal. Babies are puzzled by fruit, too, the first time they have it. But within a day or two practically all of them decide they love it. By the end of 2 weeks they are ready to assume that anything that comes on a spoon is wonderful. Then you can add cereal, too.

253. Starting fruit. Fruit is often the second solid added to the diet, a few weeks after babies have become used to cereal. Some doctors prefer it as the first solid food because babies usually take to it so enthusiastically.

For the first 6 or 8 months of a baby's life, the fruit is stewed, except for raw ripe banana. Apples, peaches, pears, apricots, and prunes are the usual fruits. You can use fresh or frozen fruit that you have stewed for the rest of the family, but strain or sieve it for the baby and add enough sugar to keep it from tasting sour. Or you can use canned fruit that you serve to other members of the family. Much canned fruit for adults is undesirably sweet, so pour off the excess syrup before straining it for the baby. You can buy canned fruit packed in water, or you can buy the small jars of strained baby fruits. Look at the label to make sure it is all fruit.

Fruit can be given at any one of the feedings, even twice a day, depending on the baby's appetite and digestion. The most popular time is 2 P.M. or 6 P.M.

Increase each fruit gradually as the baby learns to like it. Most babies are satisfied with half a baby jar or can. You can give the other half next day. Fruit can be kept 3 days if it is well refrigerated. Don't feed the baby out of the jar or can unless you are using it up at one meal. Saliva introduced into the container can spoil food rapidly.

Banana should be **very** ripe. It should have black spots on the skin and be tan-colored inside. Mash it fine with a fork. Add a little formula or milk if it seems too thick for your baby.

Fruit has the general reputation of being laxative. But most individuals, including infants, don't show any definite looseness or cramps from any of the fruits mentioned above, except for prunes, prune juice, and sometimes apricots. Prunes are mildly laxative for almost all babies, and this makes them a doubly valuable food for those who have a chronic tendency to constipation. For the baby who needs it and likes it that regularly, pureed prunes or prune juice can be given at one feeding and some other fruit at another feeding each day.

If your baby's bowels become loose too easily, you will probably omit prunes and apricots altogether and give other fruits only once a day.

In the second half of the first year, you can begin adding or substituting other raw fruits besides bananas: scraped apple, pear, avocado. (Berries and seedless grapes are commonly postponed until the baby is 2 years of age.)

254. Vegetables. Strained boiled vegetables are commonly added to the diet 2 to 4 weeks after a baby has gotten used to cereal or fruit or both.

The ones usually offered are string beans, peas, squash, carrots, beets, sweet potatoes.

There are other vegetables—such as broccoli, cauliflower, cabbage, turnips, onions—which, as usually cooked, are so strong-tasting that most babies don't like them and most parents don't bother to try them. However, if your family likes some of them (and they can be made much less strong by boiling in two changes of water), there is no harm in straining some and offering it to your baby, too. Corn is not given because of the large husks on the kernels.

You can serve your baby fresh or frozen vegetables, boiled and strained, and pureed in a food processor, blender, or grinder; or the ordinary canned vegetables that you serve the rest of the family, but strained or pureed; or the ones in jars pureed for babies. (I'd buy the straight vegetables rather than mixtures.) Don't feed out of the jar unless you are using the whole jar. Saliva spoils foods.

Babies are more likely to be choosy about vegetables than about cereals or fruits. You will probably find that there are one or two vegetables that your baby doesn't like. Don't urge them, but try them again every month or so. There's no point fussing over a few foods when we have so many to choose from.

It's common for undigested vegetable to appear in the bowel movements when the baby is first taking it. This is not a bad sign so long as there is no looseness or mucus, but increase slowly until the digestion learns to handle it. If a vegetable causes looseness or much mucus, omit it for the time being and try a very small amount in another month.

Beets may show up red in the bowel movement or color the urine, which is nothing to worry about if you can remember that it is caused by beets and not blood. Green vegetables often turn the bowel movement green.

Spinach causes chapping of the lips and around the anus in some babies. If it does, omit it for several months and try again.

Lunchtime—2 P.M. for a baby still on a roughly 4-hour schedule, noon for an older baby on three meals a day—is the conventional time for vegetables, but you and your baby can work out your own routine.

Work up to several tablespoonfuls as desired or half a baby jar or can. The rest, if refrigerated, can be given the next day. If you have no refrigerator, don't keep vegetables. Cooked vegetables spoil fairly rapidly.

255. Eggs. For a very long time, egg yolk was thought to be important as a valuable source of iron. Babies begin to need more iron for their red blood cells around the middle of the first year, because with their rapid growth, they begin to outgrow the limited amount that was in their bodies at birth. Milk contains practically no iron and many other foods provide very little. However, a majority of the cereals prepared for babies contain good amounts of iron. (It has recently been found that breast milk, though it contains very little iron, contains a form of iron that is unusually well digested and absorbed.)

Recent research has shown that the iron contained in egg yolk is poorly absorbed by babies' intestines. It has also been found that egg yolk may interfere with iron absorption from other sources—unless the egg yolk is taken with a source of vitamin C. Also, egg yolk contains a large amount of cholesterol, which can play a part in the development of hardening of the arteries and heart attacks later in life, especially in those with a family history of these ailments. It was always known that egg white could cause allergies in some babies, especially those with a family history.

So nowadays, eggs aren't added to the diet until 9–12 months, by which time both the yolk and the white can be given. The number of eggs is usually limited to 3–4 per week. As with all new foods, you'll want to start with a little bit at a time. If the baby doesn't seem to like the taste, you can mix it with her cereal, vegetable, or fruit. If this makes her balk at the cereal, vegetable, or fruit, don't persist. Egg can be given at breakfast, lunch, or supper.

256. Meats. Nutrition studies have shown that babies profit by meats during the first year, so many doctors recommend them as early as 6 months of age. Meats for babies are finely ground or "strained" or "scraped," so they can be swallowed easily before the baby has any teeth.

Or you can give straight jars of meats for babies such as beef, beef heart, liver, lamb, chicken, veal, pork. Don't feed the baby out of the jar unless you are using it up at one meal. Saliva introduced into the container can spoil food rapidly.

You can prepare the meat yourself. The simplest way to cook beef or lamb chop for a baby is to scrape it, while still raw, with a dull knife or tablespoon. Put this soft pulp in a custard cup and set it in a pan of slowly boiling water. Cook until the color changes. If desired, milk or water or both can be added, before cooking, to make the meat more moist. Another method is to briefly broil a piece of beef (top round, for instance) or lamb, to sterilize the surface, and then, grasping it firmly, scrape it with a tablespoon. This scrapes out the soft red meat and leaves the tough white fibers behind. A piece of liver can be plunged into boiling water, cooked until the color changes, and then pressed through a sieve. Pork should be well cooked. Or you can mince a piece of meat from a stew made for the rest of the family.

After your baby has become used to strained or scraped meat, you can give him beef that you have briefly broiled and put through a fine grinder. It is preferable not to give meat ground by the butcher, because the meat surfaces that have been handled and those that have come in contact with the grinder are mixed through the rest of the meat. Also, it may contain a lot of fat and tough fiber.

By the time the baby is used to ground beef, you can add ground or fine-minced chicken, lamb, liver, bacon, veal, and pork. Pork should always be cooked through.

If your baby doesn't seem to like meat at first, you can try adding strained fruit to sweeten it and soften the texture.

257. Dinners. There are a variety of "dinners" in jars for babies. They usually consist of small amounts of a meat and a vegetable with a larger amount of potato, rice, or barley. I think it's better to buy meats and vegetables in separate jars, so that you will know how much your baby is getting.

When there is a tendency to allergy, such mixtures may be confusing unless the baby has already taken each of the foods included in the mixture without reaction.

258. The meals at 6 months. By 6 months of age, your baby will probably be eating cereal and a variety of fruits, vegetables, and meats. A common arrangement for a moderately hungry baby is cereal for breakfast, vegetable and meat for lunch, cereal and fruit for supper. But there are no hard and fast rules. It all depends on your convenience and your baby's appetite. For instance, a not very hungry baby could be given fruit at breakfast, vegetable and meat at lunch, cereal alone at supper. A baby who tends to be constipated can be given prunes every night along with the cereal, and another fruit at breakfast or lunch. You may want the baby to have meat and vegetable at supper with the rest of the family, the cereal and fruit at lunch.

259. Puddings. Most puddings, being made of cornstarch and sugar, are not advisable for children. They don't add any new element to the diet; they take time to prepare. Fruit makes a more valuable dessert.

The more valuable puddings are those made mainly of milk (junket), milk and egg (boiled and baked custard), and milk and rice.

260. Adding potato if your baby likes it and needs it. Other starches. Potatoes are good as a source of starch at lunch for a child who is hungry or in place of cereal at supper. They also contain appreciable amounts of iron, other salts, and vitamin C, so that they have food values aside from the starch.

Potato, baked or boiled, can be introduced into the diet any time in the last half of the first year. A logical time is when the baby goes onto a three-meals-a-day schedule. When lunch is 5 hours away from supper, the starch, which a potato is mostly made of, supplies lots of energy (calories) to last through the afternoon.

A word of caution about potato. Babies are more apt to gag and rebel against it than any other food. I don't know whether this is because it is grainy or because it is sticky. So mash it very smooth at first, make it thin by mixing with plenty of milk, and offer it in very small amounts until the baby gets used to it. Flavor it with fruit or vegetable. Don't urge it if the baby continues to gag; forget about it, at least for a month, and then try again.

If your baby is getting plump and seems content with a lunch of green vegetable, meat, milk, and perhaps fruit, leave out potato. It doesn't add anything new to the diet.

You can occasionally substitute macaroni, spaghetti, noodles, or rice for potato but remember, they are refined, deprived foods. Strain or mash them fine at first.

261. Adding fish. By 10 or 12 months, you can also add the white, non-oily fish, such as flounder, haddock, and halibut, if the child likes them. You can poach them in pieces in slowly boiling water. Or you can place small pieces in a custard cup, cover with milk, and then place the cup in a pan of boiling water until the fish is cooked through. Or you can serve the baby the fish you have boiled, baked, or broiled for the rest of the family. In any case, crumble the flakes in your fingers to be sure there are no bones.

Substitute fish for meat at lunchtime. Some babies love it, and then it's a great help. But a lot of babies turn thumbs down. Don't try to force it.

The oily fish, like tuna and mackerel, are liable to be harder to digest and less appealing.

262. Home preparation of infant foods. Many parents are now interested in preparing their own infant foods, for philosophical or economic reasons. This can be safely done. The advantages are that you have control over the ingredients and the preparation method, that fresh, organically grown foods can be used, and that it is much cheaper.

There are fine books available on this subject. You'll need a food mill, blender, or food processor. You can reheat individual portions in the small compartments of a cheap egg-poaching pan, double-boiler, or microwave oven. Foods can be roasted or cooked in quantity and then pureed to a consistency that your baby currently likes. They can be moistened if necessary with water, milk, or both. They can be frozen in serving-sized portions in ice cube trays or on cookie sheets and then stored in plastic bags until they're used.

Foods for children under a year should not be seasoned. If your child is to be fed table foods, your seasoning habits may have to be modified. This is when small, hand-held food grinders come in so handy.

263. Finger foods. By the time babies are 6 or 7 months old, they want to and can pick foods up in their hands and suck and munch on them. This is good training for them as preparation for spoon-feeding themselves at about a year. If babies are never allowed to feed themselves with their fingers, they're less likely to have the ambition to try the spoon.

The traditional first finger food is a crust of stale whole-wheat bread or toast at 6 or 7 months. Babies suck at it and chew at it with their bare gums (their gums may be tingling with teething, and in that case they'll enjoy the biting). As it softens gradually with their saliva, some of it rubs or dissolves off into their mouths, enough to make them feel they're getting somewhere. Most of it goes on their hands, faces, hair, and the furniture.

By 9 months you are mashing the food instead of straining it, and you can leave unmashed some of the pieces of string beans, cauliflower, avocado, asparagus, potato, yams, and carrots. Babies will want to pick up these pieces, along with particles of meat, and put them in their mouths. They can also chew on a slice of raw apple, orange, or pear.

Average babies get their first tooth at about 7 months, and at a year may have four to six sharp biting teeth. But they probably won't get their first molars for grinding until sometime around a year and a quarter. Therefore you can't expect them to do much efficient grinding of food till then.

264. Lumpy foods by a year. Somewhere between 7 and 12 months, you want to get your baby used to lumpy or chopped foods. If a baby goes much beyond a year eating nothing but pureed things, it gets harder and harder to make the change. People have the idea that babies can't handle lumps until they get a fair set of teeth. This isn't true. They can mush up lumps of cooked vegetables or fruit and pieces of zwieback with their gums and tongue.

Some babies seem to be born more squeamish about lumps than others. But some babies and older children who gag easily on particles of food have become that way either because the parents tried to make the change to chopped foods too abruptly or too late, or because they have been forcing food when the child didn't want it.

There are two important points in shifting to chopped foods. Make the change a gradual one. When you first serve chopped vegetables, mash them up pretty fine with a fork. Don't put too much in the baby's mouth at a time. When the child is used to this consistency, gradually mash less and less. The other way babies get used to lumps is by being allowed to pick up a cube of cooked carrot, for instance, in their fingers and put it in their mouths themselves. What they can't stand is to have a whole spoonful of lumps dumped into their mouths when they're not used to it.

So start the change by 9 months. You can serve the baby the boiled vegetables and stewed fruits that you cook for the rest of the family or you can buy the chopped (junior) foods in jars or cans prepared for babies.

You don't have to make all the foods lumpy. It is necessary only that the baby get used to eating some lumps each day.

Meats should generally continue to be served ground or minced fine. Most small children dislike chunks of meat that don't chew up easily. They often chew on such a piece for a long time without getting anywhere. They don't dare try to swallow too big a piece, as adults do when they are desperate. This may lead to gagging or at least to a loss of appetite for this particular kind of meat.

Gagging is also discussed in Section 672.

265. Diet by the end of the first year. In case you are mixed up by all the things that have been added to the diet, here is a rough list of what babies are apt to be eating by the end of the year:

Breakfast: cereal (whole wheat or oats), egg (whole, soft), toast, pancakes, french toast, fruits, juice, milk.

Lunch: vegetable (green or yellow, in lumps), potato, meat or fish, fruit, small quarters of sandwiches (such

as peanut butter thinned with milk and mixed with mashed banana), squares of cheese, toast, milk.
Supper: cereal, fruit, milk.

Or they may have their "big" meal at supper with the family. Then lunch might be something starchy, such as potato or cereal, and a fruit or vegetable.

Fruit juice (including orange juice) is given daily between meals or at breakfast. Whole wheat or rye bread can be given at meals or between, with a little butter or margarine. The fruit is stewed except for banana, scraped apple, pear, avocado.

In other words, a pretty grown-up diet.

This is the age at which babies frequently eat less than their parents think they should—and thrive.

CHANGES IN SCHEDULE AND BOTTLE

266. When to omit the 10 P.M. feeding. When you give up the 10 or 11 P.M. feeding should depend most on when the baby is ready. There are two things to consider.

The first is whether your baby, let's say a boy, is ready to sleep through the night. You can't be sure that he's ready just because he always has to be waked up at 10 or 11. If you don't wake him, he may wake himself around midnight. Better wait until you have had to wake him for several weeks. Then see if he sleeps through. If he wakes hungry later in the night, feed him and go back to the evening feeding for a few more weeks.

Of course, if your baby is very small or gaining slowly or having trouble with his digestion, it may be better to keep the evening feeding going a while longer, even if he is willing to sleep through without it.

Another point is whether he is sucking his thumb a lot. If he is, it may mean that he is not getting as much sucking as he'd like from breast or bottle. If you cut out a feeding at this time, you reduce his sucking time further still. However, if he continues to be a thumb sucker in spite of all your efforts, you don't have to go on **forever** giving him the evening feeding.

For one thing, as he gets older he may refuse to wake up, no matter how hard you try, or fall asleep again as soon as he has taken a couple of ounces. I'd stop the feeding by this time anyway, whether he is sucking his thumb or not.

In a general way, then, let your baby give up his 10 P.M. feeding when he shows that he can sleep through without it and get enough sucking satisfaction without it. This will probably be between the ages of 3 and 6 months. Wait till 5 or 6 months if he is sucking his thumb much and is willing to take the evening feeding.

Most babies get themselves off the evening feeding as soon as they can. But an occasional one will continue it indefinitely, especially if the mother rushes in as soon as he first murmurs. If your baby is still waking for his feeding at 7 or 8 months, I'd try to get him over the habit. At this age he certainly doesn't need nourishment at night if he is eating well in the daytime and gaining satisfactorily. Let him fuss for 20 or 30 minutes (without going to him at all) and see if he won't go back to sleep.

When you omit the evening bottle, distribute the formula into the other four bottles. This probably makes about 7½ ounces in each bottle. But if he wants only his usual 5 or 6 ounces, let it go at that without any urging. Twenty-four ounces a day is plenty if he's satisfied.

267. If your baby loses his appetite between 3 and 9 months. A baby may take solids eagerly for the first couple of months and then rather suddenly lose a lot of his appetite. One reason may be that at this age period he is meant to slow down in his weight gaining. In his first 3 months he has probably gained close to 2 pounds a month. By 6 months he is apt to be down to a pound a month. Otherwise he would become too fat. Also, he may be bothered by teething. One baby wants to leave out a lot of his solid food; another turns against his milk. After six months, some babies refuse to be fed. If you let them have finger food while you're offering food in a spoon, it often will solve that problem.

If your baby loses a lot of his appetite, **don't** urge him. There are two things you can do. The first is to gradually remove the sugar if he's been on an evaporated- or whole-milk formula. (See Section 268.) The sugar was there in the early months principally to give him enough calories while he was on a diluted formula. He doesn't really need these sugar calories when he is eating a good helping of solid food three times a day. In fact, the very sweetness of the formula may be killing his appetite for unsweetened foods. If your baby's been on a commercial, prepared formula, you can switch to whole milk.

The other thing you can do is to go from the approximately 4-hour schedule during the daytime (6 A.M., 10 A.M., 2 P.M., 6 P.M.) to a three-meals-a-day schedule (approximately 7 A.M., 12 noon, 5 P.M.), whether or not he is still on an evening feeding (Section 269).

If a baby's appetite still doesn't revive with these two measures, it's important to get him to the doctor, to be sure that he's otherwise healthy.

268. When to remove the sugar from the formula. You can remove the sugar from an evaporated or whole milk formula gradually, when your baby is about to change over to fresh milk, sometime around 6 months of age. The time depends on his appetite. If he goes through a phase of poor appetite at the age of 5 or 6 months—or if he is gaining too much weight—that is a good time to take out the sugar or to switch to whole milk if he's been on a commercial, prepared formula.

Remove the sugar gradually, so that he doesn't notice any sudden change in taste. You can remove about a quarter of a tablespoonful a day from the formula until there is none left.

269. When to put the baby on three meals a day. This depends on when your baby is ready for it. It may be anywhere between the ages of 4 and 10 months. A three-meal schedule means about 5 hours between meals. If your baby is starved at the end of 4 hours and crying with hunger, he isn't ready for a three-meal schedule, no matter how old he is. If he has to have his first feeding by 6 A.M., there's usually not much use talking about three meals a day.

On the other hand, your baby may show clearly at a certain stage that he is ready for three meals. A mother will say, "He only eats well at every other meal. If he finishes his 6 A.M. bottle, he'll eat poorly at 10, well at 2, and poorly at 6 P.M." Babies who are acting like this need to be changed to a three-meals-a-day schedule so that they will be hungry at mealtime. Otherwise they are apt to develop feeding problems.

If a baby is thumb-sucking a lot and is still ready to eat every 4 hours, this is a reason for leaving in the fourth feeding for a while longer.

Once in a while there is a baby who is no longer ready to eat every 4 hours during the daytime, but who still wakes up like clockwork for his 10 P.M. bottle. There's no problem here. You try to adjust to the baby's needs, as usual, putting him on three meals during the day and continuing to give the 10 P.M. feeding until he is ready to sleep through.

There's another problem that turns up occasionally. A baby seems to have outgrown the 4-hour schedule. He's not hungry for some of his meals. And yet he's still waking around 6 A.M., yelling with hunger. How do you put him on three meals a day and still feed him at 6 A.M.? The easiest way is to give him his milk from breast or bottle as soon as he demands it in the morning, and give him his cereal, or his cereal and fruit, a little later, as soon as it is convenient (for instance, between 7 and 8). His next meal will be lunch, around noon. Of course, the baby who is hungry early is no problem if the whole family breakfasts around 6 A.M. Some babies who wake early are quite satisfied with a bottle of diluted apple juice for the time being. Then they can have their milk along with the rest of their breakfast, later.

Another factor is the parents' convenience. Suppose they have their hands full preparing meals for their older children, and their baby is **able** to go more than 4 hours between meals, even though still willing to eat that often. These parents naturally want to get the baby onto the same three meals as the older children now, and there is no reason why they shouldn't, especially if the child isn't thumb-sucking much. There are other parents, especially with the first baby, who find the 4-hour schedule fits their own convenience better than three meals a day. There is no reason why these babies shouldn't stay on the 4-hour schedule longer than average as long as they remain hungry for their meals that often. In other words, there is no rule about making such a change in a baby's routine. It's just a matter of reasonableness and common sense. You see what the baby is ready for and fit it in with your convenience.

The hours at which a baby is fed when he goes onto three meals a day depend largely on the family's habit, somewhat on the baby's hunger. Breakfast is usually between 7 and 8, but can be later if he's willing. He gets cereal and fruit (one **or** the other if he has a small appetite) and his milk. In the middle of the morning, he probably needs something to help him last through until lunch. Apple juice, about 2 ounces, is best. If he doesn't drink apple juice, you could give him prune juice or tomato juice. If he gets **very** hungry before meals, add a piece of dry bread crust.

Lunch comes in the neighborhood of 12 o'clock. Some babies must have it by 11:30. It probably consists of a green or yellow vegetable, meat, potato, and milk. Potato is usually added at the time a baby goes on three meals a day, to give him enough extra energy to last through the afternoon. You don't bother with it if your baby has a small appetite or is getting fat. Fruit may be given at lunch, if this is the most convenient time of day or if your baby is hard to fill up. A baby should get fruit once or twice a day, but there is no harm in three times a day if it agrees with his digestion.

In the middle of the afternoon, if he needs a snack, another 2 ounces of apple juice or another fruit juice. Occasionally a mother says that it suits her baby best, for the first month or two after he gets on a regular breakfast-lunch-supper schedule, to give him an extra breast or bottle feeding at about 3 P.M. Of course, this still means four milk feedings a day, though such a baby may want only half a bottle at 3 P.M. and 6 P.M. This extra bottle or half bottle in the middle of the afternoon is called for only if the parents want the supper to be late, around 6, and if the baby has a very large appetite. Ordinarily, milk is not given between meals, because it stays in the stomach for 3 or 4 hours and takes away the appetite for the next meal.

Supper is usually given sometime between 5 and 6 P.M. when a baby goes on three meals a day. Most babies can't last beyond 5 if lunch is at 12, and some need to be fed even earlier. Supper is usually cereal, fruit, and milk.

When a baby is taking milk only three times a day, he is

probably getting a smaller total for the day than formerly, because he probably does not want more than his usual 6 to 8 ounces a meal. Don't worry about this. Don't try to tuck a few extra ounces into him at odd hours to keep up to the old 30-ounce total. Most babies are quite safe if they are taking as much as 24 ounces a day. On the other hand, if your baby is the unusual one who wants as much as 10 ounces a meal, give it to him.

270. When can you stop sterilizing the formula and bottles? If you've been in a situation where you've had to sterilize in the first place, you'll need to talk to your doctor, public health nurse, or county health department about when it's safe to stop sterilizing.

If you absolutely can't consult anyone, I'd go by the general rule that as long as you are making a 24-hour formula that contains water, you have to sterilize the formula and bottles.

271. When do you change from evaporated to pasteurized milk? The really sensible answer would be "Never." Evaporated milk is sterile, easier to store, easier to digest, less likely to cause allergy. It's only slightly less convenient to serve. When the baby is off formula, you merely mix equal parts of evaporated milk and boiled water (if you've been sterilizing) or tap water in the cup or bottle just before feeding.

With all the advantages of evaporated milk, why are most babies changed to pasteurized milk? It's rarely at the insistence of the doctor. It's usually the strong wish of the parents. I think there are several reasons for this. Proud parents delight in seeing their babies make advances, and for some reason the change from evaporated to pasteurized milk seems as important to them as learning to walk or becoming toilet-trained or entering school. Also, some parents who don't like the taste of evaporated milk seem to assume that the baby will turn against it, too, just as soon as he is old enough to have any discrimination. The parents are sure this moment has come the first time he takes less than his usual amount of formula. I don't think there is any evidence that babies prefer pasteurized milk, but I've rarely been able to convince a parent of this. Also, it **seems** a lot easier to a parent to pour pasteurized milk out of a quart container than to mix evaporated milk with water, though I don't think it takes half a minute less. Anyway, there's no medical reason why a baby needs to change, so keep him on evaporated milk as long as you are willing to.

Weaning from Bottle to Cup

READINESS FOR WEANING

272. When are babies ready for weaning to cup? For years I was baffled by the fact that some breast-fed babies and some bottle-fed ones show less interest in suckling by 5 or 6 months. Instead of nursing eagerly for 20 minutes, as they used to, they stop after 5 minutes to flirt with their parents or play with their bottles or with their own hands. These babies will go on being somewhat casual toward breast or bottle at 8, 10, 12 months, though they'll take it as long as it's offered, in most cases. They like to take milk from the cup, and they continue to do so.

But there are other babies who—quite the opposite—become **more** attached to their bottles at 6, 8, and 10 months than they ever were before. The parent of one of these will say, "Oh, how she loves her bottle! She watches it all the time she's taking her solid food. When it's time, she snatches it eagerly. She strokes it lovingly all the time she's drinking it and murmurs to it. She's very suspicious about milk from the cup, though she took it willingly before 6 months." Many of these babies continue to be very dependent on the bedtime bottle until 1½ or 2 years of age—unable to settle down or go to sleep without it—and are still firmly opposed to milk in the cup or glass. (It's interesting that they are quite willing to take water or juices from the cup.)

I finally realized that it is the babies who are allowed to take their bottles to bed by themselves who become **more** attached to their bottles in the second half of the first year. The bottle becomes a precious comforter at bedtime, reminding children of their early months, when their greatest pleasure and security came from their intensely close relationship with their parents. Their bottle in this sense becomes a parent substitute. Whereas children who are still taking their bottle in their parent's lap, at 5 or 6 or 7 months, develop no such attachment to it because their real parent is right there. So the way to keep babies from forming a lasting dependence on the bottle is to refrain from giving them the bottle to take to bed. Other examples of this same kind of dependence—on a soft toy or a pacifier—are explained more fully in Section 383.

273. Starting sips of milk from the cup by 5 months. It's a good idea to begin offering babies a sip of milk from the cup each day by the time they're 5 months old. You aren't going to try to wean them to the cup right away. You only want to accustom them, at an age when they're not too opinionated, to the idea that milk comes in cups, too.

Pour half an ounce of the formula into a small cup or glass once a day. They won't want more than one sip at a time, and won't get much at first, but they'll probably think it is fun. For breast-fed babies, pour half an ounce of pasteurized milk or breast milk into a cup. It isn't usually necessary to boil this if it is pasteurized, but your doctor is the one to advise you on this point.

274. Helping a baby to like the cup. Say your baby, a boy, is 6 months old and wants to grab everything and put it in his mouth. Give him a small, narrow, empty glass (4-ounce plastic juice glasses are available in many grocery stores) or cup that he can hold easily by himself and pretend to drink from. Or a baby's mug with two handles. When he does it fairly well, put a few drops of milk in the cup. Increase the amount as he gains in skill. If he takes to the idea of drinking by himself at 6 months, he is much less likely to turn against the cup at 7 or 8 months. If he stops drinking from the cup by himself for a few days, resist the temptation to pick up the cup and offer it to him, as this might only make him balky. Remember that in the early months of cup drinking he'll probably want only one swallow at a time. Many babies don't learn to take several gulps in succession until they are 1 to 1½ years old. One good practice place is the bathtub.

Children between 1 and 2 who are suspicious of the old cup they have always been offered may be delighted with a new cup or glass of a different shape or color. Changing to cold milk sometimes changes their minds. Some parents have found that adding a little cereal to the cup of milk makes it different enough to be acceptable for drinking. The cereal can gradually be removed a few weeks later.

There are special cups designed for weaning that have a lid with a flat spout. The lid keeps the milk from spilling and the spout goes into the baby's mouth. The baby can later use it without lid and spout. Some parents like them because they prevent spilling for the first few months of cup drinking, until the baby gains skill. Other parents object that a baby may first balk at the transition from bottle to weaning cup and even object again to the change to cup or glass without a spout. There are weaning cups with two handles, which are easier for a baby to hold, and others with a weighted base.

WEAN THE BABY GRADUALLY

275. Take it easy and follow your baby's lead. Perhaps your baby, a girl, is 9 to 12 months old and is becoming a little bored with her bottle and likes milk from the cup. Gradually increase the amount in the cup. Give her the cup at every meal. This leaves less and less in the bottle. Then leave out the bottle that she takes least interest in, probably the lunch or breakfast one. In a week, give up the second bottle if she's progressing, and then the third. Most babies love their supper bottle most and are slowest in giving it up. Others feel that way about the breakfast bottle.

Willingness to be weaned doesn't always increase steadily. Misery from teething or a cold often makes babies want more of the bottle for the time being. Follow their needs. The trend that made them start to give up the bottle before will set in again when they feel better.

276. The reluctant weaner. Babies who are reluctant to give up the bottle at 9 to 12 months may take one sip from the cup and push it away impatiently. Or they may pretend they don't know what it's for; they let the milk run out at the sides of their mouths, smiling innocently. They may relent a little at 12 months but it is more likely that they'll remain suspicious till 15 months or even later. Put an ounce of milk in a small glass that they can handle and just set it on the tray every day or so, hoping that they'll drink it. If one sip is all they take, don't even try to give them two. Act as if it doesn't make any difference to you.

When suspicious babies do start to take a little milk from the cup, you must still be patient, because it will probably take several more months before they are ready to give up the bottle altogether. This applies particularly to the supper or bedtime bottle. Many late weaners insist on a bedtime bottle till about 2 years of age.

277. Sometimes it's the parent who delays weaning. Sometimes a baby is kept on the bottle longer than she needs to be because her parents worry about the fact that she isn't taking as much from the cup as she used to take from the bottle. Let's say that at 9–12 months she's drinking about 6 ounces from the cup at breakfast, 6 ounces at lunch, and about 4 ounces at supper, and that she's not especially eager for the bottle but if her mother gives it to her at the end of the meal she is willing to take a few ounces more that way. I think that a baby of 9–12 months who is taking as much as 16 ounces a day from the cup, and not acting as if she misses the bottle, might better be off the bottle altogether. If she is kept on it now, she may become **less** willing to give it up at that suspicious age between 12 and 15 months.

Another problem may develop for the parent who uses the bottle as a pacifier during the second year. Whenever the child has a crying spell in the daytime or wakes at night, mother or father kindheartedly makes another bottle. The child may get as many as eight bottles in the 24 hours—a total of 2 quarts of milk. This naturally takes away most of the appetite for meals, and the child is then likely to develop a severe anemia. (There's practically no iron in milk.)

It's important from a nutritional point of view that children not take more than a quart of milk a day. And from the point of view of emotional development, they should feel that they are being encouraged by their parents to grow out of babyhood. One of the most important ways parents achieve this is by helping children to give up bottles, one by one, as soon as they feel able to do so.

Daily Care

THE BATH

278. Before any feeding. It's usually most convenient in the early months to give the bath before the 10 A.M. feeding, but before any feeding is all right (not after a feeding, because you want the child to go to sleep then). The father may be home in time to give the bath before the 6 P.M. or 10 P.M. feeding. By the time your baby is on three meals a day, you may want to change to before lunch or before supper. As the child gets older still and stays up for a while after supper, it may work out better to give the bath after supper, especially if she needs her supper early. Bathe her in a reasonably warm room—the kitchen, if necessary.

279. A sponge bath if you prefer. Though it's the custom to give a complete tub or sponge bath every day, it certainly isn't necessary more than once or twice a week in cool weather, so long as the baby is kept clean in the diaper area and around the mouth. On the days when you don't give him a full bath, give a sponge bath in the diaper area. The tub bath is apt to be frightening at first to the inexperienced parent—the baby seems so helpless, limp, and slippery, especially after having been soaped. Babies may feel uneasy in the tub at first, because they can't be well supported there. You can give a sponge bath for a few weeks until you and your baby feel more secure, or even for months—until the child can sit up—if you prefer. It is sometimes advised that a tub bath not be given until the navel is healed. Check with your doctor.

You can give a sponge bath on a table or in your lap. You'll want a piece of waterproof material under the baby. If you are using a hard surface like a table, there should be some padding over it (large pillow or folded blanket or quilt) so that the baby won't roll too easily. (Rolling frightens young babies.) Wash the face and scalp with a washcloth and clear warm water. (The scalp can be soaped once or twice a week.) Lightly soap the rest of the body when and where needed with the washcloth or your hand. Then wipe the soap off by going over the whole body at least twice with the rinsed washcloth, paying attention to creases.

280. The tub bath. Before starting the bath, be sure you have everything you need close at hand. If you forget the towel, you'll have to go after it holding a dripping baby in your arms.

Take off your wristwatch.
An apron keeps your clothes drier.
Have at hand:

- soap
- washcloth
- towel
- absorbent cotton for nose and ears if necessary
- lotion or powder if you use either
- shirt, diaper, pins, nightie

The bath can be given in a washbowl, dishpan, kitchen sink, or enamelware tub. (See Section 68.) The regular bathtub is hard on a parent's back and legs. For your own comfort, you can put a dishpan or enamelware tub on a table, at which you sit, or on something higher like a dresser, at which you stand. You can sit on a stool at the kitchen sink. The water should be about body temperature (90°–100°F). A bath thermometer is a comfort to the inexperienced parent but is not necessary. Test the temperature with your elbow or wrist. It should feel comfortably warm. Use only a small amount of water at first, an inch or two deep, until you get the knack of holding the baby securely. A tub is less slippery if you line it with a towel or diaper each time.

Hold the baby so that her head is supported on your wrist,

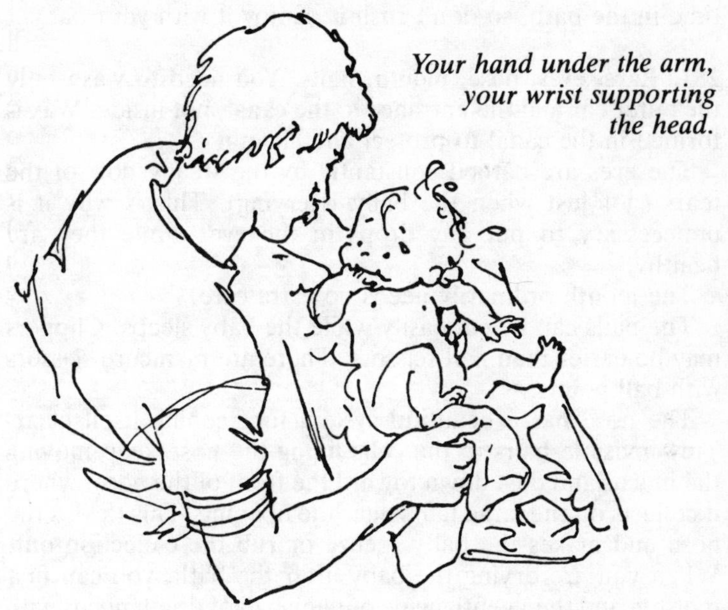

Your hand under the arm, your wrist supporting the head.

and the fingers of that hand hold her securely in the armpit. Wash the face first, with a soft washcloth, without soap, then the scalp. The scalp needs to be soaped only once or twice a week. Wipe the soap suds off the scalp with a damp washcloth, going over it twice. If the washcloth is too wet, the soapy water may get into the eyes and sting. (There are shampoos for babies that do not sting the eyes as much as ordinary shampoos.) Then soap the rest of the body, arms, and legs, using the washcloth or your hand. (It's easier to soap your hand than a washcloth when your other hand is occupied.) If the skin gets dry, try omitting the soap except for once or twice a week.

If you feel nervous at first for fear you'll drop the baby in the water, you can soap her while she is on your lap or on a table. Then rinse her off in the tub, holding her securely with both hands.

Use a soft bath towel for drying, and blot rather than rub. If you begin giving the tub bath before the navel is completely healed, dry it thoroughly after the bath with sterile cotton.

Most babies, after a few weeks' experience, have a wonderful time in the bath, so don't rush it. Enjoy it with your baby.

281. Ears, eyes, nose, mouth, nails. You need to wash only the outer ear and the entrance to the canal, not inside. Wax is formed in the canal to protect and clean it.

The eyes are bathed constantly by the steady flow of the tears (not just when the baby is crying). This is why it is unnecessary to put any drops in the eyes while they are healthy.

The mouth ordinarily needs no extra care.

The nails can be cut easily while the baby sleeps. Clippers may be easier than nail scissors. There are manicure scissors with ball points.

The nose has a beautiful system for keeping itself clear. Tiny invisible hairs in the cells lining the nose keep moving the mucus and dust down toward the front of the nose, where it collects on the large hairs near the opening. This tickles the nose and makes the baby sneeze or rub the collection out. When you are drying the baby after the bath, you can first moisten and then gently wipe out any ball of dried mucus with the corner of the washcloth, or with a piece of absorbent cotton that has been twisted into a point and then wet, or if necessary, with cotton carefully wrapped around the end of a toothpick or matchstick so that the wood does not protrude. You can also buy prepared cotton swabs. Don't fuss at this too long if it makes the baby angry.

Dried mucus obstructing the nose. Sometimes, especially when the house is heated, enough dried mucus collects in the noses of small infants to partially obstruct the breathing. Then each time they breathe in, the lower edges of the chest are pulled inward, or "retracted." The lips may even become slightly blue. An older child or adult would breathe through the mouth, but most babies can't leave their mouths open. If your baby's nose becomes obstructed at any time of day, you can first moisten and then remove the mucus as in the previous paragraph.

282. Lotion or powder? It's fun to apply lotion or powder to a baby after a bath, and the baby likes it, too, but neither is really necessary in most cases. (If it were, Nature would provide it.) Powder is helpful if the baby's skin chafes easily. It should be dusted on your hand first—away from the baby, so that she won't breathe a cloud of powder—and then rubbed gently on her skin. It should be applied thinly, so that it won't form lumps. Plain cornstarch powder is safest and cheapest. (Don't use zinc stearate powder; it's irritating to the lungs.) A baby lotion may be helpful when the skin is dry or there is a mild diaper rash. Baby oils (which are different from lotions) and mineral oil have been less often used since it has been shown that they sometimes cause a mild rash.

THE NAVEL

283. The healing of the navel. When still in the mother's womb, the baby is nourished through the blood vessels of the umbilical cord. Just after birth, the doctor ties it and cuts it off close to the baby's body. The stump that's left withers and eventually drops off, usually in about 2–3 weeks, though it may take several weeks. When the cord falls off, it may leave a raw spot, which takes a number of days, occasionally a number of weeks, to heal over. If healing is slow, the raw spot may become lumpy with what's called granulation tissue, but this is of no importance. The raw spot should merely be kept clean and dry, so that harmful germs will not infect it. If it is kept dry, a scab covers it until it is healed. Nowadays most doctors recommend that no dressing be put over the navel while it heals. In this way it is likely to stay driest. It is sometimes recommended that the baby not be given a tub bath until the navel is completely healed, but this rule is not essential if the navel is wiped dry with sterile cotton. It is wise to keep the diaper below the level of the unhealed navel, so that it doesn't keep it wet.

If the unhealed navel becomes moist and discharges, it should be protected more carefully from constant wetting by the diaper, and cleaned each day with alcohol. The doctor may recommend touching it with an antiseptic powder or powdered alum to hasten drying and healing. Or, he or she may cauterize (seal) it with a chemical (silver nitrate).

If the navel and the surrounding skin become red, infection is present and you should get in touch with your doctor right away. Until you can reach the doctor, you should apply continuous wet dressings (Section 799).

If the scab on the unhealed navel gets pulled by the clothing, there may be a drop or two of blood. This amount is of no importance.

284. Umbilical hernia. After the skin of the navel heals over, there is usually still an opening in the deeper, muscular layer of the abdomen where the umbilical vessels passed through. When the baby cries, a small part of the intestine is pushed through this hole (umbilical ring) and it makes the navel puff out somewhat. This is called an umbilical hernia. When the ring is small, the protrusion of the hernia is never much larger than a pea and the ring is likely to close over in a few weeks or months. When the ring is large, it may take months or even years to close and the protrusion may be larger than a cherry.

It used to be thought that the closing of the umbilical ring could be hastened by putting a tight strap of adhesive across the navel to keep it from protruding. It is now believed that strapping makes no difference. It is much easier not to bother with the adhesive, which always became soiled, soon loosened, and left raw places on the skin.

You don't have to worry about the protrusion of the hernia. It rarely causes any trouble, as other hernias sometimes do (Section 778). There is no need to try to keep the baby from crying.

In the well-padded older child or adult, the fat over the abdomen is thick enough to make the navel appear to be at the bottom of a hole. This is rarely the case in the first 2 or 3 years of life. The folds of skin of the navel (looking something like a rosebud) stand right out on the full abdomen. This prominence of the skin folds of the navel should not be confused with a hernia. A hernia can be felt underneath the skin folds, like a small, soft balloon. A hernia makes the navel stick out farther than it would otherwise.

If an umbilical hernia is still large at 6 or 8 years, and showing no decrease, surgical repair is often recommended.

THE PENIS

285. Circumcision and other ways to care for the penis. Should a baby boy be circumcised? If not, what care should be given the penis (the genitals)? There is no single answer.

Circumcision means the cutting off of the sleeve of skin called the foreskin, which normally covers the head of the penis at birth. In approximately 96 percent of all boys, the separation of the foreskin and the glans (the head of the penis) will be incomplete at birth. Because of this incomplete separation, it is normal for the newborn boy's foreskin to be non-retractable. By age 3 the foreskin will spontaneously become retractable in over 90 percent of boys.

The skin of the head of the penis secretes a white waxy material called smegma, which lubricates the head of the penis for intercourse, and also prevents adhesions forming between the head and the foreskin.

Circumcision is performed on the eighth day of life as a ritual in the Jewish religion and before puberty as a ritual in the Muslim religion—in both cases, according to a covenant made between Abraham and God. It has also been performed in some other parts of the world for various reasons, most often as a puberty rite, celebrating the passage from childhood to adulthood. It has been very commonly performed in the United States in the twentieth century for reasons of "cleanliness." This refers to the prevention of the accumulation of smegma under the foreskin which occasionally becomes mildly inflamed or infected. It also refers to a previous medical belief, no longer generally held, that the wives of uncircumcised men more often develop cancer of the cervix.

Formerly, there were three choices in the care of the penis in early infancy:

1. Leave the foreskin alone;
2. Forcible retraction of the foreskin daily at the time of the bath (done first by the doctor which makes the

foreskin bleed and is painful for the parent as well as the baby); and
3. Circumcision.

I used to lean toward routine circumcision at birth to avoid the possibility of circumcision at 2, 3, 4, 5 years of age. It was fairly often performed in earlier generations because a boy was masturbating, on the theory that itching due to infection under the foreskin was the cause of the masturbation. Circumcision in young childhood is disturbing emotionally because it fits in with the childhood notion that the penis may be cut off as punishment for masturbation. (See Section 582.)

Now that circumcision is not recommended to stop masturbation and now that the theory about cervical cancer has been disproved, there is no excuse for the operation—except as a religious rite. And retraction is painful and unnecessary. So, I strongly recommend leaving the foreskin alone.

286. Why circumcision is harmful after infancy. The question of circumcision is often raised later in childhood, either because there has been an irritating infection beneath the foreskin or because the child is masturbating. In the days before the importance of the child's emotions was recognized, it seemed logical to circumcise for either of these reasons. The parents or the doctor might say, "Maybe he's masturbating because there is discomfort from a little infection." The trouble is that this theory often puts the cart before the horse. We know now that a boy, especially between 3 and 6, often becomes nervous about his penis for fear some injury might happen to it (explained in Section 573). This worry may **cause** him to handle himself and produce a little irritation. If this should be the real sequence of events, you can see that an operation on the penis would be a bad thing for his fears. The danger of psychological harm from circumcision is greatest between 1 and 6 years, but there is some risk up through adolescence.

287. Erections. It is common for boy babies to have erections of the penis, especially when the bladder is full or during urination. This has no importance.

THE FONTANEL

288. The soft spot on the top of a baby's head is where the four pieces of bone that make up the top of the skull have not yet grown together. The size of the fontanel at birth is different in different babies. A large one is nothing to worry about, and it's bound to be slower to close than a small one. Some fontanels close as early as 9 months and slow ones not till 2 years. The average is at 12 to 18 months.

If the light is right, you can see that the fontanel pulsates at a rate between the breathing rate and the beat of the heart.

Parents worry unnecessarily about the danger of touching the soft spot. Actually, it is covered by a membrane as tough as canvas, and there is very little risk of hurting a baby there.

CLOTHING, FRESH AIR, AND SUNSHINE

289. Room temperature. The hardest question for a doctor to answer, in a book or in the office, is how much covering to put on a baby. All the doctor can give are some rough guides. Babies under 5 pounds don't have a very good system for keeping the body at the right temperature and have to be in an incubator. Between 5 and 8 pounds they don't usually need to be heated from the outside. They can take care of themselves in a comfortable room, say 65° to 68°F.

By the time they weigh 8 pounds, their heat regulator is working well and they are getting a layer of fat that helps them stay warm. Now their room for sleeping can be allowed to go down to 60°F in cool or cold weather.

A room temperature of 65° to 68°F for eating and playing is right for babies weighing over 5 pounds, just as it is for older children and adults.

290. Clothing. Babies and children who are reasonably plump need less covering than an adult. More babies are overdressed than underdressed. This isn't good for them. If a person is always too warmly dressed, the body loses its ability to adjust to changes, and is **more** likely to become chilled. So, in general, put on too little rather than too much and then watch the baby. Don't try to put on enough to keep the hands warm, because most babies' hands stay cool when they are comfortably dressed. Feel the legs or arms or neck. Best guide of all is the color of the face. Babies who are getting cold lose the color from their cheeks, and they may begin to fuss, too.

When putting on sweaters and shirts with small openings, remember that a baby's head is more egg-shaped than ball-shaped. Gather the sweater into a loop, slip it first over the back of the baby's head, then forward, stretching it forward as you bring it down past the forehead and nose. Then put the baby's arms into the sleeves. When taking it off, pull the baby's arms out of the sleeves first. Gather the sweater into a loop as it lies around the neck. Raise the front part of the loop up past the nose and forehead (while the back of the loop is still at the back of the neck), then slip it off toward the back of the head.

A cap in which to sleep in very cold weather should be of knitted acrylic, so that if it slips over the face the baby can breathe through it.

291. Practical coverings. It is better to use all-acrylic blankets or bags when a baby is sleeping in a cool room (60°–72°F). They have the best combination of warmth and washability. Knitted shawls tuck and wrap more easily than woven blankets, especially when the baby is up, and because they are thinner you can adjust the amount of covering to the temperature more exactly than with thick blankets. Avoid coverings that are heavy, such as solid-feeling quilts.

Sleep bags can't be kicked off, as blankets can; sleep walkers are sensible by the time a baby can stand.

In a warm room (over 72°F) or in warm weather, a baby really only needs cotton covering. There are now cotton thermal blankets said to be adaptable to cold or warm temperatures.

All blankets, quilts, sheets should be large enough to tuck securely under the mattress, so that they will not work loose. Waterproof sheets and pads should either be large enough to tuck in securely or should be pinned or tied down at all corners so that they will not come loose. The mattress should be firm and flat enough so that the baby will not be lying in a depression. A carriage mattress should fit well, so that there is no space around the edge in which the baby might get wedged. Use no pillow in crib or carriage.

292. Fresh air. Changes of air temperature are beneficial in toning up the body's system for adapting to cold or heat. A bank clerk is much more likely to become chilled staying outdoors in winter than a lumberjack, who is used to such weather. Cool or cold air improves appetite, puts color in the cheeks, and gives more pep to humans of all ages. A baby living continuously in a warm room usually has a pasty complexion and may have a sluggish appetite.

In cold weather the air contains much less moisture. When this air is heated in a house it becomes relatively drier still, especially when the temperature rises above 72°F. Dry, hot air dries and hardens the mucus in the nose and parches the air passages generally. This makes the baby uncomfortable and probably lowers the ability to resist infections.

It's good for a baby (like anyone else) to get outdoors for 2 or 3 hours a day, particularly during the season when the house is heated.

When babies are sleeping indoors during cold weather, I think it is preferable that their window be open wide enough (and the radiator turned off) so that the temperature falls to about 60°F.

When they are awake, and with the family, the room temperature should be kept between 68° and 72°F.

Most people accustomed to heated houses let the temperature gradually get hotter all winter, without noticing it, and come to demand excessive heat. One way to counteract this in a private house is with a thermostat, which turns the furnace down when the desired temperature (70°F) is reached. In an apartment or private house without a thermostat, the parents should hang a house thermometer in a prominent place and glance at it several times a day until they become so attuned to a range of 68° to 70°F that they notice a higher temperature without looking.

The problem of providing cool enough air for a baby is further complicated by the inexperienced parents' natural anxiety, and protectiveness. They tend to keep their baby in a too hot room and too well covered, besides. Under these conditions some babies even develop heat rash in winter.

I think there's a general tendency to overdress babies, even among experienced parents. A normal baby has as good a "thermostat" as an adult, as long as he isn't put into so many layers of clothing and covering that his thermostat isn't allowed to work properly.

293. Taking the baby out of doors. I grew up and practiced pediatrics in the northeastern part of the United States, where most conscientious parents take it for granted that babies and children should be outdoors 2 or 3 hours a day when it isn't raining and the temperature isn't far below freezing. Children love to be out and it gives them pink cheeks and good appetites. So I can't help but believe in the tradition. I have to admit, though, that there is no such tradition in other parts of the country.

An 8-pounder can certainly go out when it's 60°F or above. The temperature of the air is not the only factor. Moist, cold air is more chilling than dry air of the same temperature, and wind is the greatest chiller. Even when the temperature is below freezing, a 12-pound baby can be comfortable in a sunny, sheltered spot for an hour or two.

In winter the best time to have the baby out is in the middle of the day (between the 10 A.M. and 2 P.M. feedings in the early months). If you live in the country or have your own yard, you can put your baby out for even longer than 3 hours in reasonable weather. Let the sun fall on the face for a short time if this does not make the baby uncomfortable (see Section 294 on sunbathing).

As babies grow older, are awake for longer periods, and appreciate company more, I wouldn't keep them out **all by themselves** for more than an hour when they are awake. By the second half of the first year, children are entitled to have people nearby most of the time they're awake, even though they're amusing themselves. It's fine for them to be out for 2 or 3 hours with a parent or when they're asleep.

If you live in a city and have no yard to park the baby in, you can push the child in a carriage. Long woolen or thermal underwear (or tights, slacks, woolen stockings for the mother) and boots make parents' lives a lot more pleasant during this period. If you enjoy being out and can afford the time, the more the better.

In summer, if your house gets stifling hot and you can find a fairly cool place outdoors, the longer the baby stays out when asleep the better. If your house stays cool, I would still try to have the baby out for a couple of hours a day, but in the first part of the morning and the end of the afternoon.

When your baby first goes on three meals a day, you may need to shift the hours outdoors somewhat to suit your own and his convenience. But the general principle of trying to get him out for 2 or 3 hours a day remains the same. As he gets nearer to a year old, he becomes more interested in his surroundings. He may refuse to go to sleep after lunch if he is being pushed around in his carriage. Then you may have to let him have his nap in his crib after lunch. That leaves very little of the afternoon for an outing, especially in winter. You might keep him out for 1 to 2 hours in the morning and an hour in the afternoon. What part of the morning you take him out also depends on when he takes his morning nap. Some babies in the last part of the first year fall asleep right after breakfast, others not until the end of the morning. If your baby won't sleep while he is outdoors, you have to fit in the outings when he is awake.

294. Sunshine and sunbaths. Direct sunshine contains ultraviolet rays, which create vitamin D right in the skin. On general principles it's sensible for babies and children to be in the sun for part of the time. There are three cautions. Exposure to sunshine should be increased very gradually to avoid burns, especially where the sun is hot and the air is clear. Second, excessive exposure is probably unwise even when the skin has been gradually tanned. The reason the skin becomes tanned is to protect the body from the effects of too much sun. In other words, the body can't use more than a moderate amount. Excessive amounts may be harmful to the skin. Third, a severe sunburn is just as dangerous as a heat burn. When you put babies out to sleep in a carriage, you must take into account how much sunshine they will get on the skin, especially if you are putting them in a new spot in a season when the sun is bright.

In summer you can begin exposing babies' bodies to the sun as soon as the weather is warm enough and as soon as they weigh about 10 pounds. This means that they are plump enough so that they won't get chilled when they are partly undressed outdoors. In cooler weather you may be able to expose the legs alone. You have to wait longer to expose the face, until the eyes are no longer bothered by the bright light. This varies in different babies. When you do expose the face, turn the baby so that the top of the head is toward the sun. Then the eyebrows will shield the eyes.

In winter you can, if you wish, give your baby sunbaths at an open window if the room is warm enough and the wind does not blow on the child.

Begin with 2 minutes and increase the exposure gradually—adding 2 minutes each day is fast enough. Divide the time between back and stomach. I wouldn't suggest going beyond 30 or 40 minutes of full exposure, especially in summer. In warm weather it is important that babies not get overheated during their sunbath. Put them on a pad on the floor or on the ground where the air will cool them, not down inside a bassinet or carriage. If they become flushed, they're too hot.

When the sunshine is intense, as at the beach, babies should be in the shade **all** the time the first day or two, and even then they may get enough reflected glare to give their tender skins a burn. A baby old enough to sit up and crawl around needs a hat at the beach or any equally sunny place. Remember that the redness of sunburn doesn't show up until several hours after the damage is done. (See Section 798.)

Babies and children should never be put to sleep directly in front of an air conditioner because that could lower their body temperatures to dangerous levels.

SLEEP

295. How much should a baby sleep? Parents often ask this question. Of course, the baby is the only one who can answer it. One baby seems to need a lot, and another surprisingly little. As long as babies are satisfied with their feedings, comfortable, get plenty of fresh air, and sleep in a cool place, you can leave it to them to take the amount of sleep they need.

Most babies in the early months sleep from feeding to feeding if they are getting enough to eat and not having indigestion. There are a few babies, though, who are unusually wakeful right from the beginning, and not because anything is wrong. If you have this kind of baby, there's nothing you need to do about it.

As babies get older, they gradually sleep less and less. You're apt to notice it first in the late afternoon. In time they become wakeful at other periods during the day. Each baby develops a personal pattern of wakefulness and tends to be awake at the same time every day. Toward the end of the first year, most babies are down to two naps a day; and between 1 and 1½ years, they will probably give up one of these. It is only during infancy that you can leave the amount of sleep entirely up to the baby. A child by the age of 2 is a much more complicated being. Excitement, worries, fear of bad dreams, competition with a sister or brother may keep children from getting the sleep they need.

296. Going to bed. Many babies easily get used to the idea that they always go to bed and to sleep right after a meal. Many other babies are very sociable after meals. You can choose which routine fits best with the schedule of the whole family. It is good for babies to get used to falling asleep in their own beds, without company, at least by the time any 3-month colic is over.

Most babies can get accustomed to either a silent home or an average noisy one. So there is no point tiptoeing and whispering around the house at first—you'd only be training the baby to be easily wakened by unexpected sounds. The infant and child who, awake or asleep, is used to ordinary household noises and human voices usually sleeps right through a visit of talking, laughing friends, a radio or TV tuned to a reasonable level, even somebody's coming into the room.

297. On back or stomach? A majority of babies seem, from the beginning, to be a little more comfortable going to sleep on their stomachs. This is particularly true of the baby who develops colic; the pressure on the abdomen seems to partly relieve the gas pains.

Others either don't care at first or prefer sleeping on their backs. There are two disadvantages to babies sleeping on their backs. If they vomit, they're more likely to choke on the vomitus. Also, they tend to keep the head turned toward the same side—usually toward the center of the room. This may flatten that side of the head. It won't hurt the brain, and the head will gradually straighten out, but it may take a couple of years. If you start early, you may be able to get them used to turning the head to both sides by putting the head where the feet were the time before, each time you put them to bed. Then if there is one part of the room they like to look at, they will turn the head in each direction half the time. Within a few weeks babies usually develop such a strong preference for their usual position, stomach or back, that it's quite a struggle to change them.

I think it is preferable to accustom babies to sleeping on the stomach from the start if they are willing. They may change later when they learn to turn over.

The one objection that is raised against sleeping on the stomach, by some orthopedic (bone) specialists, is that if a baby has a tendency to turn the feet in too much or out too much, this may be accentuated by having the baby lie on the stomach. Others reply that even if this is true, the in-turning or out-turning will be outgrown in any case after the child has been walking for a while. Ask your baby's doctor.

Some physicians recommend that, to avoid the disadvantages of back or stomach sleeping, a baby should be taught to sleep on his side with the aid of firm pillows. In my experience this is very difficult to accomplish; the baby always slides away from the pillow and ends up on the back or stomach. By

6 months, however, some babies begin to sleep on their sides by preference.

298. See if you can train the baby to sleep later or be happy in bed in the morning. In the middle part of the first year, most babies become willing to sleep a little later than the uncivilized 5 or 6 A.M. waking hour that they all love at first. However, most parents develop such a habit of listening for their babies in their sleep and jumping out of bed at the first murmur that they never give the children a chance to go back to sleep if they're willing, or to become accustomed to amusing themselves for a while. As a result, parents may find themselves still getting up before 7 A.M. when the child is 2 or 3 years old. And a child who has been used to early company for so long will demand it.

So if you like to sleep till 7 or 8, use your alarm clock again instead of your baby. Set the alarm 5 minutes later than he usually wakes, and every few days move it 5 minutes later still. If he wakes before the alarm, he may go back to sleep without your hearing him or he may learn to stay awake contentedly for a longer and longer period. If he fusses, wait a while to see if he quiets down. Of course, if he works himself up to indignant crying and it persists, you've got to get up. But try again in another month.

299. Out of the parents' room by 6 months if possible. Children can sleep in a room by themselves from the time they are born, if convenient, as long as the parents are near enough to hear them when they cry. If they start with their parents, 6 months is a good age to move them, for they have the strength to take care of themselves pretty well, and they don't yet have set ideas about where they want to be. Otherwise there is a chance that they may become dependent on this arrangement and be afraid and unwilling to sleep anywhere else. The older they are, the harder it may be to move them.

Another trouble is that young children may be upset by the parents' intercourse, which they misunderstand and which frightens them. Parents are apt to think there is no danger if they first make sure the child is asleep. But children's psychiatrists have found cases in which the child awakened and was much disturbed without the parents ever being aware of it.

Whether children should sleep in a room by themselves or with another youngster is largely a practical matter. If it's possible, it's fine for children to have a room of their own, especially as they grow older, where they can keep their own possessions under control and have privacy when they want it. The main disadvantage of two young children in the same room is that they are apt to wake each other up at the wrong times.

300. The parents' bed. Sometimes a small child is going through a period of waking up frightened at night—perhaps coming repeatedly into the parents' room, perhaps crying persistently—and is taken into the parents' bed with them so that they can all get some sleep. This seems like the most practical thing to do at the time, but it usually turns out to be a mistake. Even if the child's anxiety lessens during the following weeks, he is apt to cling to the security of his parents' bed, and there is the devil to pay getting him out again. So **always** bring him promptly and matter-of-factly back to his own bed. I think it is a sensible rule not to take a child into the parents' bed to sleep for any reason (even as a treat when one parent is away on a trip).

If a child is ill or anxious enough to want to be in the parents' bed for the entire night, it would be wise to consult the doctor. But comfort the child in his own room: Sit down beside his crib or bed—in the dark—and reassure him that you are there and that there is no need to fear. Sit with him until he goes to sleep.

Letting your child come into your bed for a cuddle in the morning is a different story. This is a fine way for parents and children to have a special warm and loving time together, so long as it doesn't make either parent uneasy, by stirring up sexual feelings. And if a child, especially in the 3- to 6-year old period, makes persistent sexual advances, which isn't likely if both parents are in the bed, the parent can easily change position or get out of bed, as if to start the day's work, without making an issue of it.

PLAY PERIODS

301. Being companionable with your baby. Be quietly friendly with your baby whenever you are with him. He's getting a sense of how much you mean to each other all the time you're feeding him, bubbling him, bathing him, dressing him, changing his diapers, holding him, or just sitting in the room with him. When you hug him or make noises at him, when you show him that you think he's the most wonderful baby in the world, it makes his spirit grow, just the way milk makes his bones grow. That must be why we grown-ups instinctively talk baby talk and waggle our heads when we greet a baby, even grown-ups who are otherwise dignified or unsociable.

One trouble with being an inexperienced parent is that part of the time you take the job so seriously that you forget to enjoy it. Then you and the baby are both missing something.

Naturally I don't mean that you should be talking a blue streak at him all the time he's awake, or constantly joggling him or tickling him. That would tire him out, and in the long run would make him tense and spoiled. You can be quiet nine-tenths of the time you are with him. It's the gentle, easy-going kind of companionship that's good for him and good for you. It's the comfortable feeling that goes into your arms when you hold him, the fond, peaceful expression on your face when you look at him, and the gentle tone in your voice.

302. Companionship without spoiling. It's good for a baby during his play periods to be somewhere near his parents (and brothers and sisters, if any) so that he can see them, make noises at them, hear them speak to him, have them show him a way to play with something occasionally. But it isn't necessary or sensible for him to be in a parent's lap or arms or to have his mother or father amusing him much of the time. He can be enjoying their company, profiting from it, and still be learning how to occupy himself. When new parents are so delighted with their baby that they are holding him or making games for him most of his waking hours, he may become quite dependent on these attentions and demand more and more of them. See Sections 342 and 343.

303. Things to watch and things to play with. Young babies begin waking earlier and earlier, especially at the end of the afternoon. At such times they want something to do and they want **some** companionship. At 2, 3, and 4 months, they enjoy looking at bright-colored things and things that move. Outdoors, they are delighted to watch leaves and shadows. Indoors, they study their hands, pictures on the wall. There are bright-colored plastic shapes on strings that you can suspend between the top rails of the crib. Place them just within arm's reach—not right on top of babies' noses—for the time when they begin reaching. You can make mobiles yourself—cardboard shapes covered with colored paper that hang from the ceiling or from a lighting fixture and rotate in slight drafts (they aren't strong enough for playing with or healthful for chewing)—or you can hang suitable household objects within reach—spoons, plastic cups, for instance.

Remember that eventually everything goes into the mouth. As babies get toward the middle of their first year, their greatest joy is handling and mouthing objects: collections of plastic objects linked together (made for this age), rattles, teething rings, animals and dolls of cloth, household objects that are safe in the mouth. Don't let a baby or small child have objects or furniture that have been repainted with outdoor paint containing lead, or thin celluloid toys that can be chewed into small, sharp pieces, or small glass beads and other small objects that can be choked on. Take the metal whistles out of rubber animals.

Each afternoon when the baby becomes bored with his crib, put him in the playpen near where you are working or sitting. If you are going to use a pen, the baby should become accustomed to it at 3 or 4 months, before he has learned to sit and crawl and before he has had the freedom of the floor. Otherwise he considers it a prison from the start. By the time he can sit and crawl, he has fun going after things that are a few feet away, handling larger objects like cooking spoons, saucepans, strainers. When he becomes bored with the playpen, he can sit in a bouncing chair or a chair–table arrangement. It's good for him to end up with some free creeping.

304. Use of the playpen. Back in Section 93 I mentioned the differences of opinion on playpens. I have usually suggested a playpen on purely practical grounds as a great help, especially for the busy mother, from about 3 months on. Set up in the living room or the kitchen, where the mother is working, it gives babies the company that they can't have in their own rooms and a chance to see everything that is going on without the danger of being stepped on or spilled on. Later they have fun by the hour putting toys out onto the floor and getting them back again. When they are old enough to stand up, the pen gives them a railing to hold onto and a firm foundation under their feet. In good weather they can sit safely in the playpen on the porch and watch the world go by.

The net playpens are becoming more popular than the wooden ones mainly because they are so much lighter to move around.

Even if they are willing, babies should not be kept in pens all the time. They should have times for explorative crawling, while the parent pays attention. They should, every hour or so, be played with, hugged, perhaps carried around in a chest carrier for a spell while the parent works. As babies get to be 12, 15, 18 months they tolerate the playpen for shorter and shorter periods.

305. Walkers, swings. A walker or a swing is useful after babies have learned to sit and before they learn to walk. It will keep them happy for quite a while, exercise them, and keep them from getting into as much trouble as they would creeping. However, I wouldn't keep babies in a walker or swing all the time they're up. They need chances to creep, explore, stand, walk.

In one kind of walker with springs, babies can jounce up and down before they learn to walk around. But walkers don't help babies learn to walk any faster. Also, they can be dangerous if you haven't checked to be sure that your house is safe for your baby in a walker. They can pull a baby forward on an incline or down stairs. And they also increase the baby's height which allows her to reach things she couldn't otherwise have reached. Some pediatricians and orthopedists object to a walker if a baby toes in or out excessively when using one. Ask your doctor.

There are swings on standards, for indoors or out, some with windup motors, swings for doorways, swings with springs in which a baby can bounce.

The springs of a spring swing or of a bouncer should have covers to prevent finger injury, or the coils should not be more than ⅛ inch apart.

THE BOWEL MOVEMENTS

306. The gastrocolic reflex. The bowels are apt to move soon after a meal in most individuals because the filling of the stomach tends to stimulate the intestinal tract all the way down. This hookup is called the gastrocolic reflex. The movement is more apt to occur after breakfast because of the abrupt resumption of stomach and intestinal activity after the long night's quiet.

Sometimes this reflex works very actively in the early months of life, especially in a breast-fed baby, who may have a movement after every nursing. More inconvenient still is the pattern of the occasional babies who begin to strain soon after the start of each feeding, produce nothing, but keep straining so hard, as long as the nipple is in their mouths, that they can't nurse. You have to let their intestines quiet down for 15 minutes and try again.

307. Meconium. For the first day or so after birth, the baby's movements are composed of material called meconium, which is greenish-black in color and of a smooth, sticky consistency. Then they change to brown and to yellow. If a baby hasn't had a movement by the end of the second day, the doctor should be notified.

308. The breast-fed baby may have many or few movements. A breast-fed baby usually has several movements a day in the early weeks. Some have a movement after every nursing.

They are usually of a light-yellow color. They may be pasty or they may have the consistency of thick cream soup. They are practically never too hard. Many breast-fed babies change from frequent to infrequent movements by the time they are 1, 2, or 3 months old. Some then have one movement a day, others a movement only every other day or even further apart. This is apt to alarm a parent who has been brought up to believe that everyone must have a movement every day. But there is nothing to worry about so long as the baby is comfortable. The breast-fed baby's movement stays just as soft, even when it is passed every 2 or 3 days.

Some of these breast-fed babies who have infrequent movements begin to push and strain a lot when 2 or 3 days have gone by. Yet the movement is like creamed soup when it does come out. The only explanation I can make for this is that the movement is so liquid that it doesn't put the right kind of pressure on the inside of the anus, where the movement comes out. Adding a little solid food to the diet usually helps, even though the baby doesn't otherwise need solid food yet. Two to 4 teaspoonfuls of pureed prunes daily (stewed or canned) generally work well. There is no call for cathartics in this kind of difficulty. I think it is better not to use suppositories or enemas regularly, for fear the baby will come to depend on them. Try to solve the problem with prunes or other solid food.

309. The bottle-fed baby's movements. The baby fed cow's milk formula usually has between one and four movements a day at first, though an occasional baby has as many as six. As he grows older, the number tends to decrease to one or two a day. The number is unimportant if the consistency of the movement is good and if the baby is doing well.

Cow's-milk movements are most often pasty and of a pale-yellow or tan color. However, some young babies always have stools that are more like soft scrambled eggs (curdy lumps with looser material in between). This is not important if the baby is comfortable and gaining well.

The commonest disturbance of the bowel movements in the baby on cow's milk is a tendency to hardness. This is discussed in the section on **constipation** (Section 354).

A very few bottle-fed babies have a tendency to loose,

green, curdy movements in the early months. This is usually worse as more sugar is added to the formula. A severe case needs a lot of supervision by the doctor. If you are completely out of reach of a doctor, you can omit the sugar from the formula altogether. However, if the movements are always just a little loose, it can be ignored, provided the baby is comfortable, gaining well, and the doctor finds nothing wrong.

310. Changes in the movements. You can see that it doesn't matter if one baby's movements are always a little different from another baby's, as long as each is doing well. It's more apt to mean something, and should be discussed with the doctor, when the movements undergo a real change. If they were previously pasty and then turn lumpy, slightly looser, slightly more frequent, it may be a spell of indigestion or a mild intestinal infection. If they become definitely loose, frequent, greenish, and the smell changes, it is almost certainly due to an intestinal infection, whether this is mild or severe. When a bowel movement is delayed and then comes unusually firm, it sometimes means the beginning of a cold, sore throat, or other disease, but not necessarily. (The infection makes the intestine more sluggish, just as it's apt to diminish the appetite.) Generally speaking, changes in the number and color of the movements are less important than changes in the consistency and smell.

Mucus in the bowel movements is common when a baby has diarrhea, and it is just another sign that the intestines are irritated. Similarly, it may occur in indigestion. It can also come from higher up, from the throat and bronchial tubes of a baby with a cold, or of a healthy newborn baby. Some babies form a great deal of mucus in the early weeks.

When a **new vegetable** is added to the diet (less frequently in the case of other foods), part of it may come through looking just the same as it went in. If it also causes signs of irritation, such as looseness and mucus, give much less the next time. If there is no irritation, you can keep on with the same amount or increase slowly until the baby learns to digest it better. Beets can turn the whole movement red.

A bowel movement exposed to the air may turn brown or it may turn green. This is of no importance.

Small streaks of blood on the outside of a bowel movement usually come from a crack, or "fissure," in the anus, caused by hard bowel movements. The bleeding is not serious in itself, but the doctor should be notified so that the constipation can be treated promptly. This is important for psychological as well as physical reasons (Section 438). **Larger amounts of blood** in the movement are rare and may come from malformations of the intestines, from severe diarrhea, or from intussusception (Section 775). The doctor should be called or the child taken to a hospital immediately.

Diarrhea is discussed in Section 361–363.

DIAPERS

311. Diapering. How to fold a cloth diaper depends on the size of the baby and of the diaper. The only important things in putting it on are to have the most cloth where there is the most urine, and not to have so much diaper bunched between

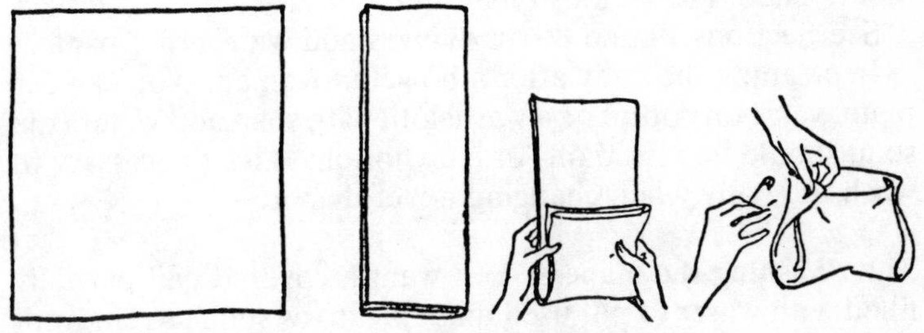

One way to fold a diaper.

the legs that they are kept widely separated. With a full-size newborn baby and the usual large square or rectagonal diapers, you can fold as in the pictures. First fold lengthwise so that there are three thicknesses. Then fold about one-third of the end over. As a result, half of the folded diaper has six layers, the other half three layers. A boy needs the double thickness in front; a girl needs the thickness in front if she lies on her abdomen, in back if she lies on her back. When you put in the pin, slip two fingers of the other hand between the baby and the diaper to prevent sticking the child. You can also buy prefolded diapers.

Most parents change the diapers when they pick the baby up for feeding and again before they put the child back to bed. Parents who are very busy, though, have found they can save time and laundry by changing only once at each feeding, either before or after. Most babies are not bothered by being wet. But a few are extra sensitive and have to be changed more often. If children have sufficient covers over them, the wet diaper does not feel cold. It is when wet clothing is exposed to the air that evaporation makes it cold.

If a baby drenches the diaper and the bed, it may be worthwhile using two diapers at a time. The second one may be too bulky if put on the same way as the first. You can pin it around the waist like an apron. Or it can be folded to make a thick but narrower panel down the middle of the first diaper. A third diaper can be used too.

Disposable diapers are particularly handy for traveling. But many parents use them all the time, despite their expense and environmental disadvantages, because they are so convenient. There are various types and sizes.

See Sections 79 and 80 on **diapers** and **waterproof pants.**

In cleaning the baby after a bowel movement, you can use plain water on cotton or a washcloth with soap and water (the soap should be rinsed off) or baby lotion. It isn't necessary to wash the baby when changing a wet diaper.

312. Washing the diapers. You want a covered pail partially filled with water to put used diapers into as soon as removed. If it contains soap or detergent, this helps in removing stains. Be sure the soap is well dissolved, to prevent lumps of soap from remaining in the diapers later. When you remove a soiled diaper, scrape the movement off into the toilet with a knife, or rinse it by holding it in the toilet while you flush it (hold tight).

You wash the diapers with mild soap or mild detergent in washing machine or washtub (dissolve the soap well first), and rinse two or three times. The number of rinsings depends on how soon the water gets clear and on how delicate the baby's skin is. If your baby's skin isn't sensitive, two rinsings may be enough.

If your baby has a tendency to diaper rash, you may need to take additional precautions—at least at the times the rash appears, and perhaps regularly. Bacteria that sometimes collect in diapers manufacture ammonia from the urine. This ammonia is the main cause of diaper rash. These bacteria are not completely removed by washing. They must be destroyed if there is much diaper rash, either by boiling the diapers or by adding ½ to 1 cup of clear vinegar to an extra rinse (the diapers should come from the dryer smelling slightly of vinegar). Some clothes washers and dryers effectively kill these bacteria, depending on the heat. (Diapers that go to the diaper service are sterilized.)

Sunshine is a potent destroyer of many bacteria. There is probably less chance of diaper rash if you hang the diapers (and also the other things that are wet by the urine: nighties, shirts, sheets, pads, waterproof sheeting, waterproof pants) in the sun to dry. See Section 366 on diaper rash.

If the diapers (and other clothes) are becoming hard, unabsorbent, and gray with soap deposit (the same as the ring in the bathtub) you can soften them and clean them by using a water conditioner. Don't use a fabric softener—they leave a coating which decreases the absorbency of diapers.

Immunizations

313. Keep a record with you. It's a good idea to keep a record (signed by your doctor) of all your children's immunizations (and sensitivity to drugs, if any) in your home, and to carry it with you when the family goes on trips. It's also valuable if you move or if you change doctors. To be sure, you can always write or phone the doctor who gave the immunizations, but this is often impossible to do in a hurry during an emergency. The commonest emergency is when a child away from home receives a wound that calls for extra protection against tetanus (lockjaw). Then it is very important for the attending doctor to know for certain whether the child has received tetanus immunizations. If a child has been fully immunized, very few wounds will require extra protection against tetanus.

314. Diphtheria, pertussis (whooping cough), tetanus immunizations (DPT). Immunizations against these three diseases are usually given together in a combined form (three materials in one shot). They should be started very early, preferably at 2 months of age. Three shots are given (each shot containing diphtheria, pertussis, and tetanus materials), most commonly 2 months apart. However, if the interval between shots is longer than 2 months, the effect is just as good.

The protection from the three shots is usually very high, but after a few months it begins to taper off. So a booster shot is given a year later (at 15 to 18 months of age) to bring the protection back to a high level, and again at 4 to 6 years of age. Further immunizations against tetanus and diphtheria are given every 10 years thereafter.

These combined immunizations often cause a reaction (on

account of the whooping cough material), consisting of fever, crankiness, loss of appetite, or soreness around the injection, which usually starts 3 or 4 hours after the shot. The doctor can prescribe medication to relieve the symptoms. The baby should feel better the next day. If the baby has a fever after that, it should not be blamed on the immunization; it is due to some new infection. These shots do not cause cough or cold symptoms.

It is common for a firm lump, or "knot," to remain in the thigh or arm where the child has received a shot. It remains for several months and is nothing to worry about.

Now we should discuss the three materials that go into these combined immunizations.

315. Pertussis (whooping cough) vaccine is one of the materials that goes into DPT immunizations. It is made from killed whooping cough germs. It may not give complete protection from whooping cough, but if an immunized child does catch the disease it is apt to be mild. Whooping cough is a dangerous disease for babies, and this is one reason the immunizations are started so early in infancy.

It takes two or three shots and some time before the vaccine stimulates the body to build a high resistance. So no immediate help can be expected from a first shot given after a child has already been exposed to the disease. Boosters are given at 15 months and 4 to 6 years.

316. Diphtheria toxoid is another of the materials that goes into DPT shots. The poisonous substance from diphtheria germs, called diphtheria toxin (which is what does the damage when a person has the disease), is treated chemically so that it is changed to a nonpoisonous substance—a toxoid. Diphtheria toxoid, when injected, can stimulate the body to build protection against diphtheria toxin. It is recommended that a child have three shots in early infancy and boosters at 15 months, 4 to 6 years, and then every 10 years. In this way he is almost certainly protected against diphtheria.

317. Tetanus toxoid is the third material that goes into DPT shots. It is made from the poisonous substance (tetanus toxin) in tetanus germs, and when several shots are injected they stimulate the body to **slowly** build its own, long-lasting protection against tetanus. The tetanus toxin is treated chemically so that it is changed to a nonpoisonous substance—a toxoid—which is what is given in the injections.

Tetanus, or lockjaw, is a serious infection that sometimes gets into a wound. The germs occur most commonly in soil and other places where horse manure and cow manure have been. The germs can still be found fairly regularly in city streets. A wound is more liable to be infected with tetanus if it is deep. A deep puncture from a nail in a barnyard is therefore the riskiest kind. Lots of people think that the rust on a nail brings the danger of tetanus. This is not true. The important thing is where the nail has been.

Nowadays if children who have already built their own protection as a result of tetanus **toxoid** injections receive a dangerous wound, the doctor may give another toxoid booster to be sure the protection is high. However, it is usually unnecessary to give a booster more often than every 5 years. But a doctor who has no proof that toxoid immunizations have been given has to give tetanus immune globulin (human) for temporary protection in order to play it safe. That is why you should carry a record of a child's immunizations with you when you are away from your own doctor.

The protection children build up from tetanus toxoid develops slowly and reaches a safe level only after the second shot. Therefore, there is no use **starting** this method at the time they get a dangerous wound. They need a shot of immune globulin to give them immediate protection.

A booster shot is given at 18 months, another between 4 and 6 years, at entrance to school, and then every 10 years. In addition, a child who gets a dangerous wound may need another toxoid injection, especially if it is 5 years since the last one.

318. Tetanus immune globulin (human). When there is no record of previous injections to prove that a person just injured has built her own protection by means of tetanus toxoid shots, she can be protected temporarily by an injection of the serum of a human being who surely has an immunity.

But when a person "borrows" the immunity of another person, this lasts only for a few weeks—enough to cover the present injury.

If injured children or adults have not already built their own protection from toxoid immunizations, or if proof of these is lacking, it is often hard to decide whether immune globulin is necessary—for instance, when a wound is not very deep and when there is a question whether any tetanus germs could have gotten in. It's a matter that has to be decided each time between the parents and the doctor. Treatment isn't usually given for cuts and scratches that a child receives indoors.

319. Oral Poliovirus Vaccine (Sabin vaccine) should be given to all babies, beginning at 2 months of age or as soon thereafter as possible. It is a live virus that has been grown on living cells in a laboratory and is taken by mouth. There are three types of virus that cause polio and a person has to take all three types of vaccine to be completely protected.

It's recommended that a child receive orally a trivalent (3-type) vaccine, the first dose at 2 months of age, the second at 4 months, the third at 6 months. A fourth dose is given a year later (18 months), a fifth at entrance to school (4 to 6 years). The vaccine is tasteless and is dropped directly onto the tongue.

If there has been delay between doses, the only risk is during the period of delay; the protection will eventually be just as high, provided the correct number of doses is given. The vaccine can be given at the same time as shots against diphtheria, pertussis, and tetanus.

Inactivated polio vaccine (Salk vaccine) is given to children who have a low resistance to infection or who are living with persons with a low resistance to infection because of the presence of some chronic illness or special drugs used for that illness. Your doctor will tell you if you're in a special situation requiring this vaccine.

320. Measles vaccine is fortunately available now and should be given to every healthy child, without exception, after the first birthday, preferably at age 15 months, or as soon thereafter as possible. Though most people think of measles as harmless because they suffered no bad consequences, it can have serious complications—ear infections, pneumonia, encephalitis, even permanent brain damage. That's why the vaccine is important. The vaccine is made of live measles virus which has been rendered mild in its effect by being grown for a long time on live chick embryo or other types of tissue. It is not given until after a year of age, so that the immunity which babies may have inherited from their mothers will have a full opportunity to wear off first. The vaccine stimulates the body to build its own immunity, which will last for life.

Though the reactions to the measles vaccine (which is really a mild case of measles) are much less severe than having regular measles itself, still, one child in ten has fever as high as 103°F, beginning about a week after the immunization and lasting 1 to 5 days, and one child in ten has a mild rash.

Preceding or at the time of measles vaccination, a tuberculin tine test should be given (Section 757). This is because regular measles or measles vaccination may cause a slight, unnoticed tubercular infection to spread.

Measles vaccine is often given with vaccines for mumps and rubella ("German measles" or "3-day measles") in a combined form.

321. Mumps vaccination is recommended at the age of 1 year or older, principally because of the rare occasion in which inflammation of the testicles in adolescent boys and men, an occasional complication of mumps, results in sterility. The vaccines for mumps, rubella ("German measles"), and measles are often given together in a combined form.

322. Rubella ("German measles") vaccine. Rubella is a relatively harmless disease except in the first 3 months of pregnancy when it fairly often causes fetal abnormalities. To prevent these tragedies it is recommended that all children be given rubella vaccine at 1 year of age or, if it was not done then at any age up to adolescence. (From adolescence onward, vaccination itself, during the first 3 months of a pregnancy, may cause fetal abnormalities. So vaccine should not be given from adolescence on, if there is any chance that the woman is pregnant.) Vaccination before a year may do no good if babies have inherited a temporary immunity from their mothers. The reason for vaccinating males is so that they won't be passing the disease to their mothers in childhood or to their wives in adulthood.

The vaccines for rubella, mumps, and measles are often given together in a combined form.

323. Vaccination against smallpox is no longer recommended routinely because the disease has been almost eradicated throughout the world. If you are going to travel outside the United States, you should check with your doctor or your local health department about whether or not you may need a vaccination to enter a country through which you plan to travel.

Vaccination is dangerous for children with eczema and other skin rashes because they may get severe reactions. Such children should not even come in contact with anyone who has a fresh vaccination for fear that some of the vaccination pus might be accidentally wiped off on them and accidently cause vaccination.

If vaccination should ever become necessary for a child with a rash because of close exposure to smallpox, it should be accompanied by an injection of vaccinia immune globulin (human).

Vaccination should never be given to children with immune deficiencies of the cellular type.

324. From time to time, some parents are alarmed and confused by stories in the newspapers and on television about a few children who have had bad reactions to a particular vaccine. Some of these parents then decide not to give their children **any** immunization, for fear that the immunization will make the child sicker than the disease would have. I think this is a bad mistake, because we know that in the vast majority of cases the disease is much more dangerous to many more children than the rare bad reaction to an immunization. If a story you see or read or hear about starts to worry you, talk to your doctor right away.

325. Recommended immunization schedule.

Age	*Vaccines*
2 Months	1st DPT and 1st polio
4 Months	2nd DPT and 2nd polio
6 Months	3rd DPT and 3rd polio
15 Months	M-M-R*
18 Months	4th DPT and 4th polio
4–6 Years	5th DPT and 5th polio
14–16 Years	Tetanus–diphtheria (No pertussis after age 6)

*Measles-mumps-rubella combined vaccine will protect against all three diseases with only one shot.

Problems of Infancy

CRYING IN THE EARLY WEEKS

326. What does it mean? This is usually an important question with a first baby. Let's assume it's a girl. As she grows older, crying is much less of a problem because you worry less, you know what to expect from her at different times of the day, you are able to distinguish between different cries, and she has fewer causes for crying.

Several questions pop into your mind: Is she hungry? Is she wet? Is she sick? Does she have indigestion? Is a pin sticking into her? Is she becoming spoiled? Parents are not apt to think of fatigue, but it's one of the commonest causes. It is fairly easy to answer these questions, one by one.

But there is a lot of fretting and crying that can't be explained by any of these reasons. In fact, by the time they are a couple of weeks old, almost all babies—especially first babies—get into fretful periods that we can give names to but can't explain exactly. When the crying is regularly limited to one period in the evening or afternoon, we can call it **colic** (if there is pain, distension, and gas) or **periodic irritable crying** (if there is no distension). If the baby is fussing off and on, any old time of the day or night, we can sigh and say that she is just a **fretful baby** at this stage. If she's unusually tense and jumpy, we use the term **hypertonic baby.** But we don't know the meaning of these patterns of behavior. We only know that they commonly occur and that they gradually peter out—

usually by 3 months of age. Maybe they are different variations of one condition. In a vague way we can sense that the age period between birth and about 3 months is one of adjustment of the baby's immature nervous system and immature digestive system to life in the outside world and that a smooth adjustment is harder for some babies to achieve. Anyway, the important thing to remember is that these most common types of crying in the early weeks are temporary and are not a sign of anything serious.

327. Hunger? Whether you're feeding your baby on a fairly regular schedule or according to her desire, you soon get an idea of what her pattern is like—at what times of day she wants more to eat, at what times she's apt to wake early. This should help you to decide whether unusual crying is due to hunger. If a baby took less than half her usual amount at her last feeding, it **may** be the reason why she's awake and crying in a couple of hours instead of in 3 or 4 hours. But not necessarily. A baby who has taken much less than her usual amount may, just as often, sleep contentedly for the full 4-hour period.

If a baby took an average amount at her last feeding and wakes crying before 2 hours, it is even less likely that she is hungry. (If she wakes within an hour, especially in the evening or afternoon, it's most apt to be colic.) If it's 2½ or 3 hours after the last feeding, then consider hunger first.

Could it be that she has outgrown her formula or the breast-milk supply, or that the breast supply is decreasing? A baby doesn't outgrow the formula all of a sudden, from one day to the next. She will have been finishing every bottle for several days and looking around for more. She begins to wake and cry a **little** earlier than usual, not a lot. In most cases, it's only after she has been waking early from hunger for a number of days that she begins crying **after** a feeding.

Normally the breast-milk supply increases as the baby demands it. The more complete and more frequent emptying of the breast stimulates it to greater production. Of course, it is possible for a mother to have less breast milk occasionally if she is fatigued or worried.

I'd sum it up with the following rule of thumb: If a baby has been crying hard for 15 minutes or more and if it's more than

2 hours after the last feeding—or if it's less than 2 hours after a **very small** feeding—give her another feeding. If this satisfies her and puts her to sleep, it's the right answer. If it's less than 2 hours after a **full** feeding, it's unlikely that she's hungry. Let her fuss or cry for 15 or 20 minutes more, if you can stand it, or give her a pacifier, and see if she won't go back to sleep. If she's crying harder than ever, there's no harm trying a feeding.

(Don't start giving a bottle the first time you suspect the breast milk is insufficient; give the breast.)

328. Is the baby sick? Babies catch colds and they catch intestinal infections during their early months, but these show themselves in running noses, coughs, or loose bowel movements. Other infections are pretty rare. If your baby is not only crying but **looks different** in general appearance and color, take her temperature and report to the doctor. Often a baby who is going to become sick is very irritable. There may be a day, or part of a day of unusual irritability; then after a nap or in the evening, the baby develops fever and is obviously ill.

329. Is she crying because she's wet or has had a bowel movement? A very few young babies seem uncomfortable when wet or soiled. Most don't mind at all. You can change her anyway.

330. Is it a safety pin? This doesn't happen once in a hundred years, but you can look to be sure.

331. Is it indigestion? You can try bubbling the baby again even though you got a bubble up before. Indigestion with spitting and loose, curdy green stools is discussed in Section 352, colic in Section 336.

332. Is she spoiled? Though older babies can be spoiled (Section 341), I think you can assume that in the first 3 months your baby is not crying because she's spoiled.

333. Fatigue? When young babies have been awake an unusually long while or when they have been stimulated more than usual by being with strangers or by being in a strange place or even by being played with by their parents, they may react by becoming tense and irritable. Instead of being easier for them to fall asleep, it may be harder. If the parents or strangers then try to comfort them with more play, more talk, more jouncing, it may make matters worse.

Some young babies seem to be made in such a way that they can **never** drift peacefully into sleep. Their fatigue at the end of every period of being awake produces a tension that is a sort of hump they must get over before falling asleep. They have to cry. Some of them cry frantically and loudly. Then gradually or suddenly the crying stops and they are asleep.

So if your baby is crying at the end of a wakeful period and after she has been fed, try assuming first that she's just tired and put her to bed. Let her cry for 15 to 30 minutes if she has to. Some babies fall asleep faster if left in the crib, and this is the method to strive for in the long run. Another baby who has become overfatigued relaxes sooner if kept in gentle motion—by being pushed back and forth in a bassinet that has wheels or by being rocked in the carriage or by being held in the arms or in a carrier and walked quietly, preferably in a darkened room. I would try walking a baby occasionally during an unusually tense spell (or rocking her in a rocking chair), but I wouldn't go on week after week always putting her to sleep this way. She might become more and more dependent on it and demand more of it. You'd surely resent it sooner or later.

334. Fretful babies. Almost all babies have at least a few fretful spells during the early weeks, especially first babies. A few babies are excessively fretful—on certain days or a good part of the time. These fretful periods may alternate with unusually long stretches during which they sleep like a log and are almost impossible to wake. We don't really know what the cause is, whether it is indigestion because of an immature digestive system or whether it is the irritability and instability of a nervous system that hasn't settled down yet. This tendency doesn't mean anything serious and it passes with time, but it's hard on the parents while it lasts.

There are various things you can try: Try a pacifier between feedings. Try swaddling the baby snugly in a receiving blanket. Some parents and experienced nurses insist that fretful or tense babies are much happier if they sleep in a small space—a small bassinet, a car carrier, even a cardboard carton fitted with a folded pad or blanket for a mattress and lined with a blanket. If you have a carriage or can borrow a cradle, you can see whether motion soothes your baby. A car ride works like magic with many fretful babies, but the trouble may return as soon as you get home, or even at every red light. A hot water bottle may comfort her (Section 337). You can also try music. Read Section 338 on getting some relief yourself.

335. Hypertonic babies are those who are unusually tense and restless during the early weeks. Their bodies don't relax well. They startle excessively at slight noise or on any quick change of position. If, for instance, they are laid on their back on a firm surface and roll to one side, or if they are held too loosely in the arms, or if the person carrying them moves them too suddenly, they may almost jump out of their skins. They may hate a tub bath for a couple of months. Hypertonic babies may also have colic or periodic irritable crying.

Hypertonic babies usually do best on a quiet regime; quiet room, few visitors, low voices, slow movements in handling them, a firm hold in carrying them, a big pillow (with a waterproof cover) to lie on while being changed and sponge-bathed so that they won't roll, swaddling in a receiving blanket most of the time, lying on the stomach in bed, a small confining bassinet (Sections 334 and 337).

336. Three-month colic and "periodic irritable crying." In this section I am describing two somewhat similar conditions that may be related to each other. The first is colic (sharp pains in the intestine). The babies' abdomens become distended with gas, they pull up or stiffen their legs, scream piercingly, and may pass gas by rectum. The second condition I call "periodic irritable crying." These babies, even though they have had plenty to eat, cry miserably for several hours at one regular time of day without definite signs of pain or gas. They may be pacified as long as you hold them and carry them about. One baby has colic, another has irritable crying, a third seems to have a mixture. The two conditions may be related to each other, because both commonly start around 2 to 4 weeks of age and are usually over by the time the baby is about 3 months old. Both conditions cause trouble most often between 6 P.M. and 10 P.M..

The commonest story is this: The baby was said to be well behaved and quiet in the hospital, but a few days after going home she suddenly has a crying spell that lasts for 3 or 4 hours straight. The parents change her, turn her over, give her a drink of water, but nothing works for long. After a couple of hours, the parents wonder if she is hungry ahead of time, because she seems to be trying to get everything into her mouth. The parents warm up a bottle or the mother begins to nurse and she takes it eagerly at first, but before it's finished she lets go and cries again. The screaming often continues for the full 4-hour interval between feedings. After she has finished her next regular bottle, she may be miraculously relieved.

Lots of babies have just a few attacks scattered through the early months. At the other extreme is the infant who has trouble every night until 3 months old (that's why the severer cases have always been called 3-month colic). In a rare case severe colic can last 6 months or even longer.

Some babies are very regular about their colic or irritable crying. They sleep like angels after every feeding but one, and always scream from 6 P.M. to 10 P.M. or from 2 P.M. to 6 P.M. Other babies spread their unhappiness through a longer period, and the parents say, "My baby sleeps like a lamb all night, but cries off and on for half the day." This is not so bad as the baby who sleeps all day and cries half the night. Another starts out being restless in the daytime and then gradually shifts to night, or vice versa. The crying of colic most often begins after a feeding, sometimes right after, sometimes half an hour or so later. In this way it is different from the crying of the hungry baby, which usually occurs **before** the feeding.

Parents are distressed to have their baby so unhappy and think that something is terribly wrong. They wonder how long the child can keep this up and not become exhausted. They wonder how long **they** can stand it. The strange thing is that colicky and irritable babies usually prosper from the physical point of view. In spite of hours of crying, they continue to gain weight, not just average-well but better than average. They are hungry babies. They gulp down their whole feeding and always seem to be demanding an increased amount.

When a baby turns colicky, the mother's first thought is apt to be that his feeding is wrong. If he is on the breast, she thinks her milk is to blame. If he is on a formula, she wonders if it needs some fundamental change. Changing the formula may bring about improvement in some cases, but not in most. It is plain to see that the quality of the feeding is not the main cause of colic. Otherwise why should the baby be able to digest it perfectly four out of five feedings a day, and get into trouble only in the evening? Colic occurs with breast milk, with cow's milk, and with all kinds of formulas. Once in a while, orange juice is suspected of being the cause. Some breast-fed babies with colic seem to get better if their mothers stop drinking cow's milk. It's at least worth a trial for a week.

We don't know the basic cause of most colic or irritable crying. One guess is that both conditions are due to a periodic tension in the baby's immature nervous system. Some of these babies are hypertonic all the time (Section 335). The fact that the trouble is commonest in the evening or late afternoon suggests that fatigue plays a part. Many babies up to the age of 3 months are on edge just before falling asleep. Instead of being able to slip peacefully off, they must let out at least a few piercing cries.

337. The treatment of colic. The most important thing is for the mother and father to recognize that the condition is fairly common, that it doesn't seem to do the baby any permanent harm, that, on the contrary, it occurs most often in babies who are developing and growing well, and that it will probably be gone by the time the baby is 3 months old, if not before, leaving the child none the worse for wear. If the parent can accept the condition in a fairly calm and resigned way, the battle is half won.

Some colicky babies (the hypertonic ones) seem to be definitely better when they lead quiet, calm lives—sleeping in a quiet room, being handled slowly and gently, being talked to softly, not seeing any visitors (at least closely), not being tickled or rough-housed in any way, avoiding noisy places outdoors, and perhaps, in an extreme case in a city, not going outdoors at all till the colic improves. The colicky baby, like others, must have company and cuddling and be smiled at, but it can be done gently. It is important to get the bubble up after feedings. The parents should keep closely in touch with the doctor.

But suppose it is not possible to get in touch immediately with the doctor. What home remedies are useful?

In many cases, a **pacifier** is by far the most effective remedy (Sections 394–396).

Colicky babies are usually more comfortable on their stomachs. They may get more relief still by being laid across the mother's or father's knees or a hot-water bottle, and massaged on the back.

Hot-Water Bottle. You should be able to rest the inside of your wrist against the hot-water bottle without discomfort. Then, as an extra precaution, wrap it in a diaper or towel before laying the baby against it or half on it.

Should you pick babies up, or rock them gently, or carry them around while they have colic? Even if it makes them stop crying, won't it spoil them? We aren't as scared nowadays of the danger of spoiling babies as we used to be. If babies are comforted when they are miserable, they usually don't go on demanding that comfort when they **aren't** miserable. If babies are screaming with colic or irritability, and picking them up or rocking them seems to help them, then do it. If, however, holding them makes them feel no better, it's just as well not to get them used to being held so much (Section 340).

Babies who are unusually miserable or unusually tense need especially to be under close medical supervision. Most of them improve steadily as they grow older, but the first 2 or 3 months may be rough on them and on their parents.

338. It's hard on the parents of a fretful, hypertonic, colicky, or irritable baby. If your baby is colicky or irritable, she may be soothed when you first pick her up. But after a few minutes she's apt to be screaming harder than ever. She thrashes with her arms and kicks with her legs. She not only refuses to be comforted—she acts as if she were angry at you for trying. These reactions are painful for you. You feel sorry for her, at least in the beginning. You feel increasingly inadequate, because you're not able to do anything to relieve her. Then as the minutes go by and she acts angrier and angrier, you feel that she is spurning you as a parent and you can't help feeling mad at her underneath. But getting angry at a tiny baby makes you ashamed of yourself, and you try hard to suppress the feeling. This makes you more tense than ever.

Every parent gets angry at such times, and there's no need to feel guilty. If you can admit the feeling and laugh about it with your spouse, you will be able to stand it more comfortably. The other thing to remember is that the baby is not mad at you. She doesn't know yet that you are a person or that she is a person. She's just a bundle of organs and nerves during her first month. Some kind of pain is spreading through her system and it automatically sets all her limbs to thrashing, just as a tap on the knee automatically makes the leg kick.

If you have the bad luck to have a baby who cries a great deal from colic or irritability or fretfulness, despite your own and your doctor's efforts, you have to think of yourself, too. You may be the kind of parent who isn't bothered too much after you have found out that there is nothing seriously wrong with her and after you have done all that you can to make her happy. That's fine, if you are made that way. But many parents get worn out and frantic listening to a baby cry, especially when it's the first. It is particularly difficult for the mother if she is with the baby constantly. She should make a great effort to get away from home and the baby for a few hours at least twice a week—oftener if it can be arranged. It's best if the parents can go out together. Hire a sitter or ask a friend or neighbor to come in and relieve the mother. If you're like most other parents, you hesitate to do this. "Why should we inflict the baby on somebody else? Besides, we'd be nervous being away for so long." But you shouldn't think of a vacation like this as just a treat for you. It's very important for you, for the baby, and for your spouse that you do not get exhausted and depressed. If you can't get anyone to come in, the parents can take turns one or two evenings a week to go out to visit or see a movie. The baby doesn't need two worried parents at a time to listen to her. Try also to get friends to come in and visit you. Remember that everything that helps you keep a sense of balance, everything that keeps you from getting too preoccupied with the baby, helps the baby and the rest of the family in the long run.

SPOILING IS NOT COMMON

339. I emphasized way back in Section 3 that it's not true—as some people and some doctors say—that babies are always looking for opportunities to get their parents under their thumbs. They do have legitimate needs—for food, for playthings, for physical affection, for comforting when in pain, for reassurance when frightened, for a response to their sociable advances, for an always dependable love, for confidence that when they ask for **reasonable** help or **reasonable** pleasure, their parents will pay attention and give some kind of fair reply. To satisfy such needs as these will not spoil a baby or a child.

To be specific, about a sleep disturbance for example, if a baby who has generally slept well unexpectedly wakes crying at night, the parents should of course go to him promptly, to comfort him, and find out if possible what the cause is.

However, there are a few situations—not in the first month or two—in which a baby becomes accustomed to an excessive amount of attention, because of some physical distress or because the parents are overly eager, anxious, or submissive, and then he may have trouble giving it up.

340. Can you spoil a baby? This question comes up naturally in the first few weeks at home if a baby, let's say a boy, is fussing a lot between feedings instead of sleeping peacefully. You pick him up and walk him around and he stops crying, at least for the time being. Lay him down, and he starts all over again. I don't think you need to worry much about spoiling in the first month or even the first 3 months. The chances are great that such a young baby is feeling miserable inside. If he stops fussing when picked up, it's probably because the motion and distraction and perhaps the warm pressure on his abdomen from being held make him forget his pains or tensions at least temporarily. Even if you decide later that he has been somewhat spoiled from an early age, you can usually undo the harm in a few days, in the first 4 or 5 months.

341. You can be a little more suspicious by 3 months. By the time babies are about 3 months old, the commonest causes of physical misery—colic, irritable crying, fretfulness—are over in a great majority of cases. (A very few babies go on having severe colic until 4 or 5 months old.) You notice that the baby who was previously colicky no longer wakes suddenly with cramps and distension. The baby who suffered from irritable crying or fretfulness no longer has distinctly miserable spells that contrast with comfortable periods. Naturally, some of these babies who have been held and walked a great deal for 3 months straight are mildly spoiled. They want their walking and their company anyway. Now it's sensible to become a little less tenderhearted. I don't mean that you should turn severe all of a sudden. But when it's bedtime you can tell your baby cheerfully but firmly that he has to sleep and that you have to go, even if he yells for a few minutes. The more severe form of this problem is discussed in Section 383.

342. A parent who's too eager to amuse. A mild kind of spoiling occurs when parents or grandparents are so delighted with the new baby they are regularly playing with him most of the time he's awake—carrying him around or dancing with him or jouncing him on their knees or playing pat-a-cake or making him laugh. (Everyone does these a little.) Gradually the baby forgets how to amuse himself. He feels bored, deserted, and miserable when left alone and cries for attention. What started out as fun for the parents becomes an endless chore.

343. A parent who feels tense and anxious. Let's take the example of a mother who can't stand to hear her baby fret, even for a minute, and carries him most of the time he's awake. By the age of 6 months he cries immediately and holds out his arms to be picked up just as soon as she puts him down. Housework has become impossible. She can't help resenting her slavery, but she can't tolerate the indignant crying either. This situation—which is rare—is different from that of a mother in our society, or in a simpler one, who **willingly** picks up her baby at the slightest whimper, or carries him in a sling all day even if he doesn't fret. I suspect that the tense parent's original anxiety was communicated to the baby and made him uneasy, and certainly he feels her increasing resentment; the combination sets up a tug-of-war.

344. Some causes of spoiling. Why does a parent get involved in these ordinary types of spoiling? In the first place, it usually happens with the first baby and all of us come near it with our first. For most people a first baby is the most fascinating plaything in the world. If an adult can be obsessed for a while with a new car, it's easy to see why a baby is all-absorbing for months. But delight is not the only factor. Parents are apt to project all the hopes and fears they've had about themselves onto their firstborn. There's the anxiety, too, the unfamiliar sense of being entirely responsible for the safety and happiness of a helpless human being. The baby's crying makes a powerful demand on you to do something. With your second baby you have more assurance and a sense of proportion; you know that children have to be denied some things for their own good, and you don't feel guilty about being hardhearted when you know for sure it's right.

But some parents are more easily drawn into spoiling than others—for instance, parents who have had to wait a long time for a baby and suspect that they may not be able to have another; parents with too little confidence in their own worthiness who become willing slaves to a child and expect her or him to be all the things they felt they never could be; parents who have adopted a baby and feel that they have to do a superhuman job to justify themselves; parents who have studied child psychology in college or nursing or medicine or have worked professionally in the field and feel doubly obligated to prove their capability (actually, it's a tougher job when you know the theory); parents who are ashamed when they've felt cross at the baby and try to even things up by giving him anything he wants; parents who feel too angry or guilty when they hear a baby crying and find the tension unbearable. See also Section 554 on overprotection.

Whatever the underlying factor, all these parents are a little too willing to sacrifice their own comforts and their own rights, too anxious to give their babies anything they ask for. This might not be too bad if babies knew what was sensible to ask for. But they don't know what's good for them. It's their nature to expect firm guidance from the parents. This comforts them. When the parents are hesitant it makes babies uneasy. If parents always anxiously pick babies up whenever they fuss—as if it would be terrible to leave them there—the babies, too, get the feeling that this would be terrible. And the more parents submit to the babies' orders, the more demanding the children become. (A human being of any age finds himself or herself imposing on a person who is too submissive.)

345. How do you unspoil? The earlier you detect the problem, the easier it is to cure. But it takes a lot of willpower and a little hardening of the heart. To get yourself in the right mood you have to remember that, in the long run, unreasonable demandingness and excessive dependence are worse for babies than for you and get them out of kilter with themselves and with the world. So you are reforming them for their own good.

Make out a schedule for yourself, on paper if necessary, that requires you to be busy with housework or anything else for most of the time the baby is awake. Go at it with a great bustle—to impress the baby and to impress yourself. Say you are the mother of a baby boy who has become accustomed to being carried. When he frets and raises his arms, explain to him in a friendly but very firm tone that this job and that job **must** get done this afternoon. Though he doesn't understand the words, he does understand the tone of voice. Stick to your busy work. The first hour of the first day is the hardest. One baby accepts the change better if his mother stays out of sight a good part of the time at first and talks little. This helps him to become absorbed in something else. Another adjusts more quickly if he can at least see his mother and hear her talking to him, even if she won't pick him up. When you bring him a plaything or show him how to use it, or when you decide it's time to play with him a bit at the end of the afternoon, sit down beside him on the floor. Let him climb into your arms if he wants, but don't get back into the habit of walking him around. If you're on the floor with him, he can crawl away when he eventually realizes you won't walk. If you pick him up and walk him, he'll surely object noisily just as soon as you start to put him down again. If he keeps on fretting indefinitely when you sit with him on the floor, remember another job and get busy again.

346. Chronic resistance to sleep in infancy—going-to-bed type. This is a difficulty that develops insidiously. In most cases it grows out of a case of colic or irritable crying. It can be thought of as a form of spoiling. A baby girl has been miserable with colic most evenings for her first 2 or 3 months. Her parents have found that she is more comfortable when they carry her around. This makes them feel better, too. But by the time she is about 3 or 4 months old, it gradually dawns on them that she doesn't seem to be in so much pain or misery any more—her cry is now angry and demanding. She wants her walking because she's used to it and thinks she's entitled to it. She almost glares at her mother when she sits down for a well-needed rest as if to say, "Woman, get going!"

A baby who becomes engaged in a nightly struggle to keep parents walking has to really train herself to stay awake, and she succeeds step by step as the months go by—first to 9 P.M., then to 10, 11, even midnight. Her parents say her lids often close and her head droops while they're carrying her, but that as soon as they start to lay her down she wakes with an indignant yell.

Such a sleep problem is exhausting to baby and parents. The baby is apt to become more irritable in the daytime, too, and may eat less well. The parents can't help getting more and more irritated and resentful. A baby shouldn't be able to put adults through a performance like this every night. They know it but don't know what to do about it. Even a baby senses, I think, that she shouldn't be able to get away with such tyranny.

The habit is usually easy to break once the parents realize that it is as bad for the baby as it is for them. The cure is simple: Put the baby to bed at a reasonable hour, say good night affectionately but firmly, walk out of the room, and don't go back. Most babies who have developed this pattern cry furiously for 20 or 30 minutes the first night, and then when they see that nothing happens, they suddenly fall asleep! The second night the crying is apt to last only 10 minutes. The third night there usually isn't any at all.

It's hard on the kindhearted parents while the crying lasts. They imagine the worst: that the baby's head is caught in the slats of the crib, or that she has vomited and is lying in a mess, that she is at least in a panic about being deserted. From the rapidity with which these sleep problems can be cured in the first year, and from the way the babies immediately become much happier as soon as this is accomplished, I'm convinced that they are only crying from anger at this age. It's important not to tiptoe in to be sure the baby is safe or to reassure her that you are nearby. This only enrages her and keeps her crying much longer. Some parents find it very helpful to set a kitchen timer (for themselves) for 20 or 30 minutes, so that they can look at the timer when they're convinced that the baby has been crying for hours. See Section 554 on overprotection.

If the several nights of crying will wake other children or anger the neighbors, you can muffle the sound by putting a rug or blanket on the floor and a blanket over the window. Soft surfaces of this kind absorb a surprising amount of the sound.

It's sometimes worthwhile to explain the program to touchy neighbors in order to reassure them that it will take only a few nights and to ask their indulgence.

347. Waking-in-the-night type. In this form the baby goes to bed and to sleep like an angel but develops a habit of waking in the middle of the night, most often in the second half of the first year or early in the second year. Sometimes it starts from an ear infection that wakes him with real pain. When the doctor makes the diagnosis the parents may feel guilty that they hadn't suspected a physical disease. So when the baby stirs and whimpers on succeeding nights, they hurry in, apprehensively, to comfort him, though it's actually very unlikely that the pain has recurred. I suspect that the baby catches some of their anxiety and, in addition, enjoys all this partying in the middle of the night. Sometimes the wakefulness seems to start during a painful stage of teething. All babies, like older people, half wake a number of times each night to shift position. When they have been picked up and treated to company and a snack for several nights, I imagine they learn to rouse themselves from half awake to wide awake, to have more fun.

In a few cases a baby may come to wake not just once, but several times, to stay awake longer and longer each time, to demand not just company but to be walked, and to resist being put back to bed by furious crying.

Most cases can be cured easily. The baby has to learn that there is nothing to be gained by waking and crying. This can usually be accomplished in 2 or 3 nights by letting her cry and not going to her at all. It is apt to be 20 to 30 minutes the first night (it may seem much longer), 10 minutes the second night, none the third.

One additional requirement is necessary, in my experience. The baby must not see the parents when she wakes up. If she sees them, even though they pretend to be asleep, this angers her and stimulates her to keep up the crying indefinitely. It is essential to put her bed in a different room from theirs, at least for a few nights, until the habit is broken, no matter how inconvenient this may be. If this is absolutely impossible, a screen or curtain can be rigged to prevent her seeing the parents. Read the other suggestions in the previous section.

At a clinic in Los Angeles which specializes in the common behavior problems of infants and small children, the staff are consulted frequently about sleep problems. They believe that these waking-in-the-night problems between 6 and 18 months are primarily due to separation anxiety (Section 551), and that the best treatment is for the parent to go into the baby's room, sit down beside the crib without turning on the light, and keep murmuring something reassuring such as "Don't worry, Mommy is right here. Go back to sleep now," until the baby does so. This treatment will probably need to be repeated for several nights. Certainly if it works it will be easier on parents and child than letting the child cry for 2 or 3 nights. If the baby simply won't go back to sleep or if the waking continues for weeks, you can use the less tender-hearted method.

348. The spoiled baby who vomits. Some babies (and young children) vomit easily when enraged. The parent is apt to be upset and shows it by anxious looks, by rushing to clean up, by being more sympathetic afterward, by being quicker to come to the baby at the next scream. This lesson is not lost on children, and they are likely to vomit more deliberately the next time they're in a temper. And they also come to be frightened by the vomiting they induce, because their parents are frightened by it. I think it is essential that parents harden their hearts to the vomiting if the baby is using it to bully them. If they are trying to get the baby over a refusal to go to bed, they should stick to their program and not go in. They can clean up later after the baby has gone to sleep.

COMMON KINDS OF INDIGESTION

Consult the doctor promptly about any change in your baby's digestion. Don't try to diagnose it yourself—there is too much chance of error. There are many other causes of vomiting, cramps, and loose movements besides those mentioned here. This discussion is primarily to help parents to adjust to a few common types of mild chronic indigestion of early infancy, after the doctor has made the diagnosis.

349. Hiccups. Most babies hiccup pretty regularly after meals in the early months. It doesn't seem to mean anything, and there is nothing that you need to do, aside from seeing if they have a bubble. If a drink of warm water stops the hiccups, there's no harm in giving it.

350. Spitting and vomiting are common. The word "spitting" is popularly used when the stomach contents spill gently out of the baby's mouth, usually in small amounts. The muscle valve at the upper end of the stomach just doesn't hold the contents down well, the way it does in an older child or adult. Any movement may cause the spitting: joggling, squeezing too tightly, laying the baby down, or just the digestive motions of the stomach itself.

Most babies do considerable spitting during the early months, and this usually means nothing. Some spit several times after every feeding. Others do it only occasionally. (Milk stains can be more easily removed from sheets, diapers, and clothing if they are first soaked in cold water.)

The word "vomiting" is used when the stomach contents are ejected with enough force to propel them at least a few inches away from the mouth. It alarms new parents when their baby first vomits a large amount of milk. But this is not serious in itself if the baby seems otherwise healthy. There are a few babies who vomit a large amount as often as once a day, especially the hypertonic babies (Section 335) and especially in the early weeks. Naturally, if your baby spits or vomits regularly even though continuing to gain, you should discuss it with the doctor—particularly if there are other signs of indigestion. It is worthwhile taking extra care to bring up the bubble. In most cases the spitting goes right on, no matter how you change the formula or decrease the quantity.

The question occurs to you: If babies have vomited what seems like their whole feeding, should they be fed again right away? If they seem happy enough, don't feed them, at least until they act very hungry. The stomach may be a little upset, and it is better to give it a chance to quiet down. Remember that the amount vomited usually looks larger than it actually is. There are babies who you would swear are vomiting most of every feeding but who still go on gaining satisfactorily.

Whether or not the spit-up milk is sour and curdled is not important. The first step in digestion in the stomach is the secretion of acid. Any food that has been in the stomach for a while is acidified. The effect of acid on milk is to curdle it.

Occasionally the valve between the esophagus (the tube that leads from the mouth to the stomach) and the stomach isn't as strong in a baby as it is in most other babies. This baby might then be more likely to vomit if she's put down in a horizontal position right after a feeding, because the milk leaks out from the stomach back up into the esophagus. In these situations, the baby won't be gaining weight as well as you want her to and the doctor may suggest keeping the baby in an infant seat for 30 minutes after each feeding. This will usually prevent the milk from leaking through this valve (you may hear the name "Gastro-Esophageal Reflux" applied to this condition).

In most babies the tendency to spitting is greatest in the early weeks and months, and decreases as they get older. Most have stopped it altogether by the time they can sit up. Occasionally it goes on until the child is walking. Once in a while babies only start spitting when they are several months old. Sometimes teething seems to make it worse for a while. Spitting is messy and inconvenient but not important if the baby's gaining well and is happy.

All that I have been saying about how common it is for babies to spit and to vomit occasionally doesn't mean that you never have to take vomiting seriously. A baby who begins vomiting all feedings right after birth must be watched carefully by the doctor. Usually it's due to mucus in the stomach and clears up in a few days, but once in a great while it's more serious, especially if there is green bile in it, and requires prompt medical or surgical treatment.

351. Worrisome vomiting in pyloric stenosis. Another uncommon form of vomiting is most apt to begin when the baby is several weeks old. It is called pyloric stenosis. In this condition, the valve leading from the far end of the stomach into the intestines will not open up satisfactorily to let the food through. It is more common in boy babies. The food is vomited out with great force (projectilely), so that it lands at a distance from the baby's mouth. The vomiting may occur during or shortly after the feeding. It doesn't mean that your baby has this condition if he has projectile vomiting once in a while. But if he has projectile vomiting as often as twice a day, he **must** be under careful medical observation. If the diagnosis is definite, an operation will probably be necessary. The operation is a very simple one and the baby usually only has to be in the hospital for a few days at the most.

If your baby has not been a vomiter and then suddenly

vomits a large amount for the first time, it's a good idea to take his temperature to make sure that the child is not sick. Many different infections start with vomiting in a baby. If there is no fever and the baby looks entirely normal, don't worry. If the baby seems sick in any other way or vomits again, call the doctor.

Vomiting that comes on suddenly later in infancy, especially if there is pain or if there is green bile in the vomitus, may mean obstruction of the intestines, as in intussusception (Section 775) or strangulated hernia (Section 778). It requires immediate attention.

352. Mild indigestion and gas. In 3-month colic, babies have regular spells of misery that seem to have more to do with the time of day than with what they are having to eat. But other babies may develop a spell of indigestion that's more continuous. Common symptoms are discomfort and fretting, passing gas by rectum, increased spitting and vomiting, bowel movements that are partly loose, partly curdy, and perhaps greenish. These cases are more likely to be improved by changes in the formula than are cases of 3-month colic. If you have a doctor or can reach one, you should, of course, consult her or him about the baby's indigestion even if the baby is gaining. It is absolutely necessary to consult a doctor if a baby is having trouble and not gaining weight.

CONSTIPATION

353. What's constipation and what isn't? Generally speaking, constipation refers to hard, dry stools, which are difficult to pass. It's not the number of bowel movements each day which determines whether or not a baby (or older child or adult) has constipation.

One baby always has a bowel movement at the same time of day, another at a different time each day. One is just as healthy as the other. There is no advantage to be gained by trying to make the irregular baby regular. In the first place, it can't usually be done. In the second place, there's a danger, in the long run, of upsetting babies emotionally if you keep trying to get a movement out of them when they aren't ready.

It isn't constipation when a breast-fed baby has a movement only every other day, because the movement is still very soft, and there is no reason why a baby needs to have a movement every day. Perhaps you could call it a kind of constipation when the baby strains unsuccessfully to get this liquid movement out, but it's not the ordinary kind.

354. Hard movements with the bottle-fed baby. One type of constipation is when the movements of a baby on cow's milk become hard and formed. They may be uncomfortable for the baby to pass. Consult your doctor about this. If you cannot reach a doctor, there are two remedies you can try. The simplest is to change the sugar in the formula to one that is more laxative. If you have been using light corn syrup, change to the dark. If this is not sufficient or if the baby has been on granulated sugar, use brown sugar. (You use the same amount as you were using of granulated sugar or corn syrup.) This kind of constipation is also helped by adding prune juice or pureed prunes to the baby's diet. You can start with 2 teaspoonfuls of the prunes (stewed or canned) or the juice (homemade, from stewed prunes, or canned prune juice) at the 6 P.M. feeding. If this isn't enough, increase to 4 teaspoonfuls of prunes or juice, or even more. Some babies get cramps from prunes or prune juice, but most take it all right.

355. Chronic constipation is less common in the older baby or child, especially those taking a varied diet including whole grain cereals, vegetables, and fruits. If your child becomes constipated, take it up with the doctor—don't try to treat it yourself, because you aren't sure what it is due to. It's very important, whatever treatment you use, that you do not get children concerned about their bowel function. Don't get into serious conversations about it with them, or connect it with germs or their health or how they feel. Don't encourage them to keep track of their movements, or seem to pay too much attention to them yourself. Avoid enemas. Do what the doctor recommends as matter-of-factly, cheerfully, and briefly as possible, whether it's diet, medication, or exercise, without going into the whys and wherefores with the child; otherwise you may turn the child into a hypochondriac.

But suppose you are unable to consult a doctor, and your little boy, otherwise healthy, gradually gets into a spell of constipation. (Naturally, if there is any symptom of illness, you get your baby to the doctor or hospital somehow.) Give him more fruit or vegetables, if he likes either, two or three times a day. If he likes prunes or figs, serve them every day. Fruit and vegetable juices help, too. See that he has plenty of exercise. If he is 4 or 5 or older, and in spite of your efforts with diet continues to have rather constipated and irregular movements that don't hurt him, relax until you can get a doctor's help.

Mineral oil is not considered safe for a baby. If he chokes on it, some may get breathed into the lungs and possibly cause a chronic kind of pneumonia.

356. Hirschsprung's disease. This is a rare but total type of constipation which is present from birth and causes a progressive distension of the abdomen. It is caused by a congenital absence of the nerves which normally cause the intestinal muscles to contract, in a certain section of the large intestine. Diet has no effect. To cause any movement, enemas may have to be given. This type of constipation needs intensive investigation and perhaps surgical treatment.

357. Psychological constipation. There are two varieties of constipation that are largely psychological in origin and that start most frequently between the ages of 1 and 2. If children at this age have one or two painfully hard movements, they may tend to hold back for weeks or even months afterward for fear of being hurt again. If they hold the movement in for a day or two, it's apt to be hard again, and this keeps the problem going. It's discussed in Section 438. Occasionally when a parent goes at toilet training in too overbearing a manner, small children, being in an independent stage in their development, automatically resist and hold the movement back, which leads to constipation. This is discussed in Section 428.

358. Painful movements and BM softeners. Painfully hard movements should be treated promptly in a child of 1, 2, or 3 years, to avoid the vicious circle of withholding and further constipation.

There are several preparations with which you can soften a small child's BMs. Neo-Cultol (Fisons Corp.) is a chocolate-flavored mixture of acidophilus bacilli and mineral oil for the relief of constipation. A teaspoonful each evening is usually enough to keep the movements soft. Another satisfactory preparation is Colace (Mead Johnson Co.)—in the syrup form—of which the dose for a 1- or 2-year-old would be 1 or 2 teaspoonfuls. A third medication is mineral oil. It is irritating to the lungs when choked on, so should not be given to children until they can take a medication cooperatively, sitting up. It has another disadvantage: As you increase the dose from 1 teaspoonful to 2 and perhaps 3, it may first not be sufficient and then may begin to leak out, which may worry the child who is trying to stay clean. But it may be useful enough if you are in a situation in which you can't get Neo-Cultol or Colace.

None of these medications will act as a cathartic to soften and hurry an already hard movement. (A carthartic is a medicine which makes the intestinal muscles contract and cause a bowel movement.) They will only keep movements from becoming hard. They should be given every day for at least a month to a child who has developed painfully hard movements—to allow the child to become confident that the painful hardness will not recur—then reduce the dose gradually. But if the hardness returns, the medication should be given regularly for another month or for as long as is necessary.

359. Temporary constipation is common during illness, especially if there is fever. In former days parents and doctors often felt it was the most important symptom to treat and that children couldn't begin to recover until they were "cleaned out." Some people even believed that the constipation was the main cause of the illness. It's more sensible to realize that any disease that can make a person feel sick all over is apt to affect the entire stomach and intestinal system, slowing down the bowels, taking away the appetite, perhaps causing vomiting. These symptoms may appear several hours before any others. If you are delayed in reaching a doctor, you needn't feel that valuable time is being lost.

If you **have** to treat a sick child without a doctor, don't worry too much about the bowels. It's better to do too little than too much. If a child isn't eating anything, there isn't much for the bowels to move. Fluids can be offered frequently.

360. Spastic constipation. In this kind of constipation, the movement comes out as a collection of small hard balls. It occurs on a cow's-milk formula or on a regular solid-food diet. The sections of the large intestine go into spasms and hold small pieces of the bowel movement until they become dried into little balls. Nobody knows why the intestines of some people have this tendency. It may be due to nervous tension in some cases. It is often hard to cure. Sometimes it is helped by changes in the formula or diet, but frequently not. A child may outgrow spastic constipation at any age. If there is a delay in consulting a doctor, you can try the suggestions in Section 358.

DIARRHEA AND DEHYDRATION

361. Looseness and diarrhea in babies. A doctor thinks of diarrhea as meaning a significant loss of body fluid through the bowels. Therefore, movements that are only mildly loose and that are only slightly more frequent than usual are not diarrhea. So we'll call that looseness. A baby's intestines are sensitive the first year or two. They may be upset not only by the germs that cause diarrhea in older individuals but by one or another vegetable, by cold germs, and by other germs that don't affect older children and grown-ups at all. This is why we try to protect babies from infections in others, prepare their milk so carefully, make formula changes gradually, add new foods slowly.

If the movements have been good but suddenly become loose, you should assume that the baby has a mild intestinal infection, even though it is only caused by a nose cold. There are usually other changes, too. The stools are likely to be more numerous. The color often changes, most commonly to greenish. The odor is usually different.

Most intestinal infections are mild and can be cured easily if they are treated early. An infection should be considered **severe** if **any** of the following symptoms are present: watery stools; pus or blood in the stools; vomiting; fever of 101°F or more; the baby looks prostrated or has sunken eyes with gray circles under them.

Even for a mild infection you ought to get in touch with the doctor promptly, because the sooner treatment is started, the lighter the disease will be and the quicker over. If the baby has any of the symptoms that point to a severe infection with diarrhea, it is vitally important to get to the doctor or to take the baby to a hospital, even if this involves a long trip.

Two rare types of chronic diarrhea are discussed in Section 776.

362. Treatment of looseness, until you can consult a doctor. It will often be several hours before you can get advice from the doctor, and in the rare case of a baby who is hundreds of miles from nowhere, it may not be possible to reach one at all. So the following emergency suggestions are given. But they should not encourage any parents to treat diarrhea or looseness themselves if they can possibly consult a doctor.

The baby who is on the breast alone should continue to nurse. If the baby wants less than usual, so much the better—it gives the intestines more rest. Omit any solids the baby is taking until you can talk to the doctor or the looseness is cured. Most cases do well with breast milk.

If your baby is on formula alone and develops a looseness, dilute each bottle in half until you can speak to the doctor. If the bottles have already been prepared with the usual formula, pour off half the quantity, add an equal amount of water. Make one or two extra bottles with the formula you are pouring off. If you are just making the formula, do it the usual way but put only half the usual amount into each bottle and then add an equal amount of water. Make one or two extra bottles with the remaining formula, weakened the same way. This method of weakening a formula may sound wasteful, but it's safer than getting all mixed up in more complicated arithmetic. Besides, it's convenient to have an extra bottle or two of formula. A baby whose formula has been weakened may suddenly get very hungry.

Let the baby take as little of each bottle as satisfies her. But if on this weak formula she gets hungry more often, feed her more frequently. If you **have** to continue to treat her yourself, try to keep her on half-strength formula until the movements have been normal or nearly normal for a whole day and until she is hungry for more. If she isn't hungry enough to demand a stronger formula, it's probably a sign that she's still ill and that it's safer not to increase yet. If a looseness isn't much improved in 3 or 4 days, you should consider it more serious and make a greater effort to reach the doctor.

If a baby on both formula and solid foods develops a looseness, omit all solids until you consult the doctor or until the looseness is over. If the baby is not hungry for the formula or has not improved in a day, dilute the formula as in the paragraph above. When the baby is well, get the formula back to normal first before resuming the solids. In putting the solids back, go slowly. Ripe banana, applesauce, rice cereal, and toast are good to start with. Add only one more type of food each day. Give one-third the usual amount the first day, two-thirds the second day, the full amount the third day. Resume the usual foods in something like the following order: (1) applesauce; (2) white cereal; (3) meat; (4) vegetables; (5) potato or other starch; (6) other fruits. For example, the first day you might give a third of the usual serving of applesauce; the second day two-thirds of the usual amount of applesauce and a third of the usual serving of meat. Naturally, you don't add any foods at this time that the baby was not taking before.

363. Emergency treatment of severe intestinal infection, until you can reach a doctor. If a baby develops any of the symptoms pointing to a severe infection (very loose or watery stools, pus or blood in the stools, vomiting, fever of 101°F or more, prostration, or sunken eyes), give only a special formula made without milk as follows:

water . . . . .1 quart
corn syrup or granulated sugar. . .1 level tablespoonful

Special formulas for diarrhea, in liquid and powdered form, are widely available in drugstores and many large grocery stores. They contain various salts in the proper quantities, in addition to sugar.

Give 1 to 4 ounces every 2 or 3 hours if the baby is awake and wants it, until you can talk to the doctor. If you are compelled to go on treating the illness yourself, keep your child on this special formula alone for 24 to 48 hours, depending on how soon the bowel movements improve in appearance. Then proceed **very** gradually. I will list the possible stages in increasing the diet. If recovery is rapid, advance one stage each day. If slow, take 2 days for each step.

Stage 1. You now want to use a diluted milk formula with the lowest possible amount of fat and sugar. (If you're not sterilizing, you don't have to use boiled water.)

If your baby has been on fresh whole milk, dilute it in half with an equal amount of boiled water. No added sugar.

If your baby has been on a prepared commercial formula, dilute it in half. With the concentrated form, instead of 13 ounces of formula and 13 ounces of boiled water, use 7 ounces of formula and 19 ounces of boiled water. With the powdered form, instead of 15 level tablespoonfuls of powder and 30 ounces of water, use 7 level tablespoonfuls and 30 ounces of water.

If you have been using an evaporated milk formula, let's say 13 ounces of milk and 19 ounces of water plus sugar or syrup, use 6 ounces of evaporated milk, 24 ounces of boiled water, and no sugar or syrup.

If you have been using a powdered milk formula with sugar or syrup, cut the number of tablespoonfuls of powder in half and omit the sugar or syrup.

Whatever kind of diluted formula you have made, you might put only about two-thirds of the usual amount into each bottle, since the baby may not want the usual volume; then you can use the remainder to make a couple of extra bottles, in case she has to be fed more often. Let her take just as little at each feeding as satisfies her; better too little than too much.

Stage 2. If you have been using, in Stage 1, a diluted evaporated milk or fresh whole milk formula, keep it diluted (because it has fat in it) but add 2 tablespoonfuls of syrup or sugar.

If you have been using a diluted prepared formula, keep it diluted (because it contains fat) and add 1 tablespoonful of syrup or sugar.

Stage 3 (if the bowel movements are normal). The usual formula.

Stage 4 and after. Add solids gradually, as in the last section.

If the movements become somewhat looser, drop back two stages. If the diarrhea becomes severe again, go all the way back to the special formula without milk and make a greater effort to get to a doctor.

When diarrhea is improving, the first movement of the day is apt to look better, and a later one not so good. This in itself should not discourage you, but it shows that it is safer to see what the afternoon movements are like before strengthening the formula or adding to the diet. A sympathetic parent who is told to cut a baby's formula or diet way down during diarrhea is apt to cry out, "But my child will be hungry." Maybe so, maybe not. But it's kinder to make babies a little unhappy for a day or two than to let their diarrhea get worse, for in the latter case you would have to starve them for longer in the end.

By the time a child is 2 or more, there is much less chance of severe or prolonged diarrhea. Until the doctor can be reached, the best treatment is bed rest and such fluids and soft solids as water, skimmed milk, gelatin, junket.

364. Dehydration (excessive loss of body water). This can become a problem, especially in severe diarrhea. If your baby begins to show any signs of dehydration, you have to get her to a doctor or to a hospital as soon as possible. These are some signs of dehydration that you can watch for: diapers being wet less than every 6 to 8 hours; no tears when the baby cries; no saliva in the baby's mouth; a sunken appearance to the soft spot on the top of the head; and sunken eyes.

RASHES

Consult the doctor about all rashes. It's easy to be mistaken.

365. Bluish mottling. Babies who have pale skins often show a bluish mottling of the skin of the body when undressed.

366. Diaper rash. Most babies have sensitive skins in the early months. The diaper region is particularly apt to suffer. You may bring your baby home from the hospital with a sore behind. This doesn't mean that the hospital has been neglectful, but only that this baby's skin needs extra care. The commonest forms of diaper rash are collections of small red pimples and patches of rough, red skin. Some of the pimples may become mildly infected and develop whiteheads (pustules) on them. If the rash is bad, raw spots may appear.

In the early months the rash is thought most often to be caused simply by the effect of constant wetness on a tender skin. Almost all babies develop a few spots of diaper rash from time to time. If it is slight and goes away as fast as it came, no special treatment is necessary. It is wise to discontinue the use of waterproof pants while there is any rash.

If a baby in the early months tends to have a persistent rash, it is necessary to discontinue the use of waterproof pants, at least while the rash remains. Try the diaper liners that keep the skin drier. After the bath or after washing the diaper area, wipe off all the soap with clear water on a washcloth. (Soap can sometimes be irritating or even favor infection when it hardens on the skin the way it hardens on the tub in a ring.) When the skin really needs a protective coating, use petroleum jelly or an ointment which combines petroleum jelly and lanolin. These are relatively durable compared to powder, lotion, and oil, which get wiped off easily. If the rash is worse in the folds than on the prominences it is probably a **seborrheic** rash; this usually responds to a steroid ointment, which your doctor may prescribe. If there are many pimples with pus in them and especially if the baby develops fever, this may be a rash caused by the **staphylococcus.** Your doctor may need to prescribe an antibiotic. A **yeast** rash will have bright red spots which often come together to form an area which is solidly red, bordered by the red spots. A special ointment will have to be prescribed by the doctor for this rash also.

As a baby grows older, the skin becomes less easily irritated by urine. Diapers that go to the diaper service are sterilized there. When diapers are simply washed at home, there is no sterilization and some of the bacteria in them stay alive. There is a particular type of bacteria named "ammonia-genes" which manufactures ammonia out of urine and which is not readily killed by soap or detergent. It may accumulate in the diapers, the nightclothes, and the bedclothes. The ammonia will be noticed especially in the morning when the blanket is turned back. It may even make your eyes water. When there is a bad diaper rash after 6 months of age and particularly after a year, it is usually caused by ammonia. See Section 768 for sore on the end of the penis.

If a diaper rash is severe and persists, especially if there is the smell of ammonia in the nightclothes, add ½–1 cup of clear white vinegar to the last rinse water for the diapers, nightclothes, the bedclothes, and everything that gets wet with urine. The clothes should smell slightly of vinegar when they come out of the dryer.

A simple and inexpensive antiseptic is the ordinary hypochlorite laundry bleach used in the normal manner (one cup of bleach per load, added to the water before the diapers or other clothing are added). Another suggestion is to resume the diaper service, even though you don't need that many diapers; this doesn't take care of sterilizing the nightclothes and bedclothes though, if the rash is caused by ammonia. Drying diapers (and night- and bedclothes) in the sun is a good way to kill most bacteria.

When a rash is bad, and especially if there are a lot of pustules (whiteheads), it usually works better not to use an ointment but to expose the whole diaper area to the air for several hours a day, keeping the baby in a warm room. You can cover the chest and the legs with 2 separate light blankets. Fold a diaper underneath the baby to catch some of the urine. Exposing a bad diaper rash to the air is the surest method of curing it, whether there are pustules or not.

If your baby has a tendency to develop bad diaper rash easily and frequently, you can experiment to see which precautions, used regularly, work best and with least effort: drying the diapers in the sun, or using vinegar in the last rinse, or boiling the diapers, or using ointment. Used regularly, one or the other of these or a combination may do the trick. If it seems necessary, you can change diapers not only before and after feedings but also midway between feedings.

Diapers from a diaper service are usually sterilized, so there is no point in boiling them again. Some diaper services also use a special antiseptic in the last rinse to discourage any growth of bacteria after the diaper has been wet by the baby.

Irritating bowel movements during an attack of diarrhea sometimes cause a very sore rash around the anus. The treatment is to try to change the diaper just as soon as it is soiled, clean the area with oil, and apply a thick covering of an ointment made with petroleum jelly and lanolin. If this does not work, the diaper should be left off and the diaper area exposed to the air.

367. Mild face rashes. There are several mild face rashes that babies have in the first few months that aren't definite enough to have names but are very common. First of all, there are minute shiny white pimples without any redness around them. They look like tiny pearls in the skin. They will surely go away as the baby gets older. Then there are collections of a few small red spots or smooth pimples on the cheeks. These may last a long time and get a parent quite upset. At times they fade and then get red again. Different ointments don't seem to do much good, but these spots always go away eventually. Less common is a rough, red patch on the cheeks that comes and goes.

Salmon patches are flat, pink-to-red, irregularly shaped spots on the eyelids or forehead ("angel kisses") or the nape of the neck ("stork bites"). The facial spots almost always disappear completely. The spots on the neck may continue into adulthood. **Mongolian spots** are blue-gray patches in the skin in dark-skinned babies. They're usually around the buttocks and may be scattered in other areas. They almost always disappear completely in the first two years. There may also be **splotchy red patches** which are a ¼–½ inch in diameter, some of them with a tiny white pimple head. They come and go on different parts of the face. (If there are larger, pus-filled blisters or pimples, this is an infection and needs to be reported promptly to the doctor.) **Strawberry birthmarks** are tiny at the beginning and usually grow and stick out from the surface of the skin during the first 6 months or so. Almost all of them will disappear by age 2. No treatment is necessary.

Babies in the early weeks often have white blisters in the middle part of their lips from sucking. Sometimes the blisters peel. These clear up in time and need no treatment.

368. Prickly heat. Prickly heat is very common in the shoulder and neck region of babies when hot weather first begins. It is made up of clusters of minute pink pimples surrounded by blotches of pink skin. Tiny blisters form on some of the pimples, and when they dry up they give the rash a slightly tan look. Prickly heat usually starts around the neck. If it is bad, it can spread down onto the chest and back and up around the ears and face. It seldom bothers a baby. You can pat the rash several times a day with a bicarbonate of soda solution (1 teaspoonful of bicarbonate of soda to 1 cup of clean water) on absorbent cotton. Another treatment is dusting with cornstarch powder. It is more important to try to keep the baby cool. Don't be afraid to take off a baby's clothes in very hot weather.

369. Cradle cap. Cradle cap is a mild disorder of the skin of the scalp. It is quite common in the early months. It appears as scalp patches that look dirty. The best treatment is daily washing with soap and water. You can try oiling the patches and then washing with a mild dandruff shampoo and brushing out the scales that come from the patches. Cradle cap rarely persists beyond the early months.

Eczema is discussed in Section 733.

Impetigo and other common rashes are discussed in Section 740.

MOUTH AND EYE TROUBLES

370. Thrush. Thrush is a mild fungus infection of the mouth. It looks as if patches of milk scum were stuck to the cheeks and tongue and roof of the mouth. But, unlike scum, it does not wipe off easily. If you do rub it off, the underlying skin bleeds slightly and looks inflamed. Thrush usually makes babies' mouths sore. They show the discomfort when they are trying to nurse. A baby's mouth is more apt to become infected with thrush if the rubber nipples are handled carelessly. But it also occurs in babies who are taken care of to perfection. If you suspect it, consult the doctor promptly for diagnosis and treatment. If there is a delay in getting medical advice, it is helpful to have the baby drink half an ounce of boiled water that's been allowed to cool, or suck it from a piece of sterile absorbent cotton, after the milk. This washes the milk out of the mouth and gives the thrush fungus less to live on.

Don't be fooled by the color of the inner sides of the gums where the upper molar teeth are going to be. The skin color here is normally very pale, and is sometimes mistaken for thrush by mothers who are on the lookout for it.

Cysts on the gums. Some babies have one or two little pearly white cysts on the sharp edge of their gums. They may make you think of teeth, but they are too round and they don't make a click on a spoon. They have no importance and eventually disappear.

371. Discharge and tearing of the eye. Many babies develop a mild inflammation in the eyes a few days after birth. This is probably caused by an immature tear duct which is often partially obstructed. It doesn't require any treatment.

If at any later time the baby has an inflammation that makes the whites of the eyes look bloodshot or even pink, it is probably an infection, and the doctor should be called promptly.

There is another kind of very mild but chronic infection of the eyelids that develops off and on in the early months in quite a number of babies, most commonly in only one eye. The eye waters and tears excessively, particularly in windy weather. White matter collects in the corner of the eye and along the edges of the lids. This discharge may keep the lids stuck together when the baby first wakes up. The condition is caused by an obstructed tear duct. The tear duct leads from a small opening at the inner corner of the eyelids, first toward the nose, then down the side of the eye socket and into the nose cavity. When this duct is partly plugged, the tears are not drained off as fast as they form. They well up in the eye and run down the cheek. The lids keep getting mildly infected, just because the eye is not being cleansed sufficiently by the tears. The doctor should, of course, see the eyes and make the diagnosis.

The first thing to realize about this condition is that it is fairly common, not serious, and does not injure the eye. It may last for many months. The tendency is outgrown in most cases even if nothing is done. If by a year it is still bothersome, an eye doctor may clear the duct with a simple procedure. When the lids are stuck together, you can soften the crust and open them by moistening your fingers or a clean washcloth with water. The doctor sometimes advises massage of the duct, but don't do this without a doctor's directions. A plugged tear duct does not cause inflammation of the white of the eye. If the eye is bloodshot, something else is wrong and you should call the doctor.

372. Crossed eyes. It is common for a baby's eyes to turn in or out too much **at moments** in the early months. In most cases they become steady and straight as the child grows older. If, however, the eyes turn in or out **all the time or much of the time,** even in the first month, or if they are not steady by 3 months, an eye doctor should be consulted (Section 780). Many times parents think their baby's eyes are crossed when they are really straight. This is because the skin area between the eyes (over the bridge of the nose) is relatively wider in a baby than in an older person; so the amount of white of the eye showing on the inner side of the iris (toward the nose) is much smaller than the white on the outer side (toward the ear). Another reason babies' eyes sometimes appear crossed is that when they are looking at something in their hands they have to converge (cross) the eyes a lot to focus on it, because the arm is so short. They are only converging their eyes normally, the way we adults do to a lesser extent. Their eyes won't get stuck that way. If you think your baby's eyes may be crossed, you can check the image of a light as it's reflected in the baby's pupils. If the image of the light is always located symmetrically on the baby's pupils, it's unlikely that the eyes are crossed.

The main reason why it is important for infants' eyes to be examined promptly, when there is a question about whether they are straight, is because a crossed eye or a walleye will gradually become nonseeing if efforts are not begun early to make the child use it. When the two eyes do not coordinate and converge on an object, each eye will be seeing a somewhat different scene. The children will be "seeing double." This is confusing and uncomfortable for them. So automatically they learn to ignore and suppress the vision of one eye. They gradually make that eye blind—not in the sense of a physical change—it's a psychological process. If this goes on too long, it will become impossible to ever bring back the vision in that eye. This has been called "lazy eye." The eye doctor's job is to promptly put the lazy eye back to work, usually by having the child wear a patch over the good eye a large part of the time. The doctor may prescribe glasses to further encourage the coordinated use of the two eyes. Then comes the decision whether there should be an operation, in addition. Occasionally several operations have to be performed before the result is satisfactory.

Parents often ask whether it is safe to hang toys over the crib, since the baby sometimes is cross-eyed looking at them. Don't hang a toy right on top of a baby's nose, but it's perfectly all right to hang it at arm's reach.

It's not uncommon in a newborn baby for the lid of one eye to droop a little lower than the other or for one eye to look smaller. In most cases, these differences become less and less noticeable as the baby grows older. The baby's eyes should be examined, to be sure that they are straight.

SWOLLEN BREASTS

373. When the baby has swollen breasts. Many babies, both boys and girls, have swollen breasts for some time after birth. In some cases a little milk runs out. This is caused by the glandular changes in the mother just before the baby is born. Nothing needs to be done for swollen breasts in the baby; the swelling will surely disappear in time. The breasts should **not** be massaged or squeezed, since this is likely to irritate and infect them.

VAGINAL DISCHARGE

374. Girl babies may have a mucous or even occasionally slightly bloody vaginal discharge at birth. This is usually due to a response to the changing hormones in the mother's body just before birth and doesn't require any treatment.

BREATHING TROUBLES

375. Sneezing. Babies sneeze easily. Sneezing doesn't usually mean a cold unless the nose begins to run, too. It is most often caused by dust and dried mucus that has collected in a ball in the front of the nose and tickles. If the breathing is obstructed, see Section 281.

376. Faint breathing. New parents usually worry a little about a new baby's breathing because it is often irregular and at times so shallow that they can't hear it or see it. They may worry, too, the first time they hear their baby snoring faintly while asleep. Both conditions are normal.

377. Chronic noisy breathing occurs in a certain number of young babies. In one form the babies make a snoring noise in the back of the nose. It's just like a grown-up snoring, except that babies do it while they are awake. It seems to be caused by the fact that they haven't yet learned to control their soft palates. They'll outgrow it.

The commoner type of chronic noisy breathing is caused in the larynx (voice box). The epiglottis, a fleshy structure just above the vocal cords, is so soft and floppy in some babies that it is sucked down and made to vibrate. This causes a loud rattling, snoring noise during breathing in, which doctors call stridor. It sounds as if the babies were choking, but they can breathe that way indefinitely. In most cases the stridor occurs only when the babies are breathing hard. It usually goes away when they are quiet or asleep. It may be better when they lie on the abdomen. It should be discussed with the doctor, but no treatment is necessary or does any good. Stridor goes away as the baby grows older.

Noisy breathing that comes on acutely, particularly in an older infant or child, has an entirely different significance from the chronic variety. It may be due to croup, asthma, or other infection, and requires **prompt** medical attention.

Every baby with noisy breathing, chronic or acute, should be examined by a doctor.

Obstruction in the nose from dry mucus is discussed in Section 281; obstruction from moist mucus during a cold, in Section 707.

378. Breath-holding spells. Some babies get so furiously angry when they cry, and hold their breath so long, that they turn blue. When this first happens, it scares the wits out of the parents. It seldom means anything except that the baby has that kind of temperament. (It's often a baby who's unusually happy at other times.) The doctor should be told about it so that at the next visit he or she can make sure that everything is all right physically; otherwise nothing needs to be done. It's not a reason for keeping babies from ever crying. If you pick them up every time they cry they're likely to get spoiled.

COMMON NERVOUS SYMPTOMS

379. Babies who startle easily. Newborn babies are startled by loud noises and by sudden change in position. Some are much more sensitive than others. When you put babies on a flat, hard surface and they jerk their arms and legs, it's likely to rock the body a little. This unexpected motion is enough to make sensitive babies nearly jump out of their skins and cry with fright. They may hate the bath because they are held so loosely. They need to be washed in their parent's lap and then rinsed in the tub, while held securely in both hands. They should be held firmly and moved slowly at all times. They gradually get over this uneasiness as they grow older. See Section 335 on the hypertonic baby.

380. The trembles. Some babies have trembly moments in the early months. The chin may quiver, or the arms and legs may tremble, especially when the baby is excited or is cool just after being undressed. This trembling is nothing to be disturbed about. It is just one of the signs that the baby's nervous system is still young. The tendency passes away in time.

381. Twitching. Some babies twitch occasionally in their sleep, and once in a while there is one who twitches frequently. This, too, usually disappears as the baby grows older. Mention it to the doctor as something to check.

Comforters and Thumb-sucking

This chapter is about the wide variety of things and methods that small children use to comfort themselves with, when they are tired or unhappy: a stuffed animal or a piece of fabric to stroke, a pacifier, thumb, or bottle to suck, a habit like rocking or head rolling.

From the age of 6 months onward, when they first begin to feel somewhat separate from the parents, they use these sucking, stroking, or rocking habits at tired or unhappy moments to bring back the complete, enveloping security which the parent formerly provided.

SIX-MONTH INDEPENDENCE AND THE NEED FOR COMFORTERS

382. The first sense of separateness. We believe that at about 6 months of age babies begin to realize dimly that they are separate persons. Perhaps it would be more accurate to say that their unfolding instincts make them begin to insist on a slight physical separateness from the parent who takes the major part of their care and on their right to do some things for themselves; and that they then become aware of the importance of this separateness to themselves. I am thinking of the way many 6-month-olds show impatience with being cuddled in their parent's arms any longer, during bottle or solid-food feedings; they try to sit up straight instead. They want to hold on to their own bottle. They may even try to get their parent's hand off it by jerking it sideways. From now on—until they are fully mature adults—children will continue to insist on a gradually increasing independence, emotional as well as physical.

383. Comforters to recapture the security of early infancy. But the young child over 6 months old, when very tired or frustrated, craves to slip back to early infancy, when being fed in a parent's arms was all there was to paradise. (Psychologists call this tendency to retreat under stress "regression"; even the competent adult may become childishly helpless or demanding when ill.) On the other hand, they are unwilling to give up the precious bit of independence which they have achieved since they were tiny. This is where various comforters come in. By means of them, the infant attains pleasure and security without giving up independence. Thumb-sucking or pacifier-sucking reminds them of the pleasure of being fed from breast or bottle in their parent's arms. Stroking a cuddly toy animal or a cherished blanket or diaper recalls the good sensation when they gently stroked their mother's clothing or the blanket they were wrapped in during feeding. (Puppies and kittens have an instinct to stroke their mother's breasts when nursing, which helps to make the milk flow. The human infant's impulse to stroke while nursing is perhaps a remnant of the same instinct in our prehuman ancestors.) When they rock themselves against a stuffed chair back or roll their heads from side to side in bed, they are creating again the rhythmic soothing they experienced as fretful young infants when their parent rocked or walked them.

The little girl (or boy) recreates certain comforting aspects of her parents out of the cuddly toy and her thumb for example; **but** it's not a parent who can envelop her or control her; it's a parent **she** can control. (It's interesting to see how a young child will sometimes abuse the object which is so precious to her; she will slap it crossly or slam it heartlessly against the furniture.)

Why do I make such an issue over comforters? Partly because it gives us an understanding of the great psychological importance to children of establishing independence, which they begin to do by 6 months, and of the meaning of regression. But also, in a very practical way, it explains a number of perplexing things about early childhood. For instance, I think that thumb-sucking in the **first** half year of infancy is simply an expression of babies' need to suck, especially when they're hungry. But after 6 months thumb-sucking becomes something else: a reminder of early infantile comfort, which children now need only when they're sleepy or upset. That is to say, the thumb becomes a comforter, such a precious comforter that most children won't give it up again until 3, 4, or 5 years of age.

Similarly the pacifier changes its meaning after the age of 6 months, from a satisfier of the sucking need to a comforter at regressed times of day. But the pacifier is not usually as precious as the thumb; most children will give it up at 1 or 2 years of age if the mother does not continue to encourage its use. (A child is apt to suck thumb or pacifier, not both.)

The meaning of the bottle changes, too. I think that the reason that many babies become more and more attached to the bottle after 6 months is that their parents have fallen into the habit of handing them their bottle to drink by themselves in bed. In this way the bottle becomes a precious comforter; if children become intensely attached to it in this way, they are apt to remain very attached to it until 1½ or 2 years of age, whereas the bottle given while the child is sitting in the parent's lap cannot become a precious comforter in place of the parent—because the parent is right there.

Some children do not adopt any stroking comforter such as a cuddly toy or piece of cloth, nor a sucking comforter such as a precious bottle, pacifier, or thumb. I don't know why. I haven't been able to see any psychological differences between those who do and those who don't. I don't know of any important reason to encourage children to adopt a precious comforter or to discourage them, except for certain practical considerations in regard to the bottle in bed (Section 238 and 272) and the pacifier (Section 395).

384. The strokable comforter. In my experience the children who are thumb suckers are more likely than the non–thumb suckers to become attached to a strokable comforter also. It's as if they regress (slip back) to early infancy through the thumb-sucking pleasure and then want to add the pleasure of stroking something, too.

Some children develop an intense attachment to an object which lasts for several years; others develop only a mild attachment which weakens after a while; still others shift from one object to another.

When the attachment to a cuddly toy or piece of cloth is intense, it is apt to raise practical problems for the parents. The child may want to carry the object at all times, everywhere. It is going to become increasingly dirty and eventually tattered. Usually the child objects vigorously to a washing or cleaning of the object and will reject a substitute altogether. If the object gets lost the child will be in real despair and will probably be unable to go to sleep for hours.

I think it is unfair (and it's usually impossible) to try to break a child's attachment to a comforter after it has been well formed. However, I've known a couple of parents who were ingenious and firm enough to keep the problem within bounds because they felt very strongly about this: They insisted from the beginning that the object must stay in the child's room, or at least in the house.

It is better to sneak a blanket or diaper away from the child at night, at regular intervals, for washing and drying **before** it ever gets gray, so that it won't change so drastically in color and smell. (The smell of a comforter may be an important part of it to some children.) Better still would be to acquire a duplicate and identical toy or piece of cloth, and to keep substituting the clean one from time to time, without the child knowing. The trouble is that you usually don't realize when the toy is bought for the 3- or 6-month-old that it's going to become priceless to the baby at 15 months. It is impossible to wash and dry most animals overnight. You can do a fair job of washing the surface with soap and water on a washcloth or brush. Dry with an electric fan. (Don't use cleaning fluid; you won't be able to get it all out by morning.) Some stuffed animals, depending on what they're stuffed with, can be put into an old nylon stocking (to hold them together) and put through the washer and dryer that way.

Is there any harm in letting a child become dependent on a cuddly comforter and take it to bed? None that I know of except the parents' distress at its dinginess. There is no way to prevent its happening anyway. Almost all children will receive soft toys during the first year and it's usually not until they're 15 or 18 months old and begin to insist on carrying one object with them that their parents realize what has happened.

Children will probably outgrow the dependence at some time between 2 and 5 years of age. (A few will cling longer.) It's wise for the parent to remind them in an encouraging tone—a couple of times a year, not every week—that someday they'll be a big girl or boy and won't need it any more. This kind of hint and confidence helps them to outgrow it as soon as they are able.

THUMB-SUCKING

385. The meaning of thumb-sucking. The main reason that young babies suck their thumbs seems to be that they haven't had enough sucking at the breast or bottle to satisfy their sucking need. Dr. David Levy pointed out that babies who are fed every 3 hours don't suck their thumbs as much as babies fed every 4 hours, and that babies who have cut down on bottle-feeding time from 20 minutes to 10 minutes (because the nipples have become old and soft) are more likely to suck their thumbs than babies who still have to work for 20 minutes. Dr. Levy fed a litter of puppies with a medicine dropper so that they had no chance to suck during their feedings. They acted just the same as babies who don't get enough chance to suck at feeding time. They sucked their own and each other's paws and skin so hard that the fur came off.

All babies aren't born with the same amount of instinct to suck. One baby never nurses more than 15 minutes at a time and yet never once has put a thumb in the mouth, and another whose bottles have always taken 20 minutes or more thumb-sucks excessively. A few begin to thumb-suck in the delivery room, and they keep at it. I suspect that a strong sucking instinct runs in some families. We now know that some babies suck their thumbs while they're still in the uterus and some are even born with sucking blisters on their hands or arms.

You don't need to be concerned when babies suck their thumbs for only a few minutes just before their feeding time. They are probably doing this only because they're hungry. It's when babies try to get their thumbs just as soon as their feeding is over, or when they suck a lot between feedings, that you have to think of ways to satisfy the sucking craving. Most babies who thumb-suck start before they are 3 months old.

I might add here that the thumb-, finger-, and hand-chewing that almost all babies do from the time they begin to teethe (commonly around 3 or 4 months) should not be confused with thumb-sucking. Naturally, the baby who is a thumb sucker is sucking at one minute, chewing at another, during his teething periods.

If your baby girl begins to try to suck her thumb or finger or hand, I think it's preferable not to stop her directly but to try to give her more opportunity to suck at the breast or the bottle or the pacifier. The most effective method by far to prevent thumb-sucking is the ample use of the pacifier in the first 3 months (Section 395), if the parents are willing. In addition there are two other matters to consider: the number of feedings, and how long each feeding takes.

386. The time to pay attention to thumb-sucking. The time to pay attention to thumb-sucking is when babies first try to do it, not when they finally succeed. I make this point because there are lots of babies who, for the first few months of their lives, haven't much control over their arms. You see such babies struggling to get their hands up, and searching around with their mouths. If by good luck they get their fists to their mouths, they suck them vigorously as long as they happen to stay there. These babies, just as much as the skillful thumb suckers, are showing a need to suck longer at the breast or bottle.

The very young baby needs help most, because the sucking need is strongest in the first 3 months. From then on it tapers off. In most babies I think it's about gone by 6 or 7 months.

The thumb-sucking which persists after 6 months is a comforting device, not an expression of sucking need. See Section 383.

387. Thumb-sucking in breast-fed babies. I have the impression that breast-fed babies are less apt to be thumb suckers. This is probably because mothers are inclined to let them go on nursing as long as they want to. A mother doesn't know whether her breast is empty, so she leaves it up to the baby. When a baby, say a boy, finishes a bottle, it's done. He stops because he doesn't like to suck air or because his parent takes away the bottle. The first question, then, about a breast-fed baby who is trying to suck his thumb is: Would he nurse longer if allowed to? If so, let him nurse for 30 or even 40 minutes at times if this is convenient for you. (To go beyond 40 minutes is too time-consuming.) A baby gets most of the milk from a breast in 5 or 6 minutes; the rest of the time he's satisfying his craving to suck, lured on by a small trickle of milk. In other words, if he nurses for 35 minutes, he gets only slightly more milk than if he had nursed for 20. A breast-fed baby, allowed to nurse as long as he wants, may vary surprisingly. He is satisfied with 10 minutes at one feeding and wants as much as 40 minutes at another. This is an example of how breast-feeding is adaptable to a baby's individual needs.

If a baby being nursed on one breast each feeding doesn't want to nurse any longer, there's nothing that you can do to make him. But if he is getting **both** breasts at each feeding and begins to suck his thumb, there are two methods you can try to make him nurse longer. See if he can be satisfied with one breast at each feeding, nursing as long as he will. If his hunger can't be satisfied that way, then at least let him nurse longer at the first breast. Instead of taking him off in 10 minutes, let him stay on for 20, if he will. Then put him to the second breast for as long as he wants.

388. Thumb-sucking in bottle babies. With the average bottle-fed baby, thumb-sucking is most likely to begin at about the time he learns to finish the bottle in 10 minutes instead of in 20. This happens because babies get stronger as they get older, but the rubber nipples get weaker. Bottles with plastic screw-on caps have nipples with a special opening near the edge for air intake. You can slow down this kind of bottle by screwing the cap on tighter. This partly blocks the air intake, keeps more of a vacuum in the bottle. The next thing to do is to get new nipples, leave the holes as they are, and see if that lengthens the bottle time. Of course, if the nipple holes are **too** small, some babies stop trying altogether. Try to keep the nipple holes small enough so that a bottle takes 20 minutes anyway, at least during the first 6 months. In this discussion, I am talking about the actual number of minutes that the baby is sucking. Naturally, it wouldn't help to lengthen the feeding time by pausing in the middle of the feeding.

389. With a thumb sucker, it's better to go slowly in omitting feedings. It's not just the length of each feeding, but also the number or frequency of feedings in the 24 hours that determines whether a baby satisfies the sucking instinct. So if a baby is still thumb-sucking even though you have made each breast or bottle feeding last as long as possible, it is sensible to go slowly in dropping other feedings. For example, if a 3-month-old baby seems willing to sleep through the 10 P.M. feeding but is doing a good deal of thumb-sucking, I would suggest waiting a while longer before dropping it—perhaps a couple of months, provided the baby is still willing to drink when awakened.

390. The effect on the teeth. You may be worried about the effect of thumb-sucking on the baby's jaws and teeth. It is true that thumb-sucking often pushes the upper front baby teeth forward and the lower teeth back. How much the teeth are displaced depends on how much children suck the thumb and, even more, on what position they hold their thumbs in. But dentists point out that this tilting of the baby teeth has no effect on the permanent teeth that begin coming in at about 6 years of age. In other words, if the thumb-sucking is given up by 6 years of age—as it is in a great majority of cases—there is very little chance of its hurting the permanent teeth.

But whether thumb-sucking displaces the teeth or not,

many parents prefer to have their child give it up as soon as possible. The suggestions I have been making are the ones that I think will end thumb-sucking soonest.

391. Why not use restraints? Why not tie babies' arms down or put aluminum mittens over their hands to keep them from thumb-sucking? This would frustrate them a great deal, which theoretically is not a good idea. Furthermore, it usually doesn't cure the baby who is thumb-sucking a lot. We have all heard of despairing parents who use elbow splints or metal mitts or bad-tasting paint not just for days but for months. And the day they take off the restraint, the thumb pops back in the mouth. To be sure, there are some parents who say they have had good results from using such restraints. But in most of these cases, the thumb-sucking was very mild. Many babies do a little thumb-sucking off and on. They get over it quickly, whether you do anything or not. I think, myself, that restraints only make the confirmed thumb sucker do it more in the long run.

392. Thumb-sucking in the older baby and child. Up to now we have been talking about how thumb-sucking begins in the early months. But by the time a baby, say a girl, is 6 months old, thumb-sucking is turning into something different. It is a comforter that she needs at special times. She sucks when she is tired or bored or frustrated, or to put herself to sleep. When she can't make a go of things at the more grown-up level, she retreats to early infancy when sucking was her chief joy. This need for comforters is discussed in Section 383.

Even though thumb-sucking satisfies a different need after the age of 6 months, it's of course the baby who first sucked the thumb to satisfy the sucking need who goes on doing it now for comfort. It's very rare for a child beyond the age of 6 months or 1 year to begin to thumb-suck for the first time.

There is no point worrying about lengthening the sucking time of the 6-month-old or 12-month-old. Is there anything that the parents need to do? I don't think so, if the child is generally outgoing, happy, and busy, and sucks mainly at bedtime and occasionally during the day. In other words, thumb-sucking by itself is not a sign of unhappiness or maladjustment or lack of love. In fact, most thumb suckers are very happy children. (And the children who are **severely** deprived of affection don't thumb-suck.) On the other hand, if a little girl is sucking a great deal of the time instead of playing, parents should only ask themselves whether there is anything they ought to do so that she won't **need** to comfort herself so much. Another girl may be bored from not seeing enough of other children or from not having enough things to play with. Or perhaps she's having to sit in her carriage for hours. A boy of 1½ may be at loggerheads with his mother all day if she is always stopping him from doing all the things that fascinate him instead of diverting him to playthings that are permissible. Another boy has children with whom he can play and freedom to do things at home, but he's too timid to throw himself into these activities. He thumb-sucks while he watches. I give the examples only to make it clear that if **anything** needs to be done for excessive thumb-sucking, it is to make the child's life more satisfying.

Elbow splints, mitts, and bad-tasting stuff on the thumb only make the child miserable and don't stop the habit any more often in older children than they do in small babies. I think that they tend to prolong the habit. The same applies to scolding a child or pulling his thumb out of his mouth. I remember the story of Anne, who finally stopped sucking her thumb of her own accord at 3. Six months later her Uncle George, who had been the member of the family who used to nag her about it, came back to the house to live. Anne's thumb-sucking began again the minute he entered the house. You often hear the recommendation that you give children a toy when you see them thumb-sucking. It certainly is sound to have enough interesting things around for them to play with so that they won't be bored. But if every time their thumb goes in the mouth you jump toward them and poke an old toy into their hands, they'll soon catch on. What about bribing? If your child is one of the rare ones who is still thumb-sucking at the age of 5, and you are beginning to worry about what it will do to the permanent teeth when they come in, you will have a fair chance of succeeding if the bribe is a good one. A girl of 4 or 5 who wants to get over her thumb-sucking may be helped by having her fingernails painted like a woman's. But practically no child of 2 or 3 has the willpower to deny an instinct for the sake of reward. You're apt to make a fuss and get nowhere.

So if your boy (or girl) is thumb-sucking, see to it that his life is good. In the long run it will help him if you remind him that someday he will be grown-up enough to stop. This friendly encouragement makes him want to stop as soon as he is able. But don't nag him. Most important of all, try to stop thinking about it. If you keep on worrying, even though you resolve to say nothing, the child will feel it and react against it. Remember that thumb-sucking goes away all by itself in time. In the overwhelming majority of cases, it is over before the second teeth appear. It doesn't go away steadily, though. It decreases rapidly for a while, and then comes back partway during an illness or when the child has a difficult adjustment to make. Eventually it goes for good. It rarely stops before 3 years. It usually peters out between 3 and 6.

Most of the babies who go on thumb-sucking until they are 1 or more years old do some kind of stroking at the same time. One little boy rubs or plucks a piece of blanket, or diaper, or silk, or a woolly toy. Another strokes an earlobe or twists a lock of hair. Still another wants to hold a piece of cloth right up close to his face and perhaps stroke his nose or lip with a free finger. These motions remind you of how younger babies used to be gently feeling their mother's skin or clothing when they were suckling at the breast or bottle. And when they press something against their faces, it looks as though they were remembering how they felt at the breast. These habits are discussed in Section 383.

393. Ruminating. Sometimes babies or young children get in the habit of sucking and chewing on the tongue until the last meal comes up (somewhat the way a cow's does), a practice known as ruminating. It's a rare condition. Some cases begin when thumb-sucking babies have their arms restrained. They turn to sucking their tongues instead. I would certainly advise letting such babies have the thumb back immediately, before the ruminating becomes a habit. Be sure, also, that the baby has enough companionship, play, and affection. It is said that the meals stay down better when they consist entirely of solids. That means cooking the milk into the cereals and puddings. Other cases of rumination occur in families in which there is marked disturbance in the parent–child relationship.

THE PACIFIER

394. A pacifier is helpful for fretfulness or to prevent thumb-sucking. A pacifier is a "blind" nipple (without a hole in it) attached to a disk that rests against the baby's lips to keep the nipple from being pulled entirely into the mouth. On the back of the disk is a ring by which the pacifier can be held by the baby.

One satisfactory style is made of one piece of soft rubber, which means that it won't bother the face if the baby goes to sleep on it and, more important, the baby won't be able to pull the nipple off the disk and choke on it. The only trouble with this shape of pacifier is that the long nipple may reach the back of the throat and gag a young baby. There is also a pacifier that has a short nipple with a ball-shaped end. Some newborn babies take this one better, probably because it's smaller and softer. Another type has the nipple flattened on one side; claims have been made by the manufacturer for the good effects of this design; however, there is no scientific evidence.

A baby who has periods of mild irritability can often be entirely quieted by having a pacifier to suck. We don't know whether this is because the sucking soothes some vague discomfort or simply keeps the baby's mouth busy. For colic, in which the pain is much more definite, the pacifier usually gives at least partial relief.

Irritable crying and colic are about over in most cases by 3 months or so, and the use of the pacifier can then be stopped so that it won't become a long-lasting habit.

395. The pacifier, if used right, is an efficient way to prevent thumb-sucking. Most of the babies who use the pacifier freely for the first few months of life never become thumb suckers, even if they give up the pacifier at 3 or 4 months.

Some would say then: What's the use of a pacifier to avoid

thumb-sucking when pacifier-sucking is just as unattractive? The answer is that babies who become regular thumb suckers in their first 3 months (and about half of all babies do) will continue to be thumb suckers until 3, 4, or 5 years of age, sometimes longer. By contrast, a majority of the babies who become pacifier suckers are ready to give it up by 3 or 4 months. Whereas they used to suck it eagerly for long periods, they now spit it out soon after it's put in their mouths, or even immediately. Most of the rest give it up by 1 or 2 years of age. This is a lot younger than the thumb is given up.

Another advantage is that pacifier-sucking is less likely to push the teeth out of position than thumb-sucking.

396. Parents' reluctance to start and reluctance to stop the pacifier. There are two problems that interfere with the most efficient use of the pacifier. In many cases where its use would be helpful, the parents are reluctant to use it at all or, more often, come around to trying it so late that the baby, who would have taken to it in the first weeks, won't take to it now. The parents' reluctance is natural enough. A majority of people dislike the appearance of a pacifier bobbing around in a baby's face, especially in one old enough to be walking around; and that face is apt to have a faraway, "dopey" expression when the baby is sucking the pacifier. But though many parents reject the pacifier when the doctor suggests it, they often change their minds a few weeks later, after learning from a friend or relative how well it can work.

The second problem is that the parents who have used the pacifier successfully for fretfulness or colic are apt to develop such a dependence on it—for comforting the baby any time there is a whimper—that they can't get over the habit of popping it into baby's mouth many times a day, even after the infant is old enough to be ready to give it up (usually between 2 and 4 months). Then the baby is apt to develop, at 5, 6, 7 months, a dependence that lasts until a year or a year and a half.

Pacifier-sucking (like thumb-sucking) up to 3, 4, 5 months of age is a way in which a baby who needs extra sucking can get it. But by 3 or 4 months the sucking need is decreasing. Many babies begin to spit the pacifier out; their regular nursing apparently gives them all the sucking they want. By 5 or 6 months the sucking need may be about gone (as is shown most clearly in the way some breast-fed babies now express disinterest in nursing). So if a parent continues to offer the pacifier after about 4 months, either because the baby is one of the minority who hasn't had enough of it yet, or because it has become a habit that the parent can't stop, the pacifier-sucking becomes a comforting habit which the baby may then not be willing to give up until 1, 1½, 2 years of age.

If a baby isn't willing to give up the pacifier—at any age—I don't think it's right to take it away. But I think there are very good reasons to stop offering it at 3 or 4 months to babies who are showing, by spitting it out soon after it is put in their mouths, that they really don't need it or want it any more. The relatives who don't approve of pacifiers will quiet down. There won't be any displacement of the teeth.

How would you use the pacifier to prevent thumb-sucking? In the first place, many babies—perhaps 50 percent—never try to thumb-suck at all or do it only casually and for brief periods. In these, there is nothing to prevent and no need to get involved with the pacifier (unless there is colic). On the other hand, you have to decide not on the basis of what your baby, say a boy, is actually accomplishing, but from what he is **trying** to do. If he tries after meals to get his thumb in his mouth and sucks eagerly when he succeeds, then there is good reason to consider the pacifier.

What age to start? If the baby becomes used to the thumb over a period of weeks or months, the chances are that he will refuse the pacifier. He has learned to enjoy not only the sensations in his mouth but the sensations in his thumb. So if you are going to use a pacifier, start it in the first few days and weeks of life.

What times of day? The logical time to offer the pacifier is whenever the baby is searching around with his mouth and trying to suck on thumb, fingers, wrist, clothing, or anything else he can reach. In the early months, a baby is seldom awake except before and after feedings, so these are the usual times. But if he's awake between feedings, I'd give it to him then, too. The idea is to give it to him not as little as possible, but as much as he can use it in the first 3 months, so that he will be satisfied and give it up as soon as he can.

I think it is preferable to remove the pacifier when the baby begins to be drowsy, if he doesn't object too strongly, or just as soon as he is asleep. A baby who is accustomed to having a pacifier in his mouth when asleep may, if it falls out, wake and cry unhappily until it is replaced. This can happen a dozen times a night—especially when a baby who has previously slept on his back learns to turn over on his abdomen—and it can be an awful nuisance.

You will know the baby is ready to give up the pacifier when he begins to spit it out soon after it's put in his mouth, or when he just seems happy without it. I wouldn't try to get him off the pacifier in one day, though. Take a week or two to cut down and don't be afraid to increase again for a day or two if he seems to have a special need for comforting. But decrease again when he's willing.

If your baby is still on the pacifier after 5 or 6 months and wakes several times a night because he's lost it, put several in his bed at bedtime so that there's a better chance of his finding one by himself. Or pin one to his nightie sleeve. (Don't put a long cord on a pacifier to hang it around the baby's neck or tie it to the crib bar. This can be dangerous, as the cord can become wrapped around the baby's finger, wrist, or neck.)

When a baby has a few teeth, he can pull the nipple of an old, tired pacifier off the disk or chew pieces out of the nipple. These pieces may cause serious choking if swallowed the wrong way. So buy new pacifiers when the old ones become at all weak or crumbly.

RHYTHMIC HABITS

397. Rocking, jouncing, head rolling, head banging. In rocking, a baby sitting in a chair or couch rocks hard against the back and lets it bounce her forward again. I call it jouncing when a baby gets on her hands and knees and rhythmically jounces down against her heels. This usually moves the crib across the room until it bangs monotonously against the wall. A baby may roll her head from side to side while lying on her back in bed. Head banging, in which a baby bangs the back of the head or forehead against the head of the crib, is of all these habits the most distressing to the parents. It makes them wonder whether the baby has any brains to start with and whether, if she does, she'll injure them.

What's the meaning of these rhythmic movements? I don't think we know all the answers but we have some ideas. These habits usually appear in the second half of the first year in the age period when babies naturally acquire a sense of rhythm and try to sway in time to music. (Is this to help them learn the rhythm of walking?) I think they are commoner in boys, who belong to the tenser sex. They are mainly carried out, like thumb-sucking or the stroking of a soft toy, when the child is tired, sleepy, or frustrated. So I think they come under the heading of comforters and may represent the wish to regress to the period of early infancy when the child was rocked and carried a lot. Read Sections 382–384.

If your baby boy bangs his head, you can pad his crib to keep him from bruising himself. One parent solved the baby's head-banging problem by sawing the headboard out of the crib and tacking a piece of canvas in its place. For the jouncing baby who rattles the whole house, you can put the crib on a carpet and tack the carpet to the floor, or tie some kind of homemade pads, preferably of rubber, onto the feet of the crib. Or you can put the crib against the wall, where it's going to end up anyway, and place a big wad of padding between the crib and the wall.

In any case, I would not scold the baby or try to restrain him.

The Development of Babies

WATCHING THEM GROW

398. They're repeating the whole history of the human race. There's nothing in the world more fascinating than watching a child grow and develop. At first you think of it as just a matter of growing bigger. Then, as the infant begins to do things, you may think of it as "learning tricks." But it's really more complicated and full of meaning than that. The development of each child retraces the whole history of the human race, physically and spiritually, step by step. Babies start off in the womb as a single tiny cell, just the way the first living thing appeared in the ocean. Weeks later, as they lie in the amniotic fluid in the womb, they have gills like fish. Toward the end of the first year of life, when they learn to clamber to their feet, they're celebrating that period millions of years ago when our ancestors got up off all fours. It's just at that time that babies are learning to use their fingers with skill and delicacy. Our ancestors stood up because they had found more useful things to do with their hands than walking on them.

Children in the years after 6 give up part of their dependence on parents. They make it their business to find out how to fit into the world outside their family. They take seriously the rules of the game. They are probably reliving that stage of prehuman history when our wild ancestors found it was better not to roam the forest in independent family groups but to form larger communities. Then they had to learn self-control, how to cooperate with each other according to rules and laws, instead of depending on the eldest of the family to boss them around.

As you watch your own baby grow, remember the advice in Section 4 of this book. Your appreciation of your child's development will be increased by reading such books as *Childhood and Adolescence* by L. Joseph Stone and Joseph Church,* and *The Magic Years* by Selma H. Fraiberg.** They tell not just what a child will probably do at different age periods, but something about what it means. Understanding what children are up to is the first step in learning to get along with them.

399. Slow developers. You watch your child, perhaps a boy, grow with a mixture of strong feelings. When he is coming along speedily, you are proud of him and proud of yourself for having produced him. As he shows his delight in his new accomplishments and in discovering the amazing world around him, you live over again the pleasantest part of your own childhood. But always you find that you are quick to worry if there are any signs that he is failing to keep up with his own progress or to keep up with other children you know about. You feel not only anxious but vaguely guilty. That's the way all good parents are made. Anything the slightest bit out of line makes them wonder whether they are caring for their child properly, whether they have given him a worthy inheritance, whether something they were made to feel guilty about in their own past is affecting him. The Bible speaks ominously of the sins of the father being visited on the children, and many of us parents were warned in similar words in our own upbringing.

Usually, slow development has nothing to do with inadequate care or inherited defects or the sins of the parents (real or imaginary).

Every child's development is different from every other child's and is a complex mixture of patterns, as was explained in Section 4. These are determined mainly by inheritance—

*New York: Random House, 4th edition, 1979.

**New York: Scribners, 1968.

normal inheritance, not faulty inheritance. Slow or fast walking, teething, talking, early or late puberty development, tallness or shortness, tend to run in families. But all these characteristics vary in the same family, because each family's inheritance is a great mixture.

Motor development covers such skills as holding the head erect, sitting, creeping, standing, walking. We have average statistics for each of these, but the variations are great among babies who are entirely healthy and normal.

There are a few rare diseases that interfere with motor development, but these can usually be diagnosed by a doctor. The overwhelming majority of cases of slow motor development—more than 9 out of 10—are simply a matter of normal variation.

Development of intelligence. It's particularly important for parents of a child who is slow in motor development to know that there is very little connection between this and intelligence. More than nine out of ten of the babies who are distinctly slow in motor development turn out to have normal intelligence. Incidentally, the development tests that are sometimes given in infancy (particularly in cases for adoption) are mainly tests of motor ability and social responsiveness. They reveal whether a baby has had a disease or injury to the brain and whether a baby has suffered emotionally from neglect. But aside from these conditions, they do not tell in the first year anything about what the child's intelligence will be in the future. Intelligence, which has to do with such abilities as reasoning and memory, cannot begin to be tested reliably until about 2 years of age.

Intelligence, in contrast to motor development, has a lot more to do with environment than with inheritance. Babies born to parents with low intelligence but adopted into average or bright families tend to develop an intelligence like that of their adoptive parents.

Social and emotional development may depend somewhat on the temperament that babies are born with—whether they are quiet or active, for instance—but most of all they depend on what experiences they have. There is no evidence that specific disturbances like untruthfulness, meanness, and delinquency are inherited.

Babies who are slow in development certainly need to be checked regularly by their doctor to be sure that there is no disease or condition that needs correcting. This is especially true if they are not only slow in motor development but also unresponsive to the people and things around them. Then they should have at least one consultation with a pediatrician, an eye specialist, and a hearing specialist.

400. They're wrapped up in themselves the first 2 or 3 months. In the period up to 2 or 3 months, babies haven't much contact with the outside world. Most of the time they seem to be listening to what their insides tell them. When they get the message that all is well, they are very peaceful. When the message is about hunger, or indigestion, or tiredness, they feel wholeheartedly wretched because there's nothing to distract them. It's an irritable period for some babies. One has colic, another has spells of irritable crying, a third always screams for a few minutes just before falling asleep.

As babies get beyond the 3-month period, they take a lot more notice of the world around them. They turn their heads in all directions, all by themselves, and seem pleased with what they see.

401. How a baby feels about strangers. You can get an idea of how a baby goes from phase to phase in development by watching the reaction to strangers at different ages. This is how it goes in a doctor's office for a typical baby, let's say a girl, until she's about a year old. At 2 months she doesn't pay much attention to the doctor. As she lies on the examining table, she keeps looking over her shoulder at her mother. The 3-month-old is the doctor's delight. She breaks into a body-wiggling smile just as often as the doctor is willing to smile and make noises at her. By about 5 months, the baby may have changed her mind. When the doctor approaches, she stops her kicking and cooing. Her body freezes, and she eyes him intently, suspiciously, maybe for 10 or 20 seconds. Then her abdomen begins to rise and fall rapidly. Finally her chin puckers, and she begins to shriek. She may get so worked up that she cries long after the examination is over. This is a sensitive period, when a baby may take alarm at anything unfamiliar, such as a visitor's hat or even her father's face if he hasn't been able to be with her and take care of her. Probably the main cause of this behavior is that she is now smart enough to distinguish between friend and stranger. If your baby is sensitive about new people, new places, in the middle of the first year, I'd protect her from too much fright by making strangers keep at a little distance until she gets used to them, especially in new places.

Some babies accept strangers in a fairly casual way until the end of the first year. But then everything changes. I think 13 months is the most suspicious age of all. The typical baby at this age scrambles to her feet when the doctor approaches and tries to climb off the table and onto her parent. She cries furiously, buries her face in her parent's neck, ostrich fashion. Every once in a while she stops just long enough to peer over her shoulder at the doctor, with looks like daggers. She usually stops crying and struggling soon after the examination is over. A few minutes later she may be happily exploring the office and even making friends with the doctor. There is more about handling the sensitiveness of the 1-year-old in Section 458.

402. A baby starts by using the head. It's a gradual process by which a baby learns to control his body. It starts with the head and gradually works down to the hands, trunk, and legs. Just as soon as he's born, he knows how to suck. And if something touches his cheek—the nipple or your finger, for example—he tries to reach it with his mouth. He's ready to do his part in nursing. If you try to hold his head still, he becomes angry right away and twists to get it free. Probably he has this instinct to keep from being smothered.

Parents ask, "When does he begin to see?" We now know that babies can begin to see much earlier than we used to think. They can tell the difference between faces and other objects in the first few days of life. In fact, careful experiments have shown that most babies will actually imitate different facial expressions within the first few days of life. In the early months they can't coordinate their two eyes very efficiently and often are cross-eyed momentarily.

We also now know that newborn babies hear and smell much better than we used to think. For example, a baby may startle all over when he hears a loud noise. And by one week of age, he can tell his own mother's nursing pad by its smell.

403. He smiles early, because he's a social being. Somewhere between 1 and 2 months of age, your baby smiles at you one day when you are talking and smiling to him. It's an exciting moment for you. But think what it means about his development. He knows little at this age; he can't use his hands or even turn his head from side to side. And yet he already knows that he's a sociable being, that it's nice to have loving people around, that he feels like responding to them. And if he's handled with plenty of affection and sensible firmness, he'll go on being friendly and reasonable just because it is his nature.

404. Using his hands. As soon as they are born, a very few babies can put their thumbs in their mouths any time they want to. But most can't get even their hands to their mouths with any regularity until they are 2 or 3 months old. And because their fists are still clenched tight, it usually takes them longer still to get hold of a thumb separately. But at about 2 or 3 months, many babies will spend days just looking at their hands, bringing them up until, surprised, they bang themselves in the nose—only to stretch their arms out and start all over again.

But the main business of hands is to grab and handle things. A baby seems to know ahead of time what he's going to be learning next. Weeks before he can actually grab an object, he looks as if he wants to and is trying. At this stage, if you put a rattle into his hand, he holds onto it and waves it. Around the middle of the first year, he learns how to reach something that's brought within arm's reach. At about this time, he'll learn how to transfer an object from one hand to the other. Gradually he handles things more expertly. In the last quarter of his first year, he loves to pick up tiny objects, like a speck of dust, carefully and deliberately.

405. Right- and left-handedness. The subject of handedness in children is a somewhat confusing one. Some babies stay ambidextrous for the first year or so and then gradually become right- or left-handed. Others show an early preference for the right or left hand that seems permanent. Others use one hand predominantly for several months and then shift to the other.

Scientists who are interested in handedness believe that it is an inborn trait that will sooner or later become evident in each individual, with approximately 10 percent of all people being left-handed. Handedness tends to run in families, so that some families will have several "lefties" and others may have none. Many specialists believe that forcing a left-handed child to become right-handed may cause stuttering or reading difficulties or emotional problems, so it seems best not to try to influence any baby or small child, for fear of confusing a possible left-hander.

If your baby seems ambidextrous, as he is likely to be when he first begins to hold things in the middle of the first year, or right-handed, then assume he is right-handed, hang his first crib toy nearer his right hand, and favor his right hand as you hand him toys and finger foods and, later, a spoon. But if from the very beginning he has a definite preference for the left or if later he begins to insist on using his left, I wouldn't argue or fight with him but leave him to his preference.

406. Rolling over and sitting up. The age when babies roll over, sit up, creep, stand up, or walk is more variable than the age when they get control of their head or arms. A lot depends on temperament and weight. A wiry, energetic baby is in a great rush to get moving. A plump, placid one is willing to wait until later.

A baby, by the age he first tries to roll over, shouldn't be left unguarded on a table for as long as it takes you to turn your back, unless he is secured with a strap. By the time he can actually roll over, it is not safe to leave him even in the middle of an adult's bed. It is amazing how fast such a baby can reach the edge.

Most babies learn to sit steadily (after being helped up) between 7 and 9 months. Some normal, intelligent ones wait till as late as a year. But before babies have the coordination to succeed, they want to try. When you take hold of their hands, they attempt to pull themselves up. This eagerness always raises the question in the parents' mind: How young can I prop my baby up in the carriage or high chair? Doctors feel that in general it's better not to prop babies straight up until they can sit steadily by themselves for many minutes. This doesn't mean that you can't pull them up to a sitting position for fun, or sit them in your lap, or prop them on a slanted pillow in the carriage, just as long as the neck and back are straight. It's the curled-over position that's not so good for long periods.

This brings up the question of a **high chair.** It is of greatest advantage when babies are eating meals with the rest of the family. On the other hand, falling out of a high chair is a common accident. If babies are to be eating most of their meals by themselves, I think it is preferable to buy a low chair–table arrangement. If you are going to use a high chair, get one with a broad base (so that it doesn't tip over easily) and a strap to buckle the baby in. Don't leave babies alone in a high or low chair after they have learned to creep or stand.

407. A toy or food while being changed. One of the things babies never learn is that they ought to lie still while being changed or dressed. It goes completely against their nature. From around 2 or 3 months, when they learn to roll over, until about a year when they can be dressed standing up, they struggle or cry indignantly against lying down, as if they have never heard of such an outrage.

There are a few things that help a little. One baby can be distracted by a parent who makes funny noises, another by a small bit of zwieback or cracker. You can have a special fascinating toy, like a music box, that you offer at dressing time only. Distract your baby just before you lay her down, not after she starts yelling.

408. Creeping (crawling). Creeping (some prefer the word crawling) can begin anytime between 6 months and a year. Some perfectly normal babies never creep at all; they just sit around until they learn to stand up. There are a dozen different ways of creeping, and babies may change their style as they become more expert. One first learns to creep backward, another somewhat sideways. One wants to do it on hands and toes with legs straight, another on hands and knees, still another on one knee and one foot. The baby who learns to be a speedy creeper may be late in walking, and the one who is a clumsy creeper, or who never learns to creep at all, has a good reason for learning to walk early.

409. Standing. Standing usually comes in the last quarter of the first year, but a very ambitious, wiry baby may do it as early as 7 months. Occasionally you see one who doesn't stand until after a year who seems to be bright and healthy in all other respects. Some of these are plump, easygoing babies. Others just seem to be slow getting coordination in their legs. I wouldn't worry about such children so long as the doctor finds that they are healthy and so long as they seem bright and responsive in other ways.

Quite a number of babies get themselves into a jam when they first learn to stand up but don't yet know how to sit down again. The poor things stand for hours until they are frantic with exhaustion. The parents take pity on their little boy and unhitch him from the railing of his playpen and sit him down. But instantly he forgets all about his fatigue and pulls himself to his feet again. This time he is crying within a few minutes. The best that a parent can do is to give him especially interesting things to play with while he's sitting, wheel him in the carriage longer than usual, and take comfort in the fact that he'll probably learn how to sit down within a week. One day he tries it. Very carefully he lets his behind down as far as his arms reach and, after a long moment of hesitation, lets go. He finds that it wasn't such a long drop and that his seat is well padded.

As the weeks go by, he learns to move around hanging on, first with two hands, then with one. Eventually he has enough balance to let go altogether for a few seconds when he is absorbed and doesn't realize what a daring thing he's doing. He is getting ready for walking.

410. Walking. Lots of factors determine the age when a baby walks alone: ambitiousness, heaviness, how well she can get places by creeping, illnesses, bad experiences. A baby just beginning to walk when an illness lays her up for 2 weeks may not try again for a month or more. Or one who is just learning and has a fall may refuse to let go with her hands again for many weeks.

Most babies learn to walk between 12 and 15 months. A few muscular, ambitious ones start as early as 9 months. A fair number of bright children, without rickets or any other physical disease, do not begin until 18 months or even later.

When a baby begins to walk, it raises a lot of minor problems, like shoes and discipline, but these are taken up in later sections.

You don't have to do anything to teach your child to walk. When her muscles, her nerves, and her spirit are ready, you won't be able to stop her. I remember a mother who got herself into a jam by walking her baby around a great deal before he was able to do it by himself. He was so delighted with this suspended walking that he demanded it all day long. Her back was almost broken.

A parent of an early walker may wonder whether it won't be bad for the baby's legs. As far as we know, children's physiques are able to stand whatever they're ready to do by themselves. Babies sometimes become bowlegged or knock-kneed in the early months of walking, but this happens with late walkers as well as with early walkers.

411. Feet and legs. All babies have feet that look flat the first couple of years, partly because they haven't built their arches yet, partly because their feet are so plump. As they learn to stand and walk, they exercise the muscles that help create the arch of the foot. (See next section.)

How straight the legs, ankles, and feet grow depends on several factors, including the pattern of development babies are born with. Some babies seem to have a tendency to knock-knees and ankles that sag inward. The heavy child is more apt to develop these conditions. Other babies seem to be born with a tendency to bowlegs and toeing in. I think this is especially true of the very active, athletic ones. Another factor may be the position babies keep their feet and legs in. For instance, you occasionally see a foot that becomes turned in at the ankle because the baby always sits with that foot tucked under in that position. It is sometimes suspected that babies have been made to toe in by always lying on their stomachs with their feet pointed toward each other, or by pushing themselves in a walker with the outside edges of their feet.

All babies toe out to some degree when they start to walk, and then gradually bring the front part of the feet in as they progress. One starts with the feet sticking right out to the side, like Charlie Chaplin, and ends up toeing out only moderately. The average baby starts toeing out moderately and ends up with the feet almost parallel. The baby who starts out with feet almost parallel is more apt to end up toeing in. Toeing in and bowlegs often go together.

The doctor at the regular examinations watches the ankles and legs from the time the baby begins to stand up. This is one reason why regular visits are important during the second year. If weak ankles, knock-knees, bowlegs, or toeing in develops, the doctor may recommend corrective measures. If there is any suspicion of rickets (soft bones due to insufficient vitamin D—a rarity nowadays in the United States), the doctor may have an X-ray picture taken.

412. Shoes: when and what kind? In most cases there's no need to put anything on babies' feet until they're walking outdoors. Normally their feet stay cool just the way their hands do, and this doesn't bother them. In other words, there's no necessity for knitted booties or soft shoes in the first year unless the house or the floor is unusually cold.

After a baby is standing and walking, there's a real value in leaving the child barefoot most of the time when conditions are suitable. The arches are relatively flat at first. The baby gradually builds the arches up and strengthens the ankles by using them vigorously in standing and walking. (I suppose the reason that the soles of the feet are ticklish and sensitive under the arch is to remind us to keep that part arched up off the ground.) Walking on an uneven or rough surface also fosters the use of the foot and leg muscles. When you always provide a baby with a flat floor to walk on and always enclose the feet in shoes (with their smooth insides), especially if the soles are stiff, you encourage the child to relax the foot muscles and to walk flat-footed.

Of course, a child who is walking needs shoes outdoors in cold weather and when walking on pavements and other surfaces that are hazardous. But it's good for a child to continue to go barefoot indoors till the age of 2 or 3, and outdoors, too, in warm weather at the beach, in the sandbox, and in other safe places.

Doctors most commonly recommend semisoft soles at first, so that the child's feet have a better chance to move. The important thing is to have the shoes big enough so that the toes aren't cramped, but not so big that they almost slip off. Socks should always be large enough, too.

Small children outgrow their shoes at a discouragingly fast rate, sometimes in 2 months, and parents should form the habit of feeling the shoes every few weeks to make sure they are still large enough. There must be more than **just** enough space for the toes, because as the child walks, the toes are squeezed up into the front of the shoe with each step. There should be enough empty space in the toe of the shoe, as the child stands, so that you can get about half your thumbnail onto the tip of the shoe before running into the child's toe. You can't judge while the child is sitting down; the feet fill more of the shoe when a person is standing up. Naturally, the shoes should be comfortably wide, too. There are soft adjustable shoes which can be let out a full size. It's important to have a non-skid sole. You can rough up a smooth sole with coarse sandpaper.

But if your baby's feet and legs are strong, you can get medium-soft shoes, even inexpensive ones if they fit well and are large enough. Sneakers are considered satisfactory by many doctors as long as they don't cause sweating. The feet are pudgy the first couple of years, and as a result low shoes sometimes do not stay on so well as high shoes.

413. Talking. Most babies begin to use a few sounds that mean something when they are in the neighborhood of a year old. But there are perfectly normal children who wait months longer. It seems to be largely a matter of temperament or personality. Your friendly, outgoing baby just naturally wants to talk young. The quiet, observer type seems to want to spend a long time solemnly watching the world go by before feeling like saying anything about it.

The atmosphere around babies and the way they are handled are important, too. If parents, under nervous tension, are always silent when they do things for their child, she feels the lack of communication and remains in her own shell. At the other extreme, if the adults in a family are going at a baby too hard, talking at her and bossing her continually, she may feel uncomfortable and unresponsive whenever people are around. She's not at an age when she can talk back or go out for a walk to get away from it all. People young and old feel like talking when they are around easygoing, sympathetic friends. The only difference with a baby is that she has to have more desire in order to learn the words in the first place.

It's sometimes said that certain children haven't learned to talk because the whole family waits on them hand and foot, gives them everything before they've had time to realize that they want it. This kind of service might slow babies down a little in learning new words, but I don't think it would make them silent unless the family were also keeping after them too much and squelching their outgoingness.

Once in a while you suspect that a baby is slow to pick up words because a parent talks in long sentences and the child never has a chance to grab hold of a single word at a time to learn. This isn't common, because it comes instinctively to most people to use single words at first with a baby, or to stress the important word in a phrase.

Does slow talking point to slow mental development? This is apt to be the first awful thought that occurs to parents. It is true that some children who are mentally slow are late talkers, but plenty of them use words at the regular age. Naturally, the child who is **severely** retarded, who can't sit up, for instance, until 2, will be really delayed in talking also. But the fact is that a great majority of the late talkers, even those who don't talk much until 3, have normal intelligence, and some of them are unusually bright.

I think you can guess what to do if your child is a late talker. Don't fret about it and don't jump to the conclusion that she's stupid. Show her comfortable affection, and try not to boss her too much. Give her chances, if possible, to be around other children where she can make her own way. Talk to her with simple words in a friendly manner. Encourage her to ask for things by name, but try to avoid angry demands that she speak.

All babies start out mispronouncing most of the words that they use, and gradually improve. But one continues to have trouble with one sound and another with another. Some of these mispronunciations are apparently due to real clumsiness of the tongue or other parts of the speech apparatus. After all, some grown-ups still lisp, no matter how hard they try. Other mispronunciations seem to be due to quirks in the child's feelings. A child clings to the mispronunciation of one word long after learning to make the same sound correctly in another word. Minor delays like this are not important if the child is generally well adjusted and outgoing, and is growing up in other respects. It's all right to correct a child occasionally in a friendly way. It's a mistake to be too serious or argumentative about it.

What about the child who has such clumsy speech at 3 or 4 or 5 or older that other children can't understand her and make fun of her? In the first place, she needs to have her hearing checked by a specialist. She might go to a speech expert if there is one who knows how to get along with a small child easily and can make the lessons appeal to her. But whether or not an expert is available, such a child needs regular association with other children as close to her own age as possible, preferably in a good nursery school, until she's ready for the grades. A good teacher can protect the child with a defect from the scorn of the other children in tactful ways, and, being less worried about it, can often coach her in talking more easily than the parent. Some grade schools have trained speech teachers.

Deliberate baby talk comes up most often in the child who feels a younger member of the family is getting too much admiration and affection, and is therefore jealous (see Section 540). There is another kind of affected baby talk in the child who has no rivals to worry about. I am thinking, for instance, of the little girl with corkscrew curls and fancy clothes who is the only child of a doting family. They are so pleased with her as a plaything that they forget she has to grow up. They keep talking baby talk to her long after it is natural, and show her that they love her best when she acts babyish and "cute." You can't blame her for playing up to them. But she will have a tough time when she gets around children her own age, because they won't think she's cute; they'll think she's awful.

TEETHING

414. Age of teething means little. Teething is quite different in different babies. One chews things, frets, and drools for 3 or 4 months before each tooth comes through, and makes life miserable for the whole family. In another case, a mother discovers a tooth one fine morning without ever having suspected that her baby was teething.

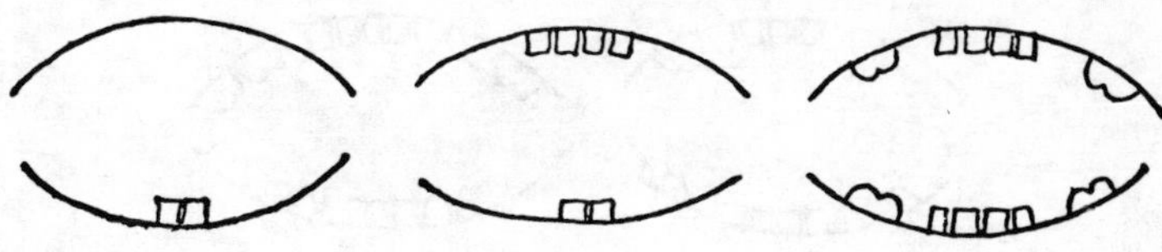

One baby gets the first tooth at 3 months, another not till a year. Yet both are healthy, normal infants. It is true that certain diseases once in a while influence the age of teething. But this is rare. In a baby who is reasonably healthy, the age of teething is simply a matter of the pattern of development the child was born with. In one family most of the children teethe early, in another late. You can't decide your baby is extra bright for teething early, or generally backward for teething late.

415. How the average baby's teeth come through. The average baby gets the first tooth around 7 months, but has been drooling, biting, and having periods of fretfulness from the age of 3 or 4 months. Since babies get twenty teeth in their first 2½ years, it is easy to see that they are teething most of that whole period. This also explains why it's so easy to blame every ailment on teething.

In the olden days it was the custom to blame teeth for colds, diarrheas, fevers. Of course, these conditions are caused by germs and not by teething. However, in some babies it looks as though teething lowers resistance, making it **easier** for an infection to start at that time. But if your baby becomes sick while teething, or has a fever as high as 101°F, a doctor is needed to diagnose and treat the disease just as much as if the baby had gotten sick when not teething.

Usually the first two teeth are the lower central incisors. ("Incisor" is the name given to the eight front teeth, which have sharp cutting edges.) After a few months come the four upper incisors. The average baby has these six teeth, four above, and two below, when about a year old. After this there's usually a pause of several months. Then six more teeth are apt to come in, without much pause in between—the two remaining lower incisors, and all four first molars. The molars

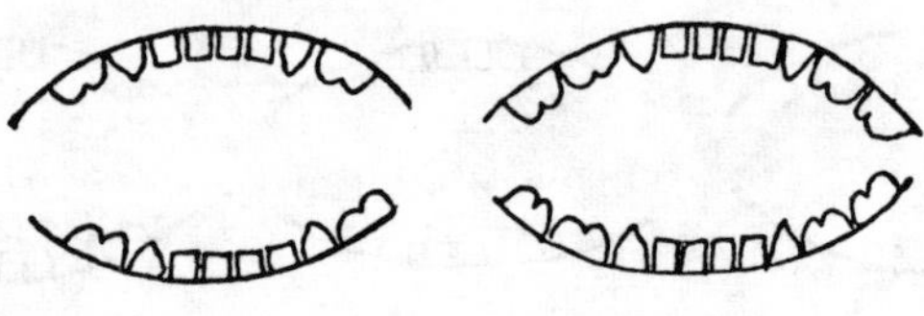

don't come in next to the incisor teeth but farther back, leaving a space for the canine teeth.

After the first molar teeth, there is a pause of several months before the canines (the pointed "dog teeth") come through in the spaces between the incisors and the molars. The commonest time is in the second half of the second year. The last four teeth in the baby set are the second molars. They come in right behind the first molars, usually in the first half of the third year.

416. Wakefulness with teething. The first four molar teeth, which in the average baby come through between a year and a year and a half, are more likely to cause babies trouble than the others. They may be cranky and lose their appetites for days at a time. They may wake crying a number of times each night. This can be quite a problem if they don't fall asleep again quickly. A small bottle or cup of milk may seem to be the easiest way to pacify them. Is this risky? In most cases, the baby stops waking when the teeth are through. But an occasional baby develops a persistent habit of waking, especially if picked up for the bottle and given a sociable time (Section 347). Therefore, I think it's preferable not to get into the habit of giving a night feeding at this age or of picking babies up, if they quiet down in a few minutes by themselves.

The coming of the first teeth, in the middle of the first year, may cause waking, too.

Refusal to take bottle or breast during teething is discussed in Section 133.

417. Let the baby chew. Sometimes parents think it's a duty to keep their baby from putting things in her mouth and chewing. This notion will surely drive the parents and the baby frantic in time. Most babies **must** put things in their mouths, off and on, at least from 6 months to 15 months. The best that a parent can do is to provide chewable objects that are dull enough so that if the baby falls with them in the mouth they won't do too much damage. Rubber teething rings of various shapes are good, but any piece of rubber that the baby can hold easily will do. You have to be careful about toys made from thin brittle plastic. Babies sometimes break off and swallow small bits or choke on them. You also have to be careful that the baby doesn't gnaw the paint off furniture and other objects if there is any danger that the paint is made with lead. Nowadays practically all babies' furniture and painted toys are painted with lead-free paint. You have to think about objects that have been repainted at home or that were never expected to be chewed by babies. Some babies prefer a certain kind of cloth for chewing on. Or, you can tie an ice cube or a piece of apple in a square of cloth. (One pediatrician I know suggests giving the child a frozen bagel to chew on.) Let them have what they seem to want as long as it's not dangerous. You don't have to fret about the germs on a teething ring or a favorite piece of cloth. They are the baby's own germs, anyway. Of course, it's a good idea to wash the teething ring with soap after it has fallen on the floor or after the dog has gotten it. If the baby chews on a piece of cloth, you can boil it occasionally. Some babies love to have their gums firmly rubbed at times. Don't use any medicine without the doctor's recommendation.

418. What makes good teeth. The first thing to realize is that the crowns of all the baby teeth (the parts that will show) are formed in the gums before birth. In other words, they are made from what the mother eats during her pregnancy. Research shows that among the food elements necessary to make strong teeth, the following are particularly important: calcium and phosphorus (milk and cheese), vitamin D (vitamin drops and sunshine), vitamin C (vitamin drops, oranges, other citrus fruits, raw tomatoes, cabbage). Other factors are probably necessary, too, including vitamin A and some of the B vitamins.

The baby's permanent teeth, the first of which won't appear until the child is about 6 years old, already **are being formed within a few months after birth.** Babies at this age are, of course, getting plenty of calcium and phosphorus from their milk diet. They should get C and D vitamins by the time they are a month old. (These are usually added in the form of concentrated drops if they're not in the formula.)

419. Fluoride in the water makes stronger teeth. One element known to be valuable in the **formation** of a child's teeth is fluoride—a minute amount in the diet of the mother while she is pregnant, and in the diet of the baby and small child while the permanent teeth are being formed. There is much less tooth decay in those parts of the country where fluoride occurs naturally in the water. It is now added, in minute, safe amounts, to the water of many progressive communities as a public health measure. If there is no fluoride in the water, the mother's physician or dentist can prescribe a minute daily dose for the mother during her pregnancy and for the child after birth. The dentist can give a child part of the benefit by painting fluoride on the teeth and recommending fluoride toothpaste. Whenever it is proposed that fluoride be added to a city's water supply, it makes some citizens anxious. They discover literature that claims fluoridation is harmful, and they may invite speakers from other cities, who are known as opponents of fluoridation, to testify against it. Since some of the statements are very alarming, they raise questions in the minds of all citizens. It is well to remember that intensive and extensive studies were made by responsible scientists before artificial fluoridation was ever proposed and that all the possible dangers and objections were carefully checked. Then committees of experts of the American Public Health Association, the American Dental Association, the American Medical Association, and the United States Public Health Service reviewed the evidence before publicly recommending fluoridation. If you're not sure about whether or not your water has enough fluoride, you can call the information number on your water bill. Adequate fluoridation is 0.7–1.0 ppm (parts/million).

It gives you a better perspective to realize that similar alarm was raised about vaccination, diphtheria immunization, and chlorination of water before these procedures became generally accepted.

420. Decay is favored by frequent contact with sugars and starches. Dental scientists haven't yet been able to find all the answers to decay (caries) of the teeth. The diet of the pregnant mother and of the baby are important in the formation of the teeth. Heredity probably plays a part.

But some teeth that look strong later decay. Dentists believe that the principal cause of tooth decay is lactic acid. This lactic acid is manufactured by bacteria that live on sugars and starches that are in contact with the teeth. The more hours of the day there are starches and sugars on the teeth, the greater the number of bacteria there are and the more lactic acid is produced to dissolve the enamel of the teeth and create holes. That is why frequent between-meal sucking of lollipops, eating of sticky candy and dried fruit, drinking of sodas, and nibbling of cookies and crackers (which so often stick to the teeth) are particularly liable to cause decay.

When children go on taking bottles in the second year and falling asleep with a mouth full of milk, there sometimes occurs a rapid decay of the teeth. That's why a baby should never be put to bed with a bottle of milk—or juice.

Of course, most fruits contain some sugar, and even vegetables contain a little. But the sugar is diluted and as a result is washed away sooner. And the rough fibers of fruit have a brushing action on the teeth. All of us eat starches to a greater or lesser extent, but we usually take them only at meals and many of them—especially those containing roughage, such as whole grains and potatoes—don't stick long to the teeth. It's the frequent between-meal eating of sugars and starches which stick that is particularly hard on the teeth.

421. Care of the teeth. It is sometimes recommended that babies' teeth be brushed when they have their first set of molars. For most babies this would be in the first half of the second year. I think, myself, that there is something to be said for waiting until children are nearly 2. At this age, they have a passion to copy everything they see done around them. If a 2-year-old girl sees her parents brush their teeth, she one day grabs one of their brushes and insists on trying it herself. This is a good time to buy her a brush and let her go to it. Naturally, she won't be very efficient at first, but you can help her tactfully. Perhaps I am making too much of a point of this, but it's a good example of a basic truth. Three-quarters of the things that we think we must impose on children as unpleasant duties are things that they enjoy learning to do themselves at a certain stage of their development, if we only give them a chance.

The main purpose of brushing the teeth is to remove the lumps and puddles of food from around the teeth. **The logical**

Children want to do grown-up things.

time is after meals, three times a day. (Hang toothbrushes in the kitchen as well as in the bathroom.) Most important is after supper, so that the teeth are clean for the long night period when the mouth is quiet and the saliva is flowing slowly.

422. Dental examination twice a year from the age of 3. It's wise to begin taking a child to the dentist every 6 months, beginning at 3 years old. This is the period when tooth decay is apt to start. The time to fill cavities is when they are small. This saves the teeth, and it hurts the child less. Even if your child doesn't have a cavity at the 3- or 3½-year-old visit to the dentist, it is worth the expense for two reasons. It's insurance that the teeth are healthy. It gets the child used to going to the dentist without fear. This confidence makes a big difference when the time comes for the first filling.

Parents sometimes think that they don't have to worry about decay of the baby teeth because they are all going to be lost anyway. This is wrong. A decayed tooth may cause the child pain, and it sometimes leads to infection of the jaw. And if a baby tooth is so decayed or causes so much pain that it has to be pulled, it leaves a space in the jaw that allows nearby teeth to grow out of position. Then there isn't enough room for the permanent tooth when it's ready to come through. Remember that the last baby teeth are not lost until the child is 12 years old. So they need just as careful care as the permanent ones.

423. The permanent teeth. The permanent teeth begin to appear when the child is about 6 years old. The 6-year-old molars come through farther back than the baby molars. The first baby teeth to be lost are the lower central incisors. The permanent incisors, pushing up underneath, destroy the roots of the baby teeth, which get loose and then fall out. The baby teeth are lost in about the same order they come in: the incisors, the molars, the canines. The permanent teeth that take the place of the baby molars are called bicuspids. The substitution of the new teeth is completed somewhere around 12 to 14 years of age. Meanwhile, the 12-year-old molars have come through behind the 6-year molars. The "18-year molars," or "wisdom teeth," come considerably later (sometimes never).

When teeth come through crooked or out of place, there is some tendency for them to straighten out later, how much one cannot tell ahead of time. Your regular dentist, who should be seeing your child's teeth every 6 months, can advise you whether special treatment is needed for this.

When the permanent teeth come in they are often behind the baby teeth and later move forward. They have jagged edges which later wear down. They're yellower than baby teeth.

Toileting

BOWEL CONTROL

424. What does it mean? Learning to use the toilet is an important forward step for children in several ways. They gain control of two apertures of the body that previously functioned automatically, and this gives them a lot of pride; in fact, they're so proud at first that they try to perform every few minutes. They are accepting the first serious responsibility assigned by their parents. Successful cooperation on this major project will give parents and child a new confidence in each other. And the child who was previously a lighthearted messer with food and BM now begins to take satisfaction in cleanliness. You may think of this shift as primarily meaning no more soiled diapers. That's important, all right. But the preference for cleanliness that a child gains at around 2 years means a lot more than that. It's actually the foundation for a lifelong preference for unsticky hands, for clean clothes, for a neat home, for an orderly way of doing business. It's from their toilet training that children get some of their feeling that one way of doing things is right and another way is not; this helps them to develop a sense of responsibility and to become systematic people. So toilet training plays a part in the formation of children's characters and in building the basic trust between them and their parents.

425. What is readiness for training? The first year. In the first year a baby shows very little awareness of bowel function, and doesn't participate—in a voluntary sense—in moving the bowels. When the rectum becomes sufficiently full, and particularly after a meal when the muscular activity of the stomach stimulates the entire intestinal tract, the movement presses against the inner valve of the anus and causes it to open somewhat. By means of a nerve reflex this stimulates a squeezing, pushing-down action of the abdominal muscles. The baby, in other words, does not decide to push the way an older child or adult does, but pushes automatically.

During the first year there is a small amount of readiness for partial training in some babies in the sense that they always have their first movement of the day within 5 or 10 minutes after breakfast. If parents wish to do so, they can sit such babies on the potty seat every day just in time to "catch" the movement. After a few weeks of this, the nervous system becomes "conditioned," as the psychologists call it, so that they automatically begin to push as soon as they feel the toilet seat under them. This is only a small degree of training, because the babies are not really conscious of the bowel movement or of what they themselves are doing. They are not cooperating knowingly.

It's believed that babies who have been "caught" early in this way are more apt to rebel later through prolonged soiling or bed wetting. I don't recommend any training efforts in the first year.

426. Signs of readiness. In the first half of the second year, children gradually become more conscious of when a bowel movement occurs. They may pause in what they are doing or change facial expression momentarily, though they are nowhere near ready to notify a parent.

They are likely, if they have had chances to see their BM—formed in the diaper or lying on the floor, or if it has been caught in the potty—to develop a distinctly possessive feeling for it. They are proud of it, just as they are proud of their nose or their navel at this stage. They may sniff the smell appreciatively, as they have been taught to sniff a flower.

One aspect of this possessiveness, as those parents have discovered who have succeeded in "catching" movements early in the second year, is a reluctance about giving up the BM to the pot and to the parent. Another aspect is anxiety about seeing the BM flushed away in the toilet. To small children this is as disturbing as if they saw their arm being sucked down the toilet.

427. Indirect signs of readiness. Beginning in the second year other aspects of readiness appear that we don't ordinarily associate with toilet training. Children now feel the impulse to give presents, and take lots of satisfaction from this—though they usually want them right back again. (Their contradictory feelings may show in the way they hold out one of their toys to a visitor but refuse to let go of it.)

It's at this age that children become fascinated with putting things in containers, which is an element in using the potty. When they get interested in putting away their toys and clothes, they've gained the further idea that certain things belong in certain places.

Gradually they want to imitate more and more of the activities of their parents or older brothers and sisters. This drive can play an important part in training.

They take great pride in learning any skill that they can carry out independently and they enjoy being praised for their accomplishments.

428. Balking. Children in past decades, who had taken to the idea of using the potty seat early in the second year, often suddenly changed their pattern. They sat down willingly but never had a movement as long as they sat there. Right after getting up they moved their bowels in the corner or in their pants. Parents sometimes said, "I think my child has forgotten what it's all about." I don't believe children forget that easily. I think that their possessive feeling about the movement has become temporarily stronger for some psychological reason and that they are simply unwilling to give it up. Early in the second year they have an increasing urge to do everything for themselves, in their own way, and toileting may seem too much the parents' scheme. So they just hold the movement in—at least until they can get away from the seat, which symbolizes giving it up and giving in.

If the resistance persisted for many weeks children might hold back not only when on the seat but for the rest of the day if they could manage it. This was a psychological type of constipation.

Balking is more apt to occur in the first half of the second year than in the second half. This is a reason for waiting until about the middle of the year to start training, and for letting children feel that it is **they** who have decided to control their bowels and bladders, rather than that they are giving in to parental demands.

429. Greater readiness between 18 and 24 months. Around 18 to 24 months, a majority of children show more definite signs of readiness. They have a greater awareness of when a movement is coming or being passed. They may stop playing for a few seconds or they may act a bit uncomfortable afterward. They may make some kind of sign or sound to the parent, to indicate that the diaper is soiled, as if they'd like to be cleaned up. This notification is more likely to appear if the parent has been suggesting that the child notify. Usually it takes a little longer, plus some encouragement from the parent, before children will become sufficiently aware of the approaching movement—before it has been passed—to be able to notify in time to be helped to the toilet.

The positive pride in the movement, including its smell, and the enjoyment of messing in it if the opportunity arises are characteristic reactions of the earlier period and can, in the latter half of the second year, be changed relatively easily into an aversion and a preference to be clean. I don't think it's wise or necessary to give a child a strong disgust reaction about his bowels or any other body function. But the readiness for a preference for cleanliness is part of what helps a child to become trained and stay trained.

430. The adult toilet or a child's seat on the floor? A few babies become accustomed from the start to a baby's toilet seat attached to the adult toilet seat. If such an arrangement is used, it's preferable to have an attached footrest so that the child can feel more steady. The parents should also build a sturdy box-shaped structure to serve as a step, so that the child can learn to climb up on the seat alone.

It's a sensible precaution during the second year for the parent to wait until the child has gone away from the bathroom before flushing the toilet. Most 1- to 2-year-olds are fascinated with the flushing at first and want to do it themselves. But later some of them become frightened by the violent way the water flushes the movement away and then they are afraid to sit on the seat. They probably fear that they might fall in and disappear likewise.

I myself think it's preferable to use a child's seat on top of a potty, close to the floor, up to 2½ years. Children feel more friendly toward a small piece of furniture that is their own and that they can sit down on by themselves. Their feet can stay on the floor, and there is no height to make them feel insecure. Until 2½ years, I'd empty the potty and flush the toilet after the child has gone away.

Don't use the urine guard for boys which comes with the seat. It too often hurts a boy when he is getting on or off—then he won't use the seat again.

431. A philosophy of training. Dr. T. Berry Brazelton, a pediatrician who has long been interested in toilet training, has worked out the following philosophy and method, which I'll summarize in my words. By now he has advised this method for over two thousand children in his practice, and 80 percent of them achieved success at bowel and urine training —abruptly and simultaneously—at an average age of 28 months. They gained night control at an average age of 3 years. These are excellent results by any standards.

Dr. Brazelton's basic principle is that children should become trained of their own free will—no coercion at all; in this way they can be trained most easily, and there will also be the least likelihood of later soiling and bed-wetting problems. (In his cases, only 1½ percent were still bed-wetting at 5 years of age. This contrasts with a figure of 15 percent at the age of induction into the army in one European country noted for its vigorous toilet-training philosophy.) He advises parents to use tactful suggestions and flattery, but no disapproval because of failure. No pressure to sit down on the seat if the child has any disinclination. No detention on the seat—even for a second—when the child wants to get up.

So the children decide to gain control, of their own free will, when they feel able, because they want to be grown up.

The method requires of the parents that they have trust in their children's desire to mature, and a willingness to wait without impatience.

432. Further readiness. Before starting any training the parents should be able to see one or more of the signs of readiness mentioned in Sections 426, 427, and 429.

The child should also be far enough past the first wild excitement of learning to walk so that she can sit down quietly at times.

The child should also not be in a violently negativistic phase in which she explodes in a tantrum whenever any suggestion is made.

It would be extra helpful if she could understand and talk about the need to go to the bathroom, though this is not essential.

433. Familiarity with the potty seat. The first step in training should not be to take the child's diaper off (let's say it's a girl) and sit her on the seat. That's too strange and sudden. It's much better, after buying her a potty seat, to let her get used to it for at least a week as an interesting piece of furniture of her own, to sit on with all her clothes on, rather than (to exaggerate the contrast) a mysterious contraption her parents will use to get her possession away from her.

You can lead your child to it, explaining that it is her very own and suggesting casually that she try it—now or later. (Children at this age are easily alarmed by being hurried or pushed into an unfamiliar situation.) You can show your children how you sit on the grown-up toilet seat (with **your** clothes on). But leave out the idea of BM or urine until the child feels friendly and comfortable about the seat just as a place for sitting. One new idea at a time is enough.

Let the child get up and leave the seat immediately if she wants to. The experience will be helpful, no matter how brief it is. The child should think of sitting on the seat not in any sense as an imprisonment but as a voluntary ritual that she is proud to carry out.

If the child has not been willing to sit down in a week, allow longer.

434. The second stage, after the child has become friendly and comfortable about her seat, is to introduce the idea of depositing a BM or urinating there. You can explain how Mommy and Daddy use their toilet that way, and perhaps one or two of the child's older acquaintances. It may help to have your child watch a friend perform. (If she has an older brother or sister she will probably have watched and learned already.)

What about the parents demonstrating, if there are no friends? Some child psychiatrists feel that it is better for parents not to uncover their genital regions in front of their children, but a demonstration of bowel moving could be carried out without too much uncovering (Section 590).

After the idea of depositing the BM or urine in the potty under the seat has been discussed a couple of times, you can take off the child's diaper, at a time when she is most likely to have a movement, lead her to her seat, and suggest that she try it. Don't push her if she doesn't want to. Try another time or another day. Some day, when the movement does go into the potty, this will help her greatly to understand and cooperate.

Continue this once-a-day ritual for about a week. In addition, right after she has had a movement in her diaper, take it off, lead her to her seat to sit down, and show her the movement in the diaper. Explain again that Mommy and Daddy sit on their seat to have their BMs, that she has her own seat, and some day she will do her BM in it—just like them. (All this repetition is monotonous for an adult, isn't it!)

If in a couple of weeks you have had no success in catching a movement or a urination, drop the business for a few weeks and then try gently and briefly again.

435. Flushing. At this stage don't flush the BM from the diaper down the toilet until the child has lost interest each time, and gone on to something else. The sight of their possession being flushed away is too frightening to many children—even though they may be fascinated to watch.

436. When the child takes an interest. If the child begins to be interested and cooperative, take her to her seat two or three times a day, especially if she gives the slightest signal of her readiness to urinate or have a BM.

If she allows herself to be "caught," for example, after a meal, or when she has been dry for a couple of hours, praise her for being so grown up ("just like Daddy" or Mommy, brother, sister, or admired friend). But don't overdo it. At this age a child doesn't like to think of herself as too compliant.

437. Going by themselves. When you're sure your child is ready for the next step, let her play for periods without any clothes on from the waist down. Put the potty seat near her, indoors or out, explaining that this is so that she can go all by herself. If she is not resistant, you can remind her every hour or so that she may want to go all by herself. If she gets bored or resistant or has an accident, put her back in diapers and wait.

438. Fear of painfully hard movements. Sometimes a child gradually or suddenly gets into a spell of unusually hard movements that are painful to pass. (Not all hard movements are painful.) The collections of small hard pellets—the result of what is sometimes called spastic constipation—are rarely painful. It's usually the hard movement in one large piece, with a wide diameter, that is to blame. As it is passed, it may tear a tiny slit, or "fissure," in the edge of the stretched anus, which may bleed a little. When a fissure has occurred, it is likely to be stretched open again each time another movement is passed. This is quite painful, and the fissure may thus be kept from healing for many weeks. You can easily see how a child who has once been hurt may dread a repetition and fight against toileting again. It may become a vicious circle, because if the child succeeds in holding back the movement for several days, it is more likely to be hard.

It's important to notify the doctor promptly if a child begins to have hard movements, particularly in this sensitive second year, so that the doctor can consider a change in the diet or a medication to keep them soft. Adding prunes or prune juice to the diet every day, if the child likes them, usually works. More whole-grain wheat and oats in cereal, bread, and crackers may help some. If you have such an emergency and cannot reach a doctor soon, you can use a BM softener (Section 358). It may also help to have the child sit in warm water in the bathtub with the legs in a cross-legged position for a couple of times a day for 10–15 minutes. An ointment containing a mixture of petroleum jelly and lanolin can be gently dabbed onto the anal area as often as necessary.

It helps to keep reassuring the child for a while that you know she is worried for fear another movement will hurt the way the previous one did, but that she doesn't need to worry any more because the movements are now kept soft by the medicine.

A child who remains frightened and resistant or seems to continue to have pain should be examined by the doctor for the possibility that a fissure has been created and is not healing.

439. Backsliding on bowel control after urine control is achieved. Many children, more often boys, when they train themselves for urine, stop giving up their BMs on the potty. They apparently can't give in to all of their parents' requests at once. If you push or cajole at this point you may make the child retain his BM inside, which may lead to painful hard BMs, adding a potent new reason for holding back. Use stool softeners (Section 358) and tell the child he can wait to do his BM until he has a diaper on.

URINE CONTROL

440. Simultaneous bowel and bladder control. The rightness of Dr. Brazelton's approach is shown by the fact that when children feel ready to control themselves, they usually achieve bowel and urine control almost simultaneously. In other words, by the first part of the third year, there is sufficient readiness—in terms of awareness and of physical competence—for both bowel and bladder control. All that is further necessary is the child's wish to be grown up in these respects; no special or additional effort is required on the parent's part to achieve urine control.

441. Attitudes toward BMs and urine. There are interesting differences in children's attitudes toward their BMs and their urine that may help you to understand their behavior.

Bladder control tends to be slightly slower than bowel control because it's easier for the anal sphincter (valve) to hold onto a solid than for the urethral sphincter to hold onto urine. (The anal sphincter becomes much less effective during diarrhea, as you know.)

Children rarely make an issue of daytime urination. It seems that urine doesn't matter to them as a possession the way BMs do. On the other hand, bed-wetting at night may express a variety of kinds of protest and excitements.

Bladder function tends to mature by itself, irrespective of training efforts. The bladder empties itself frequently in the first year. But by 15 to 18 months it begins to retain urine for a couple of hours, even though no training has been started. In fact, an occasional baby becomes spontaneously dry at night by a year of age.

The bladder retains urine for longer periods during sleep than during wakefulness, and dryness may be discovered after a 2-hour nap months before daytime control is achieved.

There may continue to be occasional "accidental" wettings in the daytime for several months after children have gained general control of urine, when they are preoccupied with play and don't want to be bothered to interrupt it.

442. Training pants. After your child is successfully controlling her BMs and bladder, put her in training pants that she can pull down by herself. This further step in independence will lessen the chance of backsliding. But don't use pants before the child is generally succeeding; they won't do any good for a child who is not succeeding, and you will have wasted their reinforcing value.

443. Inability to urinate away from home. It sometimes happens that a child around 2 has become so well trained to her own potty chair or toilet seat that she can't perform anywhere else. You can't urge her or scold her into it. She will probably wet her pants eventually, for which she shouldn't be scolded. If she is painfully full, can't let go, and you can't get home, put her in a hot bath for half an hour. This will probably work. Keep this possibility in mind when you take her traveling, and bring along her own seat if necessary. It's better to get a child used early to urinating in different places, including outdoors. There are portable urinals for boys and for girls to which they can become accustomed at home and which can then be taken along when they visit. Some children are more comfortable in diapers when they're away from home or can be reassured that they can have the choice of diapers when leaving home.

444. Standing up to urinate comes later. Parents are sometimes worried because a 2-year-old boy won't make the change to urinating standing up. It isn't necessary to make an issue of this. He'll get the idea sooner or later, when he has a chance to see older boys occasionally or his father once or twice. Some boys will urinate in a can or urinal which is held for them, as a step toward urinating in the toilet. See Section 590 on parental nudity.

445. Staying dry at night. Many parents assume that the only reason a child learns to stay dry through the night is that the parent toilets her late in the evening. They ask, "Now that she is reasonably dry in the daytime, when should I begin to toilet her at night?" This is a mistaken idea, and it makes night dryness sound like too much of a job. It's closer to the facts to say that a child just naturally becomes dry at night when her bladder becomes mature enough, provided she isn't nervous or rebellious (Section 761). This is shown clearly by the fact that one baby in a hundred regularly stays dry at night from the age of 12 months, although the parents have made no training effort at all and although the child wets throughout the day. And a few children, late in the second year or early in the third, become dry at night before they have much control in the daytime. The reason the bladder can retain urine for longer periods during sleep than in the daytime is that when a person is quiet and asleep, the kidneys automatically produce less urine and make the urine more concentrated.

Most children become dry at night around 3 years of age. Boys tend to be later than girls, high-strung children later than relaxed ones. Sometimes slowness in becoming dry seems to be a family trait.

I don't think it is necessary for parents to do anything special about night training. The natural maturing of the bladder plus the idea that the child gets in the daytime—that urine belongs in the toilet—takes care of most cases. Of course, it helps a little if the parents share in children's pride when they begin to have dry nights.

Some parents prefer to take a more active part and begin toileting children at 10 P.M. It may be possible to hasten night dryness a bit in this way, since a bladder that is emptied in the evening is not so full in the early morning. But I wouldn't do this until 6 or 8 months after daytime control is achieved. If, after that lapse of time, your child expresses a wish to leave her diaper off at night, you can act pleased that she wants to try, and let her.

Some children wake easily in the evening and perform readily. Others are hard to wake or have trouble performing or become very upset. I think if the parents run into any trouble, they should call it off.

One-Year-Olds

WHAT MAKES THEM TICK

446. Feeling their oats. One year old is an exciting age. Babies are changing in lots of ways—in their eating, in how they get around, in what they want to do, and in how they feel about themselves and other people. When they were little and helpless, you could put them where you wanted them, give them the playthings you thought suitable, feed them the foods you knew were best. Most of the time they were willing to let you be the boss, and took it all in good spirit. It's more complicated now that they are around a year old. They seem to realize that they're not meant to be baby dolls the rest of their lives, that they're human beings with ideas and wills of their own.

By 15 to 18 months, many children's behavior makes it clear that they're heading for what is often called "the terrible twos." When you suggest something that doesn't appeal to them, they feel they **must** assert themselves. Their nature tells them to. They just say "No" in words or actions, even about things that they like to do. The psychologists call it "negativism"; many parents call it "that terrible **no** stage." But stop and think what would happen to children who never felt like saying "No." They'd become robots. You wouldn't be able to resist the temptation to boss them all the time, and they'd stop learning and developing. When they were old enough to go out into the world, to school and later to work, everybody else would take advantage of them, too. They'd never be good for anything.

447. The passion to explore. They're demon explorers. They poke into every nook and cranny, finger the carving in the furniture, shake a table or anything else that isn't nailed down, want to take every single book out of the bookcase, climb onto anything they can reach, fit little things into big things and then try to fit big things into little things. Tired-out parents call this "getting into everything," and their tone of voice says that the child's a nuisance. They probably don't realize what a vital period this is for a baby. Babies **have** to find out about the size and shape and movableness of everything in their world and test out their own skill before they can advance to the next stage, just the way they'll have to go through the grades before they can go to high school. That they "get into everything" is a sign that they're bright in mind and spirit.

Incidentally, you've probably realized by now that they are never quiet while they're awake. It isn't nervousness—it's eagerness. They're made that way so that they will surely keep learning and practicing all day long.

AVOIDING ACCIDENTS

448. One year is a dangerous age. Parents cannot prevent all accidents. If they were careful enough or worrisome enough to try, they would only make a child timid and dependent.

449. Prevention of car accidents. Diseases used to be the major cause of death in babies and children, and parents lived in dread of them. Now most of the diseases have been eliminated or tamed.

Half the deaths of children are now caused by accidents. And the greatest cause of accidental death is automobile accidents. But it's hard to get parents to take them seriously —until a tragic accident has occurred.

Adult seat belts and shoulder straps are unsuitable and dangerous for small children. Every baby should be strapped into an approved carrier and every child from 20 to 40 pounds should be strapped into an approved safety seat for every ride, no matter how short. (Most crashes occur within a few miles of home.)

After they weigh about 45 to 50 pounds children should use adult belts with shoulder straps.

See Section 71 for the government's standards for children's car seats. There are now laws in many states which make it illegal for a small child to be improperly restrained.

Some parents excuse failure to use safety seats or belts on the basis that their children refuse to wear them. This excuse isn't worth a nickel. All children will do whatever their parents really insist on. Parents should begin using a carrier for their infant's first ride and never make an exception after that. If you begin making exceptions, a child will argue every time, and that's exhausting—for child and parent.

From the time your child begins walking on the sidewalk, teach him that he only steps off the curb when you are holding his hand. Sooner or later, his natural impulse to be independent will make him try to yank away, but don't let him until he's about 5 years of age and shows he has the sense to look both ways and uses good judgment before crossing.

450. Fires and burns. Next to automobiles, fires and burns are the commonest cause of accidental death in young children. Don't leave them alone in a house, even for 15 minutes. Take them with you if you have to go out. Keep matches in a truly inaccessible place or in a childproof container. Smoke and fire detectors should be in every home.

Children's sleep clothing is now made fire retardant by law. But the fire-retarding chemical will be washed away if **nonphosphate** detergent or soap or chlorine bleach is used. So use a citrate-based detergent.

Have a dry chemical fire extinguisher in the kitchen.

Make a habit of turning pot handles so they won't protrude from the stove.

Don't use tablecloths or mats that a small child can pull off the table.

Coffee burns are the commonest ones seen in many doctors' offices. Never drink hot coffee with a small child in your lap. And be sure that cups of hot coffee aren't near the edge of the table where a toddler can reach them.

Open heaters, floor furnaces, poorly insulated ovens, easily opened broilers are dangerous.

Curtains and towels blowing against a heater start many fires.

Renew worn electric cords. Tape tightly the connections between cords and extension cords.

Use electric outlet covers on all unused outlets.

You should turn the thermostat down on your hot water heater to somewhere between 120 degrees and 125 degrees F. (At 160 degrees F or higher, a small child will receive a scald burn in one second or less!)

451. Drowning. This is the third cause of accidental death in young children, the second in older children. It never seems possible until it happens. The best rule I know is to have children wear a life preserver at the beach, at a lake, near a swimming pool (even wading pools are dangerous) or when on a boat, until they can swim a quarter mile. They will argue and fight against it, but they will give in if they see that you are calmly sure it's the right thing and that you won't make exceptions.

There are life preservers now which are comfortable and not bulky.

Drowning of babies occurs in tubs and sinks. Don't leave them for a second.

452. Other safety tips. A great majority of serious accidents can be easily prevented if you know where the common dangers lie and are sensible in avoiding them. Here is a list:

Low chair–table combinations are safer than **high chairs.** If you use a high chair, it should have a broad base so that it won't tip, a harness to hold a climbing baby, a latch to keep the child from raising the tray. A **baby carriage** should have a harness for a baby who has reached the climbing age. There should be gates at the top and sometimes at the bottom of **stairs,** including porch stairs, until the child can go up and down steadily. **Windows** that a child can climb up to should have guards, or be opened only at the top.

A baby or small child who still puts things in the mouth should not have **small objects** like buttons, beans, peas, or beads to play with, or nuts or popcorn to eat, because they are easily breathed into the windpipe and cause choking. Take away a pencil or other **sharp object** if a small child keeps it in the mouth when playing or running.

As a matter of habit, always feel the temperature of a **bath** just before you put a child in, even if you remember doing it earlier. Hot faucets sometimes cause burns. Don't touch, or let a child touch, electrical equipment while in a bath or while holding onto a faucet. Don't leave pails of hot water on the floor.

Put bulbs into empty lamp sockets if they are within reach.

There are **door stops** and **safety knobs** that will keep children from opening forbidden doors, and adaptable **latches** and **locks** for medicine and kitchen cabinets.

Keep **matches** in containers in high places that are impossible for even a determined 3- or 4-year-old to reach.

Keep dangerous **tools** and power tools out of reach.

Be extremely cautious in backing a **car** down the driveway.

Wells, pools, cisterns should be well protected.

Put **broken glass, opened cans,** into a covered hard-to-open receptacle. Use a can with a slot in the top for used **razor blades.**

Don't let babies go close to a **strange dog** at an age when they are likely to startle or hurt the animal.

Plastic bags from the cleaner still cause suffocation of babies.

So do **unused refrigerators.**

Babies and small children hang themselves on **curtain cords, telephone cords, long ties** on caps and sacks.

Power mowers amputate fingers and throw stones viciously. If you have a rotary mower, trade it in.

Exposed springs on walkers, jumpers, and hobby horses can amputate fingers.

Guns should be locked up, and ammunition should be locked away in a different place.

453. Now's the time to put poisons out of reach. A fifth of all accidental poisonings occur in the second year of life. In a recent year, the Poison Control Center in a medium-sized city received 50,000 assistance calls, 90 percent of which were for children. Children in this exploring and tasting age will, when the spirit moves them, eat almost anything, no matter how it tastes. They especially love pills, good-tasting medicines, cigarettes, and matches. You will be surprised to read the list of the substances that most frequently cause dangerous poisoning in children:

Aspirin and other medicines
Insect and rat poisons
Kerosene, gasoline, benzene, and cleaning fluids
Lead in paint that a child has chewed off something (Most indoor paint and toy paint contains no lead. The danger is from outdoor paint on windowsills, porches, etc., and from outdoor paint that has been used at home to repaint toys, cribs, and other furniture.)
Liquid furniture and auto polish
Lye, alkalis used for cleaning drains, bowls, ovens
Oil of wintergreen
Plant sprays

Now is the time to inspect your house with an eagle eye—or, rather, a baby's eye. Put all **medicine** safely out of reach **immediately after each use.** Put bold, additional, clear labels on all medicines so that you won't use the wrong one. Flush medicine down the toilet after an illness is over. It's unlikely you'll use it again. It may deteriorate anyway. It's confusing to have old medicines mixed in with others still in use.

Federal and state laws now require that all medicines dispensed by a pharmacist come in childproof containers. Don't change a medicine to another container.

Don't change **any** substance from the container it came in to a container in which something else comes: plant spray in a Coke bottle, for instance, or oven cleaner in a cup. This is a frequent cause of serious accidents.

Somewhat dangerous in the bathroom are shampoos, hair tonics, home permanent and beauty preparations.

Find inaccessible places in the kitchen and utility room for cleaning fluids and powders; detergents; drain, bowl, and oven cleaners; ammonia; washing soda; bleach; wax remover; metal polish; borax; mothballs; lighter fluid; shoe polish. Get rid of rat poisons, insect pastes and poisons—they are too dangerous.

In the basement or garage find truly safe places for turpentine, paint thinners, kerosene, gasoline, benzene, insecticides, plant sprays, weed killers, antifreeze, car cleaners, and polishes. When discarding containers, be sure that they are completely empty and then rinse them.

Plant poisons. We adults think of plants and flowers as merely beautiful. Crawling babies and small children think of them as something to eat. This is a dangerous combination of attitudes, for many plants or flowers—over 700 of them—can cause illness or death. The best rule is to have no plants or flowers in the house or in the garden until children are past the eat-everything stage, and can accept prohibition. At least place plants high out of reach. Watch small children when they are around plants and flowers away from home. Here is a **partial** list of potentially fatal plants: caladium, diefembachia, philodendron, elephant's ear, English ivy, hyacinth, daffodil, narcissus, mistletoe, oleander, poinsettia, rosary pea, castor bean, delphinium, larkspur, belladonna, foxglove, lily of the valley, azalea, laurel, rhododendron, daphne berries, goldenchain, hydrangea, jessamine berries, privet (hedges), yew, gimson weed (thorn apple), morning glory seeds, mushrooms, nightshade. Your local Poison Control Center or health department can tell you whether a plant in your house or yard is poisonous if eaten.

Syrup of ipecac (See Sections 119 and 808). If you're in a situation where you want to get your child to vomit, you can give 1 tablespoon of syrup of ipecac, followed by a glass or two of water. It's also important to try to keep your child moving because this will tend to get the stomach to empty faster. If you have a Poison Control Center in your town or city, keep its telephone number attached to your phone.

454. Protect them from frightening sounds and sights. Babies at a year may become fascinated with one thing for several weeks on end—for instance, the telephone, or planes overhead, or electric lights. Let them touch and become familiar with objects that are not dangerous or disturbing. However, in some cases children are half frightened of the object. Then it's wiser for the parents not to play up to their interest, or, if it's something dangerous, not to dwell on the danger. Better to distract them with something else than to increase their awe.

At this age babies may be frightened by strange objects that move suddenly or make a loud noise, such as folded pictures that pop up from a book, the opening of an umbrella, a vacuum cleaner, a siren, a barking, jumping dog, a train, even a vase of rustling branches.

Try not to have these startling things too close to 1-year-olds until they get used to them. If the vacuum cleaner bothers them, try not to use it for a while, at least while they're nearby. Then try it the first time when they are some distance away.

455. Fear of the bath. Between 1 and 2 years, a child may become frightened of the bath, because of slipping under water, or getting soap in the eyes, or even seeing and hearing the water go down the drain. To avoid soap in the eyes, soap with a washcloth that is not too wet and rinse several times with a damp but not dripping washcloth. There are also special shampoos for children that sting less. Babies who are afraid to get into the bathtub shouldn't be forced at all. You can try a dishpan, but if your baby is afraid of that, give a sponge bath for several months, until the child's courage comes back. Then start with an inch of water and remove the baby before you pull the stopper.

If your baby, toward the end of the first year, begins to fight having the food washed off the face and hands with a cloth after meals, set a pan of water on the tray and let the child dabble the hands while you wash the face with your wet hand.

Fear of strangers is discussed in Sections 401 and 458, fear of the flushing toilet in Sections 426 and 430.

INDEPENDENCE AND OUTGOINGNESS

456. A baby gets more dependent and more independent at the same time. This sounds contradictory. A parent complains of a year-old boy, "He's getting to cry every time I go out of the room." This doesn't mean that he is developing a bad habit, but that he's growing up and realizing how much he depends on his parents. It's inconvenient, but it's a good sign.

But at the very age when he is becoming more dependent, he is also developing the urge to be on his own, discover new places, make up to unfamiliar people.

Watch a baby at the creeping stage when his parent is washing the dishes. He plays contentedly with some pots and pans for a while. Then he gets a little bored and decides to explore in the dining room. He creeps around under the furniture there, picking up little pieces of dust and tasting them, carefully climbing to his feet to reach the handle of a drawer. After a while he seems to feel the need of company again, for he suddenly scrambles back into the kitchen. At one time you see his urge for independence getting the upper hand, at another the need for security. He satisfies each in turn. As the months go by he becomes more bold and daring in his experiments and explorations. He still needs his parents, but not so often. He is building his own independence, but part of the courage comes from knowing he can get security when he feels he needs it.

I am making the point that independence comes from security as well as from freedom, because a few people get it twisted around backward. They try to "train" independence into children by keeping them in a room by themselves for long periods even though they are crying for company. I think that when the issue is being forced this hard, a child is not learning anything very good.

So babies at around a year are at a fork in the road. Given a chance, they gradually become more independent: more sociable with outsiders (grown-ups and children), more self-reliant, more outgoing. If they're confined a great deal, kept away from others, used to having only parents, often just one parent, hovering over them (Section 554), they are apt to become tied to that parent, more timid with strangers, wrapped up in themselves. How is independence encouraged?

When a baby has learned to walk, it's time to let him out of his carriage on his daily outings. Never mind if he gets dirty;

he should. Try to go to a place where you don't have to be after him every minute and where he can get used to other children. If he picks up cigarette butts, you have to jump, take them away, and show him something else that's fun. You can't let him eat handfuls of sand or earth because it irritates his intestines and may give him worms. If he puts everything in his mouth, try giving him a hard cracker or some clean object he likes to chew on, to keep his mouth busy. Keeping an able-bodied walking baby tucked in his carriage may keep him out of trouble, but it cramps his style and hinders his development. Some parents find a harness is very practical for shopping and walks at this age. It shouldn't ever be used for hitching him in one place. See Section 89.

457. Let them out of the playpen when they insist. One child is willing to stay in the playpen, at least for short periods, as late as a year and a half. Another thinks it's a prison by the time he's 9 months. Most like it well enough until they learn to walk, around the age of a year and a quarter. I'd say let your

Let her out when she's had enough.

baby out of the pen when he feels unhappy there. I don't mean at the first whimper, for if you give him something new to play with, he may be happy there for another hour. Outgrowing the pen is a gradual process. At first he gets sick of it only after a long spell. Gradually he gets impatient earlier. It may be months before he objects to being put in at all. In any case, let him out each time he's sure he's had enough.

458. Get them used to outsiders. At this age a baby's nature tells him to be leery and suspicious of strangers till he has had a chance to look them over. But then he wants to get closer and eventually make friends, in a 1-year-old fashion, of course. He may just stand close and gaze, or solemnly hand something to the newcomer and then take it back, or bring everything movable in the room and pile it in the person's lap.

Many adults don't have the sense to let a small child alone while he sizes them up. They rush up to him, full of talk, and he has to retreat to his parent for protection. Then it takes longer for him to work up his courage to be friendly. I think it helps for a parent to remind a visitor in the beginning, "It makes him bashful when you pay attention to him right away. If we talk for a while, he'll try to make friends sooner."

When babies are old enough to walk, give them plenty of chances to get used to strangers and make up to them. Take them to the grocery store a couple of times a week. If possible, take them every day where other small children play. They aren't able to play **with** the others yet, but at times they want to watch. If they are used to playing near others now, they will be ready for cooperative play when the time comes, between 2 and 3. If they've never been around other children by 3, it will take them months just to get used to them.

HOW TO HANDLE THEM

459. They're very distractible, and that's a big help. Year-old babies are so eager to find out about the whole world that they aren't particular where they begin or where they stop. Even if they're all absorbed in a ring of keys, you can make them drop it by giving them an egg beater. Their distractibility is one of the handles by which their wise parents guide them.

460. Arranging the house for a wandering baby. When you tell parents that their baby girl has outgrown the playpen or the crib and that they ought to let her on the floor, they are apt to look unhappy and say, "But I'm afraid she'd hurt herself. At the least she'd wreck the house." Sooner or later she must be let out to roam around, if not at 10 months, at least by 15 months, when she's walking. And she's not going to be any more reasonable or easier to control then. At whatever age you give her the freedom of the house, you have to make adjustments, so it's better to do it when she is ready.

How do you keep a year-old baby from hurting herself or the household furnishings, anyway? First of all, you can arrange the rooms where she'll be so that she's allowed to play with three-quarters of the things she can reach. Then only a quarter have to be forbidden. Whereas, if you try to forbid her to touch three-quarters of the things, you will drive her and yourself mad. If there are plenty of things she can do, she's not going to bother so much about the things she can't do. Practically speaking, this means taking breakable ashtrays and vases and ornaments off low tables and shelves and putting them out of reach. It means taking the valuable books off the lower shelves of the bookcases and putting the old magazines there instead. Jam the good books in tight so that she can't pull them out. In the kitchen, put the pots and pans on the shelves near the floor and put the china and packages of food out of reach. Parents of one baby boy filled a lower bureau drawer with old clothes, toys, and other interesting objects and let the baby explore it, empty it, fill it, to his heart's content.

461. How do you make them leave certain things alone? This is the main problem between 1 and 2 years. There are always a few things that you have to teach them to let alone. There have to be lamps on tables. They mustn't pull them off by their cords or push tables over. They mustn't touch the hot stove, or turn on the gas, or crawl out a window.

462. "No" isn't enough at first. You can't stop a boy (or girl) by just saying "No," at least not in the beginning. Even later, it depends on your tone of voice and how often you say it and whether you really mean it. It's not a method to rely on heavily until he has learned from experience what it means—and that you mean it. Don't say "No" in a challenging voice from across the room. This gives him a choice. He says to himself, "Shall I be a mouse and do as she says, or shall I be a man and grab the lamp cord?" Remember that his nature is egging him on to try things and to balk at directions. The chances are he'll keep on approaching the lamp cord with an

Better to remove and distract him than just to say, "No, no!"

eye on you to see how angry you get. It's much wiser, the first few times he goes for the lamp, to go over promptly and whisk him to another part of the room. You can say "No" at the same time to begin teaching him what it means. Quickly give him a magazine, an empty box, anything that is safe and interesting. There's no use tossing him a rattle that he was bored with months ago.

Suppose he goes back to the lamp a few minutes later? Remove him and distract him again, promptly, definitely, cheerfully. Say, "No, no," at the same time that you remove him, adding it to your action for good measure. Sit down with him for a minute to show him what he can do with the new plaything. If necessary, put the lamp out of reach this time, or even take him out of the room. You are tactfully but firmly showing him that you are absolutely sure in your own mind that the lamp is not the thing to play with. You are keeping away from choices, arguments, cross looks, scoldings—which may not do the job and which are likely to get his back up.

You might say, "But he won't learn unless I teach him it's naughty." Oh, yes, he will. In fact, he can accept the lesson more easily if it's done in this matter-of-fact way. When you disapprovingly waggle a finger from across the room at babies who haven't yet learned that **no** really means **no,** your crossness rubs them the wrong way. It makes them want to take a chance on disobeying. And it's no better if you grab them, hold them face to face, and give them a talking-to. You're not giving them a chance to give in gracefully or forget. Their only choice is to surrender meekly or to defy you.

I think of a Mrs. T. who complained bitterly that her 16-month-old daughter was "naughty." Just then Suzy toddled into the room, a nice girl with a normal amount of spunk. Instantly Mrs. T. looked disapproving and said, **"Now remember,** don't go near the radio." Suzy hadn't been thinking of the radio at all, but now she had to. She turned and moved slowly toward it. Mrs. T. gets panicky just as soon as each of her children in turn shows signs of developing into an independent person. She dreads that she won't be able to control them. In her uneasiness, she makes an issue when there doesn't need to be any. It's like the boy learning to ride a bicycle who sees a rock in the road ahead. He is so nervous about it that he keeps steering right for it.

Take the example next of a baby who is getting close to a hot stove. A parent doesn't sit still and say, "No-o-o," in a disapproving voice, but jumps and gets the baby out of the way. This is the method that comes naturally if the parent is really trying to keep the child from doing something, and not just engaging in a battle of wills.

463. Take lots of time or be masterful. A mother of a 1¾-year-old boy takes him with her every day to the grocery store. But she complains that instead of walking right along, he wanders up the walk and climbs the front steps of every house they pass on the way. The more she calls to him, the more he lingers. When she scolds him, he runs in the opposite direction. She is afraid he is turning into a behavior problem. This baby isn't a behavior problem, though he may be made into one. He's not at an age when he can keep the grocery store in mind. His nature says to him, "Look at that walk to explore! Look at those stairs!" Every time his mother calls to him, it reminds him of his new-felt urge to assert himself. What can the mother do? If she has to get to the store promptly, she can take him in his stroller. But if she's going to use this time for his outing, she should allow four times as long as if she were going alone, and let him make his side trips. If she keeps moving slowly, he'll want to catch up to her every once in a while.

Here's another tight spot. It's time to go in for lunch, but your small daughter is digging happily in the dirt. If you say, "Now it's time to go in," in a tone of voice that means, "Now you can't have any more fun," you get resistance. But if you say cheerfully, "Let's go climb the stairs," it may give her a desire to go. But suppose she's tired and cranky that day, and nothing that's indoors has any appeal. She just gets balky right away, disagreeably balky. I'd pick her up casually and carry her indoors, even if she's squealing and kicking like a little pig. You do this in a self-confident way, as if you were saying to her, "I know, you're tired and cross. But when we have to go in, we have to." Don't scold her; it won't make her see the error of her ways. Don't argue with her, because that won't change her mind; you only get yourself frustrated. A small child who is feeling miserable and making a scene is comforted underneath by sensing that the parent knows what to do without getting angry.

464. Dropping and throwing things. Around the age of 1 year, babies learn to drop things on purpose. They solemnly lean over the side of the high chair, and drop food on the floor, or toss toys, one after the other, out of the crib. Then they cry because they haven't got them. Are these babies deliberately trying to make monkeys out of their parents? They aren't thinking about parents. They are fascinated by a new skill and want to practice it all day long, the way an older child wants to ride a new two-wheeler. If you pick up the dropped object, they realize it's a game that two can play and

Dropping is a new skill.

are more delighted. It's better not to get in the habit of picking up dropped toys right away. Put babies on the floor or ground when they get in this dropping mood. You don't want them throwing food out of the high chair in any case, but they won't start until their appetite is pretty well satisfied. Take the food away promptly and firmly when they start dropping, and put them down to play. Trying to scold a baby out of dropping things leads to nothing but frustration for the parent.

NAP HOURS ARE CHANGING

465. Naptimes are shifting in most babies around the age of a year. Some who were taking a nap at about 9 A.M. may refuse it altogether or show that they want it later and later in the morning. If they take it late, they are unready for their next nap until the middle of the afternoon, and this probably throws off their bedtime after supper. Or they may refuse the afternoon nap altogether. A baby may vary a lot from day to day at this period, and even go back to a 9 A.M. nap after 2 weeks of refusing it, so don't come to final conclusions too soon. You have to put up with these inconveniences as best you can, realizing that they are temporary. With some babies who are not ready to sleep in the first part of the morning, you can remove the need for the before-lunch nap by putting them in their beds anyway, around 9 in the morning, if they are willing to lie or sit quietly for a while. Of course, another kind of baby only gets in a rage if put to bed when not sleepy, and nothing is accomplished.

If a baby becomes sleepy **just** before noon, it's the parent's cue to move lunch up to 11:30 or even 11 for a few days. Then the long nap comes after lunch. But for a while, after cutting down to one nap a day, whether morning or afternoon, the baby may get frantically tired before suppertime. As a doctor friend of mine put it, "There's a stage in a baby's life when two naps are too many and one is not enough." You can help babies through this period by giving them supper and putting them to bed for the night a little earlier for the time being.

Don't get the idea from this section that all babies give up their morning nap in the same way or at the same age. One is through with it at 9 months; another craves it and benefits by it as late as 2 years.

THEY'RE APT TO CHANGE THEIR EATING HABITS

466. They get more choosy for several reasons. Somewhere around a year babies are apt to change their feeling about food. They become more choosy and less hungry. This is not surprising. If they kept on eating and gaining the way they did when they were little babies, they'd turn into mountains. Now they seem to feel that they have time to look the meal over and ask themselves, "What looks good today and what doesn't?" What a contrast to their behavior at 8 months! In those days they felt they were starved to death when mealtime came around. They'd whimper pathetically while their parent tied the bib, and lean forward for every bite. It wouldn't matter much what was served. They were too hungry to care.

There are other reasons, aside from not being so hungry, that make them choosy. They're beginning to realize, "I'm a separate person with ideas of my own," so they become definite in their dislikes of a food that they were doubtful about before. Their memory is getting better, too. They probably realize, "The meals here are served up pretty regularly, and they stay around long enough for me to get what I want."

Teething often takes away children's appetites, especially when the first molars are on their way. They may eat only half their usual amount for days, or occasionally refuse an entire meal. Finally, and perhaps most important, there is the fact that appetite **naturally** varies from day to day and week to week. We grown-ups know that one day we grab a big glass of tomato juice and another day split pea soup looks better. It is the same way with children and babies. But the reason you don't see this variation more often in infants under a year is that most of the time they are too hungry to turn anything down.

467. Dr. Davis's experiments in appetite. Dr. Clara Davis wanted to find out what children would eat if left to their own desires and given a variety of wholesome foods to choose from. She didn't start with older children for fear they would have already developed prejudices about food. So she picked three babies, 8 to 10 months old, who had never had anything to eat but breast milk. She took them to live at a place where they could be watched carefully. And this is how they were fed: At each meal a nurse would place before them six to eight serving dishes containing a variety of wholesome, unrefined foods. There were vegetables, fruits, eggs, cereals, meats, whole grain bread, milk, water, and fruit juices. The nurse was told, "Don't help the babies till they show you what they want." The 8-month-old baby would lean forward and dip a fist into a dish of beets and then try to eat it off the hand. Now the nurse was permitted to offer a teaspoonful of beets. Then she must wait until the baby showed a choice again. Another spoonful of beets or maybe applesauce.

Dr. Davis discovered three important things. First, babies who chose their own diet from a variety of natural foods developed very well; none of them got too fat or too thin. Second, every baby, over a period of time, chose what any scientist would agree was a well-balanced diet. Third, from meal to meal and day to day, the appetite varied a lot. Each separate meal wasn't well balanced. For several meals in a row a baby might feed largely on greens, then change about and go more heavily for starches. Sometimes a baby would go on a real jag and, for instance, make a whole meal of nothing but beets, perhaps four times as much beets as a grown-up would consider a polite amount. And after this spree there wouldn't be any bellyache, vomiting, or diarrhea. A baby would sometimes drink as much as a quart of milk in addition to a full meal, and at the next meal want very little milk at all. One baby, on several occasions, ate as many as six hard-boiled eggs in addition to a full meal. Dr. Davis kept track of the beef intake of a baby boy over a period of many days. He would go along for a while eating an average portion of beef, and then his appetite for beef would begin to increase. He might work up to four times as much beef as we would ordinarily think proper, keep up that rate for several days, and then taper off. The way this craving for beef gradually increased and then decreased suggested to Dr. Davis that there was a real bodily need for something in that beef that influenced the appetite for days. Dr. Davis eventually carried out the experiment with many older children, too, even hospital patients, and found that the results were just as good.

468. What parents can learn from Dr. Davis. The good results from this experimental method of feeding don't prove that parents ought to serve their child six to eight dishes at each meal, like the hors d'oeuvres in a Swedish restaurant. But it does show that they can trust an unspoiled child's appetite to choose a wholesome diet if they serve a reasonable variety and balance of those natural, unrefined foods **that the child enjoys eating at present.** It means that they can allow larger amounts than usual of a food the baby's appetite craves without worrying about the consequences. Even more important, it means that they don't have to worry when their child develops a temporary dislike of a vegetable.

It is hard for us moderns to have this kind of confidence in our children's appetites. We have heard so much about what the scientists say we **ought** to eat that we have forgotten that our bodies have known a lot about this for millions of years. Each kind of caterpillar knows for sure what sort of leaves it can eat and refuses all others. The deer travels for miles to the salt lick when its body craves salt. The robin knows what is good for it without ever attending a lecture. It is not surprising that people should also have some instinctive knowledge of what is good for them. I don't mean that children or grown-ups will **always** eat what's best for them, and I don't mean that parents don't need to know what makes a balanced diet. If a parent didn't know any better than to offer only doughnuts and coffee at every meal, there would be no chance for a child to pick a well-balanced diet out of this selection, no matter how sound the instincts were. It is important for parents to know the values of vegetables, fruits, milk, meat, eggs, whole grain cereal, so that they can offer a variety that covers all their child's needs. But it is just as important for them to know that children's instincts are sound to start with, that their appetite naturally varies, that they will probably try to pick a well-balanced diet in the long run if they aren't given too many prejudices.

469. Let them give up certain vegetables for a while. Your 1-year-old daughter suddenly turns against the vegetable that she loved last week. **Let** her turn against it. If you don't make a fuss today, she will probably come back to it next week or next month. But if you insist on her taking it when she seems to dislike it, you only make her set her mind that that particular food is her enemy. You turn a temporary dislike into a permanent hate. If she turns down the same vegetable twice in succession, leave it out for a couple of weeks. It is naturally irritating to a parent to buy a food, prepare it, serve it, and then have it turned down by an opinionated wretch who loved the same thing a few days ago. It is hard not to be cross and bossy at such a time. But it is worse for the child's feeling about food to try to force or urge it. If she turns down half her vegetables for a while, as is common in the second year, serve her the ones that she does like. This is the wise and pleasant way to take advantage of the great variety of fresh, frozen, and canned vegetables that we have. If she turns against all vegetables for a while but loves her fruit, let her have extra fruit. If she is taking enough fruit, milk, and her vitamin drops, she is not missing anything that's in vegetables. (See Section 494 for vegetable substitutes.)

470. What to do if they are tired of cereal. Many babies get fed up with cereal sometime in the second year, especially for supper. Don't try to push it in. There are many substitutes you can offer, which are discussed in Sections 496 and 497. Even if they give up **all** starches for a few weeks, it won't hurt them.

471. Don't be alarmed if they want less milk at times. Milk is a very valuable food. It provides good amounts of most of the elements that are important for a child's diet, as is explained in Section 488. But it is helpful to remember that in the parts of the world where there are no cows or goats, children get these substances from other foods after their nursing period is over. It's also good to know that an average of a pint and a half (24 ounces) a day safely covers the needs of almost every child between 1 and 3 who is taking a reasonable diet otherwise. Many children between the ages of 1 and 2 want to cut down to this amount or less, at least temporarily. If parents worry and set to work to urge or force a larger amount, the children are apt to become steadily more disgusted. In the long run, they take less milk than if they had been let alone.

Don't keep offering the cup again after they have shown that they're not interested. Every time they have to decline it makes them more determined they don't want it. If they drop down to an average of 8 ounces a day, wait a few days and see if they don't increase again.

If they go on for weeks drinking less than a pint and a half, there are many other ways that milk can be used in the diet; these are discussed in Section 489. Milk in any of these forms is just as nutritious as when it comes straight from the cow.

If a child goes on for a month or so averaging less than a pint and a half of milk **in all forms,** report it to the doctor who may prescribe calcium in some other form until the child's appetite for milk comes back.

472. Be wary of feeding problems now. The reason for discussing the natural variations in a child's appetite at this age is an important one. Feeding problems start more commonly between 1 and 2 years than at any other period. Once a child becomes balky, once a parent becomes worried and angry, the fat's in the fire. The more the parent frets and urges, the less the child eats. And the less the child takes, the more anxious the parent is. Meals become agonizing. The problem may last for years. The tension that grows up between parent and child causes other behavior problems, too.

The best way to keep children eating well is to let them go on thinking of food as something they want. Allow them to eat a larger than usual amount of one wholesome food, less or none of another, if that's the way they feel. When making up meals, select a well-balanced diet, but select it from among the wholesome foods that they really enjoy. Expect their tastes to change from month to month. If you cannot consult a doctor about additions to diet, look ahead to Sections 488–498 for new foods and those to substitute for the ones your child is leaving out temporarily.

The chances are great that if you don't make a battle of it, your child will eat a reasonably balanced diet from week to week, though it may be somewhat lopsided from meal to meal or day to day. If it stays unbalanced for weeks, you should discuss the problem with a doctor, even if it is difficult to reach her or him.

473. Standing and playing at meals. This may be quite a problem even before the age of a year. It comes about because the baby is less ravenous for food, more interested in all kinds of new activities, like climbing, handling the spoon, messing in the food, tipping the cup upside down, dropping things on the floor. I've seen a 1-year-old fed a whole meal standing up backward in the high chair, or even being

Time to finish the meal.

followed around the house by long-suffering parents with a spoon and dish in their hands.

Fooling at meals is only a sign that children are growing up and that parents are sometimes more keen about children eating than the children are. It's inconvenient and irritating, and it's apt to lead to feeding problems, too. I wouldn't let it go on. You'll notice that children climb and play when they're partly or completely satisfied, not when they're really hungry. So whenever they lose interest in food, assume they've had enough, let them down from the chair and take the food away. It's right to be firm, but you don't need to get mad. If they immediately whimper for the meal, as if to say they didn't mean they weren't hungry, give them one more chance. But if they show no regret, don't try to give them the meal a little later. If they get extra hungry between meals, give them a little more than usual between meals, or give them the next regular meal early. If you **always** stop the meal casually when they lose interest, they will do their part by paying attention when they are hungry.

Now I want to state a reservation. Babies around a year have a powerful urge to dip their fingers into the vegetable, or squeeze a little cereal in their hands, or stir a drop of milk around on the tray. This isn't fooling. They may be opening their mouths eagerly for food at the same time. I wouldn't try to stop them from experimenting just a little bit with the feel of food. But if they try to turn the dish over, hold it down firmly. If they insist, keep it out of reach for a while or stop the meal.

474. Let them feed themselves early. The age at which babies feed themselves depends largely on the adults' attitude. Dr. Davis, in her experiments on what diets babies choose, found that some infants were efficiently spoon-feeding themselves **before the age of a year.** At the other extreme, overprotective parents swear that their 2-year-olds couldn't possibly feed themselves at all. It all depends on when you give them a chance.

Most babies show an ambition to manage the spoon by a year, and if they have opportunity to practice, a lot of them can do a good job without help by 15 months.

Babies get some preparation for spoon-feeding way back at

Feeling is learning.

6 months, when they hold their own bread crust and other finger foods. Then at around 9 months, when they get chopped foods, they want to pick up each piece and put it in their mouths. Babies who have never been allowed to feed themselves with their fingers are apt to be delayed in taking to spoon-feeding.

A polite baby of 10 to 12 months may just want to rest a hand on his mother's or father's when being fed. But most babies, when the urge comes, try to yank the spoon out of their parent's hand. Don't think this has to be a tug of war; give the baby that spoon and get another to use yourself. The baby soon discovers that it's more complicated than just getting possession of the spoon. It takes weeks to learn how to get a speck of food on the spoon, and weeks more to learn not to turn it upside down between the dish and the mouth. When babies become bored with trying to eat, and stir or slop the food instead, it's time to move the dish out of reach, perhaps leaving a few crumbs of meat on the tray for them to experiment with.

Even when they're trying very hard to feed themselves correctly, they make plenty of accidental messes, and this you've got to put up with. If you're worried about the rug, put a big plastic tablecloth under the chair. It helps to use a hot-water plate with partitions. This keeps the food warm, is harder to pick up, and has straight sides to push the food against. Baby spoons with looped handles are meant to be easy to hold, but I think they are more difficult than small spoons with straight handles.

There is now a spoon in which the bowl swivels in the handle so that it will stay level.

When your 1-year-old can feed herself, let her take over completely. It isn't enough to let the baby have a spoon and a chance to use it; you've got to gradually give her more **reason** to use it. At first she tries because she wants to do things for herself. But after she sees how complicated it is, she's apt to give up the whole business if **you keep on rapidly feeding her anyway.** In other words, when she begins to be able to get a speck to her mouth, you ought to let her have a few minutes alone with the food, at the beginning of the meal when she's hungriest. Then her appetite urges her on. The better she gets at feeding herself, the longer she should have at each meal to do it.

By the time she can polish off her favorite dish in 10 minutes, it's time for you to be out of the picture. This is where parents often go wrong. They say, "She can eat her own meat and fruit all right now, but I have to feed her her vegetable, potato, and cereal still." That's a little risky. If she's able to manage one food, she has skill enough to manage the others. If you go on feeding her the ones she doesn't bother with, you build up a sharper and sharper distinction between the foods **she** wants and the foods **you** want her to take. In the long run, this takes away her appetite for **your** foods. But if you put thought into serving as well-balanced a diet as possible from among the foods she is presently enjoying and let her feed herself entirely, the chances are great that she will strike a good balance from week to week, even though she may slight this or that food at certain meals.

Don't worry about table manners. Babies want to eat more expertly, more neatly, all by themselves. They want to graduate from fingers to spoon and from spoon to fork, as soon as they feel equal to the challenge, just as they want to try everything else difficult that they see others doing. Dr. Davis noticed this in the babies she was observing, and they weren't coached at all. She pointed out that puppies show the same urge to learn eating manners without teaching. In the beginning, they stand in a pan of milk and dip their faces. First, they learn to keep their feet out; next, to lap the milk without dipping their faces; finally, to lick their whiskers politely at the end.

I have been making quite a point about letting children learn to feed themselves somewhere between the ages of 12 and 15 months, because that is the age when they want to try. Suppose a parent keeps a baby from doing it at this age, and then at 21 months declares, "You big lummox, it's time for you to feed yourself." Then the child is apt to take the attitude, "Oh no! It's my custom and my privilege to be fed." At this more advanced stage, trying to manage a spoon is no longer exciting. In fact, the child's whole sense of what's proper rebels against it, and the parents have lost the golden opportunity.

Don't take this all so seriously that you think there is only one right age, or worry because your baby is not making sufficient progress, or try to force the issue. That would only create other problems. I'm only making the point that babies want to learn this skill earlier than many parents realize, and that it is important for parents to gradually give up feeding as the child is able to take over.

Elements in the Diet

Before we talk about the everyday foods that children can eat, we ought to discuss the more important chemical substances that foods are composed of, and what the body uses them for.

You can compare a child's body, in one way, to a building under construction. A lot of different materials are needed to build it and to keep it in repair. But a human being is also a machine that's running. It requires fuel for energy, and other substances to make it work properly, just as an automobile needs gasoline, oil, grease, water.

PROTEIN

475. Protein is the main building material of the body. The muscles, heart, brain, kidneys, for instance, are largely made of protein (aside from water). The structure of bones is protein, filled in with minerals, much the way a collar is made stiff with starch. The child needs good food protein to continually increase the size of every part of the body, and also to repair wear and tear.

Most natural foods contain protein, some much, some little. Meat, poultry, fish, eggs, milk are the foods richest in it. They are the only foods that supply "complete proteins"—that is to say, they contain the complete variety of protein elements (the essential amino acids) that the human body needs. That is why a child should be averaging a pint and a half of milk daily and also receiving meat (or poultry or fish) daily, and 3–4 eggs a week. Next in importance are the proteins in whole grain cereals, nuts (including peanut butter), and mealy vegetables (soy and other beans, peas). Mealy vegetables are also called legumes. These grain and vegetable proteins are "incomplete." Whole wheat, for example, contains some essential protein elements; beans contain others. If a child is eating a variety of whole grains, nuts, and mealy vegetables, they will supplement the proteins from the meats, fish, eggs, milk but will not entirely take their place.

Vegetarian diets for children should include dairy products. Adolescents can be on strictly vegetarian diets in which whole grains and legumes (mealy vegetables), or nuts and legumes, can be combined to provide all the essential amino acids of "complete protein." But this diet is too bulky for children. They require the addition of dairy products, with their rich supply of the essential amino acids, to fill out or complement what they get from vegetables and grains. If you want to have your child on a vegetarian diet, talk to your doctor or a dietician about how to do this in a way that won't interfere with your child's growth. There are a number of good books available, some of which include a variety of recipes.

MINERALS

476. Minerals of many kinds play a vital part in the structure and in the working of every part of the body. The hardness of bones and teeth depends on calcium and phosphorus. The substance in red blood cells that carries the oxygen to all regions of the body is made partly of iron and copper. Iodine is necessary in the functioning of the thyroid gland.

All natural unrefined foods (fruits, vegetables, meats, whole grains, eggs, milk) contain a variety of valuable minerals. But the refining of grains and the prolonged cooking of vegetables in a lot of water removes a great deal. The minerals most likely to be insufficient in the diet are calcium, iron, and, in certain areas, iodine. Calcium occurs in small amounts in vegetables and some fruits, but plentifully in milk (and cheese). Iron (to prevent anemia) is supplied by green, leafy vegetables, meats, fruits, whole grains, but more abundantly by egg yolk and liver. Iodine is missing in some inland regions where the drinking water, vegetables, and fruits lack it, and seafood is not available. Table salt is iodized for people in those areas, to prevent goiter. Fluoride has been discussed in Section 419.

VITAMINS

Vitamins are special substances that the body needs in minute amounts in order to work right, somewhat the way any machine needs a few drops of oil, or a gasoline motor depends on a tiny electric spark.

477. Vitamin A is necessary to keep healthy the linings of the bronchial, intestinal, and urinary systems, and various parts of the eyes, including that which enables us to see in dim light. The body gets it plentifully from milk fat, egg yolk, green and yellow vegetables, vitamin drops. Probably the only people who receive too little are those on starvation diets or those who cannot absorb it because of serious intestinal disease. There is no reason to believe that the person on a decent diet will catch fewer colds by taking more and more vitamin A. Excessive amounts of vitamin A can be harmful to children. Be careful to read the labels on jars of baby foods such as carrots and sweet potatoes. You may discover levels of vitamin A as high as 800 percent of the minimum daily requirement.

478. Vitamin B complex. Scientists used to think that there was just one vitamin B, which had several actions in the body. But when they studied "it," it turned out to be a dozen different vitamins. However, these mostly occur in the same foods. Since the B vitamins are not yet all known or understood, it is more important for people to eat plenty of the natural foods they mostly occur in than to take them separately in pill form. The four known to be most important for human beings are called by their chemical names now: thiamin, riboflavin, niacin, pyridoxine. Every tissue in the body needs these four vitamins.

Thiamin (B_1) occurs in fair amounts in whole grain, milk, eggs, liver, meat, and certain vegetables and fruits. It is destroyed by long cooking, especially when soda is used. People are apt to receive an insufficient supply of it when they eat a lot of refined starches and sugars. Lack of thiamin can cause poor appetite, slow growth, fatigue, stomach and intestinal troubles, neuritis. (However, there are many different causes of all these symptoms, and thiamin deficiency is not the most common one.)

Riboflavin (also known as B_2) occurs abundantly in liver, meat, eggs, milk, green vegetables, whole grains, yeast. So a deficiency is only likely if a person's diet consists mainly of refined starches and sugar. Deficiency causes cracks in the corners of the mouth and outer lip, skin, mouth, and eye troubles.

Niacin (nicotinic acid) occurs abundantly in about the same foods as riboflavin. Deficiency causes mouth, intestinal, and skin troubles (it looks like a chronic sunburn which turns rough and scaly) which are part of the disease called pellagra.

Pyridoxine (B_6) is widely distributed among foods, so symptoms of deficiency (neuritis, convulsions, anemia, rash) occur only in the rare individual who has an inherited need of extra amounts.

Cobalamine (B_{12}) is widely distributed among animal foods, including milk, but absent in the vegetable kingdom. Deficiency causes pernicious anemia. (Strict vegetarians who aren't eating dairy products have to take their B_{12} in pill form.)

479. Vitamin C (ascorbic acid) occurs most abundantly in oranges, lemons, grapefruit, raw and properly canned tomatoes and tomato juice, raw cabbage. It occurs in fair amounts in several other fruits and vegetables, including potatoes. It is included in many vitamin preparations. It is easily destroyed in cooking. It is necessary for the development of bones, teeth, blood vessels, and other tissues, and plays a part in the functioning of most of the cells in the body. Deficiency is commonest in babies living on cow's milk without orange or tomato juice or vitamin C medicine, and shows itself in painful hemorrhages around the bones and in swollen, bleeding gums. This condition is called scurvy. There is no scientific proof that large doses of vitamin C prevent or cure colds.

480. Vitamin D is needed in large amounts for growth, particularly of the bones and teeth. It helps get calcium and phosphorus, which are in the food in the intestines, absorbed into the blood and deposited in the growing parts of the bones. That's why it should be added to the diet of children, especially in the period of rapid growth in infancy. Ordinary foods contain only a small amount. The sun's rays shining on the fat in people's skins manufacture vitamin D right there, and that's how they naturally get it when they live outdoors and wear few clothes. When they live in colder climates, they cover up their bodies with clothes and live indoors. The sun's rays in these regions are more slanting and are shut off by soot in the air and by window glass. Various fish liver oils and synthetic preparations are then the best source of vitamin D. (Fish store it in their livers by eating minute plants that float on the surface of the ocean. Sunshine manufactures it in these plants.) Vitamin D deficiency results in soft, bent bones, poor teeth, weak muscles and ligaments. This is called rickets.

Fully grown people probably receive enough vitamin D from the small amounts in eggs, butter, fish, and from a little sunshine. But children who are not getting lots of sunshine should drink milk containing vitamin D, or take a special preparation of vitamin D, summer and winter, until they have reached full height in adolescence. Mothers need extra vitamin D during pregnancy and breast-feeding.

WATER AND ROUGHAGE

481. Water provides no calories or vitamins, but it is vitally important in the makeup and working of the body. (A baby's body is 60 percent water.) A child should have a chance to drink water between meals in very hot weather, but otherwise she gets all she needs in milk, juices, and formula. Most foods are largely composed of water, too, and that is how people receive most of their daily needs.

482. Roughage means the fibers in vegetables, fruits, and grains (bran, for instance) that our intestines can't digest and absorb. The roughage passes on in the bowel movement, unused in one sense but useful in another. It provides part of the bulk in the bowel contents that helps to stimulate the intestines to function. A person who stays on a bland diet, let's say milk and broth and eggs, is apt to become constipated from having too little substance left in the lower intestines. It is now suspected that the major factor in cancer of the large intestine is the slow passage of food caused by the lack of roughage in our overly refined diets.

FATS, STARCHES, SUGARS

483. Fuel. So far we have discussed the building materials of the body and the other substances that are necessary to make the system work right. But we haven't considered fuel. The body, being a sort of engine, requires constant fueling just as an automobile needs gasoline. When a person is asleep, the heart still beats, the intestines contract, the liver, kidneys, and other organs keep working. This is like an automobile in neutral with the motor idling. When the person wakes up, moves around, works, runs, she or he burns more fuel just as the automobile does. Most of the food children eat is used up daily for fuel, even when they are growing rapidly.

The fuel substances are starch, sugar, fat (and, to a slight degree, protein). A starch is composed of a chemical combination of sugars. In the intestines, it is broken up into sugars before it is absorbed into the body. Because starches and sugars are so closely related, they are lumped together under the term **carbohydrates.**

484. The body's fat. When a person eats more fat, sugar, starch, and protein than is needed for fuel, the extra is converted into fat and stored under the skin and in other regions. Eating too little "fuel" causes the body to use up some of its own fat and become thinner. The "fat pad," which all people have to a greater or lesser degree, serves not only as a storehouse of fuel but helps, like a blanket, to keep a person warm.

485. Calories. The fuel value of food is measured in calories. Water and minerals have no calories; that is, they have no fuel or energy in them. Fat is rich in calories; an ounce of it has twice as many calories as an ounce of starch, sugar, or protein. Butter, margarine, vegetable oil, which are almost entirely fat, and cream and salad dressings, which contain a lot of it, are therefore very high in calories.

Sugars and syrups are also very high in calories, because they are wholly carbohydrates and contain no water or undigestible roughage.

Grains (which we eat as cereals, breads, crackers, macaroni, puddings, etc.) and starchy vegetables (such as potatoes, beans, corn) are high in calories because of the large proportion of starch in their makeup.

Meats, poultry, fish, eggs, cheese are high in calories because of their combination of protein and fat. Most of us do not receive as many daily calories from these foods as we do from grains and starchy vegetables, because we eat them in smaller amounts. Milk is a fine source of calories because of its sugar, fat, and protein, and because it is easily taken in good amounts.

Fresh and stewed fruits in general provide a fair number of calories because of the natural sugar they contain. Bananas and dried fruit are richer in calories (comparable to potatoes).

Vegetables vary from moderately high to low in calories (mostly in the form of starch and sugar). The vegetables with a moderately high number of calories are white and sweet potatoes, corn, and such beans as soy, navy, baked, and lima. The vegetables that provide a fair number of calories are peas, beets, carrots, onions, parsnips, squash, beet greens. Vegetables low in calories are string beans, cabbage, cauliflower, celery, spinach, tomatoes, lettuce, Swiss chard, broccoli, asparagus.

SENSIBLE DIET

486. Keep a balanced attitude. You don't judge foods on calories alone, or on vitamins alone, or on minerals alone. Everybody in the long run needs a balance of low- and high-calorie foods as well as a balance in other respects in the diet. If a person takes one aspect of diet too seriously and forgets the others, it's apt to lead to trouble. An adolescent girl acquires a fanatical zeal to reduce, leaves out all the foods in which she has heard there are more than a few calories, tries to live on vegetables, juices, fruit, and coffee. She is bound to be sick if she keeps on. Serious-minded parents who have the mistaken idea that vitamins are the whole show and that starches are inferior serve their child carrot salad and grapefruit for supper. The poor child can't get enough calories out of that to satisfy a rabbit. A plump mother from a plump family, ashamed of her son's scrawniness, serves him only rich foods. These depress his appetite further. Taking them in small amounts, he is apt to be deprived of minerals and vitamins. Read Sections 499–506 on America's deteriorating diet.

487. A simple guide to diet. The whole business of diet sounds complicated, but it needn't be. Fortunately, parents don't have to figure out the perfect diet for their child. The experiments of Dr. Davis and others have shown that children's own appetites seek a well-balanced diet in the long run (Section 467), **provided** they haven't been urged or given prejudices against foods, and provided they are offered a reasonable variety of wholesome, natural, unrefined foods. The parents' job is to have a general idea of the kinds of foods that combine to make a good diet, and which ones can be substituted for those that the child has lost the taste for. All foods can be divided into four groups: the milk group, the meat group, the vegetables and fruits group, and the breads and cereals group. Roughly speaking, the following are required every day:

1. Milk (in any form), preferably 1½ pints.
2. Meat or poultry or fish.
3. An egg 3–4 times a week.
4. Vegetable, green or yellow, one or two times, some of it raw.
5. Fruit, two or three times, at least half of it raw, including orange juice (extra fruit can substitute for vegetable and vice versa).
6. Starchy vegetable, one or two times.
7. Whole grain bread, crackers, cereals, one to three times.
8. Vitamin D (in milk or in drops).

Now we are ready to discuss actual foods.

Foods and Meals

MILK

488. Milk after a year. Milk contains almost all the food elements that a human being needs: protein, fat, sugar, minerals, and most of the vitamins. Children who are taking a well-balanced diet except for milk are likely to get enough of **most** of these elements from other foods. The exception is calcium. Milk is the only food that contains a lot of it. That is why you would like a child to average between 1½ and 2 pints a day, in some form.

Remember, though, that many children want less one day or one week, more the next, and that the surest way to keep them liking it is to let them take less temporarily when they feel that way. When children cut down, don't urge them. If they aren't back to a pint and a half in a few weeks, think of all the other ways you can serve milk.

489. Substitutes for plain milk. Precooked and dry cereals absorb a lot of milk in preparing. There are all the milk puddings from junket to rice pudding. Yogurt is made of milk. Various soups can be mixed with milk instead of water. Baked macaroni, scalloped and mashed potatoes, and many other cooked dishes can be made with milk.

What about flavoring milk? It is better to avoid flavoring if the child takes a reasonable amount of milk in other forms. But if necessary milk can be made into cocoa or hot chocolate, or served cold, flavored with a little chocolate syrup.

However, chocolate upsets some small children, so it is preferable to delay it until the age of 2, and to start very gradually. Milk can be flavored with vanilla or any of the commercial cereal-and-malt preparations sold for this purpose. With any flavoring, avoid making the milk really sweet, for fear of spoiling the appetite. Sipping a drink through a straw or glass tube may make it seem like a treat.

A flavored drink is likely to lose some of its appeal, anyway, when the novelty wears off. This is especially apt to happen if a parent begins to urge it the first time the child takes less than a glassful. It can't be repeated too often that when a parent says, "Drink a little more of your chocolate milk" (or anything else), it begins to take away a child's appetite.

Cheese is a useful form of milk. An ounce of most varieties contains about the same amount of calcium as 8 ounces of milk. But there are two important exceptions. You need three times as much cream cheese (3 ounces) to supply the amount of calcium in an 8-ounce glass of milk. Cottage cheese provides still less; in fact, it takes 10 ounces of cottage cheese to supply the calcium in 8 ounces of milk.

Cottage cheese, having little fat, is the most easily digested, and so it can be eaten in larger amounts, mixed with grated raw vegetables or a little fruit or applesauce. Other cheeses, being rich in fat, should be started gradually, and the child will probably want only small amounts. They can be served as spreads, or grated into other foods, or in pieces.

If children don't want to take milk in any form (or are allergic to it), they should be receiving calcium in some other form that the doctor prescribes.

Butter or fortified margarine should be added very gradually to vegetables and to bread around the age of a year. The digestive system needs time to adjust to increased amounts of fat.

Normally, growing children over the age of a year should be drinking 2 percent milk to decrease their butterfat intake, unless your doctor advises otherwise. Butter, cream, and ice cream intake should be limited for children of all ages because of the likelihood that they contribute to arteriosclerosis and coronary heart disease, especially in families which are particularly susceptible. (See Section 506.)

MEATS, FISH, EGGS

490. Meats. Most babies by the age of a year will be eating ground or fine-minced beef, chicken, lamb, liver, bacon, veal, ham, and pork when these are served to the rest of the family, or they can continue having them as junior foods from jars or cans. Bacon contains little protein so should not be counted on regularly as a meat. Most of the fat should be trimmed off meats. Pork is an excellent source of vitamins. It should be thoroughly cooked, so that it is white all through, not pink. Incompletely cooked pork is the source of the dangerous disease trichinosis. Frankfurters, bologna, and other "luncheon meats" contain nitrates and too much fat and salt and what meat is in them is of poor quality. They should be avoided altogether.

Many young children who love the taste of meat turn against it if it isn't cut up or ground finely enough. They become a little frightened and gag easily at lumps that don't easily turn to mush. So continue to mince fine or grind the meats until the child is 5 or 6.

491. Fish of the white, non-oily varieties, such as cod, haddock, halibut, flounder, can be started at the age of a year, baked, boiled, or broiled. It should be carefully crumbled with the fingers to remove bones. The more oily fish and canned fish may be added gradually at 2. (Canned tuna fish comes packed in water as well as oil. The type packed in water is easier for children to digest.) Some children love fish, and then it makes a fine substitute for meat once or twice a week. But many others stay firmly opposed even after several trials. Don't urge it.

492. Eggs. Eggs are equally valuable hard-boiled, soft-boiled, scrambled, fried, cooked into foods, or served in drinks. It is desirable for babies (starting at 9–12 months) and young children to have 3–4 eggs a week if they like them, for protein.

If children dislike most meats and fish, or you cannot get

them, their protein needs will probably be covered by 1½ to 2 pints of milk daily and 3–4 eggs a week, since they are getting some protein in their whole grains and vegetables. Peanut butter is a popular source of protein.

If children dislike eggs or are allergic to them, it is more important for them to have meat regularly.

See Section 506 on eggs and heart disease.

VEGETABLES

493. Varieties of vegetables. The baby during the first year has probably had most of the following vegetables: spinach, peas, onions, carrots, asparagus, chard, squash, tomatoes, beets, celery, potatoes.

Before a year the change should have been made gradually from pureed to a coarser, lumpy consistency. (Naturally, some pureed and finely mashed vegetables can still be served.) Peas should be mashed slightly to avoid their being swallowed whole.

Sweet potatoes or yams can be used at times instead of white potatoes, beginning at a year. If you have been sticking to the easily digested vegetables up to the age of a year, you can try gradually the less popular and sometimes less digestible ones, such as lima beans (mashed), broccoli, cabbage, cauliflower, turnips, parsnips. Much of their strong taste can be removed by changing the cooking water twice, though this destroys some of the vitamins. Some children like them and digest them well, but many won't touch them. Wait until 2 years to serve corn in the kernel. Young children don't chew it; it comes through unchanged. Use only tender corn. When cutting it off the cob, don't cut too close. Then each kernel will be cut open. At 3 or 4, when you start corn on the cob, slice down the center of each row of kernels, so that they are all open.

The more easily digested raw vegetables are usually started between 1 and 2 years for the child with a good digestion. The best are peeled tomatoes, lettuce, sliced string beans, shredded carrots, scraped chopped celery. They should be well scrubbed. Go slowly at first and see how they are digested. Orange juice or sweetened lemon juice can be used for dressing.

Raw vegetable juices can be started at the same time. Raw vegetables and vegetable juices are not only as good as cooked vegetables for the child who digests them well—they are better, because the vitamins have not been partly destroyed by heat, and minerals and vitamins have not been dissolved out in the cooking water.

If a child has temporarily turned against plain vegetables, remember vegetable soups: pea, tomato, celery, onion, spinach, beet, corn, and the soups that contain a large amount of mixed vegetables.

Some commercially prepared vegetable soups are very high in salt, so you need to read the label carefully. Almost all commercially prepared soups need to be diluted with equal amounts of milk or water. If they're given to children in the undiluted form, right out of the can, they can be harmful because the salt is too highly concentrated.

494. Temporary substitutes for vegetables. Suppose a child has refused vegetables in any form for weeks. Will the nutrition suffer? Vegetables are particularly valuable for various minerals and vitamins, and also for roughage. But a variety of fruits supply many of the minerals and vitamins, and the same amount of roughage. The child who is taking vitamin drops, milk, meat, and egg is getting the other salts and vitamins that fruits do not provide so well. In other words, if your child dislikes all vegetables but likes fruits, don't fuss. Serve fruit two or three times a day and forget about vegetables for a few weeks or even months. If you don't make an issue of them, the chances are great that the child's appetite will swing around to them again in time.

FRUITS

495. Fruits. A baby during the first year has probably had stewed or canned applesauce, apricots, prunes, pears, peaches, pineapple and raw, ripe banana, apple, pear, avocado. By a year some of these should be served in a lumpy consistency. Canned fruits, such as pears, peaches, pineapple, put up for adults are not so desirable because they are heavily sweetened with syrup. At least pour the syrup off. Many canned fruits are now available in a syrup made only from fruit juice, without added sugar.

Raw fruits, such as oranges, peaches, apricots, plums, seedless grapes, and melons are usually added between the ages of 1 and 2 years for children with a good digestion. When the peel is left on, the fruit should be washed to remove chemicals used in spraying.

It is usually recommended to wait until the age of 2 to add cherries and raw berries (strawberries, raspberries, blackberries, blueberries, huckleberries, loganberries). Strawberries sometimes cause a rash. Small children swallow berries whole and pass them that way, so mash them until your child chews well. Remove cherry pits until the child can separate them in the mouth.

Dried fruits, such as prunes, apricots, figs, dates, can be given unstewed at age 2, chopped in salads or whole for nibbling. They should be well washed unless the package states they are ready for eating raw. These dried fruits stick to the teeth for a long time, so they should not be used frequently or the teeth should be brushed promptly.

CEREALS AND SUPPERS

496. Cereals. Babies at a year should be taking one or a variety of the precooked, whole grain cereals, and also cooked oatmeal and cooked whole wheat cereals that the rest of the family eats. If they like these, continue to serve them once or twice a day indefinitely.

Remember that young children like their foods either firm or else quite soft and runny. They are apt to dislike pasty consistencies. So keep cereal mixtures thin.

If you see signs of boredom with one, try another that your child may not have been so keen about before.

There are also the dry cereals, some of which are wholesome, some not. Whole wheat and oat cereals are the valuable ones, because they are rich in vitamins, minerals, and protein. Corn and rice are less valuable. I wouldn't buy cereals that are not whole grain. Cereals coated with sugar are junk foods and their manufacturers are irresponsible. Tell your children firmly, when they beg, that you won't buy them.

497. Breads are cereals. If a child is sick of the ordinary cereal for breakfast, you can serve bread, toast, rolls, or buns made of whole or cracked wheat, rye, oatmeal, or banana. A cereal in baked form is just as valuable as one that has been boiled. The fact that it is not hot makes no difference in its food value or digestibility. Spread with butter or margarine (starting with a small amount for the 1-year-old). You can also spread with pureed fruit or yogurt if it makes the bread more appealing.

498. Lunch or supper, whichever is the simpler meal. In the family in which I was brought up the young children had a light supper at 5:30 and were in bed by 6:45. Then our parents had a quiet, dignified dinner. When I practiced pediatrics in New York City, most of the families for whom I was doctor followed this same pattern. So I automatically think of supper as the light meal for children. This is generally not true, for throughout most of this country the children have their main meal in the evening with their parents; for them lunch is the light meal.

Many parents complain that they get in a rut about the lighter meal, lunch or supper, and can't think how to vary it. A good rough rule is to serve:

1. A filling dish with plenty of calories, **and**
2. Either a fruit or vegetable.

Breads and sandwiches of several kinds can be the filling dish as babies grow older. When they're only a year old, they make slow work of bread, and they always pull a sandwich apart to get at the filling. But nearer to 2 years, they can handle these well. You can use rye bread, whole wheat bread, oatmeal bread, or banana bread to start with, and by the age of 2 add pumpernickel or nut bread. Spread with a little butter, margarine, cottage or creamed cheese.

Sandwiches can be made with a wide variety of other foods, plain or in combination: raw vegetable (lettuce, tomato, grated carrot, or cabbage), stewed fruit, chopped dried fruit, peanut butter, egg, canned fish, minced poultry, and meats. Cheese can be used as a spread or grated, and later in thin slices. Creamed cheese or a little yogurt can be combined with many of the substances listed above.

A fairly substantial dish is a broth or soup containing lots of barley or brown rice, or a vegetable soup, plain or creamed, with a couple of handfuls of whole wheat toast cut into small cubes to toss in.

A poached or coddled or scrambled egg can be given on toast or with toast crumbled into it. Or serve with bread on the side.

Simple whole grain crackers (the unsalted type) can be served plain, or with a spread, or in a bowl of hot or cold milk. (Graham crackers have few calories.) Bread and toast in slices or pieces can also be served in a bowl of cold or hot milk.

Potato is a good filling dish if the child is fond of it.

Cooked, precooked, or dry cereal for supper can be made more appealing by adding sliced raw fruit, stewed fruit, chopped dried fruit or a little brown sugar, honey, or molasses.

Instead of a filling first course followed by stewed or raw fruit, you can serve first a cooked green or yellow vegetable, or a vegetable or fruit salad. Then follow with a milk-pudding dessert: custard, baked or boiled, or bread pudding. A banana makes an excellent filling dessert.

There are some children who never want and never seem to need much starch. They are able to get enough calories from milk, meats, fruits, vegetables to gain weight reasonably. They also get their B-complex vitamins from these foods. In other words, grains and other starches are the things you least need to worry about in your children's diet. Let them go without them for weeks if they are doing well otherwise.

LESS VALUABLE AND UNDESIRABLE FOODS

499. America's deteriorating diet. It is sad that the richest country in the world, which consumes the lion's share of the world's protein, also contains millions of people who are on grossly deficient diets. Some of these millions can't afford to buy—for themselves or for their children—the right ingredients. Other millions have enough money but, prodded by advertising, enamored of sweets, and disinclined to listen to warnings, they feed themselves and their children large amounts of junk that is undermining health. The harm comes principally from the excessive proportion of sugar, refined starches, animal fats, and salt in our diets.

Bottled pop, soda fountain concoctions, candy, gum, the sugar coating on dry cereals, rich cookies and crackers and pastries all take away our appetites for better foods, rot teeth, favor obesity, and, in those with a family tendency, favor premature death through diabetes and arteriosclerosis.

I mean that we ought to take much more seriously the deterioration of the American diet. We should serve our children wholesome meals made up largely of vegetables, fruits, whole grains, and lean meats. We should keep junk foods out of our homes and do everything we can to help our children avoid them outside the home.

See Section 482 on lack of roughage.

500. Cookies, cakes, rich crackers, pastries. They quickly satisfy a child's appetite, but give him practically no minerals, vitamins, roughage, or protein. They are sometimes called "deprived" foods. They cheat children by making them feel well fed when they are being partly starved, and by spoiling their appetites for better foods.

You don't have to be so suspicious of rich, refined foods that you stop your children from eating cake at a birthday party. It's the steady diet of such foods that deprives them of nutrition. There's no sense starting them at home when there is no need.

Filled pastries, such as custard and cream pies, eclairs, cream puffs, have an additional danger. Harmful bacteria grow readily in these fillings if they are not kept well refrigerated. They are a frequent cause of food poisoning.

501. Highly sweetened foods are also undesirable in the diet. They quickly satisfy the appetite, take it away for better foods, and favor obesity and decay of the teeth. Give children their cereal and fruits without extra sugar. **Jellies, jams, most canned fruits** contain excessive amounts of sugar, and it's best not to get in the habit of serving them. If occasionally it is convenient to give them canned peaches because the rest of the family is having them, pour off the syrup or buy canned fruit packed in fruit juice without added sugar. Raisins, dates, dried prunes, and figs are also believed to be hard on the teeth when eaten regularly because they stick to the teeth for such a long time. Brush teeth after meals, anyway.

502. Candy, sodas, sundaes bring up special problems because they are often eaten between meals, when they have their worst effect on appetite and teeth, and because so many other children are eating them. You have to let a child have a serving of good ice cream when the rest of the family or the gang is enjoying it. But it's sensible to avoid sweets between meals, and to avoid candy even at the end of meals. Candy, particularly, is suspected of favoring decay of the teeth because it keeps the mouth syrupy for some time.

It's easy enough to keep young children from the candy habit by not having it around the home, and to avoid sodas and sundaes by not buying them. It is more difficult with the school-age child who has found out all about these delights. But I would encourage parents to explain the bad effects of sweets on the teeth and make a flat rule against them.

503. Craving for sweets is often caused by parents. Children like sweets, for one reason, because their hungry, growing bodies recognize the extra calories in them. But it is not certain that unspoiled children want a lot of them. A few small children actually dislike all sweet foods. Dr. Clara Davis in her experiments in letting children choose their own diets from a variety of **natural** foods found that in the long run they wanted only a reasonable amount of the sweeter foods.

I think much of the exaggerated craving for sweets is caused unwittingly by parents. A parent, trying to get a child to finish a vegetable, says, "You can't have your ice cream until you've finished your spinach," or, "If you eat up all your cereal, I'll give you a piece of candy." When you hold back on food (or a prize of any kind), it whets the desire. This has exactly the opposite effect from what the parent wants: The child gets to despise spinach and cereal, and to want ice cream and candy more and more. I'd say jokingly that the only safe way to bribe a child about food is to say, "You can't have your spinach until you've eaten your ice cream." Seriously, though, **never** hold back on one food until another is eaten. Let your children go on thinking their plain foods are just as good as the sweet ones. If one day they catch sight of their dessert first and ask for it, let them have it right away, willingly.

504. Corn, rice, and refined wheat are less valuable than whole wheat and oats. Corn and rice are relatively low in vitamins and valuable proteins (even before they are refined) compared with oats, rye, and whole wheat. And when any grain is refined, much of its vitamins, minerals, and roughage are removed in the process. Therefore, the foods not to serve to children are refined (white) wheat cereals, white bread, macaroni, spaghetti, noodles, crackers (aside from whole wheat crackers), rice, corn meal, corn cereals, hominy. Then there are the desserts made from these grains: cornstarch, rice, tapioca puddings. When rice is used for cereal, puddings, and as a substitute for potato, you should use the unpolished brown rice. Enriched white bread has had some of the original B-complex vitamins restored, but it does not contain all the values in whole wheat bread by far.

505. Coffee and tea are not good drinks for children because they take the place of milk and because they contain the stimulant caffeine. (Cola and other sodas and chocolate drinks also contain caffeine, as well as excess sugar.) Most children are stimulated enough already. It's easier and safer not to get started with these beverages.

506. Avoiding later coronary heart disease. Arteriosclerosis is appearing in younger and younger adults—occasionally even in children—in rich countries like America.

Probably the most significant causative factor is a chemical and metabolic tendency that favors arteriosclerosis, and that runs in certain families. Families that have a history of early heart attacks and strokes should have their children tested in infancy to see whether they are susceptible. If they are, they should be on preventive diets all their lives.

Even though the final scientific word has not been said on the causes of arteriosclerosis, I think it is wise for all parents to keep their children's diets within sensible limits. I'd try to avoid obesity in infancy (Section 674) and in later childhood (Section 675). When my children were entering adolescence I'd limit eggs to one a week, avoid the meats that contain a lot of fat (steaks, fatty hamburger, frankfurters, sausages, minced "luncheon meats" in loaves, such as bologna and salami). I'd cut the visible fat off servings of beef, lamb, ham, and pork. I'd serve only skim milk (except for small children in the family), corn-oil margarine for butter; omit cakes, pastries, cookies. In other words, proteins should be lean meats, poultry, and fish; desserts should be fruits. To lessen the chance of obesity I'd keep out of the house sweet carbonated drinks, sugary dry cereals, sweet crackers, and candy.

FROZEN FOODS

507. Frozen foods are just as good for children as fresh and canned foods, if used correctly. Freezing a food breaks it down chemically, just as cooking it does. It is then in a state in which both people and germs can digest it better. In other words, a cooked or a frozen food spoils more rapidly than an ordinary raw food because poisonous bacteria can live and multiply in it more easily.

Foods that spoil easily when kept long out of the refrigerator are milk, foods made with milk (puddings, pastry fillings, creamy salad dressings), vegetables, poultry stuffing.

FEEDING BETWEEN MEALS

508. Use common sense between meals. Many young children, and some older ones, too, need a snack between meals. If it's the right kind of food, given at a sensible hour, presented in the right way, it shouldn't interfere with meals or lead to feeding problems.

Fruit and fruit and vegetable juices are easily and quickly digested and are least likely to favor tooth decay. Milk stays in the stomach much longer and is therefore more apt to take away appetite for the next meal. Occasionally, though, you see children who never can eat very much at one meal and get excessively hungry and tired before the next; they may thrive when given milk between meals. Its slow digestibility is what keeps them going, and they have a better appetite for the next meal because they're not exhausted.

Cakes, cookies, pastry, and salty and fried snack foods have three disadvantages: they are rich in calories, poor in other food values, and hard on the teeth. Even crackers and bread stick to the teeth for some time, and so are not ideal for a regular between-meal diet.

For most children the snack is best given midway between meals, or not closer than 1½ hours before the next one. Even here there are exceptions. There are children who receive juice in the middle of the morning but still get so hungry and cross before lunch is ready that they pick fights and refuse to eat. Getting a glass of orange or tomato juice the minute they get home, even though it is 20 minutes before lunch, improves their disposition and their appetite. So you see that what and when to feed between meals is a matter of common sense and doing what suits the individual child. Plenty of children can get along without any food between meals, and this is best of all for the teeth.

Parents may complain that their child eats badly at meals

but is always begging for food between meals. This problem doesn't arise because the parents have been lenient about food between meals. Quite the contrary. In every case that I have seen, the parents have been urging or forcing the child to eat at mealtimes and holding back on food at other times. It's the pushing that takes away the appetite at meals. After months of it the very sight of the dining room is enough to make the child's stomach revolt. But when the meal is safely over (though little has been eaten), the stomach feels natural again. Soon it's acting the way a healthy empty stomach is meant to act—it's asking for food. The treatment, then, is not to deny children food between meals but to let mealtime be so enjoyable that their mouths water then, too. What is a meal? It's food specially prepared to be appetizing. When a child finds it less appealing than snacks, something has gone wrong.

MEALS

509. Suggested guide for meals. (See Section 487.)

Breakfast

1. Fruit or fruit juice
2. Cereal
3. Egg (3–4 times a week)
4. Milk

Lunch or supper (the lighter meal)

1. A filling dish, such as:
   cereal (whole wheat or oats)
     or bread or sandwiches (whole grain)
     or potato
     or soup with crackers, toast, barley
     or a milk pudding
2. Vegetable or fruit, raw or cooked
3. Milk

Dinner or lunch (the full meal)

1. Meat or fish or poultry

2. Green or yellow vegetable (cooked or raw)
3. Potato
4. Raw fruit
5. Milk

Vitamin preparation daily
Fruit or tomato juice between meals if needed
Bread (whole grain) at meals if desired

Most children won't need a vitamin preparation after they reach their first birthday, if they're taking a reasonably well-balanced diet. Check with your doctor.

Of course, this is just a guideline and you can vary the meals according to your child's preferences and your family's routines.

Managing Young Children

PLAY AND OUTGOINGNESS

510. Play is serious business. When we see children building with blocks, pretending to be airplanes, learning to skip rope, we're apt to think, in our mixed-up, adult way, that these are just amusements, quite different from serious occupations such as doing lessons and holding a job. We are mixed up because most of us were taught in our own childhood that play was fun but that schoolwork was a duty and a job was a grind.

The baby passing a rattle from one hand to the other or learning to crawl downstairs, the small child pushing a block along a crack on the floor, pretending it's a car, are hard at work learning about the world. They are training themselves for useful work later, just as much as the high school student studying geometry. Children love their play, not because it's easy, but because it's hard. They are striving every hour of every day to graduate to more difficult achievements and to do what the older kids and grown-ups do.

The parents of a 1-year-old boy complain that he gets bored with hollow blocks and only wants to fit pots and pans together. One reason is that he knows already that his parents play with pots and pans and not with blocks. That makes pots and pans more fun. It must be for this reason that some 1-year-olds are fascinated with cigarettes.

511. Simple toys are best. Children usually love simple toys best and play with them longest. This isn't because children are simple—it's because they have so much imagination. There are two very different kinds of toy trains. One is made of metal painted to look real, and it's meant to run on a track. The other is made of plain, flat wooden blocks that link together easily. All that **young** children can do with the realistic train is push one car along the floor. It's too hard to put the cars on the track or hitch them together. They can't even put anything in the passenger coach until the top breaks off. After a while they get bored. The wooden block cars are different. Children can link a string of them together and admire the long train. Two make a trailer truck. They can pile small blocks on top, call it a freight train, and make deliveries. When they are bored with dry land, the blocks become separate boats or a string of barges with a tug. Children can go on like this forever.

Sometimes parents with little money to spend feel sad that they can't buy a shiny automobile for their children to pedal or a playhouse. But think what children can do with a large carton. By turns it's a bed, a house, a truck, a tank, a fort, a dolls' house, a garage. Don't take this idea so seriously that you never get your children a really fine plaything. The time will come when they want a three-wheel bike or an express cart with all their hearts, and you will want to buy it for them if you can. I only mean that simple things come first. Add the fancier toys as you can afford them and as you find out what your children really enjoy.

The baby, before he can use his hands, loves to watch bright-colored objects that hang on a string tied across the sides of his crib and that move slightly in the draft. In the last half of the first year, he loves objects to handle and rattle and chew, such as the newer plastic toys (small rings on a big ring, for example). There's no paint to come off, and there's no danger from chips, as there is with thin celluloid toys.

Around a year to a year and a half, the child is fascinated with putting one thing into another, and pushing or pulling it around. The block that runs on wheels and has holes for pegs is a favorite, but a plain box with a string is as good. As a matter of fact, pushing comes before pulling, and that's why the bell on wheels, pushed with a stick, is so popular. Hollow blocks don't interest a child as long as pots, pans, strainers, and spoons.

Soft dolls and woolly animals are loved by most children throughout the early years. Others see no sense in them.

As children get toward the age of 2, they're more interested in copying. First, it's the immediate things that mother and father do, like sweeping, washing dishes, and shaving. As they grow beyond 2, their imaginations become more creative. This is the period for dolls and dolls' furniture, trucks and cars, and above all, blocks. Blocks piled on top of each other are the Empire State Building; end to end they make a train. They can be laid out on the floor in the outline of a house or boat to sit in, and so on indefinitely. A good-size bag of wooden blocks of different shapes is worth ten toys to any child up to 6 or 8.

512. Let children play at their own level. A grown-up playing with a child often is tempted to make the play too complicated. Parents who have bought their small child a doll with a whole wardrobe of clothes would like to dress the doll just right, beginning with the underclothes. But the little child may want to start with the red overcoat. A mother buys her small, sick daughter a box of crayons and a book of outline pictures to color. She picks up an orange crayon and rubs it back and forth across the page, not trying to keep within the lines, not worrying that she's using orange for sky and grass. It's hard for a parent not to say, "Oh, no, not like that. See, you do it this way." Or a father who has never had enough chance to play with trains produces a whole set for his 3-year-old at Christmas. The father can't wait to get started. He fits the tracks together. But the child has grabbed one of the cars and has shot it across the room, smack against the wall. "No, no!" says Father. "You put the car on the track like this." The child gives the car a push along the track, and it falls off at the curve. **"No, no,"** says Father. "You have to wind up the engine and let the engine pull the car." But the poor child hasn't the strength to wind up the engine or the skill to put the cars on the track and doesn't care about realism yet. After the father has been impatient for 15 minutes, the child gets a strong dislike for tin trains and an uncomfortable feeling of not being able to measure up to his father's expectations and wanders off to do something else.

Children become interested in dressing dolls properly, coloring carefully, playing trains realistically, each at a certain stage of development. You can't hurry them. When you try, you only make them feel incompetent. This does more harm than good. Your children love to have you play with them if you are willing to play at their level. Let **them** show **you** how. Help them if they ask for it. If you've bought them a toy that is too complicated, either let them misuse it in their own way or tactfully hide it until they're older.

513. Generosity can't be forced. When children begin to play around each other at 1½, 2, 2½, they are apt to grab things from each other without much ceremony. **Small** children who have a possession never give it up to be nice. They either hang on like grim death, perhaps whacking at the attacker, or they give it up in bewilderment. Parents, seeing these goings-on, are sometimes horrified.

If your girl (or boy), around 2, always seems to be the grabber, it doesn't mean that she's going to be a bully. She's too young to have much feeling for others. Let her grab sometimes. If she's doing it constantly, it may help to let her play part of the time with slightly older children who stand up for their rights. If she always intimidates a certain child, better keep them separated for a while. If your child is hurting another or looks as if she were planning murder, pull her away in a matter-of-fact manner and get her interested in something else. It's better not to heap shame on her—that only makes her feel abandoned, and more aggressive.

If the child goes on being unusually aggressive when she's 3 or older and doesn't seem to be learning anything about cooperative play, it's time to look into her adjustment at home. It's in these early, less serious problems that a family social agency or a child guidance clinic can help a parent and child most easily and most thoroughly (Sections 633 and 634).

If your child at 2 doesn't give up her possessions, she is behaving normally for this age. She will come around to generosity **very** gradually, as her spirit grows up and as she learns to enjoy and love other children. If you make her give up her treasured cart whenever another child wants it, you only give her the feeling that the whole world is out to get her things away from her—not just the children but the grown-ups, too. This makes her **more** possessive, instead of less. When a child is reaching the stage when she's beginning to enjoy playing with others, somewhere around 3, you can help to make a game of sharing. "First Johnny has a turn pulling the cart and Catherine rides in it. Then Catherine pulls the cart and Johnny has a turn to ride in it." This makes sharing fun instead of an unpleasant duty. Timidity is discussed in Section 517.

514. Helping a first child to be outgoing. Most first children grow up happy and well adjusted like most second children in a family. But a few of them have a harder time adjusting to the outside world.

Parents are apt to say, "The second baby is so easy. She doesn't cry. She is rarely a serious problem. She plays contentedly by herself, and yet she is so friendly if you go near her." When she's several years older, the parents say, "The second is such a friendly, outgoing child that everybody just naturally loves her. When we're walking down the street, strangers smile at her and stop us to ask how old she is. They only notice the older one afterward, to be polite. You can see that it hurts the older one's feelings. He craves attention much more than the second."

What makes the difference? One trouble is that the first baby in some families gets more fussing over than is good for him, especially after the age of 6 months, when he begins to be able to amuse himself. The parents may be noticing him, suggesting things to him, picking him up, more than is necessary. This gives him too little chance to develop his own interests. He too seldom makes the first greeting, because the parents are speaking to him first. He may be shown off to other grown-ups too much. A little of this is harmless; a steady diet of it makes him self-conscious. When the first child is sick, the parents naturally hang over his bed with more concern and anxiety than they will show after they have had longer experience. When he is naughty, they are more apt to take it seriously and to make a fuss about it.

A steady flow of fussy attention toward a child tends to spoil him somewhat for the outside world in two ways. He grows up assuming that he is the hub of the universe and that everyone should automatically admire him whether he is being attractive or not. On the other hand, he hasn't been practicing how to make his own fun or how to be outgoing and appealing to people.

Of course, the answer is not to ignore a first child. He needs affection and responsiveness in good measure. But let him play his own games as long as he is interested and happy, with the least possible interference, bossing, scolding, and anxious concern. Give him a chance to start the conversation sometimes. When visitors come, let him make up to them himself. When he comes to you for play or for affection, be warm and friendly, but let him go when he turns back to his own pursuits.

Another factor that sometimes seems to make a first child unsociable is too serious an attitude on the parents' part. It isn't that the parents are grim people; they can be easygoing with their friends and their later children. They are just trying too hard with the first.

You know what I mean if you have ever seen tense people trying to ride a horse for the first time. They sit stiff as china dolls, don't know how to accommodate to the horse's movement, and are apt to be unnecessarily bossy. It's hard work for the horse and the rider. Experienced riders know how to relax, how to give in and conform to some of the horse's motions without losing their seat, how to direct the horse gently. Bringing up a child isn't much like riding a horse, but the same spirit works in both jobs.

A similar example is the young military officer or executive who is put in charge of others for the first time. If he isn't too sure of himself, he may be unnecessarily solemn and strict in the beginning, for fear he won't keep control. The more experienced person isn't afraid to be friendly and reasonable.

You may say, "The trouble is that I **am** inexperienced." But you don't have to have experience to do a wonderful job with a baby—all you need to start with is a friendly spirit. A child won't throw you the way a horse might (at least not until he's much older), and he won't laugh at you the way a squad of soldiers might. Don't be afraid to relax, to be agreeable. Better too easygoing than too stiff.

EARLY CHILDHOOD

515. The control of aggression. Is gun play good or bad for children? For many years I emphasized its harmlessness. When thoughtful parents expressed doubt about letting their children have pistols and other warlike toys, because they didn't want to encourage them in the slightest degree to become delinquents or militarists, I would explain how little connection there was. In the course of growing up, children have a natural tendency to bring their aggressiveness more and more under control provided their parents encourage this. One- to 2-year-olds, when they're angry with another child, may bite the child's arm without hesitation. But by 3 or 4 they have already learned that crude aggression is not right. However, they like to pretend to shoot a pretend bad guy. They may pretend to shoot their mother or father, but grinning to assure them that the gun and the hostility aren't to be taken seriously.

In the 6- to 12-year-old period, children will play an earnest game of war, but it has lots of rules. There may be arguments and rough-housing, but real fights are relatively infrequent. At this age children don't shoot at their mother or father, even in fun. It's not that the parents have turned stricter; the children's own conscience has. They say, "Step on a crack; break your mother's back," which means that even the thought of wishing harm to their parents now makes them uncomfortable. In adolescence, aggressive feelings become much stronger, but well-brought-up children channel them into athletics and other competition or into kidding their pals.

In other words, I'd explain that playing at war is a natural step in the disciplining of the aggression of young children; that most clergymen and pacifists probably did the same thing; that an idealistic parent doesn't really need to worry about producing a scoundrel; that the aggressive delinquent was not distorted in personality by being allowed to play bandit at 5 or 10, he was neglected and abused in his first couple of years, when his character was beginning to take shape; that he was doomed before he had any toys worthy of the name.

But nowadays I'd give parents much more encouragement in their inclination to guide their child away from violence. A number of occurrences convinced me of the importance of this.

One of the first things that made me change my mind was an observation that an experienced nursery school teacher told me about. Her children were crudely bopping each other much more than previously, without provocation. When she remonstrated with them, they would protest, "But that's what the Three Stooges do." (This was a children's TV program made from old movie "shorts," full of violence and buffoonery, which had recently been introduced and which immediately became very popular.) This attitude of the children showed me that watching violence can lower a child's standards of behavior. Recent psychological experiments have shown that being shown brutality on film stimulates cruelty in adults, too.

What further shocked me into reconsidering my point of view was the assassination of President Kennedy, and the fact that some schoolchildren cheered about this. (I didn't so much blame the children as I blamed the kind of parents who will say about a President they dislike, "I'd shoot him if I got the chance!")

These incidents made me think of other evidences that Americans have often been tolerant of harshness, lawlessness, and violence. We were ruthless in dealing with the Indians. In some frontier areas we slipped into the tradition of vigilante justice. We were hard on the later waves of immigrants. At times we've denied justice to groups with different religious or political views. We have crime rates way above those of other, comparable nations. A great proportion of our adult as well as our child population has been endlessly fascinated with dramas of Western violence and with brutal crime stories, in movies and on television. We have had a shameful history of racist lynchings and murders, as well as regular abuse and humiliation. In recent years it has been realized that infants and small children are being brought to hospitals with severe injuries caused by gross parental brutality.

Of course, some of these phenomena are characteristic of

only a small percentage of the population. Even the others that apply to a majority of people don't necessarily mean that we Americans on the average have more aggressiveness inside us than the people of other nations. I think rather that the aggressiveness we have is less controlled, from childhood on.

To me it seems very clear that in order to have a more stable and civilized national life we should bring up the next generation of Americans with a greater respect for law and for other people's rights and sensibilities than in the past. There are many ways in which we could and should teach these attitudes. One simple opportunity we could utilize in the first half of childhood is to show our disapproval of lawlessness and violence in television programs and in children's gun play.

I also believe that the survival of the world now depends on a much greater awareness of the need to avoid war and to actively seek peaceful agreements. There are enough nuclear arms to utterly destroy all civilization. One international incident in which belligerence or brinkmanship was carried a small step too far could escalate into annihilation within a few hours. This terrifying situation demands a much greater stability and self-restraint on the part of national leaders and citizens than they have ever shown in the past. We owe it to our children to prepare them very deliberately for this awesome responsibility. I see little evidence that this is being done now.

When we let people grow up feeling that cruelty is all right provided they know it is make-believe, or provided they sufficiently disapprove of certain individuals or groups, or provided the cruelty is in the service of their country (whether the country is right or wrong), we make it easier for them to go berserk when the provocation comes.

But can we imagine actually depriving American children of their guns or of watching their favorite Western or crime programs? I think we should consider it—to at least a partial degree.

I believe that parents should firmly stop children's war play or any other kind of play that degenerates into deliberate cruelty or meanness. (By this I don't mean they should interfere in every little quarrel or tussle.)

If I had a 3- or 4-year-old son who asked me to buy him a gun, I'd tell him—with a friendly smile, not a scowl—that I don't want to give him a gun for even pretend shooting because there is too much meanness and killing in the world, that we must all learn how to get along in a friendly way together. I'd ask him if he didn't want some other present instead.

If I saw him, soon afterward, using a stick for a pistol in order to join a gang that was merrily going "bang-bang" at each other, I wouldn't rush out to remind him of my views. I'd let him have the fun of participating as long as there was no cruelty. If his uncle gave him a pistol or a soldier's helmet for his birthday, I myself wouldn't have the nerve to take it away from him. If when he was 7 or 8 he decided he wanted to spend his own money for battle equipment, I wouldn't forbid him. I'd remind him that I myself don't want to buy war toys or give them as presents; but from now on he will be playing more and more away from home and making more of his own decisions; he can make this decision for himself. I wouldn't give this talk in such a disapproving manner that he wouldn't dare decide against my policy. I would feel I'd made my point and that he had been inwardly influenced by my viewpoint as much as I could influence him. Even if he should buy weapons then, he would be likely to end up—in adolescence and adulthood—as thoughtful about the problems of peace as if I'd prohibited his buying them, perhaps more so.

One reason I keep backing away from a flat prohibition is that it would have its heaviest effect on the individuals who need it least. If all the parents of America became convinced and agreed on a toy-weapons ban on the first of next month, this would be ideal from my point of view. But this isn't going to happen for a long time, unless one nuclear missile goes off by accident and shocks the world into a banning of all weapons, real and pretend. A small percentage of parents—those most thoughtful and conscientious—will be the first ones who will want to dissuade their children from war toys; but their children will be most apt to be the sensitive, responsible children anyway. So I think it's carrying the issue unnecessarily far for those of us who are particularly concerned about peace and kindliness to insist that our young children demonstrate a total commitment to our cause while all their friends are gun toters. (It might be practical in a neighborhood where a majority of parents had the same conviction.) The main ideal is that children should grow up with a fond attitude toward all humanity. That will come about basically from the general atmosphere of our families. It will be strengthened by the attitude that we teach specifically toward other nations and groups. The elimination of war play would have some additional influence, but not as much as the two previous factors.

I feel less inclined to compromise on brutality on television and in movies. The sight of a real human face being apparently smashed by a fist has a lot more impact on children than what they imagine when they are making up their own stories. I believe that parents should flatly forbid programs that go in for violence. I don't think they are good for adults either. Young children can only partly distinguish between dramas and reality. Parents can explain, "It isn't right for people to hurt each other or kill each other and I don't want you to watch them do it."

Even if children cheat and watch such a program in secret, they'll know very well that their parents disapprove, and this will protect them to a degree from the coarsening effect of the scenes.

516. Naughty words. Sometimes at 3, more often at 4, children go through a phase of reveling in bathroom words. They gaily insult each other with expressions like, "You great big duty," and "I'll flush you down the toilet," and think they are very witty and bold. You should consider this a normal development. You can tell children to stop it if you don't like it, or you can let them have their fun until you've had enough.

As they grow older, all normal children who have a chance (as they should) to be around other children learn swear words and "dirty" words. Long before they know what the words mean, they know that they are naughty. Being human, they repeat them to show that they are worldly wise and not afraid to be a little bad. It's usually quite a shock to conscientious parents to hear these words coming from the mouths of their supposedly sweet innocents. What's a good parent to do? It's better not to jump out of your skin or act horribly shocked. For timid children this has too strong an effect; it worries them, makes them afraid to be around children who use bad words. But most children who find they have shocked their parents are delighted, at least secretly. Some of them go on cussing endlessly at home, hoping to get the same rise. Others, stopped at home by threats, use all their bad language elsewhere. The point is that when you tell children that just by making certain sounds they have the power to scandalize the whole world, it's like handing them a full-size cannon and telling them, "For goodness' sake, don't set it off." On the other hand, I don't think that you have to sit mute and just take it. You can just tell them firmly that you and most people don't like to hear those words and you don't want them to use them.

517. Timidity. A first child, say a girl, who has not had much chance to play with other children is apt, at 2 years of age, to let them take her toys away from her and push her around. She may just look perplexed or she may run crying to her parents each time. This is apt to worry the father and mother. In most cases it is a temporary state of affairs caused by inexperience. If she continues to play near children regularly, the chances are great that as the months go by she will learn how to get mad and stand up for her rights. It's wise for her parents not to show too much concern or sympathy, not to fight her battle for her, not to tell her she must share, but to suggest casually that she go and get the toy back.

The second or third child in a family rarely has this problem, probably because she's had to stand up for her rights from the age of 1 year.

If there is one aggressive child who regularly bullies your child and your child is becoming more intimidated rather than less as the weeks go by, it may be wise for a couple of months to take her somewhere else to play, where she will have more chance of finding her courage.

If a child goes on past 3 or 4 being easily picked on, it's a good idea to consult a child guidance clinic or a family social agency to try to find out what's wrong.

518. Biting humans. It's natural for babies around 1 year to take a bite out of their parent's cheek. Their teething makes them want to bite anyway, and when they feel tired they're even more in the mood for it. I don't think it means much, either, when a child between 1 and 2 bites another child, whether it's in a friendly or angry spirit.

After 2 or 2½ it depends on how often the biting occurs and how the child is getting along otherwise. If a girl is generally happy and outgoing but occasionally takes a bite when she gets in a fight, it's of no great importance. But if she is tense or unhappy much of the time and keeps biting other children for no good reason, it's a sign that something is wrong. Perhaps she is being bossed and disciplined too much at home and is in a frantic, high-strung state. Perhaps she has had too little chance to get used to other children and imagines they are dangerous and threatening to her. Perhaps she is jealous of a baby at home and carries over the fear and resentment to all other small children, as if they were competitors, too. If the cause and the cure are not easy to see, a children's psychiatrist will be able to help (Section 633).

Some parents who have been bitten ask if they should bite back. Parents can control their child better by staying in charge as a friendly boss than by descending to her age level to battle with bites, slaps, or shouts. Besides, when you bite or slap a 1-year-old, she's apt to keep it up, either as a fight or a game. And if you just look reproachful, you bring out her meanness. The only thing you need to do is to keep from being bitten again, by drawing back when she gets that gleam in her eye, showing her clearly that you don't like it and won't let it happen.

519. Comforting a hurt child. When a child is hurt he wants to be comforted and his parent feels like comforting him. This is natural and right.

Sometimes parents who are particularly anxious for their children to grow up brave and uncomplaining fear that comforting them will turn them into complainers. But a secure child isn't made dependent by ordinary comforting.

The child who is a crybaby over small hurts and aches has had a more complicated past. She may have been made **generally** dependent by all kinds of fussing and overprotection. Sometimes one of the parents is a person who, without realizing it, has a rather severe, critical attitude toward her at most times and shows tenderness mainly when she is hurt or ill. Your move here is not to be more severe when she's in trouble but to show that you enjoy and love her when she's all right. In another case a parent has an exaggerated horror of injuries, and the child has caught some of this anxiety.

It has been a tradition in many families to make boys ashamed of showing pain or fear. (I was brought up that way.) But this tends to teach them to repress and deny feelings of all kinds, including tenderness, and may, through the rest of life, interfere with good relationships with family, friends, and fellow workers.

Just don't exaggerate the hurt. End the comforting as soon as possible. Expect children to want to be braver and need comforting less for small injuries as they grow older.

PARENTS AS COMPANIONS

520. Children need friendly, accepting parents. Boys and girls need chances to be around their parents, to be enjoyed by them, and if possible, to do things with them. Unfortunately, a working parent is apt to come home wanting most of all to slump down and read the paper. If he understands how valuable his companionship is, he will feel more like making a reasonable effort. I say **reasonable** because I don't think the conscientious father (or mother, either) should force himself beyond his endurance. Better to play for 15 minutes enjoyably and then say, "Now I'm going to read my paper," than to spend all day at the zoo, crossly.

Sometimes a father is so eager to have his son turn out perfect that it gets in the way of their having a good time together. The man who is eager for his son to become an athlete may take him out at an early age to play catch. Naturally, every throw, every catch, has its faults. If the father is constantly criticizing, even in a friendly tone, the boy becomes uncomfortable inside. It isn't any fun. Also, it gives him the feeling of being no good, in his father's eyes and in his own. A boy comes around to an interest in sports in good time if he's naturally self-confident and outgoing. Feeling approved of by his father helps him more than being coached by him. A game of catch is fine if it's the son's idea and if it's for fun.

A boy doesn't grow spiritually to be a man just because he's born with a male body. The thing that makes him feel and act like a man is being able to copy, to pattern himself after, men and older boys with whom he feels friendly. He can't pattern himself after a person unless he feels that this person likes him and approves of him. If a father is always impatient or irritated with him, the boy is likely to feel uncomfortable not only when he's around his father but when he's around other men.

So a father who wants to help his son grow up comfortable about being a man shouldn't jump on him when he cries, scorn him when he's playing games with girls, or force him to practice athletics. He should enjoy him when he's around, give him the feeling he's a chip off the old block, share a secret with him, take him alone on excursions sometimes.

The child with only one parent, temporarily or permanently, is discussed in Sections 847, 848 and 849.

The parents' part in discipline is discussed in Section 57.

There's more on the parents' relations with son and daughter in Sections 563, 565, and 566.

521. A girl needs a friendly father, too. It's easy to see that a boy needs a father to pattern himself after, but many people don't realize that a friendly father plays a different but equally important part in the development of a girl. She doesn't exactly pattern herself after him, but she gains confidence in herself as a girl and a woman from feeling his approval. In order not to feel inferior to boys, she should believe that her father would welcome her in backyard sports, on fishing and camping trips, in attendance at ball games, whether or not she wants to accept. She gains confidence in herself from feeling his interest in her activities, achievements, opinions, and aspirations. Later, when she has boyfriends, it's important for him to welcome them, even if he secretly doesn't think they are quite good enough for her.

By learning to enjoy the qualities in her father that are particularly masculine, a girl is getting ready for her adult life in a world that is half made up of men. The way she makes friendships with boys and men later, the kind of man she eventually falls in love with, the kind of married life she makes, are all influenced strongly by the kind of relationship she has had with her father throughout her childhood.

522. Parents should go lightly on rough-housing and teasing. Lots of parents enjoy rough-housing with their young children, and most children love it, too. But children easily become overexcited by it, and this sometimes leads to nightmares. It's good to remember that at 2 and 3 and 4, children's loves and hates and fears get out of control easily. And young children can't distinguish too clearly between real and pretend. For them, a father who is pretending to be a bear or a prizefighter really becomes one for the time being. This is usually too much for a small child to take. So rough-housing should be mild and good-natured and brief—even when the child begs for more. Most important is that it shouldn't be a pretend fight or a pretend chase. Let it just be simple acrobatics. Stop, anyway, if a child gets worked up.

When people feel irritated at each other, they can't simply hit or insult each other. But according to the rules, it's all right to kid each other a little. So they learn to be kidders. Then when parents feel mildly irritated at their children, they may try to work it off as kidding. Children feel humiliated when laughed at, and don't know how to tease back. Teasing is too strong for young children.

GOING TO BED

523. Keeping bedtime happy. Three or four factors can make the difference between the child who goes to bed willingly and the one who stalls and argues.

Keep bedtime agreeable and happy. Remember that it is delicious and inviting to tired children if you don't turn it into an unpleasant duty. Have an air of cheerful certainty about it. Expect them to turn in at the hour you decide as surely as you expect them to breathe. It's good for children to be able to persuade parents to change their minds once in a while about bedtime (Fourth of July, for instance). But bedtime comes

too often for regular argument. It usually works best to have the nap come right after lunch, before children have had time to become absorbed in play. The relationship between supper and bedtime is usually more complicated because of the bath and the working parent's coming home.

Until children are at least 3 or 4, and in any case until they are responsible enough to like to get themselves to bed, lead them rather than push them with words. Carry the very small child affectionately. Lead the 3- or 4-year-old by the hand, both of you still chatting about what you were talking about before.

Small children are comforted by having a certain amount of ritual about going to bed. For example, the dolly is put in her bed and tucked in. Then the teddy bear is put in the child's bed. Then the child is tucked in and kissed. Then the parent pulls down the shade or puts out the light. Try not to rush going to bed, no matter how much of a hurry you are in. (On the other hand, it isn't wise to let the child keep lengthening the rituals.) Keep it peaceful. Tell or read a story regularly if you have time. It shouldn't be scary. Most children are helped in going to bed by having a cozy toy animal or doll for company in bed.

524. How much sleep does a child need anyway? You can usually trust an infant to take what rest he needs. By the time a child is 2 or more, you can't leave it all to him to decide. He may need more sleep but be kept from getting it by tenseness of different kinds: loneliness, fear of being left alone, fear of the dark, fear of nightmares, fear of wetting his bed, excitement from stimulating experiences. He may be all keyed up from competing with an older brother, or burned up with jealousy of a younger sister. He may be on edge each evening because there is always a tug of war with his parents about when he is to go to bed or because he is worrying about his schoolwork or the TV thriller he has been watching. The prevention of these various troubles is discussed elsewhere. I bring them up here only to point out at the start that you can't say that the child doesn't need more sleep just because he won't take it.

The average 2-year-old needs 12 hours of sleep at night and 1 to 2 hours of nap. The nap or rest usually shortens as he grows from 2 to 6, and bedtime at night stays the same. Between the ages of 6 and 9, the average child can usually give up an hour of his night's sleep, half an hour at a time, and, for instance, go to bed at 8 P.M. if he's getting up at 7 A.M. By the age of 12, he will probably have been able to clip off two more half hours and go to bed at 9 P.M. These are average figures. Some children need more, others less.

Many children stop going to sleep at naptime around the age of 3 or 4, but most of them still need a real rest or at least a quiet play period indoors after lunch until they are 5 or 6. Many wise schools provide a rest period through the sixth grade. It all depends on the individual child's temperament and activity.

Going-to-bed problems and sleep problems in infancy are discussed in Sections 346 and 347; around 2 years of age, in Sections 551 and 553; after 3, in Section 568.

DUTIES

525. Let them enjoy their duties. How do children learn to perform various duties? By their very nature, they start out feeling that dressing themselves, brushing their teeth, sweeping, putting things away are exciting and grown-up things to do. If their parents succeed in keeping on good terms with them as they grow older, they enjoy going on errands, carrying packages, raking the lawn, because they still want to have a part in important jobs and to please their mother and father. Most of us (including the authors) aren't able to bring up our children so well that we get cooperation all the time, but if we realize that children prefer to be helpful, we are less likely to make household tasks sound like unpleasant duties or to assign them when we're irritable.

Children can't be expected always to be responsible about their duties—even at 15 years. (Most adults lapse into irresponsibility at times, too.) They have to be reminded. If you can find the patience, try to make the reminder matter-of-fact, polite, as if you were speaking to an adult. It's the nagging, belittling tone that kills all pride in a job. It also helps a lot to assign children tasks that they can do in the company of other members of the family, whether it's dish-drying or lawn-mowing. Then the grown-upness of the task and the fun of helping spur them on.

526. Dressing themselves. Between the ages of 1 and 1½ years, children begin to try to undress themselves. (They pull the toe of the socks directly toward their stomachs, which makes it stick.) By about 2, they can do a pretty good job of stripping themselves. Now they try hard to put on their clothes, but get all tangled up. It probably takes them another year to learn to put the easier garments on right, and another year still (till about 4 or 5) to handle the trickier jobs, like laces and buttons.

This period from 1½ to 4 years requires a lot of tact. If you don't let them do the parts they are able to, or if you interfere too much, it's apt to make them angry. If they never have a chance to learn at the age when it appeals to them, they may lose the desire. Yet if you don't help them at all, they'll never be dressed and they may get frustrated at their own failure. You can help them tactfully in the jobs that are possible. Pull the socks partway off so that the rest is easy. Lay out the garment that they're going to want to put on, so that they'll start straight. Interest them in the easier jobs while you do the hard ones. When they get tangled up, don't insist on taking over but straighten them out so that they can carry on. If they feel that you are with them and not against them, they are much more cooperative. It takes patience, though.

527. Putting things away. When your daughter (or son) is very young and you still expect to pick up and put things away after she is through playing, you can do it as part of the play, with enthusiasm. "The square blocks go here, in big piles, and the long blocks go there. Over here let's pretend there's a garage, and all the cars go here to sleep at night." By the time she is 4 or 5, she has fallen into the habit of putting things away and enjoying it. Many times she does it without any reminder. But if she still needs help at times, join in sociably.

If you say to a 3-year-old, "Now put your things away," it sounds unpleasant. Even if she enjoys doing it, you are handing her a job that practically no 3-year-old has the perseverance to carry through. Furthermore, she's still at a very balky stage.

Cheerfully helping a child to put things away not only develops a good attitude in her but is easier for the parent than long arguments.

528. Dawdling. If you ever see a parent trying to get a dawdling child going in the morning, urging him, warning him, scolding him to get out of bed, to get washed, to get dressed, to eat his breakfast, to start for school, you will vow that you will never get in that fix. The dawdling child wasn't born that way. He was made that way gradually, in most cases, by constant pushing. "Hurry up and finish your lunch." "How many times do I have to tell you to get ready for bed?" It's easy to fall into the habit of prodding children, and it builds up an absentminded balkiness in them. Parents say they have to nag or the child won't get anywhere. It's a vicious circle, but the parent starts it, especially an impatient parent or one who doesn't leave enough time to allow for children's slow speed.

In the early years, before a child is capable of carrying out directions, lead him through his various routines. As he gets old enough to want to take over responsibilities, step out of the picture as fast as you can. When he slips back and forgets, lead again. When he goes to school, let him think of it as his job to get there on time. It may be better to quietly allow him to be late to school once or twice, or to miss the bus and school altogether and find out for himself how sorry he feels. A child hates to miss things even more than his parent hates to have him miss them. That's the best mainspring to move him along.

You may have the impression that I think children should not be held to any obligation. On the contrary. I think they should sit down at table when a meal is ready and get up in the morning at the proper time. I'm only making the point that if they're allowed to use their own initiative most of the time, reminded in a matter-of-fact way when they've clearly failed to do something on their own, not prodded unnecessarily in advance, not pushed too much, they usually want to do these things.

529. Let them get dirty sometimes. Small children want to do a lot of things that get them dirty, and they are good for children, too. They love to dig in earth and sand, wade in mud puddles, splash in water in the washstand. They want to roll in the grass, squeeze mud in their hands. When they have chances to do these delightful things, it enriches their spirit, makes them warmer people, just the way beautiful music or falling in love improves adults.

Small children who are always sternly warned against getting their clothes dirty or making a mess, and who take it to heart, will be cramped. If they become really timid about dirt, it makes them too cautious in other ways also, and keeps them from developing into the free, warm, life-loving people they were meant to be.

I don't mean to give the impression that you must always hold yourself back and let your children make any kind of mess that strikes their fancy. But when you do have to stop them, don't try to scare them or disgust them; just substitute something else a little more practical. If they want to make mud pies when they have their Sunday clothes on, have them change into old clothes first. If they get hold of an old brush and want to paint the house, set them to work (with a pail of water for "paint") on the woodshed or the tiled floor of the bathroom.

530. Good manners come naturally. Teaching children to say "How d'do" or "Thank you" is really not the first step. The most important thing is to have them like people. If they don't, it's hard to teach them even surface manners.

The second step is to avoid making them self-conscious with strangers. We're apt, especially with our first child, to introduce him right away to a new grown-up and make him say something. But when you do that to a 2-year-old, you get him all embarrassed. He learns to feel uncomfortable just as soon as he sees you greeting somebody, because he knows he's about to be put on the spot. It's much better in the first 3 or 4 years, when a child needs time to size a stranger up, to draw the newcomer's conversation **away** from him, not **toward** him. A child of 3 or 4 is likely to watch a stranger talking to his parent for a few minutes and then suddenly break into the conversation with a remark, "The water came out of the toilet all over the floor." This isn't Lord Chesterfield's kind of manners, but it's real manners because he feels like sharing a fascinating experience. If that spirit toward strangers keeps up, he'll learn how to be friendly in a more conventional way soon enough.

The third, and probably most important, step is for children to grow up in a family whose members are considerate of each other. Then they absorb kindliness. They want to say "Thank you" because the rest of the family say it and mean it. They enjoy shaking hands and saying "Please."

Certainly it is also necessary to teach children just how to be polite and considerate. If it's done in a friendly spirit, they are proud to learn. More important, everybody likes children with sensibly good manners and resents those who are rude or thoughtless. So the parents owe it to children to make them likable. The appreciation they get makes them more friendly in turn.

When you coach children about manners, try to do it when you're alone with them rather than in the embarrassing presence of outsiders.

DISCIPLINE

531. Some common misunderstandings about discipline. A great deal of study has been given to the psychology of children in the past half-century by educators, psychoanalysts, child psychiatrists, psychologists, and pediatricians. Parents have been eager to read the results; newspapers and magazines have obliged by publishing them. We have learned a great deal, bit by bit: that children need the love of good parents more than anything else; that they work hard, all by themselves to be more grown-up and responsible; that many of the ones who get into the most trouble are suffering from lack of affection rather than from lack of punishment; that children are eager to learn if they are given school projects that are right for their age and are taught by understanding teachers; that some jealous feelings toward brothers and sisters and occasional angry feelings toward parents are natural and that a child does not need to feel deeply ashamed of them; that a childish interest in the facts of life and in some aspects of sex is quite normal; that too harsh a repression of aggressive feelings and sexual interest may lead to neurosis; that unconscious thoughts are as influential as conscious ones; that each child is an individual and should be allowed to be so.

All these ideas sound commonplace today, but when they were first expressed they were very startling. Many of them ran counter to beliefs that had been held for centuries. It is not possible to change so many ideas about the nature and needs of children without mixing up a lot of parents. Parents who have had a very comfortable childhood and who are very stable people have been least confused. They may have been interested in hearing about these new ideas, and they may have agreed. But when it came to actually managing their children, they did it in much the same way they were brought up themselves. And it has been successful with their children, as it had been with them. This is the natural way to learn child care—from having been a child in a reasonably happy family.

The parents who have had more trouble with the new ideas are usually those who haven't been too happy about their own upbringing. Many of them have felt both resentful and guilty about the strained relations that existed at times between themselves and their parents. They haven't wanted their own children to feel that way about them. So they have welcomed new theories. They have often read meanings into them that went beyond what the scientists intended—for instance, that **all** that children need is love; that they shouldn't be made to conform; that they should be allowed to carry out their aggressive feelings against parents and others; that whenever anything goes wrong it's the parents' fault; that when children misbehave the parents shouldn't become angry or punish them but should try to show more love. All of these misconceptions are unworkable if carried very far. They encourage children to become demanding and disagreeable. They make children feel guilty about their excessive misbehavior. They make parents strive to be superhuman. When the bad behavior comes, the parents try to suppress their anger for a while. But eventually they have to explode. Then they feel guilty and bewildered. This leads to more misbehavior on the child's part. (See Section 532.)

Some parents who are very polite people themselves allow their children to be surprisingly obnoxious, not only to themselves but to outsiders as well. They don't seem to see what is going on. Some of these situations, when studied carefully, reveal that the parents had always been compelled to be much too good in their own childhood and to suppress all their natural resentments. Now they get a subtle glee from letting their own flesh and blood act out all the disagreeableness they themselves had to bottle up, pretending all the time that this is all according to the best modern theories of child rearing.

532. How feelings of guilt in the parents lead to discipline problems. There are many situations in which parents may always feel a bit guilty toward one child or another. Some of them were mentioned in Sections 31 and 32. There are other obvious cases: the mother who goes to work without first settling in her own mind whether she will be neglecting her child; parents who have a child with a physical or mental handicap; parents who have adopted a baby and can't get over the feeling that they have to do a superhuman job to justify themselves in taking over someone else's child; parents who have been brought up with so much disapproval that they always feel guilty until they are proved innocent; parents who have studied child psychology in college or a professional school, who know about all the pitfalls, and who yet expect to have to do a superior job because of their training.

Whatever the cause of the feeling of guilt, it tends to get in the way of easy management of a child. The parents are inclined to expect too little from the child, too much from themselves. They are often still trying to be patient and sweet tempered when their overworked patience is really exhausted and the child is, in fact, getting out of hand and needs some definite correction. Or they are vacillating when the child needs firmness.

A child, like an adult, knows when she is getting away with too much naughtiness or rudeness even when her parents are trying to close their eyes to it. She feels guilty inside. She would like to be stopped. But if she isn't corrected, she's likely to behave worse and worse. It's as if she were saying, "How bad do I have to be before somebody stops me?"

Eventually her behavior becomes so provoking that the parents' patience snaps. They scold or punish her. Peace is restored. But the trouble with parents who feel guilty is that they are too ashamed of losing their temper. So instead of letting well enough alone, they try to undo the correction or let the child punish them in return. Perhaps they permit the child to be rude to them right in the middle of the punishment. Or they take back the penalty before it has been half paid. Or they pretend not to notice when the child begins misbehaving again. In some situations if the child does not retaliate at all, a parent begins to subtly provoke her to do so—without realizing, of course, what she or he is up to.

All of this may sound too complicated or unnatural to you. If you can't imagine a parent letting a child get away with murder or, worse still, encouraging it, it only shows that you don't have the problem of guilt feelings. Actually, it isn't a rare problem. A majority of conscientious parents let a child get out of hand occasionally when they feel they have been unfair or neglectful. But they soon recover their balance. However, when a parent says, "Everything this child does or says rubs me the wrong way," it's a pretty good sign that the parent feels overly guilty and is chronically submissive and permissive, and that the child is reacting to this with constant provocation. No child can be that irritating by accident. If parents can determine in which respects they may be too permissive and can firm up their discipline, they may, if they are on the right track, be delighted to find that their child becomes not only better behaved but much happier. Then they can really love their child better, and the child in turn responds to this.

533. You can be both firm and friendly. A child needs to feel that her mother and father, however agreeable, have their own rights, know how to be firm, won't let her be unreasonable or rude. She likes them better that way. It trains her from the beginning to get along reasonably with other people. Spoiled children are not happy creatures even in their own homes. And when they get out into the world, whether it's at 2 or 4 or 6, they are in for a rude shock. They find that nobody is willing to kowtow to them; in fact, everybody dislikes them for their selfishness. Either they must go through life being unpopular, or they must learn the hard way how to be agreeable.

Conscientious parents often let a child take advantage of them for a while—until their patience is exhausted—and then turn on the child crossly. But neither of these stages is really necessary. If parents have a healthy self-respect, they can stand up for themselves while they are still feeling friendly. For instance, if your daughter is insisting that you continue to play a game after you are exhausted, don't be afraid to say cheerfully but definitely, "I'm all tired out. I'm going to read a book now, and you can read **your** book, too."

If she is being very balky about getting out of the express wagon of another child who has to take it home now, though you have tried to interest her in something else, don't feel that you must go on being sweetly reasonable forever. Lift her out, even if she yells for a minute.

534. Let children know that their angry feelings are normal. When a child is being rude to a parent—perhaps because she has had to be frustrated or because she's jealous of her brother or sister—the parent should promptly stop her and insist on politeness. But at the same time the parent can say that he knows his child is cross at him sometimes—all children get mad at their parents sometimes. This may sound contradictory to you; it sounds like undoing the correction. Child guidance work teaches us in case after case that a child is happier as well as better behaved if her parents insist on reasonably good **behavior.** But at the same time it helps a child to realize that her parents know she has angry **feelings** and that her parents are not enraged at her or alienated from her on account of them. This realization helps her get over her anger and keeps her from feeling too guilty or frightened because of it. Making this distinction between hostile feelings and hostile actions works out well in actual practice.

535. Don't say, "Do you want to . . . ?" or "OK?"; just do what's necessary. It's easy to fall into the habit of saying to a small child, "Do you want to sit down and have your lunch?" "Shall we get dressed now?" "Do you want to do wee wee?" Another common approach is, "It's time to go out now—OK?" The trouble is that the natural response of the child, particularly between 1 and 3, is "No." Then the poor parent has to persuade the child to give in to something that was necessary anyway. The arguments use up thousands of words. It is better not to offer a choice. When it's time for lunch, lead him or carry him to the table, still chatting with him about the thing that was on his mind before. When you see signs that he needs to go to the bathroom, lead him there or bring the potty chair to him. Start undoing him without even mentioning what you're up to.

You might get the idea that I am advising you to swoop down on him and give him the "bum's rush." I don't mean exactly that. In fact, every time you take a child away from something he's absorbed in, it helps to be tactful. If your 15-month-old is busy fitting one hollow block inside another at suppertime, you can carry him to the table still holding his blocks and take them away when you hand him his spoon. If your 2-year-old is playing with a toy dog at bedtime, you can say, "Let's put doggie to bed now." If your 3-year-old is chugging a toy automobile along the floor when it's time for the bath, you can suggest that the car make a long, long trip to the bathroom. When you show interest in what he's doing, it puts him in a cooperative mood.

As your child grows older, he'll be less distractible, have more concentration. Then it works better to give him a little friendly warning. If a 4-year-old has spent half an hour building a garage of blocks, you can say, "Put the cars in soon now; I want to see them inside before you go to bed." This works better than pouncing on him without warning when the most exciting part of the play is still to come, or giving him a cross warning as if you never did see anything in garages except the mess they make on the floor. All this takes patience, though, and naturally you won't always have it.

536. Don't give the small child too many reasons. You sometimes see a child between the ages of 1 and 3 who becomes worried by too many warnings. The mother of a certain boy 2 years old always tries to control him with ideas. "Jackie, you mustn't touch the doctor's lamp, because you will break it, and then the doctor won't be able to see." Jackie regards the lamp with a worried expression and mutters, "Doctor can't see." A minute later he is trying to open the door to the street. His mother warns him, "Don't go out the door. Jackie might get lost, and Mummie couldn't find him." Poor Jackie turns this new danger over in his mind and repeats, "Mummie can't find him." It's bad for him to be hearing about so many bad endings. It builds up a morbid imagination. A 2-year-old baby shouldn't be worrying about the consequences of his actions. This is the period when he is meant to learn by doing and having things happen. I'm not advising that you never warn your child in words, but only that you shouldn't always be leading him out beyond his depth with **ideas.**

I think of an overconscientious father who feels he should give his 3-year-old daughter a reasonable explanation of **everything.** When it's time to get ready to go outdoors, it never occurs to him to put the child's clothes on in a matter-of-fact way and get out. He begins, "Shall we put your coat on now?" "No," says the child. "Oh, but we want to get out and get some nice fresh air." She is used to the fact that her father feels obliged to give a reason for everything, and this encourages her to make him argue for every point. So she says, "Why?" but not because she really wants to know. "Fresh air makes you strong and healthy so that you won't get sick." "Why?" says she. And so on and so forth, all day long.

This kind of meaningless argument and explanation doesn't make her a more cooperative child or give her respect for her father as a reasonable person. She would be happier and get more security from him if he had an air of self-confidence and steered her in a friendly, automatic way through the routines of the day.

When your child is young, rely most heavily on physically removing her from dangerous or forbidden situations by distracting her to something interesting but harmless. As she grows a little older and learns the lesson, remind her by a matter-of-fact "No, no" and more distraction. If she wants an explanation or a reason, give it to her in simple terms. But don't assume that she wants an explanation for every direction you give. She knows inside that she is inexperienced. She counts on you to keep her out of danger. It makes her feel safe to have you guiding her, provided you do it tactfully and not too much.

537. Temper tantrums. Almost all babies have a few temper tantrums between 1 and 3 years. They've gotten a sense of their own desires and individuality. When they're thwarted they know it and feel angry. Yet they don't usually attack the parent who has interfered with them. Perhaps the grown-up is too important and too big. Also, their fighting instinct isn't very well developed yet.

When the feeling of fury boils up in them, they can't think of anything better to do than take it out on the floor and themselves. They flop down, yelling, and pound with their hands and feet and maybe the head.

A temper tantrum once in a while doesn't mean anything; there are bound to be some frustrations. If they are happening regularly, several times a day, it may mean that a child is getting overtired or has some chronic physical trouble. Frequent tantrums are more often due to the fact that the parents haven't learned the knack of handling the child tactfully. There are several questions to ask: Does the child have plenty of chance to play freely outdoors in a place where her parents don't have to keep chasing her, and are there things for her to push and pull and climb on there? Indoors, has she enough toys and household objects to play with, and is the house arranged so that parents don't have to keep forbidding her to touch things? Are they, without realizing it, arousing balkiness by **telling** her to come and get her shirt on instead of slipping it on without comment, **asking** her if she wants to go to the bathroom instead of leading her there or bringing the potty to her? When they have to interrupt her play to get her indoors or to meals, do they frustrate her directly, or get her mind on something pleasant? When they see a storm brewing, do they meet it head-on, grimly, or do they distract her to something else?

You can't dodge all temper tantrums. Parents would be unnatural if they had that much patience and tact. When the storm breaks, you try to take it casually and help to get it over. You certainly don't give in and meekly let the child have her way; otherwise she'd be throwing tantrums all the time on purpose. You don't argue with her, because she's in no mood to see the error of her ways. Getting angry yourself only forces her to keep up her end of the row. Give her a graceful way out. One child cools off quickest if the parents fade away and go about their own business, matter-of-factly, as if they couldn't be bothered. Another with more determination and pride sticks to her yelling and thrashing for an hour unless her parents make a friendly gesture. They might pop in with a suggestion of something fun to do, and a hug to show they want to make up, as soon as the worst of the storm has passed.

It's embarrassing to have a child put on a tantrum on a busy sidewalk. Pick her up, with a grin if you can force it, and lug her off to a quiet spot where you can both cool off in private.

Breath-holding spells, in which a child may turn blue and even lose consciousness momentarily, can be an expression of temper. They are alarming to parents, but they should try to learn to manage them sensibly, as in the discussion above, in order to keep the child from deliberately using them more and more. See Section 378.

538. Is punishment necessary? Many good parents feel that they have to punish once in a while. But other parents find that they can successfully manage their children without ever having to punish. A lot depends on how the parents were brought up. If they were punished occasionally for good cause, they naturally expect to have to punish in similar situations. And if they were kept in line by positive guidance alone, they are apt to find that they can do the same with their children.

On the other hand, there are also a fair number of poorly behaved children. The parents of some of them punish a lot and the parents of others never do. So we can't say either that punishment always works or that lack of it always works. It all depends on the nature of the parents' discipline in general.

Before we go further with the subject of punishment, we ought to realize that it is **never** the main element in discipline —it's only a vigorous additional reminder that the parents feel strongly about what they say. We have all seen children who were slapped and spanked and deprived plenty, and yet remained ill-behaved. Many chronic criminals have spent half their adult years in jail, and yet each time they get out they promptly become involved in another crime.

The main source of good discipline is growing up in a loving family—being loved and learning to love in return. We want to be kind and cooperative (most of the time) because we like people and want them to like us. (Habitual criminals are people who in childhood were never loved enough to make much difference to them, and many of them were abused, besides.) Children gradually lessen their grabbing and begin to share, somewhere around the age of 3 years, not primarily because they are reminded by their parents (though that may help some) but because their feelings toward other children—of enjoyment and affection—have developed sufficiently.

Another vital element is children's intense desire to be as much like their parents as possible. They work particularly hard at being polite and civilized and responsible in the 3- to 6-year-old period (Section 563). They pretend very seriously to take care of their doll children, keep house, go out to work, as they see their parents do. A boy tries to be grown up just like his father in interests and manners, a girl like her mother.

Though children do the major share in civilizing themselves, through love and imitation, it still leaves plenty for parents to do, as all of you know. In automobile terms, the child supplies the power but the parents have to do the steering. Children's motives are good (most of the time), but they don't have the experience or the stability to stay on the road. The parents have to be saying, "We hold hands when we cross the street," "You can't play with that, it may hurt someone," "Say thank you to Mrs. Griffin," "Let's go in now, because there is a surprise for lunch," "We have to leave the wagon because it belongs to Harry and he wants it," "It's time to go to bed so you'll grow big and strong," etc. etc. How well the guidance works depends on such factors as whether the parents are reasonably consistent (nobody can be completely consistent), whether they mean what they say (are not just sounding off), and whether they are directing or prohibiting the child for a good reason (not just because they're feeling mean or bossy).

The everyday job of the parent, then, is to keep the child on the right track by means of firmness. (You don't sit by and watch a small child destroy something and then punish him afterward.) You come to punishment (if you use it at all) once in a while when your system of firmness breaks down. Maybe your son, sorely tempted, wonders whether you still mean the prohibition that you laid down a couple of months ago. Or maybe he is angry and misbehaves on purpose. Perhaps he breaks something that's very precious to you, by foolish carelessness. Or he's slightly rude to you at a moment when you are tense about another matter. Maybe he narrowly escapes being run over because he didn't look. Indignation or righteous anger wells up in you. At such a moment you punish, or at least you feel like punishing.

The best test of a punishment is whether it accomplishes what you are after, without having other serious effects. If it makes a child furious, defiant, and worse behaved than before, then it certainly is missing fire. If it seems to break the child's heart, then it's probably too strong for him. Every child reacts somewhat differently.

There are times when a child breaks a plate or rips his clothes because of accident or carelessness. If he gets along well with his parents, he feels just as unhappy as they do, and no punishment is needed. (In fact, you sometimes have to comfort him.) Jumping on a child who feels sorry already sometimes banishes his remorse and makes him argue.

If you're dealing with an older child who is always fooling with the dishes and breaking them, it may be fair to make him buy replacements from his allowance. A child beyond the age of 6 is developing a sense of justice and sees the fairness of reasonable penalties. However, I'd go light on the legalistic "take-the-consequences" kind of punishment before 6, and I wouldn't try to use it at all before 3. You don't want a small child to develop a **heavy** sense of guilt. The job of a parent is to keep the child from getting into trouble rather than act as a severe judge after it's happened.

In the olden days, most children were spanked, on the assumption that this was necessary to make them behave. In the twentieth century, as parents and professionals have studied children here and in other countries, they have come to realize that children can be well-behaved, cooperative, and polite without ever having been punished physically—or in other ways. I have known hundreds of such children myself, and there are countries in the world where physical punishment is unknown.

When an executive in an office, or a foreman in a shop, is dissatisfied with the work of an employee, he doesn't rush in shouting and whack him on the seat of his pants. He explains in a respectful manner what he would like, and in most cases this is enough. Children are not that different in their wish to be responsible and to please. They react well to praise and high expectations.

There are several reasons to try to avoid physical punishment, I feel. It teaches children that the larger, stronger person has the power to get his way, whether or not he is in the right, and they may resent this in their parent—for life. Some spanked children feel quite justified in beating up on smaller ones. The American tradition of spanking may be one cause of the fact that there is **much** more violence in our country than in any other comparable nation—murder, armed robbery, wife abuse, child abuse.

Some parents find that putting a child in his room and telling him that he can come out when he feels ready to cooperate works well. One theoretical disadvantage is that it may make his room seem like a prison.

Avoid threats as much as possible. They tend to weaken discipline. It may sound reasonable to say, "If you don't keep out of the street with your bicycle, I'll take it away." But in a sense a threat is a dare—it admits that the child may disobey. It should impress him more to be firmly told he must keep out of the street, if he knows from experience that his parents mean what they say. On the other hand, if you see that you may have to impose a drastic penalty like taking away a beloved bike for a few days, it's better to give fair warning. It certainly is silly, and quickly destroys all a parent's authority, to make threats that aren't ever carried out or that can't be carried out. Scary threats, such as of bogeymen and cops, are 100 percent wrong in all cases.

539. Parents who can't control their children or who have to punish frequently need help. A few parents have extreme difficulty controlling their children. They say their child "won't obey" or that he's "just bad." The first thing you see when you watch such a parent (let's say it's a mother) is that she doesn't appear to be really trying, even though she wants to and thinks she is. She threatens or scolds or punishes frequently. But one such mother almost never carries out a threat. Another, though she punishes, never in the end **makes** the child do what she said he had to do. And another makes him obey once, but 5 minutes later and 10 minutes later she lets him get away with it. Another laughs in the middle of a scolding or punishment. Another just keeps shouting at the child that he's bad or asks a neighbor, right in front of the child, whether she ever saw a worse one. Parents like these unconsciously expect the child's bad behavior to go right on and can do nothing effective to stop it. They are inviting it, without realizing it. Their scolding and punishing are only an expression of frustration. In their complaints to neighbors they are only hoping to get some comforting agreement that the child is truly impossible. Frustrated parents like these have often had an unsatisfactory childhood during which they never received sufficient assurance that they were basically good and well behaved. As a result they don't have enough confidence in themselves or in their children. They need a lot of help from an understanding doctor or a child guidance clinic or from a family social agency (Sections 633 and 634).

JEALOUSY AND RIVALRY

540. Jealousy can be helpful as well as hurtful. It is a strong emotion even in grown-ups. It can be more disturbing to the very young child because he doesn't know just what has hit him.

If it is intense, it may sour his outlook on life for quite a while. But jealousy is one of the facts of life and can't be completely prevented, so parents shouldn't expect to accomplish the impossible. However, they can do a great deal to minimize it and to help the child convert it into other feelings that are painless and constructive. If he comes to realize that there is no reason to be so fearful of a rival, it strengthens his character so that he will be better able to cope with rivalry situations later in life, at work, and at home.

541. Helping the child to feel more grown-up at this time. A great majority of young children react to a baby's arrival by yearning to be a baby again, at least part of the time, and this is quite normal. They want a bottle occasionally. They may wet their bed and pants, and they may soil themselves. They may relapse into baby talk and act helpless about doing things for themselves. I think a parent is wise to humor the craving to be a baby **at those moments** when it is very strong. They can even good-naturedly carry a child up to his room and undress him, as a friendly game. Then he can see that he is not being denied these experiences, which he imagines are delightful but which may prove disappointing.

However, I think the parents can help the child more by appealing, most of the time, to the side of him that wants to grow up. They can remind him of how big, strong, smart, or skillful he is. I don't mean that you should give him one big over-enthusiastic sales talk but that you should hand him a sincere compliment whenever it is appropriate. From time to time the parent can refer to some aspect of the baby's helplessness in a tone of pity.

You'll notice that I'm not suggesting direct comparisons that imply that the parents definitely prefer the other child to the baby. To feel that he is the favored child may gratify a child temporarily. But in the long run he will feel insecure with parents who are partial—they might change their preference. The parents should, of course, let their love of the baby be evident. I'm only emphasizing the importance of giving the older child chances to feel proud of his maturity and to remember that there are lots of disadvantages to being a baby.

Encouraging the child to be grown up should not be pushed too hard, however. If the parent is constantly calling all the things that the child temporarily yearns to do "babyish" and all the things that he's temporarily reluctant to do "grown up" he can only come to the conclusion that he wants to be a baby for sure.

542. Turning rivalry into helpfulness. One of the ways in which a young child tries to get over the pain of having a younger rival is to act as if he himself were no longer a child, competing in the same league with the baby, but as if he were a third parent. Of course, when he's feeling very cross with the baby, he may act the disapproving parent. But if he's feeling more secure, he can be the kind of parent who teaches the baby how to do things, gives him toys, wants to assist in feeding and bathing and clothing him, comforts him when he's miserable, protects him from dangers. He tries to slip into the parental role even without much help from the parents. But the parents can assist him tremendously by suggesting how he can help them at times when it wouldn't occur to him, and by showing their real appreciation of his efforts. As a matter of fact, parents of twins who were desperate for real help have told me they were amazed to find how much honest-to-goodness help they received from a child as young as 3 years, so it doesn't all have to be pretend. Even a young child can fetch a bath towel, a diaper, or a bottle from the refrigerator. He can pretend to help the baby, "watch" him while the parents are out of sight.

A small child almost always wants to hold the baby, and parents are apt to hesitate for fear he may drop the baby. But if the child sits on the floor (on a carpet or blanket) or in a large stuffed chair or in the middle of a bed, there's little risk, even if the baby is dropped.

In such ways the parents can help a child to actually transform resentful feelings into cooperativeness and genuine altruism.

Usually the left-out feeling is more apt to be experienced by the first child when the second baby arrives, because he has been used to the spotlight and has had no practice in sharing the parents' love with others. A middle child doesn't have to decide between being a parent and being a baby, when a new one arrives. He can see that he's still just one of the children, as he has always been. I believe that the greater need of the average first child to think of himself as a parent helps to explain why so many first children later enjoy being parents and are so apt to go into professions like teaching, social work, nursing, medicine, which are concerned with caring for others.

543. Preparing the way for the baby. It is good for a child to know ahead of time that he is going to have a baby brother or sister, if he is old enough to understand such an idea at all, so that he can get used to the idea gradually. (Don't promise him it's going to be a girl or a boy; a child takes a promise like that seriously.) The question of where the baby is coming from is discussed more fully in "The Facts of Life" (Sections 583–589). Most educators and child psychologists believe that it is wholesome for a child to know that the baby is growing inside his mother and to feel it move. It's hard to explain much to a child under 2.

The arrival of the baby should change a child's life as little as possible, especially if he has been the only child up to that time. It is better to make all possible changes several months ahead of time. If his room is to be given over to the baby, move him to his new room several months ahead, so that he feels that he is graduating because he is a big boy, not because the baby is pushing him out of his own place. The same applies to graduating to a big bed. If he is to go to nursery school, he should start a couple of months beforehand. Nothing sets a child's mind against nursery school so much as the feeling that he is being banished to it. But if he is already well established in nursery school, he goes on liking it, and his satisfying life there keeps him from being as much disturbed by what's going on at home.

How a child gets along while his mother is in the hospital makes a big difference in his feelings toward her and the baby when they come home. Most important is who takes care of him. This is discussed in Sections 50 and 552.

544. When the mother brings the baby home. It's usually a hectic moment when the mother comes back from the hospital. She is tired and preoccupied. The father scurries about, being helpful. If the older child is there, he stands around feeling troubled and left out. So this is the new baby!

If it's likely to happen this way, it may be better for the child to be away on an excursion if this can be arranged. An hour later, when the baby and the luggage are in their place and the mother is at last relaxing on the bed, is time enough for the child to come in. His mother can hug him and talk to him and give him her undivided attention. Let him bring up the subject of the baby when he is ready to.

It's tactful to play down the new baby in the early weeks. Treat her casually. Don't act too excited about her. Don't gloat over her. Don't talk a lot about her. As far as is convenient, take care of her while the older one is not

A child usually feels a mixture of love and jealousy of the baby.

around. Fit in her bath and some of her feedings when he is outdoors or taking his nap. Many young children feel the greatest jealousy when they see the mother feeding the baby, especially at the breast. If he's around, he should be allowed in freely. But if he is downstairs playing happily, don't attract his attention to what's going on.

If he wants to drink from a bottle, too, I'd suggest cheerfully fixing him one. It's a little sad to see an older child trying a bottle out of envy of the baby. He thinks it's going to be heaven. When he gets up his courage to take a suck, disappointment spreads over his face. It's just milk, coming slowly, with a rubber taste. He may want a bottle off and on for a few weeks, but there's not much risk that he'll want to go on with it forever if the parents give it to him willingly and if they are doing the other things they can to help him with his jealousy.

Other people play a part in jealousy, too. When the father comes home from work, he should suppress the impulse to ask the child, "How's the baby today?" Better to act as if he has forgotten there is a baby, sit down, and pass the time of day. Later he can drift on to have a look at her when the older one is interested in something else. Grandma, who used to make a big fuss over the child, can be a problem, too. If she meets him in the front hall with a big package tied up in satin ribbon, and says, "Where's that darling baby sister of yours? I've brought her a present," then his joy at seeing her turns to bitterness. If parents don't know the visitor well enough to coach her in how to act, they can have a box of 10-cent-store presents on the shelf and produce one for the child every time a visitor comes with one for the baby.

Playing with dolls may be a great solace to the child, whether girl or boy, while his mother is caring for the baby. He wants to warm his doll's bottle just the way his mother does, and have a reasonable facsimile of the other pieces of clothing and equipment that his mother uses. But doll play shouldn't take the place of helping care for the real baby; it should only supplement it.

545. Jealousy takes many forms. If a child picks up a large block and swats the baby with it, the mother knows well enough that it's jealousy. But another child is more polite. He admires the baby for a couple of days without enthusiasm and then says, "Now take her back to the hospital." One child feels all his resentment against his mother, grimly digs the ashes out of the fireplace and sprinkles them over the living room rug in a quiet businesslike way. One with a different makeup becomes mopey and dependent, loses his joy in the sand pile and his blocks, follows his mother around, holding onto the edge of her skirt and sucking his thumb. He may wet his bed again at night or even wet and soil in the daytime. Occasionally you see a small child whose jealousy is turned inside out. He becomes preoccupied with the baby sister. When he sees a dog, all he can think of to say is, "Baby likes the dog." When he sees his friends riding trikes, he says, "Baby has a tricycle, too." He's bothered, all right, but he doesn't admit it even to himself. This child needs help even more than the one who knows exactly what he resents.

A parent sometimes says, "We found that we didn't have to worry about jealousy at all. Johnny is **fond** of the new baby." It is fine when a child shows love for the baby, but this doesn't mean that jealousy should be ignored. It may show up in indirect ways or only in special circumstances. Perhaps he's fond of her indoors but is rude when strangers admire her on the street. A child may show no rivalry for months until one day the baby creeps over to one of his toys and grabs it. Sometimes this change of feeling comes on the day the baby begins to walk.

A parent may say, "Johnny seems very affectionate with the baby. In fact, he often hugs her so tight that she cries." This isn't really an accident. His feelings are mixed.

It's wise to go on the assumption that there is always some jealousy and some affection, whether they both show on the surface or not. The job is not to ignore the jealousy or to try to forcibly suppress it or to make the child feel deeply ashamed about it, but to help the feelings of affection to come out on top.

546. How to handle different kinds of jealousy. When the child attacks the baby, a parent's natural impulse is to act shocked and to shame him. This doesn't work out well for two reasons. He dislikes the baby because he's afraid that his parents are going to love her instead of him. When they

The jealous one must be restrained, but he also needs reassurance.

threaten not to love him any more, it makes him feel more worried and cruel inside. Shaming also may make him bottle up his feelings of jealousy. Jealousy does more harm to his spirit and lasts longer if it is suppressed than if it is allowed to stay out in the open.

There are three jobs: to protect the baby, to show the child that his parents will not permit him to **carry out** his mean feelings in action, and to reassure him that his parents still love him. When they see him advancing on the baby with a grim look on his face and a weapon in his hand, they must jump and grab him, tell him firmly that he can't hurt the baby. (Whenever he succeeds in being cruel, it makes him feel guilty and more upset inside.) But they can occasionally turn the grab into a hug and say, "I know how you feel sometimes, Johnny. You wish there weren't any baby around here for Mommy and Daddy to take care of. But don't you worry, we love you just the same." If he can realize at a moment like this that his parents accept his angry feelings (not actions) and still love him, it is the best proof that he doesn't need to worry.

As for the child who spreads the ashes around the living room, it's natural for his parents to feel exasperated and angry, and they will probably reprove him anyway. But if they realize that he did it from a deep sense of despair and bitterness, they may later feel like reassuring him, too, and try to remember what they did that he just couldn't take any longer.

The child who turns mopey in his jealousy, being of a more sensitive and in-turning nature, needs affection, reassurance, and drawing out even more than the child who eases his feelings by violence. With the child who doesn't dare show directly what's bothering him, it may actually help him to feel better if his mother (or father) can say understandingly, "I know that sometimes you can feel cross at the baby, and cross at Mommy because I take care of her," and so on. If he doesn't respond after a while, the parents may want to get a temporary helper for the baby even though they decided beforehand that they couldn't afford it. If it works and helps him get back his old joy in life, it will have a permanent value far beyond the expense involved.

It is worthwhile consulting a children's psychiatrist about the child who has turned all his jealousy inside and been curdled by it, whether it takes the form of moping or of being obsessed with the baby. The psychiatrist may be able to draw the jealousy back to the surface again, so that the child can realize what's biting him and get it off his chest.

If the jealousy comes out strongly only after the baby is old enough to begin grabbing the older one's toys, it may help a great deal to give him a room of his own, where he can feel that he and his toys and his buildings are safe from interference. If a separate room is out of the question, the parents or a carpenter can build him a big chest or cupboard for his things, with a mighty padlock. Not only does this protect his toys, but having a key of his own in his pocket and a grown-up lock to open gives him a great sense of being important.

Should he be urged or compelled to share his toys with the baby? Not compelled. A suggestion that he give the baby a plaything that he has outgrown may appeal to him a lot and foster his generosity. But generosity that has any meaning must come from inside, and a person must feel secure and loving first. Forcing a child to share his possessions when he is insecure and selfish makes those traits stronger and more lasting.

Generally speaking, jealousy of the baby is strongest in the child under 5, because he is much more dependent on his parents and has fewer interests outside the family circle. The child of 6 or more is drawing away a little from his parents and building a position for himself among his friends. Being pushed out of the limelight at home doesn't hurt so much. It would be a mistake, though, to think that jealousy doesn't exist in the older child. He, too, needs consideration and visible reminders of love from parents, particularly in the beginning. The child who is unusually sensitive or who has not found his place in the outside world may need just as much protection as the average small child. Even the adolescent girl, with her growing desire to be a woman, may be unconsciously envious of her mother's new parenthood.

There's one caution that I'd like to add here that may sound contradictory. Conscientious parents sometimes worry so much about jealousy and try so hard to prevent it that they make the older child less secure rather than more so. They may reach the point where they feel positively guilty about having a new baby, feel ashamed to be caught paying any attention to her, fall all over themselves trying to appease the older child. If a child finds that his parents are uneasy and apologetic toward him, it makes him uneasy, too. It reinforces his own suspicion that there is dirty work afoot and inclines him to be more mean to both baby and parents. In other words, the parents should be as tactful as possible to the older child but should not be worried or apologetic.

547. Doesn't the new baby need some attention, too? We have certainly been thinking exclusively about the older child's jealousy of the baby and even talking about ignoring the baby at times for the sake of the other child. New babies need attention and affection, too. But in their early days and months, they do sleep a good deal, and the minutes of the day when they're ready for fondling are few. This fits in with the needs of the older child. It's in the early days and months that he needs extra attention and demonstrations of affection. If the job is done well in the beginning, he gradually accustoms himself to the baby and loses his alarm. By the time the baby needs a full share of the family's attention, the older child should feel secure enough to permit it.

548. Jealousy between older children. There is almost bound to be some jealousy, and if it is not severe, it probably helps children to grow up more tolerant, independent, and generous.

In a general way, the more agreeably parents get along with each other and with the children, the less jealousy there is. When all the children are satisfied with the warm affection they receive, they have less reason to begrudge attention to their brothers and sisters.

Basically, the thing that makes each child secure in the family is the feeling that his parents love him and accept him for himself, whether he is boy or girl, smart or dull, handsome or homely. If they are comparing him with his brothers or sisters, either openly or in their thoughts, he senses it, feels unhappy inside, resentful toward the other children and the parent.

A harassed mother who is trying hard to treat her jealous children with perfect justice may say, "Now, Susie, here's a little red fire engine for you. And Tommy, here is another, just exactly the same, for you." But each child, instead of being satisfied, suspiciously examines both toys to see if there is any difference. Her remark has called attention to their rivalry. It's as if she said, "I bought this for you so you wouldn't complain that I was favoring your brother," instead of implying "I bought this for you because I knew you'd like it."

The fewer the comparisons, complimentary or uncomplimentary, between brothers and sisters, the better. Saying to a child, "Why can't you be polite like your sister?" makes him dislike his sister, his mother, and the very idea of politeness. And if you say to an adolescent girl, "Never mind if you don't have dates like Barbara. You're much smarter than she is, and that's what counts," it doesn't help her feelings.

It generally works better if parents keep out of most of the fights between children who can stand up for themselves. When they concentrate on pinning the blame, it leaves one warrior, at least, feeling more jealous. To a greater or lesser degree, children squabble because of their jealousy, because each would like to be favored by the parents. When parents are always ready to take sides, in the sense of trying to decide who is right and who is wrong, it encourages them to quarrel soon again. Each one hopes each time to win the parents' favor and to see the other scolded. If parents have to break up a fight, to save life or to prevent rank injustice or to restore quiet for their own sake, it's better to simply demand an end to the hostilities, to refuse to listen to arguments, to act uninterested in discrimination (unless it is quite clear that one child was outrageously to blame), and to concentrate on what's to be done next and let bygones be bygones. In one case they can casually but firmly suggest a compromise, in another case distract the children to a new occupation. Or the children can be separated and each sent to a neutral, not very interesting location.

Two-Year-Olds

WHAT THEY'RE LIKE

549. The 2-year-old learns by imitation. In a doctor's office a girl solemnly places the stethoscope bell on different spots on her chest. Then she pokes the ear light in her ear, and looks a little puzzled because she can't **see** anything. At home she follows her parents around, sweeping with a broom when they sweep, dusting with a cloth when they dust, brushing her teeth when they do. It's all done with great seriousness. She is making giant strides forward in skill and understanding by means of constant imitation.

She may be quite dependent around 2. She seems to realize clearly who it is that gives her her sense of security, and shows it in different ways. A mother complains, "My 2-year-old seems to be turning into a mother's girl. She hangs onto my skirts when we're out of the house. When someone speaks to us, she hides behind me." It's a great age for whining, which is a kind of clinging. A 2-year-old may keep climbing out of bed in the evening to rejoin the family, or calling from her room. She may be timid about being left anywhere by her parents. She's apt to be upset if a parent or other member of the household goes away for a number of days or if the family moves to a new house. It's wise to take her sensitivity into account when changes in the household are being considered.

550. Two is the age to encourage sociability. At 2, children don't play much **with** each other, cooperatively. However,

Playing near and watching come before playing together.

they love to watch each other's occupations and enjoy playing alongside each other. It's worth a lot of trouble to bring a 2-year-old every day if possible, or at least several times a week, to where other children are playing. Two-and-a-half- or 3-year-old children won't get the hang of sharing, of rough and tumble, unless they've already spent months becoming used to other children.

WORRIES AROUND TWO

551. Fear of separation. Many normal children develop a fear of being separated from the parent beginning around the age of a year. (See Section 456.) This expresses, I suspect, their new recognition of how much their sense of security depends on being near the parent. This is probably the same instinct that makes the young of other species, such as sheep and goats, follow close after their mothers and bleat when separated. It's natural that lambs and kids feel this anxiety from birth, because they can walk right away. But human babies acquire the anxiety at about the age of a year when they finally learn to walk, so that if they wander away, they'll soon feel the urge to get back.

Here's what happens occasionally when a sensitive, dependent child, say a boy, of 1¾, 2, 2¼—particularly an only child—is separated abruptly from the parent who has spent the most time with him. Perhaps it is the mother and she has to go out of town unexpectedly for a couple of weeks. Or she decides that she has to go to work, and arranges for a stranger to come in and take care of the child during the day. Usually the child makes no fuss while the mother is away, but when she returns, he hangs onto her like a leech and refuses to let the other person come near. He becomes panicky whenever he thinks his mother may be leaving again. Separation anxiety is worst at bedtime. The terrified child fights against being put to bed. If his mother tears herself away, he may cry in fear for hours. If she sits by his crib, he lies down only as long as she sits still. Her slightest move toward the door brings him instantly to his feet.

In some of these cases there is also worry about urinating. The child keeps saying "Wee wee" (or whatever word he uses). His mother brings him to the bathroom, he does a few drops, and then cries "Wee wee" again just as soon as he is back in bed. You might say that he just uses this as an excuse to keep her there. This is true, but there is more to it. Children like this one are really worried that they might wet the bed. They sometimes wake every 2 hours during the night thinking about it. This is the age period when the parents are apt to be showing disapproval when there is an accident. Maybe the child figures that if he wets, his parents won't love him so much, and will therefore be more likely to go away. If so, he has two reasons for fearing to go to sleep.

552. Avoiding fears at this age. Children who from infancy have been around different people and who have been allowed to develop independence and outgoingness are less apt to develop such fears.

If your child is between 15–18 months and 2 years, be careful about drastic changes. If it's almost as easy for either or both parents to wait 6 months for a trip or for the nonworking parent to take a job, better wait, especially if it's your first child. If neither parent can be at home with the child, arrange for her to get thoroughly used to the person who is going to take care of her, whether it's a friend, a relative, a sitter, or family day care worker. (If the child is going to be staying at the other person's house, it's even more important for her to get used to the new person and the new place by gradual steps.) Allow 2 weeks anyway. Let the new person just be around the child for a number of days without trying to take care of her, until she trusts and likes her or him. Then let that person take over gradually. Don't leave her for a full day at first. Start with half an hour and work up. Your quick reappearance reassures her that you always come back soon. Don't go away for a month or so after you have moved or after another member of the household has left. A child at this age needs a long time to adjust to each of these changes separately.

553. How to help a fearful 2-year-old. If your child has become terrified about going to bed, the safest advice, but the hardest to carry out, is to sit by the crib in a relaxed way until she goes to sleep. Don't be in a hurry to sneak away before she is asleep. It alarms her again and makes her more wakeful. This campaign may take weeks, but it should work in the end. If your child was frightened because one of you left town, try to avoid going away again for many weeks. If you **have** taken a job for the first time since the child was born, say good-bye each day affectionately, but cheerfully and confidently. If you have an anguished, unsure-whether-you're-doing-the-right-thing expression, it adds to the child's uneasiness.

Making the child more tired by keeping her up later or omitting her nap may help a little but usually won't do the whole job. A panicky child can keep herself awake for hours even though she's exhausted. You have to take away her worry, too.

If your child is worried about wetting, keep reassuring her that it doesn't matter if she does wee wee in bed—that you'll love her just the same.

554. Overprotectiveness increases children's fears. A child who is frightened by separation—or anything else—is very sensitive to whether her parents feel the same way about it. If they act hesitant or guilty every time they leave her side, if they hurry into her room at night, their anxiety reinforces her fear that there really is great danger in being apart from them.

This may sound contradictory after I've said that a parent must reassure a frightened 2-year-old by sitting by her bed as she goes to sleep and by not going away on any more trips for a number of weeks. I mean that parents must give her this special care the way they give special consideration to a sick child. But they should try to be cheerful, confident, unafraid. They should be looking for signs of the child's readiness to give up her dependence, step by step, and encourage her and compliment her. This attitude of theirs is the most powerful factor in getting her over her fear.

This connection between overprotective feelings in the parents and overdependence in the child applies to many other fear situations, sleep problems, and spoiling problems in infancy and childhood.

Overprotective feelings occur mostly in very devoted, tenderhearted parents who are too inclined to feel guilty when there is no realistic need for it (Sections 32 and 532). Most important of all, in a majority of cases, is the parent's inability to admit that she or he is sometimes resentful or angry toward the child (Section 25).

The parent and child who are afraid to recognize that there are naturally moments when they have mean feelings toward each other, when each wishes that something bad would happen to the other, have to imagine instead that **all** the dangers in the world come from somewhere else, and grossly exaggerate them. The child who is denying the meanness in her parents and in herself places it all in bogeymen or witches or robbers or dogs or dinosaurs or polio or lightning, depending on her age and experience. And she clings tightly to her parents—for protection for herself and to reassure herself that nothing is really happening to them. And a mother, for instance, may suppress her occasional mean thoughts and exaggerate the dangers of kidnappers or whooping cough or home accidents or inadequate diet. She has to stay close to the child to make sure the dangers don't strike, and her anxious expression convinces the child that her own fears are well founded.

Of course, the answer is not for parents to take out all their angriest feelings on the child or to let her be abusive toward them. Neither of these would help. But it certainly is helpful for parents to recognize the inevitability of their occasional mean feelings toward their child and to admit them jokingly to each other. It helps to clear the air if a parent occasionally admits to a child how angry she or he felt—especially if the angriness was not quite fair—and it doesn't interfere with good discipline if it's done in a sensible way. It's good to say to a child once in a while, "I know how angry you feel toward me when I have to do this to you."

When it comes to the management of children's fear, a lot depends on how important it is for them to get over it in a hurry, from a practical point of view. There's no great necessity for anxious children to be hurried into making friends with dogs or going into deep water in the lake or taking a bus trip by themselves. They'll want to do these things as soon as they dare. On the other hand, if they have already started in nursery school, I think it's better to insist that they go unless they're deeply terrified. At night children should not be allowed to come into the parents' bed; they should be trained to stay in their own bed. A school-age child with a phobia must get back to school sooner or later; the longer it is put off the harder it is. In these various separation fears, it is wise for parents to try to see whether their own protectiveness is playing a part and to overcome it. Both steps are difficult to accomplish alone, and the parents are certainly entitled to help from a child guidance clinic or family agency (Sections 633 and 634).

555. Mild bedtime difficulties. I don't want to leave the impression that every 2-year-old who objects to being put to bed should be sat with. Far from it. Severe separation anxiety is rare, but mild reluctance to being separated is very common. There are two varieties. The first consists of trying to keep the parent in the room. A boy will urgently say, "Wee wee!" though he went to the bathroom just a few minutes ago. This puts the parent in a quandary. She knows it's an excuse, but on the other hand she wants to encourage cooperation from the child by being cooperative herself. So she says, "Once more." As soon as he's back in bed and she starts to leave, he cries, "Drink of water!" looking as pathetic as a person dying of thirst. If his parent complies, he keeps alternating these two requests all evening. I think that such a child is feeling just **slightly** worried about being left alone. Usually the best and most practical way for the parent to reassure him is to remind him in a friendly, firm, and breezy tone that he's just had a drink and been to the bathroom, and then to say good night and leave the room without hesitation. If parents allow themselves to be detained or look troubled and uncertain, it's as if they were saying, "Well, maybe there **is** something to be nervous about." Even if a child whimpers and cries for a few minutes, I think it is wiser not to go back. It's much easier on the child to learn the lesson right away with a little unhappiness than to have the struggle drag on for weeks.

The other type of mild bedtime anxiety is when a 2-year-old learns to climb out of his crib soon after being put to bed and appears at the parents' side. He's smart enough to be very charming at such a time. He's happy to chat or to be cuddled—things he has no time for during the day. This makes it very hard for the parents to be firm. But firm they have to be, and promptly, too. Otherwise, repeated climbing out of bed may develop into an unpleasant battle lasting an hour or more every night.

When a climbing-out-of-bed problem in a 2-year-old has gotten completely out of hand, parents sometimes ask if it is all right to lock the child's door. I don't like the idea of a child crying himself to sleep at a locked door. In this situation, I think you need to talk to the child's doctor or other counselor to find out what needs to be done to get things under control.

I think it's sensible to keep 2-year-olds in the crib as long as they have not learned to climb out of it, even if another crib has to be bought for a new baby. I've heard too many stories of 2-year-olds who became evening wanderers just as soon as they were graduated to youth beds. By the time they can climb out of the crib, it doesn't make any difference.

When a child is afraid to go to bed, some people try to solve the problem by having either an older or younger brother or sister sleep in the same room, but it is as likely to cause a problem for an older brother or sister. Surprisingly, having a baby in the room may do the trick.

556. Children use separation anxiety to control. A child clings to his mother (or father) because he has developed a genuine fear of being separated from her. But if he finds that she is so concerned about his fear that she will always do anything he wants for reassurance, he may begin to use this as a whip. There are 3-year-olds, for instance, who are anxious about being left at nursery school and whose parents not only stay at school for days but stay close to the children and do what they ask, to reassure them. After a while you can see that such children are exaggerating their uneasiness because they have learned to enjoy bossing their parents around. A parent can say, "I think you are grown up now and aren't afraid to be in school. You just like to make me do what you want. Tomorrow I won't need to stay here any more."

CONTRARINESS

557. Balkiness between 2 and 3. In the period between 2 and 3, children are apt to show signs of balkiness and other inner tensions. Babies begin to be balky and "negativistic" way back when they are 1 year old, so this is nothing new. But it reaches new heights and takes new forms after 2. The 1-year-old Johnny contradicts his parents. The 2½-year-old Johnny even contradicts himself. He has a hard time making up his mind, and then he wants to change it. He acts like a person who feels he is being bossed too much, even when no one is bothering him. He is quite bossy himself. He insists on doing things just so, doing them his own way, doing them exactly as he has always done them before. It makes him furious to have anyone interfere in one of his jobs, or rearrange his possessions.

It looks as though the child's nature between 2 and 3 is urging him to decide things for himself, and to resist pressure from other people. Trying to fight these two battles without much worldly experience seems to get him tightened up inside, especially if his parents are a little too bossy. It's similar to the 6- to 9-year-old period, when the child tries to throw off his dependence on his parents, takes over a lot of responsibility for his own behavior, becomes overfussy about how he does things, and shows his tenseness in various nervous habits.

It's often hard to get along with a child between 2 and 3. That's why this period is often referred to as "the terrible twos." Parents have to be understanding. The job is to keep from interfering too much, from hurrying him. Let him help to dress and undress himself when he has the urge. Start his bath early enough so that he has time to dawdle and scrub the tub. At meals let him feed himself without urging. When he is stalled in his eating, let him leave the table. When it's time for bed, or going outdoors, or coming in, steer him while conversing about pleasant things. Get things done without raising issues. Don't be discouraged; there's smoother sailing ahead.

558. The child who can't stand two parents at once. Sometimes a child around 2½ or 3 can get along with either parent alone, but when the other one comes onto the scene she flies into a rage. It may be partly jealousy, but at an age when she's sensitive about being bossed and trying to do a little bossing herself, I imagine she feels outnumbered when she has to take on two important people at once. It's more often the father who is particularly unpopular at this period, and he sometimes gets the feeling he's pure poison. He shouldn't take it too seriously. It will help the child to play with her father alone, at times, so that she can know him as an enjoyable and loving person, not just an intruder. But the child must also learn that the parents love each other, want to be with each other, and will not be bullied by her.

STUTTERING

559. Stuttering is common between 2 and 3. We don't entirely understand stuttering (or stammering), but we know several things about it. It often runs in families, and it's much commoner in boys. This means that it is **easier** for certain individuals to develop it. Trying to change a left-handed child to right-handed sometimes appears to start it. The part of the brain that controls speech is closely connected to the part that controls the hand that a person naturally prefers. If you force him to use his wrong hand, it seems to confuse the nervous machinery for talking.

We know that a child's emotional state has a lot to do with stuttering. Most cases occur in somewhat tense children. Some stutter only when they are excited or when they are talking to one particular person. Here are some examples. One little boy began to stutter when a new baby sister was brought home from the hospital. He didn't show his jealousy outwardly. He never tried to hit or pinch her. He just became uneasy. A girl of 2½ began to stutter after the departure of a fond relative who had been with the family a long time. In 2 weeks the stuttering stopped for the time being. When the family moved to a new house, she was quite homesick and stuttered again for a period. Two months later the father was called into the army. The family was upset, and the little girl started again. Parents report that their children's stuttering is definitely worse when they themselves are tense. I think children who, during too much of the day, are being talked to and told stories, urged to talk and recite, shown off, are especially liable. Stuttering may start when a parent decides to be stricter in discipline.

Why is stuttering so common between 2 and 3? There are two possible explanations. This is the age period when a child is working very hard at his talking. When he was younger, he used short sentences that he didn't need to think out: "See the car,"—"Wanna go out," etc. But when he gets past 2, he tries to make up longer sentences to express new ideas. He starts a sentence 3 or 4 times, only to break off in the middle because he can't find the right words. His parents, worn out by his constant talking, don't pay too much attention. They say, "Uh huh," in an absentminded way while they go about their business. So the child is further frustrated by not being able to hold his audience.

It is also possible that the balkiness that is a part of this rather tense stage of development affects his speech, too.

560. What to do for stuttering. You may be especially distressed if you yourself or some relative has had a lifelong struggle to overcome stuttering. But there is no cause for alarm. I think nine out of ten of the children who start to stutter between 2 and 3 outgrow it in a few months' time if given half a chance. It's only the exceptional case that becomes chronic. Don't try to correct the child's speech or worry about speech training at 2½. Look around to see what might be making him tense. If he was upset by being separated from you for a number of days, try to avoid further separations for a couple of months (Sections 552 and 553). If you think you have been talking to him or urging him to talk too much, try to train yourself out of it. Play with him by **doing** things instead of by always **talking** things. Is he having plenty of chance to play with other children with whom he gets along easily? Does he have toys and equipment enough, indoors and out, so that he can be inventing his own games without too much bossing? I don't mean that you should ignore or isolate him, but when you're with him be relaxed and let him take the lead. When he talks to you, give him your attention so that he doesn't get frantic. If jealousy is upsetting him, see whether you can do more to prevent it. Stuttering in most cases lasts a number of months, with ups and downs. Don't expect it to go right away; be content with gradual progress. If you can't figure what, if anything, is wrong, talk it over with a children's psychiatrist. A "tongue-tie" (when the frenum, the fold of skin that runs from the middle of the underside of the tongue to the floor of the mouth, appears to be too short to allow free movement of the tongue) has nothing to do with stuttering, and should not be cut.

Some schools and hospitals have special speech classes or clinics, in which older children can receive special training.

This is often helpful, but by no means always. It is most valuable for the school-age child who wants assistance. For the child who is of a distinctly nervous type, it might be better to consult a children's psychiatrist first to see if it's possible to discover and remove the causes of tenseness (Section 633).

NAIL BITING

561. Nail biting is a sign of tenseness. It is more common in relatively high-strung, worrisome children. They start to bite when they are anxious—for instance, while waiting to be called on in school, while watching a scary episode in a movie. It isn't necessarily a serious sign in a generally happy, successful child, but it is always worth thinking over.

Nagging or punishing nail biters usually doesn't stop them for longer than half a minute, because they seldom realize they are doing it. In the long run, it may increase their tension. Bitter medicine on the nails rarely helps.

The better course is to find out what some of the pressures on the child are and try to relieve them. Is she being urged or corrected or warned or scolded too much? Are the parents expecting too much in the way of lessons? Consult the teacher about her school adjustment. If movie, radio, and TV adventures make her much more jittery than the average child, she'd better be kept away from the worst programs.

A child beyond the age of 3 may be helped by a manicure set if it is offered in a cooperative spirit.

Three to Six

DEVOTION TO THE PARENTS

562. Children at this age are usually easier to lead. Boys and girls around 3 have reached a stage in their emotional development when they feel that their fathers and mothers are wonderful people and want to be like them.

The automatic balkiness and the hostility that were just below the surface in the 2½-year-old period seem to lessen after 3 in most children. The feelings toward the parents aren't just friendly; they are warm and tender. However, children are not so devoted to their parents that they always obey and behave well. They are still real people with ideas of their own. They want to assert themselves, even if it means going against their parents' wishes at times.

While I'm emphasizing how agreeable children usually are between 3 and 6, I ought to make a partial exception for 4-year-olds. There's a lot of assertiveness, cockiness, loud talk, and provoking that comes out around 4 years in many children and that requires a firm hand in the parent.

563. Children strive now to be like their parents. Back at 2 years of age children were eagerly imitating their parents' activities, whether it was mopping the floor or hammering a pretend nail. The focus was on the use of the mop or the hammer. By 3 years of age they want to be totally like their parents as people. (See Section 47.) They play at going to work, tending house (cooking, cleaning, laundering), caring for children (using a doll or a younger child). They pretend to go for a drive in the family car or to step out for the evening. They dress up in their parents' clothes, mimic their conversation, their manners, and their mannerisms. This process is sometimes called identification.

Identification is a lot more important than just playing. It's how character is built—much more by what children perceive in their parents, and model themselves after, than by what the parents try to teach them in words. It's how their basic ideals and attitudes are laid down—toward work, toward people, toward themselves—though these will be modified later as they become more mature and knowing. It is how they learn to be the kind of parents they're going to turn out to be 20 years later, as you can tell from listening to the affectionate or scolding way they care for their dolls.

It's at this age that a girl becomes more aware of the fact that she's female and will grow up to be a woman. So she watches her mother with special attentiveness and tends to mold herself in her mother's image: how her mother feels about her husband (for example: lord and master, worm, or beloved partner) and about the male sex in general; about women (confidants or competitors); about girl and boy children (if the child of one sex is more favored than the other or if each individual is appreciated for herself or himself); toward work and housework—whether chore or challenge.

The little girl is not about to become an exact replica of her mother but she will surely be influenced by her in every respect.

A boy at this age realizes that he is on the way to becoming a man and therefore attempts to pattern himself predominantly after his father: how his father feels toward his wife and the female sex generally, toward other men, toward his boy and girl children, toward outside work and housework.

Though the predominant identification is with the parent of the same sex there's also, at this empathetic age, a degree of identification with the parent of the opposite sex. This is how the two sexes come to understand each other well enough to be able to live together.

564. Boys and girls now become fascinated with all aspects of babies. They want to know where they come from. When they find out that babies grow inside their mothers they are eager to carry out this amazing act of creation themselves—boys as well as girls. They want to take care of babies and love them, the way they realize they were cared for and loved. They will press a younger child into the role of a baby and spend hours acting as father and mother to him, or they'll use a doll.

It's not generally recognized that little boys are as eager as girls to grow babies inside themselves. When their parents tell them that this is impossible, they are apt to refuse to believe it for a long time. "I will too grow a baby," they say, really believing that if they wish something hard enough they can omnipotently make it come true. In some nonindustrial, isolated parts of the world, when a woman goes into labor her husband does, too, and is taken to the men's labor hut, moaning and writhing, by his sympathetic male friends.

565. Boys become romantic toward their mothers, girls toward their fathers. Up to this age, a boy's love for his mother has been predominantly of a dependent kind, like that of a baby. But now it also becomes increasingly romantic, like his father's. By the time he's 4, he's apt to insist that he's going to marry his mother when he grows up. He isn't clear just what marriage consists of, but he's absolutely sure who is the most important and appealing woman in the world. The little girl who is growing normally in her mother's pattern develops the same kind of love for her father.

These strong romantic attachments help children to grow spiritually and to acquire wholesome feelings toward the opposite sex that will later guide them into good marriages. But there is another side to the picture that creates unconscious tension in most children at this age. When people, old or young, love someone very much, they can't help wanting that person all to themselves. So, a little boy of 3 and 4 and 5 becomes more aware of his possessive devotion to his mother; he also becomes aware of how much she already belongs to his father. This irritates him underneath, no matter how much he loves and admires his father. At times he secretly wishes his father would get lost, and then he feels guilty about such disloyal feelings. Reasoning as a child does, he imagines that his father has the same jealous and resentful feelings toward him.

The little girl, if she is developing normally, develops the same possessive love for her father. She wishes at times that something would happen to her mother (whom she loves so much in other respects) so that she could have her father for herself. She may even say to her mother, "You can go away for a long trip, and I'll take good care of Daddy." But then she imagines that her mother is jealous of her, too, and subconsciously worries about this. Children try to push these scary thoughts out of their minds, since the parent, after all, is so much bigger and stronger, but they are apt to come to the surface in dreams. We believe that these mixed feelings—of love, jealousy, and fear—toward the parent of the same sex are the main cause of the bad dreams that little children of this age are so apt to have—of being chased by giants, robbers, witches, and other frightening figures.

These fears of children—that their parents are angry with them—get mixed up with their worries about why boys and men are shaped differently from girls and women. This will be discussed in Section 573.

Since all small children, we believe, go through this phase, it shouldn't make parents worry unless a child becomes excessively fearful or antagonistic to the parent of the same sex or much too close to the parent of the opposite sex. In that case, it's wise to get the help of a child guidance clinic.

566. The attachment isn't meant to become too complete. This romantic attachment to the parent of the opposite sex in the years between 3 and 6 is what you might call Nature's way of molding children's feelings in preparation for their eventual life as wife and mother or husband and father. But it wouldn't do for the attachment to go so far or get so strong that it lasts through life or even through childhood. Nature expects that children by 6 or 7 will become quite discouraged about the possibility of having the parent all to themselves. The unconscious fears about the parent's supposed anger and about genital differences will turn their pleasure in dreaming about romance into an aversion. From now on, children will shy away from kisses by the parent of the opposite sex. Their interests turn with relief to impersonal matters such as schoolwork and science. They try now to be just like the other children of their own sex rather than like their parents.

DEVOTION TO THE PARENTS

The previous intense attachments to the two parents will have served their main constructive purpose and will be progressively repressed and outgrown. (Freud called this shift the resolution of the Oedipus complex.)

A father who realizes that his young son sometimes has unconscious feelings of resentment and fear toward him does not help the boy by trying to be too gentle and permissive with him or by pretending that he, the father, doesn't really love his wife very much. In fact, if a boy was convinced that his father was afraid to be a firm father and a normally possessive husband, the boy would sense that he himself was having his mother too much to himself and would feel really guilty and frightened. And he would miss the inspiration of a confident father, which he must have in order to develop his own self-assurance.

In the same way a mother, even though she knows that her young daughter is sometimes jealous of her, best helps her daughter to grow up by being a self-confident mother who doesn't let herself be pushed around, who knows how and when to be firm, and who isn't at all afraid to show her affection and devotion to her husband.

It complicates life for a boy if his mother is a great deal more permissive and affectionate toward him than his father is. The same is true if she seems to be closer and more sympathetic to her son than she is to her husband. Such attitudes have a tendency to alienate a boy from his father and to make him too fearful of him. In a corresponding manner, the father who is putty in his daughter's hands and is always undoing the mother's discipline, or the father who acts as if he enjoys his daughter's companionship more than his wife's, is being unhelpful not only to his wife but to his daughter. This interferes with the good relationship that a daughter should have with her mother in order to grow up to be a happy woman.

Incidentally, it is entirely normal for a father to be a bit more lenient toward his daughter and a mother toward her son, and for a son to feel a little more comfortable with his mother and a daughter with her father, because there is naturally less rivalry between male and female than between two males or two females.

In the average family there is a healthy balance among the

feelings of father, mother, sons, and daughters that guides them through these stages of development without any special effort or conscious thought. I bring these points up only to give some clues for those families whose relationships have gotten out of kilter—families in which, for instance, the parents are constantly at odds about disciplining the children, or a boy is becoming timid toward all boys and men, or a girl is excessively defiant of her mother.

567. Parents can help children through this romantic but jealous stage by gently keeping it clear that the parents do belong to each other, that a boy can't ever have his mother to himself or a girl have her father to herself, but that the parents aren't shocked to realize that their children are mad at them sometimes on this account.

When a girl declares that she is going to marry her father, he can act pleased with the compliment but he can also explain that he's already married and that when she grows up she'll find another man her own age to marry.

When parents are being companionable together, they needn't and shouldn't let a child break up their conversation. They can cheerfully but firmly remind her that they have things to talk over and suggest that she get busy, too. Their tactfulness will keep them from prolonged displays of affection in front of her (as it would if other people were present), but they don't need to spring apart guiltily if she comes into the room unexpectedly.

When a boy is being rude to his father because he's feeling jealous, or to his mother because she's the cause of his jealousy, the parent should insist on politeness. And the converse is equally true if a girl is being rude. But at the same time the parents can ease the child's feelings of anger and guilt by saying that they know that the child is cross at them. See Section 534.

568. Sleep problems at 3, 4, and 5. Many of the sleep problems in 3-, 4-, and 5-year-old children that have been studied in child guidance clinics are found to be caused by romantic jealousy. The child wanders into the parents' room in the middle of every night and wants to get into their bed because subconsciously she doesn't want them to be alone together. It's much better for her as well as for the parents if they promptly and firmly, but not angrily, take her back to her own bed. (See Section 300.)

CURIOSITY AND IMAGINATION

569. Children's curiosity at this age is intense. They want to know the meaning of everything that meets their eyes. Their imagination is rich. They put two and two together and draw conclusions. They connect everything with themselves. When they hear about trains, they want to know right away, "Will I go on a train someday?" When they hear about an illness, it makes them think, "Will I have that?"

570. A little imagination is a good thing. When children of 3 or 4 tell a made-up story, they aren't lying in our grown-up sense. Their imagination is vivid to them. They're not sure where the real ends and the unreal begins. That is why they love stories that are told or read to them. That is why they are scared of violent TV programs and movies and shouldn't see them.

You don't need to jump on a child for making up stories occasionally, or make him feel guilty, or even be concerned yourself, so long as he is outgoing in general and happy with other children. On the other hand, if he is spending a good part of each day telling about imaginary friends or adventures, not as a game but as if he believes in them, it raises the question whether his real life is satisfying enough. Part of the remedy may be finding him children the same age to play with and helping him to enjoy them. Another question is whether he is having enough easygoing companionship with his parents.

Children need hugging and piggyback rides. They need to share in parents' jokes and friendly conversations. If the adults around them are undemonstrative, they dream of comfy, understanding playmates as the hungry man dreams of chocolate bars. If the parents are always disapproving, children invent a wicked companion whom they blame for the naughty things they have done or would like to do. If children are living largely in the imagination and not adjusting well with other children, especially by the age of 4, a psychiatrist should be able to find out what they are lacking.

Occasionally a parent who has always lived a great deal in her or his imagination and who is delighted to find how imaginative the child is overfills the child with stories, and they both live for hours in fairyland. The games and stories that the other children make up are poor in comparison to those of the parent. The child may be weaned away from interest in real people and things and have a harder time later adjusting to the world. I don't mean that a parent should be afraid of fairy stories or of a little make-believe, but only that it should be in moderation.

571. Why does an older child lie? The older child who tells a lie to deceive is a different problem. The first question is: Why does the child have to? Everyone, grown-up or child, gets in a jam occasionally when the only tactful way out is a small lie, and this is no cause for alarm.

A child isn't naturally deceitful. When a girl lies regularly it means that she is under too much pressure of some kind. If she is failing in her schoolwork and lying about it, it isn't because she doesn't care. Her lying shows that she does care. Is the work too hard for her? Is she confused in her mind by other worries so that she can't concentrate? Are her parents setting too high standards? The job is to find out what is wrong, with the help of the teacher, or the guidance teacher, or the school psychologist, or a psychiatrist (Section 633). You don't have to pretend that she has pulled the wool over your eyes. You might say gently, "You don't have to lie to me. Tell me what the trouble is and we'll see what we can do." But she won't be able to tell you the answer right away because she probably doesn't know it herself. Even if she knows some of her worries, she can't break down all at once. It takes time and understanding.

FEARS AROUND THREE, FOUR, AND FIVE

572. Imaginary worries are common at this age. In earlier sections we discussed how anxieties are different at different age periods. New types of fear crop up fairly often around the age of 3 or 4—fear of the dark, of dogs, of fire engines, of death, of crippled people. Children's imaginations have now developed to the stage where they can put themselves in other people's shoes and picture dangers that they haven't actually experienced. Their curiosity is pushing out in all directions. They want to know not only the cause of everything but what these things have to do with them. They overhear something about dying. Quickly they want to know what dying is, and as soon as they get a dim idea they ask, "Do I have to die?"

These fears are commoner in children who have been made tense from battles over such matters as feeding and toilet training, children whose imaginations have been overstimulated by scary stories or too many warnings, children who haven't had enough chance to develop their independence and outgoingness, children whose parents are too protective (Section 554). The uneasiness accumulated before now seems to be crystallized by the child's new imagination into definite dreads. It sounds as if I mean that any child who develops a fear has been handled mistakenly in the past, but I don't mean to go that far. I think that some children are born more sensitive than others; and all children, no matter how carefully they are brought up, are frightened by something. Read Section 565 about children's feelings about their parents.

If your child develops a fear of the dark, try to reassure her. This is more a matter of your manner than your words. Don't make fun of her, or be impatient with her, or try to argue her out of her fear. If she wants to talk about it, as a few children do, let her. Give her the feeling that you want to understand but that you are sure nothing bad will happen to her. Naturally you should never threaten her with bogeymen or policemen or the devil. Avoid movies and scary TV programs and cruel fairy stories. The child is scared enough of her own mental creations. Call off any battle that you might be engaged in about feeding or staying dry at night. Keep her behaving well by firm guidance rather than by letting her misbehave and then making her feel guilty about it afterward. Arrange to give her a full, outgoing life with other children every day. The more she is absorbed in games and plans, the less she will worry about her inner fears. Leave her door open at night if that is what she wants, or leave a dim light on in her room. It's a small price to pay to keep the goblins out of sight. The light, or the conversation from the living room, won't keep her awake so much as her fears will. When her fear subsides, she will be able to stand the dark again.

Sometimes children use a phobia increasingly to control their parents. See Section 556.

Realize ahead of time that questions about death are apt to come up at this age. Try to make the first explanation casual, not too scary. You might say, "Everybody has to die someday. Most people die when they get very old and tired and weak and they just stop being alive." Some parents like to express it in religious terms: "He was very, very sick, and God took him to Heaven to take care of him." Remember to hug her and smile at her and remind her that you're going to be together for years and years.

Since this is the age period when children are normally apt to get somewhat confused about death and sleep, it's especially important not to refer to death as "going to sleep." This most often comes up when a family pet is very ill and is brought to the veterinarian to have its life ended. Many parents refer to this as the pet having been "put to sleep." I think it's much better to explain that the veterinarian gave the pet a special kind of medicine which made the pet's heart stop beating, without causing any pain, and that this made the pet be dead.

All healthy people of every age have some degree of fear and resentment of death. There is no way to present the matter to children that will get around this basic human attitude. But if you think of death as something to be met eventually with dignity and fortitude, you'll be able to give somewhat the same feeling about it to your child.

Many parents wonder what to do about allowing a child to

attend the funeral of a relative or close friend of the family. I think that if a child wants to attend a funeral and the parents are comfortable enough with the idea so that they can prepare the child for what will happen at the funeral, then children from the age of 3 onward can attend funerals and even accompany the family to the cemetery for the burial. It's important that an adult whom the child knows well is with the child at all times, to answer questions and, if necessary, to take the child home if the child becomes too upset.

A fear of an animal is common at this period, even in children who have had no bad experiences. Don't drag them to a dog to reassure them. The more you pull them, the more you make them feel they have to pull in the opposite direction. As the months go by, they themselves will try to get over their fear and approach a dog. They will do it faster by themselves than you can ever persuade them. That reminds me of fear of the water. Don't ever pull a child, screaming, into the ocean or pool. It is true that occasionally a child who is forced in finds that it is fun and loses the fear abruptly, but in more cases it works the opposite way. Remember that the child is longing to go despite the dread of it.

With fears of dogs and fire engines and policemen and other concrete things, a child may try to get used to the worry and overcome it by playing games about it. This acting-out of a fear is a great help if the child is able to do it. A fear is meant to make us act. Our bodies are flooded with adrenaline, which makes the heart beat faster and supplies sugar for quick energy. We are ready to run like the wind or to fight like wild animals. The running and the fighting burn up the anxiety. Sitting still does nothing to relieve it. If children with a fear of a dog can play games in which they pound the stuffing out of a toy dog, it partly relieves them. If your child develops an intense fear, or a number of fears, or frequent nightmares, or frequent sleepwalking which puts him in physical danger, you ought to get the help of a children's psychiatrist (Section 633).

573. Fear of injury. I'd like to discuss separately the fear of bodily injury in the age period between 2½ and 5, because there are special things you can do to prevent or relieve it. Children at this age want to know the reason for everything, worry easily, and apply dangers to themselves. If they see a crippled or deformed person, they first want to know what happened to that person, then put themselves in the other's place and wonder if that injury might happen to themselves. Children develop these fears not only about real injuries. They even get mixed up and worried about the natural differences between boys and girls. If a boy around the age of 3 sees a girl undressed, it may strike him as queer that she hasn't got a penis like his. He's apt to say, "Where is her wee wee?" If he doesn't receive a satisfactory answer right away, he may jump to the conclusion that some accident has happened to her. Next comes the anxious thought, "That might happen to me, too." The same misunderstanding may worry the little girl when she first realizes that boys are made differently. First she asks, "What's that?" Then she wants to know anxiously, "Why don't I have one? What happened to it?" That's the way a 3-year-old's mind works. They may be so upset right away that they're afraid to question their parents.

This worry about why boys are shaped differently from girls shows up in different ways. I remember a boy just under 3 who, with an anxious expression, kept watching his baby sister being bathed and telling his mother, "Baby is boo-boo." That was his word for hurt. His mother couldn't make out what he was talking about until he got bold enough to point. At about the same time he began to hold onto his own penis in a worried way. His mother was unhappy about this and assumed it was the beginning of a bad habit. It never occurred to her that there was a connection between these two developments. I remember a little girl who became worried after she found out about boys, and kept trying to undress different children to see how they were made, too. She didn't do this in a sly way; you could see she was fearful. Later she began to handle her genitals. A boy 3½ first became upset about his younger sister's body, and then began to worry about everything in the house that was broken. He would ask his parents nervously, "Why is this tin soldier broken?" There was no sense to this question, because he had broken it himself the day before. Everything that he saw damaged seemed to remind him of his fears about himself.

It's wise to realize ahead of time that normal children are

likely to be wondering about things like bodily differences between 2½ and 3½, and that if they aren't given a comforting explanation when they first get curious, they're apt to come to worrisome conclusions. It's no use waiting for them to say, "I want to know why a boy isn't made like a girl," because they won't be that definite. They may ask some kind of question, or they may hint around, or they may just wait and get worried. Don't think of it as an unwholesome interest in sex. To them it's just like any other important question at first. You can see why it would work the wrong way to shush them, or scold them, or blush and refuse to answer. That would give them the idea they are on dangerous ground, which is what you want to avoid. On the other hand, you don't need to be solemn as if you were giving a lecture. It's easier than that. It helps, first of all, to bring the child's fear out into the open by saying that he (or she) probably thinks a girl had a penis but something happened to it. Then you try to make it clear, in a matter-of-fact cheerful tone, that girls and women are **made** differently from boys and men; they are **meant** to be that way. A small child gets an idea more easily from examples. You can explain that Johnny is made just like Daddy, Uncle Harry, David, and so on, and that Mary is made like Mommy, Mrs. Jenkins, and Helen (listing all the individuals that the child knows best). A little girl needs extra reassurance because it's natural for her to want to have something that she can see. (I heard of a little girl who complained to her mother, "But he's so fancy and I'm so plain.") It will help her to know that her mother likes being made the way she is, that her parents love her just the way she's made. This may also be a good time to explain that girls when they are older can grow babies of their own inside them and have breasts with which to nurse them. That's a thrilling idea at 3 or 4.

This is also the age period in which there is naturally a great interest in physical mastery of all kinds (hopping, running, climbing—watch any group this age in the playground) which makes body intactness very important and being broken very upsetting. This explains why a child at the age of 2½ or 3, for example, can get so upset about a broken cookie, refusing a cookie that's in two pieces and demanding a whole one.

574. The fear of nuclear war is almost universal among children and is realistic. Young children express it as fear that their parents will be killed and worry about who will take care of them then. Older children see the direct danger to themselves. Adolescents are moved to pessimism, asking what is the use of studying or maintaining their health if they are to die before they become workers and parents.

Parents can give their children partial reassurance if they can say, "Yes there is a danger but it need not happen if we will all work politically for peace. We vote for the candidates for president, senator, and congressman who are for a nuclear freeze, disarmament, and peaceful settlement of disputes. We write to our officials, not just once but often. We belong to peace groups and attend demonstrations. You can help by writing letters and attending demonstrations, too."

Children who are too young to write letters or understand demonstrations can be reassured by being told that their parents and other adults are working hard to prevent nuclear war from ever happening.

DIFFERENT CAUSES FOR HANDLING THE GENITALS

575. In the infant it's wholesome curiosity. Babies in the last part of the first year discover their genitals the way they discovered their fingers and toes, and handle them the same way, too. The 1¼-year-old girl, sitting on the potty, explores herself with definite curiosity for a few seconds at a time. This won't come to anything or start a bad habit. You can distract her with a toy if you want, but don't feel that you've **got** to. It's better not to give her the idea that she is bad or that her genitals are bad. You want her to go on having a wholesome, natural feeling about her entire body. If she is scared about any part of herself, it draws her attention to it, gets it on her mind, and may have bad results later. Furthermore, if you try to stop a year-old baby by saying, "No, no" or slapping her hand, or yanking it away, it's apt to make her more determined.

576. At 3 it's related to their feelings. Children between 3 and 6 are surprisingly grown up in lots of ways. They love intensely and romantically those who are close to them, especially their parents.

We realize now that there is a childish kind of sexual feeling at this period, which is an essential part of normal development. (In former times people believed that nothing of this sort occurred until adolescence, probably because they wanted to avoid recognizing it in their children as long as possible.) Children of 3, 4, and 5 are physically affectionate. They cling to their favorite grown-ups and lean against them. They are interested in each other's bodies, occasionally have the desire to see and touch each other. This is one reason why they like to play doctor.

If you realize that this early interest in sex is a natural part of the slow process of growing up and that it occurs to a degree in all wholesome children, you can take a sensible view of it. If a child is not preoccupied with sex, is generally outgoing, unworried, and has plenty of other interests and playmates, there is no cause for concern. If not, the child needs to be helped.

577. A lot at 3 may be due to worry. In Section 573 there were examples of children in the neighborhood of 3 years who handled themselves a great deal, in a preoccupied manner, after they became worried about why girls aren't made the same as boys. It's important for parents to know that the fear that something will happen or has happened to the genitals is one of the commonest causes of **excessive** handling or masturbation in young childhood.

To tell such children that they'll injure themselves makes matters worse. To tell them that they're bad and that you won't love them any more gives them a new fear. The wise thing is to try to take away the fear as soon as you see it developing. If the parents of the little boy who said, "Baby is boo-boo," had known that this misunderstanding and this worry are common, they could have started to reassure him the first time he said it. The same thing applies to the parents of the little girl who anxiously tried to undress the other children.

578. After 6 there's a stronger effort to control it. Between the ages of 6 and puberty, it seems as if children, by their own nature, make an effort to suppress the impulse to masturbate or to become involved in sex play with others. Children get the idea that masturbation is considered wrong, whether their parents have told them so or not, and this is the period when their conscience is becoming strong. But it doesn't stop altogether in all children, and it's still perfectly normal if it continues. A child may be drawn into it in the group because the others are doing it. It's a time in life when they're striving with might and main to become just like the others.

579. It may be a sign of tenseness and worry at any age. At any age there are a few children who handle their genitals a great deal, sometimes in public. They hardly seem to be aware of what they are doing. They are usually tense or worried children. They aren't nervous because they are masturbating; they are masturbating because they are nervous. The job here is to find out what's causing the tenseness, instead of attacking the masturbation directly. An 8-year-old boy is terrified that his ill mother is going to die. He can't put his mind on schoolwork but absentmindedly handles his genitals in school as he gazes out the window. Another child is thoroughly maladjusted, doesn't know how to get along with other children, has no close connection with the world around her. Cut off from the outside, she must live within herself. Such children and their parents need the help of a psychiatrist or child guidance clinic (Section 633).

Many children hold their genitals when they need to urinate, especially the procrastinators, and this has no special significance.

580. To disapprove or not. The parents and child psychiatrists who are opposed to showing disapproval of masturbation and other sex play reason that masturbation doesn't do any physical or psychological harm (which is correct), so why risk any chance of sexual maladjustment by instilling guilt or fears.

The opposite reasoning goes that all of us grew up with some degree of anxiety and guilt about sex; that it is, in fact, built into our species through the resolution of the Oedipus complex (Section 566). If parents are made uncomfortable by something their children are doing the children are well aware of this and made uneasy by it. Then it is better for all concerned for the parent to try to inhibit it, just as in the case of other disapproved behavior. Furthermore, many parents still have strong religious or moral objections and they don't want their own children to be playing with others who have no inhibitions.

I personally have no religious or rational moral objection to masturbation and other kinds of sex play and I wouldn't be really shocked by discovering them in my child. But I wouldn't like to have my child masturbate in public view or to feel free to engage others in sex play. Part of my discomfort would come from not wanting the neighbors to disapprove of my child. So I would try to inhibit him gently—not scare him or shame him—by saying, "It isn't polite," or "Most fathers and mothers don't want their children to play this way," or "I don't like to see you do it," or "That kind of play is for grown-ups, not for children."

I think parents should take the stand that they themselves feel right about. When you discover your small child in some sort of sex play alone or with others, you'll probably be at least a little bit surprised and shocked, even if you don't disapprove. If you do disapprove, it's better to be matter-of-fact, the way you are about lesser matters. Then shoo the children out to some other activity. That's usually enough to stop sex play for a long time in normal children. It's sensible for parents who disapprove to keep some track of a group of small children who are in a period of interest in sex, and see that they have plenty of other things to do. The principal reason is that some children are upset and worried by what is done and said, especially if there is an older child with an exaggerated interest leading them on. Naturally, parents should not become suspicious snoopers or make unsupported accusations.

581. Why there is more at adolescence. Among adolescents there tends to be an increased urge to masturbate for reasons that are easy to understand. Glandular changes are taking place that affect not only the body but the thoughts and emotions. Children become increasingly aware of their sexual and romantic feelings, not because they want to but because their glands say they have to. Yet many of them are nowhere near ready, in the early part of adolescence, to express these feelings openly. When they are more grown up, the same impulses find expression in dates, romantic companionship, dancing, and flirting. Later still, they lead to falling in love in earnest and marriage.

Some conscientious adolescents feel excessively guilty and worried about masturbation, even when it's just a thought, and need reassurance. Children who seem to be generally happy and successful, doing well in school, and getting along with friends can be told that all normal young people have these desires and that a great majority do masturbate. This won't take away all the feeling of guilt, but it will help. On the other hand, adolescents who are wrapped up in themselves, or unable to enjoy friendships, or getting into trouble with schoolwork, need help from someone who understands adolescents well. The best person would be a children's psychiatrist. If that's not possible, talk to the guidance teacher or counselor in the high school. In an unhappy child, frequent masturbation, or preoccupation with it, is only one symptom of a larger problem.

582. Why threats are harmful. Most of us heard in childhood the threat that masturbation would lead to insanity. This belief is untrue. It grew up because certain adolescents and young adults who are becoming seriously mentally ill masturbate a great deal. But they aren't becoming insane because they are masturbating. The excessive masturbation is just one symptom of the nervous breakdown. This is an example of the fact that frequent masturbation is due to something else going wrong in the child's life or spirit. The job is to find the cause.

What's wrong with telling children that masturbation will make them sick, or injure their genitals, or mark them as evil people? First of all, none of these things is true. In the second place, and more important, it's risky and it's wrong to put deep fears into a child's mind. The self-confident, tough-minded child may not be much affected by these threats. But the sensitive child takes them to heart, and may develop a morbid fear of anything sexual, which could interfere with a normal adult adjustment.

"THE FACTS OF LIFE"

583. Sex education starts early whether you plan it or not. It is common to think that sex education means a lecture at school or a solemn talk by a parent at home. This is taking too narrow a view of the subject. A child is learning about "the facts of life" all through childhood, if not in a good way then in an unwholesome way. Sex is a lot broader than just how babies are made. It includes the whole matter of how men and women get along with each other, and what their respective places are in the world. Let me give you a couple of bad examples. Suppose a boy has a father who is disagreeable and abusive to the mother. You can't educate the boy with a lecture at school telling him that marriage is a relationship of mutual love and respect. His experience tells him differently. When he learns about the physical side of sex, whether it's from a teacher or from other children, he will fit it into the picture he has of a man being disagreeable to a woman. Or take the example of a girl who grows up feeling unwanted because she thinks her parents prefer her younger brother. She is going to resent men, because she believes that they get all the breaks—that women are always the victims—and that this situation cannot be changed. It won't matter how many books or talks you give her about sex and marriage. Whatever she hears or experiences she will fit into the pattern she has fixed in her mind: it's the man taking advantage of the woman who is helpless to alter the pattern. Even if she marries, she won't adjust to it.

So children begin their sex education as soon as they can sense how their mother and father get along with each other in general, how they feel about their sons and daughters, and as soon as they become aware of differences between their bodies and their parents' bodies and those of opposite-sexed brothers, sisters, and playmates.

584. Children ask questions around 3. Children begin to get more exact ideas about the things that are connected with sex around the ages of 2½, 3, 3½. This is the "why" stage, when curiosity branches out in all directions. They probably want to know why boys are made differently from girls (which is discussed in Section 573). They don't think of it as a sex question. It's just an important question. But if they gain the wrong impression then, it will become mixed up with sex later and give them distorted ideas.

585. Where do babies come from? This question is also pretty sure to come up in the period around 3. It's easier and better to begin with the truth, rather than tell a fairy story and have to change it later. Try to answer the question as simply as they ask it. For instance, you can say, "A baby grows in a special place inside the mother, called the uterus or womb." You don't have to tell them more than that for the time being if it satisfies them. But maybe in a few minutes, maybe in a few months, they want to know a couple of other things. How does the baby get in and how does it get out? The first question is apt to be embarrassing to the parent, who may jump to the conclusion that they are now demanding to know about conception and sex relations. Of course, they have no such idea. They think of things getting into the stomach by being eaten and perhaps wonder if the baby gets in that way, too. A simple answer is that the baby grows from a tiny seed that was in the mother all the time. It will be months before they want to know what part the father plays. Some people feel that children should be told at the time of their first questions that the father contributes by putting his seed in the mother, too. Perhaps this is right, especially in the case of the little boy who feels that the man is left out of the picture. But most experts agree that at 3 or 4 years it is not necessary to try to give an exact picture of the physical and emotional sides of intercourse. It's more than children bargained for, you might say, when they asked their question. All that's necessary is to satisfy their curiosity at the level of their understanding.

To the question of how babies get out, a good answer is something to the effect that when they are big enough they come out through a special opening that's just for that purpose, called the vagina. (It's just as well to make it clear that it is not the opening for bowel movements or for urine.)

586. Why not the stork? You may say, "Why isn't it easier and less embarrassing to tell them about the stork?" There are several reasons. We know that a child as young as 3, who has a pregnant mother or aunt, may have a suspicion of where the baby is growing from observing the woman's figure and from bits of conversation overheard. It's apt to mystify and worry him to have his parent nervously telling him something different from what he suspects is the truth. Even if he doesn't suspect anything at 3, he is surely going to find out the truth or the half-truth when he's 5 or 7 or 9. It's better not to start him off wrong and have him later decide that you're something of a liar. And if he finds that for some reason you didn't dare tell him the truth, it puts a barrier between you, makes him uneasy. He's less likely to ask you other questions later, no matter how troubled he is. Another reason for telling the truth at 3 is that children at this age are satisfied with simple answers. You get practice for the harder questions that come later.

Sometimes small children who have been told where the baby is growing confuse parents by talking as if they also believed the stork theory. Or they may mix up two or three theories at the same time. This is natural. Small children believe part of everything they hear because they have such vivid imaginations. They don't try, like grown-ups, to find the one right answer and get rid of the wrong ones. You must also remember that children can't learn anything from one telling. They learn a little at a time, and come back with the same question until they feel sure that they've gotten it straight. Then at every new stage of development they're ready for a new slant.

587. A step at a time usually satisfies. Realize ahead of time that your child's questions will never come in exactly the form or at the moment you expect. A parent is apt to visualize the scene at bedtime when the child is in a confidential mood. Actually, the question is more apt to be popped in the middle of the grocery store or while you are talking on the street with a pregnant neighbor. If it does, try to curb that impulse to shush the child. Answer on the spot if you can. If that is impossible, say casually, "I'll tell you later. These are things we like to talk about when other people aren't around." Don't make too solemn an occasion of it. When children ask you why the grass is green or why dogs have tails, you answer in an offhand way that gives them the feeling that it is the most natural thing in the world. Try to get the same spirit of naturalness into your answers about the facts of life. Remember that even if this subject is charged with feeling and embarrassment for you, it is a matter of simple curiosity to them. If you feel your embarrassment is too obvious, you can say something like, "I get embarrassed talking about these things because my parents always said it was wrong to think or talk about sex. I don't agree with them at all, but I haven't had much practice so it still is hard for me." The question, "Why don't babies come until you are married?" or "What does the father do about it?" may not come until children are 4 or 5 or older unless they observe animals. Then you can explain that the seed comes out of the father's penis and goes into the uterus, a special place different from the stomach, where the baby will grow. It may be some time before they try to visualize this situation. When they are ready for that, you can bring in something in your own words about loving and embracing.

A young child is very apt to stumble on some evidence of menstruation and to interpret this as a sign of injury. A mother should be ready to explain that all women have this discharge every month and that it doesn't come from a hurt. Something about the purpose of menstruation can be explained to a child of 4 or older.

588. The child who hasn't asked. What about the child who has reached the age of 4 or 5 or more and hasn't asked any questions at all? Parents sometimes assume that this means the child is very innocent and has never thought of these questions. Most people who have worked closely with children would be inclined to doubt this. It is more likely that the child has gotten the feeling, whether the parents mean to give it or not, that these matters are embarrassing. You can be on the lookout for indirect questions and hints and little jokes that a child uses to test out parents' reactions. I think of several examples. A child of 7 who was not supposed to know anything about pregnancy kept calling attention to his mother's large abdomen in a half-embarrassed, half-joking way. Here was a good chance, better late than never, for the parents to explain. A little girl who is at the stage of wondering why she isn't made like a boy sometimes makes valiant efforts to urinate standing up. The parents then have an opportunity to give a reassuring explanation, even though the child hasn't asked a direct question. There are occasions almost every day, in a child's conversation about humans and animals and birds, when a parent on the lookout for indirect questions can help the child to ask what she or he wants to know.

589. How the school can help. If the mother and father have answered earlier questions comfortably, children keep on turning to parents as they grow older and want more exact knowledge. But the school has a chance to help out, too. Many schools make a point of letting children in kindergarten or first grade take care of animals, such as rabbits, guinea pigs, or white mice. This gives them an opportunity to become familiar with all sides of animal life—feeding, fighting, mating, birth, and suckling of the young. It is easier in some ways to learn these facts in an impersonal situation, and it supplements what children have learned from parents. But what they find out in school they probably want to discuss and clear up further at home.

By the fifth grade, it is good to have biology taught in a simple way, including a discussion of reproduction. At least some of the girls in the class are entering the puberty stage of development and need some accurate knowledge of what is happening. The discussion from a somewhat scientific point of view in school should help the child to bring it up more personally at home.

590. How much modesty in the home? In less than a century, Americans have made a full swing from the excessive modesty of the Victorian period to the partial nudity of bathing suits and to complete nudity in quite a few homes today. Most people agree (and I certainly do) that today's casual attitude is a lot healthier. Nursery school teachers, children's psychiatrists and psychologists generally agree that it's wholesome for **young** children of both sexes to see each other undressed at times in the home, at the beach, and in the bathroom of a nursery school.

However, there's evidence from the work of child psychiatrists and guidance clinics that at least some young children get upset by regularly seeing their parents naked. The main reason is that young children's feelings for their parents are so intense. A boy loves his mother much more than he loves any little girl. He feels much more rivalrous with his father and more in awe of him than he feels toward any boy. So the sight of his mother may be a little too stimulating, and the chance to compare himself so unfavorably with his father every day may make him feel like doing something violent to his old man. (Nudist fathers have told me about their 3- and 4-year-old sons making snatching gestures at the father's penis during morning shaving.) Then the boy feels guilty and fearful. A little girl who regularly sees her father nude may be too much stimulated.

I don't want to claim that all children are upset by parental nudity. No statistical study has been made, but since we know that it's a possibility, I think it's a little wiser for parents to give their children the benefit of the doubt and, as a general rule, keep reasonably covered and keep children out of the bathroom while a parent is bathing or using the toilet. This doesn't have to be carried to extremes. A parent is caught off guard occasionally and shouldn't then act shocked or angry. It's only necessary to say, "Will you wait outside until I get dressed?" After the age of 6 or 7, most children begin to want a little more privacy for themselves, at least at times, and I think it's good to respect this.

DAY NURSERY, NURSERY SCHOOL, MONTESSORI SCHOOL, DAY CARE CENTER

591. Most children would benefit from group experience in the age period between 2 or 3 and kindergarten, but it certainly isn't necessary in every case. It is particularly valuable for the only child, for the child without much chance to play with others, for the child who lives in a small apartment, for the child whose parents find her or him difficult to manage for any reason. Every young child by the age of 3 needs other children of the same age, not just to have fun with but also to learn how to get along with. This is the most important job in a child's life. Children need space to run and shout in, apparatus to climb on, blocks and boxes and boards to build with, trains and dolls to play with. They need to learn how to get along with other grown-ups besides their parents. Few children nowadays have all these advantages in their own home. Good group care is crucial to the parents as well as to the child in the growing number of families in which both parents work outside the home.

592. Day nurseries. In the nineteenth and early twentieth centuries there were day nurseries in which children from birth to 6 years could be given custodial care when their mothers had to work because their husbands had died or deserted them or taken to drink. In general no training or understanding was required of the staff and no limit set on the number of children to be assigned to each staff member. Some children suffered impairment of their intellectual and emotional development partly as a result of receiving too little attention and affection, and nurseries got a bad name; but part of the impairment was undoubtedly due to the demoralized homes from which these children came.

Day nurseries, operated openly as charities, have largely disappeared. Some of them upgraded their staffs and aims and became nursery schools or day care centers. However, there are still many unlisted nurseries run for profit by people with no training and no knowledge of children's needs.

593. The Montessori schools. Maria Montessori, an Italian physician, was impressed with the eagerness of preschool children to learn skills if they were given suitable equipment with which to work. Experimenting over a period of years in the last part of the nineteenth century she developed a large series of objects which required gradually increasing amounts of skill and maturity to manipulate; for example, colored cards to be matched for color, cubes of various sizes to be arranged in order, two flaps of cloth with eyelets to be laced together, laces to be tied in a bowknot, etc. After a child mastered one skill, she was given the object that required the next greater amount of skill. Over a period of 2 or 3 years, starting at 2 or 3 years of age, a child would advance by small steps to the beginning stages of reading, writing, and arithmetic. Each child worked alone and set her own pace. In Dr. Montessori's method there was no emphasis on social relationships or on spontaneous, creative play. She originally developed her method for developmentally disabled children.

There were thousands of Montessori schools in America early in the twentieth century. When the American nursery school movement gained momentum in the 1920s and 1930s, the Montessori schools were superseded here.

The Montessori method with its emphasis on the learning of definite skills leading up to reading and writing was reintroduced into America in the 1950s in response to a widespread concern about getting children started earlier on their academic careers and advancing them more rapidly. I myself felt that this concern was a thoughtless hysteria brought about by the unexpected success of the Soviet Union in launching the first two spacecraft, long before the United States was ready.

Nowadays there are thousands of Montessori schools all over the country. Since there is no group which licenses Montessori schools or controls the program that is actually carried out in each school, these schools vary tremendously. A few of them still follow quite closely the original model of Dr. Montessori. But the great majority of them have a mixture of her methods and the methods developed by the American nursery school movement.

594. The American nursery school concept was developed in the early twentieth century, not for the custodial care of children of working mothers and not just to prepare children specifically for the three Rs of elementary school. The aim was to give children of 3 and 4, for one-half or two-thirds of the day, under trained teachers, a variety of valuable experiences which would help them grow up in all respects and make them more sensitive, capable, and creative people: dancing and making rhythm music, painting easel pictures from their own inspiration, finger painting, clay modeling, block building, and vigorous outdoor play. They digest their life experiences and prepare for adulthood through the care of dolls and the playing-out of family dramas—their parents' and their own.

Ideally, there are quiet corners for individual play for when a child feels the need. The aim is to develop a very broad variety of capabilities—academic, social, artistic, musical, and muscular. The emphasis is on initiative, independence, cooperation (discussing and sharing instead of fighting for play equipment), and on playing-out the child's own ideas.

595. Cooperative preschools. Some parents who can't afford a nursery school join together and raise enough money among them to hire a well-trained head teacher who, perhaps with one or two other trained teachers, directs a preschool, using the parents as assistants to the teachers. These parents have the opportunity to learn from the trained teachers and to have a kind of contact with their own child and with other children which they otherwise wouldn't have.

596. Day care center is a term used in recent years to specify care of the children of working parents during their working hours (often 8 A.M. to 6 P.M.), occasionally subsidized by government agencies or private companies. It brings to all-day care the advantages of the nursery school—an educational philosophy, trained teachers, and full educational equipment.

The concept of the day care center came in during World War II when the federal government wanted to encourage mothers with even young children to work in war industries. It is primarily for the care of children from the ages of 2 or 3 years to 5 years. But it often includes the care of kindergarteners and first and second graders from the time their regular school classes are over (e.g., 12 noon) until they are picked up by their parents at 5 or 6 P.M. Basic is the requirement that at least the head teachers be trained, qualified nursery school teachers. Parents, other neighborhood adults, high school and college students are sometimes utilized as assistants. It's important to plan ahead for what you'll do if your child is sick and can't go to her day care center.

See Section 51 for a discussion of day care for children under the age of 2 or 3 years.

597. Play and playing-out in nursery schools and day care centers. The use of words like "play" and "playing-out" gives some people the idea that it's all just for amusement, without any serious purpose. Nothing could be farther from the truth. Most play is very serious for young children. It is their way of imitating and practicing adult activities so that they can master them and mature. Playing-out tense situations from their parents' lives and their own lives is their way of mastering their strong emotions. They may have been frightened by the doctor so they become doctors themselves and plunge needles into a doll. (This is getting over an anxiety by what's known in psychology as turning passive into active.) They've been painfully jealous of a brother or sister and have been made to feel guilty about it. To reassure themselves that they're getting past such dangerously "bad" behavior, they invent dramatic situations where they are parents and punish their doll child for jealous, mean behavior.

All children mature emotionally by sorting out their feelings in play. The nursery school makes it easier by providing a wealth of equipment and friends to play parts in each other's dramas.

In play, children also learn how to get along with other children and adults of different personalities, how to enjoy give-and-take, how to solve conflicts. Play in the yard on swings, jungle gyms, tricycles, and wagons teaches body coordination and social cooperation.

The cooperativeness, initiative, and creativity which children develop in a good nursery school or day care center will help to prepare them socially, emotionally, and intellectually not only for kindergarten and the elementary grades but also for their careers as adults. This is not an exaggeration, I feel.

598. Choosing the type of preschool. Some of the Montessori schools that have been established in America in the past twenty years have borrowed liberally from the activities of the American nursery school movement. So the differences in actual schools belonging to the two categories may sometimes not be great.

In advising parents about choosing between available preschools, I'd emphasize the importance of trained teachers who enjoy, understand, and can lead children, and ample opportunities for creative work and imaginative play. How the teachers get along with the children is really what makes the school. Within each category—nursery schools, Montessori schools, and day care centers—there are great differences in quality and spirit. Visit—for several hours, over several days—the preschool you are considering, until you are satisfied.

How can you tell whether a nursery school, Montessori school, or a day care center is a good one? Space indoors and out, equipment, small places where one or two children can play quietly away from the group, enough teachers and assistants (one for every five children) are all important.

But most significant is the attitude of the teachers, and the children's response. Are the teachers fussing over mechanical matters, talking to the whole group at once, and giving frequent lectures? Do they act harassed?

Or are they spending most of their time with individual children, helping them with their requests and frustrations, looking them in the eye and smiling at them, encouraging them to find their own answers, to create their own pictures and buildings and dramatic situations?

Are the children relaxed? Do they trust the teachers and turn to them for help? Do they cooperate with other children and get involved in few fights? A friendly relationship between teachers and children will show in the relationships between the children.

I am in favor of government support for all preschools or day care centers—of good quality—for all children whose parents wish them, staffed with selected trained teachers. However, my own preference for the care of children under the age of 2 or 3 is for a family kind of care. Preferably, the mother and father between them would care for the children at least half of their waking hours by means of adjustments of the parents' work schedules. The rest of the day, whether this means 2 hours or 8 hours, the child could be cared for by a live-in or live-out caregiver, or in "family day care" in another family. (See Section 52.)

599. When to start preschool. Some preschools and day care centers start with 2-year-olds. This may work very well **if** the child is fairly independent and outgoing (many are still quite dependent up to 2½ or 3), **if** the class is small (not more than 8), and **if** the teacher is so warm and understanding that she quickly makes children feel secure.

But certain children are really too immature to be in such a large group at 2, especially when it's for all day. They are still dependent on their parents, timid with other children, and tending to withdraw into themselves or to cling to the teacher. I don't mean that such children should be kept tied to their parents forever. They need every opportunity to be around where other children play so that they can become accustomed to them, interested in them, and wean themselves from their dependence. But this takes a little time. If you are in doubt about your child's readiness for nursery school or day care center, talk it over with a good nursery school teacher.

600. The first days at preschool or day care center. The 4-year-old who is outgoing takes to preschool like a duck to water and doesn't need any gentle introduction. It may be quite different with a sensitive 3-year-old who still feels closely attached to a parent, say the mother. If she leaves him at school the first day, he may not make a fuss right away, but after a while he may miss her. When he finds she isn't there, he may become frightened. The next day he may not want to leave home. With a dependent child like this, it's better to introduce him to school gradually. For several days his mother might stay nearby while he plays, and then take him home again after a time. Each day the mother and child stay for a longer period. Meanwhile, he is building up attachments to the teacher and other children that will give him a sense of security when his mother no longer stays. Sometimes a child seems to be quite happy for several days, even after his mother has left him there. Then he gets hurt and suddenly wants her. In that case, the teacher can help the mother decide if she should come back for a number of days. When a mother is staying around the school, she ought to remain in the background. The idea is to let the child develop his **own** desire to enter the group, so that he forgets his need for his mother.

Sometimes the mother's anxiety is greater than the child's.

If she says good-bye three times over, with a worried expression, it gives him the idea, "She looks as if something awful might happen if I stay here without her. I'd better not let her go." It's natural for a tenderhearted mother to worry about how her small child will feel when she leaves him for the first time. Let the nursery school teacher advise you. She's had a lot of experience.

A child who starts with some genuine anxiety about separating from the parent may learn what a control this gives over a highly sympathetic parent, and then exploit this control progressively. (See Section 552.)

When a child becomes reluctant or fearful about returning to a school with understanding teachers, I think it is usually better for the parents to act quite confident and firm and explain that everybody goes to school every day. In the long run, it's better for the child to outgrow dependence than to give in to it. When the child is having great difficulty separating from his mother at school, it often works better to have the father take him for a few weeks. If the child's terror is extreme, the situation should be discussed with a psychiatrist or child guidance clinic. The connection between overprotectiveness and fears is discussed in Section 554.

601. Reactions at home. Some children make hard work of preschool in the early days and weeks. The large group, the new friends, the new things to do get them keyed up and worn out. If your child is too tired at first, it doesn't mean that she can't adjust to school, but only that you have to compromise for a while until she is used to it. Discuss with her teacher whether it would be wise to cut down her school time temporarily. In one case, coming to school in the middle of the morning is the best answer. Taking the easily tired child home before the end of the school day works less well because she hates to leave in the middle of the fun. The problem of fatigue in the early weeks is further complicated in the all-day school by the fact that a certain number of children are too stimulated or nervous to go to sleep at naptime at first. Keeping the child at home 1 or 2 days a week may be the answer to this temporary problem, too. Some small children starting nursery school preserve their self-control in school in spite of fatigue, but let loose on the family when they come home. This calls for extra patience and a discussion with the teacher.

A well-trained preschool teacher ought to be, and usually is, a very understanding person. A parent shouldn't hesitate to talk over the child's problems with the teacher, whether or not they are connected with school. A teacher gets a different slant and has probably faced the same problems before in other cases.

602. How to get preschools. You may say, "I believe in the importance of my child's going to preschool, nursery school, or day care center but there is none in my community." Such schools aren't easy to start. Well-trained teachers, plenty of equipment, indoor and outdoor space are all necessary and all cost money. Good schools are never cheap, because a teacher can satisfactorily take care of only a small number of children. They have most commonly been formed on a private basis, with the parents paying the full expense; or by churches, which provide the space; or by colleges, for the training of students in child care. In the long run, a sufficient number of preschools and child care centers will be created, and operated with government funds, only if the citizens of the community convince the government that they want them, and vote for candidates for office who make a pledge to work for them.

From Six to Eleven

FITTING INTO THE OUTSIDE WORLD

603. There are lots of changes after 6. Children become more independent of their parents, even impatient with them. They're more concerned with what the other kids say and do. They develop a stronger sense of responsibility about matters that **they** think are important. Their conscience may become so stern that it nags them about senseless things like stepping over cracks. They are interested in impersonal subjects like arithmetic and engines. In short, they're beginning the job of emancipating themselves from the family and taking their places as responsible citizens of the outside world.

Back in Section 566 I mentioned Freud's explanation of what happens in children's unconscious feelings that makes them change so much. Between 3 and 5 years they were, generally, cozy, affectionate family children who proudly patterned their activities, table manners, and speech after their parents. The girl was trying all day to be like her admired mother and she had a strong romantic attachment to her father. For the boy it was the other way around. But the possessive, romantic feelings bring an increasingly uncomfortable sense of rivalry with the parent of the same sex. The unconscious fear of this parent's resentment and worry about genital differences eventually cause a turning away from open expressions of feeling and a reversal of many feelings. The former pleasure in romantic daydreaming turns to aversion. Children may now squirm when a parent tries to kiss them. Their aversion spreads to include children of the opposite sex.

They groan when there are love scenes in movies. This is what makes them so eager, we believe, to turn to such impersonal and abstract subjects as reading, writing, arithmetic, mechanics, science, nature study. This is part of the explanation of why children are so emotionally ready for schoolwork at this age.

Another way of viewing the psychological changes that take place in children about 6 or 7 is to see how they are related to the evolution of humans from their prehuman ancestors. Each individual passing through the 6- to 12-year-old period is retracing, I think, that particular stage of evolution. Millions of years ago our prehuman ancestors used to acquire full growth and full instincts by about 5 years of age. In their attitude toward family life, when full grown, they were probably much like our 5-year-old children: happy to continue to live with their family, even after growing up, happy to give obedience to the elders of the family, striving to be like them and learn from them. In other words, these prehumans were tied together for life by close personal family ties. It was only much later in the course of evolution that our ancestors developed the ability to become more independent of their parents, learned to live in a larger society by means of cooperation, rules, self-control, thinking things out. It takes years for each individual to learn how to get along in this complicated, grown-up way. Probably that's the reason human beings are held up so long in their physical growth. The infant increases rapidly in size like an animal, and so does the older child in the puberty period. But in between they slow down more and more, particularly in the 2 years just before puberty development begins. It's as if their nature were saying, "Whoa! Before you can be trusted with a powerful body and full-grown instincts, you must first learn to think for yourself, control your wishes and instincts for the sake of others, learn how to get along with your fellows, understand the laws of conduct in the world outside your family, study the skills by which people live."

604. Independence from parents. Children after 6 go on loving their parents deeply underneath, but they usually don't show it so much on the surface. They're cooler toward other adults, too, unless they're sure they're swell people. They no longer want to be loved as a possession or as an appealing child. They're gaining a sense of dignity as individuals, and they like to be treated as such.

From their need to be less dependent on their parents, they turn more to trusted adults outside the family for ideas and knowledge. If they mistakenly get the idea from an admired science teacher that red blood cells are larger than white blood cells, there's nothing their parents can say that will change their minds.

The ideas of right and wrong that their parents taught them have not been forgotten. In fact, they have sunk in so deep that they now think of them as their ideas. They are impatient when their parents keep reminding them what they ought to do, because they know already and want to be considered responsible.

605. Bad manners. Children drop the extra-grown-up words out of their vocabulary and pick up a little tough talk. They want the style of clothes and haircut that the other kids have. They may leave their shoelaces untied with the same determination with which people wear party buttons during a political campaign. They may lose some of their table manners, come to meals with dirty hands, slump over the dish, and stuff more in their mouths. Perhaps they kick the leg of the table absentmindedly. They always throw their coats on the floor. They slam doors or leave them open. Without realizing it, they are really accomplishing three things at once. They're shifting to their own age for their models of behavior. They're declaring their right to be more independent of parents. They're keeping square with their own conscience, because they're not doing anything that's morally wrong.

These bad manners and bad habits are apt to make good parents unhappy. They imagine that the child is forgetting all that they taught so carefully. Actually, these changes are proof that children have learned for keeps what good behavior is—otherwise they wouldn't bother to rebel against it. It will come to the surface again when they feel they have established their independence. Meanwhile, understanding parents can be reassured that their child is growing up normally.

I don't mean that every child is a hellion during this age

Manners may seem to be lost.

period. One who gets along happily with easygoing parents may show no open rebelliousness at all—most girls show less than boys. But if you look carefully, you will see signs of a change of attitude.

What do you **do**? After all, children must take a bath once in a while, get neatened up on holidays. You may be able to overlook some of the minor irritating ways, but you should stick to your guns in matters that are important to you. When you have to ask them to wash their hands, try to be matter-of-fact. It's the nagging tone, the bossiness, that they find irritating and that spurs them on unconsciously to further balkiness.

606. Gangs and clubs. This is the age for the blossoming of clubs and gangs. A number of kids who are already friends decide to form a secret club. They work like beavers making membership buttons, fixing up a meeting place (preferably hidden), drawing up a list of rules. They may never figure out what the secret is. But the secrecy idea probably represents the need to prove they can govern themselves, unmolested by grown-ups, unhampered by other more dependent children.

It seems to help children, when they're trying to be grown-up, to get together with others who feel the same way. Then the group tries to bring outsiders into line by making them feel left out or by picking on them. It sounds conceited and cruel to grown-ups, but that's because we are accustomed to using more refined methods of disapproving of each other. The children are only feeling the instinct to get community life organized. This is one of the forces that makes our civilization click.

607. Helping children to be sociable and popular. These are some of the early steps in bringing up children to be sociable and popular: not fussing over them in their first years; letting them be around other children their size from the age of a year; allowing them freedom to develop independence; the fewest changes possible in where the family lives and where they go to school; letting them, as far as possible, associate with, dress like, talk like, play like, have the same allowance and other privileges as the other average children in the neighborhood, even if you don't approve of the way they are brought up. (Of course, I don't mean letting them take after the town's worst scoundrel. And you don't have to take your child's word about what the other children are allowed to do.)

How happily people get along as adults in their jobs, in family and social life depends a great deal on how they got along with other children when they were young. If parents give children high standards and high ideals at home, these form part of their character and show up in the long run, even though they go through a period of bad English and rough manners in the middle period of childhood. But if parents are unhappy about the neighborhood they live in and the companions their children have, give them a feeling that they are different from the others, discourage them from making friends, the children may grow up unable to get along comfortably with anyone. Then the high standards won't be of much use to the world or to themselves.

If a boy is having trouble making friends, it helps most if he can be in a school and in a class where the program is flexible. Then the teacher can arrange things so that he has chances to use his abilities to contribute to class projects (Section 620). This is how the other children learn to appreciate his good qualities and to like him. A good teacher who is respected by the class can also raise a child's popularity in the group by showing that she or he appreciates that child. It even helps to put him in a seat next to a very popular child, or to let him be partners with him in marching, going on errands around the school, etc.

There are things that the parents can do at home, too. Be friendly and hospitable when your child brings others home to play. Encourage him to invite them to meals and then serve the dishes that they consider "super." When you plan week-end trips, picnics, excursions, movies, and other shows, invite another child with whom your child wants to be friends (not necessarily the one you would like him to be friendly with). Children, like adults, have a mercenary side, and they are more apt to see the good points in a child who provides treats for them. Naturally, you don't want your child to have only "bought" popularity; that kind won't last anyway. But what you are after is to prime the pump, to give him a chance to break into a group that may be shutting him out because of the natural clannishness of this age. Then, if he has appealing qualities, he can take over from that start and build real friendships of his own.

SELF-CONTROL

608. They become strict about some things. Think of the games children enjoy at this age. They're no longer so interested in make-believe without any plan. They want games that have rules and require skill. In hopscotch, jacks, and mumblety-peg, you have to do things in a certain order, which becomes harder as you progress. If you miss, you must penalize yourself, go back to the beginning, and start over again. It's the very strictness that appeals. This is the age for starting collections, whether it's stamps or cards or stones. The pleasure of collecting is in achieving orderliness and completeness.

At this age children have the desire at **times** to put their belongings in order. Suddenly they neaten their desk, put labels on the drawers, or arrange the piles of comic books. They don't keep their things neat for long. But you can see that the urge must be strong just to get them started.

609. Compulsions. The tendency toward strictness becomes so strong in many children around 8, 9, and 10 that they develop nervous habits. You probably remember them from your own childhood. The commonest is stepping over cracks in the sidewalk. There's no sense to it, you just have a superstitious feeling that you ought to. It's what a psychiatrist calls a compulsion. Other examples are touching every third picket in a fence, making numbers come out even in some way, saying certain words before going through a door. If you think you have made a mistake, you must go way back to where you were absolutely sure that you were right, and start over again.

The hidden meaning of a compulsion pops out in the thoughtless childhood saying, "Step on a crack, break your grandmother's back." Everyone has hostile feelings at times toward the people who are close to him, but his conscience would be shocked at the idea of really harming them and warns him to keep such thoughts out of his mind. And if a person's conscience becomes **excessively** stern, it keeps nagging about such "bad" thoughts even after he has succeeded in hiding them away in his subconscious mind. He still feels guilty, though he doesn't know what for. It eases his conscience to be extra careful and proper about such a senseless thing as how to navigate a crack in the sidewalk.

The reason a child is apt to show compulsions around the age of 9 is not that his thoughts are more wicked than previously, but that his conscience is just naturally becoming stricter at this stage of development. He is now worrying, perhaps, about his suppressed desire to hurt his brother or father or grandmother when they irritate him. We know that this is an age when the child is also trying to suppress thoughts about sex, and these sometimes play a part in compulsions, too.

This is also an age period in which compulsions are a way of keeping the world of one's playmates under control. Now they're free of constant adult supervision and control, and while this feels great in many ways, it's also scary in many ways.

Mild compulsions are so common around the ages of 8, 9, and 10 years that it's a question whether they should be considered normal or a sign of nervousness. I wouldn't worry too much about a mild compulsion, like stepping over cracks, in a child around 9 years who is happy, outgoing, doing well in school. On the other hand, I'd call on a psychiatrist for help (Section 633) if a child has compulsions that occupy a lot of his time (for instance, excessive hand-washing, precautions against germs) or if he is tense, worried, unsociable.

"Step on a crack, break your grandmother's back."

610. Tics. Tics are nervous habits such as eye-blinking, shoulder-shrugging, facial grimacing, neck-twisting, throat-clearing, sniffing, dry coughing. Like compulsions, tics occur most commonly around the age of 9, but they can come at any age after 2. The motion is usually quick, and it is repeated regularly and always in the same form. It is more frequent when the child is under tension. A tic may last off and on for a number of weeks or months and go away for good, or a new one may take its place. Blinking, sniffing, throat-clearing, dry coughing often start with a cold but continue after the cold is gone. Shoulder-shrugging may begin when a child has a new loose-fitting garment that feels as if it were falling off. Children may copy a tic from another child, but they wouldn't have picked it up if there hadn't been a tenseness already waiting in them.

Tics are more common in tense children, with fairly strict parents. There may be too much pressure at home. Sometimes the mother or father is going at the child too hard, directing him, correcting him, whenever he is in sight. Or the parents may be showing constant disapproval in a quieter way, or setting standards that are too high, or providing too many activities such as dancing, music, and athletic lessons. If the child were bold enough to fight back, he would probably be less tightened up inside. But being, in most cases, too well brought up for that, he bottles up his irritation, and it keeps backfiring in the tic.

The child should not be scolded or corrected on account of his tics. They are practically out of his control. The whole effort should go into making his home life relaxed and agreeable, with the least possible nagging, and making his school and social life satisfying. Tics must be distinguished from general restlessness.

TELEVISION, MOVIES, AND COMICS

611. Brutality in television, movies, and comics. Back in Section 515 I said that I believed that parents should keep their children from watching brutality on television, and the same goes for movies. Comic books are not quite as corrupting because what is shown does not seem as real, but the same principles apply.

If we rule out the comics and other stories that are brutal and obscene, there is still the question—for parents with high aspirations—whether the other kinds, which are merely vulgar or preposterously heroic or filled with fighting which is not particularly brutal, will hurt their children's characters or ruin their taste for good literature. I don't think there is much to worry about in these respects. I've known hundreds of children who went through a long stage of fascination with comics of these types and who finally outgrew them.

612. Obscenity. As children become old enough to buy comic books and other literature, and to go to movies, the problem of obscenity also comes up. There used to be considerable protection for children in the precensorship of movies in Hollywood and in the various states, and also in the respect for obscenity laws on the part of film exhibitors and sellers of literature. However, the Supreme Court has removed the ban on all but the most deliberate pornography, so parents must now be the guardians. The problem of obscenity on TV is also increasing, especially on cable channels.

I explained in Section 16 that the idealism and creativity of human beings is related to the inhibition and sublimation of sexuality which takes place all through childhood but particularly in the 6- to 12-year-old period, more so when the parents set high standards. To be specific, I believe potentialities of children for productivity in their future life work and for achieving soundly spiritual marriages may be impaired—at least slightly—if they get a consistently coarse picture of sexuality in childhood. I'm not referring here to a few accidental, unfortunate glimpses, despite the parents' best efforts, such as we all experienced. I mean that children shouldn't get the impression that their parents view sex crudely or that their parents don't care what impression their children get from others.

I believe that parents should let their children go only to

movies and buy only literature which the parents know for sure—from reviews or from neighbors—have a moral and spiritual tone of which they approve.

613. The hours for watching television should be limited. There is a problem with children who are glued to the set from the minute they come in, in the afternoon, until they are forced to go to bed at night. They don't want to take time out for supper or for homework or even to say hello to the family. There's also the temptation to parents to let their children watch endlessly since it keeps them so quiet. It's better for the parents and child to come to a reasonable but definite understanding about which hours are for outdoors, for homework, for meals, and for programs, and then for everyone to stick to the bargain. Otherwise the parents are apt to be nagging children about their duties whenever they catch them at the set, and the children are turning it on whenever they think the parents aren't paying attention. The same is true for video games and cable TV. Action for Children's Television, 26 Austin Street, Newtonville, MA 02160, is a national consumer organization which can provide you with many practical suggestions and general guidance in sensibly managing the way your family watches and uses television.

Some adolescents and adults can work just as well with the radio on (they say better), though this is less likely with talking programs than with musical programs. There is no objection to this if children are keeping up with their homework.

614. Fearfulness about movies and television. Movies are a risky business under the age of 7. You hear of a program, let's say an animated cartoon, that sounds like perfect entertainment for a small child. But when you get there, you find, three out of four times, that there is some episode in the story that scares the wits out of little children. You have to remember that a child of 4 and 5 doesn't distinguish clearly between make-believe and real life. A witch on the screen is just as alive and terrifying to a child as a flesh-and-blood burglar would be to you. The only safe rule that I know is not to take a child under 7 to a movie unless you, or someone else who knows small children well, has seen it and is **positive** that it contains nothing upsetting. Don't even take an older child who gets frightened easily to the movies.

There are sensitive children who are also upset by fairy stories, adventure stories, and Western dramas on television. They shouldn't be allowed to watch them.

STEALING

615. Taking things in early childhood. Small children of 1, 2, and 3 take things that don't belong to them, but it isn't really stealing. They don't have any clear sense of what belongs to them and what doesn't. They just take things because they want them very much. It's better not to make small children feel wicked. The parent needs only to remind them that the toy is Peter's, that Peter will want to play with it soon, and that "you have lots of toys at home."

616. What stealing means in the child who knows better. Stealing that means more occasionally crops up in the period between 6 and adolescence. When children at this age take something, they know they are doing wrong. They are more apt to steal secretly, to hide what they have stolen, and to deny that they have done it.

When parents or teachers find that a child has stolen something, they are pretty upset. Their impulse is to jump hard on and fill the child with a sense of shame. This is natural enough, since we have all been taught that stealing is a serious crime. It scares us to see it coming out in our child.

It is essential that children know clearly that their parents disapprove of any stealing and insist on immediate restitution. On the other hand, it isn't wise to scare the daylights out of them or act as if you will never love them again.

Let's take first the boy around 7 who has been carefully brought up by conscientious parents, who has a reasonable number of toys and other possessions, and who gets an allowance. If he steals something, it's apt to be small amounts of money from his mother or from classmates, or his teacher's pen, or a pack of trading cards from another child's locker. Often there's no sense to the stealing because he may own these things anyway. We can see that he's mixed up in his feelings. He seems to have a blind craving for something, and tries to satisfy it by taking an object he doesn't really need. What does he really want?

In most cases, the child is at least slightly unhappy and lonesome. He probably doesn't have as close a relationship with his parents as he used to. He may not feel completely successful in making friends with children his own age. (He may feel this way even though he is actually quite popular.) I think the reason that stealing occurs more often around 7 is that children at this age may be feeling particularly distant from their parents. Then, if they haven't the knack of making equally warm and satisfying friendships, they get into a no-man's-land and feel isolated. This explains why some children who steal money use it all to try to buy friendship. One passes out dimes and nickels to classmates. Another uses it to buy candy for the class. It's not just that children are drawing away a little from the parents. The parents are apt to be more disapproving of them at this less appealing age.

The early part of adolescence is another period when some children become more lonely because of increased self-consciousness, sensitiveness, and desire for independence.

A craving for more affection probably plays some part in stealing at all ages, but there are usually other individual factors, too, such as fears, jealousies, resentments. A girl who is deeply envious of her brother may repeatedly steal objects that are linked in her unconscious mind with boys.

617. What to do for the child who steals. If you are pretty sure that your child (or pupil) has stolen something, tell him so, be firm about wanting to know where he got it, insist on restitution. In other words don't make it easy for him to lie. (If parents accept lies too easily, it's as if they were condoning the theft.) The child should take the object back to the child or store from which it was taken. If it's a store, it may be tactful for the parent to go along to explain to the salesperson that the child took it without paying and wants to return it. A teacher can return an article to its owner to spare the child from public shame. In other words, it's not necessary to humiliate the child who steals, only to make it crystal-clear that it can't be permitted.

It is time to think over whether the child needs more affection and approval at home, and help in making closer friendships outside (Section 607). This is the time to give him, if possible, an allowance of about the same size as that of the other children he knows. It helps him to establish himself as one of the gang. The parents should get help from a child guidance clinic or a children's psychiatrist if the stealing persists or if the child seems maladjusted in other ways (Section 633).

The next type of stealing is entirely different. There are plenty of neighborhoods where the kids think of swiping things as the daring thing to do. It's not proper, but it's not vicious and it's not a sign of maladjustment. I think of it as a sort of group testing-out of the individual conscience. The children of conscientious parents who live in such a neighborhood may need an understanding talk, but should not be treated as criminals because they joined in one of these adventures. They were only obeying a normal instinct to make their place in the group. The cure lies in a clear-cut reprimand and making sure that the parents aren't modeling this kind of behavior by talking (even boasting at times) about such things as cheating on their income taxes or charging personal phone calls to their business phones.

Finally, there is the stealing of the aggressive child or adult who has little conscience or sense of responsibility. A person gets this way only through a childhood quite lacking in love and security. The only hope is in good psychiatric treatment and being able to live with kind, affectionate people.

Schools

WHAT A SCHOOL IS FOR

618. The main lesson in school is how to get along in the world. Different subjects are merely means to this end. In the olden days, it used to be thought that all a school had to do was make children learn to read, write, figure, and memorize a certain number of facts about the world. I heard a great teacher tell how, in his own school days, he had to memorize a definition of a preposition that went something like this: "A preposition is a word, generally with some meaning of position, direction, time, or other abstract relation, used to connect a noun or pronoun, in an adjectival or adverbial sense, with some other word." Of course, he didn't learn anything when he memorized that. You learn only when things **mean** something to you. One job of a school is to make subjects so interesting and real that the children want to learn and remember.

You can go only so far with books and talk. You learn better from actually living the things you are studying. Children pick up more arithmetic in a week from running a school store, in making change, and keeping the books than they learn in a month out of a book of cold figures.

There's no use knowing a lot if you can't be happy, can't get along with people, can't hold the kind of job you want. The good teacher tries to understand each child in order to help each pupil overcome weak points and develop into a well-rounded person. The child who lacks self-confidence needs chances to succeed. The troublemaking show-off has to learn how to gain the recognition he craves through doing good work. The child who doesn't know how to make friends needs help in becoming sociable and appealing. The child who seems to be lazy has to have her or his enthusiasm discovered.

A school can go only so far with a cut-and-dried program in which everyone in the class reads from page 17 to page 23 in the reader at the same time and then does the examples on page 128 of the arithmetic book. It works well enough for the average child who is adjusted anyway. But it's too dull for the bright pupils, too speedy for the slow ones. It gives the boy who hates books a chance to stick paper clips in the pigtails of the girl in front. It does nothing to help the girl who is lonely or the boy who needs to learn cooperation.

619. How schoolwork is made real and interesting. If you start with a topic that is real and interesting, you can use it to teach all manner of subjects. Take the case of a third-grade class in which the work of the year revolves around Indians. The more the children find out about Indians, the more they want to know. The reader is a story of the Indians, and they really want to know what it says. For arithmetic they study how the Indians counted and what they used for money. Then arithmetic isn't a separate subject at all but a useful part of life. Geography isn't spots on a map; it's where the Indians lived and traveled, and how life on the plains is different from forest life. In science study the children make dye from berries and dye cloth, or grow corn. They can make bows and arrows and Indian costumes.

People are sometimes uneasy about schoolwork's being too interesting, feeling that a child needs to learn, most of all, how to do what's unpleasant and difficult. But if you stop to think of the people you know who are unusually successful, you'll see that in most cases they are the ones who love their work. In any job there's plenty of drudgery, but you do the drudgery because you see its connection with the fascinating side of the work. Darwin was a wretched student in all his subjects in school. But in later life he became interested in natural history, performed one of the most painstaking jobs of research that the world has ever known, and worked out the theory of evolution. A boy in high school may see no sense in geometry, hate it, and do badly in it. But if he is studying to be a navigator of planes and sees what geometry is for, realizes that it may save the lives of the crew and passengers, he works at it like a demon. The teachers in a good school know well that every child needs to develop self-discipline to be a useful adult. But they have learned that you can't snap discipline onto children from the outside, like handcuffs; it's something that children have to develop inside, like a backbone, by first understanding the purpose of their work and feeling a sense of responsibility to others in how they perform it.

620. How a school helps a difficult child. A flexible, interesting program does more than just make schoolwork appealing. It can be adjusted for the individual pupil. Take the case of a girl who had spent her first 2 years in a school where teaching was done by separate subjects. She was a girl who had great difficulty in learning to read and write. She had fallen behind the rest of the class. Inside, she felt ashamed about being a failure. Outwardly she wouldn't admit anything except that she hated school. She had never gotten along too easily with other kids anyway, even before her school troubles began. Feeling that she was a dumbbell in the eyes of the others made matters worse. She had a chip on her shoulder. Once in a while she would show off to the class in a smarty way. Her teacher used to think that she was just trying to be bad. Of course, she was really attempting, in this unfortunate way, to gain some kind of attention from the group. It was a healthy impulse to keep herself from being shut out.

She transferred to a school that was interested in helping her not only to read and write but to find her place in the group. The teacher learned in a conference with her mother that she used tools well and loved to paint and draw. He saw ways to use her strong points in the class. The children were all painting together a large picture of Indian life to hang on the wall. They were also working cooperatively on a model of an Indian village. The teacher arranged for the girl to have a part in both these jobs. Here were things she could do well without nervousness. As the days went by, she became more and more fascinated with Indians. In order to paint her part of the picture well, in order to make her part of the model correctly, she needed to find out more from the books about Indians. She **wanted** to learn to read. She tried harder. Her new classmates didn't think of her as a dope because she couldn't read. They thought more about what a help she was on the painting and the model. They occasionally commented on how good her work was and asked her to help them on their parts. She began to warm up. After all, she had been aching for recognition and friendliness for a long while. As she felt more accepted, she became more friendly and outgoing.

621. Linking school with the world. A school wants its pupils to learn firsthand about the outside world, about the jobs of the local farmers and businesspeople and workers, so that they will see the connection between their schoolwork and real life. It arranges trips to nearby industries, asks people from the outside to come in and talk, encourages classroom discussion. A class that is studying food may have an opportunity, for example, to observe some of the steps in the collecting, pasteurizing, bottling, and delivery of milk, or in the transportation and marketing of vegetables.

High school and college students have further opportunities to learn about the world by attending summer work camps. A group of students and teachers may work in a factory or in a farming area, discuss together and come to understand better the problems of various occupations and industries and how they are solved.

622. Democracy builds discipline. Another thing that a good school wants to teach is democracy, not just as a patriotic motto but as a way of living and getting things done. A good teacher knows that she (or he) can't teach democracy out of a book if she's acting like a dictator in person. She encourages her pupils to decide how they are going to tackle certain projects, and the difficulties they later run into let them help figure out among themselves which one is to do this part of the job and which one that. That's how they learn to appreciate each other. That's how they learn to get things done, not just in school but in the outside world, too.

Actual experiments have shown that children with a teacher who tells them what to do at every step of the way do a good job while she is in the room, but when she goes out a lot of them stop working, start fooling. They figure that lessons are the teacher's responsibility, not theirs, and that now they have a chance to be themselves. But these experiments showed that children who have helped choose and plan their own work, and have cooperated with each other in carrying it out, accomplish almost as much when the teacher is out of the room as in. Why? They know the purpose of the job they are on and the steps ahead in accomplishing it. They feel that it is their job, not the teacher's. Each one wants to do a fair share because each is proud to be a respected member of the group and feels a sense of responsibility to the others.

This is the very highest kind of discipline. This training, this spirit, is what makes the best citizens, the most valuable workers, and even the finest soldiers.

623. Cooperating with other child specialists. Even the best of teachers can't solve all the problems of their pupils alone. They need the cooperation of the parents through parent–teacher association meetings and individual conferences. Then parent and teacher will understand what the other is doing, share what they know about the child. The teacher should even be able to get in touch with the child's scoutmaster, minister, doctor, and vice versa. Each can do a better job by working with the other. It's particularly important in the case of a child with a chronic ailment that the teacher know just what it is, how it's being treated, what she can do or watch for in school. It's just as important for the doctor to know how the disease is affecting the child in school hours, how the school can help, and how treatment can be prescribed so as not to work against what the school is trying to accomplish with the child.

There are children who have problems that the regular teacher and the parents, no matter how understanding, can solve better with the help of specialists in child guidance. Few schools as yet have a psychiatrist. Some, though, have guidance counselors, psychologists, or visiting teachers, trained to help children, parents, and classroom teachers in understanding and overcoming a child's school difficulties. Where there is no guidance counselor or psychologist, or when the teacher finds that the problem is deep-rooted, it is wise to turn to a private children's psychiatrist or to a child guidance clinic, if such is available.

624. How to work for good schools. Parents sometimes say, "It's all very well to talk about ideal schools, but the school that my child goes to is pretty cut-and-dried, and there's nothing I can do about it." That may or may not be true. When towns and cities do have superior schools, it is because the parents there know their value and have fought for them. But a neighborhood group in a larger city may find itself powerless against the bureaucracy of the central board of education and the indifference of municipal officials who serve special interests rather than the people generally. An important reform would be to replace each central board of education with a number of neighborhood boards made up of representatives of local parents and teachers, the people who care most about children's education.

Parents can join their local parent–teacher association, go to meetings regularly, show the teachers and principals and superintendents that they are interested and will back them up when they are using sound methods. They can also vote and campaign for the election of local officials who will work for constant improvement in the schools and actively support school bond issues.

There are lots of people who don't realize how much fine schools can accomplish in developing useful, happy citizens. They object to increasing the school budget for smaller classes, better-paid teachers, carpentry shops, laboratories, and afternoon recreation programs. Not understanding the purpose or value of these proposals, they naturally think of them as "unnecessary frills" just to amuse children or make jobs for more teachers. Even from a strictly cash point of view, that's penny-wise and dollar foolish. Money spent **wisely** for better child care pays back the community a hundredfold. First-rate schools that succeed in making each child feel she or he really **belongs,** as a useful and respected member of the group, reduce drastically the number of individuals who grow up irresponsible or criminal. The value of such schools shows even more in all the other children (who would never be criminals anyway) who take their places in the community as better workers at their jobs, more cooperative citizens, happier individuals in their own lives. How better can a community spend its money?

TROUBLE WITH LESSONS

625. There are many causes for failure in schoolwork. Individual problems are more common when a school is using rigid teaching methods, when the attitude toward the children is regimenting and harsh, when the classes are too large for individual attention.

In children themselves there are various reasons for poor adjustment. On the physical side, there are eye defects, deafness, occasionally fatigue or chronic illness. On the psychological side, there is the child unable to read because of a special difficulty in recognizing words, the child who is too nervous and worried about other things, the one who can't get along with teacher or pupils. There is the child who is too smart and the one whose intelligence isn't up to the work. (The slow child is discussed in Section 865.)

It doesn't do any good to scold or punish the child who is having difficulties. You have to try to find out where the trouble lies. Consult with the principal or teacher. Get the help of the school guidance counselor if there is one. Have the child tested by the school psychologist if that seems the next step. Consult a child guidance clinic or a private psychiatrist or psychologist if no specialists are available at the school (Section 633). The Association for Children with Learning Disabilities, 5225 Green Street, Pittsburgh, PA 15236 may be able to direct you to diagnostic and remedial facilities. Have the child examined physically, including vision and hearing.

626. The extra-bright child. In a class in which everyone does exactly the same lessons, the child who is smarter than others of the same age may be bored because the work is too easy. The only solution seems to be to skip a grade. This may not work out too badly if the child, say a boy, is large for his age and advanced socially. But if not, he's apt to become socially isolated and lost, especially when his classmates get to the adolescent years. He may be too small to compete in games or be popular at dances. He's apt to have younger interests than the other members of his class, which keep him from mixing easily. What good is it for him to enter high school or college at a very young age if he is going to turn into a lonely person?

It is much better in most cases for the bright child to stay in a class that is close to him in age, provided the school has a flexible program that can be "enriched" for the pupils who are more advanced. He, for instance, is the one to read the more difficult reference books in the library. When a bright child is working for marks and to please the teacher, the other kids are quick to call him "Smarty" and "Teacher's Pet." But if he is working on group projects, they appreciate him all the more because of the extra help he can provide.

Even if you think your daughter is extra smart, never try to get her into a more advanced grade than the school advises. Usually a teacher knows best about placement. It's cruel for a child to be placed beyond her capacities. In the end she does poorly or is left back again later.

That brings up the question of teaching a bright child to read and figure at home before starting first grade. A parent may say that the child is asking questions about letters and numbers and practically insisting on being taught. This is true to a degree with some children, and there is no harm in casually answering their questions.

But there is another side to it in many such cases. It often turns out that the parents themselves are more ambitious for their children than they perhaps realize, more eager to have them excel. When they are playing childish games or roughhousing, the parents pay only a normal amount of attention. But when the children show an interest in reading at an early age, the adults' eyes light up and they help enthusiastically. The children sense their delight and respond with greater interest. They may be weaned away from the natural occupations of their age and turned into scholars before their time.

Parents wouldn't be good parents if they weren't delighted with their children's fine qualities. But it's necessary to distinguish between which are the children's interests and which are the parents' eager hopes. If parents who are naturally ambitious can honestly admit this to themselves and be on guard against using their ambition to run their children's lives, the children will grow up to be happier, abler, and more of a credit to their parents. This applies not only to early reading and writing but to putting pressure on a child at any age, whether it's in schoolwork, music lessons, dancing lessons, athletics, or social life.

627. Poor schoolwork because of "nervousness." All kinds of worries and troubles and family frictions can interfere with a child's schoolwork. Here are some examples, though they don't cover all the possibilities by any means:

A 6-year-old girl who is burned up with jealousy of a younger brother may be tense, "distracted," unable to pay attention, and make sudden attacks on other children for no good reason.

A boy may be worried about illness at home or a threatened separation of the parents or misunderstandings about sex. In the early grades especially, he may be afraid of a bully or a barking dog on the way to school, of the school janitor, of a severe-looking teacher, of asking permission to go to the toilet, of reciting before the class. These seem like small matters to an adult, but to a timid 6- or 7-year-old they may be terrifying enough to paralyze his thinking.

The girl around 9 years old who is nagged and corrected excessively at home may become so restless and tense that she can't keep her mind on anything.

"Lazy" children who won't try to do their lessons usually aren't lazy at all. The young animals of all species are born to be curious and enthusiastic. If they lose that, it's because it's been trained out of them. Children **appear** to be lazy in school for a number of reasons. Some are balky from having been pushed too much all their lives. You find them eager enough about their own private hobbies. Sometimes children are afraid to try in school (or anywhere) for fear of failing. This may be because the family has always been critical of their accomplishments or set too high standards.

Strange as it may seem, occasionally children may do poor schoolwork from being overconscientious. They keep going over the lesson that they've already learned or the exercises that they've already finished for fear that something is incomplete or incorrect. They're always behind, fussing.

The child who has been severely deprived of love and security in the early years typically reaches school age as a tense, restless, irresponsible creature with little ability to get interested in schoolwork or to get along with teachers or pupils.

Whatever the cause of a child's difficulty in school, the problem should be attacked from two directions. Try to find the underlying cause, as suggested in Section 625. But whether or not you can discover what's bothering the child inside, it should be possible for teacher and parents, by sharing their knowledge of a child, to use his interests and good qualities to draw him gradually into the group and the things they are working on.

628. Poor reading because of slow development of visual memory. To you and me the word "dog" looks entirely different from the word "god." Most young children, when they are just beginning to read, think these words look much the same because each spells the other backward. They occasionally read "was" for "saw" and "on" for "no." In writing they sometimes reverse letters, especially those like small "b" and small "p," which are confused with "d" and "q." But as the months go by, they learn to perceive and remember more accurately and these mistakes become infrequent by the end of second grade.

But there are about 10 percent of children—most of them boys—who have much more than the average difficulty recognizing and remembering the appearance of words. They continue to reverse many words and letters for several years. It takes them a lot longer to learn to read reasonably well and some of them remain poor spellers for life, no matter how much they are drilled.

Such children quickly get the idea that they are **dumb** and often come to hate school because they cannot keep up with the others. They need to be reassured by parents and teachers that this is a special memory problem (just the way some children can't carry a tune); that they are not stupid and not lazy; that they will learn to read and write and spell as soon as they are able.

Most of these children can be helped by extra practice in **phonics,** in which they **sound** the letters and the syllables of words, and point at them with their fingers at the same time. In this way, they can make up for some of their weakness in recognizing words visually. If the school can't provide extra help, the parent should consult the teacher or principal about whether it would be desirable to try tutoring outside of school hours, either with a tactful tutor or a very patient parent. It is also sensible to consider a checkup by a child psychiatrist or guidance clinic; especially if the child has other emotional problems, since these can play a large part in a reading disability. But before you do anything complicated, have the child's vision and hearing checked by physicians, the vision by an ophthalmologist or oculist (they are the same), the hearing by an otologist.

629. Helping children in their lessons. Sometimes a teacher advises that a child is falling behind and needs extra tutoring in a subject, or the parents have the idea themselves. This is something to be careful about. If the school can recommend a good tutor whom you can afford, go ahead. Too often parents make poor tutors, not because they don't know enough, not because they don't try hard enough, but because they care too much, are too upset when their child doesn't understand. If a child is already mixed up in lessons, a tense parent is the last straw. Another trouble is that the parents' method may be different from that being used in the class. If already baffled by the subject in school, the chances are that the child will be **more** baffled when it's presented in a different way at home.

I don't want to go so far as to say that a parent should **never** tutor a child, because in an occasional case it works very well. I'd only advise a parent to talk it over thoroughly with the teacher first, and then quit right away if it isn't a success. Whoever is tutoring the child should keep in touch with the teacher, at regular intervals.

What should you do if children ask for help with their homework? If they are puzzled once in a great while and turn to you for clarification, there's no harm in straightening them out. (Nothing pleases parents more than to have a chance occasionally to prove to a child that they really know something.) But if children are asking you to do their work for them because they can't understand it, better consult the teacher. A good school prefers to help children understand, and then let them rely on themselves. If the teacher is too busy to straighten your son out, you may have to lend a hand; but even then help him to understand his work, don't do it for him.

630. School phobia. Occasionally a child, let's say a girl, develops a sudden and unexplainable fear of going to school. This often happens after she has been absent for a few days because of an illness or accident, especially if the illness began or the accident happened at school. Typically, the child hasn't any idea of what it is she fears at school. Child guidance studies of such cases show that often the real cause has little to do with school. An unusually conscientious child may have become more dependent on her mother because of feelings of guilt over unconscious antagonistic feelings toward her (Section 554). The illness at school and staying at home have brought this nearer the surface. If the child is freely allowed to stay home, her dread of returning to school usually gets stronger. It's increased by her fear that she is behind in her work and that the teacher and other children will criticize her for her absence. So it usually works best for the parents to be very firm about getting her back to school promptly and to refuse to be dissuaded by physical complaints or to try to get the doctor to excuse her. (Of course, she needs to be checked by the doctor for any physical complaints.) The child and parent should have child guidance help if this can possibly be arranged. The child guidance clinic usually considers such a case an emergency, knowing how time makes it worse (Section 633).

631. The child who can't eat breakfast before going to school. This problem comes up occasionally, especially with first- and second-graders, at the beginning of school in the fall. It's the conscientious children who are so overawed by the big class and the sovereign teacher that they can't eat the first thing in the morning. If parents force them to, they are only too likely to vomit on the way to school or after they're there. This adds a feeling of disgrace to their troubles.

The best way to handle this is to let the children alone at breakfast time; let them take only fruit juice and milk if that is all they can comfortably swallow. If they can't drink, let them go to school empty. It's not ideal for children to start the day hungry, but they'll become relaxed and able to eat breakfast sooner if you leave them alone. Such children usually eat fairly well at lunch, and then make up for all they've missed with a huge supper. As they get used to school and their new teacher, their stomachs gradually become hungrier at breakfast time, provided they don't have to struggle against their parents, too.

Even more important for the child who is timid at the beginning of school is for the parent to talk things over with the teacher so that the latter can understand and work to overcome the difficulty at school. The teacher can make a special effort to be friendly and help the child, in the projects he is working on, to find a comfortable place in the group.

632. Parent and teacher. It's easy to get along with a teacher if your son is the teacher's pride and joy and doing well in class. But if the child is having trouble, the situation is more delicate. The best parents and the best teacher are all very human. All take pride in the jobs they are doing, and have possessive feelings toward the child. Each, no matter how reasonable, secretly feels that the child would be doing better if the other would only handle him a little differently. It's helpful for the parents to realize at the start that the teacher is just as sensitive as they are, and that they will get further in a conference by being friendly and cooperative. Some parents realize that they are scared of facing a teacher, but they forget that just as often the teacher is afraid of them. The parents' main job is to give a clear history of the child's past, what his interests are, what he responds to well, what badly, and work with the teacher on how best to apply this information in school. Don't forget to compliment the teacher on the parts of the class program that are a great success with the child.

Occasionally, a child and teacher just don't "fit" temperamentally, no matter how hard they both work at it. In these cases, the school principal will be involved in making the decision to move the child to another class.

CHILD GUIDANCE

633. Psychiatrists, psychologists and child guidance clinics. Parents are apt to be confused about what psychiatrists and psychologists are for and what the difference between them is. A children's **psychiatrist** is a physician trained to understand and treat all kinds of behavior problems and emotional problems of children. Back in the nineteenth century, psychiatrists were mainly concerned with taking care of the insane, and for that reason some people are still reluctant to consult them. But as psychiatrists have learned how serious troubles usually develop out of mild ones, they have turned more and more attention to everyday problems. In this way they do the most good in the shortest time. There's no more reason to wait to see a psychiatrist until children are severely upset than to wait until they are in a desperate condition from pneumonia before calling the regular doctor. In larger cities there are child psychiatrists in private practice. Ask your family doctor.

Psychologist is a very general title used for people, not physicians, who specialize in one of the many branches of psychology. Psychologists who work with children are trained in such subjects as intelligence testing and aptitude testing, and the causes and treatment of learning and behavior problems in school.

In a **child guidance clinic** (or children's psychiatric clinic) a child's case may be in the hands of a psychiatrist, a psychologist, or a social worker who gets to know the child and where his worries are coming from, helps him to understand and outgrow them. A psychologist may perform mental tests to see what the child's weak points and strong points are, or to give the child remedial teaching if, for instance, there is a reading problem. A psychiatric social worker may visit the school to find out from the teacher more exactly what difficulties the child is having there, and to give the teacher the benefit of the understanding of the problem that has been gained in the clinic. Another staff member has interviews with the parents to find out more about the child and to help the parents in management. Some child guidance clinics are connected with hospitals; others are independent.

In a few cities there are child guidance clinics connected with the board of education, staffed with psychiatrists, psychologists, social workers, to deal with all kinds of behavior problems. Some states have traveling clinics that visit different communities. Many other school systems, local and state, have psychologists for the testing and remedial teaching of children who are having school problems.

In a city you can inquire about a child guidance clinic, or a private children's psychiatrist, or a psychologist for testing, through your regular doctor or a large hospital, through the school principal or superintendent, through a social service agency. Or you can look in the telephone book to see if there is a local Mental Hygiene Committee or Society. If you have no luck or live in a smaller place, you can write to the National Association for Mental Health, 1800 No. Kent St., Rosslyn Station, Arlington, VA 22209, and they will tell you the nearest place where you can get help. If there is no child guidance clinic, a family social agency may be able to give you the guidance you need.

Psychiatrists, psychologists, and social workers all may do psychotherapy with children and their families, and get equally good results.

Someday I hope there will be child guidance clinics connected with all school systems, so that children, parents, and teachers will be able to ask for advice on all kinds of minor problems as easily and as naturally as they can now inquire about immunizations and diet and the prevention of physical disease.

634. Family social agency. Most cities have at least one family social agency, and some large cities have Catholic, Jewish, and Protestant agencies. They are staffed by social workers trained to help parents with all the usual family problems—child management, marital adjustment, budgeting, chronic illness, housing, finding jobs, finding medical care.

Many parents have grown up with the idea that a social agency is for destitute people only and mainly provides charity. This is the opposite of the truth today. The modern family agency is just as glad to help solve small problems as large ones (they're easier), as glad to assist families who can afford to pay a fee as those who can't (that way they can expand their services).

If you have a problem with a child and you can make an appointment soon with a private child psychiatrist or a child guidance clinic, that may be the most direct approach. But if there is no clinic available or if there is a long waiting list, it may be wiser to consult a family agency. If the problem is one that they can deal with satisfactorily, they will continue with your case. If they think it requires child guidance treatment, they may be able to expedite an appointment.

Inquire at the United Way or, in a rural area, at County Welfare.

Adolescence

PHYSICAL CHANGES

635. Puberty development in girls. By **puberty development** I mean the 2 years of very rapid growth and development that come before "maturing." A girl is said to mature at her first monthly period. In the boy there is no such clear-cut event. So let's discuss puberty development in the girl first.

The first thing to realize is that there is no regular age at which puberty begins. The largest number of girls begin their development at around the age of 10 and have their first period about 2 years later, at 12. But a fair number begin their development as young as 8. Late developers may not even begin until 12. There are extreme cases of girls starting as early as 7 or as late as 14.

The fact that a girl starts her puberty development much earlier or later than average usually doesn't mean that her glands aren't working right. It only means that she is working on what you might call a faster or slower timetable. This individual timetable seems to be an inborn trait. Parents who were late developers are more apt to have children who are late developers, and vice versa. Adequacy of nutrition throughout childhood is another factor. In earlier times, when blue collar workers' families got poor diets, the average age of maturity in girls was 16.

Let's trace what happens in the case of the average girl who starts her puberty development at 10. When she was 7 years old, she was growing 2 to 2½ inches a year. When she was 8 years old, her rate of growing slowed down to perhaps 1¾ inches a year. Nature seemed to be putting on the brakes. Suddenly, at about 10, the brakes let go. She begins to shoot up at the rate of 3 or 3½ inches a year for the next 2 years. Instead of putting on 5 to 8 pounds a year as she used to, she now gains between 10 and 20 pounds a year, without becoming fatter. Her appetite becomes enormous to make this gain possible.

But other things are happening, too. At the beginning of this period her breasts begin to develop. First the areola (the dark area around the nipple) enlarges and gets slightly puffed out. Then the whole breast begins to take shape. For the first year and a half it has a conical shape, but as her first menstrual period nears, it rounds out into more nearly a hemisphere. Soon after the breasts begin to develop, the pubic hair starts to grow. Later, hair appears in the armpits. The hips widen. The skin changes its texture.

At 12 the average girl has her first menstrual period. By now she has a woman's body. She has acquired most of the height she will ever have. From this time on, her growing slows down rapidly. In the year after her first period she will grow perhaps 1½ inches, and in the year after that perhaps three fourths of an inch. In many girls the periods are irregular and infrequent for the first year or two. This is not a sign that something is wrong; it seems only to represent the body's inexperience.

636. Puberty begins at different ages. We have been talking about the average girl, but only a certain number of girls come near the average in any one particular. Many start their puberty development earlier than the average and many later. The child who begins at 8 is naturally apt to feel awkward and self-conscious when she finds herself the only girl in her class shooting upward and acquiring the shape of a woman. This experience isn't painful to every early developer. It depends, of course, on how well adjusted she was before and on how ready and eager she is to grow up. The girl who gets along well with her mother and wants to be like her is inclined to be pleased when she sees she is growing up, whether or not she is ahead of her schoolmates. On the other hand, the girl who resents being a girl—for instance, because of jealousy of her brother—or the child who is afraid to grow up is apt to be resentful or alarmed by early signs of womanhood.

Also bothered is the girl on a slow timetable. The 12-year-old who has shown no signs of puberty development has seen practically all her classmates grow rapidly taller and develop into women. She herself is still in the period of extra slow growth that precedes the puberty spurt. She feels like an underdeveloped runt. She thinks that she must be abnormal. She needs to be reassured, to be told that her growth in height and her bodily development will be coming along just as surely as the sun rises and sets. If her mother and other relatives were late developers, she needs to be told that, too, in explanation. She can be promised that when her time comes, she will have 7 or 8 more inches of height before she stops growing altogether.

There are other variations besides the age at which puberty development begins. In some girls the pubic hair growth comes months before the breasts start to develop. And once in a while hair in the armpits is the earliest sign of change instead of a late one. The length of time between the first signs of puberty development and the coming of the first period is usually about 2 years, but the girls who begin developing young are apt to have a shorter, quicker period of development, occasionally less than a year and a half. On the other hand, the girls who begin their puberty development later than average are more apt to take longer than 2 years to reach their first menstrual period. Occasionally one breast begins to develop months before the other. This is fairly common and nothing to worry about. The earlier-developing breast tends to stay larger throughout the puberty stage of development.

637. The average boy starts 2 years later than the girl. The first thing to realize about puberty development in boys is that the **average** boy begins 2 years later than the average girl, at 12 in contrast to her 10. The earlier developers among boys begin as early as 10, a few younger still. Plenty of slow developers start as late as 14, and there are a few who wait longer. The boy may grow in height at double the rate he was

Adolescence comes at different ages.

growing before. The penis, the testicles, and the scrotum (the sac in which the testicles lie) all develop rapidly. Pubic hair begins to grow early. Later comes the hair in the armpits and on the face. The voice cracks and deepens.

At the end of about 2 years' time, the boy's body has fairly well completed its transition to that of a man. In the following 2 years, he will creep up 2 or 2½ inches altogether and then practically stop.

The boy, like the girl, may go through a period of some physical and emotional awkwardness as he tries to gain control of his new body and new feelings. The way his voice keeps breaking down and up is an example of how he is both boy and man and yet not either.

This is a good moment to mention the difficulties of social life in school during puberty development and adolescence. The boys and girls in a class are of approximately the same age. And yet between the ages of 10 and 14, particularly, the average girl is two full years ahead of the average boy in development—towering over him in size and more grown up in interests. She's beginning to want to go to dances and be treated as if she were glamorous, while he is still an uncivilized little boy who thinks it would be shameful to pay attention to her. During this whole period it is better for social functions to include different age groups for a better fit.

The boy who is on a slow timetable of development, who is still a "shrimp" at 14 when most of his friends have turned into grown men, usually needs reassurance even more than the slow-developing girl. Size and physique and athletic ability count for a lot at this age. What happens sometimes is that the boy, instead of being reassured that he will start developing in time and grow something like 8 or 9 inches in the process, is taken by his worried parents on a hunt for a doctor who will give gland treatment. This helps to convince him that something is really wrong with him. There are glandular preparations that bring on the signs of puberty at whatever age they are given. They may well cause a boy to end up shorter than he normally would have been by stopping his bone growth prematurely. I'm against tampering with Nature in such a vital matter.

638. Skin troubles in adolescence. Puberty changes the texture of the skin. The pores enlarge and secrete more oil. Blackheads are formed by the combination of oil and dust and dirt. These plugs enlarge the pores further. Then it is easy for ordinary germs to get in under a blackhead and cause a small infection or pimple.

Adolescent children have a tendency to be self-conscious anyway, and to worry about any defects in their appearance. They fret about pimples and are apt to finger them and squeeze them. The trouble is that when a pimple is broken, the germs are spread in large numbers onto the surrounding skin and onto the fingers. Then the child touches another part of the face, inoculating the germs into other blackheads and starting new pimples. Squeezing a pimple often makes it larger and deeper and therefore more likely to leave a scar. Some adolescents, worried about sex, imagine that their pimples are caused by guilty thoughts or masturbation.

Parents commonly accept their children's pimples fatalistically, assuming that nothing but time will bring a cure. This is too pessimistic a view. With modern methods of treatment, great improvement can be made in many cases and some improvement can be made in others. Children are entitled to all the help they can get from their regular doctor or a skin specialist, for the sake of improving their present appearance and spirits, and to prevent the permanent scars that sometimes develop. In some situations a physician may prescribe an antibiotic or a medicine related to Vitamin A.

Whatever the specific methods are that the doctor prescribes, there are also general measures that are believed to be helpful. Vigorous daily exercise, fresh air, and direct sunshine seem to improve many complexions. It has been the common practice to recommend thorough washing of the face twice a day, though skin specialists have doubts about it in some cases. The usual procedure is to thoroughly but gently clean the face with a washcloth and soap (or a special preparation recommended by the doctor), then rinse with hot and cold water. It is certainly important to make it clear to children why they should keep their hands away from the face at all times except when they are washing it, and why they should never squeeze a pimple. If whiteheads have formed and are bothering them, they can soak them off with pieces of wet absorbent cotton, being careful not to spread the pus around when they break. There are flesh-colored cosmetic sticks in various shades, in lipstick-like cases, for covering pimples and other blemishes. Pat the end of the stick with a finger, then pat the pimple.

Another skin change at adolescence is a more profuse and strong-smelling perspiration in the armpits. Some children, and parents, too, are not aware of the odor, but it may cause unpopularity with schoolmates. Daily washing with soap and perhaps the regular use of a suitable deodorant will control the odor.

PSYCHOLOGICAL CHANGES

639. Self-consciousness and touchiness. As a result of all the physical and emotional changes, adolescents become much more self-conscious. They may exaggerate and worry about any defect. If a girl has freckles, she may think they make her look "horrible." A slight peculiarity in the body or how it functions easily convinces them that they are "abnormal."

They may not manage their new body with as much coordination as they used to, and the same applies to their new feelings. They are apt to be touchy, easily hurt when criticized. At one moment they feel like a grown-up and want to be treated as such. The next they feel like a child again and expect to be cared for.

640. Rivalry with parents. It isn't often realized that the rebelliousness of adolescents is mainly an expression of rivalrousness with parents, particularly the rivalry of son with father and girl with mother, which first developed back in the 4-to 6-year-old period. This rivalrousness becomes much more intense in adolescents because they have stronger emotions and because they sense that as an almost adult person they are ready to compete in the parents' own league, you might say. It's now their turn to challenge the world, to fascinate the opposite sex, to be the heads of families. So they feel like elbowing the has-been parents off the seat of power. Subconsciously the parents sense this and, understandably, don't feel too gracious about it.

Rebellious rivalry takes many forms. A mountaineer's son may suddenly at the age of 16 become angry at his father in an argument and, without premeditation, knock him down. He then realizes that it's no longer dignified to stay on in his father's house, so he abruptly leaves home to look for a job. Another boy may continue to get along well enough on the surface with his father but he displaces his defiance onto the school authorities or the police.

In families with children in college, parent and child are apt to be so self-disciplined that they keep their anger under control and deal with each other by reasonableness. A child from such a background, feeling angry rivalrousness underneath, may have difficulty finding a legitimate complaint against the considerate parent. In families like this, rivalry is sometimes expressed unconsciously through unexpected school failure—in high school or college or graduate school—even though the child has a high degree of intelligence, conscientiousness, and an excellent previous school record. The student, more often a boy, is sincere in saying he has no idea why he can't study or hand in papers or take examinations, whichever the problem may be. When such a youth seeks counseling, it may be discovered that, especially if he is planning to work in the same field as his father, he is afraid **unconsciously** either that he will ignominiously fail to come up to his father's level or, conversely, that he might outstrip his father and make him very angry. (The failing girl student may have the same problem in relation to her mother's or father's field of work.) In either case the school failure is the worst kind of blow to the parents; but the child, who has no conscious control, doesn't have to feel responsible for it. (Some, not all, of the youths who leave school because of unexpected failure find that they regain their academic efficiency and a heightened ambitiousness after working at a job for a couple of years; that is, they outgrow the unconscious fear. A more direct way of dealing with this problem is psychotherapy.)

Other children may express their anxious competitiveness by steering very clear of their parent's occupation though some of them swing around to it later when they have matured enough to overcome the irrational fear.

Psychoanalysis has also revealed that many boys who feel overawed by their fathers suppress their resentment and antagonism toward him and displace it onto their mothers, flaring up at her over quite reasonable requests or imagined slights.

An adolescent girl is, on the average, much less often overawed by her mother than a boy is by his father, so her rivalrousness is more apt to be expressed openly around the house, not often in academic failure. A girl can even be flirtatious with her father right under her mother's nose or reproach her mother for not being nice enough to her father. Few boys would dare taunt their fathers in such ways.

If youths were not rebellious, they would lack the motive to leave home and make their own way in the world. Rivalrousness also provides the motive power for young people who try to improve the world, find new methods that will supersede the old, make discoveries, create new art forms, displace old tyrants, right wrongs. A surprising number of scientific advances have been made and masterpieces of various arts created by individuals just on the threshold of adulthood. They were not smarter than the older people in their fields and they were admittedly less experienced. But they were critical of traditional ways, biased in favor of the new and the untried, and that happened to be enough to do the trick. This is how the world makes progress.

Some unknown parent once said, "Oh, to be only half as wonderful as my child thought I was, and only half as stupid as my teenager thinks I am."

641. Identity. A central problem for the adolescent and the young adult is to find out what kind of person she or he is going to be, doing what work, living by what principles. It's partly a conscious but even more an unconscious process. Erik Erikson has called this the identity crisis and it is exemplified in J.D. Salinger's *The Catcher in the Rye* (New York: Bantam Books, 1977).

Youths have got to separate themselves emotionally from their parents in order to find out who they are and what they want to be. Yet they are basically made from their parents—not just in the sense that they have inherited their genes from them but that they have been deliberately patterning themselves after them all their lives. So they must pry themselves apart. The eventual outcome will be influenced by three factors: the pull of their dependency, the intensity of their rebelliousness, and the kind of outside world they find and what it seems to ask of them.

In groping to find this identity adolescents may try out a variety of roles: dreamer, cosmopolitan, cynic, leader of lost causes, ascetic.

As adolescents try to emancipate themselves from their parents, they are apt to have a great need to find compensation in intimate ties to friends of the same age; more often ties to those of the same sex at first, because of the residual taboos against the opposite sex. These friendships, within or across the sexes, help to lend the youths some external support—like the timbers that are sometimes used to prop a building up during alterations—while they are giving up their identity as their parents' child and before they have found their own.

A boy finds himself through finding something similar in his friend. He mentions that he loves a certain song or hates a certain teacher or craves to own a certain article of apparel. His friend exclaims with amazement that he has always had the very same attitude. Both are delighted and reassured. Each has lost a degree of his feeling of aloneness, of peculiarity, and gained a pleasurable sense of belonging.

Two girls talk fast all the way home from school, talk for another half hour in front of the house of one, finally separate. But as soon as the second reaches her home she telephones and they resume the mutual confidences.

A majority of adolescents help to overcome their feelings of aloneness by a sometimes slavish conformity to the styles of their classmates—in clothes, hairdos, language, reading matter, songs, entertainers. These styles have to be different from those of their parents' generation. And if their own styles irritate or shock their parents, so much the better. It is revealing, though, that even those youths who adopt extreme styles to differentiate themselves from their parents must still conform to the styles of at least a few of their friends.

A majority of adolescents become ashamed of their parents for a few years, particularly when their friends are present. This is partly related to their anxious search for their own identities. Partly it is the extreme self-consciousness of the age period. Most of all it is the intense need to be just like their friends and to be accepted totally by their friends. They fear that if their parents deviate in any way from the neighborhood pattern, they, themselves, might be rejected by their own friends. What youths choose to deplore in their parents is sometimes ludicrous. But the parents shouldn't accept discourtesy. Their best cue, when they find themselves with their children's friends, is to be agreeable but not talk too much. It's most important, from their children's point of view, that they not try to talk or act as if they are young themselves.

Youths in trying to achieve emotional independence are on

the lookout for evidences of hypocrisy in their parents. To the extent that their parents are obviously sincere in their ideals, their children feel under obligation to continue to adhere to them. But if they can find hypocrisy, this relieves them of the moral duty to conform. It also gives them a welcome opportunity to reproach their parents.

642. Demands for freedom and fear of freedom. A common reproach of adolescents is that their parents don't allow them enough freedom. It's natural for children nearing adulthood to insist on their rights, and their parents need to be reminded that they are changing. But parents don't have to take every claim at its face value. The fact is that adolescents are also scared of growing up. They are unsure about their capacity to be as knowledgeable, masterful, sophisticated, and charming as they would like. But their pride won't allow them to recognize this. When they're unconsciously in doubt about their ability to carry off some challenge or adventure, they're quick to find evidence that their parents are blocking their way. They reproach them indignantly, or blame them when talking with friends. Parents can particularly suspect this unconscious maneuver when their children suddenly announce a plan of their group for some escapade—like an evening at an unsavory roadhouse—which is way beyond anything they've done before. They may be asking to be stopped.

643. Withdrawal, eccentricity, radicalism. It sometimes takes youths 5 to 10 years to truly find their own positive identity. Meanwhile they may be stalled at a halfway stage characterized by a passive resistance to and withdrawal from ordinary society (which they equate with their parents) or by an excessively rebellious radicalism.

They may decline to take an ordinary job, and may emphasize unconventional dress, grooming, acquaintances, residence. These seem like evidence of vigorous independence to them. But these by themselves don't add up yet to a positive stand on life or a constructive contribution to the world. They are essentially a negative protest against the parents' conventions. Even when the striving to be independent shows up only in the form of eccentricities of appearance it should be recognized as an attempted step in the right direction, which may go on to a constructive, creative stage later. As a matter of fact, the young people who have to strain so visibly to be free are apt to come from families with unusually strong ties and high ideals.

Other youths, who are idealistic and altruistic in character, often take a sternly radical or purist view of things for a number of years—in politics or in the arts or in other fields. Various tendencies of this age period operate together to draw them into these extreme positions—heightened criticalness, cynicism about hypocrisy, intolerance of compromise, courageousness, willingness to sacrifice, in response to their first awareness of the shocking injustices—most of them unnecessary—of the society they live in. A few years later, having achieved a satisfactory degree of emotional independence from parents and having found out how to be useful in their chosen fields, they are more tolerant of the frailties of their fellow men and more ready to make constructive compromises. I don't mean that they all become complacent conservatives. Many remain progressive, some remain radical. But most become easier to live with, work with.

644. Sexuality and romance are strained for the adolescent for several reasons. (I use the word **sexual** when I put the emphasis on glands and crude inborn instinct, the word **romantic** when I mean the tender, highly personal, idealistic aspects of love between the sexes, which are mainly learned during a childhood spent with parents whose love is of this kind. I realize that this usage has various inaccuracies; also that to call anything romantic nowadays makes it seem to some people insipid or bogus.) The adolescent has emerged from two earlier, contradictory phases which were described briefly way back in Section 16 and described in more detail in the chapters "Three to Six" and "From Six to Eleven." Between 3 and 6 years the child grew spiritually by overidealizing the two parents and became interested in romance, sex, and babies. Between 6 and 12, through a complex interaction of emotions, the child repressed much of the interest in romance and sex, turned away from parents and became absorbed in the impersonal outside world of schooling, social adaptation, laws, and legends.

In adolescence the glandular pressures compel the child to be preoccupied with sexual and romantic interests again. But the revived sexual drives will continue to be in conflict with the earlier taboos for several more years, causing internal embarrassment and guilt, and external awkwardness. The simplest example is the young adolescent's shyness in dealing with the opposite sex.

The conflicting emotions also cause trouble in the child's relations with the parents. When the rush of strong romantic feeling first wells up in early adolescence, it first starts—like a spring flood running down a dry riverbed—toward the parent of the opposite sex. Yet the adolescent realizes subconsciously that this is not right at all. So the initial job at this age is to steer the feelings away from the parent toward someone outside the family. The child actually covers up the positive feelings toward a parent with negative ones. This is at least a partial explanation of why a boy so often picks fights with his mother and why a daughter may be surprisingly antagonistic toward her father at times.

At first the adolescent girl (and it is equally true of the adolescent boy) doesn't know at all clearly where her feelings belong. She becomes generally intense and romantic in her attitudes toward different kinds of people. Yet she may be nowhere near the time where she can show these feelings toward an individual of the same age and opposite sex, especially if she is shy and idealistic. She may develop a great admiration for a teacher of the same sex, or a heroine of fiction. It's only gradually that the barriers between the sexes are broken down. Perhaps the adolescent first dares to think romantically of someone in Hollywood. Then boys and girls in the same school can dream about each other; but it may take some further time before the shy ones can show their interest face to face.

Even after an adolescent's instincts have broken through the inhibitions of the earlier period and involved her in dating, a portion of this energy will still be held in reserve and invested in idealistic yearnings. Some part of this will ensure that her attitude toward the opposite sex is romantic and idealizing. But another part, even at this relatively late stage of development, will still be sublimated into aspirations which on the surface seem unrelated to sex or even romance—to create things of beauty, for example, or to make a great contribution to humanity.

In the very beginning of her interest in members of the opposite sex the adolescent may be unable to recognize any sexual feeling toward a person for whom she feels respect and tenderness, only for those who seem debased in some way. (For a few individuals this dissociation unfortunately lasts for life.)

Before children have become secure about their sexuality or integrated it into their personality, it remains a rather awkward, compelling, crude, separate instinct. They feel a nagging curiosity about what sex is in the ultimate and a compulsion to find out by experimentation. These feelings run counter, of course, to their idealistic emotions. In fact, they may be tenderly in love with one person and still find themselves impelled to make advances—hesitant or bold—to others, in a rather impersonal, promiscuous spirit.

Children in the early teens are apt to experience a series of intense infatuations, in each of which the sense of being in love is intense. But they can fall out of love as quickly as they fall in. They discover that they and their beloved really have little in common. Sometimes the reason is that one or both have changed. More often it's that they had originally fallen in love with the ideal they saw in each other, which had little to do with the reality. As the years pass they become more cautious, and more realistic about what kind of person they need and can get along with. As they gradually mature they also have more to give to each other—a vital ingredient of true love.

645. The right slant at adolescence. You might get the idea from articles that it's easy for parents if they are wholesome people to talk about sex with their adolescent children. This is simply not so. Adolescents' acute awareness of their sexuality and their rivalry with their parents make such a discussion embarrassing in many cases, especially between son and father. Many fathers and sons can't get to it at all, nor can quite a few mothers and daughters. Then the information—or misinformation—comes from friends, older brothers or sisters, books. A sound book made available by a parent can be helpful, either alone or, better still, backed up by the parent's answers to questions.

646. Girls. A girl needs to be told by the beginning of puberty development (average age 10 years) that during the next 2 years her breasts will develop, hair will grow in the genital region and under the arms, that she will grow rapidly in stature and in weight, that her skin will change its texture and may become liable to pimples, that in about 2 years she will probably have her first menstrual period. (These changes are discussed in Sections 635-639.) How you tell her about her menstrual periods makes a difference. Some mothers emphasize what a curse they can be. But it is a mistake to stress that part to a child who is still immature and impressionable. Other mothers emphasize how delicate a girl becomes at such times and how careful she must be. This kind of talk makes a bad impression, particularly on those girls who have grown up feeling that their brothers got all the advantages or who have been inclined to worry about their health. The more doctors and women's educators have learned about menstruation, the more convinced they have become that girls and women can live perfectly normal, healthy, vigorous lives right through their menstrual periods. It is only the occasional girl who has cramps severe enough to keep her out of activities, and there are now good treatments for cramps.

When a girl is on the threshold of womanhood, it's good for her to be looking forward to it happily, not feeling scared or resentful. The best thing to emphasize about menstruation is that the uterus is being prepared for the growing of a baby.

It helps put the child in the right mood during the months she is waiting for her first period to give her a belt and a box of napkins. This makes her feel as if she is grown up and ready to deal with life rather than waiting for life to do something to her.

Boys, by the time they begin the stage of puberty development (the average age is 12 years), need to be told about the naturalness of erections and nocturnal emissions. Nocturnal emissions, which are often called "wet dreams," are an ejaculation of semen (the fluid stored in the prostate gland) during sleep, often in the course of a dream of a sexual nature. Parents who know that nocturnal emissions are certain to occur, and also that there will at times be a strong urge to masturbate, sometimes tell the boy that these things are not harmful if they don't happen too often. I think it's a mistake for a parent to set a limit, even though it may sound sensible. The trouble is that adolescents easily become worried about their sexuality, easily imagine they are "different" or abnormal. Being told, "This much is normal, that much is abnormal," is apt to make them more preoccupied with sex. Boys need to be told that it's equally normal to have many or few nocturnal emissions and that occasionally a perfectly normal boy will have none at all.

The same advice applies to sexual dreams and masturbation in girls.

647. Keep the tone wholesome. It's preferable, just as in earlier childhood, for talk about sex to come up easily from time to time rather than be one big solemn lecture. The parent has to be willing to bring it up early in puberty, though, since the child so often doesn't do so.

One mistake that is easy to make, especially if the parents themselves were brought up in fear of sex, is to concentrate on all the dangerous aspects of sex. A nervous mother may make her daughter so scared of becoming pregnant that the poor girl has a terror of boys under all circumstances. Or the father may overfill his son with dread of venereal disease. Of course, the child who is moving into adolescence should know how pregnancy takes place and that there is a danger of disease in being promiscuous, but these disturbing aspects of sex shouldn't come first. The adolescent should think of it as primarily wholesome and natural and beautiful.

What worried parents find hard to believe, but what people who have studied young people know well, is that the happy, sensible, successful adolescents rarely get into trouble with sex. All the common sense, self-respect, and kindly feeling toward people that they have built up through the years keep them on an even keel even when they are sailing through an entirely new phase of development. To turn it around the other way, the adolescents who get into trouble with the wrong kind of companions are usually children who for years have been mixed up within themselves and with others.

The danger of scaring a child about sex is partly that you make a sensitive child tense and apprehensive at the time, partly that you may impair her or his ability to adjust to marriage later.

648. Parental guidance of adolescents. Being a wise parent to adolescents has always been a difficult job. If children are made of good stuff they are bound to feel rivalrous and rebellious, whether or not the parent is being reasonable. The job is greatly complicated in the twentieth century by the fact that parents have all read psychology of one kind or another and have been made uneasy about the theoretical possibility of doing harm by well-intentioned efforts. This is too bad, because in most cases it's better to do the supposedly wrong thing with an air of confidence than the supposedly right thing with a hesitant or apologetic manner. Then there's also the fact that many children today have the bit in their teeth and have their parents on the run.

Most adolescents are not the enemies of parents, though. They are reasonable a good part of the time. This is remarkable considering the inner emotional storms they are experiencing and the dozens of new adjustments they are having to make between their new selves and the new life they are being called on to live, the heavy academic schedules that most of them are carrying.

The first and most important point, by far, is that adolescents need and want guidance from their parents—and even rules—no matter how much they argue against them. (Their pride won't let them admit the need openly.)

Trusted schoolteachers and child guidance workers have all heard adolescents say, "I wish my parents would make definite rules for me, like my friend's parents do." They sense that it's one aspect of parents' love to want to keep their children from misunderstandings and embarrassing situations out in the world, from giving the wrong impression or gaining an unfortunate reputation, from getting into trouble through inexperience.

This doesn't mean that parents can be arbitrary or overbearing. Adolescents have too much dignity and indignation for that; they want to discuss the issues on an adult-to-adult basis. If the argument comes out a draw, though, the parents shouldn't be so scrupulously democratic that they assume the child is as likely to be right as they are; the parents' experience should be presumed to count for a lot. In the end, the parents should confidently express their judgment, and, if appropriate, their explicit request. They owe their child this clarity and definiteness.

But, parents ask, what if the child openly defies the request or quietly disobeys? If the child–parent relationship is half-way sound, the child will not defy or disobey in the early years of adolescence, and may not even in the later years. In the later years the parents may even consider it wise on occasion to give a youth permission to go against the parents' judgment; this doesn't mean that the parents have no confidence that their judgment is right.

Parents' attitudes should indicate, without necessarily saying so in words, that they realize the youth will be out of their sight most of the time and therefore will be complying because of conscience and respect for the parents, not because the parents can make a young person obey or because they can watch their child at all times.

Even if an older adolescent defies or disobeys a parental direction, this does not mean that the direction did no good. It certainly helps inexperienced persons to hear all sides. If they decide not to take their parents' direction, they may of course be making a reasonably sound decision, perhaps being in possession of knowledge or insights that the parents lack. Certainly as they progress into adulthood they must be prepared to reject advice on occasion and to take the responsibility for their decision. If young people reject their parents' direction and get into trouble, this experience will increase their respect for their parents' judgment, though they probably won't admit it.

Suppose parents don't know what to say or think about some issue. They can discuss it not only with their child but with other parents, perhaps get the PTA to have a general session on it. In some cities there have been official conferences between parents and adolescents which have led to a fairly uniform code of behavior that was a comfort to all concerned.

But individual parents should not feel bound in advance to adhere to other people's codes even if they are the only parents who disagree. In the long run parents can only do a good job if they are convinced they are doing right. And what is right for them is what they feel is right, after hearing the arguments.

649. Specific suggestions. I myself have strong opinions about the general principles of parental guidance but I'd be hesitant to convert these into arbitrary specifics. Times change. Customs vary in different parts of the country and in different groups in the same community. Individual children vary greatly in their maturity and reliability.

There are some simple rules, I think:

Adolescents, like adults, out of respect for themselves as well as others, should bathe regularly and wear clothes that are clean.

Individually and in groups they should be expected to be civil to people generally and definitely cordial to their parents, family friends, teachers, and the people who serve them. It is natural for youths to have at least a mildly hostile attitude underneath toward adults, with whom they are inevitably rivalrous, whether or not they are aware of this. But it does them no harm to have to control this hostility and be polite anyway. Their politeness certainly makes a great difference to the adults concerned.

Youths should have serious obligations in helping their families—in regular chores and in special additional jobs. This benefits youths by giving them a sense of dignity, participation, happiness, as well as helping the parents.

You can't enforce these principles. I'm only saying that parents are entitled to express them in discussions with their children. It will help adolescents to hear their parents' principles, even if they won't conform.

650. Adolescents' styles of clothes and hairdos are partly their way to conform to the standards of their peers; and most teenagers need this conformity in order to feel secure and accepted. Some choose certain styles to confirm their own sense of themselves and their individuality. It can also be a way to defy parents, neighbors, or school. In this case, they may be deliberately attempting to provoke and outrage adults as a challenge to these authorities. Parents can be most helpful to teenagers by trying to understand their behavior and then helping them to understand themselves. If you explain why you object to certain styles, you may be able to convince your children to change without your having to end up with an "or else" order. On the other hand, the teenager who feels free to discuss and argue with parents may end up convincing the parents to see and accept the teenager's point of view. Adults tend to be slower than youths in accepting new styles. What may horrify or disgust us one day may later become quite acceptable for ourselves as well as our children. This was true with the long-hair styles and dungarees introduced by youths in the sixties, and the pants for girls that so upset school authorities at one time.

651. Dating. As you well know, there has been a style since the 1950s of early dating, much of it not based on love but on social custom. It provides social security at parties, confidence about one's popularity, and a sense of being grown up. But it often fosters physical intimacy long before there is much capacity for a generous love, mutual respect, or even real communication, and it plays a part in the great increase in teenage pregnancies. Pregnancies without love, and exposure to the punitive attitudes of many people, may have a disillusioning and embittering effect on sensitive individuals.

By contrast, when a mature girl and boy are becoming more deeply in love because they are right for each other, the physical desire increases, but it is always integrated with and under the control of the tender and generous feelings.

College psychiatrists report that a common problem nowadays is the students who do not feel ready yet for full sexual experience (about half the students) but are made to think that they are therefore sexually abnormal, by the taunts of their bolder classmates.

It's reassuring for teenagers to know that it is normal for many young people brought up with ideals to feel reserved about sex and the opposite sex and to want to wait until they are quite sure of their love for a person before they go far in lovemaking.

652. Parental supervision of dating. I think parents are entitled to discuss with their young adolescent children the hour at which they expect to come home from parties and dates, where they are going and with whom, and who is to drive. If the child asks why they want to know, they can answer that good parents feel responsible for their children, at least up to the time when they go away to college or to work; society expects them to maintain that responsibility. "Suppose," parents can say, "there is some accident which delays you. We ought to know where to inquire or to search." Or the parents can say, "If there were a family emergency we would want to be able to reach you." (Parents should tell their children where **they're** going and when they expect to be home, for the same reasons.) Incidentally, if there is a delay or a change in plan, adolescents (and parents) should call home to explain, before they are overdue. The fact that, with the agreement of their children, the parents set a certain hour, and are waiting for them then, reminds children that the parents are genuinely concerned with their conduct and safety. When children have a party at home, the parents should be there.

Parents can't dictate to their adolescent children or talk down to them. But they can have mutually respecting, adult-to-adult discussions. Young people never have been willing to be guided beyond a certain point by their parents, but that doesn't mean that they haven't benefited from discussions.

653. Teenage pregnancy. In earlier times a young girl who became pregnant was thought of as at least mildly delinquent because she had disobeyed her parents and her own principles. Now the greatly relaxed sexual standards and, to a lesser extent, the knowledge of how pregnancy can be prevented, have brought about great increases in the frequency of full sexual activity at earlier ages, and pregnancy among unmarried teenagers and youths. To adults the most surprising, almost incomprehensible aspect of this is that only a minority of the teenagers who are sexually active practice birth control, even when they have been well instructed through the efforts of parents and physicians. (The same is true in Sweden, where birth control is taught thoroughly and specifically in all schools and where the various devices are available.)

Why won't they take responsibility for their sexual activity? There are various overlapping explanations. To be prepared means to some of them that they expect repetition of intercourse, which many of them are not quite ready to admit; they prefer to think of each episode as an unexpected outburst of passion which won't be repeated. Some say that since they (or friends) have had intercourse a number of times without pregnancy, they assume that they are somehow immune. Others think that withdrawal is a reliable prevention. Some who are having conflicts with parents think of themselves as unloved, and they picture themselves as loving and being loved intensely by a baby. Some teenagers become sexually involved with a person whom they have come to love more or less tenderly and idealistically. Others are responding primarily to a physical urge and to an intense curiosity about the experience of intercourse. Fairly often, these latter youths instinctively avoid experimenting with the person they might love and respect—they select instead someone with merely physical appeal.

I used to fear that if parents took the initiative in arranging for their teenage children to have specific instruction in the prevention of pregnancy, by the mother or an obstetrician for the girl, by the father or another physician for the boy—it would be taken as encouragement for early sexual experimentation and for casual, nonloving affairs. Now I'm convinced that the greater danger is of pregnancy caused by ignorance and irresponsibility. I believe that the parents must take the initiative. They must not only instruct, or arrange for instruction, but reemphasize from time to time, especially if they expect sexual activity, that people who have intercourse **must** take serious responsibility for birth control on every single occasion, both boy and girl, out of consideration for the baby, for their parents, and for their school and future lives. At the same time, parents can speak about their own ideals—that sex is as much spiritual as physical, that they, the parents, as well as many young people, think it is better for young people to wait until they are confident that their love is deep and long-lasting before having sexual relations, that delaying does not mean any lack of sexual power or normality.

654. Juvenile delinquency. This subject is too complex for more than a brief definition and a few examples. The term is confusing because it covers everything for which a youth might be hauled into court, from playing hooky to murder. The aggressiveness of boys in adolescence is such that a majority of them engage in offenses such as truancy, petty theft (hubcaps, for instance), or mischief (breaking windows in a vacant building), at one time or another in adolescence, though most of them don't get caught. Such offenses are usually of no great psychological significance if a boy commits them only once or twice, and in a group. But society has to disapprove of them firmly and parents should, too. However, repeated offenses of such kinds in the case of a boy brought up in a strict neighborhood mean either that he has a definite neurotic problem (compulsive stealing, for example); or that he has never been loved adequately and doesn't care much what his parents and society think of him; or that his parents have unconscious delinquent tendencies, despite their conventional exteriors, and are vicariously enjoying his escapades. The same kind of repeated mild delinquencies in a tough neighborhood may mean only that a youth is proving his manhood by defying the police.

Offenses that have a lot of grasping aggression in them (robbery) or destructiveness (wrecking a schoolroom at night) or cruelty (a sexual attack or beating people up for no good reason) mean that a child was raised not only without much love, but was subjected to a lot of hostility or cruelty in addition.

On the other hand, the peeping tom or the boy who cautiously tries to make a pass at a strange girl sitting next to him in a movie theater usually has no excess aggressiveness—often quite the contrary. He is restricted to an incomplete expression of sexuality because of an excessive repression and perhaps also an abnormal shyness.

Girls show on the average less aggressiveness than boys and their delinquency usually does not take the form of defying the authorities or attacking people. Instead they make their parents miserable. A moderately serious form of feminine delinquency is running away from home. It occurs in girls who are immature and unstable, and there has usually been a long history of disharmony with the parents.

An example of a more harsh and serious delinquency is when a girl engages in promiscuous sexual behavior, in her parents' community, to scandalize and enrage them, and spitefully to give the whole family a bad name. The parents call on the police to arrest her because they can't control her. Usually there are serious conflicts throughout the family and a deficiency in the parents' love of the girl.

Many people blame peer pressure for almost any kind of trouble into which an adolescent gets. I don't believe that a normal adolescent from a normal family gets into serious trouble only from peer pressure.

The main point I want to make about the more serious forms of delinquency is that they don't appear suddenly in adolescents who were well adjusted before. They occur in unstable families where relations between the parents and between child and parents have been way out of line for a long time, where there has been very little love, and where the child's behavior showed serious aberrations long before adolescence. The prevention of delinquency consists, of course, in the early counseling of the disturbed family and, more fundamentally, in a more just, more stable society.

655. Drugs. The habituation or addiction to dangerous drugs is largely confined to the period from midadolescence to about the age of 30, during which many individuals are groping for a positive identity—for a place and an active function in the world.

Serious drug abuse occurs often in youths who are somewhat immature, self-centered, passive, and have little sense of direction in life as yet. But several characteristics of normal adolescents favor experimentation with drugs:

They have a powerful curiosity to find out all there is to know about life—especially about what seem like the mysterious aspects.

Many have an impulse to sacrifice themselves, in the sense of taking wild chances, accepting dangerous dares, being proud of burning the candle at both ends, proving their courage. (This is one reason why they bravely take up smoking tobacco while older people are striving to give it up.)

At the same time they are secretly afraid of facing new, difficult situations. A drug may, like alcohol, give a promise of numbing inhibitions, erasing apprehensions, increasing courage sufficiently to get a youth over the threshold—of lovemaking, for example.

There is a particularly strong appeal to a youth to follow the style of his peers; and if that style worries or angers parents, so much the better.

656. The use of marijuana is in a distinctly different category from that of the more dangerous drugs. A large percentage of young people—even of junior high and high school age—have tried it at least a few times. There is no element of physical addiction.

Most of the young people who have used marijuana have tried it only a few times or use it much less often than daily. The uncommon individual who regularly smokes several times a day and remains in a state of mild intoxication should not be thought of as having been ruined by marijuana, I'd say, but as a person who has lost his or her sense of purpose and seeks comfort in marijuana, just as other individuals have chronically abused alcohol and other dangerous drugs.

Though marijuana has been accused of causing many kinds of physical and psychological disability, and though no one can promise that any substance will never be found harmful, the fact is that up to the time of this writing the only damage that has been proved is a lowering of sex hormone and sperm count in males who use it amply and regularly. Young people keep up with the news about marijuana and only lose confidence in adults who make exaggerated or discredited claims.

It certainly is true that marijuana is much less dangerous than tobacco and alcohol which kill or incapacitate tens of thousands each year.

In speaking to a young teenager about drugs I would say, in effect: Tobacco causes many deaths from cancer and heart disease. Most doctors have quit because of what they've seen, though quitting is difficult and painful. Alcoholism causes disease and death, and ruins millions of families. Even the mild drug marijuana makes it easier for a few heavy users to get off the track. The stage of life you will be going through now is the most difficult of all, with many changes and tensions; some people lose their drive and their sense of direction. I wish that you would wait until you are 18 or 20, when things will have settled down and you'll know more about what you want out of life, before you decide whether or not to drink, smoke tobacco, smoke pot. But of course it is you who will have to make the decision.

This advice is a lot more persuasive if the parents are not using alcohol, tobacco, tranquilizers, or stimulants.

Then I would count on my children's good sense. They might well use these various drugs at times. (Most of us parents in our youth went against our parents' requests on tobacco or alcohol, at least occasionally.)

But I would know that further lectures by me—or sharp questions or snooping—not only would do no good but would provoke and tempt my children to rebel.

I'm not advocating or justifying the use of any drug. If we had a happier society with fewer tensions—which I believe we could have—people wouldn't need to soothe themselves with any drug. I'm only suggesting to parents that there is no presently known reason to become panicky about the occasional use of marijuana.

Heroin is of course extremely dangerous from every point of view. LSD ("acid") often causes serious emotional disturbance. The abuse of amphetamine ("speed") leads to physical exhaustion and serious emotional disturbance.

Problems of Feeding and Development

THIN CHILDREN

657. Thinness has various causes. Some children seem to be thin by heredity. They come from thin stock on one or both sides of the family. From the time they were babies they have been offered plenty to eat. They aren't sickly, and they aren't nervous. They just never want to eat a great deal, especially of the rich foods.

Some children are thin because their appetites have been taken away by too much parental urging (Section 660). Other children can't eat for other nervous reasons. Children who are worrying about bogeymen, or death, or a parent's going away and leaving them, may lose a lot of their appetite. The jealous younger sister who is driving herself all day long to keep up with her older sister burns up a lot of energy and gives herself no peace at mealtime, either. As you can see, the tense child is thinned out by a two-way process. The appetite is kept down, and the restlessness uses up extra energy.

There are many children throughout the world who are malnourished because their parents can't find or afford the proper food. There are a few chronic physical diseases that cause malnutrition. But children who become thin during an acute illness usually recover their weight promptly if during convalescence they are not urged to eat until their appetite recovers.

658. Sudden loss of weight is serious. If a child abruptly loses weight he must have a careful checkup—promptly. The commonest causes are diabetes (which also produces excessive hunger and thirst and frequent urination), tumors, tuberculosis, worry about serious family tensions, obsession in adolescent girls with the need to diet. (See Section 673 on anorexia nervosa.)

659. Care of a thin child. A thin child should, of course, have regular medical checkups. This is more important if the child acts tired or has lost weight or has failed to gain a reasonable amount.

Thinness, failure to gain weight, and fatigue come more often from emotional troubles than from physical causes. If your child is nervous or depressed, try to consult a child guidance clinic or a family social agency. Talk over his situation with his schoolteacher. In any case, it's wise to think over again his relations with parents, brothers, sisters, friends, and school. If you have gotten involved in a feeding problem, try to undo it. (See Section 661.)

Eating between meals is helpful for those thin children whose stomachs never seem to want to take much at a time but are quite willing to eat often.

A healthy child may stay thin despite a large appetite, and this is probably the way she or he was meant to be. In many of these cases, the child prefers relatively low-calorie foods, like meat, vegetables and fruit, and shies away from rich desserts.

Finally, if your child doesn't seem to have any kind of problem, has been slender since infancy, but gains a reasonable amount of weight every year, relax. She or he is probably meant to be that way.

FEEDING PROBLEMS

660. Where feeding problems begin. Why do so many children eat poorly? Most commonly because so many parents are conscientious about trying to make them eat well. You don't see many feeding problems in puppies, or among young humans in places where mothers don't know enough about diet to worry.

Some children seem to be born with a wolf's appetite that stays big even when they're unhappy or sick. Others have appetites that are more moderate and more easily affected by their health and spirits. The first group seem to be cut out to be plump; the second are apparently intended to stay on the slender side. But **every** baby is born with enough appetite to keep her healthy, keep her gaining at the proper rate for her.

The trouble is that children are also born with an instinct to get balky if pushed too hard, and an instinct to get disgusted by food with which they've had unpleasant experiences. There's one further complication: a person's appetite doesn't always go out to the same things. For a while she feels like eating a lot of spinach or a new breakfast cereal. Next month it may not appeal to her. Some people always go in heavily for starches and sweets; others are fed up with a little bit. If you understand these points, you can see how feeding problems begin at different stages in a child's development. Some babies become balky in their early months if their parents often try to make them finish more of their bottle than they want, or, when the first solid food is introduced, they aren't given a chance to get used to it gradually. Many become more picky and choosy after the age of a year because they aren't meant to be gaining so fast, because they are more opinionated, and perhaps because of teething. Urging them reduces the appetite further and more permanently. A very common time for feeding problems to begin is at the end of an illness. If an anxious parent begins pushing food before the appetite returns, it quickly increases the child's disgust and gets it firmly fixed.

All feeding problems don't start from urging. A child may stop eating because of jealousy of a new baby or worries of many kinds. But whatever the original cause, the parents' anxiety and urging usually make it worse and keep the appetite from returning.

661. A cure takes time and patience. Once a feeding problem is established, it takes time and understanding and patience to undo. The parents have become anxious. They find it hard to relax again as long as the child is eating poorly. And yet their concern and insistence are the main things that are keeping the child's appetite down. Even when they reform, by a supreme effort, it may take weeks for the child's timid appetite to come back. She has to have a chance to slowly forget all the unpleasant associations with mealtime.

Her appetite is like a mouse and the parents' anxious urging is the cat that has been scaring it back into its hole. You can't persuade the mouse to be bold just because the cat looks the other way. The cat must leave the mouse alone for a long time.

662. Parents have feelings, too. And they are strong feelings by the time they have a chronic feeding problem on their hands. The most obvious one is anxiety—that the child will develop some nutritional deficiency or lose resistance to ordinary infections. The doctor tries to reassure them again and again that children with feeding problems are not more susceptible to diseases, but this is hard for them to believe.

They are apt to feel guilty, imagining that their relatives, their in-laws, the neighbors, the doctor, consider them neglectful parents. Of course, they don't. It's more likely that they understand because they have at least one child in the family who's a poor eater, too.

Then there's the inevitable feeling of frustration and angriness at a whippersnapper who can completely foil all her parents' efforts to do right by her. This is the most uncomfortable feeling of all, because it makes the conscientious parents feel ashamed of themselves.

It's an interesting fact that many parents who have feeding problems in their children recall having had a feeding problem themselves in their own childhood. They remember only too well that urging and forcing work in the wrong direction, but they find themselves powerless to do otherwise. In such cases, the strong feelings of anxiety, guilt, and irritation are partly leftovers from the same feelings implanted in the parents in childhood.

663. There's rarely danger for the child. It's important to remember that children have a remarkable inborn mechanism that lets them know how much food and which types of food they need for normal growth and development. It is extremely rare to see serious malnutrition or vitamin deficiency or infectious disease result from a feeding problem. The child's eating pattern should be discussed with the doctor at the time of checkups, of course.

664. Make mealtime pleasant. The aim is not to **make** the child eat but to let her natural appetite come to the surface so that she wants to eat.

Try hard not to talk about her eating, either with threats or with encouragement. I wouldn't praise her for taking an unusually large amount or look disappointed when she takes little. With practice, you should be able to stop thinking about it, and that's real progress. When she feels no more pressure, she can begin to pay attention to her own appetite.

You sometimes hear the advice, "Put the food before the child, say nothing, take it away in 30 minutes, no matter how much or how little has been eaten. Give nothing else until the next meal." This is fine if it's carried out in the right spirit—that is to say, if the parent is really trying not to fuss or worry about the child's eating and remains agreeable. But angry parents sometimes apply the advice by slapping the plate of dinner in front of the child, saying grimly, "Now, if you don't eat this in 30 minutes, I'm going to take it away and you won't get a thing to eat until supper!" Then they stand glaring at her, waiting. This threatening hardens her heart and takes away any trace of appetite. The balky child who is challenged to a feeding battle can **always** outlast a parent.

You don't want your child to eat because she has been beaten in a fight, whether you have been forcing her or taking her food away. You want her to eat because she feels like eating.

Start with the foods she likes best. You want her mouth to water when she comes to meals so that she can hardly wait to begin. The first step in building up that attitude is to serve for **2 or 3 months** the wholesome foods she likes best (offering as balanced a diet as possible), and to omit all the foods that she actively dislikes.

If your child has a limited feeding problem, dislikes only one or another group of foods but eats most kinds fairly well, read Sections 488–498. They explain how one food can be substituted for another until a child's appetite swings around or until she loses her suspiciousness and tenseness at meals.

665. The child who likes few foods. A parent might say, "Those children who dislike just one type of food aren't real problems. Why, my child likes only hamburgers, bananas, oranges, and soda pop. Once in a while he'll take a slice of white bread or a couple of teaspoonfuls of peas. He refuses to touch anything else."

This is an unusually severe feeding problem, but the principle is the same. You could serve him sliced bananas and a slice of enriched bread for breakfast; hamburger, 2 teaspoonfuls of peas, and an orange for lunch; a slice of enriched bread and more banana for supper. Let him have seconds or thirds of any of the foods if he asks for them and you have them. Serve different combinations of this diet for days. Hold down firmly on his soda pop. If his stomach is awash with syrup, it takes away what little appetite he has for more valuable foods.

If at the end of a couple of months he is looking forward to his meals, add a couple of teaspoonfuls (not more) of some food that he sometimes used to eat—not one he hated. Don't mention the new addition. Don't comment if he leaves it. Try this one again in a couple of weeks, and meanwhile try another. How fast you go on adding new foods depends on how his appetite is improving and how he's taking to the new foods.

666. Make no distinctions between foods. Let them eat four helpings of one food and none of another if that's the way they feel (as long as the food is wholesome). If they want none of the main course but want dessert, let them have dessert in a perfectly matter-of-fact way. If you say, "No seconds on meat until you've eaten your vegetable," or "No dessert until you've cleaned your plate," you further take away their appetite for the vegetable or the main course and you increase their desire for meat or dessert. These results are the exact opposite of what you want. (The best way to handle the dessert problem is not to serve any dessert except fruit more than a night or two a week, or ever. If a non-fruit dessert is served, it should be given to all family members without restriction.)

It's not that you want children to go on eating lopsided meals forever. But if they have a feeding problem and are already suspicious of some foods, your best chance of having them come back to a reasonable balance is to let them feel that you do not care.

I think it's a great mistake for the parent to insist that children who have feeding problems eat "just a taste" of a food they are suspicious of, as a matter of duty. If they have to eat anything that disgusts them, even slightly, it lessens the chance that they will ever change their minds and like it. And it lowers their enjoyment of mealtimes and their general appetite for all foods by one more degree.

Certainly, never make them eat at the next meal food that they refused at the last meal. That's looking for trouble.

667. Serve less than they will eat, not more. For any child who is eating poorly, serve small portions. If you heap her plate high, you remind her of how much she is going to refuse and you depress her appetite. But if you give her a first helping that is less than she is willing to take, you encourage her to think, "That isn't enough." You want her to have that attitude. You want her to get to think of food as something she is eager for. If she has a **really** small appetite, serve her miniature portions: 1 teaspoonful of meat, 1 teaspoonful of vegetables, 1 teaspoonful of starch. When she finishes, don't say eagerly, "Do you want some more?" Let her ask, even if it takes several days of miniature portions to give her the idea. It's a good idea to serve the miniature portions on a very small plate, so that the child doesn't feel humiliated by sitting in front of tiny portions of food on a huge plate.

668. Getting them to feed themselves. Should the parents feed a poor eater? A child who is given proper encouragement (Section 474) takes over his own feeding somewhere between 12 and 18 months. But if overworried parents have continued to feed him until the age of 2 or 3 or 4 (probably with a lot of urging), it won't solve the problem simply to tell him, "Stop!"

The child now has no desire to feed himself; he takes being fed for granted. To him it's now an important sign of his parents' love and concern. If they stop suddenly, it hurts his feelings, makes him resentful. He is liable to stop eating altogether for 2 or 3 days—and that's longer than any parents can sit by doing nothing. When they feed him again, he has a new grudge against them. When they try another time to give up feeding him, he knows his strength and their weakness.

A child of 2 or more should be feeding himself as soon as possible. But getting him to do it is a delicate matter that takes several weeks. You mustn't give him the impression that you are trying to take a privilege away. You want him to take over because he wants to.

Serve him his favorite foods meal after meal and day after day. When you set the dish before him, go back to the kitchen or into the next room for a minute or two, as if you had forgotten something. Be away a little longer each day. Come back and feed him cheerfully with no comments, whether or not he has taken anything himself. If he gets impatient while you are in the next room and calls you to come and feed him, come right away, with a friendly apology. He probably won't progress steadily. In a week or two he may get to the point of eating one meal almost entirely himself, and the next meal want to be fed from the beginning. Don't argue at all during this process. If he eats one food, don't urge him to try another, too. If he seems pleased with himself for doing a good job of self-feeding, compliment him on being a big boy, but don't be so enthusiastic that he smells a rat.

Suppose for a week or so you have left him alone with good food for as long as 10 or 15 minutes and he's eaten nothing. Then you ought to make him hungrier. Gradually, in 3 or 4 days, cut down to half what you customarily feed him. This should make him so eager that he can't help starting in himself, provided you are being tactful and friendly.

By the time the child is regularly feeding himself as much as half a meal, I think it's time to encourage him to leave the table rather than feed him the rest of the meal. Never mind if he has left out some of his foods. The hunger will pile up and soon make him eat more. If you go on feeding him the last half of the meal, he may never take over the whole job. Just say, "I guess you've had enough." If he asks you to feed him some more, give him two or three more mouthfuls to be agreeable and then suggest casually that he's through.

After he has taken over completely for a couple of weeks, don't slip back into the habit of feeding him again. If some day he's very tired and says, "Feed me," give him a few spoonfuls absentmindedly, and then say something about his not being very hungry. I make this point because I know that a parent who has worried for months or years about a child's eating, who spoon-fed him much too long, and finally let him feed himself, has a great temptation to go back to feeding him again the first time he loses his appetite or the first time he is sick. Then the job has to be done all over again.

669. Should the parents stay in the room while he is eating? This depends on what the child is used to and wants, and how well the parents can control their worry. If they have always sat there, they can't suddenly disappear without upsetting him. If they can be sociable, relaxed, and get their minds off the food, it's fine for them to stay (whether or not they are eating their own meal). If they find that even with practice they can't get their minds off the child's eating, or stop urging him, it may be better for them to retire from the picture at mealtime; not crossly, not suddenly, but tactfully and gradually, a little more each day, so that he doesn't notice the change.

670. No acts or bribes. Certainly the parents shouldn't put on acts to bribe the child to eat, such as a little story for every mouthful or a promise to stand on their heads if the spinach is finished. All this kind of persuasion seems at the moment to be making the child eat a few more mouthfuls. But in the long run it takes his appetite away more and more. The parents have to keep raising the bribe to get the same result. They end up putting on an hour's exhausting vaudeville for five mouthfuls.

Don't ask a child to eat to earn his dessert, or a piece of candy, or a gold star, or any other prize. Don't ask him to eat for Aunt Minnie, or to make his mother or father happy, or to grow big and strong, or to keep from getting sick, or to clean his plate. Let's state the rule more briefly: Don't ask a child to eat.

There is no great harm in a parent's telling a story at suppertime, or playing the radio if that has been the custom, so long as it is not connected in any way with whether the child is eating or not.

671. It isn't necessary to be a doormat. I have said so much about letting a child eat because he wants to that I may have given the wrong impression to some parents. I remember a mother who had been snarled up for years in a feeding problem involving her 7-year-old daughter, urging, arguing, forcing. When she understood the idea that the child probably had, underneath, a normal appetite and a desire for a well-balanced diet, and that the best way to revive it was to stop battling over meals, she swung to the opposite extreme and became apologetic. The daughter by this age had a lot of resentment in her from the long struggle. As soon as she realized that her mother was all meekness, she took advantage of her. She would pour the whole sugar bowl on her cereal, watching out of the corner of her eye to see her mother's silent horror. The mother would ask her before each meal what she wanted. If the child said, "Hamburger," she obediently bought and served it. Then the child, as like as not, would say, "I don't want hamburger. I want frankfurters," and the mother would run over to the butcher's to get it.

There's a middle ground. It's reasonable for a child to be expected to come to meals on time, to be pleasant to other diners, to refrain from making unpleasant remarks about the food or declaring what she doesn't like, to eat with the table manners that are reasonable for her age. It's fine for the parents to take her preferences into account as much as is possible (considering the rest of the family) in planning meals, or to ask her occasionally what she would like, as a treat. But it's bad for her to get the idea that she's the only one to be considered. It's sensible and right for the parents to put a limit on sugar, candy, sodas, cakes, and the other less wholesome foods. All this can be done without argument as long as the parents act as if they know what they are doing.

672. Gagging. The child beyond the age of a year who can't tolerate anything but pureed food has usually been fed forcibly, or at least urged vigorously. It isn't so much that she can't stand lumps. What makes her gag is having them pushed into her. The parents of gagging children usually say, "It's a funny thing. She can swallow lumps all right if it's something she likes very much. She can even swallow big chunks of meat that she bites off the bone." There are three steps in curing a child who gags. The first is to encourage her to feed herself completely (Section 474). The second is to get her over her suspiciousness about foods in general (Sections 664–670). The third is to go unusually slowly in coarsening the consistency of her food. Let her go for weeks—or even months if necessary—on pureed foods, until she has lost all fear of eating and is really enjoying it. Don't even serve her meats, for instance, during this time if she cannot enjoy them finely ground.

In other words, go only as fast as the child can comfortably take it.

A few babies have such sensitive throats that they gag even on pureed foods. In some of these cases, the cause seems to be the pasty consistency of the food. Try diluting it a little with milk or water. Or try chopping vegetables and fruits fine without mashing them.

673. Anorexia and bulimia. These are problems that are seen almost exclusively in adolescent girls, but on rare occasions are found in adolescent boys. There has been a sudden, major increase in their occurrence in the United States during the past 5 years or so, probably connected with their having become a fad among large groups of teenagers.

Anorexia (the medical term is anorexia nervosa) is a progressive, usually rapid loss of weight due to severe, self-imposed dieting, and these girls will lose more than 25 percent of their body weight. They have a morbid fear of gaining any weight at all, exercise constantly, and are preoccupied with the obsession that they are dreadfully fat, even when everybody else sees them as thin to the point of emaciation.

Bulimia is a problem in which girls periodically gorge themselves on enormous amounts of food and then either vomit it all up in secret or take large amounts of laxatives in order to expel everything they have eaten. These girls tend not to lose weight, but rather stay at the same weight all the time instead of gaining weight normally.

Parents—and sometimes doctors—may argue, bargain, bribe, and threaten, in a desperate attempt to get the girl with anorexia to eat and the one with bulimia to stop vomiting and taking laxatives; none of these methods works.

Both anorexia and bulimia are serious illnesses which can be life threatening and which represent major emotional disorders involving both the adolescent and the parents. A children's psychiatrist should be consulted as soon as there is any suspicion of one of these problems, even if you have to travel many miles to see one.

FAT CHILDREN

674. The treatment depends on the cause. Many people think the cause is gland trouble, but actually this is rarely the case, especially if the child's height is within the normal range. There are several factors that make for overweight, including heredity, temperament, appetite, happiness. If children come from a stocky line on both sides of the family, there is a greater chance of their being overweight. The placid child who takes little exercise has more food calories left over to store in the form of fat. The most important factor of all is appetite. The child who has a tremendous appetite that runs to rich foods like cake, cookies, and pastry is naturally going to be heavier than the child whose taste runs principally to vegetables and fruits and meats. But this only raises the question of why one child **does** crave large amounts of rich foods. We don't understand all the causes of this, but we recognize the children who seem to be born ("constitutionally") to be big eaters. They start with a huge appetite at birth and never lose it afterward, whether they're well or sick, calm or worried, whether the food they're offered is appetizing or not. They're fat by the time they're 2 or 3 months old and stay that way at least through childhood, so the time to begin dieting is right then, as soon as the tendency to overweight is evident. (See Section 138.)

675. Unhappiness is sometimes a factor. Of the excessive appetites that develop later in childhood, some at least are due to unhappiness. This happens, for instance, around the age of 7 in children who are somewhat unhappy and lonely. It is the period when children are drawing away from their close emotional dependence on their parents. If they don't have the knack of making equally close friendships with other children, they feel left out in the cold. Eating sweet and rich food seems to serve them as a partial substitute. Worries about schoolwork or other matters sometimes make children seek comfort in overeating, too. Overweight often develops during the puberty stage of development. The appetite normally increases at this time to take care of the increased rate of growth, but it's probable that loneliness plays a part in some cases, too. It is the period when children may become more turned-in and self-conscious because of all the changes they are experiencing, and this may lessen their ability to get along enjoyably with their fellows.

Obesity may become a vicious circle, no matter which factor caused it in the beginning. The fatter the child, the harder it is for her to enjoy exercise and games. And the quieter she is, the more energy her body has to store as fat. It's a vicious circle in another way, too. The fat child who can't comfortably enter into games may come to feel more of an outsider, and is liable to be kidded and ridiculed.

Fatness is complicated.

Obesity is a most serious problem for any child. Since it's apt to become a vicious circle, it should be combatted as soon as it appears. If a baby is becoming unusually plump during the first year, this shouldn't be considered cute. It should be treated with dietary shifts right away. Often it's possible to satisfy such a child fairly well with a lot of protein, vegetables, fruits, and to hold way down on starches and fats.

676. Mild overweight is common between 7 and 12. But I don't want to leave the impression that every child who turns plump is unhappy. There seems to be a normal tendency for many children, including the cheerful and successful ones, to put on extra weight in the 7- to 12-year-old period. Very few of these become excessively obese. They are just slightly overpadded. Most of them stay plump during the 2 years of very rapid puberty development and then slender down as they get further into adolescence. Many girls, for instance, become slimmer around 15 years of age without great effort. It's good for parents to know that this mild school-age obesity is common and that it often goes away later, so that they won't make too much of an issue about it.

677. Dieting is difficult. What is there to do about fat children? Right away you would say, "Diet them." It sounds easy, but it isn't. Think of the grown-ups you know who are unhappy because of their weight and who still aren't able to stick to a diet. A child has less willpower than an adult. If the parents serve the child the less fattening foods, it means either that the whole family must go without the richer dishes or that the fat child must be kept from eating the very things that child's heart craves most while the rest of the family enjoys them. There are very few fat children reasonable enough to think that that's fair. The feeling of being treated unfairly may further increase the craving for sweets. Whatever is accomplished in the dining room may be undone at the refrigerator or candy store between meals.

But the prospects of dieting are not so dismal as I have made out. Tactful parents can do a good deal to keep temptation away from their fat child without making an issue of it. They can eliminate rich desserts. They can stop having cakes and cookies around in the kitchen, and provide fresh fruit for between-meals nibbling. They can serve frequently the less fattening foods that are the child's favorites. A child who shows any willingness to cooperate in diet should certainly be encouraged to visit the doctor, preferably alone. Talking to the doctor, person to person, may give children the feeling of running their own life like a grown-up. Anyone can take dietary advice better from an outsider. Children should never take any medicine for reducing without a doctor's recommendation, and unless they can return at **regular** intervals for checkups.

Since overeating is often a symptom of loneliness or maladjustment, the most constructive thing is to make sure that the child's home life, schoolwork, and social life are as happy and satisfying as possible (Section 607).

If, despite your efforts to help, the obesity is more than mild or if the child is gaining weight too rapidly, you should certainly get medical and psychiatric assistance. Obesity is a serious problem for any child.

678. Dieting should be supervised by a doctor. Self-dieting sometimes becomes a problem and a danger in the adolescent period. A group of girls excitedly work themselves up to going on some wild diet that they have heard about. Within a few days, hunger makes most of them break their resolutions, but one or two may persist with fanatical zeal. Occasionally a girl loses alarming amounts of weight and can't resume a normal diet even when she wants to. (See Section 673 on anorexia nervosa.) The group hysteria about dieting seems to have awakened in her a deep revulsion against food, which is usually a hangover from some unsolved worry of early childhood. Another girl in the early stages of puberty declares hectically, "I'm getting **much** too fat," even though she is so slender that her ribs are showing. She may be emotionally unready to grow up and secretly disturbed by the development of her breasts. The child who becomes obsessed with dieting should have the help of a children's psychiatrist.

If dieting is being considered, the first step, for a number of reasons, is to consult a doctor. First, to determine whether dieting is necessary or wise. Second, adolescents are more apt to accept the doctor's advice than that of their parents. If it is agreed that diet is wise, it should certainly be prescribed by the doctor who will take into account the child's food tastes, the family's usual menus, in order to work out a diet that is not only sound nutritionally but practical in that particular home. Finally, since weight loss puts some strain on health, anyone who is planning to reduce should be examined at regular intervals to make sure that the rate is not too fast and that the dieter remains strong and healthy.

If it is not possible to have the supervision of a doctor, the parents should insist that children who have the bit in their teeth must take at least the following foods daily: a pint of skimmed milk, meat or poultry or fish, a green or yellow vegetable, fruit twice, and 3–4 eggs a week. Children can be assured that these foods in reasonable servings do not cause weight gain and that they are essential to prevent the muscles, bones, and organs of the body from being dangerously depleted.

Rich desserts can be omitted without risk, and should be, by anyone who is obese and trying to reduce. The amount of plain, starchy foods (cereals, breads, potatoes) taken is what determines, in the case of most people, how much they gain or lose. Any growing child needs **some,** even when trying to lose weight. It is not wise for even a fat person to lose more than a pound a week, unless a doctor is carefully supervising.

GLANDS

679. Glandular disturbances. There are several definite glandular diseases, and there are a few glandular medicines that have a definite effect on human beings. For example, when the thyroid gland is not secreting sufficiently, a child's physical growth and mental development are definitely slowed down. She is sluggish, has a dry skin, coarse hair, and a low voice. Her face may appear puffy. (Insufficient thyroid secretion may also cause obesity.) Her basal metabolism, which means the rate at which her body burns fuel when resting, is below normal. The proper dose of thyroid medication brings about remarkable improvement.

Some people who have read popular articles on glands assume that every short person, every slow pupil, every nervous girl, every fat boy with small genitals, has merely a glandular problem which can be cured by the proper tablet or injection. This enthusiasm is not justified by what is known scientifically at the present time. It takes more than one symptom to make a glandular disease. A child whose height is within the normal range is unlikely to have a glandular disease.

In many cases when a boy is heavy during the years before puberty development, his penis **appears** smaller than it really is because his plump thighs are so large in comparison and because the layer of fat at the base of his penis may hide three-quarters of its length. Most of these boys have a normal sexual development in puberty, and many of them lose their excess weight at that time. (See Sections 573 and 680 on the harm of worrying a boy about his genitals.)

Certainly every child who is not growing at the usual rate or in the usual shape, or who appears dull or nervous or out of line in any other way, should be examined by a competent physician. But if the doctor finds that the child's stature is only her inborn constitutional pattern, or that her mental state is due to real troubles in her daily life, then what she needs is assistance in her adjustment to life, not a further search for magic.

UNDESCENDED TESTICLES

680. Undescended testicles. In a certain number of newborn boys, one or both testicles are not in the scrotum (the pouch in which the testicles normally lie) but are farther up in the groin or inside the abdomen. Many of these undescended testicles come down into the scrotum soon after birth. There are other testicles which appear, on casual examination, not to have descended, but which are actually down. They are only more lively than the average in retreating back into the abdomen.

The testicles are originally formed inside the abdomen and move down into the scrotum only shortly before birth. There are muscles attached to the testicles that can jerk them back up into the groin, or even back into the abdomen. This is to protect the testicles from injury when this region of the body is struck or scratched. There are lots of boys whose testicles withdraw on slight provocation. Even chilling of the skin from being undressed may be enough to make them disappear into the abdomen. Handling the scrotum in an examination frequently makes them disappear. Therefore, a parent shouldn't decide that the testicles are undescended just because they are not usually in sight. A good time to look for them is when the boy is in a hot bath, without handling his body.

Testicles that have been seen at any time in the scrotum, even if only rarely, need no treatment because they will surely settle down in the scrotum by the time puberty development is under way.

Sometimes just one testicle is definitely undescended. Though this may require treatment, there is no cause for great concern because one testicle is sufficient to make a boy develop properly and become a father, even in the case in which the other one doesn't appear later.

If one or both testicles have never been seen in the scrotum by the time a boy is 2 years old, he should be examined by a competent pediatric surgeon. If one or both are found to be truly undescended, they should be brought down by operation at this time, to avoid damage to the testicle from remaining inside the warm body. The child can usually be brought to the hospital early in the morning and go home late on the same day. Testicles that stay in the abdomen during puberty development (which begins in the average boy at 12 years) will be sterile.

Meanwhile, it is wise to avoid unnecessarily frequent examinations and anxious looks as far as possible, for boys (and men) are easily worried about their genitals. However, any child over the age of 2 with undescended testicles will know that there is cause for concern and the situation should be explained in factual terms suitable for his age. He should be encouraged to ask questions of the parents and the doctor.

POSTURE

681. The treatment of bad posture depends on the cause. Good or bad posture is made up of a number of factors. One—perhaps the most important factor—is the skeleton the child is born with. You see individuals who have been round-shouldered from babyhood, like their mother or father before them. Some children seem to be born with a relaxed set of muscles and ligaments. They run to knock-knees no matter how much vitamin D you give them. Other children look tightly knit, in action or at rest. It's hard for them to slump. There are diseases that affect posture, such as rickets, polio, and tuberculosis of the bones. Chronic illness and chronic fatigue, from any cause, that keep children under par may make them slump and sag. Overweight sometimes produces swayback, knock-knees, and flat feet. Unusual tallness makes the self-conscious adolescent duck the head. A child with poor posture needs regular examinations to make sure that there is no physical reason.

Many children slouch because of lack of self-confidence. It may result from too much criticism at home, or from difficulties in school, or from an unsatisfactory social life. People who are buoyant and sure of themselves show it in the way they sit and stand and walk. When parents realize how much feelings have to do with posture, they can handle it more wisely.

The natural impulse of a parent, eager to have a child appear well, is to keep after posture: "Remember the shoulders," or "For goodness' sake, stand up straight." But children who are stooped over because their parents have always kept after them too much won't be improved by more nagging. Generally speaking, the best results come when the child receives posture work at school, or in a posture clinic, or in a doctor's office. In these places the atmosphere is more businesslike than at home. The parents may be able to help a boy greatly in carrying out his exercises at home, if he wants help and if they can give it in a friendly way. But the main job for them is to help the child's spirit by aiding his school adjustment, fostering a happy social life, and making him feel adequate and self-respecting at home.

Illness

FEVER

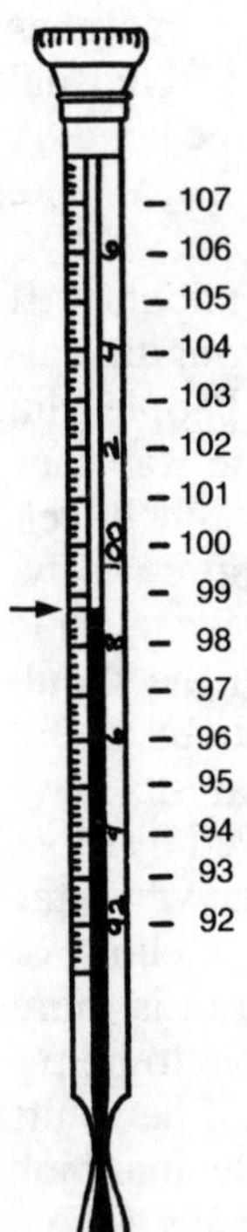

682. What's fever and what isn't? Taking the temperature is a bugaboo to many parents. They find a thermometer hard to read. They are confused by the difference between mouth, axillary (armpit), and rectal temperatures.

It might be easier for you to get someone else to show you how to read one, but here goes. Most thermometers are engraved the same. They have a long mark for each degree and a short mark for each two-tenths of a degree, that is 0.2, 0.4, 0.6, 0.8. Only the even degrees—94, 96, 98, 100, 102, 104—are numbered on the thermometer because of lack of space. There is an arrow pointing to the "normal" mark, 98.6 (ninety-eight point six). Many thermometers are marked in red above the normal point.

Reading the thermometer is very easy once you get the knack. Most thermometers are somewhat triangular in cross section, with one edge sharper than the rest. This sharp edge should point toward you. In this position the marks of the degrees are above and the numbers are below. Between them is the space in which the mercury shows. Roll the thermometer very slightly until you see the band of mercury. Don't worry too much over the fractions of degrees.

The first thing to realize is that a healthy child's body temperature doesn't stay fixed at 98.6°F. It is always going up and down a little, depending on the time of day and what the child is doing. It's usually lowest in the early morning and highest in the late afternoon. This change during the day is only a slight one, however. The change between rest and activity is greater. The temperature of perfectly healthy small children may be 99.6°F or even 100°F right after they have been running around. (On the other hand, a temperature of 101°F probably means illness whether the child has been exercising or not.) The older child's temperature is less affected by activity. All this means that if you want to know whether your child has a slight fever due to illness, you must take his temperature after he has been really quiet for an hour or more.

In most feverish illnesses the temperature is apt to be highest in the late afternoon and lowest in the morning. But there is nothing to be surprised at if a fever is high in the morning and low in the afternoon. There are a few diseases in which the fever, instead of climbing and falling, stays high steadily. The commonest of these are pneumonia and roseola infantum. A below-normal temperature (as low as 97°F) sometimes occurs at the end of an illness, and also in healthy babies and small children on winter nights. This is no cause for concern so long as the child is feeling well.

Now about the difference between mouth, axillary, and rectal temperatures. That of the rectum is highest because it is well inside the body where the body is thick. That of the mouth is lowest because the mouth is cooled by the air being breathed through the nose. There is usually less than one degree's difference in temperature between the rectum and the mouth. The temperature of the axilla is in between.

Many parents assume that the fever itself is bad and want to give medicine to bring it way down, no matter what degree it is. But it's well to remember that the fever is not the disease. The fever is one of the methods the body uses to help overcome the infection. It is also a help in keeping track of how the illness is progressing. In one case the doctor wants to bring the fever down because it is interfering with the child's sleep or exhausting the patient. In another case the doctor is quite willing to leave the fever alone, and concentrate on curing the infection.

683. The thermometer. The only difference between a mouth and a rectal thermometer is in the shape of the bulb. The bulb of the rectal thermometer is round so that it won't be so sharp. A mouth thermometer has a long slender bulb so that the mercury can be warmed more quickly by the mouth. The markings on the two thermometers are exactly the same and mean the same thing. (In other words, they are not marked differently to allow for the difference of temperature between the mouth and rectum.) You can use a clean rectal thermometer perfectly well in the mouth, and a mouth thermometer in the rectum, if inserted gently. One very popular thermometer has a bulb shape that is somewhere in between the round bulb of the rectal thermometer and the long bulb of the oral thermometer, making it convenient for using in either area.

Most thermometers register well enough in a minute in the rectum. If you watch a thermometer sometime when it is in a baby's rectum, you can see that it goes up very rapidly at first. It gets within a degree of where it is going to stop in the first 20 seconds. After that it barely creeps up. This means that if you are nervous taking the temperature of a struggling baby, you can take the thermometer out in less than a minute and have a rough idea what the temperature is.

It takes longer to register the correct temperature in the mouth—1½ to 2 minutes. This is because it takes the mouth a while to warm up after being open and because the bulb is partly surrounded by air. It takes 4 minutes to take an accurate axillary temperature but you can get a rough idea in a couple of minutes.

684. Taking the temperature. Before taking a temperature, shake the thermometer down. You hold the upper end of the thermometer (the opposite end from the bulb) firmly between

your thumb and finger. Now shake the thermometer vigorously, with a sharp, snapping motion. You want to drive the mercury at least as far as 97°F. If it doesn't go down, you aren't snapping hard enough. Until you get the hang of it, shake the thermometer over a bed or couch. Then if it slips out of your hand, it won't be broken. The bathroom is the worst place of all to shake a thermometer because of the hard surfaces.

If you are taking a rectal temperature, dip the bulb of the thermometer into petroleum jelly or cold cream. The best possible position for a baby is on the stomach across your knees. The child can't squirm out of this position very easily, and the legs hang down out of the way. Insert the thermometer gently into the rectum, an inch or less. Push it in with a light touch, letting the thermometer find its own direction. If you hold it stiffly, it may poke the baby inside. Once the thermometer is in, it is better to shift your grip off the end of the thermometer, because if the baby struggles, the twisting might hurt. Instead, lay the palm of your hand across the buttocks, lightly holding the thermometer between two of the fingers, the way it's shown in the illustration.

You can also take the rectal temperature with the child

lying on her side on the bed with her knees up a little. It is harder to find the rectum when the child is lying flat on her stomach. The worst position is with the child lying on her back. It is hard to get to her rectum, and her feet are in position to kick your hand accidentally or on purpose.

By the time the child is 1 year and older, it's psychologically preferable to take the temperature in the armpit (axilla). She is beginning to be aware of her body, her dignity, her security. She's apt to be bothered or even alarmed by having something poked into her rectum. You can get a satisfactory temperature by placing the bulb of the thermometer in her axilla and then holding her arm flat against her chest. There should be no clothes between the arm and the chest, of course, just the bulb of the thermometer. You can use a rectal or mouth thermometer in the axilla.

After the age of 5 or 6 a child can usually cooperate in keeping the thermometer bulb under the tongue and the lips closed. Then you can take the temperature by mouth or axilla, whichever is more convenient. It makes little difference if the temperature is 99.8° or 99.6°F. What the doctor will be interested in is **about** what the temperature is. When you report the temperature to the doctor, tell him what the thermometer actually says, and then add "by mouth," "by axilla," or "by rectum." I say this because sometimes a parent who has the mistaken idea that the mouth temperature is the only correct one takes a temperature by rectum, figures what the mouth temperature would be, and then tells the doctor that figure. Usually the best times to take the temperature are in the first part of the morning and late in the afternoon.

The next question is how many days to go on taking the temperature. Here is what happens occasionally. A child has a bad cold with fever. The doctor sees the child or gets reports regularly and has the parents take the temperature twice a day. Finally the fever is gone, the child is convalescing well, has only a mild cough and running nose. The doctor tells the parents to let the child outdoors as soon as the cold is gone completely. Two weeks later the parents telephone to say that they and the child are getting desperate staying indoors, that the running nose and cough have been completely gone for 10 days, that the child looks wonderful and eats well, but that the "fever" is still going to 99.6°F each afternoon. As I explained earlier, this is not necessarily a fever in an active child. The 10 days of staying indoors and worrying over the temperature have all been a waste and a mistake. When the temperature has stayed under 101°F for a couple of days, it's a good general rule to forget about the thermometer unless the doctor asks you to continue or unless the child seems sicker in any way. Children should be kept home from school until the temperature is normal for 24 hours and they are definitely feeling better, though all cold symptoms don't have to be gone. Don't get in the habit of taking the temperature when a child is well.

685. Emergency treatment of high fever. Between the ages of 1 and 5 years, children may develop fever as high as 104°F (sometimes even higher) with the onset of mild infections such as colds, sore throats, flu, just as often as with serious infections. On the other hand, a dangerous illness may never bring a temperature higher than 101°F. So don't be influenced too much, one way or the other, by the height of the fever, but get in touch with the doctor when your child looks sick or different.

If on the first day of an illness a child's temperature is 104°F or higher, and if it will be an hour or more before you can speak to the doctor, even on the telephone, it's wise, as an emergency measure, to bring the fever down a little with a wet rub and aspirin—1 tablet of "baby" aspirin (1¼ grains) under a year; 2 baby tablets (2½ grains) between 1 and 5 years; 3 baby tablets (3¾ grains) for a 6- to 12-year-old. (Be sure to keep aspirin out of your child's reach and in a childproof container.) Many doctors now recommend that a non-aspirin medicine (acetaminophen) be given for fever. Like aspirin, it comes in both solid and liquid forms and the dosage is the same as for aspirin. The medicine to bring the fever down should be given one time only, unless you still haven't reached the doctor after 3 to 4 hours, in which case you can give a second dose.

The purpose of the wet rub is to bring the blood to the surface by rubbing and to cool it by the evaporation of the water off the skin. (Alcohol has traditionally been used in a wet rub, but if it is applied very freely in a small room, too much may be inhaled. Anyway, water is just as good even if it doesn't smell so important.)

Undress the child and cover him with only a sheet or light blanket. Wet your hand in a basin of lukewarm water. Expose one of his arms and rub it gently for a couple of minutes, wetting it again any time it becomes too dry. Then put it back under the sheet. Proceed, in turn, to the other arm, each leg, the chest, the back. Take the temperature again in half an hour, and if it isn't under 104°F give the child cold fluids by mouth and place him in a tepid bath for 15 minutes or so. You prefer to keep the temperature under 104°F until the doctor comes because a small child who develops a sudden high fever the first day of an illness may become trembly or even have a convulsion (Section 785). When a child's fever is very high and he is flushed, use only light covers at ordinary room temperature, perhaps as little as a sheet. You can't get his temperature down very well if he's heavily covered.

GIVING MEDICINES AND ENEMAS

686. Giving medicine. It's sometimes quite a trick getting a child to take medicine. The first rule is to slip it into her in a matter-of-fact way, as if it has never occurred to you that she won't take it. If you go at it apologetically, with a lot of explanation, you convince her that she's expected to dislike it. Be talking about something else when you put the spoon into her mouth. Most young children open their mouths automatically, like birds in their nest.

Tablets that don't dissolve can be crushed to a fine powder and mixed with a coarse, good-tasting food like applesauce. Mix the medicine with only 1 teaspoonful of the applesauce, in case she decides she doesn't want very much. Bitter pills can be mixed in a teaspoonful of sugar and water, or honey, or maple syrup, or jam. Eye ointments and drops can sometimes be applied during sleep. They can also be given to a small child by placing him on your lap, his legs around your waist and out of kicking use, his head gently but firmly restrained between your knees and held with one hand while the medicine is put in with your other hand. (This position is also good for suctioning the nose or inserting nosedrops.)

When giving medicine in a drink, it's safer to choose an unusual fluid that the child does not take regularly, such as grape juice or prune juice. If you give a queer taste to milk or orange juice, you may make the child suspicious of it for months.

Getting a small child to swallow a whole tablet or a capsule is difficult. Try putting it in something lumpy and sticky like banana and follow the teaspoonful quickly with a drink of something she likes.

687. Don't give medicine without a doctor's advice and don't continue it without keeping in touch with that doctor. Here are some examples of why not. A child has a cough with a cold, and the doctor prescribes a certain cough medicine. Two months later the child develops a new cough, and the parents have the prescription renewed without consulting the doctor. It seems to help for a week, but then the cough becomes so bad they have to call the doctor anyway. The doctor realizes right away that the disease this time is not a cold but whooping cough, and would have suspected it a week before if the parents had called. In that case the child could have been isolated immediately and would not have exposed unnecessarily a lot of other children.

Parents who have treated colds or headaches or stomachaches a few times in the same way come to feel like experts, which they are in a limited way. But they're not trained, as a doctor is, to first consider carefully what the diagnosis is. To them, two different headaches (or two stomachaches) seem about the same. To the doctor, one has an entirely different meaning from the other and calls for different treatment. People who have been treated by a doctor with one of the antibiotics (such as penicillin) are sometimes tempted to use it again for similar symptoms. They figure that it produces wonderful results, is easy to take, and they know the dosage from the last time—so why not?

Serious reactions occasionally develop from the use of these drugs—fevers, rashes, anemia. These complications, fortunately, are rare, but they are more liable to occur the more often the drugs are used, especially if they are used improperly. That is why they should be given only when a doctor has decided that the danger from the disease and the likelihood of benefit from the medicine outweigh the risks of treatment. Even the continued use of as common a drug as aspirin can occasionally cause serious trouble. For the same reasons, you should never give the neighbor's, friend's, or relative's medicine to a child.

Cathartics (drugs to make the bowels move) should not be used for any reason—especially not for stomachache—without consulting a doctor. Some people have the mistaken idea that stomachache is frequently caused by constipation, and want to give a cathartic first of all. There are many causes of stomachache (Sections 773–775). Some, such as appendicitis and obstruction of the intestines, are made worse by a cathartic. Therefore, since you don't know for sure what is causing your child's stomachache, it is dangerous to give a cathartic.

688. Enemas, suppositories, and cathartics used to be prescribed often by physicians or simply used by parents without waiting for advice. It was assumed—without any scientific evidence—that constipation played an important part in causing illnesses, and that cure couldn't come about until the bowels were cleaned out. (When I was a child our pediatrician, making a house call for illness, always started his list of recommendations with castor oil, which I always promptly vomited.) Now, fortunately, we've outgrown that obsession. But, **rarely,** these treatments are still used, for example, a suppository for a small child afraid to push out a large, hard BM, a cathartic in preparation for certain abdominal X-rays.

Never give your child an enema, suppository, or cathartic unless your doctor has advised it.

A suppository for constipation is slipped all the way into the rectum, where it dissolves. It contains a mildly irritating material, which draws moisture into the rectum and encourages a movement.

The doctor will tell you what to put in an enema. A soapy enema is made by stirring a piece of mild facial soap in the water until it is slightly milky. This is a little irritating and is less often given to an infant. Enemas can also be made with a half teaspoonful of table salt, or a teaspoonful of bicarbonate of soda, added to an 8-ounce cup of water. The water should be at about body temperature. You can give 4 ounces to a small infant, 8 ounces to a 1-year-old, a pint to a 5-year-old.

Place a waterproof sheet on a bed and lay a bath towel over it. Have the child lie on this on the side with the legs pulled up. Have a potty close at hand.

For an infant or small child, it is easiest and safest to use a rubber ear syringe with a soft tip of the same material. Fill the bulb completely, so that you won't be injecting air. Grease the tip with petroleum jelly, cold cream, or soap; gently insert it an inch or two. Squeeze the bulb slowly and not too forcibly. The slower you put it in, the less liable it is to make the baby feel uncomfortable and expel it. The bowel contracts and relaxes in waves. If you feel a strong resistance, wait until it "gives" rather than push harder. Unfortunately, babies are apt to push as soon as they feel something in the anus, so you may not get much in.

As you pull the tip out, press the buttocks together to try to hold the water in a few minutes to do its job of softening the movement. If the water has not come out in 15 or 20 minutes, or if it has come out without much movement, you can repeat the enema. There is no danger from an enema's staying in.

With an older child who will cooperate, you can use a syringe or enema bag or enema can with a rubber tube and a small, hard-rubber tip. Don't hang the bag higher than 1 to 2 feet above the level of the rectum (the height determines the pressure). The lowest height that makes the water run in slowly causes the least discomfort and brings the best results.

689. Generic prescriptions. A generic prescription is one which doesn't use the trade name for a medicine, but uses the chemical name instead. In most cases, medicines prescribed in this way are cheaper than if they are prescribed by the advertised trade name, even though it's exactly the same medicine. You should ask your doctor about receiving generic prescriptions.

HANDLING A CHILD WITH AN ILLNESS

690. Spoiling is easy. When children are really sick, you give them lots of special care and consideration, not only for practical medical reasons but also because you feel sorry for them. You don't mind preparing drinks and foods for them at frequent intervals or even putting aside a drink they refuse and making another kind right away. You are glad to get them new playthings to keep them happy and quiet. You ask them often how they feel, in a solicitous manner.

Children quickly adjust to this new position in the household. If they have a disease that makes them cranky, they may be calling and bossing a parent like old tyrants.

Fortunately, at least 90 percent of children's illnesses are on the way to recovery within a few days. As soon as the parents stop worrying, they stop kowtowing to the child who is unreasonable. After a couple of days of minor clashes, everyone is back to normal.

But if children develop a long illness or one that threatens to come back, and if a parent has a tendency to be a worrier, the continued atmosphere of overconcern may have a bad effect on their spirits. They absorb some of the anxiousness of those around them. They're apt to be demanding. If they're too polite for that, they may just become excitable and temperamental, like spoiled actors. It's easy for them to learn to enjoy being sick and receiving pity. Some of their ability to make their own way agreeably may grow weaker, like a muscle that isn't being used.

691. Keep them busy and polite. So it's wise for parents to encourage themselves to get back into normal balance with the sick child as soon as possible. This means such little things as having a friendly, matter-of-fact expression when entering the room rather than a worried one; asking them how they feel today in a tone of voice that expects good news rather than bad (and perhaps asking only once a day). When you find out by experience what they feel like drinking and eating, serve it up casually. Don't ask timidly if they like it or act as if they were wonderful to take a little. Keep strictly away from

A child is allowed up when she feels well enough, with rare exceptions.

urging unless the doctor feels it is necessary. A sick child's appetite is more quickly ruined by pushing and forcing than a well child's.

If you are buying new playthings, look particularly for the ones that make children do all the work and give them a chance to use their imagination (blocks, sets for building, sewing, weaving, bead-stringing, painting, modeling, stamp collecting). These make demands on them and occupy them for long periods, whereas toys that are merely beautiful possessions quickly pall and only whet the appetite for more presents. Deal out one new plaything at a time. There are lots of homemade occupations, like cutting pictures out of old magazines, making a scrapbook, sewing, whittling, building a farm or town or doll's house of cardboard and masking tape or rubber cement.

If children are going to be laid up for a long time, but are well enough, get a teacher or a tutor or the best teacher in the family to start them on their schoolwork again for a regular period each day, just as soon as possible.

If they're human, they want company part of the time, and

you can join in some of their occupations or read to them. But if they want more and more attention, try to avoid arguments and bargaining. Have regular times when they can count on your being with them and others when they know you are going to be busy elsewhere. If they have a disease that isn't catching and the doctor lets them have company, invite other children in regularly to play and for meals.

The hardest part can be when the child is over her illness but not yet fully back to her old self. You have to use your best judgment about how much special consideration she still needs. It all adds up to letting children lead just as normal a life as is possible under the circumstances, expecting reasonable behavior toward the rest of the family, and avoiding worried talk, looks, and thoughts.

GOING TO THE HOSPITAL

692. How to help the child. There's no perfect way to handle the business of taking a child to a hospital. There's usually some disease or risk that worries the parents.

Between the ages of 1 and 4 years, the child is most worried about being separated from the parents. He feels as if he is losing them forever when they first leave him and at the end of each hospital visit. Between visits he may remain anxious and depressed. When the parents come to see him, he may silently reproach them by refusing to greet them at first.

After the age of 4 the child is apt to be more fearful about what's going to be done to him, the injury to his body, and the pain. It won't do for the parents to promise that the hospital will be a bed of roses, because if unpleasant things happen, the child loses confidence in his parents. On the other hand, if he is told **everything** bad that might happen, he is apt to suffer more in anticipation than he will when he is there.

The most important thing is for the parents to show all the calm, matter-of-fact confidence they are capable of, without forcing it so much that it sounds false. Unless the child has been a hospital patient before, he tries anxiously to imagine what it will be like, perhaps fearing the worst. The parents can set his mind at rest better by describing hospital life in general than by arguing with him whether it's going to hurt a lot or a little. You can tell him how the nurse will wake him in the morning and give him a bath right in bed, how the meals will come on trays and be eaten in his own bed, how there will be time to play, how he may use the bedpan or urinal instead of the bathroom, how he can tell the nurse if he needs something. You can tell him about visiting times and about all the other children to keep him company in the ward.

If he's going to be in a private room, you can talk about what favorite toys and books he's going to bring, and about renting a TV set with remote control, or whether there is a small radio to take from home or to borrow. He'll be interested in the electric button for calling the nurse.

It's fair to dwell on these everyday, pleasanter aspects of hospital life because even at the worst, the child will spend most of his time amusing himself. I wouldn't keep away from the medical program altogether, but let the child see that it's a small part of hospital life.

If he's going to have his tonsils out, you can tell him about the mask they will put on his nose, and how he will breathe and breathe until he goes into a special kind of sleep that will keep him from feeling any pain during surgery; how he will wake up in an hour and find that his throat is sore (the way it was last winter when he had tonsillitis); that you will be there when he wakes up (if that is true), or that you will come to get him the next day.

The Association for the Care of Children's Health, 3615 Wisconsin Avenue N.W., Washington, DC. 20016, (202)244-1801, is an international association of professionals who work with children in various health settings. There are also parent members. This group has a large number of books and pamphlets which are available to help parents help sick children (and their brothers and sisters) when it becomes necessary to go to the hospital. The books and booklets are low in cost and the pamphlets are free. If you have a children's hospital near you, they can tell you whether or not there is an affiliate branch of the Association in your area.

Many children's hospitals now have hospital preview programs for children whose hospitalization is planned ahead of time. The child and parents can come to the hospital a few days before the actual admission and see various parts of the hospital and have their questions answered. In many hospital preview programs, slide shows and puppet shows are used to explain ahead of time what the hospital experience is going to be like.

693. Let them tell you their worries. More important than telling your child what occurs to you, is giving him chances to ask questions and tell you what he imagines. Young children view these things in ways that never occur to adults. In the first place, they often think they have to be operated on or taken to the hospital because they have been bad—because they haven't worn their rubbers or haven't stayed in bed when sick or have been angry with other members of the family. They may imagine that their necks have to be cut open to remove their tonsils or their noses removed to get to the adenoids. Because of their worries and misunderstandings about the physical differences between boys and girls, children—particularly between 3 and 6—often fear subconsciously that an additional operation may be performed on the genitals, especially if they feel guilty about masturbation. So make it easy for your child to raise questions, be ready for strange fears, and try to reassure him about these.

694. Let them know ahead of time. If you know days or weeks ahead of time that a child will be hospitalized, it brings up the question of when to tell him. If there is no chance of his finding out, I think it is kinder to wait to tell a small child until a few days before it's time to leave. It won't do him any good to worry for weeks. It may be fairer to tell a 7-year-old some weeks ahead if he's the kind who can face things reasonably, especially if he has some suspicions. Certainly don't lie to a child of any age if he asks questions, and never lure a child to a hospital pretending it's something else.

If your child is going to have an operation and you have a choice in the arrangements, you can discuss the matter of anesthetists and anesthesia with the doctor. How a child accepts the anesthesia is apt to make the biggest difference in whether he is emotionally upset by an operation or whether he goes through it with flying colors. Often in a hospital there is one or another anesthetist who is particularly good at ensuring confidence in children and getting them under without fright. It is worth a great deal to obtain the services of such an anesthetist if you have a choice. In some cases, there is also a choice in the kind of anesthetic that the doctor is considering, and this also makes a difference to the child psychologically. Generally speaking, it is less frightening to the child to start with gas than to start with ether, which is uncomfortable to breathe. The type of anesthetic that is given by a small enema (into the rectum)—even before the child starts for the operating room—is least likely to frighten him, but is not suitable medically in all cases. Naturally, the doctor is the one who knows the factors and has to make the decision. It's when the doctor feels that there is an equal choice medically that the psychological factor should be considered carefully. You shouldn't use the expression "Put to sleep" when you explain the anesthesia to a child. That can lead to a child's developing sleep problems after surgery. Instead, explain that the anesthesia causes a special kind of sleep, from which the anesthetist will awaken the child as soon as the operation is over.

695. Visiting. The parent should stay in the hospital with a child between the ages of 1 and 5 years if at all possible, especially in the daytime. At least, a parent should visit daily. Many hospitals now have rooming-in facilities so that a parent or other adult well known to a child can stay overnight in the child's room.

Visits create difficulties with the small child. The sight of the parents reminds him how much he has missed them. He may cry heartbreakingly when they leave or even cry through the entire visiting period. The parents are apt to get the impression that he is miserable there all the time. Actually, young children adjust surprisingly well to hospital life when the parents are out of sight, even though they are feeling sick or having uncomfortable treatments. I don't mean that the parents should stay away. The child is getting security from realizing that parents always do come back when they leave. The best the parents can do is to act as cheerful and unworried as possible. If the parents have an anguished expression, it makes the child more anxious.

The chance that a child will be emotionally upset by an operation is greatest in the first 5 years of life. This is a reason for postponing an operation if the doctor feels that there is no particular hurry, especially if the child is already dependent or worrisome or subject to nightmares.

DIET DURING ILLNESS

Diet during diarrhea is discussed in Section 362.

696. Diet for a cold without fever. Your doctor will tell you what diet to use in each of your child's illnesses, taking into account the nature of the disease and the child's taste. What follows are some general principles to guide you in emergencies when you are unable to get medical help.

The diet during a cold without fever can be entirely normal. However, children may lose some appetite even with a mild cold because they're indoors, because they're not taking the usual amount of exercise, because they're a little uncomfortable, and because they're swallowing mucus. Don't urge them to take more than they want. If they're eating less than usual, offer them extra fluids between meals. There is no harm letting children drink all that they feel like drinking. People sometimes have the idea that the more fluid, the better the treatment. Excessive amounts of fluid don't do any more good than reasonable amounts.

697. Diet during fever (emergency advice until you can consult the doctor). When children have fever above 102°F with a cold, flu, sore throat, or one of the contagious diseases, they usually lose most of their appetite in the beginning, especially for solids. In the first day or two of such a fever, don't offer them solid food at all, but offer fluids every half hour or hour when they're awake. Orange juice, pineapple juice, and water are most popular. Don't forget water. It has no nourishment, but that's unimportant for the time being. It's for this very reason that it often appeals to the sick child most. Other fluids depend on the child's taste and the illness. Some children love grapefruit juice, lemonade, pear juice, grape juice, weak tea with sugar. Popsicles are a source of fluid. Older children like carbonated drinks, like ginger ale, fruit-flavored sodas, and the cola drinks. Some cola drinks contain small amounts of caffeine, a stimulant, so should preferably not be given within a couple of hours before sleep time.

Milk is hard to make a rule about. Sick babies usually take more milk than anything else. If they take it without vomiting, it is the right thing. The older child may reject or vomit it. Offer it if it is desired and held down.

When a fever continues, a child is apt to have a little more appetite after the first day or two. If your child is hungry in spite of a high fever, she may be able to take simple solids like toast, crackers, cereal, custard, gelatin, junket, applesauce, soft-boiled egg.

The foods that are usually not wanted and not well digested during fever are vegetables (cooked or raw), meats, poultry, fish, fats (such as butter, margarine, cream). However, Dr. Clara Davis in her experiments on diet found that children often crave meats and vegetables during **convalescence**—after the fever is gone—and digest them well.

One rule more important than any other is not to urge a sick child to eat anything that she doesn't want unless the doctor has a special reason for urging it. It's only too likely to be vomited, or to cause an intestinal upset, or to start a feeding problem.

698. Diet when there is vomiting (emergency advice until you can consult the doctor). Of course, vomiting occurs in many different diseases, especially at the beginning when there is fever. It occurs because the stomach is upset by the disease and is not able to handle the food. The diet depends on many factors and should be prescribed by the doctor. However, if you cannot reach the doctor immediately, you can follow these suggestions.

It's a good idea to give the stomach a complete rest for at least a couple of hours after vomiting. Then **if the child is asking for it,** give a sip of water, not more than half an ounce at first. If this stays down and she begs for more, let her have a little more, say 1 ounce in 15 or 20 minutes. Increase gradually up to 4 ounces (half a glass) if she craves it. If she has gone this far all right, you can try a little orange juice or pineapple juice or a carbonated drink. It is better not to go beyond 4 ounces at a time the first day. If several hours have gone by since the vomiting and the child is begging for solid foods, give something simple like a cracker, or a tablespoonful of applesauce. If she is asking for milk, give skimmed milk.

The vomiting that goes with a feverish illness is most apt to occur on the first day and may not continue even if the fever goes on.

Small specks or streaks of blood sometimes show in the vomited material when a child is retching violently. This is not serious in itself.

699. Avoiding feeding problems at the end of illness. If a child has a fever for several days and wants little to eat, she naturally loses weight rapidly. This worries parents the first time or two that it happens. When the fever is finally gone and the doctor says it's all right to begin working back to a regular diet, they are impatient to feed the child up again. But it often happens that the child turns away from the foods that are first offered. If the parents urge, meal after meal and day after day, the child's appetite may never pick up.

Such a child has not forgotten how to eat or become too weak to eat. At the time the temperature went back to normal there was still enough infection in the body to affect the stomach and intestines. Just as soon as she saw those first foods, her digestive system warned her that it was not ready for them yet.

When food is pushed or forced onto a child who already feels nauseated because of illness, her disgust is built up more easily and rapidly than if she had a normal appetite to start with. She can acquire a long-lasting feeding problem in a few days' time.

Just as soon as the stomach and intestines have recovered from the effects of most illnesses and are in condition to digest food again, children's hunger comes back with a bang—and not just to what it used to be. They usually are ravenous for a week or two in order to make up for lost time. You sometimes see such children whimpering for more, 2 hours after a large meal. By the age of 3, they may demand the specific foods that their starved system craves most.

The parents' course at the end of illness is to offer children only the drinks and solids they want, without any urging, and to wait patiently, but confidently, for signals that they are ready for more. If their appetite has not recovered in a week, the doctor should be consulted again.

COLDS

700. The cold virus, and the germs that make complications. Your child will probably be sick with colds ten times as much as with all other illnesses combined. We only partly understand colds at the present time. Most colds are started by a "filtrable virus." This is a germ so small that it can pass (filter) through unglazed porcelain, so small that it cannot be seen through an ordinary microscope. It is believed that the virus can cause only a mild cold with a clear nasal discharge and perhaps a light scratchy feeling in the throat. If nothing else happens, the virus cold goes away in about 3–10 days. But something else often does happen. The cold virus lowers the resistance of the nose and throat, so that other germs that cause more trouble get going, bacteria that can be seen under the microscope, such as the streptococcus, the pneumococcus, and the influenza bacillus. In these circumstances they are called secondary invaders. (In other situations, they may start infections all by themselves.) These regular bacteria are often living in healthy people's throats during the winter and spring months, but do no harm because they are held at bay by the body's resistance. It's only after the cold virus has lowered the resistance that these other germs get their chance to multiply and spread, causing bronchitis, pneumonia, ear infections, and sinusitis.

The best thing that you can do to avoid a cold is to keep away from anyone who has one.

701. Resistance to colds. Many people believe that they are more susceptible to colds when tired or chilled, but this has never been proved. People are less apt to be chilled if they have built up their resistance by regularly going out in cold weather. A bank clerk is more easily chilled when he gets outdoors than a lumberjack. That is why children of all ages should be outdoors several hours a day in winter. It's also the reason they shouldn't be overdressed outdoors or too heavily covered in bed.

Houses and apartments that are kept too hot and dry during the winter season parch the nose and throat, and this may lower resistance to germs. The air in a room that's 75°F is excessively dry. Many people try to moisten the air by putting pans of water on the radiators, but this method is almost completely worthless. The right way to keep enough moisture in the air in winter is to keep the room temperature down to 70°F or below (68°F is a good figure to aim at); then you won't need to worry about the humidity. Buy a reliable indoor thermometer. (See if it corresponds with several of the best thermometers your dealer has—an inexpensive one may be as much as 4 degrees off, which makes it useless.) Then train yourself to glance at the thermometer several times a day. Turn the heat off every time the temperature goes above 68°F. It will seem like a chore at first, but after living for a few weeks in a temperature below 70°F, you will be trained to it and will feel uncomfortable in a hotter room. If you can't control the steam heat, you can use a cold-mist humidifier to keep the air moist.

What is the effect of diet on resistance to colds? Naturally, every child should be offered a well-balanced diet. But there is no proof that a child who is already receiving a reasonable variety will have fewer colds if given a little more of one kind of food or less of another.

What about vitamins? It is true that a person who is receiving a shockingly small amount of vitamin A in the diet may be more liable to colds and other infections. But this danger doesn't apply to children who are taking a decent diet, because vitamin A is plentiful in milk, butter, eggs, vegetables.

It is believed that a child who is suffering from rickets (because of too little vitamin D) is more susceptible to the complications of colds, such as bronchitis. But if a child has no rickets and is receiving a satisfactory dose of vitamin D, there is no reason to believe that he will have fewer colds if **more** vitamin D is stuffed into him. There should be an adequate amount of vitamin C in the diet, 50 milligrams, or 2 ounces of orange juice (Section 479), but there is no proof that larger amounts will prevent more colds.

702. Age is a factor in colds. With more children in day care and nursery schools, children between 4 months and 2 years get more colds, have them longer, and with more complications. (The average is 7 a year in northern cities in the United States—more if there are children in the family attending school.) After the age of 2–3 years, the frequency and the severity grow less. Nine-year-olds are apt to be laid up only half as much as they were at 6, and 12-year-olds only half as much as at 9. This should comfort the parents of a small child who seems to be forever sick.

703. The psychological factor in colds. Psychiatrists feel quite sure that **certain** children and grown-ups are much more susceptible to colds when they are tense or unhappy. I think of a boy 6 years old who was nervous about school because he couldn't keep up with the class in reading. Every Monday morning for several months he had a cough. You may think he was putting it on. It wasn't so simple as that. It wasn't a dry, forced cough. It was a real, thick one. The cough would improve as the week went by, and by Friday it would be all gone, only to reappear again Sunday night or Monday morning. There's nothing mysterious about this. We know that one person has cold, clammy hands when nervous; an athlete may have diarrhea before a race. So it's perfectly possible that nervousness may interfere with the blood circulation of the nose or throat so that germs have a better chance to flourish there.

704. Exposure to other children. There is another factor that influences the number of colds a child has. That's the number of children he plays with, especially indoors. The **average** single child living on an isolated farm has few colds because he is exposed to few cold germs. On the other hand, the **average** child in a nursery or elementary school has plenty, even though the school is careful to exclude every child who has symptoms. People can probably give their infection to others for at least a day before they show signs of it themselves, and at times they can carry cold germs and pass them on to others without ever showing symptoms themselves. There are some lucky children who rarely catch cold, no matter how many colds there are around them.

705. Can the spread of infection in a family be checked? Most colds that are brought into a family are caught by the younger children in at least a mild form, especially if the house is small and everyone has to use the same rooms. Not only do the germs of colds and other infections get passed from one person to another in large doses on the spray of sneezes and coughs, but they also float around in the air of the room in fair numbers just from being breathed into the air. Tests have shown that a gauze mask worn over the nose and mouth doesn't keep most germs from getting into the air. All of this means that there's no great advantage in the parents' wearing a mask or in trying halfheartedly to keep young children apart. Babies catch fewer colds, and it may be worthwhile for the parents—especially one with a sore throat—to avoid sneezing, coughing, or breathing directly into a baby's face. They should wash their hands with soap before handling things that will go into the baby's mouth—the bowl of the spoon, the mouth part of a nipple, a teething ring, finger foods—to prevent the transfer of large numbers of bacteria.

Under special circumstances, it may be worthwhile to go to extra lengths to protect a baby or small child who is frail or particularly susceptible to infections—if the house is large enough so that the baby can be kept in a separate room with the door closed and if there is one adult without symptoms who can care for him. It is probably preferable that this adult, who is also mixing with the rest of the family and who is therefore carrying some germs, not sleep in the baby's room or stay there when the baby doesn't need attention.

If an outsider has any suspicion of a cold or any other illness, be very firm about not letting that person in the same house with the baby, or within a couple of yards of the carriage outdoors. Say that the doctor told you to keep people with colds away.

What about chronic nose colds or sinusitis? If a person has had such an infection for 2 weeks or more, it's probably no longer important to keep him out of the same room. I would still suggest the other precautions: hand-washing, keeping his face turned away when doing anything for the baby.

706. Skin test for anyone with a chronic cough. Anyone in a household who has a chronic cough should be examined by a doctor and have a skin test to be sure it is not tuberculosis. This rule is particularly important if there is a baby or small child in the home, or if one is expected. If you have a baby or child and are hiring a housekeeper or caregiver, she should be examined and have a skin test before becoming a member of the household.

707. Colds in the infant. If your baby has a cold during his first year, the chances are that it will be mild. He may sneeze in the beginning; his nose will be runny or bubbly or stuffy. He may cough a little. He is not likely to have any fever. When his nose is bubbly, you wish you could blow it for him. But it doesn't seem to bother him. On the other hand, if his nose is obstructed with thick mucus, it may make him frantic. He keeps trying to close his mouth and is angry when he can't breathe. The stuffiness may bother him most when he tries to nurse at the breast or bottle, so much so that he refuses altogether at times.

Bubbling and obstruction can often be relieved by sucking the mucus out with a nasal syringe. Compress the bulb, insert the tip into the nose, and release the bulb.

Extra moisture in the room (Section 711) helps prevent stuffiness. If it is severe, the doctor may prescribe the shrinking kind of nose drops for use just before nursing, or medication by mouth. In other respects the baby may not lose much appetite. Usually the cold is gone in a week. Sometimes, though, a small baby's cold can last an unbelievably long time even though it stays mild.

Of course, babies' colds **can** become severe. They can have bronchitis and other complications, but these are less common during the first year than later. If they have a frequent cough or a deep cough or a wheezy cough, they should be examined by a doctor, even if they have no fever. The same rule applies if they **look** sick with a cold. In other words, **a baby can be quite sick and not have fever,** especially in the first 2 or 3 months of life.

708. Colds and fever after infancy. Some children go on having the same mild colds, without fever or complications, that they had during infancy. It's more common, though, when children get to be over six months old, for their colds and throat infections to act differently. Here is a common story. A little girl of 2 is well during the morning. At lunchtime she seems a little tired and has less appetite than usual. When she wakes up from her nap she is cranky and her parents notice that she is hot. They take her temperature, and it's 102°F. By the time the doctor examines her, the temperature is 104°F. The child's cheeks are flushed and her eyes are dull, but otherwise she doesn't seem particularly sick. She may want no supper at all, or she may want a fair amount. She has no cold symptoms, and the doctor hasn't found anything definite except that her throat is perhaps a little red. The next day she may have a little fever, but now her nose may begin to run. Perhaps she coughs occasionally. From this point on, it's just a regular mild cold that lasts anywhere from 2 days to 2 weeks.

There are several variations of this typical story. Sometimes the child vomits at the time her fever is shooting up. This is particularly apt to happen if her parents have unwisely tried to get her to eat more of her lunch than she wanted. (Always take children's word for it when they lose their appetite.) Sometimes the fever lasts several days in the beginning, before the cold symptoms appear. One reason that the nose doesn't run at first is that fever dries it up. Sometimes the fever lasts for a day or two and then goes away without any running nose or cough taking its place. In this case, the doctor may call it grippe or flu. These terms are commonly used for infections that have no **local** symptoms (like running nose or diarrhea), only **generalized** symptoms (such as fever or a sick-all-over feeling). You suspect that this kind of 1-day fever is sometimes a cold that was stopped in its tracks: the child seems perfectly well for a day or two after her fever is gone, and then promptly starts a running nose or cough when she is taken out in cold weather.

I am making the point that children over the age of 6 months often start their colds with sudden high fever, so that you won't be too alarmed if this happens. You should, of course, always consult the doctor whenever your child falls ill with a fever because it occasionally means a more serious infection.

When children are 5 or 6, they're more apt to be starting their colds without much fever again.

Fever that begins after a cold is well under way has a different meaning entirely from the fever that comes on the first day. It usually indicates that the cold has spread or become worse. This isn't necessarily serious or alarming. It only means that the doctor should see the child again to make sure that the ears, bronchial tubes, and urinary system are still healthy.

THE HANDLING OF A CHILD WITH A COLD

709. Calling the doctor. You don't need to call the doctor when there is only a running nose or a slight cough. But you should call if new symptoms develop such as ear pain, or fever occurring several days after the cold began, which suggests some complication.

710. Treatment. Most doctors and parents don't keep a child indoors or prescribe any treatment for a simple cold.

If your child is particularly susceptible to frequent and prolonged colds or to complications such as bronchitis and ear infections, you may want to be more fussy. I have the impression from observing children's and my own colds that chilling may make a cold worse. (Experiments have proved that chilling does not cause a cold to start.) So I think it's sensible to keep a young child indoors until the cold is over, except in warm weather, and keep her evenly clothed, as much on her legs and ankles as on her chest.

711. Keeping the air moist in an overheated room. The doctor sometimes recommends humidifying or steaming the room during a cold. It counteracts the dryness of the air and soothes the inflamed nose and throat. It is particularly valuable in the treatment of a tight, dry cough, or croup.

Extra moisture is less necessary in warm weather when the heat is off.

By far the best equipment is a **cold-mist humidifier,** which blows moisture into the room. A good humidifier of this sort costs up to $30 but will be used many times and prove its worth.

An **electric steam vaporizer** gets moisture in the air by boiling water, by means of an electric heating element which fits into a large glass jar of water. It is much less expensive. But it is also less efficient in getting moisture into the child's chest, less comfortable because it heats up the room, and less safe because a small child may touch it or knock it over. If you buy one of these steam vaporizers, get a large size that holds a quart or more and turns itself off when the water boils away.

In an emergency, in the case of croup, carry the child into the bathroom and turn on the hot water in the bathtub or shower—to make steam, not to put the child into.

712. Nose drops. The doctor may prescribe nose drops. Generally speaking, they fall into two groups. There are the mild antiseptics to kill germs. Their usefulness is limited because they can't kill germs that are below the surface. The other general class of nose drops are the solutions that shrink the tissues in the nose. This opens up more space for breathing and gives the mucus and pus a better chance to drain. The main drawback is that after the tissues have been shrunk a reaction sets in and they expand again. This may leave the nose more stuffy than ever and may be irritating to the delicate membranes if it's done too often. There are three situations in which the shrinking kind of nose drops is useful. The first is when a baby is so stuffed up that she is frantic. She can't nurse without suffocating, and her sleep is interrupted. (This condition may be relieved by suction with a nasal syringe alone.) The second is in the late stages of a bad cold or sinusitis, when the nose is filled with a thick secretion that does not discharge by itself. The third is when the doctor wants to open up the eustachian tube, which connects the ear with the throat, during an ear infection.

Nose drops do a lot more good if they get back into the inner and upper passages of the nose. Suck out the mucus in the front of the nose with a nasal syringe. Then have the child lie on her back across a bed with her head hanging well down over the side. Insert the drops and try to keep her in this position for half a minute while the drops work back and up.

Medicine to take internally to shrink the nose tissues is now available.

Nose drops should be used only on a doctor's recommendation, no more often than every 4 hours. Don't use them for more than a week unless the doctor says to go on. One disadvantage of nose drops is that many small children fight them. There are only a few conditions in which nose drops do enough good to be worth getting the child all upset.

There are a number of commercial ointments for rubbing on the chest. The idea is to stimulate the skin of the chest to relieve a cough, or to help the nose with the aromatic oils that are wafted upward. There is no proof of the benefit of this kind of treatment, but if it seems to help, there is no harm in its use.

713. Cough medicines. No cough medicine can cure a cold, in the sense of killing the germs. It can only make the windpipe less ticklish, so that coughing is less frequent, or loosen up the mucus. A person who has an infection in the windpipe or bronchial tubes **should** cough once in a while to bring up the mucus and pus. It is particularly important that a baby's cough not be suppressed too much. The doctor prescribes a cough medicine to keep the cough from being so frequent that it tires the person out or interferes with sleep or irritates the throat. Any child or grown-up who has a cough that is that frequent should be under the care of a doctor who is the only one to prescribe the right cough medicine.

EAR INFECTIONS

714. Mild ear infections are common in young children. Some children have inflammation of the ears with most of their colds, and others never do. The ears are much more apt to be infected in the first 3 or 4 years of life. In fact, there is a slight ear inflammation in a majority of colds at this age, but it usually never comes to anything, and the child has no symptoms.

Usually the ear doesn't become inflamed enough to cause pain until after a cold has been going for several days. The child over 2 tells what is the matter. A baby may keep rubbing an ear or just cry piercingly for several hours. There may or may not be fever. The doctor is apt to find at this stage that there is only a mild inflammation of the upper part of the eardrum. Most ear infections of this degree get well again in a few days with proper treatment.

Any time that your child has an earache, you should get in touch with the doctor that same day, particularly if there is any fever. The drugs that are used when necessary work much better in the early stages of ear infections.

Suppose it will be several hours before you can reach the doctor. What can you do to relieve the pain? A hot water bottle or an electric heating pad helps some. Small children are impatient with them. Aspirin or acetaminophen relieves a certain amount of pain (Section 685). What will help even more, if you happen to have it on hand, is a dose of a cough medicine containing codeine that the doctor has prescribed **for that particular child.** (A medicine prescribed for an older child or adult might contain too much of the drug.) Codeine is an efficient pain killer as well as cough remedy. If the earache is severe, you can use all these remedies together, but never use more than two doses of the codeine cough medicine without talking to your doctor.

Once in a while an eardrum breaks very early in an infection and discharges a thin pus. You may find the discharge on the pillow in the morning without the child ever having complained of pain or fever. Usually, however, the drum breaks only after an abscess has been developing for several days, with fever and pain. In any case, if you find your child's ear discharging, the most that you should do is to tuck a loose plug of sterile absorbent cotton into the opening to collect the pus, wash the pus off the outside of the ear with soap and water, and get in touch with the doctor. If the discharge leaks out anyway and irritates the skin, wash the pus off and protect the skin with petroleum jelly.

It is quite common for a child's hearing to be temporarily

reduced after a few days of even a moderate ear infection. In practically all cases, this hearing loss clears up if the infection is promptly and correctly treated.

Sometimes, for a child who has had frequent, severe ear infections or fluid behind the eardrum for 4–6 months which interferes with hearing, the doctor will recommend that a minor operation be done by an ear specialist. Tiny plastic tubes are placed through the eardrums, so that the air pressure is the same on both sides of the drums. It is felt that this may reduce the chances of further infection or accumulation of fluid, and may help prevent any permanent impairment of hearing.

BRONCHITIS AND PNEUMONIA

715. Bronchitis. There are all degrees of bronchitis, from very mild with no fever, to severe. Bronchitis simply means that a cold has spread down to the bronchial tubes. There is usually plenty of cough. Sometimes you can hear faraway squeaky noises as the child breathes, and feel the vibration of the mucus as you touch the chest.

A very mild bronchitis, without fever, without much cough, without loss of appetite, is only a little more serious than a nose cold. However, if the child acts sick, or coughs frequently, or has a fever of 101°F, the doctor should be reached that same day, because modern drugs are of great benefit in cases that require them.

The young infant who has a frequent cough should be examined whether there is a fever or not, because in the first month or two of life there can be serious infections without fever. In the meantime, you don't need to worry if the baby's appetite and general appearance are satisfactory.

716. Pneumonia. Bacterial pneumonia usually comes on after a child has had a cold for several days, but it may start without any previous warning. You suspect it when the temperature climbs up to 103° or 104°F, the breathing becomes rapid, and there is a cough. Vomiting often occurs at the beginning, and there may even be a convulsion in a small child. Modern antibiotics bring about a prompt cure of the bacterial types of pneumonia if treatment is started early. Naturally, you call the doctor if your child develops a fever and cough.

More common are viral pneumonias (which many people call "walking pneumonias"). These pneumonias are often treated with antibiotics as well, because a couple of them are hard to distinguish from bacterial pneumonia. Generally, the child is less sick, though the disease may last a long time. The usual picture is a slow, but continuous improvement over a 2–4 week period.

717. Bronchiolitis. Bronchiolitis is a wheezing respiratory illness which affects infants and toddlers. It is caused by a virus, and usually the baby has a cold in addition to her cough and wheezing. Babies may become so short of breath that they cannot comfortably eat or rest. There are no medicines that cure bronchiolitis, but it is important to contact your doctor so she or he can help you with your baby's symptoms. The baby is usually better within a week, but a few babies may then wheeze with later colds.

CROUP

718. Spasmodic croup without fever. Croup is the word commonly used for various kinds of laryngitis in children. There is usually a hoarse, ringing, barking cough (croupy cough) and some tightness in the breathing.

The commonest and mildest type, **spasmodic croup without fever,** comes on suddenly during the evening. The child may have been perfectly healthy during the day or have had the mildest kind of cold without cough, but suddenly wakes up with a violent fit of croupy coughing, is quite hoarse, and is having difficulty breathing. The child struggles and heaves to get breath in. It's quite a scary picture when you see it the first time, but it's not so serious as it looks. You should call the doctor promptly for any kind of croup.

The emergency treatment of croup, until the doctor can be reached, is moist air. Use a cold-mist humidifier if you have one. See Section 711 for other ways to humidify. A small room is preferable because you can humidify it faster. If the water runs hot, you can take the child into the bathroom and run hot water into the tub (to make steam, not to put the child in). If there is a shower, that will work best of all. A 20-minute steam in the bathroom with the child sitting upright in your lap is the best first treatment.

Humidifier or vaporizer steams need to be concentrated in a makeshift tent. You can make a tent by draping sheets over a crib or small table or tacking them from the wall. When the child breathes the moist air, the croup usually begins to improve rapidly. An adult should stay awake as long as there are any symptoms of croup, wake up 2 or 3 hours after the croup is over to make sure that the child is breathing comfortably, and sleep in the same room with the child for 3 nights.

Spasmodic croup without fever sometimes comes back the next night or two. To avoid this, have the child sleep in a room in which the air has been moistened, for 3 nights. This form of croup is apparently caused by the combination of a cold infection, a child with a sensitive larynx, and dry air.

The three most important elements in treatment are the 20-minute steam in the bathroom, keeping the child upright, and plenty of fluids.

719. Croup with fever (laryngobronchitis). This is a more severe form of croup, which is usually accompanied by a real chest cold. The croupy cough and the tight breathing may come on gradually or suddenly at any time of the day or night. Steaming only partly relieves it. **A child who has hoarseness with fever or tightness of breathing with fever must be put under the close, continuous supervision of a doctor without delay.** If you cannot reach your doctor right away, find another doctor. If a doctor cannot reach you, you should take the child to a hospital.

The most severe form of croup with fever causes an

inflammation of the epiglottis (the "trap door" which covers the windpipe when you swallow food). It is caused by the hemophilus influenza germ (which goes by the nickname "H flu"). A child with H flu epiglottitis usually becomes ill very quickly, appears very sick, leans forward and is very unwilling to move his head in any direction, will be drooling, and will usually tend to make no sounds at all rather than to have a typical croupy cough. The reason for their refusal to move their heads is that they're keeping their necks in a position which gives them the most room for air to pass between the swollen epiglottis and the windpipe. Epiglottitis is a true medical emergency, and everything must be done to get the child to a doctor as quickly as possible.

720. Diphtheria of the larynx is still another cause of croup. There is a gradually increasing hoarseness, cough, difficulty in breathing, and moderate fever. There is practically no danger of this form of croup developing if a child has received diphtheria immunization.

However, with any form of croup, a child should be seen promptly by a doctor. The urgency is greatest when hoarseness and tight breathing are persisting, even mildly, and when there is fever of 101°F or more.

SINUSITIS, TONSILLITIS, AND SWOLLEN GLANDS

721. Sinusitis. The sinuses are cavities in the bones surrounding the nose. Each sinus cavity connects with the interior of the nose through a small opening. The maxillary sinuses are in the cheekbones. The frontal sinuses are in the forehead, just above the eyebrows. The ethmoid sinuses are up above the inner passages of the nose. The sphenoids are farther back, behind the nasal passages. The maxillary and the ethmoid sinuses are the only ones that are well enough developed in the early years of childhood to be infected then. The frontals and sphenoids develop gradually after the age of 6. When there is a severe or prolonged cold in the nose, the infection may spread from the nose into these various sinus cavities. Sinus infections usually last longer than simple nose colds, because they are more closed in, can't drain so well. A sinus infection may be very mild and show itself only by a chronic discharge of pus from the back of the nose into the throat (called a postnasal drip). This sometimes causes a chronic cough when the child lies down in bed or first gets up in the morning. On the other hand, sinusitis may be severe, with high fever and pain. A doctor who suspects sinusitis sometimes investigates further by X-ray pictures or by shining a light through the sinuses in a dark room. Various treatments are used, such as nose drops, nose packs, suction, drugs, depending on the case.

Whatever specific method the doctor is using, remember that the general care of the child is important, too. A sinus infection is, after all, only a more advanced and persistent form of a cold.

722. Tonsillitis. Serious tonsillitis is most often caused by the streptococcus. The child usually has high fever for a number of days and feels sick. Headache, stomach pain, and vomiting are common. The tonsils become fiery red and swollen. After a day or two, white spots or white patches appear on them. Older children may complain of such a sore throat that they can hardly swallow. Young children may be bothered surprisingly little by the sore throat.

You should consult the doctor for a case of tonsillitis, however mild. It is important to treat it promptly and thoroughly with one of the antibiotic drugs that are so effective in overcoming the infection and preventing complications. The drug should be given in a manner which will continue the treatment for 10 days. If the child continues to look washed out or to run a low fever, keep in touch with the doctor. Complications, which usually occur only in untreated cases, are rheumatic fever and nephritis (inflammation of the kidney, with smoky-colored urine).

An individual whose tonsils have been removed can still have streptococcal throat infections.

723. Other throat infections. There are all kinds and degrees of throat infections, caused by a variety of germs. The medical term for them is **pharyngitis.** Many people feel a slight sore throat at the beginning of every cold. Often the doctor, in examining a child with a fever, finds a slightly red throat as the only sign of disease. The child may or may not notice any soreness. Most of these are soon over. The child should stay indoors until the sore throat is all gone. The doctor should be called if there is any fever, or if the child looks sick, or if the throat is more than slightly sore (even if there is no fever).

The main concern with sore throats is to detect and treat promptly with drugs those caused by a dangerous streptococcus. It's wise to call the doctor in all cases of sore throat, especially if there is a fever of 101°F. The doctor will do a throat culture if there is any suspicion, or use an effective drug anyway, to prevent possible complications. See Section 722 for the precautions during convalescence.

724. Swollen glands. The lymph glands that are scattered up and down the sides of the neck sometimes become infected and swollen as a result of any disease in the throat, mild or severe. The commonest cause is tonsillitis. It can develop in the middle of the tonsillitis or a week or two later. If the glands are swollen enough to be visible, or if there is fever of 101°F or more, the doctor should certainly be called. Treatment with drugs may be called for in certain cases and is most valuable if begun early.

Slightly enlarged neck glands may last for weeks or even months after some throat infections. They can come from other causes, too, such as infected teeth, scalp infections, and general diseases, like rubella (German measles). You should consult your doctor about them. But if the doctor finds the child generally healthy, don't worry about slightly swollen glands.

TONSILS AND ADENOIDS

725. The tonsils and adenoids are meant to be there unless they are causing trouble. Tonsils and adenoids have been blamed for so many things in the present century that many people think of them as villains that have to be removed eventually, and the sooner the better. This is the wrong way to look at them. They are there for the purpose of helping to overcome infection and build up the body's resistance to germs.

The tonsils and adenoids are made of what is called lymphoid tissue, and are similar to the glands in the sides of the neck, the armpits, and the groin. Any of these glands, including the tonsils and adenoids, become swollen when there is infection nearby, as they labor to kill germs and build resistance.

726. The tonsils. In normal, healthy children, the tonsils gradually become larger until the age of 7 or 8 or 9, and then gradually decrease in size. In former times it was believed that all abnormally enlarged tonsils were diseased and should be removed. Nowadays it is believed that the size is unimportant. It is only extremely rarely that tonsils (or adenoids) need to be removed.

Recurrent tonsillitis, frequent colds, ear infections, rheumatic fever are not reasons for tonsillectomy. There is no need to remove the tonsils, even when they are large, in a child who is perfectly healthy and has few nose and throat infections. There is no reason to operate because of a feeding problem, or stuttering, or nervousness; in fact, the operation may make the child worse. (The three acceptable reasons for a tonsillectomy are severe, recurrent streptococcal tonsillitis, severe obstruction from unusually enlarged tonsils and adenoids, and an abscess in the tonsils.)

727. The adenoids. The adenoids are clusters of lymphoid tissue up behind the soft palate, where the nose passages join the throat. When they become greatly enlarged they may block this passageway from the nose and cause mouth breathing and snoring. They may prevent the free discharge of mucus and pus from the nose, and thus help to keep bad colds and sinus infections going. These conditions were usually considered reasons for removal of the adenoids in previous times. Nowadays, however, they are often successfully treated medically: with internal and external preparations to shrink the tissues, antibiotics to treat the infections.

Removing the adenoids does not necessarily make a child breathe through his nose. Some children are mouth breathers because of habit (they seem to be born that way) and not because of obstruction. And some children's noses are obstructed not by adenoids but by swollen tissues in the front of the nose (for instance, by hay fever or other forms of allergy). Removing the adenoids has little or no effect on the frequency of ear infections.

If the tonsils are removed, the adenoids are sometimes cut out, too. On the other hand, there may be reason to take out the adenoids alone if they are causing persistent obstruction, and to leave the tonsils.

The adenoids always grow back to some extent, and the body always tries to grow new lumps of lymphoid tissue where the tonsils used to be. This isn't a sign that the operation was done incompletely or that it has to be done again. It shows only that the body means to have lymphoid tissue in that region and tries hard to replace it.

In Sections 692–695 there are suggestions about handling operations.

ALLERGIES

728. Milk allergy and special formulas. Milk allergy is a lot less common than most people think it is. Young babies have many stomach complaints, but most are due to their immaturity rather than to allergy. Truly allergic babies tend to have classic allergic symptoms (see Sections 729–733) and to come from allergic families. Breast-feeding is ideal for babies from allergic families, but for babies already on formula who are having intestinal troubles, you and your doctor may want to consider switching formulas. Your doctor is most likely to recommend a soy formula (made from soybeans instead of cow's milk). A few babies will not tolerate a soy formula either, and in that case your doctor will recommend a more specialized formula based on your baby's special problems. By 1 or 2 years of age almost all babies are able to drink regular cow's milk.

729. Allergic nose troubles, including hay fever. You probably know some people who have ragweed hay fever. When ragweed pollen gets in the wind in mid-August, they start to sneeze and their noses begin to be stuffed up and itch and run. This means that the nose is **allergic,** or oversensitive, to the pollen, which doesn't bother other people at all. Some people have hay fever in spring because they are allergic to certain tree pollens. If your child develops a running, itching nose that lasts for weeks, at the same time every year, you should take it up with your doctor. From the appearance of the nose in the season and from skin tests with the suspected pollens, the physician can tell whether it's hay fever. The treatment may consist of frequent injections carried out over a long period. The doctor can usually give temporary relief with medicine.

But there are nose allergies aside from seasonal hay fevers that may be less dramatic but more troublesome. There are noses that are sensitive to the feathers in pillows, or to dog hair, or to house dust, or to any number of other substances. Such year-round allergies as these may keep a child stuffy or running at the nose, breathing through the mouth, month in and month out. The chronic obstruction may make an allergic child more susceptible to sinus infections. If your child is much bothered this way, your doctor, or an allergy specialist, may be able to find the cause. The treatment is different in each case and depends on the causes. If it's goose feathers, you change the pillow. If it's dog hair, you may have to give away the dog and substitute some other plaything. If it's something hard to avoid, like house dust, the doctor may give injections of the offending substance over a long period. "Stripping the room" may be recommended to lessen the dust there, especially if the symptoms occur mainly at night or the first thing in the morning. You remove the rugs and curtains for good and give the room a wet-mopping every day. You eliminate all wool from the room and also the stuffed toys.

You either buy dustproof coverings for the mattress and pillow, or use ones made of foam rubber, or use a canvas cot with no pillow at all.

Allergy symptoms usually can't be eliminated completely. You have to be satisfied with partial improvement.

730. Asthma. Asthma is another kind of allergy. Instead of the sensitive organ being the nose, as in hay fever, it is the bronchial tubes. When the irritating substance reaches the small bronchial tubes, they swell, thick mucus is secreted, and the passageways for air are so narrowed that breathing becomes difficult, labored, and wheezing. Coughing occurs.

When an older child has chronic asthma, it's apt to be due to substances that float in the air, such as horse dander, dog hair, molds, etc. Allergists call these "inhalants." In a very young child, allergy to foods is more likely to be the cause or to play a part. The child who has chronic asthma of more than slight degree is usually tested to discover the offending substances, and then treated. If the disease is neglected, the repeated attacks may have a harmful effect on the structure of the lungs and chest. The treatment depends on the cause and is different in each case. Foods that the child is sensitive to are eliminated from the diet. When inhalants are the cause, the treatment is much the same as in year-round allergies of the nose (Section 729).

Asthma is not simply a matter of allergy to certain substances. A person has an attack at one time and not at another, even though in the same place leading the same life. Attacks are more common at night. Season of year, climate, temperature, exercise, state of mind play a part in different cases. Colds often start an attack. Certain children are apt to have attacks of asthma (or other allergies) when they are anxious—consciously or unconsciously—about separation from a parent, for instance, or about conflict with a parent, or about conflict between the parents. They may be greatly improved when their troubles are straightened out, perhaps with a psychiatrist's help. In other words, you try to treat the whole child, not just the asthma.

The treatment of the individual attack of asthma depends a lot on how severe it is, and on what the doctor finds is helpful for that case. There are drugs given by mouth or injection or that can be inhaled in a mist form, for temporary relief when the child is having real difficulty breathing.

If your daughter (or son) develops asthma for the first time when you are out of reach of a doctor, don't be alarmed. The condition is rarely as dangerous as it looks. Keep her in bed if the breathing is very difficult. If it's winter and the house is heated, get extra moisture into the air (Section 711). If she is coughing much and you have cough medicine that was prescribed for her before, you can give her a dose. Get her occupied in play or reading while you go about your own work, or read to her yourself. If you hover over her anxiously, it keeps her more frightened and may actually make the asthma worse. If the wheezing persists or becomes worse the child must be under the care of a doctor without delay.

If your child continues to have spells, you can try stripping her room (Section 729), until you are able to consult a doctor.

It is impossible to predict about asthma. Cases that start early in childhood are more apt to clear up in a few years than those that start later. A certain number go away by the age of puberty. But sometimes hay fever takes the place of the asthma.

731. Asthmatic bronchitis should be mentioned separately. An occasional baby or small child has spells of wheezing, difficult breathing, not at any old time, as in typical chronic asthma, but only when she or he has a real cold. This tendency is most common in the first 3 years of life. It's discouraging to have a baby who regularly has this much trouble with colds, but there is a brighter side to the picture. The tendency to asthmatic bronchitis is usually well on its way to disappearing in a couple of years. The doctor should be called, of course. The infection and the cough may need treating as much as the wheezing. If the house is heated, it may help to get extra moisture in the air (Section 711). The injections and medicines to open up the bronchial tubes that are often helpful in ordinary asthma have little effect in asthmatic bronchitis.

732. Hives. Hives are considered, at least in some cases, to be due to allergy of the skin. The commonest kind consists of raised welts. They are often pale in the raised part, because the blood has been pressed out by the swelling. They itch, sometimes unbearably. A few individuals get hives repeatedly, or even most of the time. But many people have them only once or twice in a lifetime. They are occasionally found to be caused by sensitivity to some food. They also come from serum injections and at the end of certain infections. In many cases the cause cannot be discovered. On very rare occasions, hives are accompanied by swelling of the inside of the mouth and throat. If this happens, the child should be taken to a doctor immediately.

In a mild case, you can try an antihistamine medicine which you can buy in the drug store without a prescription. The pharmacist will tell you how to use it. In a more severe case, the doctor can usually relieve the attack of hives with medicine or an injection.

733. Eczema. Eczema is a rough, red rash that comes in patches. It's always associated with very dry skin. The resulting itching—and scratching—causes many of the problems of eczema. It is caused by allergy, like hay fever and asthma. In hay fever the nose is allergic (sensitive) to a pollen, like ragweed. In eczema the skin may be allergic to some food in the diet. When that food gets into the blood and reaches the skin, the skin becomes inflamed. In another case the skin may be allergic to some material, like wool, silk, rabbit's hair, or some substance, like orrisroot in powder, that comes in direct contact with the skin. A baby who has relatives who have asthma, hay fever, hives, or eczema is more likely to have eczema.

Even when eczema is primarily due to allergy to foods, irritation of the skin from the outside may play a secondary part. One baby has eczema only when the skin is irritated by cold weather, another only in hot weather from the irritation of perspiration, still another only in the diaper region from the irritation of the urine. If a baby has eczema only where wool comes in contact with the skin, it may be that the child is really allergic to wool directly, or is perhaps allergic to some food and the wool merely acts as a simple irritant.

In older children with a family history, emotional factors may play a role in producing eczema, and emotional stress may make the rash get worse from time to time.

You need a doctor, of course, to diagnose and treat the condition. The easiest eczema to describe is the kind that comes in patches of rough, red, thick, scaly skin. When eczema is mild or just starting, the color is apt to be a light red or tannish pink, but if it becomes severe, it turns a deeper red, usually itches, and the baby scratches and rubs it. This causes scratch marks and "weeping" (oozing). When the oozing serum dries, it forms crusts. When a patch of eczema is healing, even after the redness has all faded away, you can still feel the roughness and thickness of the skin.

The commonest place for eczema to begin in a young baby is on the cheeks or the forehead. From there it may spread back to the ears and neck. The scaliness looks from a distance as if salt has dried there, especially on the ears. Near a year of age, eczema may start almost anywhere—the shoulders, the diaper region, the arms, the chest. Between 1 and 3, the most typical spots are the creases in the elbows and behind the knees. Severe eczema can be a very trying disease to take care of. The baby is wild with the itching. The parents are wild trying to keep the child from scratching. It can last for months. It's important to keep the baby's fingernails clipped short. The less the baby can scratch her skin, the less chance there is of a secondary infection getting started in the scratched areas, from germs which are always on the skin. For babies who will tolerate it, making up a pair of white cotton mittens to cover the hands at night is helpful, since a lot of scratching can go on while the baby is asleep.

734. There are several angles to the treatment. What a doctor does in studying and treating a case depends on many factors, including the baby's age, the location and character of the rash, the history of what new foods were introduced before the rash began, and how he responds to different forms of treatment. Many cases can be much improved by lotions and ointments alone. In the more persistent ones, an effort is made to find what food or foods the child is allergic to. In the young infant, fresh cow's milk is occasionally found to be the cause. Then a shift to evaporated milk sometimes helps, because any food is less likely to cause allergy when it is thoroughly cooked. A few babies can be cured only by giving up real milk altogether and shifting to one of the artificial milks, such as those made from soybeans.

In severe eczema in older babies and children who are eating a number of foods, the doctor experiments carefully by eliminating various ones from the diet. In severe and persistent cases "skin testing" may be done by injecting samples of different foods. Hives develop around the injections of foods to which the child is sensitive.

When an external irritant seems to be playing a part, that needs attention, too. Wool is very commonly irritating to eczema, and it is usually eliminated from the clothing. If the eczema is all in the diaper region, it is worthwhile to take all the precautions discussed in Section 366 on diaper rashes. If cold, windy weather brings out the eczema, find a sheltered place for outings. Soap and water are sometimes irritating to eczema, in which case the baby can be cleaned with mineral oil on absorbent cotton.

If for the time being you are out of reach of a doctor and your young baby develops a severe itching eczema, it will do no harm, and it may help, to shift from a fresh-milk to an evaporated-milk formula. If you are in the same situation with an older baby who, for instance, develops a severe eczema after starting on egg, leave out the egg until you can get advice. It may take 2 weeks or more for the improvement to show. Wheat is another common offender. It is a mistake, though, for a parent to begin eliminating a **number** of foods from the diet, and not even one food should be eliminated by the parent if it is possible to get a doctor's help. The reason is this: A case of eczema varies from week to week even with the same diet. When you are changing the diet around yourself you are apt to think that first one food, then another, is the cause. Every time the eczema becomes worse again, you become more confused. The danger is that you will make the diet so lopsided that the child's nutrition will suffer. If the eczema is not bothering the baby much, don't try any changes in the diet until you can get help.

Parents are upset about a severe eczema and are impressed by the necessity of keeping the baby from scratching himself. This combination may make them afraid to cuddle and stroke him. But he needs this kind of closeness and visible affection.

The thing to remember about eczema is that it's a tendency inside the child, not an infection, like impetigo, that you can get rid of completely. In most cases you have to be satisfied if you can just keep the rash mild. A majority of the eczemas that start early in infancy clear up completely, or at least become much milder, in the following year or two.

735. Behavioral problems and allergies. In recent years, all kinds of behavioral problems in children have been blamed on "allergy"—to vague substances in the air, food additives, food colorings, etc. None of these claims has yet been proven scientifically. Many parents have brought their children to nonmedical practitioners who have performed very expensive tests and prescribed extremely complicated diets and other treatments. None of the results claimed for these approaches has been tested by the usual, accepted scientific methods. I think it's best to have a frank talk with your doctor if you think that your child has a behavior problem due to an allergy and if you feel that you want to try a method carried out by a nonmedical practitioner.

SKIN CONDITIONS

Herpes. Many parents have become frightened by newspaper and television stories about herpes. Herpes is a virus which is found worldwide, has probably existed for thousands of years, and is no more contagious than other viral diseases.

There are two main types of herpes: type I, found mostly in the mouth; and type II, mostly on the genitals. The mouth type is associated with cold sores and canker sores. It's the genital type that has received so much publicity and made people so worried.

Soap and water kills the herpes virus. So if a mother or baby-sitter with genital herpes washes her hands with soap and water after she touches her genital area, she won't pass the virus to a child she's taking care of.

If you're worried about stories you've heard or seen or read, speak to your doctor or your child's doctor.

736. Distinguishing the common rashes. This section isn't meant to make you a diagnostician. If your child has a rash, you need your doctor's help. Rashes due to the same cause vary so in different individuals that even a skin specialist sometimes has a job diagnosing them. They confuse less expert people very easily. The purpose of this section is only to give you a few general pointers about the commoner rashes of children to relieve your mind until you can reach your doctor.

Measles. Fever and cold symptoms appear 3 or 4 days before the rash begins. It consists of flat, pink spots that start around the ears and work down. The fever is high when the rash begins (Section 745).

Rubella ("German measles"). Flat, pink spots, often faint, that rapidly spread all over the whole body. Little or no fever. No cold symptoms, but swollen glands on the back of the head and neck (Section 746).

Chicken pox. Separate raised pimples. Some of these develop tiny, delicate blisters on top, which break within a few hours, leaving a small crust. The pimples come out a few at a time, beginning on the body or face or scalp. The doctor, to make the diagnosis, searches among all the crusted pimples for a few fresh tiny blisters (Section 749).

Scarlet fever. The child is sick for a day before the rash comes out, usually with headache, fever, vomiting, and sore throat. The rash, which is a red blush, starts in the warm, moist parts of the body, armpits, groin, and back (Section 752).

Prickly heat. Comes in babies in the beginning of hot weather. Starts around the shoulders and neck. It is made up of patches of many small tan-pink pimples, some of which develop tiny blisters (Section 368).

Diaper rash. All in the area that is wet with urine. Pink or red pimples of various sizes, or patches of rough, red skin (Section 366).

Eczema. Patches of red, rough skin, which in the beginning come and go. If it is bad, it becomes scaly, itchy, and crusted. Apt to start on cheeks in the very young infant, later in the first year on the trunk. Common spots after a year are behind the knees and in the elbow folds (Section 733).

Hives. Welts scattered unevenly over the entire body. They itch (Section 732).

737. Insect bites. There are many different kinds, from big, puffy swellings, the size of a half-dollar, down to a simple blood-crusted spot without any swelling. But there are two common characteristics of most bites. There is a tiny hole or tiny bump in the center where the stinger went in. And the bites are located on the exposed parts of the skin, in most cases.

Any insect bite that is itching (mosquito bite, for instance) or stinging may be partly relieved by applying a paste made by running a few drops of water into a teaspoonful of bicarbonate of soda. For a **bee sting,** remove the stinger, if visible, with tweezers and apply bicarbonate of soda. More effective for a **wasp** or **hornet sting** is to rub a drop of vinegar into the spot.

738. Scabies. Groups of pimples topped with scabs, and a lot of scratch marks from the incessant itching. Located on parts of the body that are frequently handled: backs of hands, wrists, pubic area, abdomen. Usually not on the back. It is contagious, needs treatment.

739. Ringworm. Circular patches of rough skin, most commonly about nickel size. The outer rim is made up of little bumps. In ringworm of the scalp, there are round patches of scaly skin in which the hair is broken off short. Ringworm is a fungus infection that is contagious, has nothing to do with worms, requires treatment.

740. Impetigo. In a child past infancy there are scabs or crusts, partly brown, partly honey-colored. In fact, any scabs on the face should first be suspected of being impetigo. The infection is apt to start with a pimple with a yellowish or white blister on top, most often on the face, but this soon gets rubbed off and the scab takes its place. Other spots develop on the face and on any part of the body that the hands can carry the infection to. You should have the doctor see it promptly for diagnosis and treatment. It spreads easily if neglected, and is contagious to others.

In the newborn infant, impetigo is different. It starts with a very delicate small blister that contains yellowish fluid or white pus and is surrounded by reddened skin. The blister is easily broken and leaves a small raw spot. It does not develop a thick crust as in the older child. It's apt to start in a moist place, such as the edge of the diaper or in the groin or armpit. New spots may develop. It should be treated promptly by a doctor. If you cannot reach a doctor, the best method is to carefully wipe off the blister with a piece of cotton (so as not to spread the pus onto the surrounding skin), and then leave the raw spot exposed to the air. Arrange the clothing and bedclothes so that they do not cover the spot or spots, and keep the room warmer than usual if necessary. During impetigo, disinfect the diapers, sheets, underclothing, nighties, towels, and washcloths every day. Ordinary hypochlorite bleach works well.

741. Poison ivy. Clusters of small blisters of various sizes, on reddened, shiny skin. It itches, comes on the exposed parts of the body, in spring and summer. Consult your doctor about treatment if it is extensive.

742. Head lice. It's easier to find the eggs than the lice. They are tiny, pearly-white, egg-shaped objects, each one firmly cemented to a hair. There may be itching red pimples where the hair meets the back of the neck. Look in the part line and behind the ears especially. Many people feel that head lice only occur under conditions of very poor hygiene, but they can exist in any child attending school or day care. They are very contagious and need treatment.

743. Birthmarks. Most babies have a collection of red, mottled spots on the backs of their necks when they are born. These also commonly occur in two other places: between the eyebrows and on the upper eyelids. These blotches disappear gradually in most cases, and nothing needs to be done for them.

"Port wine stains" are areas of skin that have a deep-red coloring but are flat and otherwise normal. They are similar to the red spots on the neck and eyelids mentioned in the first paragraph, but they occur on other parts of the body, are apt to be larger, deeper-colored, and more permanent. Some of them do fade, particularly the lighter-colored ones. There is no easy treatment for them.

"Strawberry marks" are fairly common. These are raised and are of an intense, deep-crimson color. They look very much like a piece of the outside of a shiny strawberry. They may be small at birth and later increase in size or they may not appear at all until after birth. They are apt to grow for a while and then stop. As the years go by, most of them shrink back to nothing without treatment. They can be treated if the doctor thinks it necessary.

"Cavernous hemangiomas" are fairly large blue-and-red marks caused by a collection of distended veins deep in the skin. Sometimes they can be removed if they are disfiguring.

Moles can be of all sizes, smooth or hairy. They can be removed surgically if they are disfiguring or irritated by the clothing. (If a mole starts to grow or get darker in color, ask your doctor to check it.)

744. Warts. There are different types of ordinary warts that develop on the hands, soles of the feet, face. They are mildly contagious and should be seen by a doctor. In addition, there is a special type known as "contagious warts." At first they are round, smooth, waxy, the size of a pinhead, and white or pink in color. They multiply, enlarge, and become concave in the center. They should be treated to avoid spreading.

MEASLES, RUBELLA, ROSEOLA

745. Measles. Measles for the first 3 or 4 days has no rash. It looks like a bad cold that is becoming worse. The eyes are red and watery. If you pull the lower lid down, you see that it is fiery red. There is a hard, dry cough that becomes frequent. The fever usually goes higher each day. The rash comes out about the fourth day, when the fever is high, as indefinite pink spots behind the ears. They spread gradually over the face and body, becoming bigger and darker-colored. The day before the rash comes out, "Koplik's spots" appear on the inside of the cheeks, next to the lower molar teeth. They are minute white spots surrounded by redness, but are hard to recognize unless you know them.

The fever stays high, the cough frequent (in spite of medicine), and the child feels pretty sick while the rash comes out fully, which takes 1 to 2 days. Then everything should improve rapidly.

You suspect a complication if the fever stays high more than 2 days from the time the rash begins, or if the fever goes down for a day or more and then comes back again. The commonest complications are ear abscesses, bronchitis, and pneumonia. You will be calling the doctor at least once during a case of measles, whether you suspect the disease or not, because of the cough and fever. You must call him back promptly or bring the child to a hospital if the fever stays up or comes back after 2 days of the rash. The complications can be serious, and unlike the measles itself, can be successfully treated by modern drugs.

During the feverish part of the disease, children almost completely lose their appetite. The most they usually take is fluids, which should be offered frequently. The mouth needs to be rinsed out three times a day. It used to be thought necessary to keep the room very dark to protect the eyes. But now it is known that there is little danger. All that is necessary is to darken the room somewhat if the light makes the child uncomfortable. The room should be kept comfortably warm to prevent chilling. Children are usually let out of bed 2 days after the fever is gone. It is safe to allow them outdoors and to play with other children a week after the rash began, provided all cough and other cold symptoms are completely gone.

The first symptoms of measles begin anywhere from 9 to 16 days after exposure. It is contagious to others from the very beginning of the cold symptoms. No one with a cold or sore throat should come anywhere near a child with measles, since it is cold germs that cause the complications. It is unusual for a person to catch real measles twice.

Measles can and should be prevented by immunization at 15 months of age. But if a child who has not been protected is exposed, the attack can still be prevented or made milder if gamma globulin is given in time. It's a good idea to prevent measles before the age of 3 or 4, because that is the time when complications are more frequent and more severe. It is also wise to prevent it in an older child who is run down or ill. Get in touch with your doctor immediately to discuss globulin while it will be effective. The protection of globulin lasts for only a couple of weeks.

746. Rubella (German measles). The rash of rubella looks much like the rash of real measles, but the two diseases are entirely separate. In rubella there are no cold symptoms (running nose or cough). There may be little sore throat. The fever is usually low (under 102°F). The person may hardly feel sick at all. The rash consists of flat, pink spots, which usually cover the body the first day. The second day they are apt to fade and run together, so that the body looks flushed instead of spotty. The most characteristic sign is swollen, tender glands on the back of the skull, behind the ears, and on the sides of the neck toward the back. These glands may swell before the rash comes out, and the swelling is apt to last some time after the disease is over. In some cases the rash is so slight that it is not noticed.

Rubella usually develops from 12 to 21 days after exposure. The child usually doesn't need to be kept in bed. A doctor should make the diagnosis, because rubella is easily confused with real measles, scarlet fever, and certain virus infections.

It is bad for a woman to have rubella during the first 3 months of pregnancy because of the chance of her baby acquiring defects from the disease. If she is exposed at this time, she should promptly discuss the situation with her doctor. A blood test will reveal whether she has had rubella in the past and is therefore protected. If she is not protected —and her exposure is definite—the doctor may recommend an injection of gamma globulin. However, its value is questionable. (It will change the blood test, though, so that it shows protection.) If gamma globulin is not given, a repeat test in 4 weeks will tell whether she did get active rubella from this exposure. (You can have rubella so mildly that nothing shows.) If the test shows she did not catch it, there is nothing to worry about. If she did, she and her doctor may want to discuss the question of abortion.

Rubella immunization should be given to all children, particularly girls, at age 15 months. Adolescent girls, who have not knowingly had the disease or the vaccine and whose blood test shows no protection, should also receive the vaccine, but it should not be given within 2 months of a possible pregnancy since the live vaccine may damage the fetus. The vaccine may produce more reaction in adults, including arthritis.

The degree of effectiveness of the vaccine—to prevent the disease, and defects in the fetus—is not yet fully proved.

747. Roseola. The proper name for this disease is exanthem subitum, but it's easier to call it roseola, short for roseola infantum. It is a less well-known, contagious disease. It usually occurs between the ages of 1 and 3, rarely afterward. The child has a steady high fever for 3 or 4 days without any cold symptoms, and usually without seeming to be very sick. (Occasionally there is a convulsion on the first day because of the fever.) Suddenly the fever falls to normal, and a pinkish flat rash, something like the rash in measles, comes out on the body. By this time the child no longer looks ill but may be cranky. The rash is gone in a day or two, and there are no complications to worry about.

748. Other infectious diseases with rashes. In recent years it has been learned that there are several kinds of respiratory diseases (colds) caused by viruses (with names like adenovirus, ECHO, Coxsackie) which often have rashes that resemble measles.

CHICKEN POX, WHOOPING COUGH, MUMPS

749. Chicken pox. The first sign of chicken pox is usually a few characteristic pimples on the body, face, and scalp. These pox are raised up like ordinary small pimples, but some of them have tiny yellow water blisters on top. The base of the pimple and the skin around it are reddened. The delicate blister head breaks within a few hours and dries into a crust. When trying to make the diagnosis, a doctor searches among all the crusted pimples to find a fresh one that still has the blister. New pox continue to appear for 3 or 4 days.

An older child or adult may feel sick and have headache the day before the pox appear, but a small child doesn't notice these symptoms. The fever is usually slight at the beginning, but may go higher the next day or two. Some children never feel sick, never have a temperature of more than 101°F. Others feel quite sick and have high fever. The pox usually itch.

You should call a physician to diagnose and treat your child if there is a rash, certainly if there is a fever or the child feels sick. (Chicken pox, for instance, can be confused with smallpox and other diseases.) The itching can be relieved by soaking in a lukewarm starch or baking soda bath for 10 minutes 2 or 3 times a day. Use a starch that dissolves in water, or bicarbonate of soda (1 cupful for a small tub, 2 for a large one). Do not rub the scabs off. The only common complication is boils, which come from infecting the pox by scratching. Wash the child's hands three times a day with soap, and keep the fingernails very short. If the child doesn't fuss about it, wearing a pair of thin, white, cotton gloves at bedtime will help prevent the damage caused by scratching during sleep.

Chicken pox usually develops between 11 and 19 days after exposure. The usual rule is to let a child out and back to school a week after the disease began, or 2 days after new pox have stopped appearing. The dried scabs are not contagious and should not be a reason for keeping the child quarantined. However, some schools insist that children stay away until all the scabs have fallen off.

750. Whooping cough (pertussis). There's nothing about whooping cough in the first week to make you suspect that disease. It's just like an ordinary cold with a little runny nose and a little dry cough. Toward the end of the week the parents usually think that the cold is about over and send the child back to school. "There was just a little cough left." It is during the second week that the first suspicion arises. Now it's noticed that the child is beginning to have long spells of coughing at night. She coughs eight or ten times **on one breath.** One night, after several of these long spells, she gags and vomits. Or maybe she whoops. The whoop is the crowing noise she makes trying to get her breath back after a spell of coughs. In these days, when whooping cough shots are so widely used, many cases never are bad enough to reach the whooping stage, and in some there isn't even vomiting. The diagnosis is then based on the character of the cough in the second week (cough, cough, cough, cough, cough, cough, cough, cough—a string of coughs in rapid succession, without a breath in between) and on the fact that there are other cases in the neighborhood.

You should never jump to the conclusion that your child has whooping cough because she or he develops a bad cough in the first few days of a cold. In fact, a bad cough in the beginning of a cold argues against the diagnosis of whooping cough.

Whooping cough lasts for weeks and weeks. In an average case, the whooping stage lasts 4 weeks, in a severe case 2 or 3 months. A doctor thinks of whooping cough whenever a dry cough lasts a month.

When there is a doubtful case and it is important to make the diagnosis, there are three laboratory tests that sometimes help. The first is a "cough plate." The doctor has the child cough into a laboratory plate containing a special gelatin on which whooping cough germs grow easily. If the germs are found the doctor is sure it is whooping cough. But not finding the germs doesn't prove that it isn't whooping cough. This test is the most reliable in the first week or two of the disease. The second test is a blood count. In some cases the result is definite, especially in the third and fourth week; in others it is no help. The third is a "fluorescent antibody" test, on material from a deep nasal swab, which is available only in certain medical centers.

Whooping cough can be a serious disease, especially in a baby under 2. It's a disease to avoid like the plague if you have a baby in the household. The main danger at this age is exhaustion and pneumonia.

Your doctor will prescribe treatment, based on the age of the child and the severity of the case. Cough medicines are always used but often have only a small influence. Most cases do better when in cold air, day and night, but naturally the child must be protected against chilling. Robust children are sometimes allowed to play outdoors throughout the disease as long as they have no fever. Naturally, they should not play with other children. Some children have many fewer coughing spells when they are kept in bed. When vomiting is a problem, frequent small meals stay down better than the regular three full meals. The safest time of all to feed children is right after they have vomited since they usually won't have another bad spell for some time. A tight abdominal binder may give relief to the exhausted abdominal muscles.

Since whooping cough is sometimes a serious disease, especially in babies and young children, it is important to call a doctor promptly when there is a suspicion. There are two main reasons: to make sure of the diagnosis, if possible; and to prescribe the right treatment. Special treatment is called for and is valuable in infants.

Quarantine regulations are different in different communities. Usually a child is kept out of school until 5 weeks after the beginning of the disease and until vomiting has stopped. The contagiousness of whooping cough does not cease suddenly after a certain number of weeks. It gradually diminishes, sooner in a light case. For home purposes, you can count a child as being no longer much danger to others when the cough has been much improved for 2 weeks. Whooping cough takes from 5 to 14 days to develop after exposure. If an infant who has not yet had whooping cough shots is exposed to the disease, a serum can be given to prevent the disease or make it lighter.

751. Mumps. Mumps is principally a disease of the saliva glands, most commonly the parotid glands, which lie in the hollow just under the lobe of the ear. First the gland fills in the hollow, then it swells the whole side of the face. It pushes the lobe of the ear upward. If you run your fingers up and down the back part of the jawbone, you can feel that the hard swelling runs forward, covering part of the jawbone.

When a child has a swelling in the side of the neck, the question always comes up, is it mumps (a specific infection of the parotid gland), or is it one of the other, rarer diseases of the parotid gland (which may recur repeatedly), or is it an ordinary swollen gland (one of the lymph glands in the side of the neck)? The ordinary lymph glands that sometimes swell after a sore throat are lower down on the neck, not tucked up under the ear lobe. The hard swelling does not cross the jawbone.

When a small child develops mumps, the swelling under the ear is usually the first thing noticed. An older child may complain of pain around his ear or in the side of his throat, especially on swallowing or chewing, for a day before the swelling begins. He may feel generally sick. There is often little fever in the beginning, but it may go higher on the second or third day. Most commonly the swelling begins on one side first, but spreads to the other side in a day or two. Sometimes it takes a week or more to spread to the other side and, of course, in some cases the second side never swells.

There are other saliva glands beside the parotids, and mumps sometimes spreads to these, too. There are the submaxillary glands, tucked up under the lower part of the jawbone. The sublinguals are just behind the point of the chin. Occasionally a person gets one of the complications of mumps without having had a swelling in any of the saliva glands.

A very mild mumps swelling may go away in 3 or 4 days. The average swelling lasts a week to 10 days.

Mumps can spread to the testicles in men and boys who have reached the age of puberty. This usually involves only one testicle. But even when both are inflamed, this does not usually cause sterility (inability to have children). Adolescent boys and men should avoid exposure. Mumps sometimes causes a special kind of mumps meningitis. The child has high fever, a stiff neck, and is delirious. This is seldom dangerous. Infection of the pancreas gland in the abdomen may cause severe abdominal pain and vomiting. The ovaries in the female may also be affected, but that rarely affects childbearing ability in later life.

Sometimes a person who believes he had mumps previously will again get a swelling of a parotid gland. Most doctors believe that one or the other such attack was caused by some other germ than the mumps virus or by a tiny stone obstructing the salivary duct; they think that a person can't have mumps twice because they believe that one attack confers immunity for life. Whether or not a person can ever have mumps twice, he can certainly catch real mumps after **thinking** he had it before. Therefore I'd advise fathers and boys who have reached puberty not to expose themselves unnecessarily when there is mumps in the family.

A mumps immune globulin (made from the blood of people who've had mumps) is available for exposed men who never received the vaccine and who don't know whether or not they've had mumps. Its value has not been proved. There is a skin test which is fairly reliable in telling whether a person is immune or susceptible and this can aid the decision whether an exposed father should take the globulin anyway.

All children, particularly boys, should receive mumps vaccine at 15 months of age. It is given in a combined shot with the measles and rubella vaccines.

You should call the doctor for a suspected case of mumps. It is important to be certain of the diagnosis. If it turns out to be a swollen lymph gland, the treatment is quite different.

Some people can't take tart-tasting foods like lemon juice during mumps (it hurts the inflamed glands), but others continue to enjoy them. So a lemon or pickle is no test of mumps.

Mumps takes 2 to 3 weeks to develop after exposure.

SCARLET FEVER, DIPHTHERIA, POLIOMYELITIS

752. Scarlet fever. It is now known that scarlet fever is not a separate disease but is a streptococcal throat infection with a rash. (See Section 722.) Scarlet fever usually begins with some of these symptoms: sore throat, vomiting, fever, headache. The rash is not apt to appear for a day or two. It begins on the warm, moist parts of the body, such as the sides of the chest, the groin, the back if the child has been lying on his back. From a distance it looks like a uniform red flush, but if you look at it more closely, you can see that it is made up of tiny red spots on a flushed skin. It may spread over the whole body and the sides of the face, but the region around the mouth stays pale. The throat is red, sometimes fiery red, and after a while the tongue usually gets red, first around the edge. You should, of course, call the doctor if your child has fever and sore throat.

Nowadays scarlet fever is not apt to be so severe as it used to be. Scarlet fever is just one form that a streptococcus infection can take, most commonly between 2 and 8 years of age. In the olden days, before it was known to be a form of streptococcus infection, scarlet fever was dreaded because cases developed far away in time and distance from other cases. Thinking that one case must come from another, people would blame the contagion on a toy that had been played with by another scarlet fever patient a year before. Now we understand that a child who develops scarlet fever probably picked up a germ from someone who just had a sore throat or was carrying the streptococcus without feeling its effect at all.

Scarlet fever should be treated promptly and carefully with one of the antibiotic drugs that shorten the disease and greatly lessen the chances of complications. The drug should be given in a form which continues for 10 days, to avoid complications (see Sections 722 and 758). The common complications are ear infections, swollen glands in the neck, nephritis (inflammation of the kidneys, with bloody, smoky-colored urine), rheumatic fever. They may begin any time in the disease, but most commonly 10 to 15 days after the fever has come down, when the child seems to be completely recovered. That is why a scarlet fever case is watched for a full 3 weeks. Report promptly any new symptoms.

Though scarlet fever may spread easily in an institution, it is not very contagious in ordinary day schools. You should not be alarmed if you receive a notice from your child's school that he has been exposed. His chances of catching it are small. (Consult your doctor about the need for throat culture or treatment.) When it does develop, it is usually within a week after exposure. After 24 hours of proper antibiotic treatment, the child is usually no longer contagious.

753. Diphtheria. Diphtheria is a serious but completely unnecessary disease. If your child is given three injections in infancy and booster shots at 18 months, 4 to 6 years, and then every 10 years, there's practically no chance of his catching it. It begins with feeling sick, sore throat, and fever. Dirty-white patches develop on the tonsils and may spread to the rest of the throat. Occasionally it begins in the larynx, with hoarseness and barking cough; the breathing becomes tight and difficult. In any case, you should call a doctor promptly when your child has sore throat and fever, or when he has any croupy symptoms. The treatment of any case of suspected diphtheria is the immediate use of serum along with other drugs. The disease develops within a week after exposure.

754. Poliomyelitis (infantile paralysis). This disease has been almost eliminated wherever polio vaccine has been systematically used. Every child should be protected in early infancy against the three types of polio, with the Sabin oral vaccine.

The disease begins, like so many other infections, with a general sick feeling (malaise), fever, and headache. There may be vomiting, constipation, or a little diarrhea. Most cases do not go on to paralysis, and a fair number of those that do recover completely. If there is any paralysis remaining after the acute stage of the infection is over, it is vitally important that the child continue to have regular, expert medical attention.

QUARANTINE

755. Quarantine or isolation for contagious diseases. In the United States, actual quarantine regulations by health departments or other government agencies are rare nowadays, except for the case of quarantine of animals being brought into the country. On general principles, I think it's a good idea to keep a child with a contagious disease in the house until he no longer has a fever and the doctor says that he no longer is contagious. I think it's sensible to keep the amount of intimate contact (kissing, hugging, and cuddling) between a child with a contagious disease and other members of the household to a minimum, except for the one person who is taking care of the sick child. This is, first of all, to prevent others—either adults or children—who have not had the disease from catching it unnecessarily. If your other children were exposed before you knew what the disease was, they will most likely catch it anyway, but it is just as well for them not to be continually overexposed. Another reason is so that they will not carry the germs to others outside the home.

To be sure, the risk of a healthy person carrying the germs to other outsiders is slight in measles, chicken pox, and whooping cough, though it occasionally occurs if less than half an hour elapses. In the case of scarlet fever, it is more important for only one adult to be in the child's room because the streptococcus that causes it can be carried in the throat for long periods. The fewer people who pick it up from the child, the less chance of its being spread around the community. Another reason for keeping sick children isolated is so that they will not be picking up new germs from others to complicate their illness.

In most places, grown-ups in the family—except those who are schoolteachers or food handlers—are not restricted from leaving the home or going to their jobs in **any** of the diseases. You have to use your own good sense, though, about visiting families who have susceptible children. The chances of your carrying the germs to other children are practically zero as long as you keep away from them. Just the same, you're not going to be very welcome if the parents are fussy, especially if the disease is one that is dreaded, such as mumps for a man or whooping cough for a baby. They'll blame you if anyone in their family catches that disease any time in the next year. On the other hand, don't hesitate to go if the disease your child has is one of the less feared ones, like measles, chicken pox, and rubella (German measles), and if you have had the disease, and if a friend who doesn't worry and whose children are out of the way asks you over for the evening.

Other children in the home who have had the disease in question are nearly always allowed to go to school during the quarantine period if it is one of the less serious diseases. The rules about brothers and sisters may be stricter for such diseases as diphtheria, meningitis, poliomyelitis, etc. The rules about other children in the family who **haven't** yet had the disease vary in different localities and in different schools. For the sake of other small children and your own conscience, keep your children away from the neighbors' small children, particularly during the period when your children may come down with a disease.

Day care centers often stay open and keep the children together after a childhood illness has appeared. The medical reason behind this is that since all the children have been exposed to the illness already, they can be observed closely instead of being sent home. Where there are working parents, a child who is sent home may be sent to friends or neighbors or other relatives, where it's likely that there won't be trained observers and where the disease can be spread to still more children.

TUBERCULOSIS

756. Tuberculosis is different in infants, children, and adults. Most people think of tuberculosis as it occurs typically in adults. A "spot," or cavity, develops in the lung and produces such symptoms as fatigue, loss of appetite, loss of weight, fever, cough, sputum.

Tuberculosis in childhood usually takes other forms. In the first 2 years of life, resistance is not so good as in later years, and there is more chance of the infection spreading to other parts of the body. That is why you never take the slightest chance of exposing a baby to a known case of tuberculosis unless the doctor and the X-ray guarantee that the person has been completely cured. It's a reason also why anyone in a household who has a chronic cough should be examined and given a tuberculin test. Also it's wise to have a new house-keeper, caregiver, or any other new member of the household tuberculin tested. If positive, an X-ray of the chest should be made.

In later childhood, tuberculous infection is more common and less likely to cause serious trouble. This is not a reason to treat it lightly or take any chances. Tuberculin tests show that in some cities as many as 10 percent of all children have had a slight infection with tuberculosis by the time they are 10 years old. Most of these cases have been so mild that no one suspected that anything was wrong at the time. An X-ray shows at most a little scar where the infection healed in the lung or in the lymph glands at the roots of the lungs.

Sometimes, however, a childhood type of tuberculosis is active enough to cause symptoms, such as fever, poor appetite, poor color, irritability, fatigue, and perhaps a cough. (There isn't much sputum, and what there is is swallowed, of course.) The infection may be in other parts of the body, such as the bones or the neck glands, but most commonly it's in the lungs and in the lymph glands at the roots of the lungs. In most of these active cases, healing gradually takes place over a period of 1 to 2 years if the child is well cared for, and only a scar is left. With proper treatment with special drugs, healing is fostered and a serious spread of infection is prevented. Children with tuberculosis are usually not contagious and frequently do not need to be separated from their families for treatment.

As children reach adolescence, they become more liable to develop the serious, adult type of tuberculosis. This should be kept in mind whenever an adolescent or young adult is rundown, tired, loses appetite or weight, whether or not there is any cough.

757. The tuberculin test. A few weeks after tubercle bacilli have gotten into the body, a person becomes "sensitized" to them. After that, if the doctor injects tuberculin (material from dead tuberculosis germs) into the skin, a red spot develops. This is a positive tuberculin test. (Nowadays the "tine test" is used for routine office tests. The tines are several tiny sharp plastic points coated with tuberculin which protrude from a plastic base and which are pressed briefly into the skin; so the more painful hypodermic needle doesn't have to be used.) The red spot shows that the body has already had experience with tuberculosis germs and reacts against them. If no red spot develops, it shows that the body has not contained the germs before. Generally speaking, if a person has ever had a tuberculous infection, he will react with a positive test result the rest of his life, even though the infection was healed long ago.

Doctors give tuberculin tests in routine examinations. The test is also made when a child isn't doing well, or has a chronic cough, or when tuberculosis is discovered in another member of the household.

If your child is ever found to have a positive tuberculin test (which is not impossible when you consider how many children are positive), you have to keep a sense of balance. There's no need to be alarmed, since a great majority of the cases discovered throughout middle childhood have either healed already or will heal gradually with care. On the other hand, you don't want to neglect any precautions.

The first step is the doctor's investigation of the child's case. X-ray of the lungs is essential in all cases to see if there are any signs of active infection or of healed scars. Sometimes the doctor orders other tests. All children who have developed a positive tuberculin test, even those without evidence of active disease, should receive specific antituberculosis drugs for at least one year. During that time, if the disease is inactive, they can live normal, active lives. The doctor may ask for further X-rays at intervals. He'll advise special precautions to avoid measles and whooping cough, which may stir up recently healed tuberculosis. Modern drug therapy is generally effective and free from serious side effects.

Aside from the affected child, the doctor checks every other member of the household (and any other adult that the child regularly comes in contact with) to discover, if possible, where the tuberculosis germs came from, and to find out if other children in the household have been infected, too. Other children should all have tuberculin tests. Any child with a positive test should be examined and have the lungs

X-rayed. It doesn't matter how healthy the other members of the household feel or how unnecessary they think all the fuss is. Many times no disease is found in any adult in the household, and it has to be assumed that the child picked up the germs from some source outside the home. On the other hand, an active case of tuberculosis is sometimes found in the least suspected adult in the house. It's a lucky thing for the person to have the disease discovered at an early stage, and it's lucky for the rest of the family to have the danger removed. No person with active tuberculosis should stay in a house with children, but should go somewhere else for drug therapy until the doctor says there is no chance of contagion.

RHEUMATIC FEVER, JOINT PAINS, AND HEART MURMURS

758. Rheumatic fever takes many forms. It is a disease that affects the joints, the heart, and other parts of the body. Doctors believe that it is a reaction in some part of the body (a joint or the heart, for instance) to a streptococcus infection in the throat. When not treated promptly and adequately, an attack is apt to last for weeks or months. Furthermore, it is a disease that has a tendency to recur again and again throughout childhood whenever the child has another streptococcal throat infection.

Sometimes it takes a very acute form with high fever. In other cases, it smolders along for weeks with only a little fever. When there is severe arthritis, it travels around from joint to joint, causing them to become swollen, red, and exquisitely tender. In other cases, the arthritis may be mild—just an aching off and on in one joint or another. If the heart is being affected severely, the child is visibly prostrated, pale and breathless. In another case, it is discovered that the heart has been damaged by some past attack that was so mild it was not noticed at the time.

In other words, rheumatic fever is an exceedingly variable disease. Naturally, you consult your doctor if your child develops any of the symptoms in a severe form. But it's just as important to have a child examined who has vague symptoms, like paleness, tiredness, slight fever, mild joint pains.

Nowadays we have several drugs that are effective in clearing up streptococcal infection in the throat—the root of the disease—and in hastening the end of the rheumatic inflammation in the joints or the heart. As a result, heart valves are no longer so likely to be damaged in the first attack. More important still, children who have had one attack of rheumatic fever can usually be kept from having further attacks—and further heart damage. They must continue indefinitely, under the doctor's continuing supervision, to take medication by mouth or by injection (to prevent new streptococcal infections) **absolutely regularly,** right into adulthood.

It is important to realize that rheumatic fever is now a preventable disease. It need not occur if children's sore throats are checked with throat cultures and if streptococcal throats are treated properly. Rheumatic fever is much less common now than formerly.

759. Joint and "growing" pains. In the olden days, it was thought natural for children to complain of growing pains in their legs and arms, and nobody worried about them.

There is, for example, the child between the ages of 2 and 5 who wakes up crying, complaining of pain around his knee or his calf. It happens only during the evening, but may recur each night for weeks on end. It is often believed to be caused by cramps in the calf muscles.

Generally, if the pains move from place to place, if there is no swelling, redness, local tenderness, or limp and if the child is entirely well otherwise, it is unlikely that a serious cause for growing pains will be found. If the pain is always in the same spot on the same limb, or if other symptoms are present, the problem should definitely be brought to the doctor's attention.

There are many other causes for pains in the arms and legs, and you can see that you need a doctor to examine, test, and decide in every case.

760. Heart murmurs. The words "heart murmur" have an alarming sound to parents. It's important to realize that a great majority of heart murmurs don't mean anything serious. Generally speaking, there are three kinds—functional (or "innocent"), acquired, and congenital.

The term **functional** or **innocent murmur** is just a clumsy way of saying that a child has a murmur that doesn't come from a congenital malformation or from rheumatic fever. These innocent murmurs are **very** common in the early years of childhood. They tend to fade out as the child reaches adolescence. Your doctor tells you about an innocent murmur in your child so that if it is discovered later in childhood by a new doctor, you can explain that it has been there all along.

Most **acquired** murmurs in childhood come from rheumatic fever, which inflames the valves and may leave scars on them afterward. This causes them either to "leak" or to obstruct the proper flow of blood. When a doctor hears a murmur in a child's heart that wasn't there before, it may mean, on the one hand, that **active** rheumatic inflammation is going on. In this case, there are other signs of infection, such as fever, rapid pulse, elevated blood count, and other abnormal tests. The doctor treats such a child with drugs until all signs of inflammation go away—even if it takes months. On the other hand, if there have been no signs of active infection for some time, the murmur may be due to old scars left over from a previous attack.

In former years, the child with an old murmur was sometimes treated as a semi-invalid for years, forbidden to play active games or sports, even though there were no signs of active infection. A doctor's tendency nowadays is to let the child who is **completely** over the stage of active inflammation go back gradually to as normal a life as possible (including the games and sports that he can do easily), if the healed scars do not noticeably interfere with the efficient working of the heart. There are two reasons for this. The muscles of the heart, as long as they are not inflamed, are strengthened by ordinary activity. Even more important is keeping the child's spirit healthy—preventing them from feeling sorry for themselves, from feeling that they are a hopeless case, that they're different from everyone else. Such children should be receiving **absolutely regular medication,** however, to prevent further streptococcus infection.

A murmur caused by **congenital heart disease** is usually

discovered at birth or within a few months afterward (occasionally not till several years later). Such a murmur is usually not caused by inflammation but means that the heart was improperly formed in the first place. The important thing is not so much the murmur itself but whether the malformation interferes with the efficiency of the heart. If it does, the baby may have blue spells, or breathe too hard, or grow too slowly.

A baby or child with a congenital heart murmur needs a careful investigation by specialists. Some cases that are serious can be cured by operation.

If a child with a congenital murmur can exercise without turning blue and without becoming abnormally out of breath, and grows at the normal rate, it is important for her emotional development that she not be thought of or treated as an invalid but that she be allowed to lead a normal life. She does need to avoid unnecessary infections and to be well cared for during illnesses, but so do all children.

These children should receive antibiotic therapy if they have to have a tooth extracted, or other operations in the mouth, to prevent germs from traveling from the mouth wound to the heart. This does not apply to the filling of tooth cavities.

URINARY DISTURBANCES

761. Late bed-wetting (enuresis). Enuresis is not a disease but a symptom. It has many causes, some of which are not well understood. It seems to run in families. Four out of five cases occur in boys, and 10 percent of boys are still wetting the bed at 12 years of age. Most of these stop wetting in adolescence. A very few cases are due to physical disease. In these there are usually symptoms, such as inability to control the urine in the daytime, that make the doctor suspicious. The great majority of cases are due to tensions of a wide variety in a child's feelings.

There are situations that upset **young** children in such a way that unconsciously they want to retreat into babyhood again. A 3-year-old who has been dry for 6 months may begin to wet again when he moves to a new house for the summer. Even though he is happy in his new surroundings, he evidently feels homesick underneath. When the children of London were removed to the country at the beginning of World War II, away from family, friends, and familiar surroundings, bed-wetting was common, even in adolescent children. It was frequent in some orphanages. Children are also apt to wet after an exciting experience, like a birthday party or an afternoon at the circus.

The commonest occasion in early childhood is the arrival of a new baby in the home.

It's important to realize that in these situations children are not wetting deliberately. After all, they are sound asleep. It is the unconscious feelings that take over at night and that express themselves in dreams. Bed-wetting often occurs during the night when a child dreams of being in a distressing situation and feels powerless to do anything. The child who wets when he is homesick or upset by the new baby may be dreaming that he is a lost baby himself, looking for the mother who will care for all his bodily needs without complaint, the way she used to.

In the case of the homesick small boy, the parents' job is to be around him a little more for a few days to ease his loneliness and help him find the joys of the new place. If there is a new baby, the job is to reassure the child that there is no need to feel displaced (Sections 541–548). There is no need to scold or shame him for wetting; he usually feels bad about it. It helps him if you express confidence that he will soon be staying dry again.

What about the child of 3 or 4 or 5 who has never become dry in the first place? (A majority of children become dry at night somewhere between 2 and 3 years of age.) In many of these cases, there has been tension over daytime toilet training. The child resisted for a long while, and the parents became more impatient. He eventually accepted daytime training, but it looks as if his resistance is continuing in his unconscious mind at night, along with a guilty feeling that he is still a naughty baby. It's wise to try to eliminate any conflict about daytime training if it still exists, and any shaming about bed wetting. In most cases, it is advisable to stop picking the child up in the evening because he is apt to interpret this as a reminder that he's only a baby. What he needs is the confidence of his parents and himself that he's growing up and that someday he will be able to stay dry all by himself.

Excitement of various kinds can play a part. A girl's romantic possessiveness toward her father may be raised to a high pitch if he responds too enthusiastically. A boy may become wildly excited every evening by rough-housing with his father (which arouses a combination of fear and pleasure) or by rough-housing with his sister (which overstimulates his aggressiveness and his unconscious sexuality).

762. A common type in boys. Some psychiatrists who have studied bed-wetting in children believe that one of the commonest types in boys (and 80 percent of children with enuresis are boys) is the following: The boy is somewhat insecure and too easily convinced that he's inadequate. He may be afraid to compete with other boys or to stand up to them. He's inclined to feel dominated by his mother. She is devoted to him, but for his particular personality she is at times too impatient, too interfering. He is too strictly brought up to fight back openly. He resists passively by procrastinating or by just being irritating. Then his mother can't help feeling more dissatisfied with him. Often in these cases the father is not giving the boy enough moral support. See Sections 57 and 519.

The measures that parents sometimes use for enuresis of this type may work in the wrong direction. To pull a groggy child out of bed (children with enuresis seem to be particularly heavy sleepers) and push him into the bathroom each night only convinces him further that he is a baby. Restricting a child's fluids after 5 o'clock usually makes him imagine he is thirsty right away (it would be the same with you and me) and almost guarantees a running argument between him and his parent all evening, which isn't good for either of them. Making a boy wash and hang out his sheets fills him with dread that other boys will learn of his disgrace. It isn't lack of shame that causes his enuresis. Any boy over 5 would give all he owns to overcome the problem. He wants to cooperate, but he has little control over the unconscious feelings that produce the wetting in his sleep.

What many a boy with enuresis needs is more confidence

that he is a competent person, and this can be gained only gradually, with help. But whether or not the parents want to or can arrange for outside help, there are a number of things the parents can do, depending on circumstances. Their general attitude should be one of encouragement. They can explain that they have learned that quite a few children have this problem but that practically all of them overcome it in time. They can express their confidence that their own child will, too.

I think it is preferable in most cases to give up such methods as getting the child up at night and restricting fluids.

Pasting gold stars on a chart is occasionally helpful for a 5-, 6-, or 7-year-old. A reward that the child has long desired—skates, bicycle, sports equipment—may be worth a try. Even better, I think, though it may not sound sensible to you, is to give, right away, a possession that the child has yearned for but that the parents have been withholding. The idea is to make the child begin to feel equal with other children, and confident of the parents' trust.

If the father has been too self-effacing at home, it helps a lot for him to take a more active part in managing his son and, if possible, to find some hobby that he can enjoy with him occasionally. If his mother has been pushing and prodding him in other areas, such as homework, or getting dressed in the morning (Section 528), she can try to ease up or turn these jobs over to the father.

763. Enuresis in girls. The commonest picture in enuresis in girls is quite different from that in most boys. The girl is more apt to be a spunky sort who is highly competitive with her brother or with her mother. (She may feel, for instance, that she can take care of her father and keep him company better than her mother can.) She may be resentful about being a girl because of the discrimination so often involved. In the case of the girl with enuresis, the job is to help her feel more comfortable about being a girl, to lessen the causes of rivalry with her brother, for her parents to show her they love her most as a girl, for her father to demonstrate that he loves her as a daughter, but that he shares his concerns and interests primarily with his wife.

764. What about psychiatric or psychoanalytic evaluation and treatment for enuresis? I am strongly in favor of treatment if a child has other problems in addition to enuresis; if a boy, for instance, has a number of fears, is timid, gets easily bullied by other boys, does poorly in school, or is in frequent conflict with his mother; if a girl is excessively rivalrous with her mother or brother or is consistently unhappy about being a girl. In these cases the psychiatric treatment is more important for the other problems than for the bed-wetting, which will probably stop in adolescence anyway. In quite a few cases the enuresis itself yields only after long therapy or not at all.

If the parents feel unclear about their child's adjustment to other children, schoolwork, teachers, or even to themselves, they could get help in evaluation from the teacher or principal, or a family social agency or a child guidance clinic. (See Sections 633 and 634.)

A drug has been used extensively for enuresis in recent years. It is very often successful at first, but less so as time goes on, and, after its use is stopped, a child may sometimes regress.

An electrical apparatus that rings a bell when the bed has been wet has been moderately successful in training children to stay dry. My own inclination would be not to use such an aggressive, mechanical method for a sensitive child who has a number of problems (psychotherapy would be more appropriate) or for a child under 5 years. It is more suited to a well-adjusted, older child who himself wants help in overcoming an embarrassing symptom.

765. Daytime wetting. Late daytime wetting (say after the age of 3) is, once in a great while, due to physical disease. In such a case, the child usually just dribbles a small amount at frequent intervals. He needs a thorough checkup by the doctor. The urine should be examined in **all** cases of late wetting.

In most cases of daytime wetting there is bed-wetting, too, and much that was said in Sections 761 and 762 about the importance of various kinds of nervousness could be repeated here.

But there are two factors that ought to be emphasized.

Most of the children who go on wetting in the daytime have a tendency to balk and to procrastinate. Watching such a child, you can see that one-half of him knows perfectly well that his bladder is uncomfortable—he's prancing around restlessly and crossing his legs. But the other half of him is absorbed in play and refuses to do anything about it. There's nothing to be concerned about if a light "accident" occurs once in a while with a small child when he's deeply absorbed. But if he's stalling and procrastinating all the time, about everything, it's usually a sign that he's being pushed and bossed too much. It's become such a habit to resist that he does it not just when his parents but when his own insides tell him there is something he ought to be doing. This is often called laziness, but actually it requires a lot of effort. It's like a car being driven with the brakes on.

A few children, even happy, well-adjusted ones, have trouble controlling the bladder when they are excited or frightened or laugh suddenly. At these times, they find themselves wetting without any warning. This is not a disease, and it's not an entirely strange thing. Many animals automatically empty the bladder when they are alarmed. The child needs only to be reassured that he has done nothing to be ashamed of.

766. Frequent urinating. Frequent urinating has several possible causes. When it develops in a child who was not frequent before, it may mean some disease, such as an infection of the urinary system or diabetes. The child and a urine specimen should be examined promptly by the doctor.

A few individuals, even calm ones, seem to have bladders that never hold as much as the average, and this may be the way they were made. But most of the children (and adults, too) who regularly have to urinate frequently are somewhat high-strung or worried. In one case it's due to a temporary strain; in another it's a chronic tendency. Even the healthy, normal athlete is apt to have to go to the toilet every 15 minutes just before a race. The parents' job, then, is to find out what, if anything, is making the child tense. In one case it's the handling at home, in another it's relations with other children, in still another it's school. Most often it's a combination of these. A common story involves the timid child and the teacher who seems severe. To begin with, the child's apprehensiveness keeps his bladder from relaxing sufficiently to hold much urine. Then he worries about asking permission to be excused. If the teacher makes a fuss about his leaving the room, it's worse still. It's wise to get a note from the doctor, not simply requesting that the child be excused, but explaining the child's nature and why his bladder works that way. If the teacher is approachable and the parent is tactful, a personal visit will help, too.

767. Difficult urination. Once in a great while a baby, usually a boy, is born with such a small urinary passage or opening that he has to push hard to pass his urine, or the urine comes in a small stream or dribble. The urinary passage needs to be enlarged promptly by a doctor. It is harmful to the inner passages and the kidneys to have the urine obstructed.

Occasionally in hot weather, when a child is perspiring a great deal and not drinking enough, he may pass his urine infrequently, perhaps not for 12 hours or more. What does come is scanty and dark and it may burn. The same thing may happen during a fever. A child in hot weather or when feverish needs plenty of chances and occasional reminders to drink between meals, especially when he is too small to tell what he wants.

A fairly frequent cause of painful urination in girls is an infection of the vagina that inflames the lower urinary passage, too. This may make her feel as if she has to urinate frequently, though she may be unable or too scared to do anything, or pass only a few drops. The doctor should be consulted and a urine specimen examined. Until a doctor can be reached, she can be relieved by sitting several times a day in a shallow warm bath to which has been added a half cup of bicarbonate of soda. After gently blotting dry the urinary region, a thick dab of petroleum jelly or an ointment containing petroleum jelly and lanolin can be applied to it to soothe and protect it.

768. Sore on the end of the penis. Sometimes a small raw area appears around the opening, or meatus, of the penis. There may be enough swelling of the tissues here to close up the meatus and make it difficult for the boy to pass his urine. This little sore is a localized diaper rash, caused by ammonia (which can be smelled in the bed in the morning). The ammonia is not passed in the urine but is manufactured from urine by bacteria in the diaper, nightclothes, and bedclothes. This ammonia sore occurs most often when the baby is over a year old and the parents have stopped the diaper service. The bacteria have accumulated in the pajamas, sheets, and pads, and they set to work making ammonia just as soon as the child wets himself in the evening. The important thing in treatment is to boil the diapers, pajamas, sheets, and pads every day or treat them with a diaper antiseptic (Section 366) as long as any sore exists. Meanwhile, the sore can be soothed and protected by frequent application of an ointment containing petroleum jelly and lanolin, especially before going to bed. If the child is in pain from being unable to urinate for many hours, he can be sat in a warm bath for half an hour. If this doesn't make him urinate, the doctor should be called.

769. Infections of the urinary tract (pyuria, pyelitis, pyelonephritis, nephritis, cystitis). Infections in the kidneys or the bladder may cause a stormy illness with a high, irregular fever. On the other hand, infection is sometimes discovered by accident in a routine urine examination in a child who hasn't felt sick at all. An older child may complain of frequent, burning urination, but most often there are no signs pointing to the urinary tract. These infections are commoner in girls, and in the first 2 years of life. Prompt medical treatment is necessary, and usually is successful.

If there is a lot of pus, the urine may be hazy or cloudy, but a little may not show to the naked eye. On the other hand, a normal child's urine may be cloudy, especially when it cools, due to ordinary minerals in it. So you can't tell definitely from looking at the urine whether it is infected or not.

If a urinary infection does not clear up satisfactorily, or if the child ever has a second urinary infection, her whole urinary system should be investigated thoroughly with special examinations. Urinary infections are more common in children who have abnormally formed urinary passages. If there is anything pointing to such an abnormality, it should be corrected before permanent harm is done to the kidneys. For this reason it is wise, after a child has had a urinary infection, to check her urine again 1 or 2 months later to make sure the infection has not come back, even though she appears well. Infections are usually treated carefully for 2 weeks. Then there are several follow-ups, over a period of time, to see whether pus or bacteria have reappeared in the urine.

It's very important to teach girls to wipe themselves from front to back, after they urinate or have a bowel movement. This prevents the bringing of germs from the anal region into the opening of the urethra (the tube between the bladder and the outside world). Wiping from back to front ("wiping up") is considered a frequent cause of repeated urinary tract infections in girls.

770. Pus in a girl's urine may not mean urinary infection. There is always the possibility that pus in a girl's urine is coming from a vaginal infection, even one so mild that there is no visible inflammation or discharge. For this reason, it should never be assumed, without further investigation, that pus in an ordinary specimen means an infection of her urinary system. The first step is to secure a "clear" urine specimen. That means to separate the labia, sponge the genital region briefly and gently with a piece of wet absorbent cotton, and blot dry with a soft towel or a piece of dry absorbent cotton, before letting her pass urine for the specimen. The important test is the culture of the specimen to see whether there are bacteria and which they are.

VAGINAL DISCHARGE

771. Treat it considerately. It is fairly common for young girls to develop slight vaginal discharges. A majority of these are caused by unimportant germs and clear up in a short time. A thick, profuse discharge that is irritating may be caused by a more serious infection and needs prompt medical treatment.

A mild one that persists for days should be examined, too. A discharge that is partly pus and partly blood is sometimes caused by a small girl's having pushed some object into her vagina, which remains there, causing irritation and infection. If this is found to be the case, it is natural and sensible for her parents to ask her to please not do this again; but it's better not to make the girl feel really guilty or to imply that she might have, or has hurt herself seriously. The exploring and experimenting she has done are not too different from what most children do at this age. As explained in Section 573, little girls may be upset about genital differences and sometimes conclude that the reason they are not like boys is because they have injured themselves in handling their genitals. Parental accusations, either about masturbation or about genital injury, may reinforce these fears.

If there is delay in reaching the doctor, the burning sensation from a slight discharge can often be relieved without fuss by sitting the child twice a day in a shallow bath to which half a cup of bicarbonate of soda has been added. Wearing white cotton panties, using white, unperfumed toilet paper, and wearing clothes that provide adequate air ventilation to the vaginal area may help in the prevention and treatment of vaginal irritation.

SOILING (ENCOPRESIS)

772. Soiling of the clothing with feces (encopresis) is, like enuresis, not a disease, but a symptom.

One type of encopresis occurs when a child has never learned bowel control. (See Sections 424–439.) Following the explanations in Sections 424 through 439, with the help of your doctor, should bring about a solution to this situation pretty easily.

A more common type of encopresis occurs in the child who has been trained and then later begins to soil his pants one or more times a week. This type almost always happens after some stressful situation has developed in the family, especially if there has been a sudden separation from an important family member. This situation can often go on for many months with the parents and the child feeling too ashamed to tell the doctor about it. Meanwhile, the parent (usually the mother) tends to work harder and harder at getting the child trained again, which may make the child more tense. In the most severe form of this kind of soiling, the child holds back his feces and develops a large amount of hard, dry stool in the rectum. From time to time, some watery feces leak out around this hard, dry (impacted) stool and soil the child's underpants. This type of soiling has to be taken care of with the child's doctor, and the sooner the better. In cases that have gone on for a long time, with much family stress, it's often necessary for the child and parents to be seen by a children's psychiatrist or psychologist or social worker, while the medical doctor prescribes whatever diet and medicine are needed.

STOMACHACHES AND UPSETS

Diarrhea is also discussed in Sections 361–363, vomiting in Sections 350, 351, and 698.

773. Call the doctor. Don't give cathartics. You certainly should get in touch with the doctor for any stomachache that lasts as long as 1 hour, whether it is severe or not. There are dozens of causes. A few of them are serious; most are not. A doctor is trained to distinguish among them and prescribe the right treatment. People are apt to jump to the conclusion that a stomachache is due either to something that has been eaten or to appendicitis. Actually, neither of these is a common cause. Children can usually eat strange foods or an unusual amount of a regular food without any indigestion.

It is wrong to give a cathartic before the doctor has seen the child because there are some stomachaches for which a cathartic is dangerous. Before you call the doctor, take the child's temperature so that you can report what it is. The treatment, until you reach the doctor, should consist of putting the child to bed and giving nothing to eat. If the child is thirsty, give small sips of water.

774. Common causes of stomachache. In the early weeks of life, stomachache is common in **indigestion** and **colic.** These are discussed in Sections 336, and 352.

After the age of a year, one of the commonest causes of stomachache is the onset of a simple **cold** or **sore throat** or **flu,** especially when there is fever. It is just a sign that the infection is disturbing the intestines as well as other parts of the body. In the same way, almost any infection may cause vomiting and constipation, especially in the beginning. A small child is apt to complain that her tummy hurts when she really means that she feels nauseated. She often vomits soon after this complaint.

Constipation is a common cause of abdominal pain. It may be dull and may recur or it may be sudden and very painful (though it may go away just as suddenly).

There are many different kinds of **stomach** and **intestinal infections** that cause stomachache, sometimes with vomiting, sometimes with diarrhea, sometimes with both. These are often loosely called "intestinal flu" or "intestinal grippe," or "a virus," meaning a contagious disease caused by an unknown germ. These infections often pass through several members of a family, one after the other. Some epidemics of intestinal flu turn out to be dysentery or paratyphoid infections. There may or may not be fever with any of them.

"Food poisoning" is caused by eating food that contains toxins manufactured by certain bacteria. The food may or may not taste queer. Food poisoning seldom occurs from food that has been thoroughly and recently cooked, because the cooking kills these germs. It's caused most often by pastries filled with custard or whipped cream, creamy salads, and poultry stuffing. Germs multiply readily in these substances if they remain out of the refrigerator for many hours. Another cause is improperly home-canned foods.

The symptoms of food poisoning are usually vomiting, diarrhea, and stomachache. Sometimes there are chills and sometimes fever. Everyone who eats the contaminated food is apt to be affected by it to some degree at about the same time, in contrast to an intestinal flu, which usually spreads through a family over a number of days.

Children with **feeding problems** often have stomachaches when they sit down to a meal or after they have eaten a little. The parents are apt to think the child has made up the stomachache as an excuse not to eat. I think that it's more likely that the poor stomach is all tightened up by the child's tense feeling at mealtimes, and that the stomachache is real. The treatment here is for the parents to handle mealtimes in such a way that the child enjoys the food. See Sections 664–671.

Children who have never had feeding problems but who have other **worries** can have stomachaches, too, especially around mealtime. Think of the child who is nervous about starting school in the fall and has a stomachache instead of an appetite for breakfast, or the child who feels guilty about something that hasn't been found out yet. All kinds of emotions, from fears to pleasant excitement, can affect the stomach and intestines. They can cause not only pains and lack of appetite, but vomiting and diarrhea and constipation. Pain in such cases tends to be in the center of the abdomen.

There are other infrequent causes of stomachache, too: chronic indigestion with gas, intestinal allergies, inflamed lymph glands in the abdomen, kidney disturbances, and so on. As you can well see, a child who has stomach pains—whether they are acute and severe, or mild and chronic—needs a thorough checkup by the doctor.

775. Appendicitis. Let me at the start contradict some common notions about appendicitis. There isn't necessarily any fever. The pain isn't necessarily severe. The pain doesn't usually settle in the lower right side of the abdomen until the attack has been going on for some time. Vomiting doesn't always occur. A blood count doesn't prove that a stomachache is or isn't due to appendicitis.

The appendix is a little offshoot from the large intestine, about the size of a short earthworm. It usually lies in the central part of the right lower quarter of the abdomen. But it can be lower down, or over toward the middle of the abdomen, or as far up as the ribs. When it becomes inflamed, it's a gradual process, like the formation of a boil. That's why a sudden severe pain in the abdomen that lasts a few minutes and then goes away for good isn't appendicitis. The worst danger is that the inflamed appendix will burst, very much as a boil bursts, and spread the infection all through the abdomen. This is called peritonitis. An appendicitis that is developing very rapidly can reach the point of bursting in less than 24 hours. That's why any stomachache that persists for as long as 1 hour should be seen by a doctor, even though 9 out of 10 cases prove to be something else.

In the most typical cases, there is pain around the navel for several hours. Only later does it shift to the lower right side. There is apt to be vomiting once or twice, but it doesn't always occur. The appetite is usually diminished, but not always. The bowels may be normal or constipated, rarely loose. After it's gone on a few hours, the temperature is apt to be elevated to 100° or 101°F, more or less, but it's possible to have real appendicitis without any fever at all. The person may feel more pain when he pulls his right knee up, or when he stretches it way back, or when he walks around. You can see that the symptoms of appendicitis vary a lot in different cases and that you need a doctor to make the diagnosis. Doctors are guided most by whether they find a tender area in the right side, as they feel deeply but gently into every part of the abdomen. You will notice that they don't ask whether it hurts every time they poke, but on the contrary try to distract the child from what they are doing. This is because many children with a pain in the stomach, especially young ones, are delighted to say, "Yes, that hurts," every time they are asked. When doctors find a tender spot in the right side of the abdomen, they are suspicious of appendicitis, but they sometimes like to have a blood count to help them decide. A raised blood count just says there is infection somewhere. It doesn't say where.

It's often impossible for the most expert of doctors to be absolutely sure whether or not a child has appendicitis. When there is much suspicion the doctor advises operation, and for a very good reason. If it is appendicitis, it is dangerous to delay. If it is not appendicitis, it is unlikely that any harm will be done by prompt operation.

There is an uncommon condition called **intussusception** in which the intestine "telescopes" into itself and becomes obstructed. The two most prominent symptoms are vomiting and intermittent abdominal cramps in a baby who has seemed otherwise healthy. In one case the vomiting is more prominent, in another the pain. The vomiting is more copious and repetitious than the usual "spitting" of a baby. The cramps are sudden and usually severe. They come a number of minutes apart, and between them the baby may be fairly comfortable. Vomiting is apt to occur and be repeated. After a number of hours (during which there may be normal or loose movements), a movement is passed containing mucus and blood—a "currant jelly" or "prune juice" stool. This condition occurs most commonly between the ages of 4 months and 2 years, though it may occur outside this age period. Though uncommon, it requires emergency medical treatment, without delay, and that is why it is mentioned here.

Also rare but serious are other types of **intestinal obstructions.** A part of the intestine gets kinked and stuck in a pocket in the abdomen—most frequently in an inguinal hernia (Section 778). There are usually vomiting and sharp cramps.

When the doctor suspects appendicitis or another serious cause for abdominal pain, he will probably do a rectal examination.

776. Chronic and intermittent diarrheas. There are several different digestive diseases that cause chronic diarrheas in infants and young children. They were once all considered the same condition. They are still not completely understood.

Cystic fibrosis. The two commonest symptoms of this disease are foul-smelling diarrhea and cough, but there is great variation in the symptoms. There may be frequent bowel movements which look normal in early infancy but become mushy, greasy, and foul-smelling after solid foods are introduced. The rectum may protrude. The intestines may be obstructed right after birth by dry meconium, and off and on again in later years by hard, dry feces (BMs). Most infants have a good or ravenous appetite in this disease. Nevertheless, malnutrition sets in because of the inability to properly digest food. Persistent bronchitis develops, but this may not be until later in childhood in a mild case.

This is a progressive, hereditary disease of certain glands, inherited from both sides of the family. The pancreas secretes insufficient digestive juices. The glands along the bronchial tubes secrete only dry mucus, in insufficient amounts, so infections can't be prevented or coped with. The sweat glands put out too much salt, which the parents may notice on kissing their baby. (The salt test is useful in diagnosis.) In severe cases, without treatment, the greatest danger in infancy and early childhood comes from bronchial infection.

The primary aim of treatment is to keep the bronchial tubes cleared out with postural drainage and antibiotic drugs as needed. The digestive symptoms are treated with a high-protein, moderate-fat diet, additional vitamins, and by adding pancreatic enzymes to the meals.

The child should be evaluated and have his treatment supervised at a special center for cystic fibrosis if at all possible. The name of the national organization is: Cystic Fibrosis Foundation, 6000 Executive Boulevard, Suite 309, Rockville, MD 20852.

Celiac disease is characterized by frequent, loose, foul-smelling bowel movements, which may appear intermittently toward the end of the first year but become chronic in the second year. There may be intermittent constipation. The appetite worsens, the abdomen becomes distended, and the nutrition suffers. The intestines are unable to handle fats. The child appears wasted and feels miserable.

The cause of the symptoms appears to be inability to digest gluten, a protein which occurs principally in wheat, but also in oats and barley.

The treatment is to remove these foods completely from the diet. However, the underlying condition in the intestine may persist and some of these children continue to have symptoms from time to time for years. It would be well to have a child with celiac symptoms under the care of a specialist in a medical center.

Other malabsorption conditions have been recognized in recent years, the best known being inability to digest certain ordinary sugars. These cause bowel movements that are loose but not foul-smelling.

Following any prolonged diarrhea there may be a problem in digestion of lactose, the sugar in milk. In the past these children were usually called allergic to milk. The problem is usually temporary; a milk substitute can be used.

777. Worms are no disgrace, but need treatment. It horrifies parents to find worms in their child's movement, but there is no reason to be distressed or to decide that the child has not been properly cared for.

Pinworms, or threadworms, are the commonest variety. They look like white threads, a third of an inch long. They live in the lower intestine, but come out between the buttocks at night to lay their eggs. They can be found there at night or in the bowel movement. They cause itching around the anus, which may disturb the child's sleep. In former days worms were thought to be the chief cause for children's grinding their teeth at night, but this is probably not so. Save a specimen of the worms to show the doctor. There is an efficient treatment for pinworms, which a doctor should supervise.

Roundworms look very much like earthworms. The first suspicion comes when one is discovered in the bowel movement. They usually don't cause symptoms unless the child has a great number of them. The doctor will prescribe treatment.

Hookworms are common in some parts of the southern United States. They may cause malnutrition and anemia. The disease is contracted by going barefoot in soil that is infested. A doctor can prescribe treatment.

HERNIAS, RUPTURES, HYDROCELE

778. Hernias, or ruptures. The commonest hernia of all, protruding navel, is taken up in Section 284.

The next commonest is what doctors call inguinal hernia. There is meant to be a small passage from inside the abdomen, down along the groin, into the scrotum (in the case of a boy), for the blood vessels and nerves that go to the testicles. This passageway has to pass through the layers of muscle that make up the wall of the abdomen. If these openings in the muscles are larger than average, a piece of intestine may be squeezed out of the abdomen and down the passageway when the child strains or cries. If the intestine goes only partway down, it makes a bulging in the groin. If it goes all the way down into the scrotum (the pouch for the testicles behind the penis), the scrotum looks very enlarged for the time being. Inguinal hernia does occur, though less commonly, in girls. It appears as a protrusion in the groin.

Rupture is a bad name for a condition like this, because it sounds as though something breaks when the intestine is pushed down during straining. This idea makes parents worry unnecessarily about their baby's crying. Actually nothing breaks. The overlarge passageway is present at the time the baby is born; it is the way he is made.

In most hernias the intestine slips back up into the abdomen when the baby or child is lying down quietly. It may push down every time he stands up, or it may go down only once in a great while when he strains hard.

Occasionally an inguinal hernia becomes "strangulated." This means that the intestine has stuck in the passage and that the blood vessels have been kinked and shut off. It is a form of intestinal obstruction. This causes abdominal pain and vomiting. It calls for emergency surgical care.

Strangulation of an inguinal hernia occurs most often in the first 6 months of life. Usually it is a hernia that has not been noticed before. The parent changes the baby because he is crying so hard and notices the lump in his groin for the first time. (The groin is the groove between the abdomen and the thigh.) It is not wise to try to push the lump down with the fingers. However, while waiting for the doctor or while driving the baby to the hospital, you can elevate his hips on a pillow and apply an ice bag (or crushed ice in a sock with a plastic bag around it) to the hernia. These procedures together may make the intestine slip back into the abdomen. You shouldn't feed the baby (breast or bottle), because it's better for the stomach to be empty if anesthesia and surgery are needed.

If you suspect a hernia in your child, you should, of course, report it to the doctor right away. Nowadays inguinal hernias are usually repaired promptly by surgery. It is not a serious operation, it is almost always successful, and the child is often out of the hospital on the same day.

779. Hydrocele, or swelling around the testicle. Hydrocele is often confused with hernia or rupture because it also causes a swelling in the scrotum. Each testicle in the scrotum is surrounded by a delicate sac that contains a few drops of fluid. This helps to protect the testicle. Quite often in newborn babies there is an extra amount of fluid in the sac that surrounds the testicle, and this makes it appear to be several times its normal size. Sometimes this swelling takes place at a later period.

A hydrocele is nothing to worry about. The fluid in most cases diminishes as the baby gets older, and then nothing needs to be done for it. Occasionally an older boy has a chronic hydrocele, which should be operated on if it is uncomfortably large. You should not try to make the diagnosis yourself. Let the doctor decide whether it's hernia or hydrocele.

EYE TROUBLES

780. Reasons for seeing the eye doctor. Children need to go to an eye doctor if their eyes turn in (cross-eyes) or out (walleyes) at any age (Section 372); if they are having **any** trouble with schoolwork; if they are complaining of aching, smarting or tired eyes; if their eyes are inflamed; if they are having headaches; if they hold their books too close; if they cock the head to one side when looking at something carefully; or if the vision is found to be defective by the chart test which should be performed by the child's regular doctor between 3 and 4 years of age, and yearly thereafter by the regular doctor or a tester at school. However, just because children can read a chart satisfactorily in school does not mean for sure that their eyes are all right. If they are having symptoms of eyestrain, they should be examined anyway. To be completely sure, it is a good idea to take a child to the oculist by the age of 4. Chart testing, at school or the doctor's, should be done each year after 5.

Nearsightedness, which is the commonest eye trouble that interferes with schoolwork, develops most often in the age period between 6 and 10. It can come on quite rapidly, so don't ignore the signs of it (holding the book closer, having trouble seeing the blackboard at school) just because the child's vision was all right a few months before.

Inflammation of the eye (conjunctivitis) can be caused by many different infections or by allergy. Most of the mild cases are caused by ordinary cold germs, and accompany colds in the nose. You should be more suspicious of inflammation when there is no nose cold. It is a good idea to get in touch with your doctor anyway, but particularly when the white of the eye becomes reddened or when there is pus.

781. Harmful fluids in the eye. If a child is accidentally squirted in the eye by something in a spray can or some possibly harmful fluid is splashed in the eye, flush the eye promptly by laying the child on the back and squeezing water freely into the eye from an eye dropper or washcloth.

782. Specks. Specks in the eye should be removed promptly. It is always preferable to let a doctor do this if possible. It is absolutely necessary to go to a doctor if the speck has not been removed in half an hour. A speck that stays imbedded over the pupil or iris for several hours may cause a serious infection. There are three methods you can try if it is difficult to reach the doctor. The first is to draw the upper eyelid down and away from the eye, holding it by the lashes. This gives the tears a chance to wash the speck out. Next, you can use an eyecup, containing a sterile 2 percent solution of boric acid (2 level teaspoonfuls of boric acid powder in a cupful of boiled water which has been allowed to cool) or ¼ teaspoon of salt in a cup of boiled water. The child tips the head down, applies the filled eyecup to the eye, straightens the head up, blinks several times with the cup against the eye. The third method is to examine the inside of the upper lid. This is where most specks lodge. You need two clean cotton swabs (the kind that come on flexible plastic sticks). Tell the child to look down and **keep** looking down. This relaxes the upper lid. Take hold of the eyelashes of the upper lid, pull the lid down as far as it goes, lay one cotton swab horizontally across the middle of the lid, and fold the eyelid back over the swab. While you hold the lid firmly folded back, reach for the other cotton swab. If you see the speck on the lid, gently wipe it off with the swab. You need a good strong light. (An inside-out eyelid looks and feels strange, but it doesn't hurt.) If you can't find the speck and the pain goes on, or if the speck is lodged on the eyeball, go to an eye doctor promptly. Don't try to remove a speck from the eyeball yourself.

783. Styes. A stye is an infection in a hair follicle of the eyelashes, and is similar to a pimple anywhere else. A stye is caused by ordinary pus germs that happen to be rubbed onto the eyelid. The stye usually comes to a head and breaks. The doctor may prescribe an ointment to promote healing and prevent spreading. An adult with a stye feels more comfortable by applying hot applications, and this may hasten its coming to a head and breaking, but it makes no great difference. A child doesn't want to be bothered. The main trouble with a stye is that one often leads to another, probably because when the first one breaks the germs are spread to other hair follicles. This is a reason for trying to keep a child from rubbing or fingering the eyelid at the time a stye is coming to a head or discharging. A child who has several styes in succession should be examined by the doctor, because styes occasionally mean that there is some condition that lowers a person's resistance.

A parent with a stye should wash her or his hands thoroughly before doing things for a baby or small child, especially if the stye has been touched, because the germs are easily passed from person to person. If possible, the parent with a stye had better not handle the baby temporarily.

784. Things that don't harm children's eyes. Watching television, sitting too close to the set, reading an excessive amount, or holding the book close will not harm the eyes. (If the book is held close, the eyes should be checked for nearsightedness, though.) However, there is some evidence that there can be exposure to harmful radiation from sitting too close to old color TV sets. I think it is best to play it safe and keep children (and adults) at least 10 feet away from such screens.

CONVULSIONS

785. A convulsion is a frightening thing to see in a child, but in most cases it is not dangerous in itself. Most convulsions stop in a short time, whether or not any treatment is used.

Telephone for the doctor. If you cannot reach one immediately, don't worry. The convulsion is usually over anyway and the child asleep by the time the doctor can get there.

Keep the child from hurting herself. Turn her on her side, to allow saliva to run out of the corner of the mouth.

Don't try to get her into a tepid bath; it won't make that much difference.

If the child has a high fever, give her a wet rub to get her temperature down. Take off her clothes. Wet your hand in water and rub one arm for a couple of minutes, then the other arm, each leg, the chest, the back. Keep wetting your hand as necessary. The gentle rubbing brings the blood to the surface, and the evaporation helps in the cooling. If the convulsions continue or if the temperature stays above 103°F, you can continue the rub. Don't cover a child with blankets when you are trying to get the temperature down.

In most convulsions, the child loses consciousness, the eyes roll up, the teeth are clenched, and the body or parts of the body are shaken by twitching movements. The breathing is heavy, and there may be a little frothing at the lips. Sometimes the urine and the bowel movement are passed.

Convulsions are brought on by irritation of the brain from a number of different causes. The causes are different at different age periods. Every convulsion should be evaluated by the child's doctor or the doctor in the emergency room. In the newborn baby they are usually not due to injury to the brain.

786. In the young child, between 1 and 5, the commonest cause is sudden fever at the onset of colds, sore throats, and flu. Fever coming on so quickly seems to make the nervous system irritable. Lots of children of this age are trembly at the start of their fevers, even though they don't have convulsions. So if your child around 2 or 3 has a convulsion at the onset of a fever, it doesn't necessarily mean that there is a serious disease, and it doesn't mean that the child is going to have more convulsions in later life. Even a convulsion attributed to fever needs to be evaluated by a physician. Convulsions are rare after the first day of fever.

787. Epilepsy is the name given to convulsions that occur repeatedly in the older child, without any fever or other disease. Nobody knows the real cause in the great majority of cases. There are two most common forms of epilepsy. In "grand mal" attacks, the person loses consciousness completely and has convulsions. In "petit mal," the attack is so brief that the person doesn't fall or lose control of herself or himself, but may just stare or stiffen momentarily.

Every case of epilepsy should be investigated by a doctor familiar with the disease. Though the condition is usually a chronic one, there are several drugs that are helpful in stopping or reducing the frequency of the spells.

There are other causes of convulsions less common than these that have been mentioned.

For information on local services, you can write: Epilepsy Foundation of America, 4351 Garden City Drive, Landover, MD 20785, phone (301)459-3700.

OTHER CONDITIONS

788. Sudden infant death syndrome ("crib death"). Every once in a while, a baby between the ages of 3 weeks and 7 months is found dead in bed. There is never an adequate explanation, even when a postmortem examination (autopsy) is done. There may have been a very slight cold, but no fever or prostration. There may be a bit of bloody foam on the baby's lips. This and the fact that some of these babies have their faces in the mattress or have their blankets over their heads have often led in the past to the conclusion that the baby suffocated. The finding of vomitus suggests that the baby may have choked to death on the vomitus.

The parents are shocked—a sudden death is much more shattering than one which follows a worsening illness. They are overwhelmed by guilt, assuming that they should have paid more attention to the cold if there was one, or that they should have noticed something, or that they should have gone in to see the child even though there was no reason to do so. But no sensible parent would call a doctor for the very slight cold that some of these children have. And if the doctor had come she or he would not have used any treatment because there would not have been any reason to do so. He or she could not anticipate the tragedy.

Though crib death has been studied extensively, there is no satisfactory, scientific explanation. There has been speculation about allergy, low blood sugar, and about sudden overwhelming infections, but no proof.

The only things that are known for sure are that crib death is not due to choking, smothering, or strangulation (the foam on the lips appears after many kinds of deaths), and that there is no known specific infection that causes this disease. It does not run in families.

It is not caused by any new development such as birth-control pills, fluoridation, cigarette smoking, bottle feeding, or modern drugs, since it occurred in Biblical times and was as common in the eighteenth century as in the twentieth. It is not caused, as was suspected earlier in this century, by an enlarged thymus gland. It is not due to injury to the spinal cord in automobile collisions. It occurs all over the world in all climates.

New theories about the cause of sudden infant death syndrome are brought out frequently. Check with your doctor. The important thing to remember is that it is **not** due to anything the parents have done or left undone. It is not preventable as far as anybody knows.

There will usually be depression in the parents lasting for many weeks, with ups and downs. They may experience difficulty concentrating and sleeping, poor appetite, heart or stomach symptoms. They may feel a strong urge to get away or a dread of being alone. If there are other children, the parents may fear to let them out of their sight, or want to shun responsibility for caring for them, or may treat them irritably. Some parents want to talk, others bottle up their feelings.

Other children in the family are surely upset whether they show ordinary grief or not. Small children may just cling, or behave badly to get their parents' attention. Older children may appear remarkably unconcerned; but psychiatric experience tells us that they are trying to protect themselves from the full force of grief and guilt. It is hard for adults to see why a child should feel guilty. But all children have resentful feelings at times toward their brothers and sisters. Their primitive unconscious thinking tells them that their hostile feelings brought about the death.

If the parents avoid talking about the dead baby, this adds to the other children's sense that they are guilty. So it is good for the parents to talk about the baby, to explain that it was a special disease of babies that caused the death and not the fault of anyone. (Euphemisms like "the baby went away," or "never woke up," add new mysteries and anxieties.) It's particularly helpful if the parents will try to respond in a gentle way to every one of the children's questions and comments, so that they will feel that it is all right to bring up their deeper worries, too.

The parents should seek some kind of counseling—from a family social agency, a guidance clinic, a psychiatrist, a clergyman—so that they can express and come to understand their overwhelming feelings.

The National Sudden Infant Death Syndrome Foundation, Incorporated, 2 Metro Plaza, Suite 205, 8240 Professional Place, Landover, MD 20785, phone (301)459-3388, has chapters in many cities, where parents can get help and comfort from others who have gone through this tragedy. The foundation prepares literature, solicits funds, and supports research.

789. Hyperactivity. A lot of attention has been given lately to the problem of the hyperactive child, especially the one who is having trouble paying attention in school.

Hyperactivity has become linked—in the minds of some physicians and teachers and in popular articles—with the concept of "minimal brain damage." This term is so vague and all-inclusive as to be almost meaningless. The terms "attention deficit disorder" and "dyslexia," as well as a number of other terms, are used by many people interchangeably with the term "minimal brain damage" to describe these children with "hyperkinesis" (hyperactivity). There is certainly such a thing as brain damage, as shown by certain kinds of behavior and neurological signs (cerebral palsy is a prime example). But there is no definite evidence of disease in a majority of children labeled "minimal brain damaged"; so the label in such cases is simply a hypothetical convenience and probably a misleading one. Furthermore, in children known to have had some brain damage at birth, hyperactivity is not a consequence.

Stimulating drugs have been used widely in recent years for children who are called hyperactive or inattentive or who are simply doing poorly in school. This has often been done without any careful evaluation of the child's intellectual, emotional, social, scholastic, or physical state. This is irresponsible medicine. The behavior and the schoolwork of some of the children treated has definitely improved, at least temporarily. But there is inadequate long-term study of the improvement. The underlying emotional and social problems still exist years later in most cases. Not enough is known about the effect of prolonged use of these drugs.

Children who are hyperactive or who are doing poorly in school are entitled to thorough investigation—by the school people, by a physician, by a clinical psychologist, and perhaps by a child psychiatrist or a child guidance clinic. There are three parts to a thorough evaluation of such situations: the physical and emotional evaluation of the child, a complete evaluation of his family situation, and an evaluation of his school performance. In advice and treatment there may be a variety of approaches. If drugs are included there should be regular follow-up.

First Aid

CUTS, BLEEDING, AND BURNS

790. Soap and pure water for cuts and scratches. The best treatment for scratches and small cuts is to wash them with soap and pure water on a piece of absorbent cotton or clean cloth. Then rinse the soap off with plenty of clear water. Ask your doctor whether the water you use is pure enough to wash wounds with. If not, you can keep a bottle of 3 percent hydrogen peroxide to use for this soaping and rinsing.

An antiseptic is less important than careful washing, and some doctors prefer that no antiseptic be used. Don't use iodine. Cover with a bandage. The only purpose of the bandage is to keep the cut reasonably clean.

For large cuts that gape open, you should, of course, consult your doctor. It is good to have expert care for cuts on the face, even when they are small, since scars are more noticeable there, and also for cuts on the hand and wrist, because of the danger of cut nerves and tendons.

Wounds that might be contaminated by any street dirt or soil that contains manure should be reported to your doctor. Manure frequently carries the germs of tetanus (lockjaw). The doctor may recommend a tetanus toxoid booster shot or antitoxin, especially for deep cuts or puncture wounds.

791. Animal bites. Get in touch with the doctor promptly. Meanwhile, first aid is the same as for cuts. The important thing is to keep track of the animal to be sure he is not developing rabies. Which animals may carry rabies varies from one part of the country to another. Dogs and cats who haven't been vaccinated are possible carriers everywhere, and so are bats. In some areas, skunks, raccoons, and foxes may be carriers. You rarely need to worry about gerbils, hamsters, or guinea pigs carrying rabies. If the animal does develop rabies or if it cannot be traced, the doctor gives the child rabies inoculations.

792. Bandaging. What you use for bandaging depends on the size and location of the scratch or cut. Small prepared sterile bandages are good for most small wounds. They won't stick on the palm. For larger cuts and scratches, use a gauze square that comes sterile in an envelope, or a folded piece of clean cotton cloth. It can be held in place by narrow strips of adhesive. (A small child can loosen a bandage in no time at all.) Any bandaging has to be snug to do any good.

Don't wrap adhesive all the way around the arm or leg (so that it overlaps itself) because this might shut off the circulation. If the foot or hand becomes at all swollen or darker in color after the leg or arm has been bandaged, it means that the bandage is too tight. It should be loosened right away. It's all right to wrap a small prepared bandage around a finger if it's not too tight. Strips of adhesive to hold a bandage in place have more chance of staying if you make them plenty long.

A wound heals quicker and is less apt to become infected if you don't disturb the bandaging too often. If it becomes too loose or dirty looking, apply a new layer on top of the old. Take a bandage off very gently. Peel the inner layer back in the same direction as the cut runs. (For instance, if the line of the cut runs up and down the arm, peel the bandage up or down the arm.) In this way there is less likelihood of pulling the edges of the cut apart. If a bandage sticks, soak it off with 3 percent hydrogen peroxide. A cut may throb the first day and night, and this doesn't mean much. If it becomes increasingly painful later, it may be due to infection. Then the bandage should be removed to see what is happening. If there is swelling or redness, the doctor should see it.

Scraped knees, after being washed, are best left unbandaged until a dry scab is formed. Otherwise the bandage gets stuck and pulls off the scab when it is changed.

If a small child has a cut near the mouth, it may stay cleaner without any bandage (to catch food and saliva). Gauze squares can also be held in place with a stretchable type of gauze that can be purchased in various widths in the drug store.

793. Bandaging a finger. A child's finger is the part most frequently bandaged and the most difficult to bandage. Use a prepared bandage wrapped around the finger if this will cover the cut. If not, wrap the finger with a sterile gauze square or a strip of clean cloth. Hold this in place with a couple of strips of adhesive that circle the finger.

Now take a narrow strip of adhesive tape about a foot long, apply one end to the base of the bandage on the palm side, run to the end of the finger, over the end, up the back side of the bandage, up the back of the hand, and halfway up the arm. When you are sticking the adhesive to the back of the hand and arm, have the child's finger and wrist partly bent over; otherwise the adhesive acts as a halter holding the finger up straight. With another piece of adhesive, circle the middle of the bandage once more, snugly, to hold it together and to keep the lengthwise strip of adhesive from coming loose.

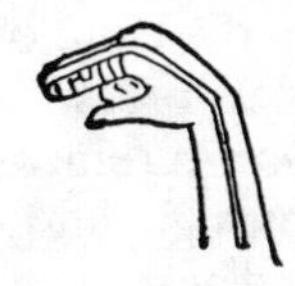

794. Bleeding (hemorrhage). Most wounds bleed a little for a few minutes, and this is good because it washes out some of the germs that were introduced. It's only profuse or persistent hemorrhage that needs special treatment.

Bleeding of the hand, arm, foot, or leg stops sooner if the part is elevated. Have the child lie down, and put a pillow or two under the limb. If the wound continues to bleed freely, press on it with a sterile gauze square or any clean cloth, until it stops or until you decide to bandage it. Clean and bandage the wound while the limb is still elevated.

If the wound was made in a clean way (with a knife, for instance) and bled freely, don't try to wash the cut but clean around it gently (soap and water, or soap and hydrogen peroxide on sterile cotton). If the wound still contains dirt, clean inside the cut, too.

When bandaging a cut that has bled a lot or is still bleeding, use a number of gauze squares (or folded pieces of clean cloth) on top of each other so that you have a thick pad over the cut. Then, when you snugly apply the adhesive or gauze roll bandage, it exerts more pressure on the cut and makes it less likely to bleed again. This is the principle of the "pressure bandage."

795. Severe bleeding. If a wound is bleeding at an alarming rate, don't wait to find the right bandages. Stop the bleeding with pressure immediately and wait for someone else to bring the bandages. Elevate a limb if possible. Make a pad of the cleanest material you have handy, whether it's a gauze square, a clean handkerchief, or the cleanest piece of clothing on the child or yourself. Press the pad against the wound, and keep pressing until help arrives or until the bleeding stops. Don't remove your original pad. As it becomes soaked through, add new material on top. If the bleeding is easing up and you have suitable material, apply a pressure bandage. The pad over the wound, made of a number of gauze squares or folded material of the cleanest available, should be thick enough so that when it is bandaged it presses on the wound. A small pad is enough for a finger, but a thick dressing is necessary for a thigh or abdominal wound. Bandage snugly with gauze bandage or adhesive tape or long strips of any kind of material. If the pressure bandage doesn't control the bleeding, continue hand pressure directly over the wound. If you have no cloth or material of any kind to press against a wound that is bleeding alarmingly, press with your hands on the edges of the wound, or even in the wound.

A great majority of even serious hemorrhages can be stopped by simple direct pressure. If you are dealing with one that can't and if you have learned in a first aid class how to apply a tourniquet, then go ahead. It's seldom necessary, though, and it's nothing that a novice should try to learn for the first time in an emergency. It **must** be loosened every 30 minutes.

796. Nosebleeds. There are a number of simple remedies for nosebleed. Just having a child sit still for a few minutes is often sufficient. To avoid his swallowing a lot of blood, have him sit up with his head bent forward, or if he's lying down, turn his head to the side so that his nose points slightly down.

Keep him from blowing his nose or from pressing and squeezing it with his handkerchief. It's all right to hold the handkerchief gently against the nostril to catch the blood, but moving the nose around helps to keep up the bleeding.

Nosebleeds usually occur from the front part of the nose. You can sometimes stop a severe hemorrhage by gently pinching the lower part of the nose for 10 minutes. Let go slowly and gently.

Cold applied to any part of the head constricts the blood vessels and helps to stop a hemorrhage. Place something cold against the back of the neck, or the forehead, or the upper lip. A cloth wrung out in cold water, an ice bag, or a cold bottle from the refrigerator will do.

If the nosebleed continues for 10 minutes in spite of these measures, get in touch with the doctor. If you have a bottle of nose drops of the kind that shrink the tissues, wet a small, loose wad of cotton with the nose drops and tuck it into the front part of the nostril.

Nosebleeds occur most frequently from blows on the nose, from picking the nose, and from colds and other infections. If a child has repeated hemorrhages from no apparent cause, he needs to be examined by the doctor to make sure he has none of the general diseases that sometimes cause nosebleeds. If no disease is found, it may be necessary to cauterize (seal) the exposed blood vessel that is always breaking. The proper blood vessel to cauterize can be discovered only right after a hemorrhage.

797. Burns. The treatment of burns has changed a lot in recent years and is continuing to change. It is a good idea to ask your doctor ahead of time what is recommended in case of emergency.

In case of a burn, put cold water (**not** ice water) on the burn as quickly as possible. Then call the doctor for instructions before doing anything else. If he is not there, ask the office to reach him and have him call you as soon as possible. Meanwhile, give first aid treatment. Then, if the burn is severe and it looks as though you can reach a hospital sooner than you will hear from the doctor, start for the hospital.

For first aid, most surgeons now advise **cold water,** which lessens pain and cleans the wound somewhat. (They no longer advise ointment or grease.) Make a pitcher of cold, clean water and dribble this on the burn even before you apply a bandage.

Ideally the bandage would be sterile gauze squares (that come in individual envelopes), held in place by gauze roll bandaging that goes round and round the burned limb or chest or head. (A small child may not want you to wrap up the eyes, nose, and mouth with circular bandaging but you can lay bandages on the eyelids and lips.)

But if you don't have proper bandages, use the cleanest cloth available to make pads over the burned areas and strips to hold them on with. Then every few minutes, dribble more cold water on the dressings—until the doctor arrives or you get the child to the hospital.

It is much safer to consult a doctor for any burns that cause blisters or raw spots. Some of the blisters are apt to break, and infection easily occurs under the edges of a broken blister.

If you have to deal with one or two small, unbroken blisters without the help of a doctor, don't open them or try to puncture them with a needle. There is less danger of infection if you leave them alone. Small blisters sometimes reabsorb without ever breaking; or if they break after several days, the new skin is pretty well formed underneath. When a blister does break, it is better to cut all the loose skin off. Use a pair of nail scissors or a pair of tweezers, both of which have been boiled for 10 minutes. Then cover with a sterile bandage. If a blister becomes infected, as shown by pus in the blister and redness around the edge, you should certainly consult your doctor. If this is impossible, cut away the blister and use wet dressings (Section 799).

Never put iodine or any similar antiseptic on a burn of any degree. It makes matters worse.

798. Sunburn. The best thing for sunburn is not to get it. Severe sunburn is painful, dangerous, and unnecessary. A half-hour of direct sunshine at a beach in summer is enough to cause a burn on a fair-skinned person who is unused to exposure.

Better to take too little sun the first days on the beach or in the country than too much. You can't tell when the skin's had enough from looking at it or feeling it. It takes hours for a burn to show. A good rule for the first few days at the beach is to keep the child's face, body, and legs covered or shaded except when he is actually going into the water. That means a hat to shade the forehead and nose, a shirt to cover the shoulders, and overalls to protect the legs, especially the back of the knees while lying on the stomach.

"Tanning" lotions that promise to make a nice tan without burning may help somewhat, but they can't protect against a large amount of sunshine. There are some lotions which prevent sunburn or tan altogether, if they're applied after every time the child goes into the water. These are helpful for unusually fair-skinned children, especially red-heads or very light blonds. Para-amino-benzoic acid (PABA) is the ingredient you should look for on the container label.

For relief of sunburn, you can apply cool water and a mild, non-aspirin containing pain reliever (acetaminophen). With a moderately severe burn, a person may have chills and fever and feel sick. Then you should consult a doctor, because sunburn can be just as serious as a heat burn. Keep sun-burned areas completely protected from sunshine until the redness is gone.

799. Wet dressings for skin infections until you reach the doctor. If a child has a boil, or an infection of the end of the finger, or around the fingernail or toenail, or an infected cut, or any similar type of infection under the skin, it should be seen by the doctor. Meanwhile, the child should be quiet, preferably in bed, with the limb elevated on a pillow.

If there is an unavoidable delay in reaching the doctor, the best first aid treatment is to apply a continuous wet dressing. This softens the skin, hastens the time when it breaks to allow the pus to escape, and keeps the opening from closing over again too soon.

You can make a solution by boiling a cupful of water and adding a teaspoonful of Epsom salts, or magnesium sulfate, or table salt.

Make a fairly thick bandage over the infection and pour enough of the cooled salt solution into the bandage to make all of it wet. Every few hours, when it begins to dry, add more solution.

You can keep it wet longer, especially at night, and keep the child's clothes and bedclothes dry, by covering the whole dressing with a piece of waterproof material, such as the plastic bags that are used to refrigerate food or plastic wrapping. Use a large enough piece to extend beyond the edges of the bandaging, and hold it in place with strips of adhesive tape. (Don't run adhesive tape tightly around an arm or leg—it may cut off the circulation.)

If a child has fever with a skin infection, or if there are red streaks running up his arm or leg, or if he has tender lymph glands in his armpit or groin, the infection is spreading seriously and should be considered a real emergency. Get the child to a doctor or a hospital, even if you have to drive all night. Modern drugs are vitally important in combating serious infections.

SPRAINS, FRACTURES, HEAD INJURIES

800. Sprains usually need examination and treatment. If your child sprains an ankle, have her or him lie down for a half hour or so and elevate the foot on a pillow. Put an ice pack over the sprained part. This keeps the deep hemorrhage and swelling to a minimum. If swelling occurs, you ought to consult your doctor, because it is possible that a bone has been cracked or broken.

A sprained knee should always be seen by a doctor and treated carefully. A neglected knee sprain in which a cartilage has been injured may not heal properly and may give trouble for years. If a child has fallen on a wrist and it remains painful, either when it is still or when it is moved, you have to suspect a fracture, even though there is no crookedness or swelling.

You can say, then, that any sprain that continues to be

painful or that swells should be examined. This is not only because of the possibility of fracture, but also because most sprains are much more comfortable if they are splinted or bandaged correctly. Many sprains and partial fractures are numb for an hour or so and then become more and more painful.

If a limb continues to be painful or if a child uses it strangely, whether or not there has been a known injury, the doctor is apt to want X-rays, often of both limbs for comparison.

801. Fractures. The brittle bones of adults really break. The softer bones of children are more apt to bend and splinter a little ("greenstick" fractures). Another type of fracture in a child is the loosening or breaking off of the growing end of a bone. This is particularly apt to happen at the wrist. (The picture that occurs when the growing end of a bone (epiphesis) becomes loosened may not be apparent at first, even on X-ray.) When a child has had a severe fracture, it is easy enough for anyone to see. But there are some common fractures that don't look especially deformed. A broken ankle can look straight enough, but there is considerable swelling and pain. A black-and-blue spot appears after a number of hours. Only a doctor can distinguish between an ankle that is severely sprained and one that is broken, and often needs an X-ray to tell. A wrist can be broken without being out of line enough for you to realize it. Finger bones are often chipped when a ball is caught on the end of the finger. There is only swelling and later some blueness. A vertebra (one of the bones in the spine) is sometimes slightly crushed when a child falls on her behind. Nothing shows outside, but she complains of pain when she curves her body forward or when she jumps and runs. In a general way, suspect a fracture if pain in a limb continues, or if there is swelling, or if a black-and-blue mark appears.

Avoid further injury in a suspected fracture. Don't move the injured limb around. Don't let the child move it. If she's in a halfway comfortable place and you can get a doctor soon, keep her quiet where she is. If she has to be moved, put some kind of splint on first.

A splint to do any good must extend far enough up and down the limb. For an ankle injury, the splint should reach to the knee; for a break in the lower leg, it should go up to the hip; for a break in the thigh, you need a board that goes from the foot to the armpit. For a broken wrist, the splint should go from the fingertips to the elbow; for a broken lower or upper arm, it should go from the fingertips to the armpit. You need a board to make a long splint. A short one for a small child can be made by folding a piece of cardboard. Move the limb with extreme gentleness when you are applying the splint to it, and try to avoid any movement where the break is. Tie the limb to the splint snugly in 4 to 6 places, using handkerchiefs, strips of clothing, or bandages. Two of the ties should be close to the break, on either side of it, and there should be one at each end of the splint. For a back injury, it is even more important to leave the patient where she is if she can possibly be made comfortable there. If she must be moved, use a stretcher or a door. In picking up a person with a back injury, keep the back straight or arched inward (so that it is in the "swayback" position). (If the injured person is on his stomach, leave him that way, but don't roll a person over from his back to his stomach.) Never let the back curve outward. That means that when picked up, or carried on a mattress or other makeshift stretcher that sags, the injured person should be kept straight or, if curved at all, curved backward. (The head should not bend forward.) For a broken collarbone (at the top of the chest in front) make a sling out of a large triangle of cloth and tie it behind the neck, so that it supports the lower arm across the chest.

If a person with a serious injury has to be kept for some time in a cold place, protect her reasonably well with blankets or with other clothing. Put a blanket under her. It is no longer considered wise to try to make a person in shock really warm with many hot blankets or hot water bottles.

802. Head injuries. A fall on the head is a common injury from the age when a baby can roll over (and thereby roll off a bed). A parent usually feels guilty the first time this happens. But if a child is so carefully watched that she **never** has an accident, she is being fussed over too much. Bones may be saved, but her character will be ruined.

If, after a fall on the head, a baby stops crying within 15 minutes, keeps a good color, and doesn't vomit, there is little chance that she has injured her brain. She can be allowed to resume her normal life right away.

When a blow on the head is more severe, the child is apt to vomit, lose her appetite, be pale for a number of hours, show signs of headache, fall asleep easily but be able to be roused. If a child has any of these symptoms, you should get in touch with your doctor who may want to examine the child or have the skull X-rayed. The child should be kept as quiet as possible for 2 or 3 days and any new symptoms reported to the doctor immediately. It's a good idea to rouse the child twice during the first night after the fall to make sure that she's not unconscious. If she is not feeling her usual self the next day, the doctor should be notified again.

If a child loses consciousness either right after a fall or later, she should certainly be examined by a doctor immediately. The same rule applies even without unconsciousness if the child continues to complain of headache, trouble with her vision, or if she vomits later.

A swelling that puffs out quickly on a child's skull after a fall doesn't mean anything serious in itself if there are no other symptoms. It is caused by a broken blood vessel just under the skin.

SWALLOWED OBJECTS AND CHOKING

803. Swallowed objects. Babies and small children swallow prune pits, coins, safety pins, beads, buttons—in fact, anything you can mention. They seem to be able to pass most of these things through their stomachs and intestines with the greatest of ease, even open safety pins or a little broken glass. The objects that are more dangerous are needles and straight pins.

If your child has swallowed without discomfort a smooth

object, like a prune pit or a button, you don't have to worry or give a piece of bread to push it along. Just watch the movement for a few days to reassure yourself that it has come out. Naturally, if the child develops vomiting or pains in the stomach, or if an object gets painfully stuck in the gullet, or if it is a sharp object such as an open safety pin or a needle that is swallowed, you should consult the doctor immediately. Never give a cathartic to a child who has swallowed an object. It won't do any good and it may do harm.

804. Choking. When a child breathes or coughs something into her windpipe and is choking, hold her upside down and slap her vigorously on the back of her chest. If she keeps on choking, try **chest thrusts** as follows:

1. Stand behind the child and slip your arms directly under her armpits, wrapping them across her chest. To get into this position for a toddler, drop to your knees.
2. Make a fist with one hand and place the thumb side of your fist against the child's chest, midway between the nipples. Grasp your fist with your other hand.
3. Press your fist into the child's chest with a quick squeeze/thrust.
4. Repeat this thrust a few times if necessary.
5. If the object is not dislodged (it usually pops across the room like a champagne cork) the whole cycle should be repeated once.

If she keeps on choking and begins to turn blue, rush her to the nearest hospital or doctor's office or call the fire department aid car if you have one in your community. Unless an aid car is coming to your house, don't wait for anything.

A sharp object stuck in the throat, like a fishbone, though very uncomfortable and gagging, is not dangerous like an object that is obstructing the breathing. You should reach the doctor as soon as possible, but it isn't a matter of life and death. Lots of times the object can't be found when the doctor examines the throat, though the child keeps saying it's there. In these cases the fishbone, or whatever it is, has been swallowed, but the child is still feeling the scratches left in the throat.

ARTIFICIAL RESPIRATION

805. Artificial respiration

If a person has drowned, first clean out the mouth. Then drain water from lungs by laying the victim on stomach for 10 seconds with hips a foot higher than head (on an incline, over your knee, a box, etc.)

A person may stop breathing because of smothering, drowning, electric shock, inhaling gas. Start artificial respiration promptly. Keep it up until he continues to breath by himself or until help comes, as long as 2 hours. **Never give it to a person who is breathing.**

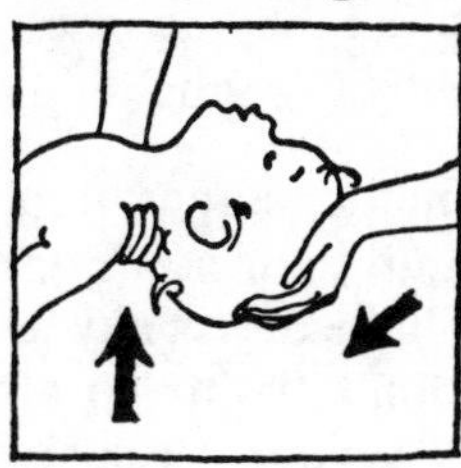

It is vital to open the air passages by raising neck, tilting head back.

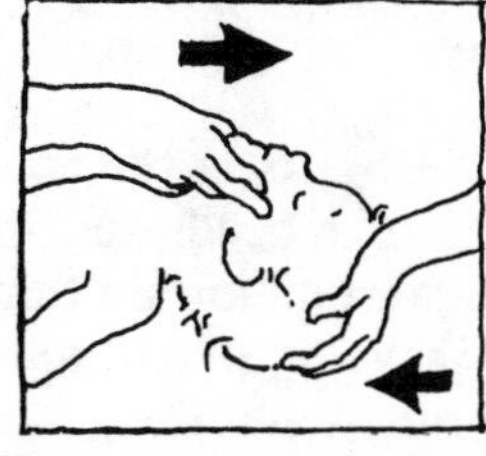

Then keep victim's chin pressed upward all the time, to keep the passages open.

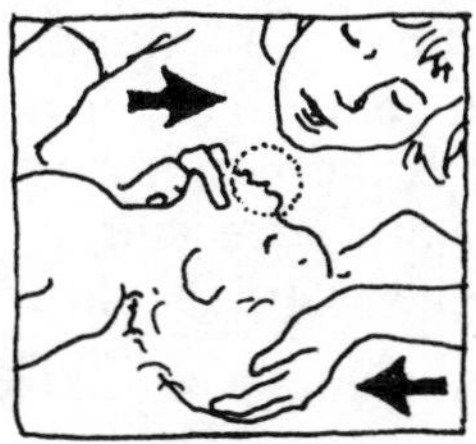

With a child's small face you can breathe into nose and mouth together. (With adult, breathe into mouth or nose, and keep the other pinched shut.)

Breathe into victim, using only mild force. (A small child's lungs cannot contain your entire exhalation.) Remove your lips, allowing the child's chest to contract while you inhale your next breath. Breathe into victim again.

Each of your breaths goes into the victim. With an adult, breathe at your natural speed. With a child use slightly quicker, shorter breaths.

Courses in cardiopulmonary resuscitation (CPR) are now offered by the Red Cross or fire department in many cities. These courses teach you how to try to start the heart beating, if it has stopped, while you are doing artificial respiration. The courses are free and take very little time. You should try to take one if it's available in your community.

OBJECTS IN THE NOSE AND EARS

806. Objects in the nose and ears. Small children often stuff things like beads and wads of paper into their noses or ears. The most important thing is not to push the object any farther in, in your efforts to take it out. Don't try to go after a smooth, hard thing. You are almost certain to push it in farther. You may be able to grasp a soft object that isn't too far in with a pair of tweezers.

With objects in the nose, have children blow their noses. (Don't try this if they are so young that they sniff in when told to blow.) They may sneeze the object out in a little while. If the object stays in, take the child to your doctor or a nose specialist. Foreign objects that stay in the nose for several days usually cause a bad-smelling discharge tinged with blood. A discharge of this kind from one nostril should always make you think of this possibility.

POISONS

Write here, and/or on a card near your telephone, the number of the nearest Poison Control or Information Center and the hospital you favor.

807. On the skin or in the eye: Flush off the skin with plenty of plain water. If you have no eye dropper, you can squeeze water from a sponge or washcloth into the eye.

808. Swallowed substances: First **telephone your doctor.** If she or he is in, the doctor will tell you what to do.

If your doctor is not in, and if it will take you less than half an hour to get to the nearest hospital emergency room, I think it is **better to start immediately,** not waste time trying to find your doctor or reach the Poison Information Center.

If it will take **more than half an hour to get to the hospital,** it may be wiser to **get advice from your Poison Information Center** if you can reach them immediately.

If you can't immediately reach them (or your doctor) and if it will take more than half an hour to get to the hospital, and if you have **syrup of ipecac, read the list** in the box below of the substances for which you should **not** induce vomiting. If what your child ingested is on this list **don't give ipecac,** but start for the hospital, no matter how long it will take.

DO NOT INDUCE VOMITING FOR THESE

kerosene	turpentine	ammonia
gasoline	liquid auto polish	lye; drain cleaners
benzene	caustic lime	liquid furniture polish
bleach	insect sprays	cleaning fluids

strong acids (sulfuric, nitric, hydrochloric, carbolic)

Petroleum products are most harmful when breathed or choked into the lungs and vomiting might cause this. Acids and caustic cleaners may burn the throat again coming up.

Do not induce vomiting in a person who is unconscious or having a convulsion.

If the **ingested substance is not on the list** in the box and if you have syrup of ipecac, give your child **a tablespoonful** (3 teaspoonfuls) followed by a glass or two of water. Then start for the hospital, taking the bottle of ipecac—in order to give a second dose in 15 minutes if vomiting has not occurred—and a saucepan to catch the vomitus, for the hospital to analyze. Take the poison container (or plant part) with you.

The aim is to get the stomach emptied as soon as possible unless the doctor is sure there is no danger from the ingested substance.

Do not delay seeking help because your child seems well. The effects of many poisons—aspirin, for instance—take hours to show.

809. Some substances which are dangerous though they may not seem so: tobacco (one ingested cigarette is dangerous for a 1-year-old); boric acid; aspirin; pills containing a combination of iron, quinine, and strychnine (a traditional tonic); plant and insect sprays; some plants; nail polish remover; perfume; dishwasher detergent.

810. Some frequently ingested substances which are only mildly harmful (call the doctor anyway): ink, mercury in liquid form from a broken thermometer, tincture of iodine, bleaches.

Special Situations

TRAVELING WITH A BABY

There are several methods of preparing and carrying formula when traveling. Which one is most convenient for you depends on the facilities you will have and on how long you will be away from a kitchen and refrigerator.

Well ahead, ask whether your doctor has any recommendations. Ask a railroad or airline whether they can provide you with refrigeration, and for how many bottles.

811. Buy prepared, ready-to-use formula in disposable bottles with disposable nipples. They have all the conveniences. They don't have to be refrigerated. There is nothing to wash or sterilize. They are expensive, but you probably will not be traveling for long. Powdered, prepared formula is cheaper. The powder and water can be measured ahead of time, in separate containers, and mixed just before you feed the baby.

812. Solid foods. Most solid foods should be in jars. The baby can be fed directly from them. Then discard them even if they are half full. Don't worry about providing everything that the baby usually gets (potatoes, for example). Just bring enough of the things your baby likes best and digests most easily. Many traveling babies do not want as much as they would be taking at home. Don't urge anything that they don't want even if they are taking much less than usual. They may want to be fed small amounts at more frequent intervals.

813. Food for a child. It's better to keep small children from drinking train water (bring some in a bottle) and eating unusual food. When buying food for them in public places, avoid particularly cakes and pastries with moist fillings, milk puddings, cold meats, cold fish, and cold eggs, creamy salad dressings (including sandwiches and salads that contain them). These are foods that are most easily contaminated with poisonous bacteria if carelessly handled or not properly refrigerated. Better stick to hot foods, fruit that you peel yourself, milk in separate containers. (Of course, you can put up your own sandwiches, such as peanut butter and jelly.) Even if you are expecting to feed a child at roadside restaurants, or in the diner, or on the meals provided in a plane, bring a bag of food for snacks or—in case meals are delayed—a box of salted crackers (said to be helpful for car sickness), cheese and hard-boiled eggs in the shell (if enjoyed), fruit, a vacuum bottle of milk, a jar of pureed prunes in case of constipation.

814. Other tips. It is worthwhile, with a baby, to travel by the best accommodations that you can afford. You will get more service on a first-class plane or railroad ticket, and if you can afford it, you will feel a lot more comfortable in a Pullman compartment when the baby is fussing.

Disposable diapers are a great help.

With a small child, don't forget to have handy the cuddly **toys** usually taken to bed. They will be an extra comfort in traveling. In addition to the favorite toys, it is wise to bring a few new playthings of the kind that take a lot of doing—miniature cars or trains, a small doll with several articles of clothing or other equipment, a coloring or cut-out book, a new picture book, cardboard houses, or other objects to fold and assemble, a pad of paper, pencil and crayons. Children of 3 or over like to pack favorite toys in their own small suitcases.

Some babies and children have trouble with ear pain when the airplane in which they're traveling begins to descend for a landing. Older children, who can understand the need to swallow to avoid the pain, can be given something to suck or chew on. Babies should be awakened as soon as the plane starts to descend, and offered the breast or bottle, to keep them swallowing. If a child has a cold, ask your doctor about long-acting medicine that can be given to keep the eustachian tubes open during the trip.

A large box of **cleansing tissues** is essential. A couple of large **plastic tablecloths** are valuable, one for protecting the mattress from bed-wetting, another to cover the carpet if a small child is eating in a hotel room or a baby is sitting on the floor, or to cover a bed on which a baby is being changed. A wet face cloth, kept in a plastic bag to retain its moisture, can be very helpful. Many people now buy prepared "wipes" that come in individual packets for traveling.

In car travel, it is wise to stop, not only at regular mealtimes, but also in midmorning and midafternoon, for a snack and for a chance for children to run around for a few minutes in a place, perhaps a field or a playground in a city park, where they don't have to be constantly warned to keep off the road.

It may be important to carry along the **toilet seat** a small child is used to.

It's vital that babies travel in cars in government-approved carriers, children under 45 pounds in government-approved seats, and that larger children, like adults, wear seat belts and shoulder straps at all times. (See Sections 71 and 449.)

If your child has a tendency to develop motion sickness, it helps for her to sit high enough to see out of the car. Your doctor can tell you about some medicines that are helpful in preventing motion sickness.

A good rule for car travel is to plan to always stop for the night by 4 P.M., so you'll have more chance of finding a motel room and avoid driving on for hours with tired children. Many drivers get the bit in their teeth about making a certain distance and refuse to stop even though it's getting late. But if they solemnly agree before the trip to a certain stopping hour, there's more chance they will be reasonable.

815. Going to restaurants with children. Most children will get restless while waiting to be served in a restaurant (except for the fast-food type). In most cities, there are a few restaurants that cater to families with small children, and they provide special activities to keep children from becoming bored. But for most other restaurants, it's best to bring paper and pencils and perhaps a coloring book or two, to keep the children occupied until the food is served. This also keeps them busy when they're finished eating and the adults feel like having a second cup of coffee. (A bored child running loose in a restaurant can be annoying to other diners and can easily become involved in an accident.) You can bring food from home for your baby.

THE PREMATURE BABY

A baby weighing much under 5 pounds will almost certainly be taken to a hospital where an incubator and expert care are available.

816. Keep the baby warm. A premature baby loses body heat rapidly when exposed to cool air, and his body's ability to make heat and to keep an even temperature is poor.

Wrap him in a warm cotton receiving blanket and then in a soft acrylic or wool baby blanket the minute he is born (even before the cord is cut) and keep him in a warm place. The cord should not be tied and cut until it stops beating. This is to make sure he receives all the blood available from the placenta. Then get him to the nearest hospital that has incubators. If the weather is not warm, use the car heater.

817. It's hard to get over your anxiety. Most premature babies develop quite normally, allowing for their prematurity. Though they gain weight slowly at first, they usually gain and grow more rapidly for a while later to make up for this. Naturally, they cannot make up for their youngness. The baby who was born 2 months early and has become "1 year old" should be thought of as really a 10-month-old.

They may need an iron prescription by the age of a month to prevent anemia.

By the time a premature baby weighs 6 pounds, he needs no more coddling or worrying than any baby, but this is very hard for the parents to believe. In the beginning the doctor probably cautioned them against being too optimistic, and only gradually became more reassuring. The baby probably had to be in an incubator, watched constantly by nurses and doctors, and probably had to be fed by tube at first. The parents might not have been able to get near him most of that time, though most hospitals are now encouraging parents to touch and, where possible, hold and feed their premature babies from the very beginning. The mother had to go home from the hospital without him, and both parents then lived a strange kind of parental life for a number of weeks, knowing in a theoretical way that they had a baby but not completely feeling as if they did. As such parents say, "Sometimes it felt like it was the hospital's baby, not ours."

It's no wonder that when the doctor finally says, "Now you can take him home," the parents may feel quite frightened and unready. They may find that they don't yet have all the clothing and equipment (the mother had counted on more time at the end of her pregnancy). They may find that one or the other has a slight cold. All kinds of small reasons seem terribly important reasons why they can't take him yet.

When the baby at last comes home, all the worries that all new parents experience—about room temperature, baby temperature, breathing, hiccups, burps, bowel movements, formula-making, schedule, crying, colic, spoiling—hit the parents of a premature baby with triple force. It may take weeks before they gain self-confidence and months before they are convinced that the baby is as healthy, husky, and advanced as any other conceived at the same time.

818. Worrisome neighbors. Meanwhile, other troubles may come from the outside. Neighbors and relatives often act more anxious, more awestruck, more preoccupied, than the parents. They question, they exclaim, they fuss until the parents can hardly stand it any longer. A few of them insist on telling the parents all the wild stories they have heard about how frail and susceptible premature babies remain. This kind of talk would be bad enough for the parents to hear if it were true. It's particularly unfortunate for them to be subjected to untruths of this sort at a time when they are trying to overcome their own anxiety.

819. Feeding. Premature babies are often discharged from the hospital when they weigh about 4 pounds. You can find out how much and how often your baby is being fed from the hospital and go on from there. By the time he weighs 7 or 8 pounds, the interval will probably be 3–4 hours if he's on a formula, 2–3 hours if he's breast-fed. If you are working toward a regular schedule, I'd encourage him to wait 4 hours by the time he weighs 9 pounds.

Somewhere between 7 and 10 pounds, most babies are ready to give up one of the night bottles. They show it by sleeping through at 10 P.M. and waking at 11 or 12.

I would encourage the parents of a premature baby to be looking for this readiness and to take advantage of it by waking and feeding the baby just before they retire, hoping that he will then sleep through till 4 or 5 A.M. By helping him to give up this feeding, they will be convinced in one more respect that he is growing up normally. Each time a feeding is dropped, the same total formula is then divided into fewer bottles.

The main thing to be on guard against in the beginning is attempting to get the baby to take more milk (and, later, more solids) than he wants. This is a great temptation because he looks so slender. You feel that if you could squeeze a little more in, he would fatten up faster and thus be better able to throw off any germs. But resistance to disease has nothing to do with fatness. Your baby, like every other, has his individual pattern of growth and an appetite to take care of it. If you push food beyond what he is eager for, you only take away his appetite and slow up his weight gaining.

A premature baby particularly needs his vitamins with regularity. The doctor has to watch him for anemia because he has inherited little iron from his mother. As with full-term babies, premature babies are not begun on solids until age 4 to 6 months nowadays. Because of the parents' anxiety about growth, it's important here, too, to be tactful, to give him plenty of time to get to like solids, and to increase them only as he shows his enthusiasm. In other words, avoid feeding problems.

820. Nursing a premature baby. Occasionally, a mother who is eager to get her premature baby off the supplemental bottles containing expressed breast milk or formula that were given in the hospital may be advised simply to stop the bottles and give only her breast. But this may prove to be too sudden for a premature baby discharged before he reaches the date when he was expected to be born. At homecoming, he may still be slightly immature and tire too easily to get all that he needs from the breast. If this is the case, or if the baby has become used to the bottle while in the hospital and needs to relearn breast-feeding, the mother can make the transition gradually. Your doctor can instruct you on how you can slowly reduce the supplements over days or weeks, while still offering the breast at feedings and expressing or pumping your milk for the bottle. The period of transition is temporary, and your baby will be able to totally breast-feed, if that is what you want, before long.

821. No other precautions. He can have a tub bath as soon as he weighs 6 or 7 pounds, and I'd encourage the parents to start them by 7 pounds. Like any baby, he can go for outings and have his window open when he weighs 8 pounds.

The parents certainly don't need to wear masks even when he first comes home. He has to get used to the ordinary family germs. He shouldn't be exposed to outsiders with colds or other infections any more than any baby or child should, but otherwise no special precautions are necessary or wise.

An organization of parents and professionals which can help you and your doctor is: Parents of Premature and High Risk Infants International, Inc., 33 W. 42nd Street, New York, NY 10036.

THE RH FACTOR

822. If you have an Rh problem in the family, you need the help of your doctor in understanding how it applies to your particular situation. This is just a very abbreviated discussion of a complicated subject for general information.

A majority of people have the "Rh-positive factor" in their blood. A minority have the "Rh-negative factor." There is no problem if a man and wife are both Rh positive or both Rh negative or if the wife is positive and the husband is negative.

But difficulty sometimes arises (unless preventive measures are taken) if the man is positive and the wife is negative. In this situation, which occurs in about one marriage in eight in the United States, some of the children inherit the Rh-positive factor from their father. Then if an Rh-positive baby is growing in the uterus of an Rh-negative mother, a little of the baby's blood may get into the mother's blood through the placenta. The mother's system may then develop protective antibodies that destroy these alien blood cells—just as we all develop antibodies against the germs of measles to destroy them if they try to attack us a second time. But if the mother develops antibodies against her baby's Rh-positive cells, her antibodies go back through the placenta into the baby's circulation and destroy some of the baby's own blood cells there. If a lot are destroyed, the baby becomes anemic soon after birth, and the material from the destroyed cells makes the infant jaundiced and sick.

A mother's blood won't develop antibodies in time to destroy blood cells in her first Rh-positive baby (unless she had a transfusion with Rh-positive blood before her pregnancy). But each Rh-positive baby may sensitize her blood to a greater degree.

Now it is known that if every such mother receives immune globulin (RhoGAM) immediately after the birth (or miscarriage) of her first (and any subsequent) Rh-positive baby, this will prevent her sensitization and there will be no Rh problem in her babies.

If the mother has already been sensitized (before this preventive measure was developed) she should be followed closely by her doctor during pregnancies. Examination of her blood and of the amniotic fluid which surrounds the baby will tell the seriousness of the situation and what treatment may be needed.

JAUNDICE

823. Jaundice. Many newborn babies develop a yellow tinge to their skin called jaundice, due to the still immature liver.

Though a little jaundice is common, occasionally the level can be high enough to be worrisome. The doctor may want to watch the degree of jaundice, which he can do with a simple blood test which measures the chemical responsible for the jaundice. Giving the baby extra fluids helps. On rare occasions, further measures are necessary. Jaundice is rarely a problem after the first 7–10 days of life.

TWINS

I once made an appeal to parents of twins to tell me what solutions they had found for their problems, so that I could pass them on. I got 200 wonderfully helpful letters. As you might expect, they showed sharp differences of opinion in some respects, great unanimity in others.

824. Help! All parents of twins agree that the work is overwhelming, especially at first, but that the rewards are great.

You need all the help you can get, for as long as you can get it. If possible, hire somebody, even though you have to go into debt. Or beg your mother or another relative to come for a month or two. When there is no room and no privacy in the house, parents have even turned the garage into a bedroom for the helper, in suitable climates. Part-time assistance is a lot better than none at all: a high school student after school, a cleaning woman or a sitter once or twice a week. Encourage the neighbors to help regularly with certain feedings. It's surprising how much assistance can be gotten from even a 3-year-old sister or brother of the twins.

This is a time—if there ever was one—for parents to show their thoughtfulness and generosity toward each other. They can work out schedules for sharing the endless work. They can give each other the extra, visible affection that parents need when they are called on to pour out unaccustomed amounts of loving care to their children.

The father may be able, in some jobs, to shorten his

outside working day for several months. He may take his vacation when the twins first come home from the hospital. (There is apt to be a longer than average hospital stay because twins are often born prematurely.)

Even if the father has to continue to work an 8-hour day he can do wonders between the time he comes home from work and leaves the next morning. I once watched the father of quintuplets—and two older children—pitch in the minute he got home, feeding solids and bottles, giving baths, changing diapers, preparing the older children's and parents' supper and washing up after supper, giving time to the older boys. On weekends he shopped, cleaned house, did laundry.

825. Laundry. Disposable diapers will be doubly convenient. Now is the time, if at all possible, to get an automatic washer and dryer. They save hours of work and produce clean sheets, pads, shirts, nighties, even in rainy weather.

The babies' wash can be done daily or every other day, depending on what suits the parents' wishes. Frequency of change of sheets and pads can be decreased by placing a small additional waterproof sheet under the baby's hips.

Laundry service, complete or partial, for the rest of the family is also an important saver of time and energy.

The diaper load can be reduced by changing diapers only once at each feeding, either before or after.

826. Shortcuts. Any parents of twins simply have to find shortcuts in housework. They can go through the house, room by room, stripping it of unessential furnishings and furniture that prolong housecleaning. Furthermore, they should clean only half as often as before. They can select clothes for the family that don't muss and soil quickly, that launder easily and that, as far as possible, don't need ironing. They can select foods that require the minimum of preparation and attention, let dishes soak clean in suds, let them drain dry.

827. The right equipment for the twins can be enormously helpful. Many parents find a single crib, with a partition across the middle designed by themselves, very practical for the first couple of months until the twins become too large and active. Cribs with springs that can be elevated save parents' backs and energy, can serve as diapering and dressing tables. An extra bassinet in which one fussing baby can be wheeled into another room helps to keep the other baby asleep. A great convenience in a two-story house is extra cribs and stores of clothing downstairs for the daytime, eliminating constant stair climbing. Much of the equipment can be borrowed or bought secondhand.

A hospital table on wheels or a tea table on wheels may be convenient, with certain room layouts, for holding stacks of diapers, clothing, sheets, etc. It can be wheeled from crib to crib or room to room.

A double baby carriage is too wide for most doors, and two babies sleeping that close together begin to disturb each other within a few months. On the other hand, a double stroller usually proves valuable for many months. A back-to-back stroller goes through doors more easily. Two car beds are useful, but remember that these are not the same as car seats. Each baby must have her own government-approved car seat. It's best to get the type that converts for larger babies rather than the one that has to be replaced when the baby weighs 20 pounds. Two inclined seats are really essential.

828. Bathing can be skimped a great deal, if care is taken. Faces can be kept clean with plain water on a washcloth. The diaper area can be washed daily with a soapy washcloth and the soap wiped off twice with a rinsed washcloth. Then, as long as the skin stays in good condition, the all-over bath can be cut down to every other day, twice a week, or even once a week. The complete bath can be given with a washcloth on a waterproof sheet (a sponge bath) if more convenient. It's hard to finish baths for two babies soon enough to avoid a lot of crying from one or both. There are several solutions: a helper to feed the baby who is bathed first; baths when both parents are available; different bath days or bath hours for different babies. If a tub bath is given (in sink, washstand, or tub) and if the babies can wait long enough, it's time-saving to bathe one right after the other in the same water. All bath equipment, clothing, crib, and bottles must be ready and close at hand before the bath is started.

829. Breast-feeding is practical and possible. From letters I received, I believe that twins are breast-fed for a number of months as often as single babies. (This proves again that there is no set limit to the amount of milk a mother can produce. The breasts supply whatever the baby or babies demand if the mother is going about it with the right method and attitude.) If the babies are too small to nurse well or if they stay in the hospital longer than the mother, then it is a job to establish the breast-milk supply by means of manual expression. But as soon as the babies can nurse at the breast, they can both be put to breast together. The mother must have a comfortable chair with good arm support. There are at least three possible positions. If the mother can half recline, or recline, a twin can lie along each of her arms. If she sits up fairly straight, with pillows at each side, the babies can lie along each side, feet toward her back, heads held up to her breasts with her hands. It's also possible to lay the babies across the mother's lap, one more or less on top of the other, but with heads at opposite sides of the mother. The underdog doesn't object in these circumstances.

830. The making and storing of formula for two is cumbersome. Twins are usually small at birth and may need feedings on the average of every 3 hours, which adds up to sixteen bottles every 24 hours. Let's assume that you don't have to sterilize. If refrigerator space is a problem, the formula can be refrigerated in two quart-size jars. Then at each feeding, two nursing bottles are filled with the correct amount of formula.

831. Feeding schedule. A great majority of parents of twins have found that it is essential to get onto a regular schedule as soon as possible and to feed both babies at once, or one right after the other. Otherwise feeding is going on at all hours of the day and night. (A few find a modified demand schedule is practical. They wait for the first baby to wake and cry, but they wake up the second baby as soon as the first is finished.) Most babies can be accustomed to regularity within a few weeks. If a baby wakes and fusses before feeding time, you stall for a while, hoping she will go back to sleep. If she gets crying hard, you may have to compromise and feed ahead of schedule, but each day you get stricter, counting on the baby's digestive system to become habituated to the schedule. A pacifier is usually a great help in keeping a baby happy until feeding time. In a few cases, with very irregular, fretful babies, scheduling doesn't work. Then it's easier to feed on demand for a few weeks, however irregularly, rather than have to listen to crying for long periods.

Twins are often premature and small. Then they may require a 3-hour schedule, at least in the daytime, until they weigh 6 or 7 pounds. If one twin is much smaller, she may require a 3-hour schedule for a few weeks while the other is fed every 4 hours, but the smaller one may still be able to go 4 hours at night.

832. How to give bottles. How do you feed bottles to two babies at the same hours if only one parent is available? A few parents have trained one cooperative baby to wake half an hour after the other. But most parents find that both babies wake together and that there is nothing more nerve-racking than to feed one while the other howls. One solution in the early weeks is to lay the twins on a sofa or bed on either side of the parent, let's say the mother, their feet toward her back; in this position she can give two bottles at the same time. Another method is to use a bottle holder for one while she holds the other, alternating babies each feeding.

But some parents find that a bottle holder (or propping a bottle on a folded diaper) doesn't work that well, at least in the early weeks. Either the baby loses the nipple and cries, or else chokes. Then the parent has to hurriedly drop the other baby, who cries, while rescuing the first. These parents find it more practical to use bottle holders or propping for both babies simultaneously, with the babies in inclined seats. They sit close by or between the babies, with both hands free to give whatever help is needed. As these parents correctly point out, they save enough time with bottle holders to be able to give the twins more and better cuddling at less hectic times.

If there is much irregularity in the early weeks in the amounts or times of feedings, it is necessary to keep a record of how much formula each baby has taken at what hour, and also data on weight and baths. Otherwise you forget too much or try to feed one twin twice and burp the one with the empty stomach. A notebook or a blackboard serves the purpose, or a cardboard clockface for each crib.

Many twins, like single babies, burp themselves if laid on their stomachs after feeding. Remember, too, that though some babies will be uncomfortable unless the bubble is gotten up, others don't seem to feel any difference and then there is no need to make the effort.

833. Feeding of solid food has to be done efficiently, too. When it's all new to the twins, many parents spoon-feed one baby while the other takes the bottle, and then reverse the process. Additional time can be saved in two other ways: You can bunch the solids so that they are all given in two feedings a day instead of three. You can also give the solids (cereal and fruit, for instance) at one of the daily feedings in the bottle of formula, with a nipple hole as large as the head of a pin. This leaves the other feeding each day in which the babies learn how to swallow solids from a spoon. By the time the twins are skillful at taking solids, they can be propped up in the corners of bassinet, crib, or armchair, and spoon-fed together. Or there is an infant feeding table that comes in twin size, with seats that can be adjusted to a semi-reclining position for babies who can't sit up yet; parents find it extremely useful.

It is a great time-saver to spoon-feed twins simultaneously. One has just time enough to swallow a mouthful while the parent is loading the spoon and offering it to the other. It may not seem hygienic or polite to use one dish and one spoon, but it's so much more practical.

With twins, there's extra reason for an early start with finger foods (bread crusts, wholesome crackers, chopped cooked vegetables, chopped meats) and for relying on them heavily. There's also reason to encourage self-feeding by spoon at least by the age of 12 months.

834. A playpen is particularly valuable for twins (it's impossible to watch two crawling babies at once), and fortunately they are happy in it for longer hours and until a later age than single babies because of each other's company. (It can even be used as a double crib in traveling.) They should be put in it for play periods by 2 or 3 months, so that they won't become accustomed to freedom first. Heavy or sharp toys must be avoided because twin babies whack each other without realizing that it hurts. Later, if they begin to be bored in the pen together, one can be moved to a walker, then the other. Such variations interest even the one in the playpen.

After the age of a year it's a great convenience to have a separate room for the twins to play in, with a gate at the door. It can be furnished so that the children can't easily hurt it or themselves (twins are ingenious, cooperative, and lightning fast in getting into mischief), and they will play happily in it much longer than a single child would.

835. Clothes and toys: similar or dissimilar? Some parents point out that since there is usually only one kind of playsuit, for instance, in a store that appeals to the parents in terms of design, warmth, price, it is difficult if not impossible to dress twins differently. And their twins, they say, usually insist on wearing similar clothes at the same time. Other parents emphasize the opposite—about dresses, for instance—that it's usually impossible to buy two of a kind, so twins are compelled to dress differently. Still other parents say that since the twins have to wear mostly hand-me-down clothes, they have to dress differently from the start and enjoy having their own distinctly different clothes.

Some parents report that they have had to buy identical toys from the start, or their twins would be rivalrous and miserable. Others say that they usually buy different toys (except for particularly precious possessions like tricycles, dolls), and that twins learn to share happily from an early age.

I suspect that the attitude of the parents makes the biggest difference. If the parents take it for granted that twins must wear different clothes most of the time and share some of their playthings, either by necessity or on principle, the twins will generally accept this. But if the parents encourage the expectation of identical clothes and toys, and especially if they give in every time the twins insist, the children may well become more insistent with time. Of course, this same principle applies to single children: if parents are firm, children accept; if parents are hesitant, children argue.

It helps twins develop a sense of individuality about their own clothes and a liking for them if each has separate drawer and closet space and if similar garments are marked with names or other markings. Similar garments of different colors preserve some of the advantages of being both twins and individuals. When one twin always has green and the other yellow, this helps everybody keep them straight.

836. Individuality. This brings us finally to the philosophical question of how much to emphasize the twinness of twins and how much to encourage the individuality, especially with identical twins. The whole world is fascinated with twins, makes a fuss over them, likes them to look alike and be dressed alike, asks the parents silly questions about them ("Which is smarter?" "Which do you love best?"). It's hard for the parents not to play up to the world's sentimental or morbid interest. Why not? The trouble is that this may give the twins the feeling that their only source of attraction is their cuteness as a look-alike, dress-alike pair. This may seem appealing at 3 years of age. But if it ends up, as it occasionally does, in twins still trying to attract attention by dressing alike at 30, so dependent on each other that they can't fall in love or marry, the result is not cute but sad.

Now, this doesn't mean that the parents should be afraid of ever dressing the twins alike or should be ashamed to enjoy the world's attention to their children. Twinness is fun for the twins **and** for the parents.

Twins, in fact, develop special strength of personality from being twins: early independence of parental attention, unusual capacity for cooperative play, great loyalty and generosity toward each other.

But to avoid overemphasis on twinness, it's wise for parents, particularly with identical or very similar twins, to keep away from very similar names (it's hard enough to call the right twin even when the names are dissimilar), to refer to them by their names rather than as "the twins," to dress them alike only part of the time, to introduce them early and regularly to other children before they become used to each other's company exclusively, to let them make separate friends to the degree they wish, to encourage the neighbors to feel free to invite one of them over to play or to a party occasionally (while the other twin has a chance to have his parents all to himself for a change).

In an occasional case, one twin becomes so dependent on the other in schoolwork that it is wise to separate them into two different classrooms. But it seems foolish and cruel to have an arbitrary rule about separation when there is no need.

837. Don't worry about favoritism. One further word of advice. Some conscientious parents become too worried at the start that they may give a bit more attention to one baby or always serve her first—because she's smaller, for instance, or more responsive. Such strict impartiality is not necessary—in fact, it encourages a too mechanical, too forced kind of attention. Every child wants and needs to be loved naturally for her own lovable qualities. She is satisfied if she knows that she has a good niche of her own in her parents' hearts and does not worry then about what love her brother or sister is getting. But in the long run she will sense the hollowness of forced attention. A legalistically equal treatment will focus her attention on her rights and make her argue for them like a lawyer. Avoid systems like "Mother puts A's shirt on first, then B's pants on first," or "Today is A's chance to sit next to Daddy."

838. Twin language. Twins often develop a private language between themselves—glances, grunts, foreign-sounding words—which may lead to delay in speaking the family's language and may even cause temporary backwardness in school. Some parents have had to insist that the twins' demands not be met unless they were expressed in English.

DIVORCE, SINGLE PARENTS, AND STEPPARENTS

Separation and divorce have become common. In the United States, there are now about a million divorces a year. While you can read about "friendly divorce" in fiction and see examples of it in movies, in real life most separations and divorces involve two people who have become very angry at each other.

839. Marriage counseling. Divorce is disturbing to all members of the family in most cases, at least for a couple of years. Of course, it may be no more upsetting than continued hostile conflict. But there is a third alternative, which is marriage counseling or family therapy or family guidance, at a clinic or a family social agency or with a private therapist. It's best, of course, if both husband and wife go into counseling on a weekly basis, for months or even several years, to get a clearer view of what has gone wrong and of the part that each partner is playing. For it's true that it takes two to make a quarrel. But if one spouse refuses to consider his or her role in the conflict, it may still be worthwhile for the other to get counseling on whether and how to save the marriage. After all, there were strong positive attractions in the beginning, and many divorced people say later that they wish they had tried harder to solve the problems and make a go of it.

It's usually true that when a couple are disagreeing, each one feels that the other is mostly to blame. Yet an outsider can often see that the trouble is not that one or the other is a villain but that neither seems to realize how she or he is acting. In one case, each spouse unconsciously wants to be pampered by the other, like an adored child, instead of being willing to contribute her or his share in a partnership. In another case, a bossy spouse has no idea how much she or he is trying to dominate the other, and the one who is being nagged may be asking for it. Very often in the case of unfaithfulness, the faithless one is not really falling in love with an outsider but, rather, running away from a hidden fear or unconsciously trying to make the spouse jealous.

840. Telling the children. Children are always aware of and disturbed by ongoing conflicts between their parents, whether or not divorce is being considered, and it is good for them to feel that they can discuss these with their parents, together or singly, in order for them to get a more sensible picture than their morbid imaginations may suggest. Since it is important for children to believe in both their parents, in order to grow up believing in themselves, it is wise for both parents to try to avoid bitterly heaping blame, which is a natural temptation. Instead, they can explain their quarrels in general terms, without pinning the blame: "We get angry about every little thing." "We quarrel about how to spend money." "It upsets Mommy when Daddy takes several drinks."

It is wise to keep children from hearing the word "divorce" shouted in anger, unless and until divorce is almost certain. Then it should be discussed, not just once but again and again. To young children the world consists of the family, which to them is mainly father and mother. To suggest breaking up the family is like suggesting the end of the world. So the divorce has to be explained much more carefully than it would be to an adult: that the children will live most of the time with, let's say, their mother; that their father will live near (or far away); he will still love them and will still be their father; they will live with him according to some schedule; and they can telephone him any time and write him letters.

Just as important as telling the children about the divorce is giving them ample opportunities—during or between discussions—to ask questions. You'll be amazed at some of the mistaken assumptions they'll make—for example, that they caused the divorce or that they may lose both parents. It is wise to get these misunderstandings straightened out as promptly as possible, but don't be surprised if young children slip back into weird misconceptions.

841. Children's and parents' symptoms. All children develop signs of tension—for a couple of years at least. In one study children under 6 most often showed fears of abandonment, sleep problems, regression in bed-wetting and temper tantrums, aggressive outbursts. Children of 7 and 8 expressed sorrow and feelings of aloneness. Nine- and 10-year-olds were more understanding about the realities of divorce; nevertheless, they expressed hostility toward one or both parents, and complained about stomachaches and headaches. Adolescents spoke of the painfulness of the divorce and of their sadness, anger, and shame. Some girls were handicapped in developing good relationships with boys.

Mothers who gain custody of the children usually find the first year or two of divorce very difficult. The children are more tense, demanding, and complaining; they are simply less attractive. The mother misses the part that the father played in making decisions, settling arguments, and sharing responsibility for plans. She is apt to feel tired out as the result of working at a job, caring for the home and the children. She misses adult companionship, including the social and romantic attention of men. Worst of all, most mothers say, is the fear that they will not be able to earn a satisfactory living and to run the family. (They should have secured an adequate child support allowance in the separation agreement, although this doesn't guarantee that it will be forthcoming, or on time.) Many women say that there is great satisfaction and compensation in the end, when they prove to themselves that they can support and run a family without help—that this gives them a sense of competence and confidence that they never had before in their lives.

One method that has proved practical and satisfying to some divorced women, for limiting expenses, sharing in the care of home and children, and having companionship, is to share a home or apartment with another divorced woman. Of course, they should know each other well before moving in together. There is no reason why men should not consider this alternative.

Some people imagine that divorced fathers without custody have a high old time, and all the dates they can arrange, with no family responsibilities except for child support payments and visitation. Actual studies show that most fathers are miserable much of the time. If they get involved in casual affairs they soon find that these are shallow and meaningless. They are unhappy not to be consulted about important and unimportant plans for the children. They miss the company of their children. Even more, they miss having their children ask for advice or for permission, which is part of what a father is for. Their children's weekend visits often settle into a combination of hamburger joint and movie, which may satisfy the children's pleasure needs but not their own or their father's need for a real relationship. Both father and children may find conversation difficult in this new situation.

842. Custody. It was assumed in the first three-quarters of the twentieth century that children's needs are best served, at least up to adolescence, by living mainly with and in the custody of the mother, unless she was clearly unfit. (It's interesting to learn that in the nineteenth and earlier centuries, when divorce was rare, custody was usually awarded to the father, on the basis that the children were property and that he was entitled to most of it.)

In recent years, there has been increasing recognition that many fathers are just as capable of nurturing children as mothers, and now more judges take this into account in awarding custody. Naturally, but unfortunately, there is intense bitterness in many divorces. This creates a rivalry between the parents over custody and keeps them from focusing on what would be best for the children, or makes them each assume that their custody would be best.

The factors to consider are these: Who has been giving most of the care (especially in the case of babies and small children who will badly miss their accustomed caregiver); the relationship of each child to each parent and each one's expressed preference, especially in later childhood and adolescence; the importance to each child of living with a particular brother or sister (apt to be strong in the case of twins).

In the past, it has usually been assumed that the divorcing parents will be adversaries at court, in regard to custody as well as to child support, alimony, and property settlement. The more this battling attitude can be avoided, especially in the case of custody, the better for the children. In recent years, there has been a movement for joint custody, to keep the noncustodial parents (more frequently the father) from getting the short end of the stick in visitation rights and, even more important, to keep that parent from feeling "divorced" from his or her children—feeling as if he or she is no longer a real parent—a feeling which often leads to a gradual withdrawal from contact with the children.

When speaking of joint custody, some lawyers and parents mean an equal sharing of the children, such as 4 days with one, 3 with the other, or one week with one and then a week with the other. This may or may not be practical for the parents, or comfortable for the children. School-aged children have to keep going to the same school, and the same may be true for nursery school. Children like and benefit from routine schedules. Five days with the mother and weekends with the father has a practical sound and is a common schedule, but the mother may well want some weekend time with the children, when she can be more relaxed, and the father may want most weekends with his children but then want occasional weekends without them. Much the same considerations may apply to Christmas and summer vacations. So any schedule is apt to require flexibility.

I myself prefer to think of joint custody as a spirit of cooperation between the divorced parents in regard to the children's welfare, which means first and foremost that they consult with each other about plans, decisions, and responses to the children's major requests, so that neither parent feels left out. (It may be very helpful to have a counselor, one who knows the children, to help the parents come to some decisions.) The second priority is to share the children's time in such a way that each parent keeps as closely in touch with them as possible, which will have to depend on such factors as the distance between the parents' dwellings, the capacity of the dwellings, the location of the school, the preferences of the children as they grow older. Obviously, if one parent moves across the continent, the visits will have to come at vacation times, though the parent can still keep in touch by letter and phone. Joint custody is only practical when both parents believe that they can subordinate what bitterness they have toward each other for the benefit of their children. Otherwise the wrangling will be continuous. Then it's better to let one parent have custody and let the judge set the rules for visitation.

843. Avoid trying to bias the children. It's vital that one parent not try to discredit or even criticize the other with the children, though this is a great temptation. Both parents feel a little guilty about the failure of the marriage, at least unconsciously. If they can get their friends, relatives, and children to agree that the ex-spouse is a no-gooder, they can lessen the guilt. So they are tempted to tell the worst possible stories about the "ex," leaving out any mention of their own contribution. The trouble is that children sense that they are made up of both parents and if they come to accept the idea that one was a scoundrel, they assume that they've inherited some of that. Besides, they naturally want to retain two parents and be loved by both. It makes them feel uncomfortably disloyal to listen to criticism.

By adolescence, children know that all people have imperfections and they are not so deeply affected by those of their parents, though they can be plenty critical. Let them find the faults for themselves. Even at that age it's better policy for one parent not to try to win the children's allegiance by criticizing the other. Teenagers are prone to turn hot and cold on slight provocation. When they become angry at the parent they've favored they may do an about-face and decide that all the unfavorable things they've heard in the past about the other parent were unfair and untrue. Both parents will have the best chance of retaining their children's love for the long haul if they let them love both, believe in both, spend time with both.

It's a mistake for either parent to pump children about what happened while they were visiting the other parent. This only makes children uneasy when they're with either parent. In the end, it may backfire and make them resent the suspicious parent.

844. Visitation time. Some divorced fathers feel shy or awkward when visitation time comes, especially if it's their sons visiting. Mothers may have the same problems, but much less often, because they commonly have custody. Besides, there is frequently greater tension anyway between fathers and their sons than between fathers and daughters. Fathers often respond by simply providing treats—meals out, movies, sporting events, excursions. There is nothing wrong with these occasionally, but fathers shouldn't think of these as essential on every visit; such behavior would signal that they are afraid of silences and will make these treats more obligatory every week. The children's visits can generally be as relaxed and as humdrum as staying in their regular home. That means opportunities for activities such as reading, doing homework, bicycling, roller skating on the sidewalk, tossing baskets, playing ball, fishing, working on hobbies such as model building, stamp collecting, carpentry. Fathers can participate in those activities they enjoy, which provide ideal opportunities for casual conversation. The children can watch their regular TV programs, but I as a father would discourage a whole weekend of viewing. And part of the time the father can be following his own interests as he would in an unbroken family.

It is vital that noncustodial parents not casually break their appointments for visits. Children are hurt when they get the impression that other obligations are more important. They lose faith in the negligent parent and in their own worth. If appointments have to be canceled, this should be done ahead of time and substitutions made if possible. Most important of all is that the noncustodial parent should not break contact progressively.

845. Dating for the parents. Children whose parents have been recently divorced consciously or unconsciously want them to get back together, and think of them as still married even though separated.

They are apt to feel that dating represents faithlessness on the part of their parent and an unwelcome intrusion on the part of the date. So it is well for parents to go slowly and be tactful in introducing their dates to their children. Let the fact that the divorce is permanent sink in for a number of months. Be alert to the children's remarks. After a while you can bring up the topic of your loneliness and drop the idea that you may want to have a friend to date. It's not that you are allowing your children to control your life forever; you are simply letting them know that dating is a possibility, and doing it in a way that is easier for them than being presented, first of all, with a person in the flesh. And when you do finally arrange to have them share a meal with the date at your home or in a restaurant, it's tactful to hold down your own physical affection for your date at first and then let it show gradually.

If you are a mother who has been living with young children who rarely or never see their father, they may beg you to marry and give them another "daddy," which is good as far as it goes; but they may and probably will show evidence of jealousy as soon as you let them see the growing closeness between you and a man, and certainly by the time you marry again.

846. Stepchildren and stepparents. It's no accident that so many fairy stories have an evil stepmother or stepfather as a villain. The step relationship is one that lends itself to mutual jealousy and hatred. A child, let's say it's a boy, had his mother all to himself after his father's death or divorce, and formed an unusually close and possessive relationship with her. Then along comes a strange man who wins his mother's heart and bed and at least half her attention. The boy cannot help but resent this intruder, no matter how appealing a personality the man has, and shows it with continuous rudeness and a hating expression. This gets under the stepfather's skin and he responds with a critical attitude and even threats of punishment. He reproaches the mother for not making the child behave and she sometimes turns on the child, which makes him feel more bitter. If she defends the child, the stepfather may show anger toward her which further convinces the child that the stepfather is a brute.

The resentment is most obvious in a young boy against his stepfather or in a young girl against her stepmother, but children can also hate a stepparent of the opposite sex, and they can show their disapproval even when they acquire a stepparent in middle age.

The main thing for new stepparents to realize is that this hostility is almost universal and that it is not a reflection on their likeableness or parenting skills. It often persists strongly for 2 or 3 years and then lessens slowly.

There are some general principles, that may or may not be helpful, and that are certainly difficult to apply. To put it the other way, a stepparent who succeeds in being loved soon is a natural genius in human relations. (Both authors have experienced the pains of the step relationship.)

It is better for the stepparent to avoid moving into the guiding and correcting role of a full parent until he or she has been accepted—this has to do with such routine matters as chores, homework, putting away playthings, bedtime, and curfews for teenagers—for you are sure to be judged a harsh intruder even if you are laying down exactly the same rules as the parent.

On the other hand, it's not good for you to be submissive when the stepchild intrudes into your territory, for instance, abusing one of your possessions or being deliberately rude. Then you can say in a friendly but firm way that you don't like abuse—of your things or yourself. Yet you can't make an issue of it every time the child glowers at you or answers less than civilly. You'd be reproving all day. So you pretend not to notice the small slights of which the child is not consciously aware.

One good rule—hard to follow—is to try to avoid showing loud hostility when you are standing up for yourself, for this gets translated, in the child's state of chronic resentment, into brutality. Another rule, more positive, is to keep looking for episodes in which the child is even slightly considerate or friendly, or for periods when at least there is no disagreeableness, and tell the child how much you've enjoyed having a good time together. In general, don't forget to be friendly and affectionate when the climate is neutral or better. Show your thoughtfulness by planning a picnic, a sporting event, a visit to the zoo or museum, or by giving an **occasional** gift that's much desired. But it's not effective to give treats or presents much more often than the full parent does; children sense it when adults are too eager, too submissive, in trying to buy approval, and scorn the giver.

THE CHILD WITH ONLY ONE PARENT

847. The fatherless child. Let's take first the example of the boy who has no father because of divorce or death or because he was born out of wedlock or because a single woman adopted him. It would be foolish to say that his father's absence makes no difference to a child, or that it's easy for a mother to make it up to him in other ways. But if the job is handled well, the child, either boy or girl, can continue to grow up well adjusted.

The mother's spirit is most important. She may feel lonely, imprisoned, or cross at times, and she will sometimes take it out on the child. This is all natural and won't hurt him too much. The important thing is for her to go on being a normal human being, keeping up her friendships, her recreations, her outside career if she has had one, at least on a part-time basis, her outside activities as far as she can. This is hard if she has a baby or child to take care of and no one to help her. But she can ask people in, and take the baby to a friend's house for an evening if he can adjust to sleeping in strange places. It's more valuable to him to have his mother cheerful and outgoing than to have his routine perfect. It won't do him any good to have her wrap **all** her activity and thoughts and affection around him.

Children, young or old, boys or girls, need to be friendly with other men if the father is not there. With babies up to the age of a year or two, a good deal is accomplished if they can just be reminded frequently that there **are** such creatures as agreeable men, with lower voices, different clothes, and different manners than women. A kindly grocer who just grins and says hello helps even if there are no closer friends. As children go on toward 3 and over—whether boys or girls—the kind of companionship they share with men is increasingly important. They need chances to be with and feel close to other men and older boys. Grandfathers, uncles, cousins, scoutmasters, men teachers at school, the minister, old family friends, or a combination of these can serve as substitute fathers if they enjoy the child's company and see him or her fairly regularly. Children of 3 or over build up an image of their father that is their ideal and inspiration, whether they remember him or not. The other friendly men they see and play with give substance to the image, influence their conception of their father, make their father mean more to them. The mother can help by being extra hospitable to male relatives, sending her son or daughter to a camp that has some men counselors, picking a school, if she has a choice, that has some men teachers, encouraging a child to join clubs and other organizations that have men leaders.

The boy without a father particularly needs opportunity and encouragement to play with other boys, every day if possible, by the age of 2, and to be mainly occupied with childish pursuits. The temptation of the mother who has no other equally strong ties is to make him her closest spiritual companion, getting him interested in her particular preoccupations, hobbies, and tastes. If she succeeds in making her world more appealing to him, easier to get along in, than the world of boys (where he has to make his own way), then he may grow up precocious, with predominantly adult interests. It's all to the good if a mother can spend time and have plenty of fun with her boy, provided she also lets him go his own way, provided she shares in his interests rather than having him share too many of hers. It helps to invite other boys to the house regularly and to take them along on treats and trips.

848. The motherless child. The example of a girl without a mother brings out other points. The father in most cases will have to stick to a full-time job; but he should scrupulously reserve the major part of his after-work hours to be with his child until her bedtime, on a regular schedule that she can usually depend on. If his social or romantic interests are pressing, he can do a lot of his entertaining at home, and get his child included in many of the invitations he receives to dine with others. (I don't mean that his child should see heavily amorous behavior, or quick switches in his attachments. Children are conservative, easily shocked in such matters.)

Though children need to be with their parents a lot and though this means, in the case of working, single parents, a large proportion of the time in the evening and on weekends, it is not necessary or sensible for the parent to spoil the child with presents and kowtowing. (See Section 45 on working parents.) In fact it's not wise for the parent to even try to be focused on the child for most of the time they are together, as if the child were a visiting prince. The child can be working on a hobby, doing homework, helping with the housework most of the time, while the parent does likewise. But this doesn't mean that they have to be out of touch. If they are in tune with each other they can chat and comment off and on, as the spirit moves. (See Section 48 on two parents, and Section 54 on care for the child after the age of 3.)

849. When a parent dies. It is important to remember that children deal with death differently at different ages, and that, on average, it takes most adults and children of all ages a year to put their lives back together again. Most children don't understand death as an irreversible, biological event until they are 9 or 10 years old. The child younger than this may not seem to be reacting very much to the death of the parent, at first, because he or she thinks the parent will come back. This is the time for the surviving parent to share his or her personal and religious beliefs about what happens after death, as a way of being supportive to the child. Fear, anger, guilt, and sadness are all present to some degree for everyone involved, and these emotions need to be expressed gradually so that everyone can get past them and get on with their lives.

It's normal for the surviving parent to turn to his or her child or children to some extent to meet some of the emotional needs that were met by the dead spouse, but it's important to remember that the children have to go on with their own emotional growth and development, and this will be interfered with if they have to act like substitute adults. It's especially tempting, for example, to think of and even tell the oldest girl or boy, "You're the woman (or man) of the family now, and I'm really depending on you." While all normal children can take on extra chores, and provide some emotional support to a distressed parent, no child can take on an adult role without serious consequences to her or his future emotional growth and development.

HANDICAPPED CHILDREN

850. Treat them naturally. Children with a handicap may need treatment of the defect. But even more they need to be treated naturally, whether the handicap is mental slowness, crossed eyes, epilepsy, deafness, shortness, a disfiguring birthmark, or a deformity of any other part of the body. This is easier said than done. A defect quite naturally upsets the parents to some degree. Here are examples of different reactions they may have.

851. Handicapped children's happiness depends on their attitude, not on their defect. A boy has been born with only a thumb and one finger on his left hand. At 2½ years he is happy and can do almost as much with his left hand as with his right. His 6-year-old sister is fond and proud of him, wants to take him with her everywhere she goes, never seems to worry about his hand. The mother, however, is very conscious of the missing fingers. She winces when she sees a strange child catch sight of his hand and stare. She thinks it is fairer to the child to keep him at home where he won't be subjected to curiosity and remarks, makes excuses when he wants to go shopping with her. Which attitude is better for him, the mother's or the sister's? We first have to answer another question. Does a defect in itself make a child seriously self-conscious and ashamed? Generally speaking, no.

Of course, all of us are slightly self-conscious, and we all focus on what we think are our weakest features. Those with defects naturally worry about them to some degree. But anybody who has known many handicapped individuals realizes that some of those with the worst handicaps are just as outgoing, happy, and unworried as anyone with sound limbs. And at the other extreme, you can probably think of one acquaintance who is miserably self-conscious, for instance, about the prominence of his ears, when actually they are not noticeable at all.

In other words, the seriousness of a defect has little to do with whether a person grows up feeling self-conscious, ashamed, unhappy.

The important factors that make a person (**with or without defects**) grow up happy and outgoing are having parents who thoroughly enjoy and approve of him, who do little worrying, urging, fussing, criticizing; having opportunities to learn the fun of give-and-take with other children from an early age. If the parents from the beginning are unhappy or ashamed about a child's appearance, always wishing he were different, overprotecting him, keeping him from mingling with others, he is apt to grow up turned in on himself, dissatisfied, feeling that he is odd. But if they take his disfiguring birthmark or deformed ear as of no great importance, act as if they consider him a normal child, let him go places like anyone else, don't worry about stares and whispered remarks—then the child gets the idea he is a regular guy and thinks little of his peculiarity.

As for the stares and pointing and whispered remarks, the child with a noticeable defect has to get used to them, and the younger the easier. If he is hidden most of the week and gets one stare on Sunday, it is more disturbing than ten stares every day, because he is not accustomed to them.

852. Children will be happier without pity. A 6-year-old boy has a birthmark that covers half his face. His parents have taken this hard and feel a lot of pity for him. They are strict with their two older daughters but excuse the boy from household tasks, let him get away with rudeness to them and meanness to his sisters. He's not too popular with his sisters or other children.

It's understandable why parents of handicapped children are inclined to feel too sorry for him for his own good and to expect too little of him. Pity is like a drug. Even if it's distasteful to a person at first, he's likely to come to depend on it. Naturally, a child with a defect needs understanding, and he often needs special handling. The slow child should not be expected to do a job that is proven to be beyond his mental development, and one with stiff hands shouldn't be criticized for poor penmanship. (On the other hand, don't sell your child short by assuming that he can't do something, or be taught to do something. It is the confidence of parents and teachers that keeps a child moving forward.) But the child with a defect can be reasonably polite, take turns, do his share of the chores. Everyone is happier and more pleasant when he knows he's expected to be considerate. The child with a handicap wants to be treated the same, held to the same rules as other children.

853. Fairness to the whole family. A 4-year-old child has been found to be very slow in her mental and physical development. The parents have taken her from doctor to doctor and clinic to clinic. Each time they hear the same story. It is not a mental defect for which there is any curative treatment, though there are many things to be done to bring her up happy and useful. The parents naturally want more than this, and they end up traveling long distances and paying exorbitant fees to a quack who promises a magical cure. As a result, the other children in the family receive less than their share of attention. Some parents, however, feel much happier spending the money and making the effort.

It certainly is right and normal for parents to want to do whatever has a reasonable chance of helping a child with a handicap. But there's another hidden factor. It's human nature for them to feel, underneath, that they are somehow to blame—even though all the doctors and books explain that the condition is a pure accident of nature. All of us in our upbringing have been made to feel guilty about things we did and things we ought to have done. If we have a handicapped child, this guiltiness left over from youth is apt to get focused on the handicap.

This unreasonable sense of guilt often drives parents, especially if they are very conscientious people, to **do something** even if it's not sensible. It's a kind of penance, though they don't think of it that way.

If parents are on the lookout for this tendency, they are better able to choose the right treatment for the child and, incidentally, spare their other children (and themselves) unnecessary deprivation.

854. Love them for themselves. A certain child at the age of 10 is distinctly shorter than average, even shorter than his 8-year-old sister. The parents feel that this is a real tragedy and keep taking him to new doctors, all of whom agree that there is no deficiency disease—he is merely a child who seems to have been born with a small pattern. The parents show their concern in other ways, too. They frequently urge him to eat more so that he will grow faster. When there is any allusion to his size compared to his sister's or to other boys', they eagerly remind him how much smarter he is.

There is enough rivalry among boys so that an individual who is short feels some disappointment anyway. But the two factors that make the biggest difference are the boy's general happiness and self-confidence, and how easily the parents accept his shortness.

Being told to eat reminds him of how worried his parents are and is more likely to take his appetite away than to improve it. Being compared favorably to his sister and friends in other qualities doesn't make him feel better about being short, and it only emphasizes the idea of competition and rivalry. There are times when the parents sense that a short child, or a homely one, or a nearsighted one, wants to be told how unimportant the handicap is. Confident reassurance is then a great help. But if the parents are the uneasy ones, always bringing up the subject, it convinces the child that he must be in a bad way.

855. Brothers and sisters take their attitude from the parents. A girl, now 7 years old, was born with cerebral palsy. Her intelligence has not been affected at all, but her speech is hard to understand and her face and limbs are constantly making strange contortions over which she has little control.

Her mother has a sensible attitude toward the handicaps. She treats her daughter the same as her younger boy except that she takes her several times a week to a special clinic, where she receives instructions in the daily activities of living—feeding, speech, toileting, walking. (Her parents are also learning how to be instructors.) Her younger brother and the children in the neighborhood are all devoted to her because of her friendly nature and enthusiasm. She gets in all their games and, though she often can't keep up, they make allowances. She goes to the regular neighborhood school. She is naturally handicapped in some ways, but since the program is flexible and the children take a part in planning and working out their projects, her good ideas and cooperative spirit make her a popular member of the class. Her father, who may be more of a worrier, thinks the girl might be happier in the long run if she were sent away to a special boarding school, among others with similar handicaps. He also fears that when the younger child grows older, he will be embarrassed by the other's peculiar appearance.

If the parents accept the handicapped child wholeheartedly and matter-of-factly, the brothers and sisters are apt to do so also. They are not too upset by the remarks of other children. But if the parents feel embarrassed and tend to conceal her, she will be on the minds of the brothers and sisters just as much as if she were in sight.

856. Changes in the parents' feelings. Many parents who discover that they have a child with a serious handicap go through much the same stages of feelings. First is the painful shock and the natural resentment. "Why does this have to happen to our family?" Then so often comes the guiltiness (discussed in Section 853). "What did I do wrong or what did I not do that I should have done?" The doctor keeps explaining, "You could not have prevented this condition." But it takes a long time for the parents to begin to feel convinced on the inside.

A difficulty that arises now and later is that various relatives and acquaintances keep coming forward with tales that they have heard of experts and new treatments all over the world. They insist that the parents consult each in turn. They act shocked when their advice is not followed. They are well meaning, but they keep the parents troubled.

The next stage is often one in which the parents become so preoccupied with the handicap and its treatment that they partly lose sight of the child as a person. They fail to enjoy all the other good qualities, which are quite unimpaired. Then as they gradually get back into focus and begin to think of their child as another nice human being who just happens to have a particular difficulty, they can't help being irritated by those relatives and friends who still can't talk about anything but the child's handicap.

It helps parents in going through these painful stages to know that hundreds of thousands of other good parents have had the same experience.

857. Most parents need some help too. Caring for a child with a handicap usually means extra effort and extra strain. To make the best plans for him requires real wisdom, which is hard to come by when you are upset and have little experience. All this adds up to the fact that you who are parents of handicapped children often need guidance and you are certainly entitled to it. I am thinking not just of medical advice. I'm thinking of opportunities to discuss the management of the child at home, the problems created for the other members of the family, the pros and cons of the local school compared with schools farther away, the frustrations and resentment of the parents themselves. To get such matters clarified usually takes many long talks, over a period of years, with a counselor who is experienced in the field and is comforting to deal with.

There are usually social workers in state bureaus for the blind, deaf, crippled, and retarded, and also on the staffs of the schools and clinics that care for such children. In a rural district there may be a county welfare worker. In cities there are social workers in family and children's social agencies. To find the right person to help you with your problems, write, if you live in the country or a small town, to the department of welfare in your state capital. If you live in the city, call the United Way or United Good Neighbors. They can tell you the right agency.

Parents of children with various handicaps have organized themselves into local chapters and national associations. There are several purposes, all worthwhile. They share their special problems and solutions. They hear talks by professionals in the field. They exert their influence to get better facilities for their children. They raise funds for research and treatment.

You should be able to get information from the national organizations listed under the various handicaps in this chapter and in other parts of the book—visual and hearing defects, mental retardation, cerebral palsy, cystic fibrosis, epilepsy.

Here are some other organizations:

Muscular Dystrophy Association of America, Inc.
810 7th Avenue
New York, NY 10019

National Hemophilia Foundation
25 W. 39th Street
New York, NY 10018

Council for Exceptional Children
1920 Association Drive
Reston, VA 22091

You can get information about special schooling from your state Department of Education, about professional resources from your state Department of Health, about financial help from your state Department of Social Welfare. These departments are all located in your state capital. Or, you can write your senator or representative in Washington, D.C.

A helpful book is *The Chronically Ill Child,* by Audrey T. McCollum (New Haven, CT: Yale University Press, 1981). (Available in paperback.)

858. Where to live, where to go to school, where to get special training. Suppose children have defects that do not interfere with getting to the regular neighborhood school and do not handicap them in learning in a regular class. Examples would be minor orthopedic handicaps, healed heart disease that does not seriously limit a child's activity, peculiarities of appearance such as birthmarks. It's best for such children to go to the regular neighborhood school. They will be living the rest of their lives among average people, and it's best for them to start out that way, thinking of themselves as average in almost all respects.

859. Regular school when possible. In previous times, it was believed that children with handicaps that interfere with ordinary classroom learning—such as impaired hearing or vision, for instance—should be sent from the start to specialized day schools in their own community or, if none were available, to specialized residential boarding schools. In more recent years it has been realized that though the education of handicapped children is extremely important, even more important are their adjustment and their happiness. This means keeping in mind the sociability they will acquire from being with unhandicapped as well as handicapped children, the wholesome view they will take of the world and themselves if they grow up thinking of themselves as normal people in most respects, the security they will gain from being part of the family. It is certainly preferable that children live at home if possible. The younger children are (especially up to the age of 6 or 8), the more they need the close, loving, understanding kind of care, the sense of really belonging, that they are more likely to get at home than in even the best of boarding schools. So there has been an increasing effort to provide for handicapped children in regular neighborhood day schools and, when appropriate, to keep them in regular classes as much of each day as is possible. This means increasing school budgets and training more specialized teachers so that local schools can have such facilities. It means in one case that the handicapped child may spend part of each day in a special class and other periods in the regular classroom with unhandicapped children. It is good for other children to know and understand the handicapped, to outgrow some of their morbid dread. In some cases a specialized teacher can coach the regular classroom teacher in how to teach a subject so that the handicapped child can comprehend and participate, or teach the child directly.

How the philosophy works out in any community or school depends on many factors: the number and skill of the special teachers, the size of classes and classrooms, the kind of handicap, the severity of the handicap, the age and previous training of the handicapped child.

860. Slightly or moderately hard-of-hearing children need primarily lip reading instruction, speech correction, and a hearing aid. With the assistance of these they can usually take their places in a regular local school.

861. Children who are more severely deaf cannot get much from a regular classroom until they have learned how to communicate with others. This requires long training at a special school for the deaf or a regular day school with a qualified teacher of the deaf. It is important for children to begin attending training programs, which are available in clinics and schools for the deaf, **in infancy,** when children's capabilities are flexible and their eagerness to learn is great. It is much better for young children to be living at home if this is at all possible, where their special needs for love and for belonging can be satisfied. If there is no local school, the family can consider moving.

There has been much controversy about whether, in order to favor lip reading and speech training, the deaf child should be prevented from using sign language and finger spelling. Parents who of course would like their child to be able to comprehend and speak in the company of hearing people and are eager that she not appear different have naturally favored the philosophy of no sign language or finger spelling.

But lip reading is an incomplete, inexact form of comprehending for even the most apt pupil. Different sounds have exactly the same mouth movements, so there has to be a lot of guessing. Many children—including bright ones—never become even fairly good lip readers, despite the most expert schooling. The teaching of speech to severely deaf children is painfully slow and often far from satisfactory. So, in most cases, it is helpful to allow and encourage **all** forms of communication for the deaf: sign language and finger spelling can supplement lip reading and speaking.

You can consult the Alexander Graham Bell Association, 3417 Volta Place, N.W., Washington, DC 20007 about local facilities.

862. Visually handicapped children may be able to get a great deal from the regular school class (or regular nursery school) even though they need some special instruction at the same time. It is amazing and inspiring to see how well even a 3- or 4-year-old blind child can get along in a class of seeing children. The inexperienced teacher, just like the parent, tends to be anxiously overprotective at first, but gradually comes to realize that overprotection is not necessary and only gets in the child's way. Of course, sensible precautions have to be taken and allowances made. The other children accept the handicapped one easily after a little questioning. They usually make allowances and give help in a very sensible manner. Information about special classes and residential schools for visually handicapped children can be obtained from your state Board of Education, or state Commission for the Blind, or the American Foundation for the Blind, 15 West 16th Street, New York, NY 10011. Children with severe visual handicaps are eligible for federal funds to help defray costs of educational materials, provided by American Printing House for the Blind, 1839 Frankfort Avenue, Louisville, KY 40206.

863. Some children with cerebral palsy and other neuromuscular problems require not special classes but highly skilled muscle treatment that is available in only a few places. Information about classes, schools, and other facilities for crippled children can be secured from your state Department of Education. The very special training that is needed for children with cerebral palsy can be secured from the United Cerebral Palsy Associations, Inc., 66 East 34th St. New York, NY 10016 or the National Easter Seal Society for Crippled Children and Adults, 2023 West Ogden Avenue, Chicago, IL 60612.

If no satisfactory training and treatment can be received where a family lives, they may consider moving.

864. Steady medical care. The parents of a child with any defect should, of course, get expert advice from a private doctor or from a good hospital clinic. If they don't feel satisfied or if the suggested treatment sounds drastic, they are entitled to request another opinion, in consultation with the first doctor. Occasionally parents who have received what sounds like good advice from one doctor will go to one or two more "just to be sure," but they are apt to be confused by minor differences in treatment or terminology and end up with more doubts than they started with.

If you have found a skillful doctor who understands your child's problems, stay with and consult her or him regularly. The doctor who has known the child and family over a period of time is in a better position to prescribe wisely than the doctor who has just been called in. Psychologically, it is apt to be upsetting to the child with a defect to be taken to one new doctor after another. If you read of a new discovery in the condition your child has, ask your own doctor about it rather than rush to the discoverer. If it has been proved to be beneficial, your own doctor will know or can find out whether it has any promise in your child's case.

865. Mental slowness. You can roughly divide cases of real mental slowness into three groups: organic, glandular, and experiential (or environmental). Organic cases are those in which there is physical brain damage, caused, for example, by insufficient oxygen reaching the brain during birth or by encephalitis. Glandular cases are due to deficient functioning of the thyroid gland; if they are diagnosed early and treated correctly, the mental deficiency may be kept to a minimum.

The remaining cases of mental slowness are experiential in the sense that there has been a low level of mental stimulation in the way the child has been reared, or some other psychological cause. Disease or injury is not a cause of this type of mental slowness. It is often difficult to distinguish between organic and experiential cases. The intelligence of the child with experiential slowness continues to develop steadily but at a slower rate than average.

If a particular child at the age of 4 years has the intelligence of the average 3-year-old, he is said to have an intelligence quotient (I.Q.) of 75 (3/4=75/100).

866. Being accepted enables them to make the most of their abilities. The behavior problems that a few slow children develop are usually due not to low intelligence but to mistaken methods of handling. If the parents feel that the child is queer or shameful, for instance, their love may not go out to him in sufficiently full measure to give him security and happiness. If they mistakenly believe that they are to blame for his condition, they may insist on unwise "treatment" of all kinds that disturbs him without benefiting him. If they jump to the conclusion that he is a hopeless case who will never be "normal," they may neglect to provide him with the playthings, the companions, the proper schooling that are needed by **all** children to bring out their best abilities. One great danger is that the parents, trying to ignore the signs that he is slow, trying to prove to themselves and the world that he is just as bright as the next child, will push him all along the line—try to teach him skills and manners before he is ready, hurry his toilet training, get him into a school class that he isn't up to, coach him at home in his lessons. The constant pressure makes him balky and irritable. Being frequently in situations in which he can't possibly succeed robs him of self-confidence.

Sadly enough, the slow child whose parents have had only an average amount of schooling and are living happily on a modest scale often makes out better than the child who is born into a college-educated family or one that has high ambitions for worldly success. The latter are more likely to assume that it's vital to get good marks at school, to go to college, to go into a profession.

There are many useful and dignified jobs that are best performed by people who have less-than-average intelligence. It's the right of every individual to grow up well-enough adjusted and well-enough trained to be able to handle the best job that he has the intelligence for.

The slow child must be allowed to develop in his own pattern, to have eating habits and toilet habits that are suitable for his stage of mental growth rather than suitable for his age. He needs opportunities to dig and climb and build and make-believe at the periods when he is ready for these activities, playthings that appeal to him, chances to play with children whom he can enjoy and keep up with (even if they are a year or more younger in age). When he goes to school, he must go into a class where he can feel that he belongs and is accomplishing something.

On the other hand, a child's progress may be slowed down by a pessimistic attitude on the part of parents and teachers. Careful educational assessment and an individually designed program may accelerate his mental growth so that he makes up for some of his retardation. Any child of whatever mental level benefits from feeling that he is loved warmly and enjoyed for his appealing qualities.

Anyone who has observed groups of slow children knows how natural and friendly and appealing most of them are—particularly the ones who have been accepted naturally at home. And when they are busy at play or schoolwork that is right for them, they have the same eager, interested attitude that average and superior children do. In other words, the "dumb" look comes more from feeling out of place than from having a low I.Q. Most of us would have a stupid look in an advanced lecture on relativity.

The child who is only mildly or moderately slow is, of course, usually cared for at home. This is the place where he, like the average child, gets the most security. It will be good for him to go to nursery school, if possible, where the teachers can decide whether he should be with his own age or younger children.

867. The care of a slow child at home. Parents, when they become convinced that a child is slow in his mental development, are apt to ask the doctor or social worker what special playthings and educational material they should buy and what special instruction they should give the child at home. This is due to people's natural tendency to think, at first, that a handicapped child is very different from other children. To be sure, a retarded child may have interests and capabilities that are not up to his chronological age; they correspond more to his mental age. He is apt to want to play with children younger than himself, and with toys suitable for that younger age. He might not begin to try to tie his shoelaces or to pick out letters at 5 or 6. He may also have difficulty in interpreting what he sees or hears. He may be awkward or hyperactive.

Parents of a child of average intelligence don't have to ask a doctor or read a book to find out his interests. Mostly they watch him playing with his own possessions and with the possessions of neighbors and sense what else might appeal to him. They observe what he is trying to learn and help him tactfully.

It's really just the same with a retarded child. You watch to see what he enjoys. You get him the playthings, indoors and out, that are sensible. You help him locate the children he has fun with, every day if possible. You teach him the skills he wants assistance with.

868. The right school placement is vital. It is wise to get the opinion and guidance of a psychologist, privately or through a child guidance clinic or through the school system, when it is suspected that a child is slow (Section 633). He should not get into a class that is way beyond him. Every day that he is unable to keep up, his self-confidence is destroyed a little, and being left back a grade or demoted hurts him. If he is only slightly slow and the school program is one in which every child can contribute according to his ability, he may be able to move along with children his own age. Otherwise, he should be in a special class. It is not advisable to delay his school attendance. Special preschool programs for slow children are being developed around the country. Many slow children need help in attending to ordinary kindergarten and school activities. Special, well-planned materials and special educational approaches are called for.

869. The more seriously retarded child. The child who at 1½ or 2 years, for instance, is still unable to sit up, who shows little interest in people or things, presents more complicated problems. He will have to be cared for as a baby for a long time. There is no one right solution. It depends on the degree of retardation, the temperament of the child, how he affects other children in the family, whether by the time he is active he can find playmates and activities to keep him happy, whether there is a special class in one of the local schools that will accept him and suit him. Most of all, it depends on whether his parents find predominantly satisfaction or strain in caring for him. Some of these questions can't be answered until the child is several years older.

870. Some parents are so constituted that they can take a retarded child in their stride. They can find ways to care for him that don't exhaust them. They are able to enjoy his agreeable qualities, not be upset by the difficulties he presents, and not become too wrapped up in his care. The other children in the family take their cue mainly from the parents in these respects. The acceptance by the rest of the family brings out the best in the retarded child and gives him a good start in life. He may be able to benefit most by living at home indefinitely.

Other parents who are equally devoted find themselves becoming increasingly tense and impatient in caring for a child with such special needs. This may impair their relationship with each other and their other children. The parents need a lot of help from a doctor who specializes in this field and who will usually be working with a team which includes a social worker and a children's psychologist or psychiatrist. This should lead either to a more comfortable attitude or to finding a more satisfactory solution in a residence elsewhere than home, preferably in a small group.

Still other parents find that they can throw themselves into the care of a seriously handicapped child without a feeling of undue strain, even with an enjoyable devotion. But an outsider can see that their sense of obligation to the child is so intense that they are not thinking enough of each other, the other children or their own normal interests. In the long run, this is not healthy for the family as a whole or even for the retarded child. The parents need help in gaining a sense of proportion and in easing up in their preoccupation (Section 857).

When the parents feel unable to cope with the problems of the retarded child, they should consult at length with a family social agency or an agency specializing in the care of retarded children. Sometimes counseling provides the practical and emotional support that the parents need. Or it may lead to the search for a foster home or small-group home for the care of the child. The tendency in recent years has been to avoid, if possible, placement in large institutions.

The National Association for Retarded Citizens, 2709 E Avenue East/P.O. Box 6109, Arlington, TX 76010 may be able to suggest local resources.

871. Down's syndrome (Mongolism). This is a special type of organic mental deficiency but there is also a disturbance of bodily growth. The eyes slant upward somewhat like an Oriental's and this is how the condition received its earlier name. There are other distinctive characteristics. Physical growth is slow, and the child does not reach full size. Intelligence develops very slowly in most cases, but in a few it develops to a fair degree. In disposition, many of these children are characteristically sweet-natured.

The chances of having a baby with this condition increase toward the end of a woman's child-bearing period. It is caused by an abnormality of the chromosomes, which develops at the start of the life of the embryo. It is not an inherited disorder. There are several distinct types of the disorder. If a mother has one such child, a study of chromosome patterns in the child and the mother should be carried out by a genetic specialist to determine how much chance there is that any future child of this mother will have the condition. The chromosome study is particularly essential if the mother is young. A special test can be done during the beginning of a pregnancy which will tell whether or not the baby has Down's syndrome. Then the parents can decide whether or not they want to continue the pregnancy.

As in other forms of mental slowness, the best course for the future depends on how the child develops, the local opportunities for classes and playmates, how difficult or how comfortable it proves for the parents to carry out their other jobs and this special one, too. Some children with Down's syndrome are reared at home enjoyably and without undue strain on parents and other children. In other cases, it turns out as the child grows older that she and the rest of the family would be happier if she were cared for in another residence, preferably in a small group. Continued counseling is helpful in arriving at the best decision.

CHILD ABUSE AND NEGLECT

872. Most parents get angry enough at their children once in a great while to want to hurt them—at a baby who continues to cry for what seems like hours when you can't find anything wrong and have done everything possible in the way of comforting her, or at a boy who has broken your precious possession right after you have asked him to put it down. Your justified rage boils up. But in most cases you have enough control to avoid hurting the child, except perhaps for a brisk slap to the willfully careless older child. (I remember when I was a medical student, picking up my own crying 6-month-old baby in the middle of the night and yelling, "Shut up!" at him, barely able to control myself from physically hurting him. He hadn't slept through the night for weeks, due to roseola followed by difficult teething, and his mother and I were exhausted and at our wits' end.) You may feel ashamed and embarrassed after such an incident. If you remember that the majority of parents have the same experience, you'll be able to talk to your spouse or the baby's doctor about it and get the support and help you deserve.

There has been a lot of study and attention given to child abuse and neglect in recent years. Abuse may be emotional, physical, or sexual. Neglect may be emotional or physical. Child abuse and neglect occur among all social classes, though somewhat more frequently among poor people whose poverty adds one more major pressure to their stressful lives. If a baby is premature, or sick in the newborn period, requiring more than the usual amount of care, she may be more likely to be abused. Girls are more often sexually abused than boys.

Most of the parents or others who abuse or neglect a child

in any way are not brutal or insane people, but they have had, on one occasion, a momentary loss of physical and emotional control.

Closer contact with a smaller number of parents who have lost control repeatedly reveals that a majority of these were abused, neglected, or molested in their own childhoods, that they have little or no physical or emotional support from family and friends, and that they tend to have unreasonably high expectations of the abused child. They profit greatly from counseling (guidance clinic, family therapy, family social agency) and especially from joining a group of parents or others with similar problems.

The purpose of the laws regarding child abuse and neglect, and the facilities provided, is not to punish the parents but to help them, through counseling, to understand and cope with the various pressures on them that they have taken out on the child, and to have more realistic expectations about the child's ability to conform. The preference is always to keep the child in her home while the parents are supported and helped. But if the risk is temporarily too great, she is placed in a foster home until the family is ready to care for her again.

At the time this is written (1985), we have all been shocked and frightened by recent revelations of sexual abuse of children. It's important to realize that a great majority of the sexual molestations of children are carried out not by depraved strangers but by family members, friends of the family, or other people already known to the children.

One recommendation that has been made is talks by police officers in schools, warning children of strangers who offer candy and rides. I fear that such talks, if carried out by insensitive authorities, could give excessive, morbid fears to millions of children and yet have very, very limited usefulness.

I would suggest instead that parents themselves carry out any warnings they think wise, depending on their evaluation of the risks. To make warnings less frightening, I would tell a young child (3 to 6 years old)—preferably when she asks some question or when the mother has discovered sex play with another young child—that an older boy may want to touch her clitoris or vagina but she doesn't have to let him. She can be told to say, "I don't want you to," and to tell her mother about it. Then the mother can add, "Sometimes a man may want to touch you, or want you to touch him, but you don't have to. Tell me. It won't be your fault." This last idea is mentioned due to the fact that children characteristically don't tell because they feel guilty, especially if the molester is a relative or family friend.

Boys can be molested as well as girls, though this occurs much less often.

In many places, parents have organized branches of a national organization for the prevention of child abuse and neglect. They prepare informational pamphlets about prevention for both parents and children, and put them into schools and libraries. And they have local celebrities, whom the children know well, make public service announcements about how children can protect themselves. These are played on the local television and radio stations.

A national organization of parents and professionals which helps with this problem is: National Committee for Prevention of Child Abuse, 332 South Michigan Avenue, Suite 1250, Chicago, IL 60604, telephone 312-663-3520. They have free booklets on child abuse, child abuse prevention, and parenting. They can tell you how to get help in your own area, and whether they have a local chapter near you. Many large cities have child abuse "hot lines" which you can call if you feel that you're losing control, and your local child welfare agency can help.

Kidnapping. There has been a lot of publicity about missing children in recent years. Many (some say most) of the children who disappear are kidnapped by a divorced, noncustodial parent who feels unfairly deprived. Many others are teenagers, most of them girls, who run away because they feel unloved or unfairly treated. Of the runaways, the young ones soon reveal that they are runaways or give themselves up. The older ones may evade detection and use this path for leaving home for good.

Some people have recommended fingerprinting in response to this. If you want your child fingerprinted, despite the extremely minute chance that it would ever be useful, I suggest that you say something such as, "I'd like you to get fingerprinted because everyone's fingerprints are different, just like pictures of people's faces, and if you should ever get lost this would help us to find you." In other words, you don't have to get involved in talk about kidnapping in order to talk about fingerprinting.

Of course, all children should be taught never to go anywhere with a stranger, no matter what the stranger tells them, as soon as the children are old enough to leave their homes by themselves.

Adopting a Child

873. A great majority of the children waiting to be adopted are older. So most of the people who want to adopt only babies or very young children will not be able to or may have to wait for a long time. These people may be tempted to adopt a baby through a lawyer or doctor who says she or he has a baby available. A lot of people think they won't have any trouble if they get a "gray market" baby this way as opposed to a "black market" baby who is clearly being adopted without any legal procedures at all. Often these people discover that they have terrible difficulties, legally and otherwise, later on, such as when the mother or parents of the baby decide that they want the baby back.

For many reasons, more unmarried parents are keeping and raising their children. Therefore, there are not as many very young children needing homes. However, there are other children waiting for parents. They are for the most part school aged. They may have a brother and sister from whom they don't want to be separated. They may have some physical, emotional, or intellectual handicap. They may be war orphans from Southeast Asia or South America or other parts of the world where recent wars have produced many orphaned children. They are as in need of love and as rewarding to parents as any other child. It's the responsibility of adoption agencies to focus their attention on finding homes for these children, even more than on finding babies for parents.

If the older child has some special need, the agency staff and physicians will be helpful in supplying adoptive parents with important information about the child. Most people have enough latent capacity to be able to take good care of children. It is the job of professionals to help inexperienced adopting parents to develop this latent capacity.

Nowadays many of the prospective adoptive parents coming to agencies already have children. They are not infertile and already have demonstrated parental ability. They come out of humanitarian motives, wanting to do something for the child.

People have various reasons for wanting to adopt. A couple should decide to adopt only if both of them love children and want one very much. All children, biological or adopted, need to feel that they belong to and are loved by both father and mother deeply and "forever," if they are to grow up secure. For an adopted child, let's say a girl, it is even worse to sense a lack of love in one or both parents. She's not so secure to begin with, having been through one or more previous separations. She knows that she was given up for some reason by her biological parents, and she may fear secretly that her adopted parents might someday give her up too. You can see then why it's a mistake to adopt when only one parent wants to, or when both parents are thinking of it only for practical reasons, such as to have extra help or to have someone to take care of them in their old age. Occasionally a woman who is afraid that she's losing her husband wants to adopt a child with the futile hope that this will hold his love. Adoption for reasons like these is unfair to the child. It usually proves to be wrong from the parents' point of view too. All too often the child who is not deeply loved becomes a behavior problem.

Single parents are being given consideration as adoptive parents. Most waiting children need parents right away. Childhood passes quickly and a permanent parent now is of more value than the possibility of two parents some time in the future. So agencies unable to find couples have chosen to use single parents. There is another good reason for this in some cases. Certain children have been emotionally bruised in such a way that it is better for them to have one parent of a particular sex. Some children have such a tremendous need for attention and care at the time of placement that the absence of a spouse who also needs attention allows the single parent to give what the child needs.

A couple should not wait until they are too old to adopt a

child. Some of them become too set in their ways. They've dreamed so long of a little girl with golden curls filling the house with song that even the best of children turns out to be a rude shock. How old is "too old"? It is not a matter of years alone, but of an individual's capacity to give what a particular child needs. It is something to discuss with the agency.

Parents who have a child who is not very happy or sociable sometimes consider adopting another to provide company. It is a good idea to talk this over with a child psychiatrist or the child-placing agency before proceeding. The adopted child is apt to feel like an outsider compared to the other child. If the parents lean over backward to show affection for the newcomer, it may upset rather than help their biological child. It is a risky business.

There is danger, too, in adopting to "replace" a child who has died. Parents need time to work out their grief. They should adopt only because they want a child to love. There is no harm in adopting one who is similar in age or sex or appearance to the child who died, but the comparison should stop there. It is unfair and unsound to want to make one individual play the part of another. She is bound to fail at the job of being a ghost, and she will disappoint the parents and become unhappy. She should not be reminded of what the other child did, or be compared with her out loud or in the parents' minds. Let her be herself. (Some of this applies also to the child who is born after an older one dies.)

874. Adopt through a good agency. Probably the most important rule of all about adoption is to arrange it through a first-rate child-placing agency. It is always risky for the adopting parents to deal directly with the biological parents or through an inexperienced third person. It leaves the way open for those parents to change their minds and to try to get their child back. Even when the law stands in the way of this, the unpleasantness can ruin the happiness of the adopting family and the security of the child. The agency helps the biological mother and relatives to make the right decision in the first place as to whether to give the baby up or not. It uses its judgment and experience in deciding which couples should be dissuaded from adopting. The agency worker helps the child and family during the adjustment period. The goal of all concerned is to help the child become a member of the family. Wise agencies and wise state laws require this adjustment before the adoption becomes final. One way to find out about the qualifications of an adoption agency is to call your State Department of Health. All state health departments have a section which licenses adoption agencies.

At what age should a child be adopted? For the child's sake, the younger the better. For a number of complex reasons this has not yet been possible for thousands of youngsters living in foster homes and institutions. Research has shown that these older children can also be successfully adopted. The age of children should not prevent their being placed. The agency helps older children and parents decide if this is right for them.

Some people worry about heredity and how it will affect a child's future. The more we have learned about personality development, including intelligence, the clearer it becomes that the most important factor by far is the environment in which the child grows up, especially the love she receives and the feeling of belonging that she acquires. There is no evidence that specific social abnormalities like immorality, delinquency, or irresponsibility are inherited.

875. Let her find out naturally. Should an adopted child be told she is adopted? All the experienced people in this field agree that the child should know. She's sure to find out sooner or later from someone or other, no matter how carefully the parents think they are keeping the secret. It is practically always a very disturbing experience for an older child, or even an adult, to discover suddenly that she is adopted. It may disturb her sense of security for years. Supposing a baby has been adopted during her first year. When should she be told? The news shouldn't be saved for any definite age. The parents should, from the beginning, let the fact that she's adopted come openly, but casually, into their conversations with each other, with the child, and with their acquaintances. This creates an atmosphere in which the child can ask questions whenever she is at a stage of development in which the subject interests her. She finds out what adoption means bit by bit, as she gains understanding.

Some adopting parents make the mistake of trying to keep

the adoption secret, others err in the opposite direction by stressing it too much. Most adopting parents have, quite naturally, an exaggerated sense of responsibility at first—as if they have to be letter-perfect to justify the fact that someone else's child has been entrusted to their care. If they go too earnestly at the job of explaining to the child that she's adopted, she begins to wonder, "What's wrong with being adopted, anyway?" But if they accept the adoption as naturally as they accept the color of the child's hair, they won't have to make a secret of it, or keep reminding her of it. They should remind themselves that, having been selected by the agency, they're probably darned good parents and the child is lucky to have found them. They should not fear the missing biological parent. Parents need to resolve these fears and anxieties or they will communicate them to the child.

Let's say that a child around 3 hears her mother explaining to a new acquaintance that she is adopted, and asks, "What's adopted, Mommy?" She might answer, "A long time ago I wanted very much to have a little baby girl to love and take care of. So I went to a place where there were a lot of babies, and I told the lady, 'I want a little girl with brown hair and brown eyes.' So she brought me a baby, and it was you. And I said, 'Oh, this is just exactly the baby that I want. I want to adopt her and take her home to keep forever.' And that's how I adopted you." This makes a good beginning because it emphasizes the positive side of the adoption, the fact that the mother received just what she wanted. The story will delight the child, and she'll want to hear it many times.

Children who have been adopted at an older age will need a different approach. They may have memories of their biological and foster parents. Agencies should help both child and parents to handle this. It is important to realize that questions will surface repeatedly during different stages of a child's life. They should be answered as simply and honestly as possible. Parents should allow the child to freely express her feelings and fears.

Between the ages of 3 and 4, like most children, she wants to know where babies come from in the beginning. The answer is discussed in Section 585. It is best to answer truthfully, but simply enough so that the 3-year-old can understand easily. But when her adopted mother explains that babies grow inside the mother's abdomen, it makes her wonder how this fits in with the story of picking her out at the agency. Maybe then, or months later, she asks, "Did I grow inside you?" Then the adopting mother can explain, simply and casually, that she grew inside another mother before she was adopted. This is apt to confuse her for a while, but she will get it clear later.

Eventually a child raises the more difficult question of why her biological parents gave her up. To imply that they didn't want her would shake her confidence in all parents. Any sort of made-up reason may bother her later in some unexpected way. Perhaps the best answer and nearest to the truth might be, "I don't know why they couldn't take care of you, but I'm sure they wanted to." During this period when the child is digesting this idea, she needs to be reminded, along with a hug, that she's always going to be yours now.

All adopted people are naturally intensely curious about their biological parents, whether they express this or not. In former times, adoption agencies told adopting parents only the vaguest generalities about the physical and mental health of the biological parents. They completely concealed their identities. This was partly to make it easy for the adopting parents to explain, "I don't know" to the extremely difficult-to-answer questions a child would ask about her origin and about why she was relinquished. And it was even more to protect the privacy of the biological parents who, in most cases, had been unmarried and who, in their subsequent separate lives, may have kept the pregnancy a secret.

Today, the courts, in recognition of the individual's "right to know," have sometimes compelled an agency to reveal the identity of the biological parents to an adopted youth (or adult) who has demanded that information. In some cases, when this has led to a visit, it has had a beneficial effect on the turbulent feelings and obsessive curiosity of the adopted individual; in others, such a visit has been disturbing to the youth and therefore to the adopting parents, as well as to the biological parents. Obviously, any such demand by an adopted youth or adult needs to be discussed at length with the agency people, with all its pros and cons, whether or not the case is ever brought to court.

876. She must belong completely. The secret fear that the adopted child may have is that her adopting parents will someday give her up as her biological parents did, if they change their minds or if she is bad. Adopting parents should always remember this and vow that they will never, under any circumstances, say or hint that the idea of giving her up has ever crossed their minds. One threat uttered in a thoughtless or angry moment might be enough to destroy the child's confidence in them forever. They should be ready to let her know that she is theirs forever at any time the question seems to enter her mind; for instance, when she is talking about her adoption. I'd like to add, though, that it's a mistake for the adopting parents to worry so about the child's security that they overemphasize their talk of loving her. Basically, the thing that gives the adopted child the greatest security is being loved, wholeheartedly and naturally. It's not the words, but the music, that counts.

EMERGENCIES

Index

INDEX

A

INDEX

C

D

G

H

J

K

L

M

Q

R

S

T

U

V

W

X

Y

Z